The Engaged Citizen

Writing and Speaking at the University of Oklahoma

The First-Year Composition Program

English 1113/1213

With selected chapters from:

Habits of the Creative Mind, First Edition
by Richard E. Miller and Ann Jurecic

FieldWorking, Fourth Edition
by Bonnie Stone Sunstein and Elizabeth Chiseri-Strater

Everything's an Argument, Eighth Edition
by Andrea A. Lunsford and John J. Ruszkiewicz

A Pocket Guide to Public Speaking, Sixth Edition
by Dan O'Hair, Hannah Rubenstein, and Rob Stewart

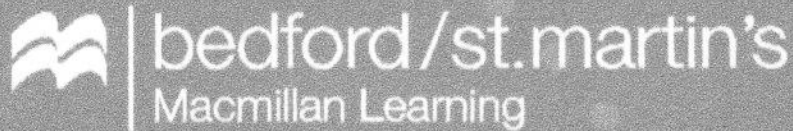

Content taken from:

Habits of the Creative Mind, by Richard E. Miller and Ann Jurecic

FieldWorking, Fourth Edition, by Bonnie Stone Sunstein and Elizabeth Chiseri-Strater

Everything's an Argument, Eighth Edition, by Andrea A. Lunsford and John J. Ruszkiewicz

Pocket Guide to Public Speaking, Sixth Edition, by Dan O'Hair, Hannah Rubenstein, and Rob Stewart

3 2 1 0 9
f e d c b a

ISBN 978-1-319-27388-0

Macmillan Learning Curriculum Solutions
14903 Pilot Drive
Plymouth, MI 48170
www.macmillanlearning.com

Mountford 7388-0 F19

Acknowledgments

Contents

PART 3: Reading and Understanding Arguments 229

First-Year Composition at the University of Oklahoma

Winner of the 2017–2018 Writing Program Certificate of Excellence

We welcome you to the award-winning First-Year Composition (FYC) Program at the University of Oklahoma. Whether you are with us one semester or two, this textbook will support you in learning to write for and speak to others.

Like all college writing programs, our priority is teaching you to write at the university level. We do not view writing as a skill dependent upon natural, unlearned talent. Instead, we view writing as a tool that anyone can learn to use well. We also believe that all writers have more to learn, and we are confident that no matter your level of achievement, our courses will offer you innovative ways to approach new writing situations and deepen your critical thinking skills. Our instructors will guide you in the development of strategic writing habits that can be adapted to your educational, professional, or social interests.

But our program has an additional purpose: enabling you to succeed *as a citizen* at productively debating issues of local and national importance. We want you to emerge from our courses with *civic empathy*, the capacity to respond to others in the public sphere with understanding and respect. We believe our job is to enable you to analyze public debates and intervene in our broken national discourse. We do so by asking you to:

- Focus on values that motivate meaningful action
- Study the ways in which groups and stakeholders are motivated by values and beliefs
- Understand and practice rhetorical listening (an element of deliberation)
- Study public issues with a local face
- Study rhetorical concepts such as stasis theory that help illuminate controversies
- Study and practice in persuading specific stakeholders
- Make a meaningful personal connection with your research and writing
- Engage in formal and informal public speaking

To support these key goals, our textbook contains materials from four separate writing and public speaking textbooks. To develop your critical thinking skills and sense of wonder and curiosity, we first ask you to read from *Habits of the Creative Mind*. A short excerpt from *FieldWorking* will support your efforts to learn from communities. Chapters from *Everything's an Argument* will develop your ability to find, analyze and use arguments when engaging with others. Finally, chapters from *A Pocket Guide to Public Speaking* will offer you a comprehensive resource for developing your formal speaking skills.

What to Expect

In order to get the most from our classes, it is important to understand your role, the role of your instructor, and the role of the FYC office in our classrooms.

Your Role:

- Come to class, fully prepared (bring assigned readings, homework, note-taking utensils, etc.). Note that attendance is required in all FYC classes.
- Complete all homework and make a good faith effort to learn from assignments
- Check your OU email and course Canvas page regularly
- Ask questions early and often
- Dedicate yourself to challenging your assumptions about writing and public speaking, recognizing that this will be a rigorous course
- Be willing to practice new writing habits and techniques
- Take class discussions and group work seriously; our program values collaboration and the more you put in, the more you will get out
- Communicate with your instructor about any difficulties affecting your ability to be successful

FYC Instructors' Role:

- Come to class with carefully prepared lesson plans that work toward unit and course learning objectives
- Encourage questions and provide answers, guidance, or next steps
- Be available during office hours to meet with you as well as respond to your emails according to the policy listed in the class syllabus
- Assign homework and classwork designed to prepare you to succeed on unit projects
- Give feedback on essay drafts at least 48 hours before final drafts are due (incomplete drafts may not receive feedback)
- Return graded unit projects within two weeks of receiving them
- Have an optimistic view of students and be invested in your success
- Check OU email regularly, list office hours/location on class syllabi, and update grades routinely on Canvas

FYC Office's Role:

- Prepare instructors to successfully teach course and unit objectives
- Design departmental policies to support instructors and students
- Mediate disputes between FYC instructors and students
- Support students and instructors during any grade appeals for FYC unit projects
- Provide a safe environment for you to share concerns about your FYC classes or instructors
- Answer questions about FYC policies or procedures
- Have an optimistic view of students and instructors
- Check fyc@ou.edu regularly and keep office hours from 9:00 a.m. to 3:00 p.m. in Cate 2, rooms 426 & 428

We look forward to working with you and wish you every success!

—The Directors and Instructors of the First-Year Composition Program

Introduction to the FYC Course Sequence

At the University of Oklahoma, the Office of First-Year Composition is dedicated to providing you with a rhetorical education that prepares you to write and speak inside and outside of the university setting, and equips you to approach writing and speaking situations as opportunities to contribute to the public good. Below, you'll find a description of our two courses and a list of the learning objectives for each.

English 1113

In English 1113, you will practice rhetorical inquiry by investigating values and worldviews, which inform our beliefs and motivate our actions. As you complete your projects, you will explore:

- How core values are formed, understood, and defined in ways specific to each person
- Arguments on social and political issues, particularly those we disagree with, and how they are informed by the values and worldview of the author
- How personal values are collectively enacted through social and political engagement
- Your experiences throughout the semester in order to compose and deliver an informative speech to classmates

As you might notice, we purposefully delay students from composing arguments that seek to persuade an audience to change their minds. Rather, through the close exploration and analysis of values and social actions, we emphasize first *understanding* the motivations of potential audiences by *listening* to what they have to say. By concentrating on listening and understanding one another instead of promoting causes, we avoid knee-jerk arguments that close off the very audience we hope to persuade. An early focus on values provides a way to understand audiences that we don't agree with, setting the stage for later persuasive projects in English 1213.

When you complete English 1113, you will be able to:

- Use writing for exploration, discovery, comprehension, problem solving, and the construction of nuanced claims
- Compose and deliver essays and speeches that demonstrate rhetorical awareness
- Engage thoughtfully with other perspectives in a manner that encourages, rather than curtails, public discussion and participation
- Respond effectively to writing tasks without being given a prescribed organizational form to follow
- Develop flexible and effective strategies for organizing, revising, practicing/rehearsing, editing, and proofreading (for grammar and mechanics) to improve development and clarity of ideas
- Find, analyze, and correctly cite primary and secondary sources to support and develop personal points of view, understand the views of others, and connect actions to values
- Analyze texts to reveal how writers and speakers make rhetorical choices in the service of an intended purpose or goal
- Define and practice revision strategies for essays and speeches that locate areas for improvement and effectively target them
- Develop considerate and constructive strategies for responding to peer work

English 1213

In English 1213, you will turn your focus to a current issue of public concern that is important and relevant to you. You will begin the semester by delivering a brief speech to your classmates that introduces your personal investment in a chosen issue as well as that issue's larger social importance. This chosen issue will serve as the basis for the four major projects of the course, in which you will:

- Synthesize research in order to explain the background, context, and current state of the issue
- Analyze at least five relevant stakeholders—individuals and groups invested in or affected by the issue—to show why the issue remains unresolved

- Write an essay designed to persuade a particular stakeholder to change their mind or their actions regarding the issue
- Deliver a 6–8 minute persuasive speech to your classmates about the issue and respond effectively to questions from the audience

In English 1213, you will learn to embrace the complexity present in public issues and recognize the different ways issues affect different people. In order to effectively persuade others, you have to first understand how to identify who is impacted and explore what they stand to gain or lose regarding a particular issue. Through cumulative research and analysis, you will learn to recognize how stakeholders argue about your issue, which helps you to determine the most effective way to intervene. When you finally craft written arguments to a particular stakeholder and deliver persuasive speeches to your classmates, you can do so ethically, with confidence and precision, speaking with—not past—your audiences.

When you complete English 1213, you will be able to:

- Explore and intervene in an issue of public interest and deliberation using writing and speaking
- Write and deliver persuasive arguments grounded in scholarly research that respond to audience needs and expectations
- Conduct relevant primary and secondary research on a subject, effectively presenting and synthesizing research findings
- Use advanced rhetorical strategies, including stasis theory, for analyzing arguments and developing ideas
- Refine speaking, writing, and visual communication skills, focusing on matters of construction, design, and delivery style
- Apply revision strategies to your writing, drawing on feedback from your instructor and classmates
- Develop considerate and constructive strategies for responding to peer work
- Serve as an active and courteous audience able to respond productively to public speaking

Our Values Enacted

The OU FYC program's core values impact the expectations that we hold for our instructors, staff, and students, as well as how we design our curriculum and department policies. We try to enact these values by creating assignments and activities that encourage you to practice these same values alongside your instructors. On the following pages, we have provided definitions of what we consider to be our most important values and explanations of how both students and instructors might exercise those values in English 1113 and 1213.

Curiosity

Curiosity is what drives us to learn more about ourselves, others, and the world around us. Curiosity motivates us to continually ask questions when we encounter unfamiliar ideas and beliefs; it leads us to new perspectives, unique ways of thinking, and novel solutions to the problems we face.

Being curious is a way to practice paying attention and actively engaging with the world around you. We believe it can be learned and developed. In your FYC classes, you will engage your curiosity by exploring what motivates you, what motivates others, and what motivates and shapes public issues, using your own questions to guide your thinking and writing. Through continued research, your curiosity will result in a deeper understanding of topics that interest you. Part of this exploration and inquiry is approaching your writing as an ongoing process that involves developing your writing and thinking, strengthening both.

Listening

Listening is an act that requires a full consideration of others' perspectives, as well as our own. To listen actively is not only to hear what others are saying—and what isn't being said—but also to pay attention to why and how they are saying it. We listen in order to understand, and we believe that listening, especially to those we may disagree with, is an important step in joining public conversations and making our own arguments.

Listening, therefore, is a form of inquiry and a form of research. In your FYC courses, you will practice this style of investigative listening in a variety of ways. Reading and analyzing texts will allow you to gain an in-depth understanding of what motivates the arguments they contain. Through interviews and observations, you will engage directly with members of the local community to determine how their values drive their public actions. And, public speaking opportunities will require that you listen attentively to your classmates deliver presentations about ideas and issues that are meaningful to them. You will demonstrate that you have listened effectively by showing that you deeply understand other perspectives.

Collaboration

We love collaboration, because we achieve more together than on our own. Collaborating helps us see the holes in our own ideas, pushes us to articulate our ideas in ways that make sense to others, and, best of all, surprises us when we create innovative solutions. Engaging in collaboration creates space where people can listen to each other and share the work of tackling a project.

You can expect to practice informal collaboration by discussing class concepts and brainstorming ideas for projects with your classmates. Formal peer review sessions will enable you to elevate your ideas, learn from your classmates' work, and help them to refine and clarify their ideas. Acknowledging the help you receive inside and outside of your classroom, you will give credit to those who have contributed to your projects through footnotes, in-text citations, and Works Cited pages. Collaboration will better prepare you to work productively and respectfully with others in public deliberation.

Public Engagement

Public engagement begins by recognizing that we are not private individuals. We live and work in communities, and it is our responsibility to make those spaces better for others. It's about advocating for the causes that matter to us, effectively contributing to the broader conversations surrounding us, and meaningfully participating in movements happening in the public sphere.

For this reason, we will be working to understand and respond to questions of public importance. You will study how others—both individuals and groups—engage with social or political causes, offering insight into what motivates their involvement. In English 1213, you will spend the semester researching a single public issue, examining its history, and analyzing key groups and individuals with a stake in it. Only after you've done this work will you enter into the conversation, seeking to persuade those who disagree with you while maintaining respect for and demonstrating your understanding of their stake in the public problem.

Thoughtful Deliberation

Deliberation, as the highest form of public engagement, offers a democratic means for determining how best to proceed on issues affecting the public. Thoughtful deliberation requires the conscientious consideration of what is at stake for others when we make decisions. When we deliberate, we refuse to reduce the outcomes of arguments to winning and losing. Curiosity, listening, collaboration, and public engagement all contribute to effective deliberation. *Curiosity* inspires us to explore all sides of an issue in-depth, and *listening* to others allows us to see how an issue impacts those beyond our own immediate circle. Deliberation also benefits from *collaboration*; a group of people working to solve a problem has a better chance of finding a superior solution than an individual working alone to solve an issue. And, in order for deliberation to even begin, we must first be *publicly engaged*—prepared to contribute to public conversations and advocate for issues we care about. As a place of intersection with all of our other values, deliberation emphasizes a conscientious approach to argument that is critical to a functioning democracy.

Further Opportunities to Develop Your Writing

After completing English 1213, you may find yourself interested in taking other courses that focus on writing prose or composing in multimedia. While you may find courses offered within your chosen major, there are plenty of opportunities to take courses that are open to all students. The following courses require only that you have successfully completed 1213.

English 1913: Writing for the Health Professions. This course prepares students for the types of writing they will do in later coursework and in medical practice.

English 2113: Intermediate Writing. The faculty who teach this course give it a theme. The course is organized around the writing of non-fiction prose.

English 2123: Creative Writing. This course serves as an introduction to imaginative writing, especially short stories and poems.

English 2133: Autobiographical Writing. This course focuses on writing essays from personal experience and reading and analyzing journals, diaries, letters, and autobiographies as models for writing.

English 3113: Nature and Environmental Writing. This course offers students a chance to read and write about the natural world and the environment. It is attractive to students in the natural sciences and in environmental studies. The course fulfills a general education requirement (Humanities—Western Civilization).

English 3153: Technical Writing. This course is generally open only to students in Engineering or one of the pure and applied sciences. It takes a user-centered approach to the forms of writing most frequently encountered in research and industry.

English 3183: Digital Composing. If you are interested in writing for media other than print, this course is for you. The course focuses on composing for websites and social media, with emphasis on delivery and design of information and effective use of graphics.

English 3233: Oklahoma Writers/Writing Oklahoma. If you enjoy writing about local and regional issues, you will enjoy this course. The course involves reading and writing about Oklahoma. The course fulfills a general education requirement (Humanities—Western Civilization).

English 4113: Magazine Editing and Publishing in the Humanities. This course introduces students to magazine writing, editing, and publishing practices, "scholarly and otherwise" in the humanities.

Please consult the current course catalog for additional course information and availability.

part 1

Habits of the Creative Mind

CHAPTER 1

Beginning

The blank screen and the blinking cursor: for most of us, the hardest moment in the writing process is getting started. To get that cursor moving, you need to have something to say, something of interest to others. But how do you just start off being interesting? Where do interesting thoughts come from? It's a mystery—or so it seems.

The three essays in this section discuss how to begin using this book to unpack this mystery. The first essay introduces learning's central paradox: when we begin to learn something new, we simultaneously have to unlearn something familiar. A beginning is also an ending. In unlearning formulaic approaches to writing pseudo-arguments, you will be on your way to learning how to think seriously about open-ended questions.

The second and third essays discuss how to use your writing to confront what is unknown to you. In some cases, this process will involve choosing to read and write about topics that are unfamiliar. In other cases, it will involve finding ways to join an ongoing conversation among experts. In every case, you will have to contend with moments of confusion and uncertainty. The more you practice confronting what is unknown to you, the more comfortable you'll become with questions that confront all kinds of complexity and with answers that never settle things once and for all.

On Unlearning

When students enter our writing classes, they often bring with them a set of rules from high school that they use to define good writing. They know that every paragraph should start with a topic sentence that states the main point of the paragraph. And they know that all good essays have five sections or paragraphs: an introduction that states the essay's thesis; three descriptive body paragraphs, each of which discusses a different example that supports the essay's thesis; and a conclusion that restates what has been said in the previous sections. And finally, they are certain that no good essay ever uses the word *I*.

Chapter 1, "Beginning," from *Habits of the Creative Mind*, by Richard E. Miller and Ann Jurecic, pp. 15–33 (Chapter 2).

I—or rather we—suspect you know these rules well, since they've been repeated in writing classrooms for decades, with good grades going to those who follow them. But do they *really* produce good writing? Think about it: When was the last time you ran across a five-paragraph essay outside of school? Try looking for one in a news source, a magazine, a book, or even a collection of essays. You might find a modified version of one in an op-ed piece, but most of the writing you find will be organized quite differently. The five-paragraph essay, it turns out, is a very limited form, one best suited to the work of making simple claims and reporting or describing supporting evidence. (It's also easy to skim and easy to grade.)

In college classes, professors often expect students' writing to do a kind of work that is simply beyond the reach of the five-paragraph essay: contending with complexity. You may have had a professor who asked you to develop an argument by working with a handful of original sources, each with a competing point of view; or to support a new interpretation of a text not discussed in class; or to synthesize a semester's worth of lectures into a thoughtful reflection on a complex problem. When professors compose assignments like these, they assume you know how to use your writing to grapple with a genuine problem, puzzle, or question related to a course; they assume you've got something else in your quiver besides the formula for the five-paragraph theme.

So why don't we just give you a new set of rules, one that is capacious enough to provide directions for handling the range of writing tasks college students confront—the response paper in introductory history, the seminar project in advanced economics, the seven-to-eight-page argument for a 300-level psychology or politics or anthropology class? As appealing as that solution is, it's not available to us, because there's not one set of rules for generating good writing that works within any single discipline, let alone across multiple disciplines. The reason for this is not that any judgment of writing quality is inevitably arbitrary, as is often supposed, but rather that writing quality is always a function of context. Thus, what makes for a good paper in a literature class doesn't always make for a good paper in a history class or an econ class, or perhaps even in another literature class taught by a different professor.

How, then, does anyone in any discipline learn how to write about complex challenges? The first step involves unlearning the rules that are at the core of the five-paragraph essay. Taking that first step may seem impossible. We can't unlearn how to walk or how to talk. These habits are so deeply ingrained that a catastrophe of some kind (either psychological or physical) is required to unseat them. And we can't unlearn how to ride a bike or how to swim; we may forget how to over time, but when we return to these activities after a long hiatus, our challenge is not to learn how to do them as if for the first time, but to remember what's involved in keeping the bicycle upright or our body afloat and moving through the water.

Writing is unlike these other activities because each act of writing is not a straightforward repetition of what you've done before. Writing something new requires that you make choices about why you're writing, whom you're writing for, what you think, and what you want your writing to accomplish. So when we say you should unlearn what you learned about writing in school, we mean that we want you to actively resist the idea that writing is governed by a set of universal rules that, if followed, will clearly communicate the writer's ideas to the reader. We can't tell you to forget what you've learned (that would have the same paradoxical effect as telling you not to think about an elephant); and we can't say you shouldn't have been taught the rules governing the five-paragraph essay because, within an educational system dominated by the industry of standardized testing, you must be able to demonstrate that you can produce writing that follows those rules. Rather, we are asking you to question the two assumptions behind the formula for the five-paragraph essay: first, that the primary purpose of writing is to produce irrefutable arguments; and second, that the best writing is immediately understandable by all.

What do we propose in place of these assumptions? That you practice the habits of mind experienced writers exercise when they compose. Experienced writers tend to be curious and attentive. They choose to engage deeply with sources, ideas, people, and the world they live in. They are mentally flexible, self-reflective, and open to new ways of thinking, attributes that allow them to adapt to unfamiliar circumstances and problems. And they are persistent, resisting distraction and disappointment, accepting the fact that writing what hasn't been written before is hard work. When you commit yourself to practicing these habits—curiosity, attentiveness, openness, flexibility, reflectiveness, and persistence—you will also be committing yourself to making a habit of creativity, the practice of inventing novel and useful connections, compelling ideas, and thoughtful prose. As you delve into Part 1 of this book, you'll see that we've designed it to give you practice developing these habits. As you work your way through, you won't be working toward mastery of a formula for good writing; you'll be working on developing the habits of mind that increase your sensitivity to context and that allow you to use your writing to explore the unknown. You'll be practicing using your writing to show to others and yourself how your mind—not *any* mind, not *every* mind—works on a problem.

PRACTICE SESSION ONE

REFLECTING

When we tell students to unlearn the writing rules they learned in high school, they often ask for something—anything—to put in the place of those rules. We start our students on a path toward developing curious and creative habits of mind by telling them that their writing should show their minds at work on a problem. But what does that look like on the page?

Before you can answer that question for yourself, you need to know what kind of thinker you are. How does *your* mind work? What are your mental habits? How do you know? To answer these questions, pay attention over the course of a week to how you write and how you read.

Take notes every day on *everything* you read and write (not just in school or for school). Pay attention to all the times you process words: reading a page, a sign, a cereal box, the screen of a phone or a computer; writing a note, a Facebook post, a text message, a school assignment, a journal entry. For each instance, take note of where and when you read or wrote. Was it quiet? Were you moving? Were you alone?

At the end of the week, consider the following questions and spend at least 30 minutes composing a reflective response about what you've observed. Is the way you read and write better described as a set of rules or as a set of habits? Whichever option you choose, explain why. If you were to teach someone to read and write *the way you do*, how would you do it? What standards would apply?

PRACTICE SESSION TWO

READING

Select a reading and read it with an eye toward seeing the habits of the writer's mind at work on the page. Read the text through once and then review it, identifying evidence of the writer's habits of mind. Where do you see signs of curiosity, attentiveness, openness, flexibility, reflectiveness, persistence, and creativity?

Next, spend at least 30 minutes jotting down notes about the habits of mind on display in the reading you selected. What do the examples you've found tell you about how the writer thinks?

WRITING

The reading you chose to work with is obviously not a five-paragraph theme, and not just because it has far more than five paragraphs! Review the reading again and think about other ways the writer breaks what you thought were rules of writing. Then write an essay that considers why the writer made some surprising choices, writing in ways you thought were discouraged, or at least risky. What do these choices tell you about the writer's habits of mind?

EXPLORE

Can curiosity and creativity be learned? Unlearned? Relearned? Francine Prose recalls learning to write—outside school—by becoming a close and careful reader. In two TED videos, Ken Robinson laments the value placed on standardization and conformity in schools in the United States and United Kingdom and asks us to reimagine schools as environments that cultivate curiosity and creativity.

Prose, Francine. "Close Reading: Learning to Write by Learning to Read." *Atlantic*. 1 Aug. 2006. Web.

Robinson, Ken. "How Schools Kill Creativity." TED. Feb. 2006. Web.

———. "How to Escape Education's Death Valley." TED. April 2013. Web.

On Confronting the Unknown

In his book *Deep Survival: Who Lives, Who Dies, and Why*, Laurence Gonzales recounts the story of seventeen-year-old Juliane Koepcke who was seated next to her mother on a flight with ninety other passengers when the plane was struck by lightning, causing it to go into a nosedive. The next thing Koepcke recalled was being outside the plane, still strapped into her seat, hurtling earthward towards the canopy of the Peruvian jungle.

What would you think if you were in her place at that moment? What strikes Gonzales is Koepcke's recollection of her thoughts as she fell. Her mind was not filled with shrieking terror, or a hastily pulled together prayer, or feelings of regret. No, Koepcke remembered "thinking that the jungle trees below looked just like cauliflowers." She was moving into her new reality. She passed out while still falling, and when she regained consciousness sometime later, she was on the ground, still strapped into her chair. Her collarbone was broken. There was no sign of anyone else. She decided that the planes and helicopters she could hear flying above would never be able to see her because of the thickness of the tree canopy so she began to walk out of the jungle.

Central to Gonzales's thesis about resiliency is that those who survive a life-threatening crisis see the future as unmapped. Thus Koepcke, falling two miles upside down through a storm, didn't think the obvious thought—that her future was already clearly mapped out. Instead, she was struck by the appearance of the Peruvian forest from above. And when she came to later, having crashed through the canopy, she didn't think—or didn't only think—the obvious thought about what lay ahead for a seventeen-year-old girl without her glasses, walking alone in a jungle, barefoot, slapping the ground with her one remaining shoe to frighten off the snakes that she couldn't see well enough to avoid. She walked for eleven days while she was, as Gonzales described it, "being literally eaten alive by leeches and strange tropical insects." On the eleventh day, Koepcke found a hut and collapsed inside. The next day, as chance would have it, three hunters came by, discovered her, and got her to a doctor.

Gonzales is interested in this question: Why did Koepcke survive this crash, while "the other survivors took the same eleven days to sit down and die"? Gonzales identifies a number of reasons, besides blind luck, for Koepcke's survival. First, rather than follow rules, she improvised. Second, although she was afraid, as the other survivors surely were, she used that fear as a resource for action. And third, while many better-equipped travelers have succumbed to much lesser challenges, Koepcke had "an inner resource, a state of mind" that allowed her to make do with what the moment offered.

As Gonzales pursues his research further, he finds other traits that resilient people share in common: they use fear to focus their thoughts; they find humor in their predicaments; they remain positive. The list goes on, but the item that most interests us is Gonzales's admonition that to survive a crisis, one must "see the beauty" in the new situation:

> Survivors are attuned to the wonder of the world. The appreciation of beauty, the feeling of awe, opens the senses. When you see something beautiful, your pupils actually dilate. This appreciation not only relieves stress and creates strong motivation, but it allows you to take in new information more effectively.

After we read this, it was hard not to ask: If it's possible for someone to be attuned to the wonder of the world when confronted by a situation that is *life threatening*, could writers in far less dire circumstances cultivate this attunement as a habit of mind?

Here's why this connection suggested itself to us: from our years teaching writing, we know how terrifying and humbling the confrontation with the blank screen and the flashing cursor can be—for beginning writers and experienced writers alike. This confrontation is not life threatening, of course, but it can nevertheless trigger fears: Do I have anything worth saying? Can I make myself understood? Will the struggle with the blank screen be worth it in the end? These questions arise because the act of writing, when used as a technology for thinking new thoughts, takes us to the edge of our own well-marked path and points to the uncharted realms beyond.

Ultimately, each time a writer sits down to write, he or she chooses just how far to venture into that unknown territory. To our way of thinking, the writing prompt, properly conceived, is an invitation to embark into unmapped worlds, to improvise, to find unexpected beauty in the challenges that arise. We know from experience, though, that learning to approach writing this way takes practice, and that without such practice, the writing produced in response to a prompt tends to reject whatever is unfamiliar and huddle around whatever is obvious and easiest to defend.

We have designed the prompts in this book to help you use your writing to bring you to the edge of your understanding, to a place where you encounter what is unknown to you. The more you practice using your writing in this way, the further you will be able to take your explorations; you'll find yourself moving from writing about what is unknown to you to what is more generally unknown, and then to what is unknowable. Making this journey again and again is the essence of the examined life; the writing you do along the way tracks your ongoing encounter with the complexity of human experience. The more you do it, the more you know; and the more you know, the more connections you can make as you work through your next encounter with what is unknown to you. You'll never make it to absolute knowledge, but the more you practice, the more comfortable you'll be with saying, "I don't know, but I'm sure I can figure it out."

Or so we say.

We can pose our position as a challenge: Can you make your writing trigger an inner journey that is akin to falling from a plane over the Amazon, with everything that seemed solid and certain just moments ago suddenly giving way, question leading to question, until you land on the fundamental question, "What do I know with certainty?"

We all can count on being faced with challenges of comparable magnitude over the course of our lives—the death of a loved one; the experience of aging, disease, separation, and suffering; a crisis in faith; a betrayal of trust. Writing, properly practiced, is one way to cultivate the habits of mind found in those who are resilient in moments of crisis: openness, optimism, calm, humor, and delight in beauty.

PRACTICE SESSION ONE

WRITING

One could say that seeing the future as unmapped is something children do, and that part of growing up is learning to have reasonable expectations about what the future holds. What interests Gonzales is how a person responds, regardless of his or her age, when disaster strikes. When the plane you're on splits in half miles above the Earth, it's reasonable to assume that your future is mapped: you are going to die. Gonzales's contention is that those who respond to disaster by suspending that sense that the future is known have, perhaps paradoxically, a better chance of surviving.

The thing is, you don't know how you're going to respond to hugely significant and unexpected events until they happen. What is the most unexpected event that has taken place in your life so far? What made it unexpected? How did you respond to this confrontation with the unknown? In the event, did you settle into the moment, or did your sense of what the future held remain constant and unshaken?

Spend at least an hour writing a profile of how you responded to the unexpected. Feel free to discuss what you would do differently if given another chance, knowing now what you didn't know then.

PRACTICE SESSION TWO

REFLECTING

The kinds of crises that interest Gonzales have a cinematic quality to them: planes split apart in midair; a hiker is trapped, miles from anyone else, with his arm pinned by a boulder; a mountain climber dangles over the edge of a cliff, his partner unable to pull him to safety. (Indeed, the last two cases have been made into major motion pictures.) But writers rarely find themselves in predicaments of this kind; their crises tend to be internal and to center on getting to the heart of a matter, finding a way to express a fugitive truth, struggling to put a new thought into words.

What has been the most striking event in your *mental* life? A crisis of faith? An existential crisis? A realization that your way of thinking about love or friendship, truth or beauty, justice or politics, or any other of the concepts that are central to human experience was grounded in a false assumption? How did you respond to this confrontation with the unknown? What happened to your experience of time while this event unfolded? Did you find yourself living from moment to moment, or did your sense of what the future held remain clear?

Spend at least an hour writing a profile of how you responded to the most striking event in your mental life. Feel free to discuss what you would do differently if given another chance, knowing now what you didn't know then.

PRACTICE SESSION THREE

RESEARCHING

Choose a reading and write an essay that describes the writer's strategies for confronting the unknown. In tales of survival and resiliency, it is common to stress the hardships confronted and overcome, as well as acts of courage and ingenuity. If these terms strike you as out of place in a discussion of a writer grappling with a question, then provide terms of your own that you find more appropriate.

EXPLORE

What constitutes "the unknown" can take many forms. Jo Ann Beard writes about a radical change in her personal circumstances. Charles Mann imagines a world where people live to be 150 years old. Neil deGrasse Tyson discusses the edge of scientific understanding. And Amy Wallace looks at the deadly consequences of responding to life's uncertainties with inaction. Whatever form "the unknown" takes, writing about an encounter with it involves a confrontation with fear and an effort to get that fear under control.

Beard, Jo Ann. "The Fourth State of Matter." *New Yorker.* 24 June 1996. Web.

Mann, Charles C. "The Coming Death Shortage." *Atlantic.* May 2005. Web.

Tyson, Neil deGrasse. "The Perimeter of Ignorance." *Natural History.* Nov. 2005. Web.

Wallace, Amy. "An Epidemic of Fear: How Panicked Parents Skipping Shots Endangers Us All." *Wired Magazine.* 19 Oct. 2009. Web.

On Joining the Conversation

The literary critic Kenneth Burke described the exchange of academic ideas as a never-ending parlor conversation. "Imagine," he wrote,

> that you enter a parlor. You come late. When you arrive, others have long preceded you, and they are engaged in a heated discussion, a discussion too heated for them to pause and tell you exactly what it is about. In fact, the discussion had already begun long before any of them got there, so that no one present is qualified to retrace for you all the steps that had gone before. You listen for a while, until you decide that you have caught the tenor of the argument; then you put in your oar. Someone answers; you answer him; another comes to your defense; another aligns himself against you, to either the embarrassment or gratification of your opponent, depending upon the quality of your ally's assistance. However, the discussion is interminable. The hour grows late, you must depart. And you do depart, with the discussion still vigorously in progress.

With this extended metaphor, Burke offers us a way to think about how to write academic arguments. Preparing to write a paper about a topic that is new to you is like entering a parlor where a "heated discussion" is already taking place. For a while, all you can do is read what others have written and try to follow the debate.

Then, after a bit, you begin to figure out what's being discussed and what the different positions, conflicts, and alliances are. Eventually, after you catch the "tenor" or drift of the conversation, a moment arrives when you feel you have something to contribute to the conversation, and you "put in your oar." And so you begin writing, even as you know that you won't have the last word—that no one will ever have the last word.

Doubtless, there is much about Burke's vision of academic writing that won't surprise you: to write, you need to understand what others have written about the problem or question that intrigues you, and you must be able to represent, analyze, and synthesize those views. You also have to be interested enough in joining the conversation to develop a position of your own that responds to those sources in compelling ways. What *is* surprising about Burke's scenario is that the conversation never ends: it is "interminable." There are no decisive arguments in Burke's parlor, or even any strongly persuasive ones; there is only the ceaseless exchange of positions.

Why, it's reasonable to ask, would anyone choose to engage in a conversation without end? To answer this question, we'd like to walk you through an example of a writer working with multiple sources to explore an open-ended question.

Magazine journalist Michael Pollan writes about places where nature meets culture: "on our plates, in our farms and gardens, and in the built environment." In his article "An Animal's Place," Pollan grapples with the ideas of Peter Singer, a philosopher and the author of an influential book, *Animal Liberation*, which argues that eating meat is unethical and that vegetarianism is a moral imperative. Pollan makes his own view on meat eating clear from the very first sentence of "An Animal's Place": "The first time I opened Peter Singer's *Animal Liberation*, I was dining alone at the Palm, trying to enjoy a rib-eye steak cooked medium-rare." He's being purposely outrageous, dramatizing his resistance to what he knows of Singer's ideas. But he hasn't yet read *Animal Liberation* and he knows that engaging with Singer's text is going to be a challenge, because it's "one of those rare books that demands that you either defend the way you live or change it."

When Pollan opens *Animal Liberation* at his table at the Palm, he transforms the steakhouse into his own Burkean parlor. Having entered the conversation late, he tries to catch "the tenor of the argument." He discovers that Singer not only opposes eating meat but also objects to wearing fur, using animals in experiments, or killing animals for sport. While these practices may seem normal today, Singer argues that they will someday be seen as expressions of "speciesism," a belief system that values humans over all other beings, and that will be looked back upon, in Pollan's phrasing, as "a form of discrimination as indefensible as racism or anti-Semitism." At the core of Singer's book is this challenging question: "If possessing a higher degree of intelligence does not entitle one human to use another for his or her own ends, how can it entitle humans to exploit nonhumans for the same purpose?"

Pollan discovers that, although Singer's ideas were far from mainstream when *Animal Liberation* was first published in 1975, Singer's campaign for animal rights has since gained many intellectual, legal, and political allies. At the time that Pollan's article was published in November 2002, German lawmakers had recently granted animals the constitutional right to be treated with respect and dignity by the state, while laws in Switzerland were being amended to change the status of animals from "things" to "beings." England had banned the farming of animals for fur, and several European nations had banned the confinement of pigs and laying hens in small crates or cages. In the United States in 2002, such reforms had not yet been addressed by legislation, but today animal rights are no longer a fringe issue.

Pollan also discovers that a crowd of scholars and writers is clustered near Singer in Burke's parlor. Among them is Matthew Scully, a political conservative and former speechwriter for President George W. Bush who wrote *Dominion: The Power of Man, the Suffering of Animals, and the Call to Mercy*, a best seller about the routine cruelty toward animals in the United States. Also present is eighteenth-century philosopher Jeremy Bentham, who argued that even though animals cannot reason or speak, they are owed moral consideration because they can suffer. Beside Bentham are legal scholar Steven M. Wise and the contemporary philosophers Tom Regan and James Rachels, and off to the side is novelist J. M. Coetzee, who declares that eating meat and purchasing goods made of leather and other animal products is "a crime of stupefying proportions," akin to Germans continuing with their normal lives in the midst of the Holocaust.

Pollan wants to resist Singer's insistence on the moral superiority of vegetarianism, but before he can build his argument, he needs to find his own allies in the ongoing conversation. He is intrigued by John Berger's essay "Why Look at Animals?" which argues that humans have become deeply confused about our relationship to other animals because we no longer make eye contact with most species. This helps Pollan to explain the paradox that, even as more and more people in the United States are eager to extend rights to animals, in our factory farms "we are inflicting more suffering on more animals than at any time in history." From sources as varied as Matthew Scully's *Dominion* and farm trade magazines, Pollan learns that these farms, also known as Confined Animal Feeding Operations, or CAFOs, reduce animals to "production units" and subject them to a life of misery.

But these sources don't particularly help Pollan to stand up against Singer's insistence that everyone who considers eating meat must choose between "a lifetime of suffering for a nonhuman animal and the gastronomic preference of a human being." Unhappy with either option before him—to refuse to pay attention to the suffering of animals in factory farms or to stop eating animals—Pollan brings a completely new voice into the parlor: not a philosopher or a writer, but a farmer. Joel Salatin, owner of Polyface Farm in Virginia, raises cattle, pigs, chickens, rabbits, turkeys, and sheep on a small farm where each species, including the farmer himself, performs a unique role in the ecosystem. The cows graze in the pasture; afterward, the chickens come in and eat insect larvae and short grass; then the sheep take their turn and eat what the cows and chickens leave behind. Meanwhile, the pigs compost the cow manure in the barn. In this system, the mutual interest of humans and domestic animals is recognized, even when the animals are slaughtered for meat. In life, each animal lives according to its natural inclinations; and when it is slaughtered, its death takes place in the open. Nothing is hidden from sight. Pollan concludes that slaughtering animals, where the process can be watched is "a morally powerful idea." Salatin convinces him that animals can have respectful deaths when they are not, as they are in factory farms, "treated as a pile of protoplasm."

Pollan's visit to Polyface Farm is transformational. He decides that "what's wrong with animal agriculture—with eating animals—is the practice, not the principle." The ethical challenge, in other words, is not a philosophical issue but a practical one: Do the animals raised for meat live lives that allow them to express their natures? Do they live good lives? Pollan decides that, if he limits his consumption of meat to animals that are raised humanely, then he can eat them without ethical qualms. Pollan is so pleased with his creative solution to the problem Singer posed that he even writes to the philosopher to ask him what he thinks about the morality of eating meat that comes from farms where animals live according to their nature and appear not to suffer. Singer holds to his position that killing an animal that "has a sense of its own existence" and "preferences for its own future" (that is, a pig, but not a chicken) is wrong, but he also admits that he would not "condemn someone who purchased meat from one of these farms."

Does this mean that Pollan has won the argument? Not really. The discussion in Burke's parlor has not ended. New voices have entered to engage with both Pollan and Singer, and new ideas have emerged about sustainability, agriculture, economics, and ethics. Curious, reflective, and open-ended thinkers continue to enter, mingle, and depart, "the discussion still vigorously in progress."

PRACTICE SESSION

REFLECTING

For this exercise, we'd like you to read Michael Pollan's "An Animal's Place" and think more about how he uses sources and what it means to be "in conversation" with words on a page or screen. Read the piece with care, taking notes about where and how Pollan uses his sources to develop his own thoughts. After reading, take at least 30 minutes to write answers to these questions about entering into a conversation with sources: Where did Pollan engage with sources in ways that surprised you? Where did he use sources in ways that you'd like to emulate? What different kinds of conversations did Pollan engage in with his sources? Why did he choose to be in conversation with some sources more than others? What have you learned from these exercises about writing "in conversation" with sources?

READING

Next, we'd like you to read Harriet McBryde Johnson's "Unspeakable Conversations." Johnson's article is also in conversation with Peter Singer, but unlike Pollan, Johnson is primarily interested in Singer's controversial views on euthanasia. Read the article with care, observing the many different ways Johnson joins in conversation with her sources. To start, you might notice sources that serve as the focus of analysis; supply background or information; provide key ideas or concepts; provide positions or arguments to grapple with; or shift the direction of the conversation.

After you've read, spend at least 30 minutes making a list of the many ways Johnson uses her source material. Notice that she may name or quote some sources explicitly, while not identifying every source of information. This is one way in which journalistic writing differs significantly from academic writing, where, of course, all sources must be cited.

WRITING

Now that you've read both "An Animal's Place" and "Unspeakable Conversations," we'd like you to compose an essay in which you enter a conversation with Pollan and Johnson and answer the question: To what extent is it possible to define what makes a "good life" (or a "good death") for humans and other animals? Use Pollan's and Johnson's essays both as sources and as models of how to join a conversation in writing.

EXPLORE

Essays about ethical quandaries invite readers to join the fray. Michael Pollan challenges philosopher Peter Singer on the ethics of eating meat. Harriet McBryde Johnson also argues with Singer, but she objects to his stance on the ethics of killing severely disabled newborns. We invite you to join those conversations, and also to see how biologist Sandra Steingraber connects the words of early environmentalist Rachel Carson, author of *Silent Spring*, to current debates about the dangers of fracking.

Johnson, Harriet McBryde. "Unspeakable Conversations." *New York Times Magazine*. 16 Feb. 2003. Web.

Pollan, Michael. "An Animal's Place." *New York Times Magazine*. 10 Nov. 2002. Web.

Steingraber, Sandra. "The Fracking of Rachel Carson." *Orion Magazine*. Sept./Oct. 2012. Web.

Curiosity at Work: Rebecca Skloot's Extra-Credit Assignment

Rebecca Skloot's best-selling book, *The Immortal Life of Henrietta Lacks,* tells the story of a poor African American woman in Baltimore who was hospitalized with cancer in 1951. Before Lacks died, a surgeon removed some of her cancer cells for research without her knowledge, and they were used to grow human cells in a lab for the first time. Lacks's cells, now known as HeLa cells, are still alive today and have been essential to medical research for more than sixty years. Every person who has received a polio vaccine or who lives in a country where polio has been eradicated, for example, is a direct beneficiary of research that used HeLa cells. And yet, before Skloot's book, few people knew of Henrietta Lacks and her immortal cells.

The path that led Skloot to write Lacks's story was long and circuitous. At age sixteen, Skloot registered for a community college biology course to make up the credit she lost when she failed the subject during her freshman year of high school. When the class was studying cell division, Skloot's teacher, Mr. Defler, told his students about HeLa cells and then wrote HENRIETTA LACKS in big letters on the blackboard. He told them that Lacks had died of cervical cancer, that a surgeon had taken a tissue sample from her tumor, and that "HeLa cells were one of the most important things that happened to medicine in the last hundred years." Before erasing the name from the board and dismissing the class for the day, Mr. Defler added one more fact: "She was a black woman."

Skloot followed her teacher back to his office, asking questions: "Where was she from? Did she know how important her cells were? Did she have any children?" Lacks's life is a mystery, Mr. Defler told her, and then he made the kind of comment teachers make: "If you're curious, go do some research, write up a little paper about what you find and I'll give you some extra credit."

That night, Skloot couldn't find any information on Lacks beyond a parenthetical reference in her biology textbook, but she didn't forget about this mysterious woman whose cells had helped protect millions from contracting polio. Some ten years later, when Skloot was working on her undergraduate degree in biology, she took her first writing course, and the teacher began by asking the students to "write for 15 minutes about something someone forgot." Skloot immediately scrawled "Henrietta Lacks" on her page and wrote about how Lacks had been forgotten by the world. Over time, Skloot resolved to write "a biography of both the cells and the woman they came from." As her commitment to her project deepened, her research became "a decade long adventure through scientific laboratories, hospitals, and mental institutions, with a cast of characters that would include Nobel laureates, grocery store clerks, convicted felons, and a professional con artist." She met Lacks's five adult children and their families, which raised new questions for her about race, ethics, and medical research, among them: If Henrietta Lacks's cells were so important to medical science and had given rise to a multibillion-dollar industry, why couldn't Lacks's children and grandchildren afford health insurance?

More than two decades after Rebecca Skloot first heard the name Henrietta Lacks, she finished her book. Putting her research skills to use once more, she tracked down the biology teacher who first told her about HeLa cells and sent him a note: "Dear Mr. Defler, here's my extra credit project. It's 22 years late, but I have a good excuse: No one knew anything about her."

Note: The quotations in this essay are from Rebecca Skloot's blog post, "What's the Most Important Lesson You Learned from a Teacher?" *Rebeccaskloot.com* 8 May 2012.

CHAPTER 2

Paying Attention

Is it possible to write without paying attention? At first the question seems absurd: How could words move from your brain to your keyboard if you weren't paying attention? Writing doesn't just happen. And yet people text while walking and even while driving, which shows that writing happens all the time without one's full attention. And of course, students can now write papers while also surfing the Net and snapchatting their friends.

Funnily enough, a common response to the mistakes that happen as a result of being distracted is the command to "pay attention." You step off the curb into oncoming traffic and are pulled back to safety by a friend just before you would have been hit. "Pay attention!" You're sitting in class daydreaming when your teacher calls on you. "Pay attention!" You're in a crowd and walk directly into a stranger. "Pay attention!" In each case, the command arrives too late: it's less helpful guidance than it is a rebuke.

We want you to think of writing not as a way of proving you *were* paying attention but as a way *of* paying attention. To this end, we've populated this chapter with essays that explore how writing can be used to train the mind to focus and the eye to see. We also explore using your writing to reflect on how you think and on how you imagine the thoughts of others. When you use writing in these ways, you are practicing being engaged with and interested in the world.

On Learning to See

When Betty Edwards started teaching high school art classes in the late 1960s, she was baffled as she watched her students having trouble drawing simple, familiar objects. If they could see that the orange was *in front of* the green bottle, why did they draw the two objects *next to* each other? Why was it that the ability of her students to express themselves verbally and to reason mathematically had improved from kindergarten to high school, but their ability to draw hadn't changed much since the third grade? And when her students eventually figured out how to produce drawings that were more accurate, why did the improvement seem to take place all at once rather than gradually?

Around the time that Edwards was pondering why students who learned easily in academic classes had so much difficulty in art class, neuroscientists Roger W. Sperry and Michael Gazzaniga began publishing reports that suggested that the two sides of the brain did different kinds of mental work. The left hemisphere, where language was typically housed, was more systematic and linear. The right hemisphere was more visual, spatial, and synthetic. Once Sperry and Gazzaniga's research got picked up by the popular press, it was reduced to a simple binary opposition: the right brain is creative and the left brain is analytical.

Edwards used this research to make sense of the difficulty her students had seeing what was right in front of them as well as the breakthroughs they experienced when they suddenly began to see differently. In Edwards's view, students were rewarded in their academic classes for being verbal and analytical thinkers; they were required, one could say, to be left-brained. But to draw well, they needed access to visual, perceptual, and synthetic thought; they needed to find a way to see with the right brain. To trigger this apparent hemispheric shift for her students, Edwards developed exercises that quieted the verbal, analytical, and systematizing thinking rewarded elsewhere in the curriculum, so that visual, creative, and associative thinking could come to the fore. As she developed these exercises, Edwards was beginning to understand that, in order to learn how to draw, her students had to stop naming what they were trying to draw and start seeing what was in front of them in a new way—as related lines and connected spaces without names. If they stopped saying "hand," for example, they could learn to stop drawing the symbol for a hand (five stick fingers at the end of a stick arm) and could instead begin to see the intricate pattern that is made by a particular hand resting on the edge of a particular keyboard.

Edwards's explanation of the brain's two dominant operational modes makes a kind of immediate, intuitive sense; indeed, it makes it sound like all you really have to do to draw is to learn how to toggle the switch between your left brain and right brain. The truth, though, is that both the brain and learning how to draw are more complicated than the model of a sharp division between left-brain and right-brain function suggests. We now know from neuroscience that it is more accurate to say that activity in the right hemisphere is *correlated* with creative and divergent thinking and that activity in the left hemisphere is *correlated* with analytic and convergent thinking. While the right part of your brain contributes a good deal to creative potential, your whole brain has to work in concert for you to engage in creative work.

In *A Whole New Mind*, Daniel Pink describes attending a drawing class based on the methods developed by Edwards and learning just how difficult it is to get the whole brain to play along with this new way of seeing. His first attempt at drawing a self-portrait while looking at his face in a mirror was simply terrible. The eyes, nose, and lips were clumsy cartoon versions of these basic components of the human face. Pink's placement of these features in his drawing was equally cartoonish and bore little relation to where the eyes, nose, and mouth are found on a real human face. Pink couldn't draw what was right in front of him, the most familiar, recognizable part of himself, because his preconceptions about faces—which his teacher called "remembered symbols from childhood"—blinded him to the actual contours of the face looking back at him in the mirror. To draw better, Pink needed to stop naming, analyzing, and judging what he saw and practice seeing and sketching lines, patterns, relationships, and relationships between relationships. He had to practice finding increments of simplicity in complex patterns of lines and spaces.

We believe that the kind of seeing Edwards aims to trigger through her teaching practice is a specific instance of the kind of seeing that lies at the core of creative thinking. Indeed, Edwards herself says that "this ability to see things differently has many uses in life aside from drawing—not the least of which is creative problem solving." So, although it surely seems contradictory, we adapted a couple of Edwards's exercises meant to restrain the dominance of language to serve our own interest in having you think differently about the role of language in the creative process.

PRACTICE SESSION ONE

WRITING

Draw a self-portrait. Start by finding a spot with a mirror and plenty of light where you can work comfortably for at least 30 minutes. Using a pencil and a blank sheet of paper, draw your face. Do your best, and don't give up before you've got all your facial features looking back at you. The drawing may look awful, and that's okay.

Next, look carefully at the shape of the features and the relationships between features and think about how and why your portrait turned out as it did. What went right? Where did you successfully transform perception into image? What went wrong? What did you *not see* as you were drawing? How did you feel while you were completing this exercise? How did you feel when you were done? Why?

As a final step, take at least 15 minutes to write an assessment of the act of seeing that generated your self-portrait.

PRACTICE SESSION TWO

REFLECTING

In the 1940s, a psychologist named Karl Duncker developed a test of problem solving that's popularly known as "the candle problem." The challenge posed to participants is to figure out how to attach a lit candle to a wall without it dripping on the floor below. To complete the challenge, participants can use only the objects pictured here:

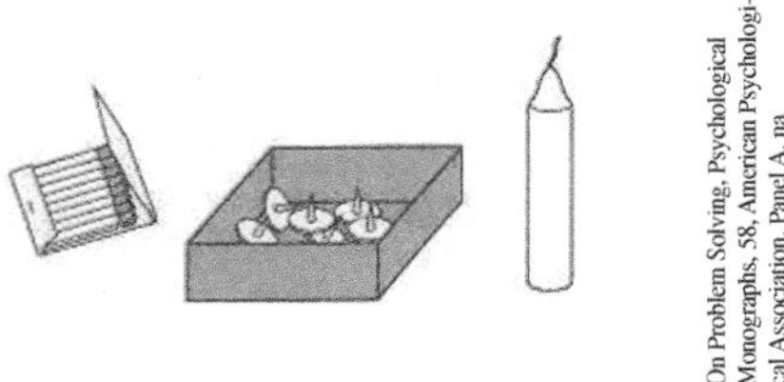

On Problem Solving, Psychological Monographs, 58, American Psychological Association. Panel A, na

FIGURE 2.1 Karl Dunker Candle Problem.

Take as much time as you need to figure out how you would solve the candle problem, and then write down your solution.

Next, watch Daniel Pink's TED talk, "The Puzzle of Motivation." Pink begins talking about the candle problem and its solution at around the two-minute mark, but we want you to listen to the talk in its entirety. Take notes while you're watching, writing down anything Pink says that surprises you.

After you've listened to Pink's TED talk, we'd like you to spend 45 minutes writing a reflective piece that considers the role seeing played in your response to the candle problem. Did solving the candle problem require a new way of seeing, a new way of thinking, or both? What do you think the implications of the candle problem are for learning?

EXPLORE

Writing about seeing is often precipitated by the experience of learning to draw. John Berger has been drawing his entire life. Adam Gopnik earned a BA and MA in art history but didn't learn to draw until middle age. A classical pianist before changing careers, Peter Mendelsund is a self-taught artist who designs book covers for a living. Each of these writers explores the relationship between how we see the world and how we put the world of our experience into words.

Berger, John. *Bento's Sketchbook: How Does the Impulse to Draw Something Begin?* New York: Pantheon, 2011. Print.

Gopnick, Adam. "Life Studies: What I Learned When I Learned to Draw." *New Yorker.* 27 June 2011. Web.

Mendelsund, Peter. *What We See When We Read.* New York: Vintage, 2014. Print.

On Looking and Looking Again

"Pay attention!"

Walk the hallways of any elementary school, and it won't be long before you hear this exasperated command. Over time, all students learn that what their teachers mean when they say "pay attention" is "sit still and be quiet." The teachers know, of course, that there's more to paying attention than being quiet, but what that "more" turns out to be is something that can't be ordered into existence by the voice of another. So students learn early on how to get their bodies to behave in class, but getting their minds to behave is another matter.

The paradox at the beginning of the process of paying attention seems irresolvable: How does mental focus emerge out of chaos, the attentive mind out of distraction? How does anyone ever learn the inner work of paying attention?

Our answer is: by practice.

But what kind of practice? How does one practice a state of mind?

The poet William Blake offers some guidance on how to think about this paradox in the opening stanza of his poem "Auguries of Innocence":

> To see a World in a Grain of Sand
> And a Heaven in a Wild Flower
> Hold Infinity in the palm of your hand
> And Eternity in an hour

On a first reading, Blake's stanza seems to offer a straightforward proposition about how to trigger a state of deep attentiveness: if you want X (to see the world in a grain of sand), then do Y (hold infinity in the palm of your hand). But if this is what it takes to pay attention, attentiveness of the kind Blake describes seems an impossibility, for how is one supposed to go about grabbing hold of infinity or experiencing "eternity in an hour"?

Perhaps we've misread the stanza. Perhaps Blake is making a statement both about what paying attention involves and what it makes possible: "To see a world in a grain of sand and heaven in a wild flower [is to] hold infinity in the palm of your hand and eternity in an hour." Read this way, Blake's verse is saying that, if you can learn to "see a world in a grain of sand" or "a heaven in a wild flower," you can gain access to realms beyond what you know and even beyond the limits of thought—you can reach the infinite and the eternal.

From Blake's poem we could conclude that the practice of writing poetry has trained Blake's mind to focus on the particular (a grain of sand, a wildflower) until it leads to something much bigger (a world, a heaven) and onward to realms beyond measure (infinity, eternity). More generally, we can say that Blake shows us that the attentive mind generates insights, connections, and beautiful objects and moves by inference, analogy, and metaphor.

Does this mean that, instead of commanding a distracted student to "pay attention" teachers should try saying, "sit still and be a poet"?

That command wouldn't work any better than the command to pay attention, of course: first, even the best poet can't be a poet on command; and second, poetry is only one possible result of paying attention.

Better by far, we think, to say, "Practice looking and looking again."

A teacher we greatly admire, Ann Berthoff, developed an exercise that we've adapted here to help you experience the kind of seeing Blake describes. To get her students to resee the natural world, Berthoff would bring to class all manner of organic objects—a starfish, the husk of a cactus, dried reeds, a pressed flower—and then have each student take one of the objects home to study for a week.

For our version of this exercise, you'll need to select your own organic object—anything from the natural world will do. You should choose something that you can hold in your hand and that you can put somewhere out of harm's way for a week.

We ask that, for seven straight days, you spend at least 10 minutes recording your *observations* of the object you've selected.

Here's an example of what a day's entry might look like, written by Erik on day five:

> Clearly the plant is dehydrated and dying, and yet, besides my dismembering it of its limbs, it still has the same form and design as it did when I first took it home. The colors of the leaves have noticeably changed, but nothing else has visibly changed as far as I can tell. Of course, the way I'm seeing this object has changed since the first day I laid my eyes upon it.

> There are definitely patterns that are quite unmistakable in and on this plant. For instance, the mini-stems that connect the buds to the stem that connects back to the entire organism: there are seven of these mini-stems, and they are all about of equal length. That is interesting. If it is sunlight the buds seek, I would think that maybe one of the mini-branches would push itself considerably farther out so as to receive more energy for its own survival. But, naturally, these buds are probably not competing for energy but rather are working together for the survival and health of the entire plant.
>
> I cannot help but draw a connection to a human body here. You can find multi facets and numerous parts and functions of parts within a single limb of a body. In fact, you can find it in one single human cell. . . . I'm reminded of a quote from Aldous Huxley [who was quoting from William Blake]: "If the doors of perception were cleansed, every thing would appear to man as it truly is, infinite." A person is not just a person with a name, a height and a weight, and a social status; each person is also composed of electricity, of a billion cells that perform who knows how many functions.
>
> My plant here, at first glance, is just a little piece of a shrub. But if you really look at it, there is a lot going on here that makes this plant what it is. Can the physical world ever be described as infinite? Do we really actually know, in an empirical sense, of anything that is infinite? Why do we have a "word" describing something that we have never experienced? Is that evidence or a suggestion from our subconscious mind, our inner spirit, our unseen self, that there is such a thing as infinity? Is there infinity present in my little piece of shrub? I don't know, but I'm willing to bet that as more powerful microscopes are developed, there will surely be more we will be able to "see" in the physical universe around us, and this will further lend credence to the idea that, yes, with a necessary perspective, it may be possible to hold infinity in the palm of your hand. You won't know it unless you have eyes to see it, or take the time to meditate on it, and even then . . . infinity is a tough thing to swallow and ascribe to what we can perceive with our five senses. But it's not impossible.

Focusing on the plant stem, Erik makes connections to the human body, to a quote he's read in Aldous Huxley, and then back to the Blake poem we used in our writing prompt. Looking closely allows Erik to see beyond the plant back into his own mind. Thinking about how the plant is organized becomes, in this instance, a way to think about how all minds organize perceptions.

PRACTICE SESSION

WRITING

Choose an organic object from the natural world, something that you can hold in your hand and that you can keep out of harm's way for a week. Then, over seven consecutive days, write for at least 10 minutes each day about what you see.

Describe how your object is put together.

What questions does your object pose?

What does it point to?

Where did it come from?

What is it a part of?

You are free to move your object, to alter it, or to interact with it in any way that furthers your effort to understand how it is put together. You can also read and do research if questions come to mind. Your goal is to see how your object is organized within itself and how it is implicitly connected with other natural objects.

Write every day.

Ponder what your observations and explorations tell you about the object.

Write even if you're stuck.

If you try to sketch your object, does that help you see aspects you would otherwise miss? What if you photograph it?

Write even if you think you've said all there is to say about your object.

There's only one rule: don't anthropomorphize your object. Don't give it a human name. Don't invent a dialogue between yourself and your object. We've found that this approach only serves to obliterate the object—it displaces the act of looking and looking again.

REFLECTING

After you've completed your seven days of writing, reread what you've written with the following questions in mind: At the end of all your looking, how would you describe the organization of your organic object? Based on what you've written, how would you describe your own way of looking? What did you see right away? What did it take you a while to see? What kinds of questions did you ask automatically? What kinds of questions emerged late in the process?

Write an essay that reflects on what this exercise of looking and looking again has helped you to recognize about seeing in general and about paying attention in particular.

EXPLORE

Looking, learning, and rethinking can turn the ordinary into something extraordinary. Rachel Carson, Annie Dillard, and Michael Pollan each look at familiar objects or places until they become strange and surprising. Carson lingers by a sea cave that appears only at the year's lowest tide. Dillard looks for hidden treasures in the natural world: monarch pupae, flying squirrels, the streak of green light that bursts from the sun at the moment of sunset. And Pollan explores an orchard with 2,500 varieties of apple trees, including an ancient species from Kazakhstan that may be the origin of all apples.

Carson, Rachel. "The Marginal World." *The Edge of the Sea.* Boston: Houghton Mifflin, 1998. 1–7. Print. (Available on Google Books via preview.)

Dillard, Annie. "Total Eclipse." *Teaching a Stone to Talk: Expeditions and Encounters.* New York: HarperCollins, 1982. 9–28. Print. (Available on Google Books via preview.)

Pollan, Michael. "Breaking Ground: The Call of the Wild Apple." *New York Times.* 5 Nov. 1998. Web.

On Encountering Difficulty

In his essay "The Mind's Eye," the neurologist Oliver Sacks confronts the conundrum of free will: "To what extent are we—our experiences, our reactions—shaped, predetermined, by our brains, and to what extent do we shape our own brains?" He is led to this conundrum by consideration of a series of cases of individuals who were born with sight but then became blind. The point that Sacks wants to make in "The Mind's Eye" is deceptively simple: how one responds to becoming blind is idiosyncratic—that is, it is unique to the individual. Sacks did not always think this was the case. Initially, he assumed that responses to going blind were determined by the structure of the human brain and thus were essentially uniform.

Sacks begins his essay by describing an extreme example of what is thought to be the typical response to going blind, where the other senses gain heightened powers as the ability to see recedes. After John Hull, blind in one eye due to cataracts at seventeen, went completely blind at forty-eight, he steadily lost access not only to his visual memories but to what Sacks terms "the very idea of seeing." In this profound state of "deep blindness," Hull claimed that spatial references such as "here" and "there" lost meaning for him. At the same time, he became what he calls a "whole-body seer," someone whose other senses have roared to life to compensate for the loss of vision and who now experiences wholly new ways of engaging with the world.

After first writing about Hull in 1991, Sacks began to hear from others whose own experiences of becoming blind conflicted with this compensatory model of how senses covered for each other. For example, Zoltan Torey's response to going blind was the exact opposite of Hull's: instead of embracing "deep blindness" when he lost his sight in an accident at the age of twenty-one, Torey cultivated the powers of his "inner eye," self-consciously laboring to hold on to his ability to think with and manipulate visual images. What Torey has done since going blind is almost unthinkable: he learned to multiply four-figure numbers by visualizing the operations as if the calculation were written on a blackboard; he taught himself to move and manipulate three-dimensional images in his mind, breaking them apart and recombining the pieces; he even single-handedly replaced the roof on his gabled home. What motivates Torey? A deep need to retain a sense of the visual.

Then there's Sabriye Tenberken, blind since twelve, who has traveled extensively in Tibet, often alone, advocating for the blind. She has cultivated a rich synesthetic inner world, one full of color and feeling, which allows her to use words to paint elaborate and fanciful descriptions of the outside world. While Torey visualizes highly detailed maps and diagrams of the real world, Tenberken delights in holding on to an inner vision that is poetic and playful.

Sacks started out looking for a neurological explanation of these varied responses to becoming blind—i.e., that whereas Hull's visual cortex had atrophied completely, Torey was able to "stave off an otherwise inevitable loss of neuronal function in the visual cortex" as a result of his mental gymnastics. But when Sacks turns his attention to people who can see, he quickly finds a similar range in the visual imagination of sighted individuals: some seeing people can hold images in their minds and manipulate them as Torey does; some, akin to Hull, cannot generate visual images or call them to mind; others can achieve the ability to visualize in great detail only through chemical enhancement.

Where does this leave us? For Sacks, the fact that both the blind and the seeing share a spectrum of possible ways to visualize the outer world illustrates the difference between brain and mind. The power to see has a physical, neurological basis located in the brain. What happens to those impulses once the brain processes them is determined not by the brain alone but by "the higher and more personal powers of the imagination, where there is a continual struggle for concepts and form and meaning, a calling upon all the powers of the self," which we would call *the mind*. Sacks continues:

> Imagination dissolves and transforms, unifies and creates, while drawing upon the "lower" powers of memory and association. It is by such imagination, such "vision," that we create or construct our individual worlds.

Thus, at the level of the individual, there will always be a measure of mystery in the adaptations that occur in response to radical change. We see this mystery as much in Hull's embrace of deep blindness as in Torey's tending the flames of inner vision—in the interplay between the hardwiring of neurology and the software of the self. Such a mystery cannot be unraveled by science alone because the self simultaneously resides in and is created by the work of the imagination as it connects and transforms the memories and associations recorded by and stored in the brain.

To put this another way, we could say that our inner lives are both created and sustained by the imagination; and further, that in times of radical change the very survival of the self depends on imagining what was previously unimaginable—that life without sight is sensually rich, for example, or that one's blindness should be fully embraced. This observation doesn't resolve the mystery, of course, but only further sharpens it: How does one cultivate an imagination capable of such adaptation? How does one learn to live with and within new forms of embodied experience?

PRACTICE SESSION ONE

RESEARCHING

If you are blind or visually impaired, skip this exercise and go to Reflecting (for blind or visually–impaired students) on the next page. If you are sighted, visit the online *Time* magazine photo gallery *Photos by Blind Photographers*. The opening blurb says that the exhibit "raises extraordinary questions about the nature of sight." What do you see when you look at these photographs taken by photographers who are legally blind? How do the words that accompany each image influence what you see? Can you unsee the words and consider the images simply as photographs? Search the Web for other works by these photographers and for the work of other blind photographers. Follow your curiosity.

REFLECTING (FOR SIGHTED STUDENTS)

How do blind photographers teach the sighted to see? Using examples of images you have collected through your research, write a reflective essay about what you've learned about blindness and the imagination.

REFLECTING (FOR BLIND OR VISUALLY-IMPAIRED STUDENTS)

Consider what the sighted could learn about perception through a representation of your experience. John Hull offers such a representation when he describes the intensity of experiencing rain as a "whole-body seer":

> Rain has a way of bringing out the contours of everything; it throws a colored blanket over previously invisible things; instead of an intermittent and thus fragmented world, the steadily falling rain creates continuity of acoustic experience....The sound on the path is quite different from the sound of the rain drumming into the lawn on the right, and this is different again from the blanketed, heavy, sodden feel of the large bush on the left. Further out, the sounds are less detailed. I can hear the rain falling on the road, and the swish of the cars that pass up and down.

Write a reflective essay that represents your experience of your environment. Does your experience strike you as idiosyncratic? That is, did your individual character, temperament, or will play a role in your perception of your environment?

PRACTICE SESSION TWO

WRITING

John Hull, Zoltan Torey, and Sabriye Tenberken help Sacks to see the power of the individual imagination in shaping how one responds to trauma. But what about ordinary, everyday problems? Does the imagination come into play when confronting a problem that is not life altering?

Choose a mundane problem that arises in the course of your day: a disagreement with a family member; difficulty finding parking; misplacing your keys. Does this sort of problem, in its solution, yield evidence of the uniqueness of each individual's imagination? Or do mundane problems call for mundane solutions? Write an essay that explores multiple ways of solving an everyday problem, and consider whether your example demonstrates the powers of the human imagination.

PRACTICE SESSION THREE

RESEARCHING

Choose an essay and, while reading it, mark the moments when the author encounters difficulty. When you're done, review the passages you've marked. Are all the difficulties of the same kind? Of the same importance? Of the same intensity?

How does the writer respond to these difficulties? Write an essay in which you examine the writer's approach to difficulty. Although you might be tempted to say that the writer's approach is simply "idiosyncratic," explore in greater detail how the writer responds to difficulty that's encountered in the world of ideas and words.

EXPLORE

Our essay on encountering difficulty works with four examples of how people have responded to losing the ability to see. The material we suggest here further complicates our discussion. Michael Finkel profiles a blind man who sees like a bat. Filmmakers Peter Middleton and John Spinney interpret John Hull's audio-diary of his journey into blindness. A photo gallery showcases images created by people who are legally blind.

Finkel, Michael. "The Blind Man Who Taught Himself to See." *Men's Journal*. March 2011. Web.

Hull, John. "Memory," "Panic," and "Rainfall." Supplements to Peter Middleton and John Spinney's "Notes on Blindness." Audio. *New York Times*. Web.

Middleton, Peter, and John Spinney, directors. "Notes on Blindness." *New York Times*. 16 Jan. 2014. Web.

Photos by Blind Photographers. Time n.d. Web.

Curiosity at Work: David Simon Pays Attention to the Disenfranchised

David Simon has excelled as a writer in many different roles: police reporter in Baltimore; author of two award-winning books, *Homicide: A Year on the Killing Streets* and *The Corner: A Year in the Life of an Inner-City Neighborhood;* screenwriter for *Homicide*, a television series based on his book of the same title; head writer for the HBO series *The Wire*; and cocreator and coproducer of the HBO series *Treme*. In 2010, he was awarded a no-strings-attached $625,000 MacArthur "Genius" Fellowship, which the MacArthur Foundation says "is not a reward for past accomplishment, but rather an investment in a person's originality, insight, and potential." Not bad for a guy who graduated from the University of Maryland with a C average.

What made it possible for Simon to move from cub reporter to chronicler of the collapse of American cities? The decades Simon spent on the beat in Baltimore made him comfortable with not knowing in advance what he was going to see or hear or report: "To be a decent city reporter, I had to listen to people who were different from me. I had to not be uncomfortable asking stupid questions or being on the outside. I found I had a knack for walking into situations where I didn't know anything, and just waiting." Simon learned to listen closely to the people of Baltimore and to pay attention to their multiple points of view. Because of the way he listened, he fell in love with the crime-ridden, impoverished city.

Why has Baltimore gone from being a major US port to a city with one of the highest murder rates in the country? This is a problem that can't be answered in a sound bite. It takes Simon five seasons of storytelling in *The Wire* to bring to light the multiple variables that work together in postindustrial capitalism to create the toxic conditions in which humans are worth less and less with every passing moment, while glistening new buildings rise on Baltimore's Inner Harbor. These rapacious economic and social forces can't be understood in isolation; they have to be seen in action, degrading the value of the lives of gang members as well as those who work in the police force, the failing shipping industry, the city government, the public school system, and the local newspapers. Like a contemporary Charles Dickens, Simon employs a large canvas, multiple intersecting plotlines, and memorable hard-luck characters to voice his critique of the widening gap between the haves and the have-nots.

In the four seasons of *Treme*, Simon continues exploring the fate of American cities, this time focusing on New Orleans after Hurricane Katrina. Looking beyond the image of New Orleans as the Big Easy, a place where the good times always roll, Simon tells stories about the city's recovery from the hurricane through the eyes of local musicians, a neighborhood bar owner, a "Big Chief" in the Mardi Gras parades, a civil rights attorney, and a jazz musician who has made good in New York. Why does he use storytelling and not journalism or the documentary form to do this work? Simon explains: "By referencing what is real, or historical, a fictional narrative can speak in a powerful, full-throated way to the problems and issues of our time. And a wholly imagined tale, set amid the intricate and accurate details of a real place and time, can resonate with readers in profound ways. In short, drama is its own argument."

Note: The first Simon quote is from Margaret Talbot's *New Yorker* article, "Stealing Life"; the second quote is from "HBO's 'Treme' Creator David Simon Explains It All for You," published in the *New Orleans Times-Picayune.*

CHAPTER 3

Asking Questions

"There are no bad questions": this is an incantation repeated year in and year out in classrooms across the country. It represents a well-intentioned effort to establish a comfortable learning environment, but it's a hard sell, since teachers and students alike know that not only are there bad questions, but there are whole categories of questions that are unwelcome in the classroom. There are questions most teachers dread—the intrusively personal question, the cynical question, and the do-you-mind-repeating-what-you-just-said question, to name a few—and there are questions most students dread, such as the teacher's guess-what-I'm-thinking question, the teacher's fill-in-the-blank question, and the question that exposes the student who asked it to ridicule.

Rather than make the demonstrably false assertion that there are no bad questions, we prefer to ask: What is a good question? In this chapter, we introduce you to two of our favorite question posers, the hosts of *Radiolab*. We also propose an alternative to the thesis-driven writing project: writing your way to a question. And we look at how to prepare for an interview-based project. Questions you hear, questions produced by your own speculative writing, questions you put to others: we give you three different contexts for considering the roles that context, expertise, research, and curiosity play in the production of good questions.

On Asking Questions

We're devoted fans of *Radiolab*, a radio show and podcast on which the hosts, Jad Abumrad and Robert Krulwich, invite listeners to join them "on a curiosity bender." Abumrad is a composer by training and won a MacArthur Fellowship in 2011 for his work on the show, while Krulwich is a science correspondent with over three decades of broadcast experience. Working together, they make the exercise of being curious about the world *sound* like an exciting adventure.

In each show, Abumrad and Krulwich assume the air of happy amateurs who delight in having simple questions open up complex realities. They typically begin with a big question—about science, the arts, medicine, philosophy, or some other aspect of human experience—and then spend an hour exploring a range of responses to the question they've posed. The questions they ask often express an open-minded wonder about the world: Why do we sleep? What is color? What is race? How do we assign blame? To help them with their explorations, they always turn to experts, but they never take what the experts have to say as the final word on the matter. They question, provoke, and at times openly disagree with their guests and with each other.

There's a common pattern in most *Radiolab* shows: Abumrad and Krulwich move back and forth between questions, big ideas, interviews, and stories, inevitably leading their listeners to new problems and new questions, and revealing in the process that the issue they started with is more complicated than it first seemed. We admire how they move from simple wonder to complex possibilities, and we like that multiple answers, insights, and solutions are entertained along the way. We also like that *Radiolab* sounds beautiful. It's important to recognize that the creative soundscapes Abumrad and Krulwich produce are more than mere entertainment. In every episode, they demonstrate how curiosity can generate beauty as well as answers and ideas.

What we admire most about *Radiolab* is that the hosts manage to express in sound and language the whole spectrum of habits of the creative mind. You can hear Abumrad's creativity as a composer in the ways he uses sound to represent ideas that might otherwise remain too abstract for listeners to grasp. You can hear how open both men are to ambiguity, the unknown, and discovery as Abumrad and Krulwich talk their way through the implications of what they're learning. You can also hear their attention to and engagement with ideas, information, and expertise in the questions they ask. And you can hear their reflectiveness as thoughts digress, reverse, and surprise. Most of all, you can hear their boundless curiosity at work in the shape and progress of each episode.

We'd like you to listen to two episodes of *Radiolab*—one scripted, one open ended—so that you can hear what curiosity as a habit of mind sounds like.

PRACTICE SESSION ONE

LISTENING

In "An Equation for Good," a chapter in *Radiolab*'s "The Good Show" podcast, Abumrad and Krulwich consider an open-ended question that has puzzled evolutionary biologists since Charles Darwin first advanced his theory that species evolve through struggle and competition. If the "fittest" survive through tooth-and-claw rivalry, how can we explain kindness, generosity, and altruism?

Find a quiet place where you can listen to "An Equation for Good" without interruption; the podcast is about 22 minutes long. Use headphones or earbuds so you don't miss a thing.

Next, listen to the podcast again, this time pausing it when necessary to write down the questions Abumrad and Krulwich ask; this is likely to take more than 30 minutes. Keep track of where each question leads. What people and sources do Abumrad and Krulwich turn to for answers? What stories do they tell? Is there a logic to the overall shape of the show? An aesthetic?

WRITING

Spend at least 30 minutes creating a visual map that illustrates the development of the hosts' thinking as "An Equation for Good" unfolds. When do their ideas move in a straight line? When do their questions cause a change in direction? Do they ever take wrong turns? If so, are any of the resulting digressions useful? By the end of "An Equation for Good," how far have Abumrad and Krulwich traveled? What do they conclude about the status of the definition of *evolution* as "the survival of the fittest"? (Note: You might want to experiment with making your map "move"; feel free to use presentation and/or animation software to bring your map to life.)

After you've created your map, pause to reflect on what you've learned. What does your map reveal about Abumrad and Krulwich's methods? Could someone else look at your map and understand what you've learned about how the show is structured? If not, how is what you've produced a map?

PRACTICE SESSION TWO

LISTENING

Next, we'd like you to listen to the *Radiolab* podcast "Secrets of Success," a conversation between Robert Krulwich and Malcolm Gladwell, author of *The Tipping Point*, *Blink*, and *Outliers*. This podcast shows how questions unfold when a curious person talks at length to a single expert, trying to understand the development and reach of the expert's ideas while also puzzling through whether to accept the expert's conclusions.

Find a quiet place where you can listen without interruption; the interview is about 25 minutes long. Don't forget your earbuds.

When you're done, set aside more than 30 minutes to listen to the podcast again, this time pausing to write down the questions and other prompts Krulwich uses to get Gladwell to explain his ideas about talent, practice, passion, and success.

WRITING

Set aside at least 30 minutes to create another map that illustrates the unfolding conversation between Gladwell and Krulwich. When does Krulwich move the discussion in a straight line? When does he seem to change direction? Do any apparent digressions end up looping back to serve the main argument? Are there other digressions that take the conversation off track? Are you convinced by Gladwell's responses to Krulwich's questions?

PRACTICE SESSION THREE

REFLECTING

After you've created maps for both "An Equation for Good" and "Secrets of Success," look at them side by side. Spend at least 30 minutes considering what they show you about how curiosity works and how understanding and arguments develop. What do you see that helps you to think about how you might compose a curiosity-driven essay or podcast about a big question like "How can we explain why humans sometimes go out of their way to help strangers?" or "Is there a secret to success?" What are some open-ended questions you'd like to read, listen, or write about?

EXPLORE

We're drawn to works of nonfiction that are question-driven. The podcast *Radiolab* asks questions about anything and everything, including time, tumors, blame, mosquitos, quicksand, and the power of music. While *Radiolab* jumps from topic to topic, the captivating podcast *Serial* devotes twelve episodes to one subject—an investigation into whether a man was wrongfully imprisoned for the 1999 murder of a Maryland teen. Law professor Ruthann Robson asks questions about a different kind of case, one that emerges after she is misdiagnosed with cancer, suffers through chemotherapy and medical mistreatment, and then considers both what her life is worth, and what matters more to her than money.

Radiolab. Podcast.

Robson, Ruthann. "Notes from a Difficult Case." *In Fact: The Best of Creative Nonfiction*. Ed. Lee Gutkind. New York: Norton, 2005. 226–44. Print.

Serial. Season One. Podcast.

On Writing to a Question

What's writing for? In school, the most common answer given to that question is, "To make a point." And so in school one practices having a point that can be succinctly stated in a thesis statement. "Writing is for making points" is itself an example of a succinct thesis statement.

We think the requirement to *start* an essay by committing to a thesis is a good way to kill curiosity. It turns writing into a mindless fill-in-the-blank exercise: Thesis? Check. Three examples? Check. Conclusion that summarizes the previous three paragraphs? Check. This approach to writing is a machine for arguing the obvious; it does not use writing as a tool for thinking new thoughts or for developing ideas that are new to the writer.

For your writing to become a mode of learning for you, you must begin in a state of not-knowing rather than committing yourself to a claim you came up with before you've done any curiosity-driven research. In the "Curiosity at Work" profiles in this book, we showcase a wide range of nonfiction writers who use writing as a mode of learning. Consider the divergent cases of Donovan Hohn and Rebecca Skloot.

Donovan Hohn, a high school English teacher, was reading a student's paper when he first learned about the plastic bath toys—yellow ducks, green frogs, blue turtles, and red beavers—that began washing ashore in Alaska and Australia in the early 1990s. Curious, he began to do some research online. Caught up in the mysteries, he left his job and traveled the earth to follow the path of the toys. He recorded his journey of discovery in his book *Moby-Duck*.

Rebecca Skloot was sixteen years old and taking a biology class when she learned that the first human cells ever grown in a lab were from an African American woman named Henrietta Lacks. Skloot wanted to know more about Lacks, but her teacher had no additional information, and at the time Skloot couldn't find anything more in the library. Many years later, when Skloot decided to become a writer, she tracked down Lacks's family and pieced together Henrietta Lacks's history and the history of her cell line. Then Skloot wrote the best-selling book *The Immortal Life of Henrietta Lacks*.

Neither of these writers began with a thesis that they then set out to prove. Rather, each started with a question and pushed past simplistic discussions of pollution or racism to develop a deeper, richer understanding of the situation's complexity. But where did the questions that Donovan and Skloot began with come from? Were the questions the result of inspiration or just dumb luck?

While there's always an element of chance in any research project, we think you learn how to ask the kinds of questions that stick with you for years by cultivating the habit of generating questions. How does this process work? Once you've developed the habit of generating questions about things that are taken for granted and about things unknown, you will find that you have many questions to choose from and many possible paths to explore. Some questions will seem more important than others, some will nag at you, and some will seem urgent; the very best questions will have all of these attributes.

To help our students develop the intertwined habits of curiosity and questioning, we've adopted a drafting strategy that throws out the familiar essay form. We ask our students instead to write frequent short papers in response to readings, and we tell them that these papers should not contain thesis statements.

At first they're baffled. How can you even begin an essay without a thesis? We tell them to just go ahead and give it a try. We instruct them to look in the assigned readings for moments when an author

- says something surprising or confusing;
- makes an unexpected connection;
- presents a provocative example;
- uses a familiar term in a new or peculiar way;
- or poses an idea or argument that is difficult to accept.

Freed from having to begin with a thesis statement, our students use their responses to readings to puzzle through surprising, confusing, or provocative passages. Consequently, when they write, they aren't reporting what the author said and then agreeing or disagreeing with it; they are focusing on interesting moments in which they sense a tension between their own thoughts, knowledge, or expectations and what an author has written.

Once they've written their way through a passage or a series of passages, we ask them to conclude their response papers with a reflection on what they've figured out over the course of developing their responses. Ideally, their exploration of moments of tension leads them to a compelling question or questions, which they pose in the final sentences of their responses. These should be questions that they can't presently answer and that require more thought, reading, and research—questions they are truly curious about and *want* to answer.

Right now you might be wondering, what's the point of writing to a question you can't answer? Isn't exposing your own ignorance the exact opposite of what you should be doing in school? Good questions!

We think there are many good reasons to use informal writing and drafting to arrive at a compelling question. When you write about passages or ideas in a text or set of texts that confuse or interest you, you are learning to use writing as a tool for thinking. And you'll see that writers discover what they think not *before* they write but *in the act* of writing. You'll also learn how to take more risks with your thinking. Ending with a question you don't know the answer to may feel uncomfortable at first—as if you're revealing a weakness. But openly confronting what you don't know is an essential part of learning to write well. Paradoxically, by writing to a question in a draft, you'll learn how to generate a truly interesting thesis. Once you've drafted a question that you're genuinely curious about, you're ready for the next step: figuring out how to respond to that question. Your response will be a thesis that's worth writing and reading about. Writing to a question also gives you practice with the essential habits of the creative mind: curiosity, openness to new ways of thinking, engagement with learning, and intellectual adventurousness.

PRACTICE SESSION ONE

REFLECTING

Are you a curious person? Do you express your curiosity most often in school, among your friends, at work, or elsewhere? You may not know the answers to these questions, so we'd like you to pay attention to your own curiosity for a week. Take notes every day, keeping an account of when, where, and how you pose questions, whether out loud to others or silently to yourself.

At the end of the week, spend at least 30 minutes reviewing your notes and learning about your own curiosity. When and where were you most curious? How often did you ask questions in classes? Did you pose more questions in one class or another? Did you ask questions as you read, jotting questions in the margins or in your notes? What was your most vivid experience of curiosity-driven learning in the past week? Was it in school or elsewhere?

PRACTICE SESSION TWO

READING

In the list of suggested readings in this essay's "Explore" section, on p. 39, each writer presents his or her central question in the article's subtitle: "What Should Medicine Do When It Can't Save Your Life?"; "Did American Conservationists in Africa Go Too Far?"; "Why Are We So Fat?"; "Is It a Crime?" Read one of the suggested readings, paying attention to how the writer answers the question posed in the subtitle. Trace how the writer's answer to the main question develops as the piece progresses.

Spend 30 minutes taking notes on how the answer to the question unfolds. Does the writer reverse or qualify your expectations? Are additional questions posed, explicitly or implicitly, that shift the direction of the writer's inquiry or reshape your understanding of the issue?

REFLECTING

In our essay, we describe how we ask our students to write to a question. Now we want you to give it a try.

Return to the reading you selected and review it, looking for moments in the argument that catch your attention—passages that are surprising or confusing, make an unexpected connection, present a provocative example, use a term in a new or peculiar way, or pose an idea or argument that is difficult to accept. Then write a draft in which you explore three or more parts of the reading that you find interesting or baffling—places where you feel friction between the text and your own thoughts, knowledge, or expectations.

In the final paragraph of your draft, reflect on what you've learned about the ideas or argument in the reading you selected, and pose a question that has emerged from your work with the passages you've chosen. The standard for assessing the quality of the question you've generated is this: Do you genuinely want to answer it?

WRITING

Having arrived at an interesting question, you can now write an essay that allows you to develop your thoughts and figure out your answer. Bring a version of your question into your essay's title or subtitle, as the writers of the suggested readings do. Then go about answering it, working with the reading you selected and the passages you wrote about, as well as any other passages that now seem relevant.

EXPLORE

At the beginning of Practice Session Two, we draw your attention to the subtitles of the essays listed below: each one poses a difficult question and each question leads readers into realms of ambiguity, uncertainty, and ethical confusion. It's unlikely these writers began with their questions already formed; they began instead with challenging cases: a pregnant mother who learns she is going to die; a conservation effort that leads to killings; a graph that shows an explosion in American obesity in the 1980s; a man who forgot to drop his toddler off at daycare and the terrible consequences that followed. Only after much reading, researching, drafting, and revising did the big issues crystalize: How should medicine treat the dying? What is the human cost of protecting endangered species? What has caused an "epidemic" of obesity? And can a terrible mistake also be a crime?

Gawande, Atul. "Letting Go: What Should Medicine Do When It Can't Save Your Life?" *New Yorker.* 2 Aug. 2010. Web.

Goldberg, Jeffrey. "The Hunted: Did American Conservationists in Africa Go Too Far?" *New Yorker.* 5 April 2010. Web.

Kolbert, Elizabeth. "XXXL: Why Are We So Fat?" *New Yorker.* 20 July 2009. Web.

Weingarten, Gene. "Fatal Distraction: Forgetting a Child in the Backseat of a Car Is a Horrifying Mistake. Is It a Crime?" *Washington Post.* 8 March 2009. Web.

On Interviewing

Creative nonfiction, defined by Lee Gutkind as "true stories, well told," is often focused on a personal profile: a portrait of a hero or villain, a talented athlete, or an attractive star. Some of the work in this genre features individuals who are distinctive because of their unusual interests or their exceptional abilities, but there is also work that focuses on those who have earned attention because of circumstance or an accident of history. We are particularly drawn to profiles of individuals contending with contingency, such as Anne Fadiman's account of a Hmong family struggling to take care of a gravely ill child in *The Spirit Catches You and You Fall Down* and Jon Krakauer's portrait of a young, idealistic college grad who dies while camping in Alaska in *Into the Wild*. We also admire writing that unveils mysterious, socially marginal figures, such as Susan Orlean's description of an eccentric Florida orchid hunter in *The Orchid Thief*; and Truman Capote's voyage into the minds of two murderers in the *locus classicus* of the creative nonfiction genre, *In Cold Blood*.

Capote, who is credited with inventing creative nonfiction, once said that the genre requires a writer "to empathize with personalities outside his usual imaginative range, mentalities unlike his own, kinds of people he would never have written about had he not been forced to by encountering them inside the journalistic situation." For Capote, the writer of creative nonfiction must go beyond the journalist's commitment to neutrally reporting verifiable information and must instead, via empathy, strive to reconstruct the assumptions, beliefs, and feelings of another person. For Capote, describing the murders was a relatively simple matter: two drifters break into a farmhouse, kill the owners and their two teenage children, and escape with nothing, having been misinformed about the presence on the property of a safe stuffed with cash. But finding a way into the murderers' inner worlds was a much steeper challenge. How could Capote understand the thinking of the men behind these unthinkable acts? And why would he even want to try?

Once the murderers were captured, Capote interviewed them repeatedly over a three-year period—during and after their trial, throughout their efforts to appeal their convictions, and up to the time of their executions. He also interviewed townspeople, family members of the deceased, family members of the murderers, police officers, jailers, and other inmates. To make sense of the minds behind this senseless act of violence, Capote had to work long and hard. What they had done was clear, but why they had done it could be understood only through painstaking research and leaps of the imagination.

Getting inside the heads of cold-blooded killers—that's the outer limit of the impetus driving creative nonfiction. The more general desire motivating work in this genre is a deep curiosity about how others make sense of the world—and those others can be just about anyone: a family caring for a child in a persistent coma; a young man dissatisfied with the emptiness of contemporary life; a guy who searches swamps for orchids and sells them in an international black market. The realm of creative nonfiction enables us to grapple with the most profound difference there is: what life is like in the mind of another.

• • • • •

The journalist's most important tool for understanding others is the interview. How does one learn to interview? The first rule is easy: be curious.

The art and craft of interviewing, like writing, takes practice. Your first few efforts might feel clumsy, but as you gain experience, conducting interviews gets easier. As you begin, these general guidelines will make the process easier and the results more useful.

Before the Interview

- Choose a time and a place for the interview that will put the interviewee at ease. You need to be able to hear each other, so select a location that doesn't distract from the conversation or invite interruptions from others.
- Draft your questions ahead of time, but before you draft them, spend time on background research. Then generate questions that your background research *can't* answer.
- Bring everything you need for note taking to the interview. You'll need paper and pencil or a laptop, of course. If the interview subject agrees to be recorded, you can also bring equipment for making an audio or a video recording. (We find that an audio recording is preferable, because the presence of a video camera often causes the interviewee to speak as if on television.) Be sure to get your subject's permission in advance to record the interview.

During the Interview Itself

- After you ask a question, pause and wait for an answer. Give your interview subject time to think. If she or he is truly stumped, ask whether you should rephrase the question.
- If your interview subject says something you don't understand or refers to something unfamiliar to you, don't be embarrassed to ask more questions.
- Listen carefully to what your interview subject says and how he or she says it.
- Give yourself permission to improvise. Your interview should feel like a conversation, not an interrogation. For this to happen, you need to be willing to stray from what you've written down and follow the interview subject down any unexpected paths the conversation has revealed.

A Cautionary Tale

A while back, we were teaching a course in which students were researching a number of nearby development projects. In one case, the developer had taken down an entire block of local businesses and was in the process of putting up a high-rise of condos and apartments. The developer agreed to meet and discuss his vision of New Brunswick with the team of students working on the case. The students did their research, and at the appointed time, they sat down with the developer in his office, the model of his redevelopment plans laid out in front of his panoramic view of the city.

The lead interviewer asked the developer about the number of apartments he anticipated renting out to students in the new high-rise.

"None," the developer told them. The high-rise wasn't being built for students.

The interview effectively ended at that point, though other questions followed. The students had done research, but their research did not help prepare them for this particular interview with this particular person. They had their one shot with a very busy local entrepreneur, and they used it to ask a question about a matter of concern to them. Unfortunately, the way their question was phrased revealed that they had not imagined a world in which students might not be the central concern. They were, in essence, asking the entrepreneur why he didn't see the world the way they did, instead of using the interview to better understand how *the entrepreneur* viewed the development project and why he viewed it that way.

To the students' credit, they realized that the interview had failed because they had not posed questions that would solicit useful material. So they started over: they drafted a whole new set of questions and requested another chance. In this instance, they were lucky enough to be granted a second interview, but interviewers can't count on their subjects giving them multiple shots, especially if, in their first shot, they seem unprepared, have chosen a poor location, or fail to show that they value the interviewee's time.

Moral?

You may only get one shot. Make it count.

PRACTICE SESSION ONE

READING

Read Gene Weingarten's "Pearls before Breakfast," which is available online at washingtonpost.com, and watch the videos embedded in the article. As you read, keep notes on the many people Weingarten interviews for his article and on how he goes about discovering what and how they think.

After you've read and thought about Weingarten's article, spend at least 30 minutes reviewing your notes and reflecting in writing on Weingarten as an interviewer. When do you think he's most successful at gathering compelling or surprising points of view? Identify instances in which Weingarten elicits a particularly important idea or revealing insight from someone he interviews. How does Weingarten use what he learns from interviews to develop his own thoughts? What does he do as an interviewer that you would like to emulate?

PRACTICE SESSION TWO

RESEARCHING

As preparation for writing a nonfiction profile, spend a week researching a little-known subculture or group at your school or in your community. The deeper the mystery, the better. (Over the years, we've had students write about underground music scenes, fire throwing—look it up!—urban gardening, religious practices, body modification, and a dance-influenced Brazilian martial art called *capoeira*.) Your research will require both observing and interviewing.

Begin by doing background research about the activity or subculture. If it's possible to attend a group activity—a performance, a practice session, a ceremony—do so. Observe, listen, and take notes. Describing the activity or subculture will be part of the challenge when you begin to write; you will need to bring the unknown and unfamiliar to light.

The other part of the challenge is getting inside the minds of the participants. You will need to interview at least one participant in depth. Conduct an interview that's at least 30 minutes long, keeping careful notes and, if your subject agrees, recording the conversation. Do your best to ask questions that invite your subject to tell stories. Try to figure out why she or he finds participation in the activity or group *meaningful*.

After you've conducted your interview, you're ready to write a profile. Compose a curiosity-driven essay that explores the subculture or group your interviewee belongs to and its meaning or value.

REFLECTING

Take at least 30 minutes to reflect on your experience as an interviewer. Review your notes and the recording you made (if there is one). Then look over the essay you wrote. Where did your use of the interview work best? What would you do differently in your next interview? What do you need to practice to get better results?

EXPLORE

There's an art to the interview. Anne Fadiman, Jon Krakauer, Janet Malcolm, and Susan Orlean each composed book-length nonfiction narratives that grew out of months, even years, of listening, learning, and asking questions. Their prose portraits display both intimate insights and evidence of the mysteries that remain after their interviews ended. We also invite you to read the transcripts of writers interviewing other writers in *The Paris Review* and *The Believer.*

The Believer. Interviews with writers from 2003 to the present. Web.

Fadiman, Anne. *The Spirit Catches You and You Fall Down.* New York: Farrar, Straus and Giroux, 1997. Print.

Krakauer, Jon. *Into the Wild.* New York: Villard, 1996. Print.

Malcolm, Janet. *The Journalist and the Murderer.* New York: Knopf/Random House, 1990. Print.

Orlean, Susan. *The Orchid Thief.* New York: Random House, 1998. Print.

The Paris Review. Interviews with writers, from 1953 to the present. Web.

Curiosity at Work: Michael Pollan Contemplates the Ethics of Eating Meat

What would history look like if it were told from the vantage point of the plant world? This provocative question drives Michael Pollan's *The Botany of Desire*, in which he considers how plants that satisfy the human desire for sweetness (apples), beauty (tulips), pleasure (marijuana), and sustenance (potatoes) have transformed the global landscape. By shifting to "a plant's-eye view," Pollan is able to see anew how the fate of the plant kingdom is inextricably linked to human desire.

In "An Animal's Place," published shortly after *The Botany of Desire*, Pollan moves from the plant world to the animal world to consider the personal, political, and moral puzzles involved in something many people take for granted: eating meat. Pollan begins his essay as a committed meat eater, one who is frustrated by the argument Peter Singer makes in *Animal Liberation* that eating, wearing, or experimenting on animals violates animals' right to live free of suffering caused by humans.

Pollan responds to his frustration with Singer by posing questions and noticing contradictions. Why is it that 51 percent of Americans believe that primates should be extended the same rights as human children, while at the same time "in our factory farms and laboratories we are inflicting more suffering on more animals than at any time in history"? Why are we so confused about our relationship to animals?

From there, Pollan's questions emerge in a steady stream. "When's the last time you saw a pig?" he asks. Is the fact that animals lack certain human characteristics a just basis for raising them for slaughter on factory farms? Pollan is especially intrigued by a question posed by eighteenth-century philosopher Jeremy Bentham, who wrote that we ought to make moral decisions about animals not by asking whether animals can reason or talk—questions that render them less than human—but rather by asking, "Can they suffer?"

And the questions keep coming. "Why treat animals more ethically than they treat one another?" "Wouldn't life in the wild be worse for these farm animals?" "Doesn't the fact that we could choose to forgo meat for moral reasons point to a crucial moral difference between animals and humans?" "What's wrong with reserving moral consideration for those able to reciprocate it?" Do "we owe animals that can feel pain any moral consideration, ... and if we do ... how can we justify eating them?" And finally, "were the walls of our meat industry to become transparent, literally or even figuratively, ... who could stand the sight?"

Pollan's train of thought leads him to a question posed in the title of critic John Berger's essay "Why Look at Animals?" Berger was concerned, says Pollan, that "the loss of everyday contact between ourselves and animals—and specifically the loss of eye contact—has left us deeply confused about the terms of our relationship to other species." Pollan agrees and concludes that if we looked animals in the eyes, and if we created the conditions in which we were also able to look without disgust or shame at how we raise and slaughter them, then we could eat animals "with the consciousness, ceremony, and respect they deserve." In two subsequent books, *The Omnivore's Dilemma* and *In Defense of Food,* Pollan has sought to better understand how to live in accordance with this insight.

Note: For additional discussion of Michael Pollan's "An Animal's Place," see "On Joining the Conversation" on **p. 11**.

CHAPTER 4

Exploring

Our first history lessons in school are often about "the explorers." Christopher Columbus discovered America; Vasco da Gama discovered the overseas route from Europe to India; Marco Polo opened trade routes in Asia. These captivating stories involve adventure, courage, bravery, and derring-do. There are skirmishes, riches beyond imagining, kings and queens—all sorts of things to fire the imaginations of the young.

Later on, we learn that these stories have been simplified and that exploration itself is rarely the process of moving peacefully through unoccupied, unclaimed territories. Some find the revision of these earlier stories to be upsetting and somehow wrong. But we believe that those who practice being curious with their writing are learning how to explore both the worlds beyond and the worlds within the self. This isn't exploration as represented in fairytales and childhood stories of questing heroes. It's the messier, more disorienting, more complicated work that making sense of human experience and human history demands.

The first essay in this chapter likens exploration in the Internet age to Alice's trip "down the rabbit hole" and invites you to use your search engines to practice chasing ideas, thoughts, and questions wherever they may lead. In the second essay, we suggest that there is an activity called "creative reading" that parallels creative writing, and in the third essay, we show you how the process of understanding others (as opposed to conquering them) requires acts of imagination, informed by research. Why would anyone want to engage in explorations of these kinds? We close this chapter with a meditation on the mystery of motivation.

On Going down the Rabbit Hole

"Down the rabbit hole": it's a strange phrase, isn't it? If you've heard it before, it's possible that the first thing it calls to mind is the scene in *The Matrix* where Morpheus offers Neo two pills: "You take the blue pill—the story ends, you wake up in your bed and believe whatever you want to believe. You take the red pill—you stay in Wonderland,

and I show you how deep the rabbit hole goes." In the inside-out world of *The Matrix*, reality is an illusion and what seems illusory—that time can be slowed down, that bullets can be dodged, that gravity only applies intermittently—is actually possible in a deeper reality.

Morpheus (the name Ovid gives the god of dreams in his long poem *Metamorphoses*) refers to "Wonderland" and "the rabbit hole" on the assumption that Neo—and those watching the film—will make the connection to Lewis Carroll's *Alice's Adventures in Wonderland*. In that story, a young girl named Alice is sitting on a riverbank, bored with how the day is going, when a rabbit carrying a pocket watch rushes past her. Alice follows the rabbit, who disappears down a rabbit hole. She sticks her head in and begins to fall down the hole, and what follows is a series of adventures that has captivated generations of readers for nearly 150 years.

Think of all that happens to Alice in the few pages that make up the first chapter of her *Adventures*: when she finally hits bottom (when she sees how deep the rabbit hole goes), the rabbit is just turning a corner in another long tunnel, so she gives chase. When she turns the same corner, Alice finds herself in a long hallway with doors on each side, all of them locked. Then she discovers a key that opens a very small door, which leads to a beautiful garden on the other side. Because she is too big to fit through the door, Alice keeps exploring the hallway. She finds a bottle with a note that says DRINK ME. Alice complies, and suddenly she's "shutting up like a telescope" until she's only ten inches tall. She wants to go into the garden but can no longer reach the key to open the small door, and so she begins to cry. She looks down, discovers another small door, opens it, and finds a small cake with the words EAT ME written on top in currants. Which Alice does, of course, leading to this statement at the beginning of the second chapter:

> "Curiouser and curiouser!" cried Alice (she was so much surprised, that for the moment she quite forgot how to speak good English); "now I'm opening out like the largest telescope that ever was! Good-bye, feet!" (for when she looked down at her feet they seemed to be almost out of sight, they were getting so far off).

Why is this idea, which is at the heart of both *The Matrix* and *Alice's Adventures in Wonderland*, so appealing? Why do we take such pleasure in imagining that there's the world we experience every day and that, just beyond this everyday world (or just beneath it, assuming rabbit holes go down), there's another world where the laws of the everyday world no longer apply? One explanation for this fantasy's appeal is that the other extraordinary world is action packed: once the rules that govern the ordinary are suspended, anything can happen—rabbits can talk; bodies can bend out of the way of approaching bullets; a boy with a scar on his forehead can fight off the forces of evil. But this isn't really an explanation so much as it is a description masquerading as an explanation. Why are we drawn to the extraordinary?

Ellen Dissanayake has spent nearly five decades exploring the allure of the extraordinary. Working in evolutionary aesthetics, a field she helped to invent, Dissanayake has concluded that humans are hardwired to seek out the extraordinary; it is, she says, in our nature to do so. In making her argument, Dissanayake sets out to establish that the desire to "make special" or to "artify" (she uses both terms interchangeably) serves a number of evolutionary purposes central to the survival of the species—the most significant being that acting on this desire provides concrete responses to anxiety and uncertainty. Over time, certain ways of making special become ritualized: the wedding ceremony or the walk across the graduation stage, for example, or the gift of flowers to someone who is sick. What we find appealing about Dissanayake's thesis is the implication that art is not the set of static images you find on a wall at a museum. Rather, it is a way of doing or making; it's the practice of making special, which can manifest at anytime—at the feast for a visiting dignitary or over coffee between friends.

Is there an art to doing research? We think so. Most handbooks will send you out to do your research with a plan, an outline, or a map of some kind. The idea behind all this preplanning is to protect you from getting lost while mucking about in the endless thicket of information that's out there. That seems sensible if you think of research only as the process of predicting and then confirming results. That is, when this approach to research is followed, it's no accident that the end results are unsurprising; the whole point of this approach to doing research is that there will be no surprises!

We invite you to envision the research process not as a voyage out onto already mapped territory but as a trip down the rabbit hole. We want you to set for yourself the goal of generating research that is extraordinary—research that proceeds by "making special," by "artifying." We want your research to lead you to write something that rewards repeated acts of attention, which, after all, is just another way of defining *extraordinary*.

What does artful, special, or extraordinary research look like? Obviously, there's no formula. But we'd like to offer an example of what it can look like with an excerpt from an e-mail we received from Chris Osifchin, a former student who wrote to us a year after graduating.

> I've been really getting into Richard Linklater lately, after watching *Dazed and Confused* (my favorite movie of all time) for about the thirtieth time. I watched his movie *Slacker* and also part of *Waking Life*, and what was interesting to me was the portrayal of nothing as everything and how it is displayed in a much more explicit manner than *Dazed*.
>
> I then saw a tweet from an awesome Website, Open Culture, directing Tweeters to the films and works of Susan Sontag. Never heard of her. Isn't it funny how connections come about? As I read more about her, and more of her pieces,

I began to make a connection between Linklater's work and Sontag. The first piece of Sontag's work that I read was "Against Interpretation." I found it fascinating, and also true to a point. The best art does not try to mean anything, it just [lies] there in the glory and awe of its creation....

Next, I read a NYT review of Sontag's first novel, *The Benefactor*, and was struck by how similar it seemed to *Waking Life*. The review even says "Hippolyte also dreams numerous repetitious dreams, ponders them endlessly, and keeps encountering Frau Anders, like a guilty conscience. The intent is to present waking life as if it were a dream. And, to present dreams as concrete as daily living." This is precisely what *Waking Life* is portraying. I think the depiction of dreams as reality and reality as dreams or any combination of those is not "without motive or feeling" as the reviewer says, but rather allows you to view things from a less interpretive point of view, as Sontag might [argue for].

Now, after reading this review, I decided to see if Linklater was influenced by Sontag. I literally searched on Google "Richard Linklater influenced by Susan Sontag." Interestingly enough, and why I decided to send this email to you, Sontag mentions Linklater's *Dazed and Confused* in an article on the Abu Ghraib torture incident, "Regarding the Torture of Others." In it, Sontag mentions the increasing brutality of American culture and the increasing acceptance of violence. Not only did this make me think of [*The Ballad of Abu Ghraib*] and reading it in your class, but it also made me think of a specific moment in *Waking Life* [here he provides the link to the YouTube clip of the moment he references]. "Man wants chaos. In fact, he's gotta have it. Depression, strife, riots murder. All this dread. We're irresistibly drawn to that almost orgiastic state created out of death and destruction. It's in all of us. We revel in it!" It seems to me that this connects very well to Abu Ghraib as a whole, not just the immediate actions of the guards. Sontag's observation that "Secrets of private life that, formerly, you would have given nearly anything to conceal, you now clamor to be invited on a television show to reveal," collides at the intersection of American fantasies played out on TV screens all the time and the real world. It's an interesting comment on American society as a whole—who would have thought that reality TV would come back to bite America in a *war*? And with the extension of reality TV that is now, what I can't think to call anything but the "reality Web" (i.e., social media/networks), it is becoming more prevalent than ever. Sontag puts it better than I have—"What is illustrated by these photographs is as much the culture of shamelessness as the reigning admiration for unapologetic brutality."

For our former student, the world of ideas, like the rabbit hole in *Alice in Wonderland*, is endlessly surprising and extraordinary. He begins by writing about rewatching Richard Linklater's movie *Dazed and Confused*, and then before he knows it, he's off on an entirely self-motivated search through film, philosophy, war, and media in search of artists and thinkers who can help him better understand our "culture of shamelessness" and "unapologetic brutality." With genuine curiosity and some practice doing research, you can transform the world of ideas, as Chris did, into an astounding place in which nearly every turn inspires a new connection and thinking itself becomes both art and play.

PRACTICE SESSION

RESEARCHING

Type the words *Ellen Dissanayake* into the Google search engine. Press return.

Everyone who does this at the same time will get the same results. We can call this "ordinary research." If you click on the Wikipedia entry for Dissanayake, you'll find yourself on a page that provides a thumbnail sketch of the author and her work. Again, in gaining this foothold on Dissanayake's work, you'll be doing what any ordinary researcher starting out would do.

It's what you do next that matters. Choose one of Dissanayake's works that you find online and read it.

Your next task is to make your research into this researcher of the extraordinary extraordinary. (We composed that last sentence with *Alice's Adventures in Wonderland* in mind.) Set aside at least an hour for exploratory research. Begin by choosing a phrase, a quotation, a reference, or a footnote from the Dissanayake work you read and doing another Google search. Read two or more of the recommended links. Then choose a phrase, a quotation, a reference, or a footnote from the second set of works and do another Google search. Repeat. Repeat. And repeat again, until you've burrowed down to an insight or a question that you yourself find extraordinary.

REFLECTING

We call the process outlined above, where you move from one linked source to the next, "drilling down." Spend at least 30 minutes reflecting on this process. As you drilled down in your research, beginning with your first search about Dissanayake and ending with an extraordinary insight or question, how did you distinguish between ordinary and extraordinary moments of discovery? What choices yielded genuine surprises? Begin a list of useful strategies to include in your repertoire as a curious researcher, a list you can add to as you continue to practice drilling down.

RESEARCHING

Write an essay about your research into the extraordinary that presents a special or artful idea, insight, or question. Don't write a schoolish "report" about your research. Instead, make something special with your words; write something that rewards repeated acts of attention.

WRITING

We challenged you to write about your research into the extraordinary in a way that rewards repeated acts of attention—just as Lewis Carroll did in *Alice's Adventures in Wonderland*, and as the writers and directors Lana and Andy Wachowski did in *The Matrix*. Now spend at least 30 minutes writing and thinking about what makes *The Matrix* or *Alice's Adventures* or another work of literature, film, or art worth returning to again and again. What did you do in your own essay to reward repeated acts of attention?

EXPLORE

A rabbit hole can open up anywhere. Tim Cahill's efforts to make sense of conflicting accounts of the Jonestown Massacre lead him into the mind of a madman. Sarah Stillman's research into the war on drugs reveals the deadly consequences of police reliance on young drug informants. David Foster Wallace, dispatched to cover a lobster festival, finds himself on an existential journey to make sense of the joys of eating creatures who have been boiled alive.

Cahill, Tim. "In the Valley of the Shadow of Death: Guyana after the Jonestown Massacre." *Rolling Stone.* 25 Jan. 1979. Web.

Stillman, Sarah. "The Throwaways." *New Yorker.* 3 Sept. 2012. Web.

Wallace, David Foster. "Consider the Lobster." *Gourmet.* August 2004. Web.

On Creative Reading

Once you've learned to read, it's easy to lose sight of just what a complicated business reading actually is. You see the letters *c-a-t*, and without effort you know that together they refer to the furry, whiskered, four-legged purring thing curled before the fire. To accomplish this seemingly simple act of translation, you have had to learn a sign system (the alphabet), a host of rules governing the combination of the signs in the given system (for example, there are vowels and consonants, and they can be put together only in certain ways), and the connection between the signifier (the word that results from the orderly combination of sounds) and the signified (the object, idea, or sensation out there in the world).

Even at this most rudimentary stage, there's an inescapable arbitrariness at the heart of the reading process: Why does *c-a-t* and not some other series of letters signify that furry thing? Why *that* sound for *that* creature? And beyond the arbitrariness of the sign system, there's an even deeper mystery: How does the child watching the parent's finger point to the letters on the page ever make the leap to that moment when the sound, the letters, and the image in the picture book suddenly connect, and meaning gets made?

Solving the mystery of how and why humans developed this ability to work with sign systems is a job for evolutionary neuroscientists, and their answer, when it comes, will apply to humans in general. We're interested in a more personal issue: Once the process of reading has been routinized and internalized, why is it that different people reading the same material reach different conclusions? Or to put this another way, why is there ambiguity? Why is there misunderstanding? What happens in the movement from decoding the characters on the page or screen to creating an interpretation of what those characters, considered in context, might mean that causes one reader's mind to go in one direction and another reader's mind to go in a different direction?

The mystery of the individual response is made clear as soon as class discussion begins. Where'd *that* idea come from? How'd the teacher get *that* out of *those* words? And because students can't see inside the teacher's mind, they often conclude that the connections the teacher is making are arbitrary and, beyond that, that anything other than the reporting of facts is "just a matter of opinion." For many students, the mystery of how teachers—and experts, in general—read is never solved. For these students, the experience of higher-order literacy, where reading and writing become ways to create new ideas, remains out of reach.

Social bookmarking, a gift from the Internet, gives us a way to make visible for others some of the previously invisible workings of the creative reader's mind. Below we walk you through an example of how using social media worked in one of our classes, and then we give you some exercises to get you on your way. Although there are any number of bookmarking tools out there for you to try, we use Diigo because it allows our students to annotate the Web pages they share with the class. They can highlight passages they want to draw attention to or pose inline questions. And just like that, two previously invisible aspects of the reading process—what people read and how they respond to what they've read—become visible and available for others to consider.

So what does *creative* reading look like in practice?

Our example comes from a creative nonfiction course we taught in which the students read *On Photography*, a collection of essays by Susan Sontag that was originally published in 1977 and that remains a touchstone in discussions of how the free circulation of images changes societal norms. We were halfway through the second essay in the collection, "America, Seen through Photographs, Darkly," and had reached the point where Sontag considers the work of Diane Arbus, who presented her subjects, whether they were at the margins of society or at its center, in ways that were strange and disturbing.

Sontag's criticism of Arbus is damning: Sontag argues that Arbus used her camera to depict all of her subjects as "inhabitants of a single village ... the idiot village [of] America." Here the class encountered a problem that runs throughout Sontag's *On Photography*: there are no photographs. For readers who already know the history of American photography, this isn't a problem; they can just call to mind some of Arbus's most famous images and judge for themselves whether or not Sontag's assessment is fair. But for readers who don't know Arbus's work, the only option is to treat Sontag's assessment as a fact.

Sontag's readers in the 1970s who wanted to know more about Arbus's work would not have had an easy time of it, but today any reader with access to the Internet can check out Arbus's images and assess the validity of Sontag's judgment. Without exerting any more effort than it takes to type "Diane Arbus" into a search engine, our students found the images Sontag refers to in her piece and more: Arbus's shots of circus freaks; the off-balance, bedecked socialites; the nudists; the giant man towering over his miniature parents; and of course, the twin girls.

Once she'd seen the pictures, our student Alice asked: "Well, how did people at the time react? We know Sontag didn't like Arbus's work, but did they?"

As so often happens in our classes, we didn't know the answer to the question our student had posed. (And in this instance, even if we had known, we wouldn't have said so.) Alice asked a good question—both because finding out the answer would end up requiring some creativity on her part and because wondering about how others see what you're seeing always serves to highlight the fact that meaning is both a public and a private matter. So we said, "That's a Canvas Collaboration moment," which is shorthand in our classes for, "See what you can find out and post the results to our class's collaborative Google Doc in Canvas."

Back in her room, Alice set off to answer her own question. She entered some search terms, cast about a bit, and then settled on a path that took her to *Athanor*, a journal published by Florida State University's Department of Art History, and an article by Laureen Trainer entitled "The Missing Photographs: An Examination of Diane Arbus's Images of Transvestites and Homosexuals from 1957 to 1965." Alice posted a link to the piece on Canvas and then highlighted a passage that struck her:

> However, the reaction to her images was intense anger, an emotional response prompted by the cultural war against sexual "deviants." Yuben Yee, the photo librarian at the MoMA, recalls having to come early every morning to wipe the spit off of Arbus's portraits. He recalls that, "People were uncomfortable—threatened—looking at Diane's stuff." Even within the art world, Arbus was thought to be photographing subject matter that was ahead of her time. As Andy Warhol, who had seen some of Arbus's portraits, commented, "drag queens weren't even accepted in freak circles until 1967." Arbus's images were not only disturbing to her audience on an aesthetic level, but her unabashed and unapologetic views of transvestites touched a deeper nerve in the people who viewed them.

Beneath this quote, Alice wrote about the difference between a time when people spat on images of transvestites in the Museum of Modern Art and her own experience looking at the images a half century later.

How did people respond to Arbus's work at the time? Alice made her way of answering this question visible to the rest of the class. She also found something that was new to her teachers, new to the class, and new to her; in so doing, she gave us a glimpse of what was going on in her mind while she was reading. Yes, it is true that she had just uncovered a piece of information. Yes, it is true that she had not yet done anything with this information. But meaningful engagement with information can happen only *after* one has had the experience of posing an open, exploratory question.

Alice kept looking—it's a requirement in our courses. The next source she posted to Canvas would likely raise the hackles of many teachers: Wikipedia! It's an outrage!

Well, actually, it isn't. If we grant that students are going to use Wikipedia (and SparkNotes and YouTube and, and, and), we can focus on how to use these sources productively rather than insist on unenforceable prohibitions.

So, Wikipedia: Is there a beneficial way to use an encyclopedia? How could the answer to that question be anything other than *yes*?

Alice posted the link to Wikipedia's Arbus entry as well as excerpts from the section of that entry that specifically concern the reception of Arbus's work. She deleted material that was not of interest to her; separated past reactions from more contemporary responses; added an inline comment that directly connected the Wikipedia entry to Sontag's argument; reordered the information so as to place the introductory material in this section of the Wikipedia entry at the end of her own citation; and eliminated entirely a passage where it is observed that "Sontag's essay itself has been criticized as 'an exercise in aesthetic insensibility' and 'exemplary *for its shallowness*'" (italics added).

All of this editorial activity gives us a much richer sense of what Alice did while she was reading. Alice amassed many examples of how the subjects of Arbus's images responded to being photographed; how anonymous viewers at MoMA responded when the photographs were first displayed; and how critics—those who were Arbus's contemporaries and those who came after her—responded to the photographs. Then she concluded her entry with the news that Arbus had photographed Sontag and her son.

Who was this last bit of information news to? Alice. The other students in the course. Her teachers. And given that Sontag herself does not reveal this fact anywhere in *On Photography*, it's safe to say that it would also be news to most, if not all, of Sontag's readers, past and present.

Alice posted this fact to Canvas without comment. She thought she was done.

But the practice of creative reading is never done. In this case there was a question hanging in the air, waiting to be asked. And because the Canvas Collaboration tool made what Alice was reading and how she was reading it visible to the members of the group and to her teachers, it became possible for us to pose the question that could keep the reading process going for Alice: What does the picture Arbus took of Sontag look like?

This question was posed in public for all the other students to see on the collaborative document, just below Alice's entry. And soon enough, Alice posted a link to the image. True, it was only a small, low-resolution image, but it was a start. Or rather, it was a continuation, an extension of a process that started with Alice asking, "How did others see Arbus?" and eventually led to her discovering an image of Sontag and her son looking back at the photographer Sontag describes as "not a poet delving into her entrails to relate her own pain but a photographer venturing out into the world to *collect* images that are painful."

This is one version of what happens when the purpose of reading shifts from the acquisition of information to the exploration of an open-ended question: reading begets more reading, one passage leads to another, and the original text is read and reread in a series of changing contexts, its meaning expanding and contracting depending on the use to which the reader puts it. This is the essence of higher-order reading. Some explorations will be more fruitful than others, and some more valuable for the individual than for a larger community of readers, but the movement from answers to questions, from information to ideas, remains the same.

PRACTICE SESSION ONE

REFLECTING

The example of creative reading we've described leads from a question about an essay to an image not included in or referenced in the original essay. We first want you to find a reproduction online of Diane Arbus's photograph of Susan Sontag. What light do you think Arbus's photograph of Sontag and her son sheds on Sontag's assessment of Arbus's work in "America, Seen through Photographs, Darkly"? Spend at least 20 minutes figuring out a thoughtful, compelling answer to this question. For the purposes of this exercise, work only with what we've provided. *Don't* seek out the rest of Sontag's essay or more information about Arbus. What does the photograph alone tell you?

RESEARCHING

As we've said, the work of creative reading is never done. What information can you find online about the image of Sontag and her son? About *their* relationship? About Sontag's fuller argument in "America, Seen through Photographs, Darkly"? About her argument in *On Photography*? Spend at least an hour researching and reading, keeping careful notes on your discoveries.

WRITING

Now you're ready to work on an extended essay about how to read Arbus's images creatively. Continue the research Alice began about how viewers have responded to Arbus's photographs in the forty years since Sontag's judgment, gathering information about one or more lines of response to the photographs. Then make an argument for how you think an Arbus photograph ought to be read. (Note: This series of exercises can be profitably executed using any visual artist.)

PRACTICE SESSION TWO

RESEARCHING

Once a day for a week, we'd like you to print out and annotate a page you've visited on the Web. We want you to mark those places in your reading where a question of *any kind* is raised for you. An unfamiliar word, data that seems not to compute, an interpretation that doesn't make sense, an odd sentence structure—wherever your reading is stopped, take note of it. At the end of a week, you'll have a profile of your own reading practice.

REFLECTING

Now that you have made a version of your own reading practice visible for you to consider, what do you see? Set aside at least 30 minutes to write down answers to these questions: What does your profile reveal about what kind of a reader you are? What habits do you practice currently? Are there instances when your experience of reading was more pleasurable than it was at other times? More productive? More useful? Was your practice of reading markedly different during any of these phases, or was the outcome entirely dependent on what you were reading at the time?

WRITING

Using your research and reflections on your reading practices, compose a portrait of yourself as a reader. Where are you now as a reader? Where would you like to be? What specific steps do you need to take to become a lifelong creative reader? Write an essay that analyzes the most important events in your experience as a reader up to the present moment.

EXPLORE

Two of our suggested readings invite you to continue the creative reading of work by Susan Sontag and Diane Arbus: journalist Franklin Foer considers Sontag's critical success alongside her changing relationship to photography, while art critic Peter Schjeldahl's brief remembrance of Arbus seeks to provide a reparative reading of her work. In our third suggested reading, Nathan Chandler uses creative reading to learn about and describe the inner workings of Anonymous—a group of highly skilled hackers who are committed to remaining unknown and unfindable.

Chandler, Nathan. "How Anonymous Works." Howstuffworks.com. Web.

Foer, Franklin. "Susan Superstar: How Susan Sontag Became Seduced by Her Own Persona." Nymag.com. 14 January 2005. Web.

Schjeldahl, Peter. "Looking Back: Diane Arbus at the Met." Newyorker.com. 21 March 2005. Web.

On Imagining Others

We've all heard the proverb "Before you judge someone, walk a mile in that person's shoes." This saying is so well known because it captures the experience we've all had of making a snap judgment that then turns out to be wrong. Understanding another person's motives requires more than just trusting your intuition, and it involves more than just reviewing the evidence about that person reported to you by your own eyes and ears. It also requires an act of imagination that gives you a glimpse of what it is like to experience life as that person does.

But is the imagination really powerful enough or trustworthy enough to approximate the experience of walking a mile in another person's shoes? In our view (that is, as seen through our eyes, when walking in our shoes), the more you practice using your imagination to gain a sense of how others see the world, the better your approximations will become. We're aware that this sense, which is by definition an *approximate* understanding, is not the same thing as *complete* knowledge. Indeed, the very act of trying to produce writing that fully renders the experience of another person can lead to a deeper appreciation for how much of anyone else's experience remains out of reach of your imagination.

One of the most ambitious efforts to imagine the lives of others is the photographer Yann Arthus-Bertrand's 7 billion Others project, which seeks to promote understanding of "what separates and what unites" the world's more than seven billion people. Prior to launching the 7 billion Others project (which began as the 6 billion Others project), Arthus-Bertrand was most famous for the aerial photographs he took for his book *Earth from Above*. From up in the sky, he says, "the Earth looks like an immense area to be shared." But back on the ground, all the local impediments to sharing the earth come back into focus—problems produced by geography, culture, language, religion, wealth, health, and opportunity. To counter this immediate sense of an unshareable world, Arthus-Betrand offers spectacular image after spectacular image in *Earth from Above* of the world's rich natural resources and of the vibrant productivity of its peoples.

Confronted with the problem of how we might better understand each other, in 2003 Arthus-Bertrand and his coworkers began filming thousands of interviews in eighty-four different countries and posting these videos on their Web site. Every interview subject responded to the same list of questions (forty-five in all) about experiences, beliefs, and hopes, a list that included these conversational prompts:

> What did you learn from your parents?
> What would you like to hand on to your children?
> What was the most difficult ordeal you have had to face in your life?
> What do you think is the meaning of life?
> Have you ever wanted to leave your country? Why?
> Have you seen nature change since your childhood?
> What does love mean to you?
> What is your greatest fear?
> What do you think happens after death?
> What did you dream about when you were a child?

Comparing the subjects' answers to these questions to our own answers reveals both what we have in common with others and what remains puzzling and mysterious about the thoughts and lives of others.

The 7 billion Others project provides us with raw material for imagining the lives of others around the globe and across the country. But one can also find the compelling mystery of otherness across the street or across the kitchen table. Imagine, for instance, how different it might be to see the world from the perspective of a parent, sibling, grandparent, or friend, or how you would perceive the world from a wheelchair, or if you couldn't see at all. (You can even find the mystery of otherness within yourself, but that's a paradox we'll consider at another time.)

In the preface to his book *What the Dog Saw*, Malcolm Gladwell captures the sense of otherness within one's own home in a vignette from his childhood. As a young boy, Gladwell would slip into his father's study and marvel at the graph paper covered with rows of penciled numbers strewn across his father's desk. Gladwell knew his father was a mathematician, but what did that mean, really? He writes,

> I would sit on the edge of his chair and look at each page with puzzlement and wonder. It seemed miraculous, first of all, that he got paid for what seemed, at the time, like gibberish. But more important, I couldn't get over the fact that someone whom I loved so dearly did something every day, inside his own head, that I could not begin to understand.

If Gladwell could "not begin to understand" what was going on in his father's mind, why did he persist in wondering about the symbols scrawled on graph paper? He persisted, he explains, because "curiosity about the interior life of other people's day-to-day work is one of the most fundamental of human impulses." Early in life, Gladwell discovered the rewards of confronting the unknown in everyday life, and he held onto his curiosity long after childhood, convinced "that everyone and everything has a story to tell." His curiosity about others' thoughts became the foundation of his career as a writer.

PRACTICE SESSION ONE

REFLECTING

Go to the 7 billion Others Web site and explore all that it makes available. Set aside at least 30 minutes to watch a few of the testimonials. Listen to how people from all over the world respond to questions about love, fear, family, and more. Then select one film on a specific topic ("After death," "Family," "Meaning of life," and so on), and watch it in its entirety.

After viewing the film, spend at least 30 minutes reflecting on what you saw and heard. Begin by reflecting on the responses of the people interviewed in the video. Then consider your own response to the topic you chose. At which points did you feel the strongest affinity with the people being interviewed? Which responses struck you as being most surprising? Does the 7 billion Others project show that there are seven billion perspectives?

PRACTICE SESSION TWO

RESEARCHING

Imagining the lives of others begins with curiosity, openness, and a commitment to listening attentively. One way to practice those habits of mind is to conduct an interview in which you listen closely and carefully to what the person being interviewed has to say. (When you conduct an interview, you should either take notes or get the interviewee's permission to record the interview.)

Option 1: Find a friend or an acquaintance—someone around your age who has a different perspective on the world than you do—and invite that person to talk with you for 30 minutes or more about one or two of the topics that most interest you from the 7 billion Others project, such as "What did you learn from your parents?" or "What do you think is the meaning of life?" Invite stories. Listen for places where your interviewee's beliefs or thoughts are different from your own, and ask questions to expand your understanding of those differences.

Option 2: Find a friend or an acquaintance who is at least twenty years older than you are, and invite that person to talk for 30 minutes or more about childhood and growing up. What was everyday life like when he or she was your age? What are the most dramatic changes that this person has observed in his or her lifetime? What does she or he miss about the past? What changes have been most welcome? Listen for places where your subject's experiences are radically different from your own, and ask questions to expand your understanding of those differences.

WRITING

After your interview, review your notes or your recording and write an essay about what it would take for you to see the world as your interview subject does. What else would you need to know about this person that you don't know from your conversation and your previous interactions? How would you know whether you had succeeded in approximating their worldview? At what point do you have to shift from what you know to what you imagine to be the case?

EXPLORE

When we imagine the experience of another person, we might focus on what it would be like to have that person's thoughts, talents, or background. With our suggested readings, we invite you to consider what it would be like either to inhabit another person's body or to be intimate friends with someone who is both enormously talented and self-destructive. Nora Ephron describes life without a plunging cleavage. Lucy Grealy describes life after half of her lower jaw was removed, at age nine, due to cancer. And Ann Patchett describes the challenges involved in being Grealy's close friend.

Ephron, Nora. "A Few Words about Breasts." *Esquire.* May 1972. Web.

Grealy, Lucy. "Mirrorings." *Harper's Magazine*. Feb. 1993. Web.

Patchett, Ann. "The Face of Pain." *New York Magazine.* 1 July 2003. Web.

On Motivation

Why write?

When posting on social media, the writer's motivation is clear: to connect with friends, or to say something others will "like." As in other kinds of "unsponsored writing," such as keeping a diary or maintaining a personal blog, the central activity is giving voice to the self. This can be pleasurable; it can teach you about yourself; it can relieve stress. While there are plenty of people who never feel the desire to engage in unsponsored writing, there's not much mystery as to why some do.

What *is* mysterious is why anyone, outside of a school assignment, voluntarily writes about anything other than the self, its interests, its desires, its travails, and so on. Why write a searching analysis of a social problem, for instance, or a book-length study of voting behaviors, or a biography of someone long dead and wholly unrelated to the writer? Why do something that requires so much time and mental energy, and for which the odds of getting published or having your work read are so low?

When cast in these terms, the motivation to write voluntarily about something other than the self does seem mysterious. But perhaps these are not the best terms for understanding how the motivation to write emerges. So let's move from the hypothetical to the particular and consider the story of how the historian Jill Lepore set out to write a book about Benjamin Franklin and ended up writing one about Jane Franklin, his virtually unknown sister. It's obvious why a historian might want to write about Ben Franklin. He's a major figure in American history; he was an inventor, an ambassador, an educator, and a philosopher; he was one of the most famous people of his time, and he interacted with others in all walks of life. If you're a scholar of American history, writing about him sounds fun.

In "The Prodigal Daughter," Lepore describes settling into reading Franklin's papers and finding herself drawn instead to the sixty-three-year-long correspondence Ben Franklin had with his younger sister Jane. Lepore discovered that Ben Franklin wrote more letters to Jane than to anyone else. "No two people in their family were more alike," Lepore came to realize, even though "their lives could hardly have been more different." Jane Franklin was nearly illiterate, and the few writing lessons her brother gave her ended after he left home when she was only eleven. Aside from letters to family and friends, the only writing she did was to record the dates of major events in a small, handmade book she called her "Book of Ages," which Lepore describes as "four sheets of foolscap between two covers to make a little book of sixteen pages." Turn the pages of this homemade book and you'll move through a list of dates and events: Jane's birth; her marriage at age fifteen; the birth of her first child, and that child's death less than a year later; the births of eleven more children and the deaths, during her lifetime, of all but one of those children.

In contrast to her brother's life, Jane Franklin's life seemed too spare and uneventful to warrant general attention. And yet when Lepore told her mother what she had learned about Ben Franklin's forgotten sister, her mother said, "Write a book about her!" Lepore thought her mother was joking. How could she write a book about a phantom? Who would want to read about her? It seemed like an impossible task, but when her mother's health began to fail, Lepore returned her attention to Jane Franklin's letters "to write the only book [her] mother ever wanted [her] to write."

Although her personal motivation for writing a book about Jane Franklin couldn't have been stronger, Lepore floundered. She tried to write a double biography that placed Jane Franklin's life story next to her brother's, but she abandoned this approach after drafting 250 pages, having found that the juxtaposition only magnified the sadness and sameness of Jane's life. Without a more compelling reason to write than pleasing her mother, Lepore put the project aside. We would say that, at this stage, Lepore had a private motive but not a public one. Her private motive was powerful enough to get her writing, but it didn't provide her with a way to present Jane Franklin's monotonous life as a puzzle, problem, or question that others might find meaningful.

Perhaps the problem was that the questions raised by Jane Franklin's life didn't merit a book-length study. Maybe what was interesting about her life could be stated much more briefly. In "Poor Jane's Almanac," a short opinion piece Lepore published in the *New York Times*, she described Jane Franklin's "Book of Ages" and the political arguments Jane had with her brother after her child-rearing days were done. By highlighting Jane's two modes of writing—the catalog of her losses and her letters to her brother—Lepore found a way to show her readers why they should be interested in her life. Jane Franklin's biography in itself isn't compelling; what is so interesting is what her life's story reveals about the connections between gender, poverty, education, and access to contraception. "Especially for women," Lepore writes, "escaping poverty has always depended on the opportunity for an education and the ability to control the size of their families," neither of which Jane had.

Lepore was stunned by the flood of letters she received in response to the *New York Times* piece. In an interview ("Out Loud: Jane Franklin's Untold American Story"), she described letters from readers about how their mothers, like Jane Franklin, swam against the "undertow of motherhood" to steal the time required to read and learn and engage with the wider world. Taken together, the mass of personal letters helped Lepore see why trying to fit Jane Franklin's life into the form of a biography hadn't worked. Lepore's readers hadn't written to her because they were moved by Jane Franklin's singular, unique life; rather, they wrote because they saw in Jane Franklin a version of their own mothers. At last, Lepore had a public motive for writing at length about Jane Franklin's life: she would use her story to show how poverty, motherhood, and limited education diminished the lives of women in the eighteenth century and rendered achievement outside the home impossible. And that's exactly what she did in *Book of Ages: The Life and Opinions of Jane Franklin*, which was nominated for a National Book Award in 2013.

We began with the question "Why write?" and have ended with a discussion of audience. How did we get here? By following the story of Jill Lepore's struggle to find a satisfying way to write about Jane Franklin's life, we've seen that the movement from a private to a public motive to write involves a shift in the imagined audience for one's writing. For personal reasons, Lepore set out to write a book about Jane Franklin with her own mother as the imagined audience; when Lepore imagined a larger audience of sympathetic readers, she realized she had to reconceive the project. It would still be about Jane Franklin, but Franklin's life story would become a case study of the challenges women in general faced in eighteenth-century America.

Given that virtually all of the writing students do in school is in response to an assignment of one kind or another, and further, that those assignments come with an external motivator (the grading system) and an intended audience (the teacher), it's highly unlikely that you have had an experience like Lepore's while writing in school. Even so, with the assignments in this book, we want you to practice imagining that the audience for your work is composed neither exclusively of your friends nor solely of those who are paid to read your work, but rather of sympathetic readers interested in seeing how your mind works on a problem. As you practice imagining a different audience for your work, you will find yourself confronting the writer's central challenge: How do I make what interests me of interest to others?

PRACTICE SESSION ONE

READING

For this exercise read Jill Lepore's "The Last Amazon: Wonder Woman Returns," or any of her other writing that is available on the Web. After you've finished reading the piece, spend at least 30 minutes considering Lepore's public motive for writing it. What is the compelling problem, question, puzzle, contradiction, or ambiguity she is exploring? At what point in the reading does she make her central project clear? What does she do to make her project compelling to her audience?

WRITING

Public and intellectual motives are often expressed as questions, or as statements that use a complicating or qualifying word such as *but*, *however*, or *or*. For example, Lepore's motive in *Book of Ages* can be expressed by this statement: Jane Franklin's life appears to be unexceptional, *but* her life provides a valuable example of how poverty, lack of education, and motherhood severely limited what women in the eighteenth-century United States could achieve.

We'd like you to spend at least 20 minutes reviewing the Lepore article you selected and defining the public motive of the article as clearly as you can in just one sentence. Experiment with restating the motive in a sentence that uses *but*, *or*, *however*, or some other complicating word. How does the statement you composed help to clarify Lepore's project for you?

PRACTICE SESSION TWO

RESEARCHING

We invite you to practice the motivating move that Lepore employs regularly. Specifically, we want you to use details about particular people or historical events to open up larger questions about cultural or social issues, such as motherhood, fatherhood, national identity, education, poverty, or economic opportunity.

To begin, write up a familiar anecdote from your family history. Then follow Lepore's example and consider how you could use the story to shed light on an interesting cultural or social problem, puzzle, or mystery that is bigger than your particular family. In other words, define a public motive for writing by using your family anecdote to rethink a larger issue or idea. Before you try to make a compelling connection, spend at least one hour doing research about the cultural or social issue that interests you.

After you've done sufficient research and feel ready to connect personal experience and public ideas, compose an essay that links your family history to the larger issue you've researched.

EXPLORE

Jill Lepore, whose work is the foundation for our discussion of how the motive to write evolves over time, explains in a recorded interview why she chose to write about Jane Franklin. George Orwell's discussion of motive differs from ours because it focuses instead on how writers are driven by ego, beauty, a desire for knowledge, and political purpose. Oliver Sacks further complicates explanations for motive because of what is now known about how malleable memory is; when memories change over time, motives for past actions can't be recalled with certainty.

Lepore, Jill. Interview by Sasha Weiss and Judith Thurman. "Out Loud: Jane Franklin's Untold American Story." Podcast audio. *New Yorker.* 30 June 2013. Web.

Orwell, George. "Why I Write." *Gangrel* 4 (Summer 1946). Web.

Sacks, Oliver. "Speak, Memory." *New York Review of Books*. 21 Feb. 2013. Web.

Curiosity at Work: Donovan Hohn Follows the Toys

Donovan Hohn was teaching high school English in New York when a student's paper inspired him to pursue his own open-ended research assignment. Hohn had asked his students to practice the "archaeology of the ordinary" by picking an artifact, researching its history, and writing up what they found. One student, who chose to write about his lucky rubber duck, came across a report from 1992 about twenty-eight thousand bath toys that fell off a container ship in the Pacific Ocean. A few years later, the report continued, beachcombers in Alaska began to notice the toys floating ashore—a plastic duck here, another there, arriving year after year. Hohn couldn't get this story out of his head. He started asking questions: Why had some of the toys ended up in Alaska? Where were the rest of the toys? Why didn't they all end up in the same place? He decided to look for answers.

"At the outset," Hohn writes in his book *Moby-Duck*, "I figured I'd interview a few oceanographers, talk to a few beachcombers, read up on ocean currents and Arctic geography, and then write an account of the incredible journey of the bath toys lost at sea." He thought he'd be able to do this work without leaving his desk. But Hohn didn't manage to stay seated for long. He discovered that questions

> can be like ocean currents. Wade in a little too far and they can carry you away. Follow one line of inquiry and it will lead you to another, and another. Spot a yellow duck dropped atop the seaweed at the tide line, ask yourself where it came from, and the next thing you know you're way out at sea, no land in sight, dog-paddling around in mysteries four miles deep. You're wondering when and why yellow ducks became icons of childhood. You want to know what it's like inside the toy factories of Guangdong. You're marveling at the scale of humanity's impact on this terraqueous globe and at the oceanic magnitude of your own ignorance.

In pursuit of answers to his growing list of questions, Hohn crossed the Northwest Passage in an icebreaker. He sailed on a catamaran to the Great Pacific Garbage Patch, a huge expanse of plastic soup—broken-down bits of bottles, toys, and packaging of all kinds—drawn together by ocean currents. He rode out a terrifying winter storm on the outer decks of a cargo ship in the middle of the Pacific, with "shipping containers stacked six-high overhead, ... strain[ing] against their lashings, creaking and groaning and cataracting with every roll." He sped on a ferry up China's Pearl River Delta to a factory where he saw bath toys being made. He learned how to say "thank you" in Inuktitut and Cantonese.

In the end, Hohn wrote a book about many things: consumer demand for inexpensive goods, the toxins in the Chinese factories where the ducks are made and in the ocean where the toys degrade, and prospects for change. His curiosity took him all the way from an absurd image of a flotilla of plastic ducks to questions about the most pressing environmental concerns the world faces today.

CHAPTER 5

Connecting

"Connect the dots": this phrase used to appear atop the pages of activity books designed to help young children practice counting while they worked on improving their fine motor skills. A child, crayon in hand, would draw a line from numbered dot to numbered dot, and at the end of the process, if the child had followed the dots in order, then voilà, there was a picture. If not, there was a mess.

No one would argue that connecting the dots is creative. The child has simply followed the directions to uncover a design. But once we move from children connecting dots to students using their own writing to connect ideas discussed in what they've been reading, we enter a realm where creativity becomes possible. Any two ideas can be connected; any claim can be made; any argument can be put forward. Under such chaotic conditions, how does one make connections that matter?

The essays in this chapter will help you to resist writing formulas that preorganize your encounters with the infinite range of connections to be made. To encourage you to practice using your writing to develop new habits for engaging with and exploring what is unknown to you, we want you to think of writing itself as the act of making connections. Writers make connections with the language they use, with the questions they choose to ask, and with the sources they choose to interview. As you experiment with making connections in each of these areas, you will be engaging directly in the creative act of making meaning: the dots you connect will be your own, and the image that results will be of your own design.

On the Three Most Important Words in the English Language

How do you know you're thinking?

This is the kind of question that stops you in your tracks. First, you think, who would ask about something so obvious? And then—well, then you're left with the challenge of putting into words a central facet of your mental life.

When we begin discussing this question in class, we are soon deep in the murk. There's involuntary mental activity, which takes place in any brain-equipped creature—for example, the turtle sunning on a log is passively monitoring the surroundings, scanning for threats. There's instinct, the lightning-quick response to inbound data—the cat pounces on whatever is rustling in the bush, killing, as the common phrase puts it, without thinking. There's dreaming, and there's daydreaming, too. There's all this involuntary mental activity going on up there that we don't control. And then there's thought, which is, in contrast, mental activity over which we have some control. So while we can't unsee what our eyes behold or unhear the sounds that enter our ears, and we can't unsmell, untouch, or unfeel, we can change how we think about what our senses are reporting. And though we can't exactly *unthink* a thought we've had, we can change that thought by *rethinking* it.

We're interested in that stretch of mental activity that you can influence. For the moment, we ask that you grant us the following proposition:

Thinking is the intentional act of making connections.

This act of connecting can take place in language, sound, and images; chefs would doubtless say it takes place in taste, and perfumers in smell. We're open to the medium; what we want to focus on is the array of connections available to the thinker.

We are pretty sure that you'll have reservations about this proposition, but we need you to suspend those reservations for the time being. Don't worry; we'll qualify and complicate it by and by—we promise.

Beginning writers, like beginning thinkers, tend to rely on one connector: the coordinating conjunction *and*. For the beginning writer, writing is the act of connecting like to like, with thoughts or observations linked together via the explicit or implicit use of *and*:

> The house I grew up in had a garden. It also had a garage. It had two floors. *And* an attic.

In this additive mode of composing, the beginning writer can expand the composition as much as the assignment requires. All that the writer needs to supply is more of the same:

> It had two chimneys. It had three bedrooms. *And* one bathroom.

In the hands of an experienced storyteller, this additive mode of composing can serve as the foundation for an episodic epic poem:

> After the end of the Trojan War, Odysseus heads home. On the way back, he and his men sack the city of Ismarus. And then they sail to the land of the Lotus-Eaters. After they escape, they encounter the Cyclops, Polyphemus. And then, and then, and then…

Beginning writers are more likely to make connections via addition (A and B and C) than via qualification (A and B but not C). The machinery of the five-paragraph theme makes no room for thinking of this kind; there's just the thesis, the three supporting examples (A and B and C), and the conclusion. Qualification muddies the waters.

It's not that beginning writers have no access to the word *but*. Indeed, when we confer with beginning writers, we often find that their minds are abuzz with qualifications, exceptions, contradictions, and confusions. However, little of this mental activity makes it onto the page because our students have been told repeatedly that the goal of writing in school is clarity. Equating *clarity* with *simplicity*, beginning writers avoid presenting anything that might complicate their efforts to produce an argument that is straightforward and to the point. When this strategy of avoiding complications is rewarded, writing's primary function is reduced to the activity of simplification, and the goal of writing in school becomes nothing more than producing "arguments" that are clear, direct, and easy to follow.

Obviously, writing has a communicative function (moving idea X from point A to point B), but this isn't writing's sole function. Writing can also serve as a technology for thinking new thoughts—thoughts, that is, that are new to the writer. We believe that this use of writing, as a heuristic for venturing into the unknown, is as important as its communicative use. Indeed, it is through learning how to use writing for discovery, comprehension, and problem solving that we come to have ideas that are worth communicating.

Beginning writers start with a thesis and then find evidence to support their position; for them, writing is the process of reporting what fits the thesis and ignoring the rest. The problem with such writing is not that it is unclear but rather that it is, from the outset, *too* clear: it says what it's *going* to say (thesis), then it says it (three supporting examples), and then it says what it said (conclusion). Reading writing of this kind is like being plunged into the great echo chamber of nothingness.

This problem is easily solved: we just insist that our students bring the coordinating conjunction *but* into their writing. Things get messy right away, and clarity, misunderstood as simplicity, gives way to qualification and complexity. At the start, some of the qualifications are silly, and others are improbable. But the qualifications become more meaningful over time, and the prose begins to engage more productively with the complexities of lived experience. The writing begins to capture the shape of a mind at work on a problem.

But* is the passkey for entry into critical thinking.

If you want to test out this assertion, we invite you to consider how different Abraham Lincoln's Gettysburg Address would be if it ended after the second paragraph:

> Four score and seven years ago our fathers brought forth on this continent, a new nation, conceived in Liberty, and dedicated to the proposition that all men are created equal.
>
> Now we are engaged in a great civil war, testing whether that nation, or any nation so conceived and so dedicated, can long endure. We are met on a great battle-field of that war. We have come to dedicate a portion of that field, as a final resting place for those who here gave their lives that that nation might live. It is altogether fitting and proper that we should do this.

Lincoln speaks at the dedication of the cemetery at Gettysburg, Pennsylvania, for the Union casualties of the Battle of Gettysburg. He invokes the nation as if it were one thing, but the nation is at war with itself. Those who have gathered for the dedication of the cemetery do so to recognize the sacrifice of those who died so that the "nation might live."

If the speech ended here, it would end with the statement that recognizing the fallen is "altogether fitting and proper." Lincoln's intent is clear: it's appropriate to recognize those who have died defending the liberties of those who are still living. He's saying aloud what everyone present already knows; the point he is making is obvious to all.

But the speech *doesn't* end here. Lincoln continues:

> But, in a larger sense, we can not dedicate—we can not consecrate—we can not hallow—this ground. The brave men, living and dead, who struggled here, have consecrated it, far above our poor power to add or detract. The world will little note, nor long remember what we say here, but it can never forget what they did here.

Everything hinges on the qualification that Lincoln introduces in the third and final paragraph of his speech. What those who are assembled are doing is "altogether fitting and proper," *but* the living do not, in fact, have the power to do what those who have died have done.

With this qualification, Lincoln is able to shift the audience's attention from an understanding of dedication as a commemorative event bounded in time to its redefinition as an open-ended activity carried out by the living in the service of a vulnerable ideal:

> It is for us the living, rather, to be dedicated here to the unfinished work which they who fought here have thus far so nobly advanced. It is rather for us to be here dedicated to the great task remaining before us—that from these honored dead we take increased devotion to that cause for which they gave the last full measure of devotion—that we here highly resolve that these dead shall not have died in vain—that this nation, under God, shall have a new birth of freedom—and that government of the people, by the people, for the people, shall not perish from the earth.

Lincoln's use of *but* at the beginning of the third paragraph of his address allows him to connect dedication as a ceremonial event to the ongoing activity of being dedicated to some higher ideal. The connection is not like to like: coming to the dedication is not the same thing as dedicating oneself to the preservation of the nation. Without the *but*, we have a speech that thanks people for coming to a battlefield; with that qualification, we have a speech that links the deaths that took place on the battlefield to a larger set of ideas, values, hopes, and aspirations.

How do you get from critical thinking to creative thinking? Here's a rubric that oversimplifies to the point of distortion:

and	Foundation for thought	Basis for black-and-white, yes/no, binary thinking
but	Foundation for critical thought	Enables qualifications, exceptions, conditions, ambiguity, uncertainty
or	Foundation for creative thought	Enables alternatives, possibilities; is future oriented

We know this table can't withstand rigorous critical examination. Indeed, we'd say the table predicts its own dismantling, since it assumes both a critical thinker who will respond to the clear-cut grid by qualifying the table's assertions and a creative thinker who will imagine other grids or other ways of modeling the relationship between coordinating conjunctions and modes of thought.

So, just like the overly simplified left brain/right brain distinction discussed in "On Learning to See" (pp. 18–22), our table doesn't fully depict how thought happens. It's just a heuristic device, a helpful strategy for identifying different mental operations; it's a way to get you to think about thinking as the process of making connections.

With those qualifications, we stand by this assertion:

> Consciously introducing *but* and *or* to your mental activity is a surefire way to generate new thinking.

It really is that simple.

PRACTICE SESSION ONE

REFLECTING

Find three images that are important to you. They can be pictures of you or pictures you took yourself; pictures from the Internet; pictures of historical events or pictures of historical importance; pictures of art objects; even advertisements. They need not all be important in the same way.

Place the images before you. What are the implicit connections between them—A and B and C? A or B or C? A and B but not C? A or B and C? The possibilities are not infinite, but they are multiple. Spend at least 5 minutes jotting down notes about the implicit connections—connections that are not openly expressed but that are capable of being understood—between the images as they are laid out before you.

When you've completed your reflections, change the order of the images. What happens to the implicit connections? Repeat the exercise above with the newly ordered images.

When you've completed these two reflections about connections, take at least 20 minutes to write a reflective account of what happened to the connections when you reordered the images. Why does their order make a difference?

PRACTICE SESSION TWO

READING

We'd like you to look at Ta-Nehisi Coates's essay "Fear of a Black President," found on the *Atlantic* Web site. Read it through once; then return to it and mark where Coates makes connections.

Make a list of explicit (expressed) or implicit (unexpressed) *and* connections that set information or ideas next to each other.

Then list connections that explicitly or implicitly use the word *but* to establish qualifications, exceptions, conditions, ambiguity, or uncertainty.

Next, list connections that explicitly or implicitly use the word *or* to point out alternatives or possibilities.

Finally, spend at least 30 minutes writing a reflective piece about the connections you listed in the *but* and *or* categories. Which connection is the most important? Which is the most surprising?

PRACTICE SESSION THREE

RESEARCHING

After our students compose the first draft of an essay, we often find ourselves saying something along the lines of, "Yes, you've chosen a promising topic (or made a valid observation), but the issue is more complicated than it first appears." Then we invite them to make their thinking more complex by connecting to new ideas or information using *but* or *or* instead of *and*. These objections, qualifications, and additions can't be pulled out of thin air, however. They have to be discovered through reading, research, and thought.

Ta-Nehisi Coates's article "Fear of a Black President" offers a sharp critique of the first term of Barack Obama's presidency. While it's easy to take a polarized position on Coates's argument by simply agreeing or disagreeing with him, it's more interesting to use his work as a starting place for thinking more deeply about the points he raises.

Select three or four passages that confuse, surprise, disturb, or otherwise interest you, and then spend at least 2 hours doing research into the events or history Coates presents. As you dig down into your research, pay attention to places where you learn things that deepen or complicate your understanding of Coates's argument and your own thinking. In other words, look for places where you can make new connections.

WRITING

Write an essay that discusses how your research has informed and altered your thinking about Coates's argument. As you write, use the "three most important words" (and variations) to present research that adds to, qualifies, contradicts, or suggests alternatives both to Coates's ideas *and* to your own previously held opinions.

EXPLORE

We've suggested that critical thinking begins with the word *but*. Roxane Gay feels she meets one definition of what it means to be a feminist, but not another. In Etgar Keret's short story, the narrator tells us about a crushed car he has in his living room, but something about the story—and the narrator—seems a little off. Physician Siddhartha Mukherjee knows the arguments for and against antidepressants, but he thinks both arguments distort what is currently known about the treatment of depression. Joyce Carol Oates knows there's a long tradition of writers gaining inspiration from the natural world, but she thinks differently about the ants crawling across her table.

Gay, Roxane. "Bad Feminist." *VQR* Fall 2012. Web.

Keret, Etgar. "Car Concentrate." Trans. Nathan Englander. *Granta*. 2 Jan. 2014. Web.

Mukherjee, Siddhartha. "Post-Prozac Nation: The Science and History of Treating Depression." *New York Times*. 19 April 2012. Web.

Oates, Joyce Carol. "Against Nature." *Antaeus* 57 (Autumn 1986): 236–43. Print.

On Writing by Formula

In math and science, a formula is a hard-and-fast rule or fact. The chemical formula for water, for example, is H_2O, and the algebraic formula that defines the equivalence of energy and mass is $E = mc^2$. The beauty of such formulas is that they remain true, regardless of when or where they are used. Formulas in cooking, which we usually call recipes, are sometimes more flexible. If you're making a cake and you use a little less flour than the recipe calls for, you'll still end up with a cake at the end of the process. But if you substitute an equal amount of baking soda for the baking powder listed in the recipe, you'll push kitchen chemistry past its point of flexibility; what comes out of the oven will look more like a plate than a cake.

If we shift our attention to human communication, we can see how cultural formulas differ from scientific formulas. When applied to culture, the primary meaning for *formula* is "a set form of words for use in a ceremony or ritual." Most events involving human communication—purchasing something in a store, sending a child to school, even quitting a job—aren't ceremonies or rituals and, thus, aren't governed by strict formulas. And, even when the focus is narrowed to a specific ceremony or ritual, the cultural formula for what to say isn't universal, like a scientific formula, but, rather, is context-specific and subject to change over time. Take the marriage vow: the formula for what to say depends on the country in which the ceremony is to occur, whether the vow is to be made in a secular or a religious setting, and, if the setting is religious, the denominations of the participants. In the Episcopal Church, for example, the formula for what the bride and groom vow has changed over time: prior to 1922, the bride vowed "to love, cherish, and obey" the groom; since 1922, brides and grooms have vowed "to love and to cherish" one another. As of 2012, Episcopal churches have the option of consecrating the wedding vows of same sex couples.

As this example suggests, cultural formulas loosely define the conventions that govern a given ritual or ceremony. How loosely? Enter a church of a different denomination or a mosque or a synagogue or an ashram and the formula for creating a marriage bond changes. And if you head over to City Hall to get married by a justice of the peace, where the ceremony is pared down to its essentials, you'll find that a formula still applies: the presiding authority oversees an exchange of vows; there's still an opportunity to seal the vows with a kiss; and there are still papers to be signed afterwards. Even in those ceremonies where the participants write their own vows, there's no escaping the convention of being heartfelt, sincere, and personal. Popular entertainment, for example, is often formulaic. Many of you are likely to be familiar with the formula for the horror film ("Don't go in there!"), and you may even recognize the formula for parodying horror films. ("I know only dumb people in horror movies go into places like this alone, but here I go." Screams follow.) Formulas like these, which build on audience expectations, can be picked up either by watching a bunch of popular horror films or by having someone who knows the formula tell it to you.

If the formulas that govern everything from wedding vows to movie plots are flexible, what about the formulas that govern the thoughtful essay? Are they similarly flexible? We'd be surprised if you thought so, since the tendency of writing teachers from elementary school onward is to represent the recipes or templates or rules of thumb for generating the kind of writing valued in school as hard and fast. We, on the other hand, would say that following these formulas does not produce writing that is thoughtful or compelling or reflective; it just produces writing that can be graded according to the degree to which it has followed the assigned formula. When the work at hand is delivering expected information back to the teacher, such as in an essay exam, formulaic writing is an entirely appropriate mode of response. But when the goal is independent thinking, original insights, or the production of writing that others will read voluntarily, writing that follows a formula is incapable of delivering the goods.

A formula for originality is a contradiction in terms. If your writing is going to help you to think new thoughts, it will be because you are using your writing to practice curiosity, creativity, attentiveness, and engagement. The only way to produce thoughtful prose is to actually be thoughtful; the only way to produce writing that is compelling is to feel compelled by ideas, events, and issues; the only way to produce writing that is reflective is to regularly engage in acts of reflection. In all of these realms, writing is not filling in blank spaces on a form; it is the act of exploring the possible.

• • • • •

At this point in our essay, we intended to demonstrate how we distinguish between writing that's formulaic and writing that's driven by curiosity. But we've discovered that a funny thing happens when you write about writing by formula: every path we've gone down to illustrate what's wrong with formulaic writing has ended up being formulaic itself. If we were teaching a class, we'd ask our students to brainstorm with us about the paths we might take after we've discussed how the meaning of "formula" changes with the context. Since we can't do that with you, our readers, we're going to ask you to join us in a thought experiment about the options available to us. We'll go through them in turn.

Show why the writing in our classes is better than the writing produced under other approaches. "Piece of cake!" we say. This was, in fact, the first path we tried. Given that we are arguing for using writing as a technology for producing thoughts that are new to the writer, it seemed only logical that we would then go on to provide our readers with an example from one of our classes that shows what "non-formulaic" writing looks like. Going in this direction felt natural, necessary, and appropriate.

It also felt familiar. And this is why, eventually, we had to admit that it didn't work. It's not that we lack examples of writing from our classes that we feel amply demonstrate the advantages of developing the habits of the creative mind. But when we tried to frame our argument about curiosity-driven writing, we found ourselves trapped in the solipsistic activity of arguing for the superiority of writing that we ourselves have assessed as superior.

There's another problem with moving the discussion of curiosity-driven writing to examples from our own classrooms; when it comes to making our case, we hold all the cards. We don't have to show you the writing that didn't succeed; we don't have to take you through the portfolios of students who didn't make progress over the course of the semester. We just have to find examples that prove our point. And then you, the reader, have only two options: you can either agree that we've proven what we've set out to prove or you can argue that our example isn't actually writing that explores new ideas and possibilities; it's just writing to a new formula.

So much for using examples from our classes in this context. Next!

Show why the writing produced in classes that emphasize formulaic writing is bad. "Easy as pie!" we say. To head off in this direction, all we needed was an exemplary five-paragraph essay. After much research, though, we had to conclude that there was no archive of "the universally agreed upon greatest five-paragraph essays in history" for us to draw on. A sample five-paragraph theme posted on a college Web site seemed promising at first, but the sample turned out to have been copied without attribution from an online paper mill. Even the paper mill sites themselves proved to be a poor source for exemplary five-paragraph essays: it turns out these sites don't claim that the writing they are selling is actually good; they just say it's what your professors are looking for.

Our inability to find a compelling example of the five-paragraph essay led us to see that we were arguing against a phantom. We can search for "prize-winning five-paragraph essays," but no prize winners come up. We can point to a testing industry that provides models for students to emulate with clear thesis statements, clear supporting evidence and analysis, and clear structures, but we can't find compelling examples of school systems or university administrations that insist that formulaic writing of any kind is ideal for conveying important thoughts. In fact, as we continued to drill down on this problem, we were surprised to discover that the critique of formulaic writing has a long history. Michelle Tremmel, writing in 2011, found more than 120 articles published over the past fifty years in professional journals for writing teachers that were "clearly against the five-paragraph theme."

Our failed search for the exemplary five-paragraph essay showed us that we had set ourselves the wrong task. We didn't need to develop an argument against writing by formula because that argument has already been made many times over—to, as far as we can determine, very little effect. Instead, we needed to ask a different question: why is it that students are taught to excel at a form of writing that the preponderance of writing teachers agree isn't actually "good writing"? Our answer to this question, when it finally came, surprised us: teaching students to produce formulaic essays and arguments has never actually been about teaching students to write like good writers. It has instead been about teaching them to be clear and rule-abiding language users.

So, in the end, we concluded that there's actually no point in delineating the limits of the five-paragraph essay or any other writing formula because learning to be a clear and conventional language user has little to do with learning to be a writer. If familiar formulas are really just recipes for clarity, without regard for the writer's thoughts and ideas, we don't need to include them in our discussion of writing at all.

Now what?

Make a joke? We believe in the power of humor to create opportunities that reason alone can't make available. And, the truth is, we are in a funny situation: two writing teachers have given themselves the worst writing prompt ever: "make an unconventional argument against convention." Our predicament is funny in the way only contradictions, paradoxes, and koans can be: there's a fugitive meaning captured by the situation we've put ourselves in that can only be understood through the experience of being caught in the trap.

So, let's admit it's funny that, in our meditation on writing by formula, we've written ourselves into two dead ends: we can't provide unconventional evidence that our approach is better and we can't find anyone who argues convincingly that good writing requires conforming to conventions. We're Don Quixote and Sancho Panza, tilting at windmills.

If we really want to shift the conversation about writing from following a formula to practicing habits of mind, we need to take a different approach. We can't look to a single piece of student writing to bear the burden of illustrating either the habits of a creative mind or the robotic prose of a student trained to produce writing that can be assessed by machines. Instead, we need to ask some new questions: What habits of mind are being encouraged by questions that ask for the faithful reproduction of the main points in a lecture? By questions that ask the writer to agree or disagree with a simple explanation for a complex event? By an assessment system that stresses clarity over shades of meaning?

We'd like you to take some time to think about these questions and to reflect on your own experiences producing writing in school. We think your reflections are likely to support our contention that the emphasis in your education has been on order, clarity, and concision more than exploration, questioning, and the joys of digression.

Change direction. Having produced three different discussions of formulaic writing, we finally wrote ourselves to an understanding of why this particular transition has been so difficult. To comprehend how writing is based in habits of mind, one must look at the work of writers who are in the habit of writing. We want our students to ask difficult questions and get lost in the rabbit holes of research; we want them to know what it's like to get trapped in dead ends and to learn to write themselves out of such impasses. When writing this way becomes a habit, one learns the art of writing oneself into awareness of the complexity of what previously seemed straightforward, obvious, or familiar.

We realized, at last, that the best way to show you the habits of experienced writers at work is to do exactly what we've done here: document just how much work goes into resisting the allure of the familiar and the easily proven.

• • • • •

So, a different direction.

Certain topics seem to invite predictable writing and thinking. One of the most clichéd topics in high school and college writing curricula is gun control. Given the differences between those who favor gun control and those who favor gun rights, it seems implausible that writers on either side of this debate could introduce anything that would alter where anyone stands on this issue. Pro/con, liberal/conservative, right/wrong. There doesn't appear to be a lot of room for movement.

How do experienced writers, who have made a habit of being genuinely curious, avoid reproducing predictable arguments when writing about long debated topics? To answer this question, let's consider the first few paragraphs of the introduction to *Reducing Gun Violence in America: Informing Policy with Evidence and Analysis*, an edited collection published soon after the mass shooting at Sandy Hook Elementary School in 2012.

> The role of guns in violence, and what should be done, are subjects of intense debate in the United States and elsewhere. But certain facts are not debatable. More than 31,000 people died from gunshot wounds in the United States in 2010. Because the victims are disproportionately young, gun violence is one of the leading causes of premature mortality in the United States. In addition to these deaths, in 2010, there were an estimated 337,960 nonfatal violent crimes committed with guns, and 73,505 persons were treated in hospital emergency departments for nonfatal gunshot wounds. The social and economic costs of gun violence in America are also enormous.
>
> Despite the huge daily impact of gun violence, most public discourse on gun policy is centered on mass shootings in public places. Such incidents are typically portrayed as random acts by severely mentally ill individuals which are impossible to predict or prevent. Those who viewed, heard, or read news stories on gun policy might conclude the following: (1) mass shootings, the mentally ill, and assault weapons are the primary concerns; (2) gun control laws disarm law-abiding citizens without affecting criminals' access to guns; (3) there is no evidence that gun control laws work; and (4) the public has no appetite for strengthening current gun laws. Yet all of the evidence in this book counters each of these misperceptions with facts to the contrary.

At first glance, the moves that Daniel W. Webster and Jon S. Vernick, co-authors of the introduction to *Reducing Gun Violence*, make here are likely to seem familiar. They establish the importance of their topic by referencing what they present as undebatable facts. Next, they discuss popular thinking about gun violence and legislation. And then they announce that their book will debunk the four major misperceptions about gun violence in turn.

This description of the way Webster and Vernick build their argument misses their most important move, though: they want to shift the context of the discussion of gun violence away from headline-grabbing mass shootings in order to focus their reader's attention on the high rate of gun violence in the United States. The research they have done documents the undeniable costs of this violence, both in lives lost and in medical expenses for the roughly one hundred thousand people injured or killed by guns in the United States every year. Webster and Vernick then point to one of the problems that limits our ability to discuss workable ways to reduce gun violence: *despite* the prevalence of gun violence in the United States, the only gun violence that gets sustained attention from the media is that which takes the form of a mass shooting.

What Webster and Vernick do next is further evidence of curiosity-driven minds at work on a problem: they detail the conclusions that reasonable people might make from how mass shootings are covered in the media; they *imagine* themselves in the place of such viewers and list the reasons why reducing gun violence seems impossible as a result. They haven't, in other words, produced an unsupportable "most people think" statement; they've made a connection between popular opinions and what mass media focuses on—namely mass shootings. In making this connection, Webster and Vernick have implicitly established a relationship of causality: because most people encounter information about gun violence in the context of mass shootings, they reach certain predictable conclusions about both the means and the possibility of curbing gun violence. Webster and Vernick promise to show how these conclusions no longer hold once the context is shifted from mass shootings to gun violence in general.

Can we imagine someone being persuaded to rethink gun violence as a result of Webster and Vernick's argument? In so doing, do we imagine someone who has thought about the issue a great deal? If this person *is* persuaded, would the change in position be consequential for the person? Does this personal change also have the potential to be consequential on a larger scale? We'd answer all of these questions in the affirmative. In fact, we'd go further and say that asking questions of this sort is a good way to start a conversation about how to distinguish writing that emerges from habits of the creative mind and writing that is done to confirm beliefs the writer already holds: the first kind of writing imagines readers who can consider multiple and conflicting ideas; the second seeks out readers who already agree.

Could a less experienced student writer produce something on gun control that made moves similar to those we found in the opening paragraphs of Webster and Vernick's introduction? We think so, but that writer would have to be genuinely interested in gun control as a question to be understood, rather than as an issue upon which one first takes a stand and then sets out in search of evidence supporting that stand. That student would have to want to spend time doing research that drilled down into questions about gun control, and that student would have to believe that staking out a position on gun control has consequences that extend far beyond the fulfillment of a paper assignment.

If such a student were working in a course that encouraged exploring questions rather than following a formula for putting together an argument, that student would have the chance to experience just how much is involved in understanding a complex issue in depth and what it means to use one's writing to think new thoughts. And this, finally, is why we believe that shifting the teaching of writing from formulas to habits matters. This shift encourages the creation of classroom practices that allow inexperienced writers to cultivate curiosity, to explore in wide-ranging ways, and to engage with the most pressing questions of our time.

Note: All definitions come from merriamwebster.com.

PRACTICE SESSION ONE

RESEARCHING

Using the Web as your archive, find an example of a persuasive essay that has been truly influential and that *actually changes your mind* on an issue. See if you can find an example written by a professional journalist or an experienced writer from a newspaper, an important magazine, or an academic journal. Spend at least 30 minutes searching for an essay that meets these criteria.

After you've found a truly persuasive essay, or after you've put in 30 minutes looking for one, take at least 20 minutes to write about your search. What challenges did you encounter? If you found a persuasive essay, was it about a topic that previously mattered to you, or was it about something you hadn't thought much about? What did you learn about persuasive writing as your search progressed? What's the value of doing this exercise?

PRACTICE SESSION TWO

READING

Select one of the readings suggested in the Explore section that follows. Read the article or essay and then return to the introductory paragraphs, rereading them with care. After that, spend at least 20 minutes taking notes on how the writer composes the introduction. How does the writer choose to launch the article? How does the writer get the reader interested in the topic at hand? How does the introduction differ from a conventional five-paragraph-essay introduction? Does it share any qualities with the introductions you learned to write in school?

REFLECTING

Review the article or essay you read for the Reading Practice Session taking notes about how the writer exercises curiosity; connects ideas, sources, and information in surprising ways; and keeps the reader interested from the beginning of the piece to the end. In other words, explore how the article or essay *works*.

Based on what you've discovered about how the piece you selected is put together, what would you say governed the writer's organizational decisions? Is the writer following a set of rules or a formula that you can identify? Has the writer broken rules you were taught? Spend at least 45 minutes writing about the relationship between the writer's curiosity and the structure he or she has used to organize the article or essay you've read.

EXPLORE

Is there a formula for writing against formula? Probably not. The essays we've suggested here demonstrate, instead, just how malleable the essay's form is. Annie Dillard writes lyrically about witnessing a natural event. James Baldwin reflects fearlessly on what it means to grow up black in America. John Branch uses a host of multimedia resources to help tell the story of a deadly skiing decision. And the reporters at Planet Money use video, taped interviews, and text to show how an ordinary t-shirt is the result of a global production process.

Baldwin, James. "Notes of a Native Son," *Notes of a Native Son.* Boston: Beacon Press, 1955. Print.

Branch, John. "Snow Fall: The Avalanche at Tunnel Creek." *New York Times.* 21 Dec. 2012. Web.

Dillard, Annie. "Total Eclipse," *Teaching a Stone to Talk.* New York: Harper Collins, 1982. 9–29. Print. (Available on Google Books via Preview.)

"Planet Money Makes a T-shirt: The World Behind a Simple Shirt, in Five Chapters." Video. *Planet Money.* National Public Radio. Web.

On Working with the Words of Others

Cite your sources.

It's hard to imagine a research assignment that doesn't include some version of this admonition. If you were to ask your teachers why it's important to provide full information about the sources you've used, they'd likely tell you one of two things: citation is a service to your readers because it allows them to follow up on ideas or information they encounter in your writing, or citation is a way of marking the boundaries between your work and the work of others. These answers aren't wrong, but they both imply that citation is primarily a means for defending yourself from skeptical readers—those who would doubt the quality of your sources and those who would suspect you of plagiarizing.

We acknowledge that documenting sources and preventing plagiarism are both worthy goals, but we fear that discussing citation only in these terms actively discourages students from participating in the most powerful educational experience there is—engaging deeply with the ideas of other thinkers. "To cite" a source means more than following a set of rules about how to list it in a footnote or on a works cited page; "to cite" also refers to the act of quoting, summarizing, or generally making use of material from sources.

We invite you to think of citation as an opportunity to demonstrate what you can *do* with the words of others. To cite sources is to bring other voices, other approaches, and other ideas into your work. It provides the material for you to carry on a conversation with writers whose work you find compelling. While you may have experience using sources as the object of analysis (for instance, when you've been asked to write about a literary text or primary document) or to supply background information, citation can serve your writing in a variety of other ways. It can contribute key ideas or concepts, provide positions or arguments to grapple with, or shift the direction of the conversation. We especially value citation that brings in a new perspective that questions or rejects the most obvious way of thinking, or that turns the issue, question, or problem you are working on so that you can see it from another angle.

With this understanding of citation in mind, every time you cite another writer you should ask: *What work do I want these words or ideas to do for my readers?*

To explore the value of this question, let's take a look at three examples that involve citation and consider what asking this question allows us to see about each writer's project.

• • • • •

1. Fareed Zakaria hosts his own show on CNN, where he discusses foreign policy and international relations. He is the author of best-selling books that consider America's fate in the altered global landscape of the twenty-first century, and he writes for *Time* magazine. On August 10, 2012, he published an editorial in *Time* entitled "The Case for Gun Control: Why Limiting Easy Access to Guns Is Intelligent and American." He was prompted to write, he says, by a mass shooting at a Sikh temple in Oak Creek, Wisconsin, that left seven dead, including the gunman, who committed suicide at the scene.

In his editorial, Zakaria refers to an influential book on the history of gun laws in the United States:

> Adam Winkler, a professor of constitutional law at UCLA, documents the actual history in *Gunfight: The Battle over the Right to Bear Arms in America*. Guns were regulated in the U.S. from the earliest years of the Republic. Laws that banned the carrying of concealed weapons were passed in Kentucky and Louisiana in 1813. Other states soon followed: Indiana in 1820, Tennessee and Virginia in 1838, Alabama in 1839, and Ohio in 1859. Similar laws were passed in Texas, Florida and Oklahoma. As the governor of Texas (Texas!) explained in 1893, the "mission of the concealed deadly weapon is murder. To check it is the duty of every self-respecting, law-abiding man."

What work does Zakaria want this citation of Winkler's work to do for his readers? Zakaria draws his readers' attention to recent scholarship, arguing that gun control in the United States has a history dating back nearly two hundred years. Zakaria clearly identifies both the author of this research and where the research can be found, should his readers care to look more deeply into this history. In referencing and summarizing work of this caliber, Zakaria is displaying his expert credentials: he knows where the best writing on gun control is, and he can succinctly represent the other author's ideas, sparing his readers the work of reading Winkler's 384-page tome on their own. So in this example, the work of citation is analogous to a display of heavy lifting.

That's one way to use citation: to digest and distill information for the reader.

There's one problem with our presenting Zakaria's writing on Winkler as exemplary of this valuable use of citation, however: the heavy lifting on display was done not by Zakaria but by Jill Lepore, whom Zakaria has failed to cite. There's an unmistakable similarity between Zakaria's paragraph and a paragraph in Lepore's April 23, 2012, *New Yorker* article, "Battleground America: One Nation, under the Gun," which she wrote in the aftermath of the shooting death of Trayvon Martin:

> As Adam Winkler, a constitutional-law scholar at U.C.L.A., demonstrates in a remarkably nuanced new book, *Gunfight: The Battle Over the Right to Bear Arms in America*, firearms have been regulated in the United States from the start. Laws banning the carrying of concealed weapons were passed in Kentucky and Louisiana in 1813, and other states soon followed: Indiana (1820), Tennessee and Virginia (1838), Alabama (1839), and Ohio (1859). Similar laws were passed in Texas, Florida, and Oklahoma. As the governor of Texas explained in 1893, the "mission of the concealed deadly weapon is murder. To check it is the duty of every self-respecting, law-abiding man."

When accusations surfaced that Zakaria had used Lepore's work without making clear that he had paraphrased and quoted from her article, CNN and *Time* suspended Zakaria pending a full review of the incident.

This appears on its face to be a clear-cut case of plagiarism. Zakaria never mentions Lepore in his piece, and he doesn't signal in any way that he is presenting her summary of Winkler's book with minor changes. He's representing Lepore's words and work as his own, which is the very definition of plagiarism. Zakaria released a statement the same day the news broke, acknowledging his responsibility for the error: "I made a terrible mistake. It is a serious lapse and one that is entirely my fault. I apologize unreservedly to her [Lepore], to my editors at *Time* and CNN, and to my readers and viewers everywhere." A week later, CNN concluded its review of Zakaria's work and determined that the error was "unintentional" and "an isolated incident." He was immediately reinstated at CNN, and he returned to *Time* after a one-month suspension.

Note that Zakaria was suspended even though his long record of publication establishes beyond a doubt that he knows how to cite in ways that do the heavy lifting for his readers; time and again, he's demonstrated that he knows how to distill long texts into concise summaries. So while we are emphasizing here that we want you to be able to (1) select an appropriately challenging source with which to work, (2) engage with an extended piece of historical scholarship, and (3) capture the author's argument succinctly, Zakaria's example shows just how important it is that you demonstrate, in *every instance*, that you are able to (4) document your sources. No one gets a free pass on that fourth requirement, no matter how long her or his record of publication!

• • • • •

2. For our second example of working with the words of others, we would like to draw your attention to Jonathan Lethem's "The Ecstasy of Influence: A Plagiarism." Early in his essay, Lethem illustrates his thesis that originality and copying go hand in hand during the artistic process by discussing his initial encounter with the John Donne quote that introduces his essay, "All mankind is of one author, and is one volume; when one man dies, one chapter is not torn out of the book, but translated into a better language; and every chapter must be so translated." Lethem tells us that he first came across this quote while watching the film *84 Charing Cross Road*. He then relates a convoluted tale of trying to track down the passage in its original context, turning first to the book and then the play on which the movie was based, before discovering, after many fruitless searches on the Web, that the film had misquoted Donne.

Lethem's story is an elegant example of how the meaning of strings of words (that is, quotations) changes as those strings of words travel through time and across media. There's just one thing about the example, though, as Lethem tells us in the "key" he provides at the end of his essay: "The anecdote [about tracking down the quote] is cribbed, with an elision to avoid appropriating a dead grandmother, from Jonathan Rosen's *The Talmud and the Internet*. I've never seen *84 Charing Cross Road*, nor searched the Web for a Donne quote." As Lethem's key makes clear, he has composed his essay almost entirely of uncited quotations and unattributed ideas to show what his essay has argued—the act of creation always involves copying, building on, modifying, and combining material from other sources. This is what Lethem means by "the ecstasy of influence": all originality depends on the writer having been deeply influenced by the ideas of others.

We are particularly taken with Lethem's description of the writing practice that guided him in "The Ecstasy of Influence," which appears at the end of the essay, in his introduction to the list of his unattributed sources:

> This key to the preceding essay names the source of every line I stole, warped, and cobbled together as I "wrote" (except, alas, those sources I forgot along the way). First uses of a given author or speaker are highlighted in red. Nearly every sentence I culled I also revised, at least slightly—for necessities of space, in order to produce a more consistent tone, or simply because I felt like it.

With his key, Lethem has turned our question on its head: What work does he want his *noncitation* of the words of others to do for his readers? We would say that his noncitation is a performance: since Lethem has subtitled his piece "a plagiarism," and he has provided a closing list of the citations he left uncited in the body of his essay, it's clear he isn't trying to pass off the work of others as his own. Rather, by the time Lethem is done with his key, he has documented that the work of being influenced by the ideas of others requires reading widely and deeply.

• • • • •

Before moving to our final example, we want to acknowledge the intentionally unconventional character of our first two examples of working with the words of others. We could have pointed to Jill Lepore's distillation of Adam Winkler's book *Gunfight* as a great example of what it means to condense a lengthy text into a concise summary. Instead, we chose to highlight Zakaria's unattributed use of Lepore's writing as an example of what it means to fail to work well with the words of others. And we could have called on any number of prominent examples to further illustrate the perils of plagiarism. But instead we chose Lethem's essay, "The Ecstasy of Influence: A Plagiarism," because it complicates the notion that the process of documenting sources of inspiration or insight could ever be complete. We have started with these examples to encourage you to be thoughtful, and even creative, about working with the words of others. The primary goal of citing others' work shouldn't be to follow the rules of documentation but to extend your own thinking and show your readers that your ideas are grounded in both verifiable facts and an ongoing conversation with sources about the issues and ideas that interest you.

• • • • •

3. For our final example, we'll look at the kind of citation that will most occupy you as a college writer: working with the words of others to complicate and enrich your own understanding of the problem, question, or mystery you've chosen to explore. To do so, we'll turn to perhaps the most generic of research topics: gun control. This was a typical research topic when we were in high school over thirty years ago, and we imagine that it will continue to be a typical research topic thirty years from now. Gun control is seen to be an ideal prompt in traditional writing classrooms, we would say, because it lends itself so easily to for-or-against arguments.

A central point of disagreement in the debate about gun control is what James Madison meant when he wrote the Second Amendment: "A well regulated Militia, being necessary to the security of a free State, the right of the people to keep and bear Arms, shall not be infringed." Did he mean that the people, as a collective, have the right to form militias for their common defense? Or did he mean that individuals have the right to own and carry guns? In our view, it is not a stretch to claim that the argument about the meaning of the Second Amendment and gun control is in part about citation. People on both sides cite the amendment, but neither side can establish, once and for all, what the amendment means. Why? Because all arguments about the amendment's meaning hinge on how one works with Madison's words. And so the for-or-against argument about gun control just gets repeated over and over again, without generating new insights or understandings on either side of the "debate."

A writer who practices curiosity, however, can reject the dead end of the for-or-against assignment. Consider, for example, the article we discussed above (the one Zakaria failed to cite), "Battleground America: One Nation, under the Gun," in which Jill Lepore engages with the question of whether the Second Amendment was originally intended to preserve the right of individuals to own guns. We're particularly interested in this article because of Lepore's adept and highly varied use of citation. As we noted earlier, her summary of Winkler's work is an example of citation as heavy lifting; she does the hard work of condensing a long text into a clear and concise overview. In the exercises at the end of this essay, we ask you to examine how else she works with the words of others, including Madison's. Our goal is for you to be able to use citation as Lepore does, to be able to work with the words of others in the service of exploring and exposing the complexity of a chosen question, problem, or mystery.

Lepore's discussion of the Second Amendment points to a problem all writers face when they work with the words of others. Simply quoting another writer's words isn't enough to make those words do the work you want them to do. There are moments when you have to analyze those words and make a case for what you think they mean. Lepore, a historian who specializes in early US history, mines documents from the country's past, including the Articles of Confederation and the Constitution, to place the Second Amendment in the context of an eighteenth-century debate about whether the states or the newly formed federal government should have the power to maintain militias. In 1776, the Articles of Confederation included the requirement that "every *state* shall always keep up a well regulated and disciplined militia," but in 1787, when the Constitution was signed in Philadelphia, *Congress* was granted the power "to provide for calling forth the Militia to execute the Laws of the Union." When Madison drafted the Bill of Rights in 1789, he was trying to appease those who worried that the Constitution had granted too much power to the federal government. His concern, Lepore argues, was to address anxieties about a permanent federal army. By citing these original sources, Lepore means to establish that there is a historical ground for arguing that the Second Amendment originally had nothing to do with individual ownership of guns.

But if Lepore's citation of the nation's foundational documents accurately depicts Madison's original intent, how does she then account for the transformation of Madison's original concern with militias and state power into a constitutional defense of private gun ownership? Here, too, Lepore keeps her attention focused on original source material. She points out that even the National Rifle Association—founded in 1871 and now the nation's most influential lobby against gun control—did not interpret the Second Amendment as preserving a personal right to bear arms until the 1970s. What prompted this change? Lepore, citing speeches by Malcolm X and Huey Newton from the 1960s, makes the surprising case that the idea that the Second Amendment guarantees the right of private citizens to own guns was first made by black nationalists and the Black Panther Party for Self-Defense. At that point in time, following the many assassinations of that decade—of President John F. Kennedy, Malcolm X, Robert Kennedy, and Martin Luther King Jr.—the NRA actually supported the Gun Control Act of 1968. Not until 1977, on the cusp of a new conservative movement, did the NRA adopt as its new motto a quote from the Second Amendment: "The Right of the People to Keep and Bear Arms Shall Not Be Infringed." The idea that the amendment protects the rights of individual gun owners only went mainstream during the presidency of Ronald Reagan, after Senator Orrin Hatch and the Subcommittee on the Constitution issued a 1982 report about the Second Amendment entitled "The Right to Keep and Bear Arms."

Can we generalize about the work Lepore wants her many citations to do for the readers of "Battleground America"? Lepore does plenty of heavy lifting, summarizing many important scholarly sources. But what we find to be exemplary is her commitment to working with the words of others who are in the position to complicate her thinking. Throughout the article, Lepore demonstrates her ability to work with primary source material to cast something familiar—in this case, the debate over the Second Amendment—in a new light. Lepore does not, in other words, use citation to simplify the historical record or to flatten an issue into those who stand on one side of the question and those who stand on the other side. Rather, she weaves her many sources together into a sinuous braid supple enough to explain why repeated and horrific acts of gun violence have not yet led to meaningful legislation curbing access to guns.

PRACTICE SESSION ONE

RESEARCHING

We emphasized the importance of working with primary sources in our essay above. We'd like you to identify the primary sources Jill Lepore cites either in her essay "Battleground America" or "the Last Amazon: Wonder Woman Returns," both of which are available through the *New Yorker* Web site. After you've identified all of Lepore's primary sources, select one of the documents she mentions and go find it. If you can't access the source online, try to find it in your library. If you're reading "Battleground America," for instance, you could look at the Constitution, examples of nineteenth-century gun laws, the speech by Malcolm X that Lepore cites, or official documents of the National Rifle Association.

Read the document you've chosen and then spend at least 30 minutes writing about how a more detailed citation from the document could have further complicated Lepore's discussion. If the first document you track down doesn't yield a compelling example, search for other primary source material; once you've found something compelling, complete the assignment.

READING

Journalists who write for popular magazines or newspapers typically don't provide in-text documentation of page numbers or a list of works cited. And it's rare to come across a footnote in the *New Yorker*, *Harper's*, or the *Atlantic*. Return to the essay you read for the previous exercise and review at least three pages, paying attention to where Lepore is clear about where she found words, ideas, and information from others and where she's not. Spend at least 20 minutes making a list of where she would need to cite her sources if she had written this article for an academic class. Also note how often you were confused or unclear about whether she had taken material from a source.

REFLECTING

After reviewing how and where Lepore documents her sources, spend at least 60 minutes writing about the different citation standards of journalism and scholarly writing. Did you find evidence that caused you to trust or to doubt Lepore as a writer? Is there any way to tell whether a citation is accurate or not *without* tracking it down and checking on it yourself?

PRACTICE SESSION TWO

READING

Now we'd like you to pay attention to the variety of ways writers work with the words of others. Select an essay from the suggested readings in the Explore section that follows. Read the essay with care.

Next, spend at least 40 minutes observing, marking, and identifying the many different ways the writer works with sources. You might notice sources used to supply background information, to provide key ideas or concepts, to provide positions or arguments to grapple with, to shift the direction of the conversation, or to serve as the focus of analysis. Where did the writer work with sources in ways that impressed, surprised, or perhaps disappointed you? Were there moments when you felt a citation didn't do the work the writer wanted it to? Did the writer cite sources in ways that you'd like to emulate?

REFLECTING

Spend at least 60 minutes writing reflectively about what you've learned from this exercise about working with the words or ideas of others.

EXPLORE

As writers, we are always working with the words of others. Our suggested readings provide examples of ways of doing this work that you might want to give a try. Christopher Chabris questions the words of Malcolm Gladwell, a writer we quote a good deal in this book. Zadie Smith argues with a contemporary cultural theorist about the nature of reality. Sarah Resnick interviews a member of WikiLeaks about the collection and distribution of classified material. And John Jeremiah Sullivan evaluates the success of a half-finished work by a writer he greatly admires.

Chabris, Christopher. "The Trouble with Malcolm Gladwell." *Slate* 8. Oct. 2013. Web.

Smith, Zadie. "The Rise of the Essay." *The Guardian* 20. Nov. 2007. Web.

Resnick, Sarah. "Leave Your Cellphone at Home: Interview with Jacob Applebaum." *n+1* 10. 10 June 2013. Web

Sullivan, John Jeremiah. "Too Much Information." *GQ*. May 2011. Web.

Argument at Work: Michelle Alexander and the Power of Analogy

A decade ago, when legal scholar Michelle Alexander first noticed a bright orange poster stapled to a telephone pole that declared, in bold letters, THE DRUG WAR IS THE NEW JIM CROW, she rejected the statement as preposterous. A Stanford Law School graduate and a former clerk for Supreme Court Justice Harry Blackmun, Alexander had good reason to trust her judgment. She didn't forget that sign, though, and after years of studying how the war on drugs had been carried out, she came to believe "that mass incarceration in the United States had, in fact, emerged as a stunningly comprehensive and well-disguised system of racialized social control that functions in a manner strikingly similar to [the pre–civil rights era, "separate but equal" laws known as] Jim Crow."

Anticipating that some readers of her book *The New Jim Crow: Mass Incarceration in the Age of Colorblindness* will share her initial skepticism about the racist character of the war on drugs, Alexander uses the government's own statistics to show that, although people of all races use and sell drugs at similar rates, "black men have been admitted to prison on drug charges at rates twenty to fifty times greater than those of white men." Over time, mass incarceration leads to mass disenfranchisement, since convicted felons, regardless of their race, lose the right to vote and the right to serve on juries and may also lose access to public housing, student loans, food stamps, and other public benefits. Excluded from the mainstream economy, prisoners who have served their time fall into a status of "permanent second-class citizenship." Given the manifest disparity in rates of incarceration, Alexander argues that "laws prohibiting the use and sale of drugs are facially race neutral, but they are enforced in a highly discriminatory fashion." And this, Alexander goes on to show, has served to create "a racial caste system."

So is the drug war a new incarnation of Jim Crow? An analogy establishes a relationship of similarity, not exact equivalence. The rhetorical strength of such comparisons is realized when they shake us out of our usual ways of thinking, shift our perspectives, make us see a connection that was previously invisible. In this instance, there is evidence that Alexander has produced an argument persuasive enough to get readers who are as skeptical as she once was to reconsider their positions. Bill Frezza, a writer for the conservative magazine *Forbes*, begins his review of Alexander's book thus: "Once in a great while a writer at the opposite end of the political spectrum gets you to look at a familiar set of facts in a new way. Disconcerting as it is, you can feel your foundation shift as your mind struggles to reconcile this new point of view with long held beliefs. Michelle Alexander has done just that in her book, *The New Jim Crow*."

The raw material for Alexander's argument—government statistics on incarceration—is readily available on the Web. Anyone can cite this data, but citation alone doesn't produce a foundation-shifting argument. Alexander drills down into the data and locates her argument in history; she is skeptical of the patterns that emerge, so she tests the connections she has made and allows the results of her research to guide her thinking. In the end, she produces an argument that invites other reasonable skeptics to see the drug war as the reimplementation of Jim Crow–style institutionalized racism.

CHAPTER

6

Practicing

How do you develop a habit? Through practice. But what is practice? When you're a kid practicing handwriting, you learn through repetition. You copy the letters of the alphabet over and over, mastering the block shapes first before moving on to cursive. With both types of writing, you practice certain physical gestures so that you can faithfully reproduce the conventional shape of each letter. This practice requires hand–eye coordination, fine motor control in your dominant hand, and symbol recognition. Once you've practiced these activities enough, you can reproduce all the letters of the alphabet quickly, without conscious thought. Then, in a very limited sense, you know how to write.

What do you practice if you want to become a writer? Aspiring writers are often given two pieces of well-intentioned advice: "write what you know" and "write every day." While we can quibble with this kind of advice, we'd rather have you think about what habits you should be developing through practice (that is, through writing every day). What does it mean to look at the world the way a writer does? What does it mean to read like a writer? What does it mean to ask questions like a writer? In posing these questions, we encourage you to see writing as a way of being curious about the world and your place in it.

On Seeing as a Writer

> The very reason I write is so that I might not sleepwalk through my entire life.
>
> —Zadie Smith, "Fail Better"

Learning how to draw, as we discussed earlier (**pp. 18–22**), means learning how to see without naming; this allows the visual, spatial, and synthesizing ways of thinking to guide the hand on the page. Quieting the verbal train of thought allows you to see like an artist, but what if you want to put what you see into words? How do you learn to see as a writer does?

Young children can be intensely observant and curious. They learn about the world by paying attention and asking lots of questions. Once we become adults, many of us stop observing so acutely and constantly—in part because so much of the previously mysterious world is now familiar to us. We go on mental autopilot during routine experiences. We see what we expect to see. And we keep our surprise and wonder in check because both take up time we don't think we have to spare.

To see as a writer does, you need to practice asking questions about what you see. So instead of quieting the verbal activity in your mind, in this process you are training yourself to question the information your eyes are reporting to you. This questioning serves two purposes: it makes you conscious of your own perspective, and it also makes clear that other perspectives are possible. And this, ultimately, is part of what seeing as a writer involves—noticing clashes, subtle tensions, or unexpected connections between differing perspectives.

What do we mean by this? Here's an example of such a conflict, which comes from the opening of an essay by Annie Stiver, a student in one of our creative nonfiction classes:

> Recently, while standing in line for a ticket at the New Brunswick train station, I witnessed a mother nudge her young son, who, after barely noticing his mother's prod, continued to look steadily at a man sitting half-awake on a bench in the corner of the station. After her eyes dropped and brows narrowed on her son, she clasped his shoulder and bent down to tell him that he is "not supposed to stare at bums." The boy turned his head forward at his mother's instruction, yet as I watched him I noticed his eyes were straining towards the right side of the room where this man was. Eventually, when it was his mother's turn at the ticket machine, the boy immediately turned his head to stare full-on at the man in tattered clothing on the train station bench. I figured that the boy was an infrequent visitor to New Brunswick.
>
> This situation got me thinking about the rate at which children are encouraged not to stare even as they are curiously struck by novel experiences and when confronted with the unexpected. How did it come to be that we are taught not to stare?
>
> A common response is that it's simply not polite to stare. But in those moments of heightened curiosity when we are told to keep our eyes from wandering on another's "business," we are, aside from being polite, affecting our own development and behavior as we repress our individual curiosities and questions about others. What happens when we stare? I would argue that staring goes beyond seeing the "other." Rather, when we stare, we are meant to think about ourselves. Watching the boy staring at the man in the

> station, I remembered the familiar feeling of when I was his age during unfamiliar and curious encounters with the unknown and unexpected. We're not staring because we want to know that our way of life is more comfortable and reassuring (we can consider this impolite), but sometimes we stare because we feel instinctively that our way of life is not quite right. When this happens, we want to ask, "Why aren't more of us staring?"

This is a great start to a thoughtful essay. Rereading this passage and thinking about the choices the student made as a writer, we see that she began with close, careful observation of the scene in the train station—a mother scolds her young son for staring at a homeless person. The writer had many choices about what perspective to take on this scene, and she chose to pay attention to the tension between what the mother says—that her son is not supposed to stare—and what he does—look again and again. In so doing, the writer stages for her readers an encounter between one perspective (staring is impolite) and another (staring is evidence of curiosity). Rather than arguing that one perspective or the other is the correct one to have on the situation, the writer responds to this common experience of a parent scolding a child with a question that the scene has raised for her:

"How did it come to be that we are taught not to stare?"

The writer pushes past the obvious answer, that it's impolite. There's something more going on here than bad behavior: the child wants to stare. The writer asks another question:

"What happens when we stare?"

Again, the writer rejects the commonplace answer. Staring that involves judgment of others is rude, she concedes, but curious children may be staring for another reason. "I would argue," she writes, "that staring goes beyond seeing the 'other.' Rather, when we stare, we are meant to think about ourselves.... Sometimes we stare because we feel instinctively that our way of life is not quite right." And this line of reasoning leads the writer to the question that drives the rest of her essay:

"Why aren't more of us staring?"

As writing teachers, we look at this student's sequence of observations, interpretations, and questions, and we see the habits of a creative mind at work.

> She began with close observation.
>
> She asked lots of questions—and not just questions about the facts (that is, questions starting with the words *what, where,* or *who*), but also questions about cause and significance (questions starting with *how* or *why*).
>
> She recognized a key concept—in this case, staring—and shifted her frame of reference to focus on what's going on when a child stares.
>
> She shifted her perspective away from the straightforward and obvious to think from a different point of view. In this case, she thought about why the child continued to look after having been told not to.
>
> Remembering her own childhood, she realized that a child may stare because her or his usual way of thinking has been unsettled. Staring—or merely looking thoughtfully—can lead to reflection about oneself and one's relationship to others.

This isn't a formula for seeing like a writer; rather, it shows that seeing like a writer means developing the habit of choosing—from what to focus on, to the terms of the description, to the connections made, to the other perspectives entertained. To see as a writer, one doesn't begin by choosing a topic or a theme, both of which are inert, but rather by practicing questioning what one sees, which is a never-ending activity.

Now we'd like you to practice looking from different perspectives at places and the people who inhabit them, with the goal of opening up new and compelling questions about what you see.

PRACTICE SESSION ONE

REFLECTING (ON PUBLIC SPACE)

Begin by selecting a familiar, common space in your community or on your campus, somewhere you've been dozens if not hundreds of times. Visit at a time of day when it's likely to be busy. Observe the space for at least 20 minutes. Take notes on what you see. Notice who uses the space and how they move through it. Move around, exploring different perspectives.

After you've spent 20 or more minutes observing, spend at least 15 minutes writing down questions that your observations have raised for you. How does the space signal that it's public? Is it welcoming and beautiful, or ramshackle and dirty? Is it used by a wide variety of people or by a more homogeneous group? How does the space itself shape the experiences of the people who use it? How does it encourage or enhance some activities and limit others? These questions are just to get you started; they should trigger other questions that are directly related to your observations.

Write a reflective essay that develops out of your observations and a few of your most compelling questions about the place you observed.

REFLECTING (ON PRIVATE SPACE)

Next, we'd like you to do a similar exercise with a more private place, one that's inside, known or used by few people, and rich in visual detail. (Avoid choosing your own room or any other place that's overly familiar; it's hard to see such places in new ways.) Spend at least 20 minutes observing and taking notes and photographs. Then spend another 15 minutes pondering your experience in the space and writing down questions that your observations have raised. Start with the basics: How does the place signal that it's private? What activities does the space encourage, and what activities does it discourage? Is it possible to have a perspective on this place that is uniquely your own?

Write a reflective essay that develops out of your observations and a few of the most interesting questions you asked about the place you observed. Your goal is to compose a piece that gives your readers a new way to see and understand this private space.

REFLECTING (ON NATURAL SPACE)

Repeat this exercise in a natural, uninhabited, and unlandscaped space. Once again, observe and take notes for at least 20 minutes. Then spend 15 minutes or more developing questions that are grounded in your particular perspective. Coming up with questions about a natural space may be hard at first, but that too is worth pondering. After you've gathered your notes and questions, write another reflective essay that develops out of one or more of your most interesting questions and shows your reader how to see and think about this place in a new way.

PRACTICE SESSION TWO

READING

In "On Seeing as a Writer," we examine how one of our students started to see as a writer. And we find our evidence in the words she chose to explain her experience in the train station. Select a passage from a reading you've already written about. What does this passage you've selected reveal about the writer's way of seeing?

Spend at least 30 minutes writing a profile of the writer's way of seeing based on what you can draw from the passage you've read. How is the way of seeing you've identified distinctive?

EXPLORE

In our essay, we ask you to consider the writer's way of seeing the world as something that is learned through practice. Mason Currey's blog, a compendium of the daily routines of writers and other creative people, makes it clear that seeing as a writer isn't a talent one is either born with or not, but a skill that arises from disciplined practice. Patrick Cavanagh asks: are artists and scientists wired to see the world differently? V. S. Ramachandran, looking at three cases of brain damaged patients, concludes that the ability to make abstractions, which all healthy brains have, arises because the essence of mental activity is the ceaseless making of connections via metaphor. And, finally, Joan Didion's famous riposte to George Orwell provides an electrifying account of how her acts of attention led her to turn to writing.

Cavanagh, Patrick. "The Artist as Neuroscientist." *Nature* 434 (March 17, 2005). 301–7. Print.

Currey, Mason. *Daily Routines: How Writers, Artists, and Other Interesting People Organize Their Days*. Blog.

Didion, Joan. "Why I Write." *New York Times Book Review*. 5 December 1976. Web.

Ramachandran, V. S. "Three Clues to Understanding Your Brain." TED. March 2007. Web.

On Reading as a Writer

In our writing classes, we have a couple of mantras about reading that we repeat throughout the semester:

> In order to learn how to write, you have to learn how to read *as a writer.*
>
> There's only one way to learn how to read well, and that's by rereading.

These mantras are connected. To read as a writer means to pay close attention to the choices other writers make. This kind of reading requires attending to lots of things at once—what the writer says, how she organizes her ideas, what types of sources she works with, and how she addresses her readers. Such multifocal reading can only be accomplished by rereading. The first time through a challenging work, you might only be able to focus on what it says; after you know how the writer gets from point A to point Z, then you can attend more carefully to the choices the writer has made along the way. As your understanding of the entire piece comes together, you can assess what works, what doesn't, and why.

If you were in a history class and were assigned Susan Sontag's essay "Looking at War," your teacher would expect you to read the essay as a student, which would entail being able to identify Sontag's thesis and to evaluate the evidence she provides to support her thesis. But if you were in one of our classes, where the focus is on becoming a writer, we would ask you to read differently: we would ask you to attend not only to Sontag's thesis and to the evidence Sontag provides in its support but also to how she presents and develops her ideas. So instead of expecting you to mark Sontag's main points with a highlighter, we would encourage you to slow down so that you can make connections, puzzle over references, and think about how the details contribute to the overarching effect of the piece.

Sontag begins her essay by telling her readers about Virginia Woolf's *Three Guineas*, a book-length essay that Woolf wrote while the Spanish Civil War was in progress. Sontag explains that Woolf framed her essay as a long-delayed response to a letter from a London lawyer who had asked her, "How in your opinion are we to prevent war?" While Woolf has sympathy for his cause, she calls into question the idea that she and the lawyer belong to the same collective "we." Even though they are both members of the same privileged social class, as a woman Woolf was denied the kind of education and professional experience that the lawyer, a man, took for granted. Woolf suggests that the two of them will only be able to find common ground by looking at photographs of war's atrocities, which are, in her view, "simply statements of fact addressed to the eye."

> However different the education, the traditions behind us, our sensations are the same; and they are violent. You, Sir, call them "horror and disgust." We also call them horror and disgust. And the same words rise to our lips. War, you say, is an abomination; a barbarity; war must be stopped at whatever cost. And we echo your words.

For Sontag, the key words in this passage from Woolf's essay are, surprisingly, "us," "our," and "we." These tiny words might seem hardly worthy of comment, but Sontag wants her readers to see what work they do in the passage she's cited. Reading as a writer, Sontag notices that, when Woolf imagines herself looking with the lawyer at photographs of the war, she uses the pronoun "our" to show that the photographs evoke the same emotional responses in both of them. They agree that the images reveal war to be an abomination and a barbarity. But this alliance between them is temporary. In the final sentences quoted above, Woolf has shifted the meaning of "we" and "our." They no longer refer to Woolf and the lawyer, but to Woolf and other women. "We" *women* "echo your words." Woolf has become the voice for what she believes is a universal female opposition to war, an opposition triggered by a shared revulsion to the realities of war as depicted in photographs.

After writing several paragraphs explicating *Three Guineas*, Sontag suddenly rejects Woolf's argument. "Who believes today," Sontag asks, "that war can be abolished? No one, not even pacifists." Why does Sontag start her own essay in this curious way? If Woolf's position is wrong, why tell her readers about it at all?

Starting her essay with Woolf allows Sontag to get three common assumptions about war and photography on the table for consideration: (1) that women are unified in opposition to war; (2) that photographs are "statements of fact"; and (3) that seeing photographs of war's brutal effects will bring about an end to war. Seventy-five years after Woolf published *Three Guineas*, Sontag sees no evidence to support the contention that women naturally oppose war, and she sees no reason to stipulate that photographs present self-evident truths. To the contrary, Sontag sets out to argue that documentary photographs of war have never given rise to a political consensus against war and will never do so. Reading Woolf's essay led Sontag to formulate her own question: If it's not the function of war photography to bring about the end of war, what *is* its function?

Our discussion of Sontag's use of Woolf's essay models the importance of both reading as a writer and rereading. These practices attune us to the choices writers make as they shape their ideas and their readers' experience.

• • • • •

We have a third mantra we repeat to our students:

Read in slow motion.

When we teach writing, we know it's more valuable for students who are learning to read as writers to read and reread a brief selection with great care than it is for them to race through a much longer text in search of some highlighter-worthy main point. Reading in slow motion means looking up unfamiliar terms, names, historical events, and images. We encourage our students to track down some of the author's sources and to read those sources as writers, which means having them explore the connections the author has made to or between those sources. We do this because we want our students to see that whatever they're reading is connected to a much larger network of meaning.

If you read Sontag's "Looking at War" in slow motion, for example, and track down the text of *Three Guineas*, you'll discover something surprising: far from being a treatise on war photography, Woolf's 144-page book includes just two paragraphs on the subject. This fact makes Sontag's decision to begin her essay with a discussion of Woolf's work curious in a different way. Is her presentation of Woolf's position a distortion? Is Sontag setting Woolf up to make her own argument look more compelling than it actually is?

After slow reading, we've decided that Sontag learned more from Woolf than she lets on. The difference between Woolf's style and Sontag's is striking: Woolf makes her arguments through stories, while Sontag makes hers with ideas, drawing on the work of preeminent thinkers in history, art, and political theory. And yet, despite her predilection for ideas over stories, Sontag arrives, late in her argument, at the idea that photographs can only "haunt us," while "narratives can make us understand." The passage that Sontag cites from *Three Guineas* at the opening of her own essay is, we realize in retrospect, a narrative. Although Sontag rejects Woolf's idea that war photography can create solidarity for peace, she recognizes that Woolf's mode of writing may well be better suited to generating insights than a discussion of abstract ideas would be.

Seeing how Sontag has used Woolf in the opening of "Looking at War" helps us to see the significance of Sontag's decision to conclude her essay by narrating a story told by a photograph. Jeff Wall's 13-by-7.5-foot photograph *Dead Troops Talk (A vision after an ambush of a Red Army patrol, near Moqor, Afghanistan, winter 1986)* shows thirteen Russian soldiers clustered on a desolate, rocky landscape. It may look at first like a documentary photograph, but it's actually a fictional scene of postbattle carnage. The men in the photograph are actors on a studio set, playing the parts of soldiers. These soldiers, it seems, have died from gruesome injuries, but most of them appear alive to each other and are talking and laughing. Sontag describes them as indifferent to the world of the living: "one could fantasize that the soldiers might turn and talk to us. But no, no one is looking out of the picture at the viewer. . . .

These dead are supremely uninterested in the living.... Why should they seek our gaze? What would they have to say to us?"

The collective "us" at the end of Sontag's essay is not Woolf's female collective "we." Rather, at the end of "Looking at War," Sontag arrives at a new "we": "this 'we' is everyone who has never experienced anything like what [the soldiers] went through." This "we," Sontag argues, can never fully understand what this photograph depicts: "We don't get it. We truly can't imagine what it was like. We can't imagine how dreadful, how terrifying war is—and how normal it becomes. Can't understand, can't imagine." Only by reading in slow motion can we appreciate that Sontag makes her point about how little most of us know of war by translating Wall's photograph into a story. This story does not try to teach us what it's like to be in a war; instead, it teaches us that without actual experience of war, we can never know how it feels or understand its horrors.

Reading as writers, we can appreciate the arc of Sontag's essay and the elegance of her argument without being compelled to reach the same conclusions. And in fact, this is exactly how Sontag responded to Woolf's *Three Guineas*: she admired the way Woolf shifted the meaning of "we" in a single paragraph and Woolf's ability to seamlessly embed a story in her larger argument, but Sontag didn't feel bound by this admiration to agree with Woolf. Rather, she did what writers do who wish to engage fully with the ideas of another: she wrote an essay of her own.

PRACTICE SESSION ONE

READING

You can use any serious text to practice reading and rereading as a writer. For now, we recommend that you read Sontag's "Looking at War," found on the *New Yorker* Web site. Start by reading the essay from beginning to end and marking key moments in Sontag's argument. Next, read the essay again, paying attention *as a writer* to how Sontag phrases and organizes her ideas, what types of sources she uses, how and where she presents major points, and how she addresses her readers. Take notes in the margins.

What's striking about how Sontag chose to approach her topic? What parts drew you in? Are there parts of the essay that confuse you, or parts where you don't know enough about photographs or history to follow her argument? Were there any points or turns of phrase that impressed you, or sections you found yourself rereading with appreciation?

Having read Sontag's essay as a writer, identify one of the significant choices Sontag made when she composed her essay, and then spend at least 30 minutes writing about that choice. As you write, quote specific passages from Sontag's work to help your reader see what you find meaningful about how Sontag writes as well as what she writes.

RESEARCHING

Next you'll return to Sontag's work to practice a specific kind of rereading— reading in slow motion.

Sontag wrote about photographs throughout her career. Despite her enduring fascination with images, she did not include photographs in books such as *On Photography* or *Regarding the Pain of Others*. "Looking at War" is an exception to Sontag's usual practice: when the essay was originally published in the *New Yorker*, it included photographs; now that it is on the *New Yorker* Web site, the images are no longer part of the essay.

The experience of reading "Looking at War" without reproductions of the photographs obviously differs from the experience of reading the text with the images. It's important to consider why Sontag typically chose *not* to reproduce photographs in her essays about photography. But it's also important to know that you are not bound by her decisions—or by the decisions of any writer. Indeed, when reading as a writer, you are always considering both what the writer says and what the writer *doesn't* say, what the writer directs you to look at and what the writer *doesn't* draw your attention to.

Working with "Looking at War," use the Web to track down the photographs Sontag references. Seek out the highest-resolution images you can find. Look at them with care. Learn about their context by reading what others have written about them. Then return to Sontag's essay and consider what additional sources might deepen your understanding of her argument. Search more; read more. Keep track of which sources you turn to and why.

WRITING

Now that you've reread "Looking at War" in slow motion, write an essay about how slow reading altered your understanding of Sontag's work. It's likely that your research enhanced your reading of Sontag's work significantly. It's also likely that new questions or confusions arose. Again, as you write, quote specific passages from Sontag's work and your sources to show what you find meaningful about what is said and how it is said.

PRACTICE SESSION TWO

WRITING

What happens if we shift the focus from photographs to paintings? The Colombian artist Fernando Botero has created over fifty paintings that are inspired by the globally circulated images of human rights abuses committed by members of the United

States Army at Abu Ghraib, in 2003. Search the Web for the highest-resolution versions of Botero's paintings you can find. Conduct your research *as a writer*, taking notes that will allow you to write an essay that is in conversation with Sontag's "Looking at War." Write an essay about the value of painting images of war in the age of digital photography.

EXPLORE

"Annotation Tuesday!" is a regular feature on *Nieman Storyboard* in which writers are interviewed about how they composed a particular essay or article. As the interviewers move through the pieces paragraph by paragraph, the writers explain their choices, often in surprising ways. We invite you to browse the archives of "Annotation Tuesday!" on the *Nieman Storyboard* Web site. We recommend, in particular or search for the interviews with writers Buzz Bissinger, Leslie Jamison, and Rachel Kaadzi Ghansa listed below.

"Annotation Tuesday! Buzz Bissinger and 'The Killing Trail.'" Interview by Elon Green. *Nieman Storyboard*. 28 Jan. 2014. Web.

"Annotation Tuesday! Leslie Jamison and the Imprisoned Ultradistance Runner." Interview by Elon Green. *Nieman Storyboard*. 2 July 2013. Web.

"Annotation Tuesday! Rachel Kaadzi Ghansa and 'If He Hollers Let Him Go.'" Interview by Elon Green. *Nieman Storyboard*. 7 Oct. 2014. Web.

On Self-Curation

The word *curate* has an interesting etymological history. According to the *Oxford English Dictionary*, *curate* entered the English language in the mid-fourteenth century as a noun signifying someone "entrusted with the cure of souls: a spiritual pastor." This nominal form of the word is linked to earlier adjectival forms in medieval Latin (*c-ur-atus*) and Italian (*curato*) and to the French noun *curé*, all of which denoted "having a cure or charge."

Some six hundred years later, *curate* made its first appearance as a verb in an English dictionary. And notice what happens to the meaning of the word when it moves from being used as a noun or an adjective to being used as a transitive verb: "to act as curator of (a museum, exhibits, etc.); to look after and preserve." So, for a very long time, a curate was a religious occupation; in the twentieth century, it became a secular activity.

Self-curation does not yet appear in the *Oxford English Dictionary* or *Merriam-Webster* or the *Cambridge Dictionary*. Nevertheless, if you search the Web for the term (with the hyphen), you'll find that this as-yet-unofficial word is currently in circulation and that it is used most frequently to refer to the conscious management of one's online life. Fancifully, we might define *self-curation* thus: "to act as curator of one's own online life; to look after and preserve an archive of one's digital existence."

We first came across the term while reading Dana Spiotta's wonderful novel *Stone Arabia*. The principle that guides the life of Nik Worth, brother of the novel's narrator, is "Self-curate or disappear." The mystery at the heart of the novel is twofold: first, what Nik has actually done is self-curate *and* disappear; and second, the self Nik has curated is an entirely fictional one. Not wanting to be remembered as an unsuccessful crank living on the margins of society, Nik spent two decades fabricating the documents, the personal journals, and the history of a forward-looking, deeply thoughtful musician. And then he left without a word. All his sister Denise can do while she waits for word from him is to make her way through the fictional journals in hopes of piecing together some understanding of what Nik had done with his life.

Nik's relationship to self-curation is pathological: he fabricates reviews of performances that never happened; he creates but never releases CDs by his fictional persona and then records the public reception of music that only he has ever heard. But Spiotta shows over the course of her novel that self-curation, understood more generally as the conscious act of placing oneself in a larger narrative, is an activity we all participate in, to a greater or lesser degree. Ada, Denise's estranged daughter, self-curates via her blog, where she foregrounds her work in documentary film. And Denise herself tries to fit the artifacts Nik has left behind into a narrative of her own life that she can understand.

In the Age of Paper, self-curation was a largely private affair. One kept a journal, perhaps, or collected shells or stamps or firearms or first editions or autographs or whatever. Now that we live in the Age of the Screen, self-curation is a largely public affair: there is the self or the selves that an individual maintains via social media; the blogging self; the photo- or video-posting self; the reviewing self. These are selves over which a person has some measure of control. And then there is the self as represented by others—via social media, via the news, via public documents.

What do you know about yourself as currently represented on the Web? Is that the version of yourself you would voluntarily give others access to? There's a practical reason for making that distinction: once something associated with your name, your face, or your work appears on the Web, it is potentially on the Web forever. Were you identified doing a keg stand on a friend's Facebook page? Did you post a comment on a local news site railing against something you now support? Have you had a run-in with the law? Any one of these events could function as a "digital tattoo" for you, ensuring that there's a public record of some past embarrassment available to anyone who is interested in digging it up. Self-curation is a practical way to counter the negative effects of the digital tattoo.

While there are good practical reasons to self-curate, we're more interested in the creative benefits that come with self-curation. If you take control of your online presence, you have the opportunity to represent yourself as a multifaceted individual with a range of interests. By self-curating as a writer, you make it that much easier for potential readers to find your work. And by making your work public, you create the opportunity to have the kind of readers all writers want—those who read voluntarily.

PRACTICE SESSION ONE

RESEARCHING

What happens when you do a Google search on your name? Do you get different results if you use Dogpile? Twitter? Facebook? Pinterest? Photobucket? Your high school's home page? Do a thorough search and document all the information about you that is publicly available on the Web. Your final dossier should include images where appropriate. Spend at least 20 minutes writing about the results of your research: What does the uncurated version of yourself, as represented on the Web, look like?

REFLECTING

What would you like people who search for you to find? What would best represent you as a thinker? A writer? A creative person? An artist? If you were to design a self-curated site, what would it include?

Spend at least 45 minutes sketching out what such a site would look like by hand or using the graphing feature on your word processing platform. Another option is to actually create a self-curated site. Regardless of which option you choose to do, you'll need to decide what tabs you would like to appear in your home page's navigation bar. Are you a writer who works in more than one genre? Have you made videos? Taken striking photographs? Started a graphic novel? Are you involved in other projects or activities that you could represent on your site? We are particularly interested in you designing a site that represents you as someone whose creativity expresses itself in production rather than consumption, so we ask that you restrict your listing of favorite books, musicians, and artists to the "About" tab on your site.

PRACTICE SESSION TWO

RESEARCHING

What happens when you do a Google search on a contemporary visual artist or writer you admire? Do you get different results if you use Dogpile? Twitter? Facebook? Pinterest? Photobucket? Spend at least 30 minutes doing a thorough search and document all the information about the artist or writer you've chosen that is publicly available on the Web. (Don't choose a celebrity, a sports star, or a politician; these figures always bring gossip, scandals, and excitable fans in their wake.) Then spend an additional 20 minutes writing about the results of your search. What does the uncurated version of the writer's or artist's self look like?

RESEARCHING

Seek out the official site or sites for the contemporary visual artist or writer you elected to research. Then take at least 45 minutes to write an essay on the difference between the official, curated self and the version of that self that emerged during your open-ended search. Drawing on your research, discuss what the artist or writer you've chosen to study might do on his or her self-curated site to engage with whatever additional unauthorized material you've discovered circulating outside the site.

PRACTICE SESSION THREE

RESEARCHING

It is now common journalistic practice to head straight to the Web in the immediate aftermath of a tragedy to see what social media can tell us about the possible victims or the possible perpetrators in the unfolding event. This practice has tended to have catastrophic results, as the pressure to be first on the scene with news has created a fertile ground for jumping to unfounded conclusions. This happened, for instance, after the tragedy in Sandy Hook and after the Boston Marathon bombing. In both cases, an innocent person was linked to the atrocity and was then quickly "convicted" online on the basis of material that was later revealed to be erroneous.

Choose a recent event that has been in the headlines and spend at least 45 minutes investigating what role social media has played in both the coverage and the interpretation of the event. Why do some responses to the event get picked up, shared, and repeated, while others are ignored? Take extensive notes, tracking key moments in the coverage of the chosen event. When you're done with your research, create a timeline that represents what you've learned about the role social media played in shaping popular understandings of the event.

WRITING

If you were to curate a site dedicated to the event you selected, what would you include? Write an essay on self-curation, the digital tattoo, and social media as they relate to the event you've chosen to research. Your piece should include your design for a site that would provide a richer understanding both of the event and of its coverage.

EXPLORE

Our suggested readings all focus on understanding how social media has changed human behavior. Ann Friedman provides a trenchant analysis of LinkedIn, the self-proclaimed largest professional network on the Web. Ariel Levy examines the role that Twitter played in the handling of the Steubenville rape trial. And Clay Shirky looks at the ways that social media is changing how citizens and their elected officials engage with each other.

Friedman, Ann. "All LinkedIn with Nowhere to Go." *The Baffler* 23 (2013). Web.

Levy, Ariel. "Trial by Twitter." *New Yorker.* 5 Aug. 2013. Web.

Shirky, Clay. "How Social Media Can Make History." TED. June 2009. Web.

Creativity at Work: Twyla Tharp and the Paradox of Habitual Creativity

The film *Amadeus* annoys dancer Twyla Tharp because it portrays Wolfgang Amadeus Mozart as a born genius. "Of course, this is hogwash," Tharp writes in her book, *The Creative Habit*. Then in large red letters she asserts, **"There are no 'natural' geniuses."**

Tharp has done her research. She knows that Mozart's father, Leopold, who was himself a composer and a musician, recognized his son's musical interest and nurtured the boy's ability by teaching him to play at a very young age. She also knows that Mozart had a strong work ethic, even as a child. And she knows that he complained in a letter to a friend that people mistakenly thought he composed without struggle; the truth was that making beautiful music took time and effort.

Tharp uses Mozart's story to begin her book about creative habits because she wants to be clear about her project: "More than anything, this book is about preparation: **In order to be creative you have to know how to prepare to be creative.**"

She understands the allure of thinking that creativity is the birthright of a lucky few, but her experience as a dancer and choreographer, as well as with the creative people who have surrounded her all her life, has shown her that creativity can be learned and that it can be taught. "There's a paradox," she writes,

> in the notion that creativity should be a habit. We think of creativity as a way of keeping everything fresh and new, while habit implies routine and repetition. That paradox intrigues me because it occupies the place where creativity and skill rub up against each other.
>
> It takes skill to bring something you've imagined into the world.... No one is born with that skill. It is developed through exercise, through repetition, through a blend of learning and reflection that's both painstaking and rewarding. And it takes time.

Tharp reminds her readers that Mozart, who certainly had a gift and a passion for music, composed *twenty-four* symphonies before he wrote a work that would endure: Symphony no. 25 in G Minor, which serves as the opening score for *Amadeus.*

What can we learn from the examples of Mozart and Tharp? Tharp distills her ideas in this simple statement: "Creativity is a habit; and the best creativity is a result of good work habits." So practice every day. Make a ritual of your practice. "The routine," Tharp writes, "is as much a part of the creative process as the lightning bolt of inspiration, maybe more."

CHAPTER 7

Planning and Replanning

When you undertake a writing project, one of the early steps in the process is to make an outline. The value of doing so seems self-evident: an outline, with its schematic representation of the argument you hope to make, shows you where you plan to go and keeps you on track so you don't get lost in a thicket of irrelevant details. But, the risk in the outline-driven approach is that anything that threatens to pull the project away from its predetermined destination can be dismissed as irrelevant: potential connections won't get explored, new information won't be pursued, and unsettling insights will be ignored.

In this chapter, we recommend curiosity-driven approach to planning that assumes replanning is an inevitable and essential part of the writing process. This doesn't necessarily mean abandoning the outline, so much as it means assuming that the outline is likely to get revised as the writing project develops. It means thinking of structure as malleable rather than inevitable; it means anticipating the possibility that revision will yield unforeseen insights that require starting the planning process over again from scratch; it means acknowledging that the failure of the original outline may well be proof that learning has occurred. The creative mind always has a plan, but that plan always includes planning on replanning.

On Structure

John McPhee, the author of twenty-nine books and a staff writer for the *New Yorker* since 1965, is one of the most prolific and influential writers of contemporary nonfiction—which he prefers to call "factual writing." He's written books about subjects as diverse as the geography of the western United States (*Annals of the Former World*); efforts to contain natural destruction caused by lava, water, and mountainside debris flow (*The Control of Nature*); people who work in freight transportation (*Uncommon Carriers*); and even a rogue American professor whose covert actions played a central role in preserving dissident Soviet art (*The Ransom of Russian Art*). While we admire McPhee's work, we draw your attention to him here because McPhee may well be the best writing teacher on the planet. His former students, who collectively have published over 430 books, include David Remnick, a Pulitzer Prize winner and editor-in-chief of the *New Yorker*; Richard Stengel and Jim Kelly, each of whom has served as managing editor of *Time*; Eric Schlosser, author of *Fast Food Nation*; and Richard Preston, author of *The Hot Zone*.

Why are McPhee's students so successful?

One reason is how McPhee trains them to think about structure. In a *New Yorker* essay simply titled "Structure," McPhee offers lessons about writing and its organization that were previously reserved for the small number of Princeton University students lucky enough to get a seat in one of his seminars. He begins the essay by describing the crisis of confidence he faced early in his career when he settled in to write a long article about the Pine Barrens of New Jersey, which he'd been researching for eight months. "I had assembled enough material to fill a silo," he recalls, "and now I had no idea what to do with it." He spent two weeks lying on his back on a picnic table, stymied by panic, unable to see a way to organize his thoughts. Finally, he realized that an elderly native of the Pine Barrens, Fred Brown, had connections to most of the topics he wanted to discuss, so McPhee decided he could begin the essay by describing his first encounter with Brown and then connect each theme to various forays he and Brown made together. Having solved his structure problem, McPhee got off the picnic table and began to write. "Structure," he says, "has preoccupied me in every project I have undertaken since."

For four decades, McPhee has taught his students that structure should be "strong, sound, and artful" and that it is possible to "build a structure in such a way that it causes people to want to keep turning pages." Nonfiction, in other words, can be as absorbing as a good novel if the structure is right. To teach his students how to find the right structure, McPhee compares preparing to write to preparing to cook.

> The approach to structure in factual writing is like returning from a grocery store with materials you intend to cook for dinner. You set them out on the kitchen counter, and what's there is what you deal with, and all you deal with. If something is red and globular, you don't call it a tomato if it's a bell pepper.

In other words, to plan the structure of a piece of writing, you have to gather all the pieces of your research and lay them out so you can see them at a glance. And as you figure out the structure, you can only work with the facts in front of you.

Before he had a computer, McPhee would type all of his notes, study them, separate them into piles so that his facts were literally in front of him. Then, he would distill them into a set of several dozen index cards. On each card he would write two or three code words that indicated to him a component of the story he wanted to tell. The codes might refer to a location (UNY for upstate New York) or to an event or anecdote ("Upset Rapid"). His office furniture at the time included "a standard sheet of plywood—thirty-two square feet—on two sawhorses." He would scatter his index cards face up on the plywood, anchoring a few pieces and moving the others around until he figured out how to organize the work in ways that were both strong and artful.

Rebecca Skloot, author of *The Immortal Life of Henrietta Lacks*, regularly uses McPhee's essay "Travels in Georgia" to teach structure to her writing students. She shows her students that, if you map the narrative of "Travels in Georgia," you can see that it spirals in time: McPhee begins in the middle of the story, goes forward briefly, and then loops backward in time. By the middle of the essay, McPhee has brought his account back to where it started, and from that point on, he moves the narrative steadily forward in time. Skloot explains that McPhee calls this "the lowercase *e* structure," and she promises that once you recognize it, you'll see it everywhere—in movies, novels, and *New Yorker* articles. (Skloot's exercise teaches her students to read as writers, a topic discussed in our essay "On Reading as a Writer.")

Like McPhee, Skloot has a story about grappling for a long time with a writing task. In her case, though, she had to figure out how to organize ten years of research that she had collected for her book. She struggled because she was writing about multiple time periods and had three different narratives: the story of Henrietta Lacks, an African American woman who developed cervical cancer and died at the age of thirty-one in 1951; the story of Lacks's cancer cells, which were cultured without Lacks's consent and continue to be used to this day in medical research; and the story of Lacks's family, especially her daughter, Deborah, who for much of her life did not know that her mother's cells were alive in medical labs all over the world.

Skloot's breakthrough in organizing her research into a readable book came when she was watching *Hurricane*, a movie about the boxer Hurricane Carter, who was falsely convicted of a triple homicide in 1966. Skloot saw that the film braided three different narratives together: the story of Carter's conviction; the story of Carter's twenty years in prison; and the story of how a Brooklyn teen and three Canadian activists successfully lobbied to have Carter's case reopened. She wrote notes about the film's scenes on colored-coded index cards—one color for each of the three storylines—and laid them out on her bed according to where the scenes occurred in the film. Then she placed the color-coded index cards for the three strands of her own book on top of the cards for *Hurricane*. She saw that the film jumped more quickly between the three strands of narrative than her book manuscript did, and that the rapidity of those jumps helped sustain the momentum of each line of the intertwined narrative. When Skloot finally realized how to weave together the pieces of her own narrative, she photographed the rows of colored index cards for posterity. (See this photograph on p. 112.)

Rebecca Skloot

FIGURE 7.1 Rebecca Skloot's note cards for *The Immortal Life of Henrietta Lacks,* arranged on her bed.

For Skloot to structure her ten years of research as a braided narrative, she had to throw a lot of material away, just as McPhee did when he was sorting the siloful of material he'd collected for his article on the Pine Barrens. Neither Skloot nor McPhee thought that time spent collecting unused research was wasted, however. McPhee's former student Eric Schlosser recalled how McPhee taught him that deciding what *not* to include is a crucial and often unrecognized step in defining structure. McPhee told him, "Your writing should be like an iceberg." What ends up on the printed page is just the tip of the iceberg, while beneath the surface is all the research, reading, and writing that was done to generate the final product. The reader may not be able to see that work, but it's there—the hidden substructure of the writer's visible work.

• • • • •

In school, the operating assumption is often that there is one structure with which students should work: introduction, body, conclusion. Note that this approach *begins* by prescribing an organizing structure, no matter what the subject or project is, whereas the examples from McPhee and Skloot show the structure emerging after the research process is finished or well underway. In line with these examples, we think that the best time for you to make decisions about structure is *after* you've formulated the question you want to answer, the problem or puzzle you want to solve, or the idea you want to explore, and *after* you've taken time to do substantial research. Once you've gathered your materials, then you can experiment. You can move the ideas around on paper or on digital index cards, testing out possibilities. You can consider whether there's an organic order to your project. You can think about how different parts of your essay seem connected and about how you can best make those connections meaningful to your readers. Then, when you've mapped a possible structure, step back and think carefully about what you see.

Imagine that your index cards define a path readers will follow as you guide them through the development of your thoughts, and consider these questions:

- What shape is the path? Is it straight and simple because you're writing a descriptive essay ("there's this and that and the other thing")? Given the assignment or your ambitions, is this structure sufficient?
- Does the path of your project take interesting turns? Is there a step that takes your thoughts in a new direction? Are there turns that might pivot on a qualifying word or phrase such as *but*, *however*, or *on the other hand*?
- Does the path turn more than once? Does it double back on itself? Does it have a "lowercase *e* structure"? Does it braid three or more strands together?
- Is there a fork in the path? Is there a moment where you entertain multiple options?
- Are there gaps? Does the path abruptly change direction or miss a step between a given section and the one that follows?
- Are there pieces or ideas that don't fit anywhere? Does it make sense to include the material as a digression that eventually leads back to the main path? Would a digression contribute to the essay's overall project?
- Is there a dead end, a place where the path hits a brick wall or goes off a cliff? If so, can you use this dead end to rethink how you've addressed your essay's question or problem?

After remapping the path of your project, step back even further and consider whether the structure you've now laid out is "strong, sound, and artful." We also recommend asking the following questions:

- Where do you see evidence of your curiosity? Your creativity? Your skill at making connections between sources and ideas? Your depth of knowledge? Your mastery of detail?
- If these aren't evident, how could you rework your project? Should you do more research? Formulate a different question or problem?
- Are there places where you ignored information that would have complicated the structure or the path? Are there places where you chose the easier route?

PRACTICE SESSION ONE

RESEARCHING

We recently discovered the *Nieman Storyboard* Web site, which we recommend for a number of reasons. It not only gathers notable examples of narrative journalism but also includes a series of "Essays on Craft" in which experienced journalists explain how they have moved a story from initial idea to final publication. In addition, there's a series called "Why's This So Good?" in which writers discuss what they value in the work of a fellow writer. You can't go wrong on *Nieman Storyboard*. Explore the site for at least 20 minutes. Then select at least three essays that intrigue you and read them.

PRACTICE SESSION TWO

READING

If you search on *Nieman Storyboard*, you'll find Adam Hochschild's piece on John McPhee's craft, "'Why's This So Good?' No. 61: John McPhee and the Archdruid." What McPhee calls "structure," Hochschild calls "engineering." Hochschild explains: "A key secret of McPhee's ability to make us care about his vast and improbable range of subject matter lies in his engineering. From the pilings beneath the foundations to the beams that support the rooftop observation deck, he is the master builder of literary skyscrapers."

As you read the essay about McPhee, pay attention to Hochschild's descriptions of the structure of his favorite works. For example, Hochschild describes *Encounters with the Archdruid* as having been built using a structure that McPhee described as:

$$\frac{ABC}{D}$$

After you've read Hochshild's essay once through, spend at least 30 minutes reviewing his descriptions of four of McPhee's other works: a profile of Thomas Hoving; the book *Levels of the Game*; and the articles "In Search of Marvin Gardens" and "A Forager." Make simple sketches to represent the structure of each of these four works.

PRACTICE SESSION THREE

READING

Select an article from the "Notable Narratives" section of *Nieman Storyboard*. Then spend at least 30 minutes making a detailed map of the essay's structure using any medium you like—a computer graphics program, pen and pencil, crayon and cardboard, or index cards on a bedspread. The map you make should highlight what surprised or impressed you about the writer's structural choices.

PRACTICE SESSION FOUR

WRITING

Go through your personal archive of papers you've written and select at least three of them. Then make a map or sketch of the structure of each one. Once you're done, step back and think about the relationship between the maps or sketches you generated for this exercise and the ones you generated for Practice Sessions Two and Three above. Your own essays will probably be shorter than Hochschild's essay or the other essays on *Nieman Storyboard*, but what other differences are there between the structure of your writing and the structure of essays by professional writers? Write an essay that uses the maps of your own writing and those you made for the previous exercises as material for speculating about the relationship between structure and thought.

EXPLORE

David Dobbs describes the structure of Michael Lewis's essay about the Greek financial crisis as "an agile manipulation of a standard trip-to-Oz story form." It can be hard to step back and see the structure of a piece of writing as a whole, but Dobbs's comparison seems obvious after the fact. To help you develop a sense for structure, we invite you to read Lewis's essay alongside Dobbs's analysis, or to read McPhee's "Structure" as well as his interview in the *Paris Review*. While Dobbs and McPhee are concerned with the big picture, the manuscript pages on Joyce Carol Oates's blog provide a more detailed picture of how a fiction writer invents and refines the shape of a novel by making sketches of towns, charts of characters, and lists of scenes and their arrangement.

Dobbs, David. " 'Why's This So Good?' No. 15: Michael Lewis' Greek Odyssey." *Nieman Storyboard*. 11 Oct. 2011. Web.

Lewis, Michael. "Beware of Greeks Bearing Bonds." *Vanity Fair*. Oct. 2010. Web.

McPhee, John. "John McPhee, The Art of Nonfiction No. 3." Interview by Peter Hessler. *Paris Review*. 192 Spring 2010. Web.

McPhee, John. "Structure." *New Yorker*. 14 Jan. 2014. Web.

Oates, Joyce Carol. "Manuscripts," "Research and Bibliography." *Celestial Timepiece: The Joyce Carol Oates Home Page*. Web.

On Revising

Every writing lesson in Part 1 of this book is implicitly connected to revision. We've repeatedly encouraged you to look and look again. (Another name for the act of reseeing is "revision.") We showed you how being curious requires that you peer around corners, disappear down rabbit holes, and explore the unknown in order to replace old assumptions or confusions with new knowledge and understanding. We showed you that creative habits of mind include being able to reflect on (that is, to resee) how you express yourself and even how you think. In a multitude of ways, reseeing and revising are fundamental practices for writers.

So why include a separate essay on revision? Two reasons, really. First, people who take writing seriously know that writing *is* revising. Indeed, the claim that "there is no such thing as good writing, only good rewriting" is so widely acknowledged by writers that it has been attributed to Robert Graves, Louis Brandeis, Isaac Bashevis Singer, William Zinsser, and Roald Dahl. Second, we know that revision is not a single stage in the writing process but a range of practices that occur throughout the writing process. The distinction is worth driving home, we've found, because many students mistakenly believe that revising is simply correcting errors and tidying up unclear sentences that a teacher marked in an essay draft. In our view this is copyediting, not revision, and it misrepresents true revision.

As writers, we know that rethinking, reseeing, and rewriting can happen at any step in producing a work of writing. In fact, before we drafted the opening paragraphs of *this* essay, we composed two different preliminary outlines and two different introductions. When we determined that neither of those versions worked, we scrapped them and started over. This example isn't an anomaly; writers regularly spiral back to rethink what they've done, entirely abandoning earlier work and beginning all over again. Moments of revision can occur as soon as you've thought your first thought or written your first word; they can occur just when you think you're writing your final sentence; and they can occur anywhere between those two points.

If revision isn't correcting grammatical mistakes and isn't a single step in a linear process, then what is it? We'd like to help you resee revision by offering descriptions and examples of a variety of ways of returning to the writing you've already completed with the goal of improving it. You won't use all of these practices every time you rewrite, but you're quite likely to use more than one as you work over what you've written.

Rethinking

As essayists and academic writers, when we contemplate a new project, we spend a lot of time reading, exploring, researching, learning, and thinking before we begin a formal draft. And yet, after composing the first pages or even the entire first draft, we may still find our work unsatisfactory because, in the process of writing about our chosen topic, we have begun to question our original position. Rethinking motivates us to revise globally—to rework our ideas rather than tinker away at surface corrections.

What's the difference between rethinking and tinkering? It's difficult to point to a published example of the former because rethinking typically occurs before publication and thus remains hidden from readers. But writer and blogger Ta-Nehisi Coates makes a practice of rethinking his opinions in public, so we'll look at a moment when he felt obligated to acknowledge that new events had shifted his perspective.

Coates's essay "Fear of a Black President" contends with a paradox at the heart of President Obama's first term in office: "As a candidate, Barack Obama said we needed to reckon with race and with America's original sin, slavery. But as our first black president, he has avoided mention of race almost entirely." To illustrate how constraining this paradox is, Coates looks at a rare public statement on race by Obama in which the president puts that topic—and his own race—at the center of the nation's attention.

On March 23, 2012, Obama was asked to comment on the shooting death of an unarmed black teenager, Trayvon Martin, that had occurred a month earlier in Florida. George Zimmerman, a member of a neighborhood watch patrol, claimed to have shot Martin in self-defense when the young man responded violently to being detained. Obama briefly addressed the uproar that followed Martin's death, saying: "When I think about this boy, I think about my own kids, and I think every parent in America should be able to understand why it is absolutely imperative that we investigate every aspect of this, and that everybody pulls together—federal, state, and local—to figure out exactly how this tragedy happened." Obama closed with the following statement: "But my main message is to the parents of Trayvon Martin. If I had a son, he'd look like Trayvon. I think they are right to expect that all of us as Americans are going to take this with the seriousness it deserves, and that we're going to get to the bottom of exactly what happened." As mild, measured, and brief as Obama's comments were, a media frenzy ensued. Radio shock jocks and cable TV pundits accused the president of lighting the match that could start a race war. Far from finding Obama's response incendiary, Coates details in "Fear of a Black President" his own frustration with Obama for making such moderate comments and for avoiding an open discussion of race.

As strong as his criticism of Obama was in "Fear of a Black President," Coates displayed his commitment to rethinking in a blog post he wrote after Obama responded to the news that George Zimmerman had been acquitted of second-degree murder and manslaughter charges on July 19, 2013. In this instance, Coates says, Obama spoke *as* an African American and *for* African Americans to explain their suffering over the verdict. We think it's worth quoting Obama's statement in full.

> You know, when Trayvon Martin was first shot I said that this could have been my son. Another way of saying that is Trayvon Martin could have been me 35 years ago. And when you think about why, in the African American community at least, there's a lot of pain around what happened here, I think it's important to recognize that the African American community is looking at this issue through a set of experiences and a history that doesn't go away.
>
> There are very few African American men in this country who haven't had the experience of being followed when they were shopping in a department store. That includes me. There are very few African American men who haven't had the experience of walking across the street and hearing the locks click on the doors of cars. That happens to me—at least before I was a senator. There are very few African Americans who haven't had the experience of getting on an elevator and a woman clutching her purse nervously and holding her breath until she had a chance to get off. That happens often.
>
> And I don't want to exaggerate this, but those sets of experiences inform how the African American community interprets what happened one night in Florida. And it's inescapable for people to bring those experiences to bear. The African American community is also knowledgeable that there is a history

> of racial disparities in the application of our criminal laws—everything from the death penalty to enforcement of our drug laws. And that ends up having an impact in terms of how people interpret the case.

Coates's blog post, "Considering the President's Comments on Racial Profiling," praises Obama for having the courage to speak out personally about the experience of racism: "No president has ever done this before. It does not matter that the competition is limited. The impact of the highest official in the country directly feeling your pain, because it is his pain, is real. And it is happening now." Coates's willingness to change his mind and express his gratitude sets him apart from many other political-opinion journalists. He's committed to presenting himself as an avid learner, and he refuses the pundit's pretense of certainty.

When you're writing for school, it may seem that you don't have the opportunity that Coates has as a blogger to rethink and rewrite; once a paper is handed in, there's usually no going back. But the truth is that every time you sit down to write, you have the opportunity to seek out new information that will complicate or alter what you were thinking before you started writing. This is the lesson we'd like you to take from Coates's work: in order to begin the process of rethinking what you've written, you need to seek out new information and be open to questioning everything, even your own certainties.

Restructuring

Often first drafts make sense to the writer, but the logic behind what has been written isn't yet clear enough for a reader to follow. This can be caused by gaps in the research or argument; lack of attention to what readers need to know and when they need to know it; too much information or too many ideas about one topic and not enough about another; or the lack of good transitions. These problems can be addressed through revision that focuses on structure.

The history of F. Scott Fitzgerald's *The Great Gatsby* reveals what a difference structural revisions can make. Fitzgerald sent the manuscript of his novel to his editor, Maxwell Perkins, who immediately saw that it was brilliant but flawed. First of all, the character of Gatsby was too physically vague. "The reader's eyes can never quite focus upon him, his outlines are dim," he wrote to Fitzgerald. "Now everything about Gatsby is more or less a mystery . . . , and this may be somewhat of an artistic intention, but I think it is mistaken." Fitzgerald's reply indicates that defining Gatsby's character was something he hadn't been able to accomplish in the first draft: "*I myself didn't know what Gatsby looked like or was engaged in* & you felt it." Perkins's second complaint about Fitzgerald's presentation of Gatsby was that the character's whole history—his apprenticeship on Dan Cody's yacht, his time in the army, his romance with Daisy, and his past as an "Oxford man"—all tumbled out in one long monologue in the penultimate chapter.

What to do? Perkins suggested that Fitzgerald reorganize the *whole* novel: "you can't avoid the biography altogether. I thought you might find ways to let the truth of some of his claims like 'Oxford' and his army career come out bit by bit in the course of actual narrative." Fitzgerald followed this advice, weaving bits of Gatsby's past more gracefully into earlier chapters. The result? *The Great Gatsby*, first published in 1925, has now sold over twenty-five million copies and is widely considered an enduring example of the Great American Novel.

Notice that Perkins's advice about revising *Gatsby* focused on creating a better experience for the reader. Notice, too, that Fitzgerald couldn't see what *The Great Gatsby* needed until he got the feedback that made it possible for him to view the novel through the eyes of another. (We discuss how to provide and how to respond to such feedback on p. 122.)

The Post-Draft Outline

While outside feedback is essential to the revision process, there is a way to defamiliarize your own writing to the point that you can make its implicit structure explicit and, simultaneously, produce a map that can direct your revisions. The way to do this is to produce a "post-draft outline," so called because, instead of making it before you begin to write your draft, you make it after the draft is completed.

The process for making a post-draft outline is straightforward: sequentially number every paragraph in your draft, and then write a one-sentence statement about the main idea or point in each paragraph. When you're done, you'll be able to see the structure of your draft as a whole, which you can then use in a variety of ways to help you assess the quality of the experience you've created for your reader.

1. Your outline gives you a snapshot of the path your draft has taken. To develop this snapshot, read the sentences of your post-draft outline in order, and then read the post-draft outline again, this time thinking through the following questions (which also appear in our essay "On Structure" on pp. 109–114):

    - Is the path a straight line? Does it proceed by a series of *and* connections (that is, there's this and this and this)?
    - Does the path turn? Is there a paragraph that qualifies what has gone before or takes the conversation in a new direction? Are there sentences or paragraphs that pivot—or could pivot—on a qualifying word or phrase such as *but*, *however*, or *although*?
    - Does the path turn more than once? Does it double back on itself?
    - Is there a fork in the path? Is there a moment where more than one option is entertained?
    - Is there a paragraph that pivots on words or phrases such as *or*, *perhaps*, or *what if* ? that introduce more than one possible outcome or position?

- Are there gaps? Does the path abruptly change direction or miss a step between a given paragraph and the one that follows?
- Are there digressions, places where there's a loop off the path that eventually returns to the main path? If the answer is yes, does each digression contribute to the essay's overall project? (Don't assume the answer to this last question is no. In restructuring, some digressions can become central to the newly organized draft.)
- Is there a dead end, a place where the path hits a brick wall or goes off a cliff, never to return? (Again, don't assume that this is necessarily a bad thing; in restructuring, there are times when dead ends can be repurposed to improve your handling of your essay's question or problem.)

After you have a sense of the path you took in your draft you can begin to sketch plans for structural revision.

2. Before you begin to rewrite, return to the draft and reassess it as a snapshot of your mind at work on a problem.

   - Where is your curiosity in evidence? Your creativity? Your skill at putting original sources into conversation? Your interest in language? Your mastery of detail? How can these be made more evident in revision?
   - Spend some time thinking about what you've left out of your draft. Are there places in the draft where you ignored ideas or information that would have complicated the journey? Where you chose to go where you were expected to go instead of where your thinking was pointing you? What can you do now to introduce ideas and information that would make your essay more interesting?
   - Could anyone else have written the draft, or is it obvious to you that it's *yours*? How can you make the essay even more your own?

By using the post-draft outline in this way, you'll be serving as your own Maxwell Perkins: you'll assess both what your draft is and what it might become through structural revision.

Letting Go

Cutting sentences and paragraphs, or cutting everything and starting over from scratch: has there ever been a writer who enjoys this part of the writing process? Has there ever been a writer of note who could skip the cross-out, the toss, the "Ctrl-A, Delete"? No. But the difference between beginning writers and experienced writers is that experienced writers have practiced encountering the newly blank screen; they know that the blinking cursor can be set in motion once again and that there are always more words out there somewhere. Beginning writers, without much practice starting over, tend to fear the blank screen and to see deleted work as wasted time rather than as an unavoidable part of letting the mind work on a problem.

To encourage our students to see letting go as a habit of creative minds, we tell a story about going to hear Nobel Prize–winning writer Toni Morrison read from a work in progress. Morrison approached the lectern, paused, and then told the audience that the year before she'd completed well over a hundred pages of the novel's manuscript, but that she stood before us that night to read from the forty or so pages she had left. What had happened? Revision happened. Morrison had set out in one direction and then had to spend a year peeling off pages and pages of what she'd written until she found work that met her standards.

The Morrison anecdote can be read as an extension of the quote we opened this essay with: "there is no such thing as good writing, only good rewriting," and all good rewriting involves letting go. We hear this idea repeated in Colette's definition of an author: "Put down everything that comes into your head and then you're a writer. But an author is one who can judge his own stuff's worth, without pity, and destroy most of it." Novelist Anne Lamott makes this point about letting go in perhaps its bluntest form in her popular book *Bird by Bird*, where she asserts that all good writers write "shitty first drafts," drafts that they know will be thrown away. "This," she says, "is how they end up with good second drafts and terrific third drafts."

While Lamott's specific recommendations may not apply to all writing or to all writers, we believe there's real value in her advice to view draft after draft as practice, as work that may never see the light of day but that is valuable nonetheless. If you give yourself sufficient time to use writing to help yourself think, knowing that you are going to get rid of most of it before anyone else sees it, then maybe, as Lamott writes, you'll find "something in the very last line of the very last paragraph on page six that you just love, that is so beautiful or wild that you now know what you're supposed to be writing about, more or less, or in what direction you might go—but there was no way to get to this without first getting through the first five and a half pages."

Getting Feedback

Most writers don't publish until after they've gotten feedback from friends, colleagues, and editors. We think that getting feedback from people whose work you admire is probably *the most important revision practice of all.*

To acheive this Kerry Walk, a teacher we admire, recommends that cover letters accompany all drafts submitted for feedback. If you were to compose such a cover letter, Walk would advise you to state:

- the main question or problem your writing seeks to address;
- the idea or point you feel you've made most successfully;
- the idea or point you feel you need help with;
- your number one concern about your paper that you'd like your reader to answer for you; and
- any questions you have about how or where to start your revision.

The advantage of a cover letter of this kind is that it gives your reader a clear sense of how you see your draft and where you think it needs work. Your reader need not agree with your assessment, but the letter gives your reader a way to gauge his or her response to what you've written and to adjust that response accordingly.

Taking a Break

The best way to see your writing with fresh eyes is to set your draft aside—for a day if that's all you have, or for longer if possible. When you pick it up again, you'll be able to see more clearly what's working and what's not. And the feedback you've received, which may have caught you off guard at first, may now seem more reasonable. The point is to give yourself time to reenergize, so that you don't resort to tinkering on the edges of your writing when you really need to be rethinking and restructuring your first draft.

Prolific writer Neil Gaiman explains taking a break also allows you to return to your work as a reader, instead of as its writer. Once a draft is done, he advises, "put it away until you can read it with new eyes.... Put it in a drawer and write other things. When you're ready, pick it up and read it as if you've never read it before. If there are things you aren't satisfied with as a reader, go in and fix them as a writer: that's revision." By "fix them as a writer," he means rethinking, restructuring, letting go of what's not working, getting feedback, writing again, polishing—doing whatever it takes to move the writing forward.

PRACTICE SESSION ONE

REFLECTING

Spend at least 20 minutes reflecting on your experiences with revision and your thoughts about trying new approaches. What is your typical approach to revision? Which of the strategies that we describe in this essay have you tried before? Which approach seems easiest for you? Which approach seems most challenging or unsettling?

Now commit to setting aside the time you need to practice revision in new ways. Make a resolution to try at least three of these strategies—rethinking, restructuring, post-draft outlining, letting go, getting feedback, taking a break—before handing in your next paper. Which three do you think you'll try?

PRACTICE SESSION TWO

RESEARCHING

Do an online image search for "manuscript revisions." You'll get many pages of results. Explore, clicking on images of manuscripts that call out to you and visiting the pages where they are embedded. Look for examples from writers you admire. Then spend at least 30 minutes examining several images carefully, taking notes on how various writers revise. What can you learn about writing and revision by looking at marked-up manuscript pages?

WRITING

Write an essay that examines three or more of the manuscript revisions you find most interesting. Explain what you've learned from these specific examples about various processes for revising.

PRACTICE SESSION THREE

WRITING

Take a final draft that you wrote recently and see if you can cut it by at least 25 percent without losing the main argument or ideas. After you've cut your original piece by a quarter, compare the original version to the shorter, revised one. What's better about the more concise version? What's better about the longer one?

Then try cutting the shortened version by 25 percent again. What happens to your argument or ideas this time?

PRACTICE SESSION FOUR

REVISING

If you have a draft you're presently working on, follow the advice in "Getting Feedback" and find a tutor, teacher, or fellow student who agrees to give you feedback. Spend at least 20 minutes writing a one-page, single-spaced cover letter that explains your concerns about the draft. Give this letter to your reader with a copy of the draft, and schedule a meeting to discuss his or her feedback.

After you've received your reader's feedback, figure out what kind of revision the feedback suggests is most necessary: Should you try rethinking, restructuring, letting go, or a combination of strategies? Then revise.

EXPLORE

The word revision refers to many practices—from rethinking and restructuring to polishing sentences. For Adrienne Rich, revision is a process of reading and writing—reseeing texts from the past to make new thoughts, stories, and poems possible. Other forms of revision, especially sentence-level editing, have become essential elements of writing due to advances in technology. Craig Fehrman describes the typewriters emergence as a writing tool at the beginning of the twentieth century. You can see examples of famous writers' manuscript revisions at the *Bad Penny Review* and the *Paris Review* Web sites. At the *Paris Review*, we recommend looking at the work of Salman Rushdie and Joan Didion.

Fehrman, Craig. "Revising Your Writing Again? Blame the Modernists." *Boston Globe*. 30 June 2013. Web.

Rich, Adrienne. "When We Dead Awaken: Writing as Re-vision." *College English* 34.1 (October 1972). 18–30. Print.

"Murdering Your Darlings: Writers' Revisions." *A Bad Penny Review*. Web.

"Interviews." *Paris Review*. Web.

(To get to the manuscript files, first select an interview; then click on the "view a manuscript page" button in the menu under the title. Zoom in on the pages to read them.)

On Learning from Failure

When we watch children building a sandcastle on a summer beach, we see creativity in action. The process seems so simple. The castle grows and becomes more elaborate—with moats, towers, turrets, and carefully laid rows of shells—until late in the day it's abandoned, to be reclaimed by the tide before morning. If we watch more closely, however, we can see that the activity of building is more than just adding more and more pieces.

When we look again we notice how often things go wrong. An unexpected wave knocks down an hour's worth of building. A toddler wanders over from a neighboring beach blanket and causes more destruction. The sand dries and walls crumble. Unless disagreements and exhaustion take over, we also see the kids recover from failures. They experiment to figure out how to build a better moat to stay the tide. The toddler is distracted by collecting shells. A bucket brigade creates a pile of wetter sand. Or the construction project is moved up or down the beach to a better location. When children are at play, often enough they react to failures as opportunities for invention. They're not afraid of failure, because the stakes are low. The point is simply to have fun.

However, once we become adults, we're likely to avoid situations where the prospect of failure is high. Whether at work or school, most of us fear tackling a complex problem in front of our peers because of the possible consequences of failing: i.e. embarrassment, shame, a lower grade, a demotion. This fear of failure stifles creativity and innovation.

Not all people respond to fear of failure in the same way, though. In fact, creative people tend to have an attitude toward failure that's more like the kids on the beach than like a typical adult trying to solve a problem at work or a student trying to figure out what the teacher wants him to say. In What the Best College Students Do, Ken Bain argues that what sets the best students apart from the rest is their willingness to acknowledge failures, to explore them, and to learn from them. Unlike less creative people, they didn't deny their mistakes or get defensive about errors.

Where does this ability to bounce back from failure come from? To answer this question, Bain points to a study that compared two groups of ten-year-olds who were each given a series of puzzles. The first eight problems required the students to make real effort, but the challenges matched the students' age and education level. The next four problems were designed to be too hard for the students to solve. Over the first eight problems, there were no differences in how the groups performed; both groups talked about the problems as they worked through them, had fun, and came up with roughly the same number of correct solutions. On the second set of problems, however, the groups' reactions differed greatly from each other. The first group got frustrated, complained, and tried to change the rules; they started to make surprisingly poor choices, shifted their focus away from the problems, and gave up. By contrast, the second group continued to encourage each other, tested different approaches, and seemed to thrive on the challenge, even though they couldn't solve the hard problems either.

What caused the divergent responses? The students were grouped by researchers based on their attitudes toward intelligence. The first group had a fixed view of intelligence and the second group believed, conversely, that with effort you could become smarter. (As shorthand, we call members of the first group the "knowers" and members of the second group the "learners.") When the knowers faced failure, they looked for an escape route, because their failures called their intelligence into question; they went into mental tailspins, reverting to strategies that might be expected from preschoolers. The learners didn't take failure personally. Because they believed they could develop intelligence, working on the problems was its own reward. Even if they never found solutions, they valued learning things along the way.

Obviously, we can't just snap our fingers and change ingrained beliefs and patterns of behavior. And we can't change the fact that in some situations, when the stakes are immediate and high, it's nearly impossible to sustain an impersonal attitude toward failure. We believe, however, that it is possible to cultivate more creative attitudes toward failure through practice, and one of the most important locations for such practice in school assignments where time is allowed for experimentation and revision—such as the writing assignments (which we call "practice sessions") provided throughout Part 1 of this book. You've probably noticed that these practice sessions ask open questions or pose messy problems that can't be responded to simply with facts or by following a formula to a right answer.

In our writing classes, we encourage students to pursue what interests them, and we're thrilled when they set aside their fears and egos and risk exploring really knotty problems. In the end, even if their efforts come to naught, these students tend to learn from their mistakes. They figure out what went wrong and decide what they'll do differently the next time.

When we learn from failure, we discover that practice never ends.

PRACTICE SESSION ONE

REFLECTING

As a thought experiment, look back at what kind of student you were in middle school and in high school. Then imagine what school would have been like for you if grades hadn't mattered to parents or college admissions committees. Would you have taken more risks as a writer and learner, or would you have worked less?

Then set aside at least 30 minutes to reflect on the kind of school that could foster an environment in which students, including you, would be willing both to work hard and to "fail big." At your college, are there classes, teachers, or majors that encourage or even require students to take creative and intellectual risks?

PRACTICE SESSION TWO

READING

In "Fail Better," an essay about writing, Zadie Smith identifies the cliché as a small-scale example of literary failure. "What is a cliché," she asks, "except language passed down by Das Mann [the Man], used and shop-soiled by so many before you, and in no way the correct jumble of language for the intimate part of your vision you meant to express? With a cliché you have pandered to a shared understanding, you have taken a short-cut, you have represented what was pleasing and familiar rather than risked what was true and strange." This isn't the usual definition of failure, but it's a useful way of thinking about how to write well. While there are occasions when settling for the pleasing, familiar, and expected is the polite thing to do, success for a writer seeking new thoughts means having written something unfamiliar, unexpected, even unsettling—productively unsettling.

We'd like you to choose a reading and look for passages in which the writer is productively disruptive, rather than pleasing and familiar.

Then spend at least 40 minutes reflecting in writing about three passages from the reading that you think are particularly risky. Was the writer's risk worthwhile? Did the writer succeed or fail in Zadie Smith's terms? How about in your terms?

PRACTICE SESSION THREE

REFLECTING

We imagine it would be pretty straightforward to ask you to write about a time when you learned from failure. So instead of asking you to write up an account of a moral or educational failure that ends in self-improvement—"and ever afterwards, I was a better person"—we'd like you to write about a time when you failed to understand a concept or idea. What were the consequences of your failure? What rewards, if any, followed from overcoming that failure?

EXPLORE

We know how failure feels: we're disappointed in ourselves and ashamed of disappointing others. Catherine Tice describes the regret and loss that has accompanied her failure to become a musician. When the British daily newspaper the *Guardian* asked seven writers to reflect on failure, however, few of them expressed regret. Most wrote about failure as an inherent part of writing, inseparable from creativity. While even these writers fall into platitudes about failure as opportunity, together their comments suggest a more nuanced view: it's possible to fail *well*—to learn from failure, to make use of it, and to continue to work. Learning from failure also concerns Paul Tough, who wonders whether schools that protect students from failure in the short term ultimately set them up for failure in the long term.

"Falling Short: Seven Writers Reflect on Failure." *Guardian.* 22 June 2013. Web.

Tice, Catherine. "A Brief History of a Musical Failure." *Granta.* 2 Oct. 2013.

Tough, Paul. "What If the Secret to Success Is Failure?" *New York Times Magazine.* 18 Sept. 2011. Web.

Curiosity at Work: Alison Bechdel and the Layered Complexity of the Graphic Narrative

When Alison Bechdel began publishing her comic strip, *Dykes to Watch Out For*, in 1983, the possibility of anyone becoming a graphic memoirist—that is, someone who tells her life story using words and images—wasn't on anyone's radar. In the 1980s, the comic form was restricted largely to "the funnies" in the newspapers and to serialized stories about superheroes sold on rotating racks in convenience stores. The readers of these stories were assumed to be mostly, if not exclusively, teenage boys. A young woman just out of college composing a comic strip that followed the lives of feminists, lesbians, and gays? Not exactly a foolproof plan for success.

And yet Bechdel, inspired by Howard Cruse's *Gay Comix*, was convinced that she could use the comic form in a new way and that she could reach a different demographic with different reading interests. While she didn't set out to produce a strip that would steadily gain popularity and influence, this is exactly what Bechdel ended up doing, by dint of her ability to unite her meticulously drawn characters (some of whom were suggested to her by her avid fans) with compelling lines of narrative that crisscrossed the genres of political commentary, melodrama, and humor. (Bechdel has described the strip as "half op-ed column and half endless, serialized Victorian novel.") And this unlikely project earned Bechdel a living and numerous awards during the twenty-five years she kept *Dykes to Watch Out For* in syndication.

Bechdel's breakout work as a graphic memoirist came in 2006 when she used her cartooning skills to tell her own coming-of-age story *Fun Home: A Family Tragicomic* (the title is a play on the fact that Bechdel grew up above a funeral home). The mystery that resides at the center of *Fun Home* is her father's apparent suicide, which occurred shortly after Bechdel left home for college. Told from the dual perspective of Bechdel as a child moving into adolescence and contending with her eccentric family in rural Pennsylvania, and Bechdel as a mature, successful cartoonist reflecting on the past, *Fun Home* provided Bechdel with a means of exploring her past that simply wasn't available to her in the comic strip form.

Bechdel's sustained attention to detail, which is evident in every cell and every word of her narrative, allows her to see all of the players in this tragicomic tale in their complex humanity: her father, who was a mortician, fastidious home restorer, strict disciplinarian, and guardian of a secret life; her mother, who was an actress, distant and miserable; her brothers; the townspeople; her first female lover in college; and herself. In an interview, Bechdel described how the graphic narrative allowed her to reproduce the multiple perspectives that are ever-present in real life: "Every moment that we're living and having experiences, we're bringing to bear all of the other experiences that we've had. This is what is exciting to me about graphic narrative, that you're able to do a layered complexity that I couldn't imagine doing with just writing."

An instant success, *Fun Home* was followed in 2012 by *Are You My Mother? A Comic Drama*, Bechdel's equally incisive exploration of her mother's life in the time before and after Bechdel's father's mysterious death. In 2014, Bechdel received a MacArthur "genius" grant in recognition of her ongoing work "changing our notions of the contemporary memoir and expanding the expressive potential of the graphic form."

CHAPTER 8

Arguing

In college, it often seems that *writing* and *arguing* are treated as synonyms. Teachers ask their students to write arguments that present interesting claims supported by evidence. But how do good, thoughtful arguments come into being? Does the act of writing move a preformulated argument from your brain to the screen? Or is an argument created through the act of writing? The distinction matters: if argument comes first, then writing is simply transcription. If writing comes first, then the argument emerges through the process of engaging with and responding to writing—one's own and the writing of others.

While it would certainly be more convenient if writing simply recorded our already-formulated thoughts, we know as writers and as teachers of writing that the best arguments emerge over time—after one has read, thought, reflected, drafted, revised, started over, and reconsidered. Thus, in this chapter we invite you to think of an argument as a compelling idea that emerges over the course of an intellectual journey. We also invite you to imagine your mental life as a drama in which there's action, excitement, and passion that can motivate your writing. And we show how three influential scholarly arguments are driven by curiosity. The emphasis throughout is on producing writing that matters.

On Argument as Journey

When professors assign papers in college classes, they typically expect their students to hand in essays that make an argument. What they mean by "an argument," however, isn't always clear to the students. Many of our students arrive in our classes believing that writing an argument is like participating in a debate: they pick a side (their thesis); they gather evidence to support the side they've chosen; and they write as if trying to show that they are right and the other side is wrong. Winning, or getting a good grade, is the goal—not thoughtfulness, not discovery, not learning.

There are contexts within which this type of writing is entirely appropriate: a legal brief, for example, or a letter of complaint. But if you listen to pundits on cable news,

Chapter 8, "Arguing," from *Habits of the Creative Mind*, by Richard E. Miller and Ann Jurecic, pp. 227–252 (Chapter 11).

follow congressional debates, or read the comment sections of online news sources, you'll see that such oppositional argumentation has become the norm in contemporary culture. In these venues, pushing ideas to their extremes, stirring up the emotions of one's allies and enemies, and scoring points with a pithy phrase or sound bite are more common than the reasoned exchange of ideas.

Because we have not found that practicing argument-as-debate leads to good academic writing—or to good journalism or good literary nonfiction—we propose, in its place, practicing argument as journey. What's the difference? In practicing argument as journey, you begin with the goal of answering a question or solving a problem (that's your destination); you ponder possible trajectories; you do research and rethink your plan; you learn more and more; you write, make mistakes, and head off in new and unanticipated directions; you make discoveries; you define a clearer purpose and path; you figure out how you want to answer your central question or solve your problem. Finally, the finished essay takes your readers on a journey to new ideas.

We'd like to walk you through an extended example of the argument as journey by looking at Elizabeth Kolbert's *Field Notes from a Catastrophe*, a book about global climate change. When Kolbert chose this topic, she knew she was stepping into contentious territory. Some people see climate change as an empirically verifiable threat to the future of life on this planet and others dismiss it as a false claim based in bad or inconclusive science. In the scientific community, the consensus is clear: global warming is a fact and it is caused by human activity—especially our reliance on burning carbon-based fuels such as coal, oil, wood, and natural gas. There is no such consensus in politics. Indeed as the scientific community has made it harder to deny that global warming is a fact, nonscientists of every stripe have shifted their doubt to the role humans play in changing the earth's climate. Given this political context, the project of writing about climate change poses a real challenge for Kolbert: if the National Academy of Sciences, which has been issuing warnings about impending environmental disaster since 1979, hasn't been able to convince people of the reality and danger of climate change and that humans have caused it, what could Kolbert—or any writer, for that matter—possibly say that would change readers' minds?

We admire *Field Notes from a Catastrophe* both because Kolbert sets out to see for herself the effects of climate change on the environment and because she takes her readers with her on a journey that is both physical and metaphysical. She seeks to examine evidence of climate change and also to contemplate why we have been so reluctant to acknowledge and act on signs of impending disaster. She begins by traveling above the Arctic Circle because the signs of warming are so striking there.

Kolbert visits the Alaskan village of Shishmaref, on an island off the coast of the Seward Peninsula, where native villagers once drove snowmobiles twenty miles out on the ice to hunt seals. By the time she gets there, the ice around the island is so soft that using snowmobiles is no longer safe, so the hunters use boats. The village, only twenty-two feet above sea level, has become so vulnerable to storm surges that the residents have decided to give up their way of life and relocate. Farther inland, near Fairbanks, Kolbert sees the effects of melting permafrost. Areas of ground that have been frozen since the beginning of the last glacial cycle are now threatened by thaw. Where the permafrost has been disturbed by the construction of buildings or roads, the land is especially vulnerable to warming; in some neighborhoods, foundations are degrading and houses are collapsing.

Kolbert then visits Iceland during the summer-melt season and meets members of the Icelandic Glaciological Society, who regularly survey the size of the country's three hundred or so glaciers. Though glaciers in Iceland continued to grow in the 1970s and 1980s, even as North American glaciers were shrinking, in the 1990s they, too, began to retreat. There have been glaciers on Iceland for two million years, Kolbert writes, but climate models predict that by the end of the next century there will be no more ice left to measure in Iceland.

Kolbert also travels to a research station on the Greenland ice sheet where scientists study ice cores drilled from the glacier. "A hundred and thirty-eight feet down," Kolbert writes, "there is snow that fell during the time of the American Civil War; 2,500 feet down, snow from the time of the Peloponnesian Wars, and, 5,350 feet down, snow from the days when the cave painters of Lascaux were slaughtering bison. At the very bottom, 10,000 feet down, there is snow that fell on central Greenland before the start of the last ice age, more than a hundred thousand years ago." Today, however, scientists at the research station are observing and measuring the gradual contraction of this massive glacier, which contains eight percent of the world's fresh water supply. If the Greenland ice sheet melts—and it is shrinking by twelve cubic miles each year—the consequences will be more than the loss of the history it contains. The ice sheet, Kolbert reports, contains enough water to raise sea levels around the world by twenty-three feet.

As Kolbert describes her physical journey, she also takes her readers on a journey through the science of climate change. Chapter by chapter, she carefully and clearly tells her readers how science explains the role humans have played in bringing about current warming trends and what these changes indicate about the future of the planet. After her account of Shishmaref, for instance, Kolbert summarizes the first major study of global warming, completed in 1979 by the National Academy of Sciences. A panel evaluated early studies on the effects of adding carbon dioxide to the atmosphere and concluded that continued increases in carbon dioxide would cause climate changes. They knew then that there was "no reason to believe that these changes [would] be negligible." If we had taken their warning seriously thirty years ago, we might have lessened the impact of climate change.

Later Kolbert explains why we should be concerned about the melting of perennial sea ice, which, unlike seasonal ice that forms and melts each year, remains frozen year-round. Back in 1979, perennial sea ice covered 1.7 billion acres—about the size of the continental United States. By the time Kolbert was writing her book in 2005, that area had shrunk by 250 million acres, an area about the combined size of Texas, New York, and Georgia. Why does this matter? Ice reflects sunlight away from the earth, while the dark open water of the ocean absorbs its heat. The more the perennial ice melts, exposing open ocean water, the more heat gets retained by the ocean, which then melts even more ice: the system feeds on itself, and the pace of warming speeds up. Small changes in the average temperature of ocean water, in other words, can lead to big changes in climate.

Having explained the science of the greenhouse effect and how industrialization—with its coal-burning factories, railroads, and power stations—started the process of global warming, Kolbert moves in her third chapter to discuss a contemporary symposium on climate change she attended in Iceland. None of the scientists at the symposium doubt that humans are responsible for warming the Earth's atmosphere. So Kolbert's journey through the science leads her and her readers to a *certainty* that too many politicians willingly deny: human consumption of carbon-based fuels has dramatically raised the level of carbon dioxide in the atmosphere and the consequences are changing life on earth.

Kolbert's journey does not end when she leaves the Arctic. She goes to England to see how climate change threatens the survival of butterflies and toads—and up to a quarter of the Earth's species. She learns how droughts long-ago caused the disappearance of ancient civilizations. She visits the Netherlands, where existing dikes will not hold back rising seawaters, so companies are manufacturing floating "amphibious" homes. She also travels to Burlington, Vermont, where a grassroots campaign to reduce greenhouse gas emissions by ten percent affirms the possibilities of local action, and also its limits. After all, whatever the residents of this small city accomplish is quickly offset by the rest of the world's continued expansion of energy use. Kolbert closes her book by arguing that humans have launched the planet into a new geological era. We should recognize, she says, that the Holocene, the epoch that began at the end of the Pleistocene about 11,700 years ago, is now over. We are in the dawn of the "Anthropocene," a "new age ... defined by one creature—man—who [has] become so dominant that he [is] capable of altering the planet on a geological scale."

It's obvious throughout *Field Notes from a Catastrophe* that Kolbert thinks we must end our destructive addiction to fossil fuels, but she knows this argument has been made before to little effect. So she doesn't use her book to tell us what to do. Instead, the journey she takes us on makes the argument that the problem is so far along and so deeply entrenched in human behavior that it may not be solvable. When Kolbert arrives at the conclusion that we have entered the Anthropocene, it's clear that her readers have to choose what to do now. Denial, disbelief, or despair is always an option, but if we have been affected by reading Kolbert's book, we may at least be willing to accept responsibility for the problem we've created, and we may decide that trying to halt the pace or lessen the effect of the catastrophe is surely better than doing nothing at all. Indeed, if we're capable of causing disaster on a global scale, we may also be smart, creative, and lucky enough to come up with ways to ameliorate the consequences of this disaster. If we're truly lucky, we may even manage to delay the end of the Anthropocene era.

PRACTICE SESSION ONE

READING

We've just described how Elizabeth Kolbert takes a physical journey that she then transforms into an intellectual journey for her readers. Now we'd like you to choose a reading and follow the author's intellectual journey. After you've read through the piece once, set aside at least 40 minutes to review it and take more detailed notes about how the journey unfolds. Pay attention to the sources—the people and texts the author cites. Step back and look at the decisions the author made about how to organize the text.

Then draw a map of the journey. When did it move straight ahead? When did you encounter turns of thought? Did the author send you off on digressions? Did they still feel like digressions after you'd followed them to their conclusions?

REFLECTING

Spend at least 30 minutes writing reflectively about your own journey as a reader of the essay you selected. After reading and then reviewing the article, how far have you traveled intellectually? Were there places where your own thinking diverged from the path the author provided? Did reading the piece allow you to think about its central problem or question in a new way? Did it change your mind?

PRACTICE SESSION TWO

RESEARCH ESSAY

After reading our description of *Field Notes from a Catastrophe*, you now have a sense of Kolbert's view of the environmental challenges we face. The world we know will change radically during our lifetimes and, as a consequence of our collective choices and actions, may eventually become a planet that is uninhabitable by humans. The facts are menacing and disturbing, and they raise an important question: Can we construct rational hope in the face of climate change, and if so, how?

To compose an essay that offers a thoughtful answer to this question, you will first need to do additional reading. If you go out to the Web, you will find more on climate change than any single person could read in a lifetime. How do you separate what's worth considering from what's not? How do you determine what's compelling? We'd like you to spend at least 60 minutes searching online for a fact or a set of facts about climate change that you find both powerful and worthy of further consideration.

Write up a discussion of the facts you've uncovered. What makes the facts you're presenting more convincing than other facts regarding climate change? In completing your write-up, you are likely to need to do more reading, since facts only become convincing when placed in context.

SPECULATIVE ESSAY

Thinking seriously about climate change inevitably affects one's sense of the future. Given the evidence you've uncovered in your limited research, would you say that it is possible to construct a rational hope about the future? What compelling evidence would you point to that either supports or undermines the grounds for rational hope? In composing your response, stick to evidence that you find persuasive: this isn't an invitation to trade in generalities about "human nature"; it's an opportunity to consider the relationship between evidence, reason, and the future. Take your reader on a journey that reveals your mind at work on this problem.

EXPLORE

Writers we admire often begin their work with a question about why an event occurred, how an idea came into being, or how a problem might be resolved; then they lead their readers through facts, analysis, and ideas to arrive at their own answers. The list below offers examples of such complex journeys. Brian Cathcart guides us through a London murder case while pondering race and injustice. Ta-Nehisi Coates considers the evolution of racism in the United States, from slavery to Jim Crow and from segregation to racist housing policies, asking whether a discussion about financial reparations might bring about necessary change. Joan Didion reflects on how a set of fixed political opinions led to the US invasions of Iraq and Afghanistan. Venkatesh Rao invites readers to consider how having resources to waste serves creativity. And Rebecca Solnit walks us through the collapsed city of Detroit where she finds hope in how nature quickly reclaims the landscape.

Cathcart, Brian. "The Case of Stephen Lawrence." *Granta.* 6 Jan. 2012. Web.

Coates, Ta-Nehisi. "The Case for Reparations." *Atlantic.* 21 May 2014. Web.

Didion, Joan. "Fixed Opinions, or the Hinge of History." *New York Review of Books.* 16 Jan. 2003. Web.

Rao, Venkatesh. "Waste, Creativity, and Godwin's Corollary for Technology." *Ribbonfarm.* 23 Aug. 2012. Web.

Solnit, Rebecca. "Detroit Arcadia." *Harper's Magazine.* July 2007. Web.

On the Theater of the Mind

If you do a search on the phrase "theater of the mind," you'll find it has been used in two ways. Starting in 1956, "theater of the mind" was used by those wishing to argue that listening to radio dramas required more brainpower than watching dramas on the newer medium of television. Radio dramas, the argument went, are superior to television dramas because they take place not in the sound studio where the voice actors and sound effects people convene, but in the imaginations of the listening audience. The phrase is now used more generally to describe what happens when words, whether read or heard, and/or images, whether seen or described, create a dramatic scene in the mind of the beholder. And so one could say that advertising, which has long made the programming on radio and television possible, is convened in the theater of the mind, where it continuously prods audiences to imagine the better life that comes from consumption. Indeed, this search exercise itself demonstrates just how much advertising dominates the theater of the mind: the top search results for this phrase are not links to definitions or discussions of the debate over whether radio is superior to television or vice versa; they are for the sixth studio album by the hip-hop artist Ludacris, which happens to be named... *Theater of the Mind*.

We'd like to hijack the phrase "theater of the mind" and use it for an entirely different purpose. We grant that words and images can create a virtual theater *in* the mind. What we're interested in, though, is considering what becomes possible when you think of the flow of thoughts in your mind as participating in an open-ended drama that quietly plays out as you think through and about the ideas that are most important to you. It's a drama not just *in* your mind but *of* your mind. And you can use your writing to make the theater of your mind available for others to experience. Indeed, we'd say that this is one way to define the practice of creativity. When you write, you also shape an experience in the minds of your readers; your words stage the unfolding of an idea or an argument or a narrative.

When scientific and philosophic treatises were presented as dialogues, it was easier to see that there are dramatic, comedic, and even tragic aspects to the exchange of ideas. Galileo's use of the telescope, for example, shows how a new technology can generate new information that, under the right circumstances, triggers an internal dialogue—in the theater of the mind—that in turn leads to a whole new way of thinking and seeing.

In 1609, with the aid of one of the world's first telescopes, Galileo began to collect evidence suggesting that the earth was not at the center of what we now call the solar system. He first published his results as a scientific treatise in 1610. In 1632, in his book *The Dialogue Concerning the Two Chief World Systems*, Galileo presented his argument for a sun-centered model of the universe as a dialogue between three fictional characters: Salviati, a scholar whose research supports the idea that the sun is at the center of the universe; Simplicio, who believes that the earth is at the center of the universe, an idea initially presented by Aristotle and Ptolemy more than a thousand years earlier; and Sagredo, an intelligent bystander who asks questions as Salviati and Simplicio debate the merits of the two diametrically opposed models. Galileo used the form of the dialogue to make his own thinking process accessible to the greatest number of readers, most of whom were not involved in studying the heavens. He staged what would otherwise be an arcane discussion about measuring the movements of celestial bodies as a dialogue for a general audience, one that serves up humor and insults along with explanations of the significance of his discovery of craters on the moon. With his dialogue, Galileo made it possible for his readers to imagine that the sun was at the center of the universe regardless of what the Bible said or what the Church held. While Galileo's 1610 treatise presented the same fundamental threat to the Catholic Church's worldview, it was the publication of *The Dialogue* that led to Galileo's trial for heresy in 1633, where he was forced to recant his argument for the heliocentric universe and was then sentenced to house arrest for the remainder of his life.

Were you expecting a happier ending?

Our second example comes from ancient Greece. Plato, Socrates's prolific student, presented his teacher's philosophical reflections as a series of dialogues. Here, too, one finds the exchange of ideas depicted not as the dispassionate, orderly laying out of the steps that lead to some deep truth but as a wayward back-and-forth between Socrates, who is forever searching after the Good, and one or more interlocutors, who are inevitably shown to know much less than they claim to know. In *The Republic*, the Platonic dialogue that explores whether or not the State has the power to produce good, law-abiding citizens, Socrates tells a story about the difference between the world as it is seen by average people and the world as it is seen by those who seek the truth.

Socrates asks his listeners to imagine a cave in which prisoners are chained to the ground, their gaze fixed on the cave wall before them. Behind them there is a fire, and between the fire and the prisoners is a pathway traveled by people carrying life-size cutouts of various objects. The fire casts shadows of the objects on the wall, and the prisoners, because they can't turn their heads, take these moving shadows to be reality. This, Socrates would have his listeners believe, is how unthinking people experience life: they mistake shadows for reality; they are prisoners to illusions.

Continuing his story, Socrates imagines a prisoner who breaks free of his chains, turns and sees the fire and the cutouts, and then walks from the cave into the sunlight. The former prisoner now sees things as they are, and he returns to the cave to tell the prisoners what he has seen. For Socrates, the freed prisoner is akin to the philosopher, and the return to the cave is the beginning of the philosopher's educational mission, which Socrates defines as turning the prisoners toward the light of the fire.

> Then education is the craft concerned with doing this very thing, this turning around, and with how the soul can most easily and effectively be made to do it. It isn't the craft of putting sight into the soul. Education takes for granted that sight is there but that it isn't turned the right way or looking where it ought to look, and it tries to redirect it appropriately.

With Socrates's allegory of the cave, we get a nested set of theaters of the mind: there's the theater in the prisoner's mind, which is inhabited by shadows; there's the theater in the philosopher's mind, where one encounters reality; and there's Plato's theater of the mind, which stages this moment when Socrates uses a story to illustrate his view of education as the process of turning from the illusory to the real.

What we find compelling about the Allegory of the Cave and *The Dialogue Concerning the Two Chief World Systems* is that they make visible what would otherwise go unnoticed—namely, that there is a drama to the life of the mind that gets expressed in the movement from confusion to clarity, a drama that gets felt in the weight and heft of the process of changing one's mind. While the dramas that played out in the theater of Galileo's mind and the theater of Socrates's mind proved to be of global significance, we all experience a true change of mind, like a genuine change of heart, as life changing, even though the significance of the change extends no further than our own worldview.

Writing plays a central role in the theater of the mind because it makes it possible for us to see our own thoughts and then to reflect on what happens when we move those thoughts out into the world. As it happens this is why Socrates so distrusted writing: unlike an embodied dialogue between a teacher and a student, with writing there's no one there but ourselves to test the veracity of our thoughts as we express them. Despite Socrates's argument against writing, his student Plato wrote a series of dialogues featuring Socrates that have been read, discussed, and argued over for the past two thousand years. Why? Because the questions Socrates poses in Plato's dialogues cut to the very essence of what it means to be human. Indeed, for Socrates, it is the ongoing engagement with the theater of one's mind, where questions about how to live a good life are posed and reposed, that separates us from all the other animals. This sentiment, succinctly captured in Socrates's oft-quoted declaration in *The Apology* that "the unexamined life is not worth living," is, we would argue, more accurately rendered as "a life lived without ongoing self-examination is not a human life." The drama of the theater of the mind commences as soon as the question "What do I think?" is given serious consideration.

PRACTICE SESSION ONE

REFLECTING

There's a quick way to test how the idea of the theater of the mind, as we've defined it, can be of use to you: write a description of the most dramatic moment you've experienced in the realm of thought. In the theater of the mind, one deals with ideas—friendship, citizenship, truth, faith, integrity, or success, for example—and the drama is in the development of a revised understanding of the idea at the center of one's self-examination. We are not asking you to write a story about how winning an award improved your self-confidence or how an act of shoplifting led to feelings of guilt. The assignment is to focus squarely on the redefinition of an *idea* and to lead your readers through your thought process to show them why the shift in definition *matters*.

PRACTICE SESSION TWO

READING

There's a maxim in argumentation that goes like this: tell them what you're going to say; say it; tell them that you said it. This is argumentation through repetition. In the context of the current discussion, we'd say that this kind of argumentation contains no drama; there's nothing for the reader to do in the theater of the mind other than accept or reject the point that is being argued.

This is not the case for any of the readings we've included at the end of this volume. Choose a reading and observe, as you read, how the writer tries to create a theater of the mind for the readers, encouraging them to think in new ways about the topic at hand.

Set aside at least 30 minutes to take notes about places where the writer dramatizes the evolution of ideas, perhaps by refining the argument, shifting directions, or introducing new and surprising information.

WRITING

After you've read and reviewed the article, draft an essay that describes how the writer moves your thinking along from the beginning of the article to the end. Is there a drama to this movement? What has the writer done to get you to shift your thinking? Does he or she succeed?

REVISING

And now for the real challenge: revise the essay you wrote in the previous exercise so that it compellingly demonstrates your experience reading the piece you've chosen and contending with its implications. In other words, create for your reader the drama of your engagement with the writer's ideas.

EXPLORE

One of the pleasures of reading and writing is exploring the theater of other people's minds. In the *Invisibilia* podcast "The Secret History of Thoughts," you can hear the "ghost boy," who spent thirteen years in a vegetative state, describe what it was like to live entirely inside his mind. Leslie Jamison discusses how her experiences as a medical actor—i.e., playing sick for doctors in training—transformed her understanding of empathy. Cheryl Strayed offers advice to a beginning writer, Elissa Bassist, about how to overcome the internal fears that prevent getting down to work. In an interview two years later, Strayed speaks with Bassist, who has completed the book she feared she would never write.

Bassist, Elissa, and Cheryl Strayed. "How to Write Like a Mother#^@%&." *Creative Nonfiction*. #47, Winter 2013. Web.

Jamison, Leslie. "The Empathy Exams: A Medical Actor Writes Her Own Script." *The Believer*. Feb. 2014. Web.

"The Secret History of Thoughts." NPR *Invisibilia*. 9 Jan. 2015. Podcast.

Strayed, Cheryl. "Write Like a Motherfucker." *The Rumpus*. 19 Aug. 2010. Web.

On Curiosity at Work in the Academy

Throughout Part 1 of this book, we've included short entries about "Curiosity at Work"—examples of how curiosity inspires creative thought and expression. In these brief essays, we emphasize the work of contemporary nonfiction writers because they do such a good job of posing compelling questions about the world. If you're a student learning to write for school, however, you may be wondering how to connect what this book teaches you about writers' habits of mind to the kinds of papers you are asked to write for classes in particular academic disciplines. We think the best way to address that connection is to show you examples of curiosity at work in academic writing so you can see how academic articles and books emerge from the very habits of mind we've been discussing.

Academic writing differs from journalistic writing and general nonfiction in important ways. Scholarly articles and books explicitly join conversations taking place in particular branches of knowledge, and they focus on questions that are of interest to others in the same discipline; philosophers ask different kinds of questions than psychologists or anthropologists or historians ask. The various fields of study also differ from each other in their methods of research, the kinds of evidence used, and the traditions that govern how arguments, ideas, evidence, and sources are presented.

Despite these differences, academic writing has much in common with nonfiction written by generalists. Each of the three academic works we discuss below begins with the author expressing curiosity about a difficult problem, puzzle, or paradox that can be addressed through research. While the authors present their work according to the conventions of their respective academic fields, they are all motivated by a desire to advance understanding about complex issues. Reviewing these examples will make it easier for you to see three of the main moves academics make in launching their writing projects. Each writer identifies an important problem, puzzle, or paradox; joins an ongoing discussion about the problem, puzzle, or paradox; and establishes the key words in that conversation. This description may suggest that we think academic writing follows a formula. But we'd say that these writers *begin* with curiosity. The conventions become useful later as the writers shape what they've discovered for an audience of specialized readers.

• • • • •

One of the most influential articles in the field of political theory is Michael Walzer's "Political Action: The Problem of Dirty Hands," which appeared in *Philosophy & Public Affairs* in 1973. (The full article can easily be found online.) In the introduction to his essay, Walzer immediately signals that he's joining an ongoing conversation. His first paragraph explains that he's interested in a disagreement about moral dilemmas that has already been addressed by three fellow philosophers—Thomas Nagel, Richard B. Brandt, and R. M. Hare. They disagree about "whether or not a man can ever face, or ever has to face, a moral dilemma, a situation where he must choose between two courses of action *both of which it would be wrong for him to undertake*" (emphasis added). More specifically, they're concerned about whether it's possible for a leader to govern "innocently." In other words, can a political leader resolve moral dilemmas without ever having to choose a course of action that is immoral?

Nagel thinks that, because dilemmas arise in which each possible course of action is morally wrong, a leader cannot govern innocently. Brandt argues that logical reasoning can be used to resolve such dilemmas and thus a leader can remain innocent. Hare agrees, arguing dilemmas of this kind can and should be resolved at a higher level of moral discourse.

Walzer is not satisfied with any of these answers. In the third paragraph of his article, he writes:

> My own answer is no, I don't think I could govern innocently; nor do most of us believe that those who govern us are innocent—as I shall argue below—even the best of them. But this does not mean that it isn't possible to do the right thing while governing. It means that a particular act of government (in a political party or in the state) may be exactly the right thing to do in utilitarian terms and yet leave the man who does it guilty of a moral wrong. The innocent man, afterwards, is no longer innocent. If on the other hand he remains innocent ..., he not only fails to do the right thing (in utilitarian terms), he may also fail to measure up to the duties of his office (which imposes on him a considerable responsibility for consequences and outcomes).

If you have trouble understanding what Walzer is saying the first time through, try reading this passage again, slowly, and look up the terms that are unfamiliar to you. If you look up *utilitarianism*, for example, you'll find that it is the principle of the greatest good for the greatest number. A utilitarian evaluates choices on the basis of how useful they are; the *right* choice to a utilitarian is one that is beneficial for more people.

With this definition in mind, you might assume that calculating the greatest good for the greatest number is a straightforward business, but Walzer thinks that making a utilitarian decision could be simultaneously the right course of action and a morally wrong one. For example, suppose a political leader could serve the greater good of his or her country by sacrificing the lives of bystanders to kill the head of a terrorist organization. Even if the political leader makes the "right" utilitarian choice to kill bystanders for the greater good of the country, she or he has still committed the immoral act of killing innocent people and now has dirty hands. If the leader refuses to commit this immoral act on behalf of the greater good and lets the terrorist live, then the leader has put his or her own citizens at risk. With this choice, the leader commits a different moral wrong and also has dirty hands.

Six pages into the article, Walzer fully lays out the paradox that leaders "who act for us and in our name are often killers, or seem to become killers too quickly and too easily." Even "good and decent people" who choose politics as a vocation, he writes,

> are then required to learn the lesson Machiavelli first set out to teach: "how not to be good." Some of them are incapable of learning; many more profess to be incapable. But they will not succeed unless they learn, for they have joined the terrible competition for power and glory; they have chosen to work and struggle as Machiavelli says, among "so many who are not good."

> They can do no good themselves unless they win the struggle, which they are unlikely to do unless they are willing and able to use the necessary means. So we are suspicious even of the best of winners. It is not a sign of our perversity if we think them only more clever than the rest. They have not won, after all, because they were good, or not only because of that, but also because they were not good. No one succeeds in politics without getting his hands dirty. This is conventional wisdom again, and again I don't mean to insist that it is true without qualification. I repeat it only to disclose the moral dilemma inherent in the convention. For sometimes it is right to try to succeed, and then it must also be right to get one's hands dirty. But one's hands get dirty from doing what it is wrong to do. And how can it be wrong to do what is right? Or, how can we get our hands dirty by doing what we ought to do?

As this last paragraph shows, Walzer doesn't rush to resolve the moral puzzle that fascinates him. Rather than being satisfied with the conclusion that successful leaders must have dirty hands, he continues to generate more and more questions: If having dirty hands is inevitable, when should dirty-handed leaders be held accountable? Does holding leaders accountable then dirty the hands of citizens in turn? Does everyone end up with dirty hands? Walzer concludes his essay without having answered any of these questions definitively. And yet, forty years after it was written, "Political Action: The Problem of Dirty Hands" is still being cited by scholars and taught in politics classes. Why? For two reasons: because Walzer's article presents the complex puzzle of "doing bad to do good" with remarkable clarity; and because Walzer's way of engaging with this puzzle is so lively and original that readers from across the political spectrum feel invited to join with him as he wrestles with the unsolvable challenge of leadership.

• • • • •

Edward Said's influential book *Orientalism* begins by making the same series of moves we saw Walzer's "Political Action" make above: in the introduction to Orientalism, Said joins an ongoing conversation about culture; he works to unsettle key terms; and he argues that we should understand a complicated puzzle in a new way. The introduction opens with Said staging his response to the following: "On a visit to Beirut during the terrible civil war of 1975–1976 a French journalist wrote regretfully of the gutted downtown area that 'it had once seemed to belong to ... the Orient of Chateaubriand and Nerval.'" The jounalist saw only what his own country had lost. The distortions of this view of Beirut inspired Said to write a book about how the East has been seen through Western eyes.

We'd like you to read the first two paragraphs of *Orientalism* and observe how Said's curiosity about the journalist's sentence leads him to intellectually creative thoughts. It will help you understand Said's project if you know that Chateaubriand and Nerval were nineteenth-century French writers who wrote extensively about their travels to the Middle East and, more specifically, about their time in Beirut.

> On a visit to Beirut during the terrible civil war of 1975–1976 a French journalist wrote regretfully of the gutted downtown area that "it had once seemed to belong to … the Orient of Chateaubriand and Nerval." He was right about the place, of course, especially so far as a European was concerned. The Orient was almost a European invention, and had been since antiquity a place of romance, exotic beings, haunting memories and landscapes, remarkable experiences. Now it was disappearing; in a sense it had happened, its time was over. Perhaps it seemed irrelevant that Orientals themselves had something at stake in the process, that even in the time of Chateaubriand and Nerval Orientals had lived there, and that now it was they who were suffering; the main thing for the European visitor was a European representation of the Orient and its contemporary fate, both of which had a privileged communal significance for the journalist and his French readers.
>
> Americans will not feel quite the same about the Orient, which for them is much more likely to be associated very differently with the Far East (China and Japan, mainly). Unlike the Americans, the French and the British—less so the Germans, Russians, Spanish, Portuguese, Italians, and Swiss—have had a long tradition of what I shall be calling *Orientalism*, a way of coming to terms with the Orient that is based on the Orient's special place in European Western experience. The Orient is not only adjacent to Europe; it is also the place of Europe's greatest and richest and oldest colonies, the source of its civilizations and languages, its cultural contestant, and one of its deepest and most recurring images of the Other. In addition, the Orient has helped to define Europe (or the West) as its contrasting image, idea, personality, experience. Yet none of this Orient is merely imaginative. The Orient is an integral part of European *material* civilization and culture. Orientalism expresses and represents that part culturally and even ideologically as a mode of discourse with supporting institutions, vocabulary, scholarship, imagery, doctrines, even colonial bureaucracies and colonial styles. …

You may need to read this passage more than once and look up terms that are unfamiliar to you to understand Said's project. You could look carefully, for instance, at what Said does with the term "the Orient." For over a century, the term seemed to be culturally neutral, but Said draws our attention to how it is deeply embedded in a Western cultural perspective that casts the East as both in service to and inferior to the West. The ways the West perceives the East, he says, have far-reaching effects. The European idea of "the Orient" is embedded in the European languages, patterns of thought, and institutional structures. If we return to the journalist's description of the "gutted downtown" of Beirut that "had once seemed to belong to . . . the Orient of Chateaubriand and Nerval," we can now see what Said wants us to see—namely, the nostalgia of a Frenchman who cannot appreciate Beirut as an Eastern city and who regrets that it no longer reflects the influence of its French colonizers. With this brief example, Said takes the first step in his journey to establish that the idea of "the Orient" is a European invention. His intellectual journey ultimately inspired a generation of scholars to document the ways that European and Americans have represented Middle Eastern, African, and Asian societies and cultures over time.

• • • • •

The two examples of academic writing we've offered so far are both focused on abstract concepts, "Orientalism" and "the problem of dirty hands," and they both address how ideas and narratives shape the way we think about politics, power, culture, and cultural difference. Our third example, from the field of sociology, is less abstract, though it too examines the power of cultural narratives. "Fetal Alcohol Syndrome: The Origins of a Moral Panic," by Elizabeth M. Armstrong and Ernest L. Abel, examines the growing concern in the 1990s about fetal alcohol syndrome (FAS) as a public health issue. The writers of this article are very direct: they begin by defining fetal alcohol syndrome and then quickly cite six articles to demonstrate that they are entering an ongoing scholarly conversation about the prevalence and danger of fetal alcohol syndrome. Although their prose is unadorned, they make clear in their introduction that they've uncovered an unexpected and serious problem.

> Fetal alcohol syndrome (FAS) is a pattern of anomalies occurring in children born to alcoholic women (Jones and Smith, 1973). The main features of this pattern are pre- and/or postnatal growth retardation, characteristic facial abnormalities, and central nervous system dysfunction, including mental retardation (Stratton *et al.*, 1996). Despite the pervasiveness of alcohol and drunkenness in human history (Abel, 1997), FAS went largely unrecognized until 1973, when it was characterized as a "tragic disorder" by Jones and Smith, the Seattle physicians who discovered it (Jones and Smith, 1973). By the 1990s, FAS had been transformed in the United States from an unrecognized condition to a moral panic characterized as a "major public health concern" (e.g. Stratton *et al.*, 1996) and a "national health priority" (Egeland

> *et al.*, 1998). In this paper, we trace this evolution, paying special attention to the ways in which this moral panic has inflated fear and anxiety about the syndrome beyond levels warranted by evidence of its prevalence or impact. To acknowledge that the current level of concern about FAS is exaggerated is not to suggest that the syndrome does not exist. One of us (E. L. A.) has spent his entire professional career researching and writing about FAS and continues to be actively engaged in its prevention.

Armstrong and Abel are curious about a paradox in the history of fetal alcohol syndrome: although the syndrome was unknown before 1973, in the space of twenty years, fetal alcohol syndrome went from being invisible to being the focus of a "moral panic." They want to understand how and why the syndrome became an urgent "public health priority."

In the pages that follow the introduction, the authors reinterpret evidence that was available to everyone at the time and yet was routinely oversimplified and misunderstood by others caught up in the moral panic. They point out, for example, that highly visible prevention efforts, such as the placement of warning labels on alcohol bottles, "are doomed to fail" because all pregnant women are not, in fact, equally at risk of giving birth to children with fetal alcohol syndrome. If, as the authors say, "a small proportion of women of child-bearing age, especially those who are most disadvantaged by poverty, bear the greatest burden of risk for FAS," then the real public health concern should be identifying and helping those women who are most at risk.

This is what it means to be creative as an academic: you show your readers how to understand a problem in a new way. Armstrong and Abel have recast a seemingly intractable public health crisis so that new ways of responding to it become imaginable.

• • • • •

These three examples of curiosity at work in the academy offer just a glimpse of how academics share their curiosity about the ways of the world with others. Academic writing poses special challenges to readers who are new to a topic or a field of study, but if you know to look for the problem, question, puzzle, or paradox that the writer is grappling with, if you can spot where the writer is joining an ongoing conversation with other scholars, and if you figure out how to define key terms and concepts, you'll be able to get your bearings, even if the language and subject matter at first seem entirely unfamiliar.

PRACTICE SESSION ONE

READING

Above we've presented examples of two kinds of curiosity-driven scholarly projects: Armstrong and Abel seek to resolve a puzzle, and Walzer and Said explore the complexity of an abstraction. For this exercise, we want you to think about other roles that curiosity can play in scholarly writing.

Begin by selecting a scholarly essay to read. You can work with one of the five articles listed in the Explore section (p. 149), or your teacher may suggest other readings. You may even be able to read an article written by one of your teachers.

Read the essay you've chosen from beginning to end, marking key moments in the argument. Then read the essay again; most academic articles need to be read more than once to be fully understood. As you reread, pay attention to how the scholar organizes ideas, works with sources, presents major points, and addresses readers. Take notes in the margins about the key moments you marked.

After you've read and reread the article with care, take at least 30 minutes to write out answers to the following questions: How did the scholar introduce his or her topic? Where did the writing draw you in? Are there parts of the essay that confused you, or sections where you didn't know enough about the topic or the sources to follow the argument? What parts of the article were particularly clear? Were there passages that prompted you to think new thoughts?

WRITING

Write an essay that reflects on how curiosity gets announced and pursued in the article you've read. Make certain to quote specific passages where you feel the focus of the scholar's curiosity is made clear. What is the status of that curiosity at the end of the article? Have the author's questions been resolved, or have they led to other questions?

PRACTICE SESSION TWO

READING

All of your teachers will have other examples of academic writing they admire. Ask some of them to recommend a few favorite academic articles, chapters, or books. Choose one and read it with an eye toward understanding the curiosity that drives the scholar's project, following the steps in the Reading section of Practice Session One: read, reread, take notes, reflect, and write. Why do you think your teacher recommended that piece of writing? Can you offer an explanation for why it has been influential?

EXPLORE

Zora Neale Hurston once wrote, "research is formalized curiosity." Although some academic prose seems dry and airless, many scholarly writers put their passion and curiosity on display. Hurston's fellow anthropologist, Ruth Behar, challenges her field to recognize ethnography as an art that engages the imagination. Douglas Hofstadter wonders about the importance of analogy in thinking, and proposes that analogy *is* cognition. Anne Harrington also examines how scientists think about thinking; she questions the assumption that neuroscience alone can account for "moral choice, existential passion, and social contracts." David Bartholomae and Shirley Brice Heath both raise questions about how teachers evaluate learning. Bartholomae insists that we rethink our assumptions about how college students learn to write academic essays, and Heath points out how strange it is that teachers judge academic ability with formulaic essays when, by design, these essays curtail "creativity, the pursuit of alternative answers, and the power of collaborative thinking in academic life."

Bartholomae, David. "Inventing the University." *When a Writer Can't Write: Studies in Writer's Block and Other Composing-Process Problems.* Ed. Mike Rose. New York: Guilford, 1985. 134–65. Print.

Behar, Ruth. "Ethnography in a Time of Blurred Genres." *Anthropology and Humanism* 32.2 (2007). 145–55. Web.

Harrington, Anne. "How to House a Mind Inside a Brain: Lessons from History." *EMBO Reports* 8, no. S1 (2007). Web.

Heath, Shirley Brice. "Rethinking the Sense of the Past: The Essay as Legacy of the Epigram." *Theory and Practice in the Teaching of Writing: Rethinking the Discipline.* Ed. Lee Odell. Carbondale: Southern Illinois UP, 1993. 105–31. Print.

Hofstadter, Douglas R. "Analogy as the Core of Cognition." Stanford Presidential Lectures in the Humanities and Arts. Web.

Argument at Work: Sonia Sotomayor and Principled Openness

On August 8, 2009, Sonia Sotomayor, who was born and raised in a working-class Puerto Rican family in the Bronx, was sworn in as the first Latina member of the United States Supreme Court. Since then, Sotomayor has written a coming-of-age memoir, *My Beloved World* (simultaneously published in Spanish as *Mi mundo adorado*), in which she describes her early years living in public housing with an alcoholic father and a distant mother, her studies at Princeton University and Yale Law School, and the steps early in her career that put her on a path to the Supreme Court.

Sotomayor credits many mentors and friends for contributing to her success, but her memoir also makes it clear that her success is due to her intellectual habits of mind, which were evident before she graduated from Cardinal Spellman High

School. As a member of that school's forensics club, Sotomayor discovered that she loved vigorous argument. She enjoyed arguing not because she was always certain of her position but because she took pleasure in the sport of rhetorical sparring and in testing her ideas against challenges.

She recalls that her manner of using argument as a tool for learning—as opposed to sticking to her original position no matter what new information and ideas she encountered—didn't always inspire the affection or admiration of her competitors. At a forensics meet during her junior year of high school, she encountered an especially hostile opponent who accused her of never being willing to take a strong stand and of thinking too much about how her position depended on context. Sotomayor thought it was valuable to be open to persuasion, but her fellow debater found it a mark of weakness because Sotomayor's position on an issue was never predictable. She accused Sotomayor of being without principles.

Sotomayor writes in her memoir's epilogue that she grappled with that accusation for decades. She concedes that she would be at fault if she truly lacked principles and had no moral center. She counts among her core values "integrity, fairness, and the avoidance of cruelty." At the same time, she reasons, "if you held to principle so passionately, so inflexibly, indifferent to the particulars of circumstance—the full range of what human beings, with all their flaws and foibles, might endure or create—if you enthroned principle above even reason, weren't you then abdicating the responsibilities of a thinking person?" Her practice as a Supreme Court justice is built on this habitual questioning and curiosity, on an openness to individual difference and a willingness to learn. She concludes: "Concern for individuals, the imperative of treating them with dignity and respect for their ideas and needs, regardless of one's own views—these too are surely principles and as worthy as any of being deemed inviolable. To remain open to understandings—perhaps even to principles—as yet not determined is the least that learning requires, its barest threshold."

part 2

FieldWorking: Reading and Writing Research

CHAPTER

9

Reading Self, Reading Cultures: Understanding Texts

Your ability to "read" involves texts, but also artifacts, cultures, and yourself. In this chapter you will:

- react and respond to readings
- explore your positions as they relate to a topic
- describe and interpret cultural artifacts
- integrate source material
- learn to work with online communities

We all read differently. Literary theorist Louise Rosenblatt suggests that a reader's main instrument for making meaning is one's self. And meaning is an intertwining of our past reading experiences, current tastes, attitudes about genres and forms, and history of teachers, mentors, friends, and relatives. No one reads exactly as you do because no one has exactly the same experiences.

> The reader performs the poem or the novel, as the violinist performs the sonata. But the instrument on which the reader plays, and from which he evokes the work, is—himself.
>
> —Louise Rosenblatt

We also read differently because we have different needs as readers, and we read differently at different times in our lives. You may have a different reaction to a book like *Charlotte's Web*, for example, when you reread it as an adult. When Bonnie read *Little Women* to her daughter, she felt connected with the character of the mother "Marmee," although as a 10-year-old reading *Little Women*, she hadn't noticed the mother at all. We bring our current lives into the reading we do.

As a reader, you have formed tastes and predispositions from your many past experiences. What are your attitudes toward reading? Are you a reluctant reader? Do you like to whip through a book quickly, or do you luxuriate in how an author uses words? Do you read novels differently than textbooks? Poetry differently than magazines and newspapers?

Online magazines and Web sites differently than print versions? Do you like to mark your own comments in the margins of a book? Do you respond to your reading in a journal? Do you like to talk with friends in a book club about what you read?

Reading as Negotiation

Meaning itself is a process of negotiation among the reader, the text, and the writer. This negotiation takes place both on and off the page. *On the* page of your mystery novel you may find yourself rereading for clues to the murder as you are reaching the conclusion of the book. But negotiation *off the page* is a less visible process. When you read a poem or hear a song, for example, the words on the page may have little meaning without your off-the-page experience. Sometimes it is through talk with others that you discover new meanings. At other times, knowing about the writer's background helps you negotiate meaning. Your understanding may come entirely through an emotional response. If no other person reads exactly like you do, it follows that no text has the same meaning for another reader. Meaning is a subjective experience.

Reading Cultures as Text and Texts as Culture

Fieldworkers research cultures in the same way as readers approach novels. As you read the following excerpt from the opening of Gloria Naylor's *Mama Day*, we'd like you to "read yourself" into this text. This bestseller about the fictional sea island of Willow Springs invites you into an entire culture—one that you may approach by "stepping out" or one that you may already know by having "stepped in." You may know something about the novel's setting, the Georgia–South Carolina sea islands. You may have vacationed there with your family or worked at one of the hotels. You may have read about or seen a movie set there. In other words, how do you situate yourself as a reader?

You probably approach any text with expectations based on your membership in different subcultures, including your readership preferences, which represent subcultures in themselves. For example, all readers of a particular mystery science fiction writer belong to a subculture, whether they know one another or not. Gloria Naylor is an African American female novelist. What other writers does Naylor remind you of? Does she make you think of other African American women writers, such as Alice Walker or Toni Morrison? If you're male, how will you approach a novel about a black matriarch? Do you think your ethnicity and gender affect the way you read, or are they irrelevant?

We chose this excerpt from a novel because it depicts a fieldworker researching his culture. Reema's boy, though fictional, represents the novice fieldworker—a position you'll take when you enter your fieldsite. He puzzles over an unfamiliar term he hears, "18 & 23," and tries to make sense of it. Notice both what he does as he researches this culture—in which he once lived—and what he forgets to do. As you read, use your subjective experiences to negotiate meaning—your personal background and your history as a reader. Add your response to that of the text. Take notes, pose questions, and write about your process of reading.

Mama Day

GLORIA NAYLOR

Willow Springs. Everybody knows but nobody talks about the legend of Sapphira Wade. A true conjure woman: satin black, biscuit cream, red as Georgia clay: depending upon which of us takes a mind to her. She could walk through a lightning storm without being touched; grab a bolt of lightning in the palm of her hand; use the heat of lightning to start the kindling going under her medicine pot: depending upon which of us takes a mind to her. She turned the moon into salve, the stars into a swaddling cloth, and healed the wounds of every creature walking up on two or down on four. It ain't about right or wrong, truth or lies; it's about a slave woman who brought a whole new meaning to both them words, soon as you cross over here from beyond the bridge. And somehow, some way, it happened in 1823: she smothered Bascombe Wade in his very bed and lived to tell the story for a thousand days. 1823: married Bascombe Wade, bore him seven sons in just a thousand days, to put a dagger through his kidney and escape the hangman's noose, laughing in a burst of flames. 1823: persuaded Bascombe Wade in a thousand days to deed all his slaves every inch of land in Willow Springs, poisoned him for his trouble, to go on and bear seven sons—by person or persons unknown.

Mixing it all together and keeping everything that done shifted down through the holes of time, you end up with the death of Bascombe Wade (there's his tombstone right out of Chevy's Pass), the deeds to our land (all marked back to the very year), and seven sons (ain't Miss Abigail and Mama Day the granddaughters of that seventh boy?). The wild card in all this is the thousand days, and we guess if we put our heads together we'd come up with something—which ain't possible since Sapphira Wade don't live in the part of our memory we can use to form words.

But ain't a soul in Willow Springs don't know that little dark girls, hair all braided up with colored twine, got their "18 & 23's coming down" when they lean too long over them back yard fences, laughing at the antics of little dark boys who got the nerve to be "breathing 18 & 23" with mother's milk still on their tongues. And if she leans there just a mite too long or grins a bit too wide, it's gonna bring a holler straight through the dusty screen door. "Get your bow-legged self 'way from my fence, Johnny Blue. Won't be no 'early 18 & 23's' coming here for me to rock. I'm still raising her." Yes, the *name* Sapphira Wade is never breathed out of a single mouth in Willow Springs. But who don't know that old twisted-lip manager at the Sheraton Hotel beyond the bridge, offering Winky Browne only twelve dollars for his whole boatload of crawdaddies—"tried to 18 & 23 him," if he tried to do a thing? We all sitting here, a hop, skip, and one Christmas left before the year 2000, and ain't nobody told him niggers can read now? Like the menus in his restaurant don't say a handful of crawdaddies sprinkled over a little bowl of crushed ice is almost twelve dollars? Call it shrimp cocktail, or whatever he want—we can count, too. And the price of everything that swims, crawls, or lays at the bottom of The Sound went up in 1985, during the season we had that "18 & 23 summer" and the bridge blew down. Folks didn't take their lives in their hands out there in that treacherous water just to be doing it—ain't that much 18 & 23 in the world.

But that old hotel manager don't make no never mind. He's the least of what we done had to deal with here in Willow Springs. Malaria. Union soldiers. Sandy soil. Two big depressions. Hurricanes. Not to mention these new real estate developers who think we gonna sell our shore land just because we ain't fool enough to live there. Started coming over here in the early '90s, talking "vacation paradise," talking "pic-ture-ess." Like Winky said, we'd have to pick their ass out the bottom of the marsh first hurricane blow through here again. See, they just thinking about building where they ain't got no state taxes—never been and never will be, 'cause Willow Springs ain't in no state. Georgia and South Carolina done tried, though—been trying since right after the Civil War to prove that Willow Springs belong to one or the other of them. Look on any of them old maps they hurried and drew up soon as the Union soldiers pulled out and you can see that the only thing connects us to the mainland is a bridge—and even that gotta be rebuilt after every big storm. (They was talking about steel and concrete way back, but since Georgia and South Carolina couldn't claim the taxes, nobody wanted to shell out for the work. So we rebuild it ourselves when need be, and build it how we need it—strong enough to last till the next big wind. Only need a steel and concrete bridge once every seventy years or so. Wood and pitch is a tenth of the cost and serves us a good sixty-nine years—matter of simple arithmetic.) But anyways, all forty-nine square miles curves like a bow, stretching toward Georgia on the south end and South Carolina on the north, and right smack in the middle where each foot of our bridge sits is the dividing line between them two states.

So who it belong to? It belongs to us—clean and simple. And it belonged to our daddies, and our daddies before them, and them too—what at one time all belonged to Bascombe Wade. And when they tried to trace him and how he got it, found out he wasn't even American. Was Norway-born or something, and the land had been sitting in his family over there in Europe since it got explored and claimed by the Vikings—imagine that. So thanks to the conjuring of Sapphira Wade we got it from Norway or theres about, and if taxes owed, it's owed to them. But ain't no Vikings or anybody else from over in Europe come to us with the foolishness that them folks out of Columbia and Atlanta come with—we was being un-American. And the way we saw it, America ain't entered the question at all when it come to our land: Sapphira was African-born, Bascombe Wade was from Norway, and it was the 18 & 23'ing that went down between them two put deeds in our hands. And we wasn't even Americans when we got it—was slaves. And the laws about slaves not owning nothing in Georgia and South Carolina don't apply, 'cause the land wasn't then—and isn't now—in either of them places. When there was lots of cotton here, and we baled it up and sold it beyond the bridge, we paid our taxes to the U.S. of A. And we keeps account of all the fishing that's done and sold beyond the bridge, all the little truck farming. And later when we had to go over there to work or our children went, we paid taxes out of them earnings. We pays taxes on the telephone lines and electrical wires run over The Sound. Ain't nobody here about breaking the law. But Georgia and South Carolina ain't seeing the shine off a penny for our land, our homes, our roads, or our bridge. Well, they fought each other up to the Supreme Court about the whole matter, and it came to a draw. We guess they got so tired out from that, they decided to leave us be—until them developers started swarming over here like sand flies at a Sunday picnic.

Sure, we coulda used the money and weren't using the land. But like Mama Day told 'em (we knew to send 'em straight over there to her and Miss Abigail), they didn't come huffing and sweating all this way in them dark gaberdine suits if they didn't think our land could make them a bundle of money, and the way we saw it, there was enough land—shoreline, that is—to make us all pretty comfortable. And calculating on the basis of all them fancy plans they had in mind, a million an acre wasn't asking too much. Flap, flap, flap—Lord, didn't them jaws and silk ties move in the wind. The land wouldn't be worth that if they couldn't *build* on it. Yes, suh, she told 'em, and they couldn't build on it unless we *sold* it. So we get ours now, and they get theirs later. You shoulda seen them coattails flapping back across The Sound with all their lies about "community uplift" and "better jobs." 'Cause it weren't about no them now and us later—was them now and us never. Hadn't we seen it happen back in the '80s on St. Helena, Daufuskie, and St. John's? And before that in the '60s on Hilton Head? Got them folks' land, built fences around it first thing, and then brought in all the builders and high-paid managers from mainside—ain't nobody on them islands benefited. And the only dark faces you see now in them "vacation paradises" is the ones cleaning the toilets and cutting the grass. On their own land, mind you, their own land. Weren't gonna happen in Willow Springs. 'Cause if Mama Day say no, everybody say no. There's 18 & 23, and there's 18 & 23—and nobody was gonna trifle with Mama Day's, 'cause she know how to use it—her being a direct descendant of Sapphira Wade, piled on the fact of springing from the seventh son of a seventh son—uh, uh. Mama Day say no, everybody say no. No point in making a pile of money to be guaranteed the new moon will see you scratching at fleas you don't have, or rolling in the marsh like a mud turtle. And if some was waiting for her to die, they had a long wait. She says she ain't gonna. And when you think about it, to show up in one century, make it all the way through the next, and have a toe inching into the one approaching is about as close to eternity anybody can come.

Well, them developers upped the price and changed the plans, changed the plans and upped the price, till it got to be a game with us. Winky bought a motorboat with what they offered him back in 1987, turned it in for a cabin cruiser two years later, and says he expects to be able to afford a yacht with the news that's waiting in the mail this year. Parris went from a new shingle roof to a split-level ranch and is making his way toward adding a swimming pool and greenhouse. But when all the laughing's done, it's the principle that remains. And we done learned that anything coming from beyond the bridge gotta be viewed real, real careful. Look what happened when Reema's boy—the one with the pear-shaped head—came hauling himself back from one of those fancy colleges mainside, dragging his notebooks and tape recorder and a funny way of curling up his lip and clicking his teeth, all excited and determined to put Willow Springs on the map.

We was polite enough—Reema always was a little addle-brained—so you couldn't blame the boy for not remembering that part of Willow Springs's problems was that it got put on some maps right after the War Between the States. And then when he went around asking us about 18 & 23, there weren't nothing to do but take pity on him as he rattled on about "ethnography," "unique speech patterns," "cultural preservation," and whatever else he seemed to be getting so much pleasure out of while talking into his little gray machine. He was all over the place—What 18 & 23 mean? What 18 & 23 mean? And we all told him the God-honest truth: it was just our way of saying something. Winky was awful, though, he even spit tobacco juice for him. Sat on his porch all day, chewing up the boy's Red Devil premium and spitting so the machine could pick it up. There was enough fun in that to take us through the fall and winter when he had hauled himself back over The Sound to wherever he was getting what was supposed to be passing for an education. And he sent everybody he'd talked to copies of the book he wrote, bound all nice with our name and his signed on the first page. We couldn't hold Reema down, she was so proud. It's a good thing she didn't read it. None of us made it much through the introduction, but that said it all: you see, he had come to the conclusion after "extensive field work" (ain't never picked a boll of cotton or head of lettuce in his life—Reema spoiled him silly), but he done still made it to the conclusion that 18 & 23 wasn't 18 & 23 at all—was really 81 & 32, which just so happened to be the lines of longitude and latitude marking off where Willow Springs sits on the map. And we were just so damned dumb that we turned the whole thing around.

Not that he called it being dumb, mind you, called it "asserting our cultural identity," "inverting hostile social and political parameters." 'Cause, see, being we was brought here as slaves, we had no choice but to look at everything upside-down. And then being that we was isolated off here on this island, everybody else in the country went on learning good English and calling things what they really was—in the dictionary and all that—while we kept on calling things ass-backwards. And he thought that was just so wonderful and marvelous, etcetera, etcetera.... Well, after that crate of books came here, if anybody had any doubts about what them developers was up to, if there was just a tinge of seriousness behind them jokes about the motorboats and swimming pools that could be gotten from selling a piece of land, them books squashed it. The people who ran the type of schools that could turn our children into raving lunatics—and then put his picture on the back of the book so we couldn't even deny it was him—didn't mean us a speck of good.

If the boy wanted to know what 18 & 23 meant, why didn't he just ask? When he was running around sticking that machine in everybody's face, we was sitting right here—every one of us—and him being one of Reema's, we woulda obliged him. He coulda asked Cloris about the curve in her spine that came from the planting season when their mule broke its leg, and she took up the reins and kept pulling the plow with her own back. Winky woulda told him about the hot tar that took out the corner of his right eye the summer we had only seven days to rebuild the bridge so the few crops we had left after the storm could be gotten over before rot sat in. Anybody woulda carried him through the fields we had to stop farming back in the '80s to take outside jobs—washing cars, carrying groceries, cleaning house—anything—'cause it was leave the land or lose it during the Silent Depression. Had more folks sleeping in city streets and banks foreclosing on farms than in the Great Depression before that.

Naw, he didn't really want to know what 18 & 23 meant, or he woulda asked. He woulda asked right off where Miss Abigail Day was staying, so we coulda sent him down the main road to that little yellow house where she used to live. And she woulda given him a tall glass of ice water or some cinnamon tea as he heard about Peace dying young, then Hope and Peace again. But there was the child of Grace—the grandchild, a girl who went mainside, like him, and did real well. Was living outside of Charleston now with her husband and two boys. So she visits a lot more often than she did when she was up in New York. And she probably woulda pulled out that old photo album, so he coulda seen some pictures of her grandchild, Cocoa, and then Cocoa's mama, Grace. And Miss Abigail flips right through to the beautiful one of Grace resting in her satin-lined coffin. And as she walks him back out to the front porch and points him across the road to a silver trailer where her sister, Miranda, lives, she tells him to grab up and chew a few sprigs of mint growing at the foot of the steps—it'll help kill his thirst in the hot sun. And if he'd known enough to do just that, thirsty or not, he'd know when he got to that silver trailer to stand back a distance calling *Mama, Mama Day*, to wait for her to come out and beckon him near.

He'da told her he been sent by Miss Abigail and so, more likely than not, she lets him in. And he hears again about the child of Grace, her grandniece, who went mainside, like him, and did real well. Was living outside of Charleston now with her husband and two boys. So he visits a lot more often than she did when she was up in New York. Cocoa is like her very own, Mama Day tells him, since she never had no children.

And with him carrying that whiff of mint on his breath, she surely woulda walked him out to the side yard, facing that patch of dogwood, to say she has to end the visit a little short 'cause she has some gardening to do in the other place. And if he'd had the sense to offer to follow her just a bit of the way—then and only then—he hears about that summer fourteen years ago when Cocoa came visiting from New York with her first husband. Yes, she tells him, there was a first husband—a stone city boy. How his name was George. But how Cocoa left, and he stayed. How it was the year of the last big storm that blew her pecan trees down and even caved in the roof of the other place. And she woulda stopped him from walking just by a patch of oak: she reaches up, takes a bit of moss for him to put in them closed leather shoes—they're probably sweating his feet something terrible, she tells him. And he's to sit on the ground, right there, to untie his shoes and stick in the moss. And then he'd see through the low bush that old graveyard just down the slope. And when he looks back up, she woulda disappeared through the trees; but he's to keep pushing the moss in them shoes and go on down to that graveyard where he'll find buried Grace, Hope, Peace, and Peace again. Then a little ways off a grouping of seven old graves, and a little ways off seven older again. All circled by them live oaks and hanging moss, over a rise from the tip of The Sound.

Everything he needed to know coulda been heard from that yellow house to that silver trailer to that graveyard. Be too late for him to go that route now, since Miss Abigail's been dead for over nine years. Still, there's an easier way. He could just watch Cocoa any one of these times she comes in from Charleston. She goes straight to Miss Abigail's to air out the rooms and unpack her bags, then she's across the road to call out at Mama Day, who's gonna come to the door of the trailer and wave as Cocoa heads on through the patch of dogwoods to that oak grove. She stops and puts a bit of moss in her open-toe sandals, then goes on past those graves to a spot just down the rise toward The Sound, a little bit south of that circle of oaks. And if he was patient and stayed off a little ways, he'd realize she was there to meet up with her first husband so they could talk about that summer fourteen years ago when she left, but he stayed. And as her and George are there together for a good two hours or so—neither one saying a word—Reema's boy coulda heard from them everything there was to tell about 18 & 23.

But on second thought, someone who didn't know how to ask wouldn't know how to listen. And he coulda listened to them the way you been listening to us right now. Think about it: ain't nobody really talking to you. We're sitting here in Willow Springs, and you're God-knows-where. It's August 1999—ain't but a slim chance it's the same season where you are. Uh, huh, listen. Really listen this time: the only voice is your own. But you done just heard about the legend of Sapphira Wade, though nobody here breathes her name. You done heard it the way we know it, sitting on our porches and shelling June peas, quieting the midnight cough of a baby, taking apart the engine of a car—you done heard it without a single living soul really saying a word. Pity, though, Reema's boy couldn't listen, like you, to Cocoa and George down by them oaks—or he woulda left here with quite a story.

BOX 1

RESPONDING TO TEXT

Purpose

We hope you found yourself reading the excerpt from *Mama Day* more than once. We did. When each of us first read it, we realized we needed to read it again. Bonnie's interest in the character of the bumbling young researcher, Reema's boy, focused her reading so that she excluded other characters. Elizabeth found herself looking at Naylor's map, imagining how close it might be to where she lives in North Carolina. As Elizabeth read the code word "18 & 23," she found herself trying to substitute other words each time she encountered it. But as we reread the text together for the purpose of writing this book, we talked about it and found ourselves discovering much more. We began to read the text in two ways: one as a parody of fieldworking and the other as a rich fictional account of a cultural group with its own codes, behaviors, stories, and rituals.

Action

Describe your own process of reading and rereading *Mama Day* in a page or two. If you're keeping a journal or a process log, you might want to use these questions to guide your response:

- What assumptions did you bring to this text? About this region's geography? This group of sea islanders? Rural families and their belief systems and values?
- What other books have you read or movies have you seen that this excerpt reminds you of? In what ways?
- How do your previous reading experiences affect the way you appreciate Naylor's writing? How would you describe Naylor's style?
- What was hard for you to understand in this text? Which words, phrases, or paragraphs made you stop and reread? How did you solve this problem?
- What stood out for you? Where in the text did you find yourself entertained? Immersed? Confused?
- What information was helpful as you read the first time? In your second reading, what did you discover that you missed the first time?
- Which of the characters interested you most, and why? Cocoa? Mama Day? Reema's boy? Sapphira Wade? The narrator?
- What details of the setting involved your imagination? When you share your response with your colleagues, notice how they might have read differently.

The kinds of questions that we list in **Box 1** can be asked of any text you read. Reading any complex text can also involve reading a culture. In the excerpt from *Mama Day*, we see culture's ordinary life in dailiness that fieldworkers always try to penetrate—catching crawdaddies, chewing tobacco, truck farming. But we also see this culture's uniqueness through Naylor's specific characters and setting.

With the character of Reema's pear-headed nameless boy, Naylor offers us a parody of a field researcher. He is an insider, born on the island, but his college education had so shaped him that he was unable, even as an insider, to do what fieldworkers need to do: listen, observe, and participate in the life of the people he studied. Even the residents of Willow Springs knew more about how to do his field-work than he did: "If the boy wanted to know what 18 & 23 meant, why didn't he just ask?" The narrator concludes that a researcher who doesn't know how to form questions would never be in a position to understand answers.

You'll need to think about how your background can affect what you see in another culture just as it does when you read a written text. What you see is affected by who you are. Your education, geography, family history, personal experiences, race, gender, or nationality can influence the way you do research. Learning to read a culture like a text is similar to learning to read a text like a culture.

Positioning: Reading and Writing about Yourself

As we conduct our fieldwork, we must be conscious of ourselves as the key instruments of the research process. When you begin to research a site, you will need to "read" yourself in the same way that you have deciphered texts, and you will want to write that perspective into your study. Had Reema's boy thought or written about his insider status, education and field training, family history, and geography, he might have asked different questions and gotten different answers. Instead of leaving out personal, subjective information, fieldworkers should write it in.

In fieldwork, **positioning** includes all the subjective responses that affect how the researcher sees data. Readers of ethnography sometimes wonder how this kind of research could be considered social "science" if the researcher is not offering "objective" data. In fact, fieldworkers achieve a type of objectivity through **intersubjectivity**, the method of connecting as many different perspectives on the same data as possible. These multiple sources encourage the fieldworker to interpret patterns and interrelationships among various accounts alongside the researcher's own account and to leave other interpretations open as well.

Being the researcher so influences your fieldwork that it would be deceptive *not* to include relevant background information about yourself in your study. From our own experiences as fieldworkers, we believe that as a researcher you position or situate yourself in relationship to your study in at least three ways: fixed, subjective, and textual.

Fixed Positions

Fixed positions are the personal facts that might influence how you see your data—your age, gender, class, nationality, race—factors that do not change during the course of the study but are often taken for granted and unexamined in the research process. Does it matter that you are middle-aged and studying adolescents? Or that you grew up on a kibbutz in Israel? Does being a middle-class African American affect the way you interpret the lives of homeless African Americans?

Our word *fixed* is problematic; nothing is truly "fixed." Sometimes fixed factors are subjected to change during the research process, and then that, too, demands the researcher's attention. If, for example, a male researcher looking at the play behaviors of preschool children becomes the father of a girl during his study, he may find himself looking at his fieldsite data through a different lens. If what originally seemed a fixed influence in the researcher's position becomes more fluid, then that process of changed perspectives would become part of the researcher's data.

Subjective Positions

Subjective positions such as life history and personal experiences may also affect your research. Someone who grew up in a large extended or blended family will see the eating, sleeping, and conversation patterns of groups differently than someone from a small nuclear family. Many people who grew up in large families confess that they learned to eat quickly at family meals because they wanted to get their fair share before the food disappeared.

Textual Positions

Textual positions—the language choices you make to represent what you see—affect the writing of both fieldnotes and the final ethnographic report. The way that you position yourself in the field with respect to the people you study—how close or how far away you focus your research lens—determines the kind of data you'll gather, the voice you'll create in your finished text, and to some extent your credibility as a researcher.

BOX 2

POSITIONING YOURSELF

Purpose

This activity will help you uncover the assumptions, preconceptions, personal experiences, and feelings that influence you as a fieldworker by writing about them throughout your research process. In this way, you will become conscious of your positioning as a researcher.

Action

Writing short commentaries regularly will help you understand how fixed, subjective, and textual positions affect your continuing research process. You can do the following exercise while considering a site or subculture you might want to research, or at any stage of the research process.

Ask yourself: What are your reasons for choosing this particular subculture? Which of your own "fixed positions" may affect what you see? What "subjective positions" do you carry into your site? Then, write a short commentary describing how your positions might affect what you'll see at your fieldsite.

Understanding Positioning: Checking In on Yourself

Throughout the process of conducting your fieldstudy, you'll need to continue to ask how who you are affects how you understand yourself and your fieldwork. Three questions can help you monitor your assumptions, stances, and blind spots:

- What surprised me?
- What intrigued me?
- What disturbed me?

These questions help provide ways of "checking in" on yourself as well as ways of interrogating the different features of your positions as you bring them to your study. This kind of monitoring will eventually help you see how your fixed and subjective positions contribute to the textual voice you'll develop as you write about your topic. Even more important, checking in will heighten your awareness of the extent to which the instrument of your data gathering is not statistical information or a computer program or an experiment but *you*—with all of your assumptions, preconceptions, past experiences, and complex feelings.

A humorous essay by Laura Bohannan about her fieldwork experience in West Africa, "Shakespeare in the Bush," illustrates the importance of checking in on yourself—on your assumptions, expectations, and feelings—throughout your research experiences. In "Shakespeare in the Bush," Bohannan, an anthropologist, exposes how she tried to import the "universal" message of *Hamlet* to the Tiv tribe she was studying in Africa.

At one point in the essay, Bohannan decides to skip summarizing the famous "To be or not to be" speech because she feels her listeners would misinterpret it. They have already approved of Claudius quickly marrying Hamlet's mother soon after her husband's murder—something Western audiences usually condemn. Bohannan then proceeds to try to explain Hamlet's father's "ghost" to her audience. She finds herself interrupted at every turn in the telling of what she had previously thought to be a "universal" and "transcultural" story:

> I decided to skip the soliloquy. Even if Claudius was here thought quite right to marry his brother's widow, there remained the poison motif, and I knew they would disapprove of fratricide. More hopefully I resumed, "That night Hamlet kept watch with the three who had seen his dead father. The dead chief again appeared, and although the others were afraid, Hamlet followed his dead father off to one side. When they were alone, Hamlet's dead father spoke."
>
> "Omens can't talk!" The old man was emphatic.
>
> "Hamlet's dead father wasn't an omen. Seeing him might have been an omen, but he was not." My audience looked as confused as I sounded. "It *was* Hamlet's dead father. It was a thing we call a 'ghost.'" I had to use the English word, for unlike many of the neighboring tribes, these people didn't believe in the survival after death of any individuating part of the personality.
>
> "What is a 'ghost'? An omen?"
>
> "No, a 'ghost' is someone who is dead but who walks around and can talk, and people can hear him and see him but not touch him."
>
> They objected. "One can touch zombis."
>
> "No, no! It was not a dead body the witches had animated to sacrifice and eat. No one else made Hamlet's dead father walk. He did it himself."
>
> "Dead men can't walk," protested my audience as one man.
>
> I was quite willing to compromise. "A 'ghost' is a dead man's shadow."
>
> But again they objected. "Dead men cast no shadows."
>
> "They do in my country," I snapped.

To appreciate the full scope of Bohannan's mistaken assumptions, read her complete essay online. As you read, you'll want to notice the ways the author monitors herself as she relates the story of Hamlet to the audience of informants she is trying to win over through her storytelling.

Bohannan's essay also raises the many ethical issues she faced in the field. Should she drink beer in the morning with her informants? Should she try to change parts of *Hamlet* to make the story more culturally relevant to her audience? Should she defend the way her own culture thinks of family relationships when clearly her audience thinks differently? Although Bohannan constructs herself textually as a bewildered fieldworker in "Shakespeare in the Bush," she also makes it clear that the ethical issues she faced are serious ones, worthy of lengthier consideration than she was able to give them in this essay.

The mental checking Bohannan does in this reading is what we are suggesting you do as well, seeing yourself as outsiders like the Tiv might see you. Try to think, as Bohannan did, about your own cultural assumptions as you encounter others in the fieldstudy.

Getting Permission

When you enter a fieldsite and make yourself known, you must follow many courtesies to make yourself and the people you're observing feel comfortable. All places in which you are a participant-observer involve an official process for "negotiating entry." As a beginning researcher, don't enter a site where you feel at risk in the subculture. For the kinds of projects this book suggests, you will not have adequate time to gain entry or insider status in an intimidating group. One of our students, for example, wanted to research a group of campus skinheads. They permitted Jake to hang out on the edges of their subculture, even allowing him to read their "code of honor," which included these statements:

- Be discreet about new recruits; check them out thoroughly.
- For prospects, we must have at least a 90-day contact period in which we can attest to your character. A probationary period and productivity report will be given.
- Outsiders need no knowledge of what goes on or is said in our meetings.
- No racial exceptions whatsoever! All members must be 100 percent white!

Early on, Jake began to realize that his research position was unworkable, that he was stuck. While the skinheads had let him into their subculture as a potential recruit, he could never fully enter their subculture or worldview. Their code of honor, which excluded minority groups, stood against his personal ethics. In an early portfolio reflection, Jake wrote, "I never hung out with them in public. I never went to an organizational meeting. I realized I was an outsider to this subculture."

Jake's negotiation experience was so dramatic that he was unable to gain full access, and so he was unable to collect the data he wanted. No matter how interested in and enthusiastic we are about a possible fieldsite, we must be conscious of our own comfort levels and even potential dangers in investigating certain groups or places.

Harvey DuMarce, another of our students, experienced difficulty negotiating entry into a fieldsite owing mainly to his own assumption that it would be easy for him to do so. He is a Native American, a Sioux, who wanted to research a gambling casino on another tribe's reservation. Because of his heritage, he assumed that he would be welcomed. But he wasn't. He had enormous difficulty finding people who were willing to talk to him, and he never really knew whether it was because of his Sioux background or because he was perceived as a student. Eventually, he had a conversation with the woman who ran the gift shop at the casino, and she introduced him to others. As his informant, she helped him gain an insider status in a place where he had assumed he already had it.

Any fieldsite you enter requires that you be conscious of your own personal assumptions and how they reflect your ethics, but you must also be respectful of the people whose lives you are watching. It is common courtesy for researchers to acknowledge time spent with informants with gestures as small as writing thank-you notes or as large as exchanging time (tutoring or babysitting, for example) or obtaining grant-funded stipends to pay them. As you work your way through the process of getting permission or "negotiating entry," be sure to follow the guidelines in the box below.

GUIDELINES FOR NEGOTIATING ENTRY

- Explain your project clearly to the people you will study, and obtain the requisite permission from those in charge.
- Let your informants understand what part of the study you'll share with them.
- Think about what you can give back to the fieldsite in exchange for your time there.

Some sites may require official documentation, as in the case of two of our students who collaborated on a study of a day-care center. The center required them to have an interview, submit a proposal describing their project, and sign a document attesting that they had reviewed all of the center's rules and procedures. Entry might be simple, laborious, or even impossible. For this reason, don't wait too long to make yourself visible to the insiders you study. One student we worked with spent over a month in the field observing a Disney store. When she attempted to get official permission to write about this store, however, she was denied entry and could not continue her project.

Once you finalize your site, you might want to check with your instructor to find out your university's policy with respect to research on human subjects.

For long-term projects, the university's **human subjects review board** usually requires that you file a proposal and submit permission forms from your informants. They are called "**informed consent** forms," and below we present a sample of one of our own forms as a model. Universities usually have less formal procedures for the kind of short-term fieldwork that you might do for a one-semester course, and often have no requirements for filing permissions. Fieldworkers, no matter what size their projects, are ethically responsible for accurately showing the voices of their informants on the page. We feel strongly that you should receive permission from all the informants whose work you audio or video record as well as from any official person at your fieldsite.

Mary Smith
Dormitory Hall
State University
City, State
Telephone number

I give my permission to Mary Smith to use my written and spoken words in her research project written for "Composition/English 102" at State University. I understand that I may read and approve the final draft of the material she uses about me in her project.

Signature: ______________________ Date: ______________

Address: ____

____

Telephone number: _____________________________________

I prefer to use this pseudonym: _________________________

FIGURE 9.1 Informed consent form

The Ethics of Fieldwork: A Brief History

Whether you're conducting a long-term project with formal permission or a classroom-based study with a short informed consent from each informant, it's important to understand a bit of the history of human subjects review for research. In 1974, the National Research Act established the National Commission for the Protection of Human Subjects of Biomedical and Behavioral Research. Members of the Commission came from diverse disciplines, including medicine, law, religion, and bioethics, and their job was to identify the basic ethical principles that should underlie research with human subjects. Prior to this time, there had been far too many cases of research that harmed its subjects. In 1979, five years after their first meeting, the Commission published what's commonly called "the Belmont Report," which identifies three basic principles relevant to the ethics of research involving human subjects:

1. **Respect for Persons** Informants should participate in research studies voluntarily and have enough information to make a decision about their participation. If you expect to interview a nurse, for example, and follow her throughout her clinical day or even meet her at home, you would need to inform her of your plan and see if she is willing and available to give you that much of her time.

2. **Beneficence** Researchers should protect informants against risk from harm and also from the loss of any substantial benefit that might be gained from research. Let's say, for instance, you're working with a punk rock band that has fallen on hard times. You write an exciting essay about their ups and downs. You sell it to a magazine. In this instance, you are profiting from their story. As an ethical researcher, you should either share the profits or not sell the story.

3. **Justice** We need to select our informants fairly, without creating undue pressure, especially for people who already experience burdens. In this country, for example, in the 1940s, the Tuskegee syphilis study used disadvantaged, rural black men to study the untreated course of a disease that is by no means confined to that population.

These three principles from the Belmont Report cover the ethics of research in the United States in all disciplines across research communities. Whether you're working in a lab on stem-cell research, studying the behavior of penguins, working in a soup kitchen, or writing about a punk rock band, the basic ethics are the same—respect for persons, beneficence, and justice.

BOX 3

FROM ETHOS TO ETHICS

Julie Cheville, Illinois State University, Normal, Illinois

Purpose

"Ethos" in speakers' or writers' texts implies their ethics, and it emerges in writing or speech as their credibility: When my students and I read *Mama Day*, many of us sympathize with Reema's boy. The tactical errors of a college student turned fieldworker hit close to home. And they raise imposing questions. How do we enter a cultural space and earn the trust of insiders? And how, as outsiders just stepping in, do we recognize the essence of identities and relationships?

I like to read this selection from *Mama Day* to students so we can concentrate less on processing language than on listening to the rich images of character and culture. I ask groups of students to notice particular "informants" so that when we finish the story, we can interpret the lives Naylor writes about without obsessing first on the question of "18 & 23." Rather than attend to the single and most obvious question, as Reema's boy does, we focus on informants' habits of mind, language, and body—all features of cultural life that answer the question implicitly.

While notetaking and recording are essential field techniques, they can become liabilities and get a fieldworker into trouble. For Reema's boy, these tools are a means to his particular end—the "truth" about "18 & 23." But in the same way that Sapphira Wade "ain't about truth or lies," the culture that memorializes her resists a single interpretation. When Reema's boy contrives his own interpretation, the residents resist him. For the descendants of Sapphira Wade, "18 & 23" represents the totality of the unsaid.

From the experiences of Reema's boy, we understand that entering the field is not about exerting oneself on others but about emerging into delicate relationships with those who guide us where they choose. In this way, our credibility, or "ethos," arises from our receptiveness to what and to whom we're introduced.

So how do fieldworkers position themselves without overriding informants' identities, relationships, and histories? This is where this excerpt from *Mama Day* invites a discussion of ethics. As you'll learn in this book, fieldworkers by profession rely on written ethical principles to monitor their interactions. These principles ensure that research involving human subjects protects the welfare of all involved. In this activity, you will research many of the professional codes that govern fieldworkers in a variety of disciplines.

Action

In small groups, analyze the online ethics statements of some of the professional organizations that monitor fieldwork. Here are a few of them:

American Anthropological Association

Association of Internet Researchers

American Folklore Society

American Psychological Association

American Sociological Association

Museum Ethnographers Group

The Society of Professional Journalists

Each group can study a single statement for principles that might have helped Reema's boy to make more sensitive choices. As a class, talk about the strengths of each association's code. From this discussion, you may either come to consensus about the code that seems most relevant to your work or create a code of your own. During fieldwork, as you encounter particular dilemmas, you will be able to use the guidelines to identify options and obligations.

Reading an Object: The Cultural Artifact

As you enter the field, you should train yourself to notice material objects—**artifacts**—that represent the culture of that site. Objects are readable texts. As you read an object, your position as researcher affects your reading just as it affects the way you read a fieldsite. You can investigate the surface details of an object, research its history, or learn about people's rules and rituals for using and making the object. Researchers—folklorists and anthropologists—use the term **material culture** to refer to those personal artifacts loaded with meaning and history that people mark as special: tools, musical instruments, foods, toys, jewelry, ceremonial objects, and clothes.

Photos: Bruce Drummond

FIGURE 9.2 South Carolina Low Country coil basket

As you look at the photographs of the basket in **Figure 9.2**, think about the kinds of questions you might want to ask the owner or the basketmaker. How is it made? How old is it? What is it used for?

On the surface, it is a woven basket with a lid. But the basket holds a coiled history, a collection of stories that belongs to its makers, its sellers, and its owners. The basket itself is an artifact produced by several interconnected cultures. It is made by African American women on the coast of South Carolina, near the city of Charleston, not far from Gloria Naylor's fictional Willow Springs. The basketmakers use natural materials (coastal sweetgrass, palmetto fronds, and pine needles) found on the southeastern coast of the United States, much like the plants their ancestors knew on the western coast of Africa. These baskets come out of a strong craft tradition of using available materials to make everyday objects. It is a tradition that daughters learn from mothers, who learned it from their mothers, who learned it from their mothers. The basketmaking technique represents a long chain of informal instruction over many generations of craftswomen. And each generation—in fact, each basketmaker herself—adds her own technique and her own circumstances to what she has learned. During their years of American slavery, for example, African American women modified kitchen implements, such as spoons, to create the tools they needed to continue making baskets according to their traditional designs.

But knowing the history of this craft and even holding the basket in your hand does not speak about the object the way the maker does. When Bonnie interviewed a basketmaker in the Charleston marketplace, a middle-aged woman named Wilma, she learned more than the observable and historical details we described here. Bonnie was already positioned by knowing the history of this craft from reading about the tradition and having heard her mentor, folklorist Burt Feintuch, lecture on exactly this topic. So when she visited Charleston, she was eager to find a basketmaker who would talk about her craft. Bonnie wanted to buy one of Wilma's baskets, one with a beautifully tight-fitting top. As they examined it together, Wilma explained the challenge of pulling the fresh sweetgrass, weaving in palmetto fronds, and keeping the pine needles fresh enough to bend. After the basket is finished, Wilma said, it is important to coil it all carefully and work it with an awl-like tool made from a spoon. Bonnie complimented her on the top.

"Oh, I didn't make this," Wilma answered as she stroked the top that fit so well. "My cousin is the only person in the family who can make a tight top. My tops just float around. She's good at making tops. I'm good at selling them." This conversation contained important firsthand information about the stories that lie inside cultural objects. The information from Wilma—about the awl-like tool made from a spoon, and the separate roles she and her cousin took—explained that the craft of basketmaking, like much folk art, is a collective endeavor that involves not only a long history of instruction but also a family of craftspeople who establish rules, determine roles, and invent new methods to carry on an old tradition. Bonnie's subjective positioning from her knowledge of folklore and her history as a basket collector affected the way she "read" Wilma's basket. And Wilma's story of her family's craft unpacked another layer of meaning and cultural knowledge.

BOX 4

READING AN ARTIFACT

Beth Campbell, Marshall University, South Charleston, West Virginia

Purpose

The everyday objects people use inside a culture are often so utilitarian and taken for granted that the members of the culture don't recognize them as being important or symbolic of their history. An outsider is more likely to notice them and wonder where the objects come from, what they're used for, who makes them, and why they're made the way they are. All of these facts become clues to the traditions, rituals, values, rules, and behavior of a cultural group.

Our colleague and friend, Beth Campbell, shares an exercise she developed for her class, using the "inscribed artifact" of the tattoo. Tattoos, while they're now almost mainstream in our culture, have a long history of cultural meanings. Beth writes:

> We often think of artifacts as connected with archaeology: potsherds, for example, or projectile points and stone tools. But things that are *inscribed* are artifacts too: cave paintings, hieroglyphics, and philosophical texts are all things made by human hands that carry significance. Some kinds of artifacts, in fact, have been with us for thousands of years. Like tattoos.
>
> Tattoos are a kind of written, or *graphic*, artifact. Some tattoos signify status; some signify affiliation with particular groups. Others call up memories; still others express the aesthetic preferences of the wearer. Some call up all of these meanings and more.
>
> For many years in the West, tattoos signified marginal lives. Sailors and soldiers had tattoos, as did prisoners, bikers, prostitutes, and equally "dangerous" others.
>
> But tattoos have clearly lost their outlaw edge; they have moved from the margins to the mainstream. Today, one in three people under thirty has at least one tattoo. Those numbers are even higher for those between the ages of eighteen and twenty-five. If you are reading this book as part of a typical, twenty-five student writing class, it's likely that at least ten of your classmates have tattoos.

Action

1. Break into small groups and pick one tattoo you'll all write about. It could belong to someone in your group, or you might also find images of tattoos on the Web.
2. Write a physical description of the tattoo. Focus on the material artifact itself and get as much detail into your description as you can. Describe the graphic or the figure itself, of course, but also describe the color, the placement, and the shading. Challenge yourself to write words that paint a picture.
3. Once you've finished, compare your description with others in your group. What did some of you catch that others missed? What did some of your group members describe really well? Pick a few of those passages and read them out loud. Talk about why they work as well as they do.
4. Now, focus on what you think these artifacts signify. Write about what you think this tattoo might mean to the person who has it. Where do you think the image comes from? What is it related to? What is she trying to do or say with this tattoo? Why do you think he got it? When you've finished that, write a little more about what this tattoo means to you. What does it bring to your mind? What would it mean if it was on your body?
5. Come back together as a group and compare the meanings you created with the meanings made by others. If you were all writing about the same tattoo, how similar were your attributions of meaning? How different? Compare some of the most interesting similarities and differences. How can people who look at the same thing in the same setting at the same time see and interpret things so differently?

The Uses of Cultural Artifacts

Your fieldsite and your informants will, of course, be the keepers of many important cultural artifacts that will offer you information and insight into their world. As a researcher, you'll want to sketch, photograph, record, or actually acquire as many artifacts as you can. As you gather them into your portfolio and begin to write about them, you'll find the ways they represent the group or place you're studying.

We love the following short story "Everyday Use," by Alice Walker, for its analysis of cultural artifacts. Even though it's fiction, it reveals the significance of objects—a quilt, butter churn, clothing, other household objects—that define a culture that one daughter has discarded and another has embraced. Dee, the daughter of the narrator, places value on her family's artifacts without recognizing their cultural meanings or functions. Here are some questions to think about while you read the story:

- What are the different values the characters place on the cultural artifacts in the story? The butter churn and its dasher? The table benches? The food? The quilts?
- How are different characters positioned to value the cultural artifacts? What subjective history affects their positioning? How do the fixed positions of age, race, and gender affect the way they see these artifacts?
- Where are the indications of the interaction between tradition and creativity? Dee's old and new names, for example? The quilts?
- How does the narrator position herself in relationship to each of her daughters? What scenes show this?
- In what kind of culture do Maggie and her mother live? What everyday details stand out for you as they would for a fieldworker? The mother's outdoor work? The role of the church in the community? The use of snuff?

Everyday Use

ALICE WALKER

for your grandmama

I will wait for her in the yard that Maggie and I made so clean and wavy yesterday afternoon. A yard like this is more comfortable than most people know. It is not just a yard. It is like an extended living room. When the hard clay is swept clean as a floor and the fine sand around the edges lined with tiny, irregular grooves, anyone can come and sit and look up into the elm tree and wait for the breezes that never come inside the house.

Maggie will be nervous until after her sister goes: she will stand hopelessly in corners, homely and ashamed of the burn scars down her arms and legs, eying her sister with a mixture of envy and awe. She thinks her sister has held life always in the palm of one hand, that "no" is a word the world never learned to say to her.

You've no doubt seen those TV shows where the child who has "made it" is confronted, as a surprise, by her own mother and father, tottering in weakly from backstage. (A pleasant surprise, of course: What would they do if parent and child came on the show only to curse out and insult each other?) On TV mother and child embrace and smile into each other's faces. Sometimes the mother and father weep, the child wraps them in her arms and leans across the table to tell how she would not have made it without their help. I have seen these programs.

Sometimes I dream a dream in which Dee and I are suddenly brought together on a TV program of this sort. Out of a dark and soft-seated limousine I am ushered into a bright room filled with many people. There I meet a smiling, gray, sporty man like Johnny Carson who shakes my hand and tells me what a fine girl I have. Then we are on the stage and Dee is embracing me with tears in her eyes. She pins on my dress a large orchid, even though she has told me once that she thinks orchids are tacky flowers.

In real life I am a large, big-boned woman with rough, man-working hands. In the winter I wear flannel nightgowns to bed and overalls during the day. I can kill and clean a hog as mercilessly as a man. My fat keeps me hot in zero weather. I can work outside all day, breaking ice to get water for washing; I can eat pork liver cooked over the open fire minutes after it comes steaming from the hog. One winter I knocked a bull calf straight in the brain between the eyes with a sledge hammer and had the meat hung up to chill before nightfall. But of course all this does not show on television. I am the way my daughter would want me to be: a hundred pounds lighter, my skin like an uncooked barley pancake. My hair glistens in the hot bright lights. Johnny Carson has much to do to keep up with my quick and witty tongue.

But that is a mistake. I know even before I wake up. Who ever knew a Johnson with a quick tongue? Who can even imagine me looking a strange white man in the eye? It seems to me I have talked to them always with one foot raised in flight, with my head turned in whichever way is farthest from them. Dee, though. She would always look anyone in the eye. Hesitation was no part of her nature.

"How do I look, Mama?" Maggie says, showing just enough of her thin body enveloped in pink skirt and red blouse for me to know she's there, almost hidden by the door.

"Come out into the yard," I say.

Have you ever seen a lame animal, perhaps a dog run over by some careless person rich enough to own a car, sidle up to someone who is ignorant enough to be kind to him? That is the way my Maggie walks. She has been like this, chin on chest, eyes on ground, feet in shuffle, ever since the fire that burned the other house to the ground.

Dee is lighter than Maggie, with nicer hair and a fuller figure. She's a woman now, though sometimes I forget. How long ago was it that the other house burned? Ten, twelve years? Sometimes I can still hear the flames and feel Maggie's arms sticking to me, her hair smoking and her dress falling off her in little black papery flakes. Her eyes seemed stretched open, blazed open by the flames reflected in them. And Dee. I see her standing off under the sweet gum tree she used to dig gum out of; a look of concentration on her face as she watched the last dingy gray board of the house fall in toward the red-hot brick chimney. Why don't you do a dance around the ashes? I'd wanted to ask her. She had hated the house that much.

I used to think she hated Maggie, too. But that was before we raised the money, the church and me, to send her to Augusta to school. She used to read to us without pity; forcing words, lies, other folks' habits, whole lives upon us two, sitting trapped and ignorant underneath her voice. She washed us in a river of make-believe, burned us with a lot of knowledge we didn't necessarily need to know. Pressed us to her with the serious way she read, to shove us away at just the moment, like dimwits, we seemed about to understand.

Dee wanted nice things. A yellow organdy dress to wear to her graduation from high school; black pumps to match a green suit she'd made from an old suit somebody gave me. She was determined to stare down any disaster in her efforts. Her eyelids would not flicker for minutes at a time. Often I fought off the temptation to shake her. At sixteen she had a style of her own: and knew what style was.

I never had an education myself. After second grade the school was closed down. Don't ask me why: in 1927 colored asked fewer questions than they do now. Sometimes Maggie reads to me. She stumbles along good-naturedly but can't see well. She knows she is not bright. Like good looks and money, quickness passed her by. She will marry John Thomas (who has mossy teeth in an earnest face) and then I'll be free to sit here and I guess just sing church songs to myself. Although I never was a good singer. Never could carry a tune. I was always better at a man's job. I used to love to milk till I was hooked in the side in '49. Cows are soothing and slow and don't bother you, unless you try to milk them the wrong way.

I have deliberately turned my back on the house. It is three rooms, just like the one that burned, except the roof is tin; they don't make shingle roofs any more. There are no real windows, just some holes cut in the sides, like portholes in a ship, but not round and not square, with rawhide holding the shutters up on the outside. This house is in a pasture, too, like the other one. No doubt when Dee sees it she will want to tear it down. She wrote me once that no matter where we "choose" to live, she will manage to come see us. But she will never bring her friends. Maggie and I thought about this and Maggie asked me, "Mama, when did Dee ever *have* any friends?"

She had a few. Furtive boys in pink shirts hanging about on washday after school. Nervous girls who never laughed. Impressed with her they worshiped the well-turned phrase, the cute shape, the scalding humor that erupted like bubbles in lye. She read to them.

When she was courting Jimmy T she didn't have much time to pay to us, but turned all her faultfinding power on him. He *flew* to marry a cheap city girl from a family of ignorant flashy people. She hardly had time to recompose herself.

When she comes I will meet—but there they are!

Maggie attempts to make a dash for the house, in her shuffling way, but I stay her with my hand. "Come back here," I say. And she stops and tries to dig a well in the sand with her toe.

It is hard to see them clearly through the strong sun. But even the first glimpse of leg out of the car tells me it is Dee. Her feet were always neat-looking, as if God himself had shaped them with a certain style. From the other side of the car comes a short, stocky man. Hair is all over his head a foot long and hanging from his chin like a kinky mule tail. I hear Maggie suck in her breath. "Uhnnnh," is what it sounds like. Like when you see the wriggling end of a snake just in front of your foot on the road. "Uhnnnh."

Dee next. A dress down to the ground, in this hot weather. A dress so loud it hurts my eyes. There are yellows and oranges enough to throw back the light of the sun. I feel my whole face warming from the heat waves it throws out. Earrings gold, too, and hanging down to her shoulders. Bracelets dangling and making noises when she moves her arm up to shake the folds of the dress out of her armpits. The dress is loose and flows, and as she walks closer, I like it. I hear Maggie go "Uhnnnh" again. It is her sister's hair. It stands straight up like the wool on a sheep. It is black as night and around the edges are two long pigtails that rope about like small lizards disappearing behind her ears.

"Wa-su-zo-Tean-o!" she says, coming on in that gliding way the dress makes her move. The short stocky fellow with the hair to his navel is all grinning and he follows up with "Asalamalakim, my mother and sister!" He moves to hug Maggie but she falls back, right up against the back of my chair. I feel her trembling there and when I look up I see the perspiration falling off her chin.

"Don't get up," says Dee. Since I am stout it takes something of a push. You can see me trying to move a second or two before I make it. She turns, showing white heels through her sandals, and goes back to the car. Out she peeks next with a Polaroid. She stoops down quickly and lines up picture after picture of me sitting there in front of the house with Maggie cowering behind me. She never takes a shot without making sure the house is included. When a cow comes nibbling around the edge of the yard she snaps it and me and Maggie and the house. Then she puts the Polaroid in the back seat of the car, and comes up and kisses me on the forehead.

Meanwhile Asalamalakim is going through motions with Maggie's hand. Maggie's hand is as limp as a fish, and probably as cold, despite the sweat, and she keeps trying to pull it back. It looks like Asalamalakim wants to shake hands but wants to do it fancy. Or maybe he don't know how people shake hands. Anyhow, he soon gives up on Maggie.

"Well," I say. "Dee."

"No, Mama," she says. "Not 'Dee,' Wangero Leewanika Kemanjo!"

"What happened to 'Dee'?" I wanted to know.

"She's dead," Wangero said. "I couldn't bear it any longer, being named after the people who oppress me."

"You know as well as me you was named after your aunt Dicie," I said. Dicie is my sister. She named Dee. We called her "Big Dee" after Dee was born.

"But who was *she* named after?" asked Wangero.

"I guess after Grandma Dee," I said.

"And who was she named after?" asked Wangero.

"Her mother," I said, and saw Wangero was getting tired. "That's about as far back as I can trace it," I said. Though, in fact, I probably could have carried it back beyond the Civil War through the branches.

"Well," said Asalamalakim, "there you are."

"Uhnnnh," I heard Maggie say.

"There I was not," I said, "before 'Dicie' cropped up in our family, so why should I try to trace it that far back?"

He just stood there grinning, looking down on me like somebody inspecting a Model A car. Every once in a while he and Wangero sent eye signals over my head.

"How do you pronounce this name?" I asked.

"You don't have to call me by it if you don't want to," said Wangero.

"Why shouldn't I?" I asked. "If that's what you want us to call you, we'll call you."

"I know it might sound awkward at first," said Wangero.

"I'll get used to it," I said. "Ream it out again."

Well, soon we got the name out of the way. Asalamalakim had a name twice as long and three times as hard. After I tripped over it two or three times he told me to just call him Hakim-a-barber. I wanted to ask him was he a barber, but I didn't really think he was, so I didn't ask.

"You must belong to those beef-cattle peoples down the road," I said. They said "Asalamalakim" when they met you, too, but they didn't shake hands. Always too busy: feeding the cattle, fixing the fences, putting up salt-lick shelters, throwing down hay. When the white folks poisoned some of the herd the men stayed up all night with rifles in their hands. I walked a mile and a half just to see the sight.

Hakim-a-barber said, "I accept some of their doctrines, but farming and raising cattle is not my style." (They didn't tell me, and I didn't ask, whether Wangero (Dee) had really gone and married him.)

We sat down to eat and right away he said he didn't eat collards and pork was unclean. Wangero, though, went on through the chitlins and corn bread, the greens and everything else. She talked a blue streak over the sweet potatoes. Everything delighted her. Even the fact that we still used the benches her daddy made for the table when we couldn't afford to buy chairs.

"Oh, Mama!" she cried. Then turned to Hakim-a-barber. "I never knew how lovely these benches are. You can feel the rump prints," she said, running her hands underneath her and along the bench. Then she gave a sigh and her hand closed over Grandma Dee's butter dish. "That's it!" she said. "I knew there was something I wanted to ask you if I could have." She jumped up from the table and went over in the corner where the churn stood, the milk in it clabber by now. She looked at the churn and looked at it.

"This churn top is what I need," she said. "Didn't Uncle Buddy whittle it out of a tree you all used to have?"

"Yes," I said.

"Uh huh," she said happily. "And I want the dasher, too."

"Uncle Buddy whittle that, too?" asked the barber.

Dee (Wangero) looked up at me.

"Aunt Dee's first husband whittled the dash," said Maggie so low you almost couldn't hear her. "His name was Henry, but they called him Stash."

"Maggie's brain is like an elephant's," Wangero said, laughing. "I can use the churn top as a centerpiece for the alcove table," she said, sliding a plate over the churn, "and I'll think of something artistic to do with the dasher."

When she finished wrapping the dasher the handle stuck out. I took it for a moment in my hands. You didn't even have to look close to see where hands pushing the dasher up and down to make butter had left a kind of sink in the wood. In fact, there were a lot of small sinks; you could see where thumbs and fingers had sunk into the wood. It was beautiful light yellow wood, from a tree that grew in the yard where Big Dee and Stash had lived.

After dinner Dee (Wangero) went to the trunk at the foot of my bed and started rifling through it. Maggie hung back in the kitchen over the dishpan. Out came Wangero with two quilts. They had been pieced by Grandma Dee and then Big Dee and we had hung them on the quilt frames on the front porch and quilted them. One was in the Lone Star pattern. The other was Walk Around the Mountain. In both of them were scraps of dresses Grandma Dee had worn fifty and more years ago. Bits and pieces of Grandpa Jarrell's paisley shirts. And one teeny faded blue piece, about the size of a penny matchbox, that was from Great Grandpa Ezra's uniform that he wore in the Civil War.

"Mama," Wangero said sweet as a bird. "Can I have these old quilts?"

I heard something fall in the kitchen, and a minute later the kitchen door slammed.

"Why don't you take one or two of the others?" I asked. "These old things was just done by me and Big Dee from some tops your grandma pieced before she died."

"No," said Wangero. "I don't want those. They are stitched around the borders by machine."

"That'll make them last better," I said.

"That's not the point," said Wangero. "These are all pieces of dresses Grandma used to wear. She did all this stitching by hand. Imagine!" She held the quilts securely in her arms, stroking them.

"Some of the pieces, like those lavender ones, come from old clothes her mother handed down to her," I said, moving up to touch the quilts. Dee (Wangero) moved back just enough so that I couldn't reach the quilts. They already belonged to her.

"Imagine!" she breathed again, clutching them closely to her bosom.

"The truth is," I said, "I promised to give them quilts to Maggie, for when she marries John Thomas."

She gasped like a bee had stung her.

"Maggie can't appreciate these quilts!" she said. "She'd probably be backward enough to put them to everyday use."

"I reckon she would," I said. "God knows I been saving 'em for long enough with nobody using 'em. I hope she will!" I didn't want to bring up how I had offered Dee (Wangero) a quilt when she went away to college. Then she had told me they were old-fashioned, out of style.

"But they're *priceless*!" she was saying now, furiously; for she has a temper. "Maggie would put them on the bed and in five years they'd be in rags. Less than that!"

"She can always make some more," I said. "Maggie knows how to quilt."

Dee (Wangero) looked at me with hatred. "You just will not understand. The point is these quilts, *these* quilts!"

"Well," I said, stumped. "What would you do with them?"

"Hang them," she said. As if that was the only thing you *could* do with quilts.

Maggie by now was standing in the door. I could almost hear the sound her feet made as they scraped over each other.

"She can have them, Mama," she said, like somebody used to never winning anything, or having anything reserved for her. "I can 'member Grandma Dee without the quilts."

I looked at her hard. She had filled her bottom lip with checkerberry snuff and it gave her face a kind of dopey, hangdog look. It was Grandma Dee and Big Dee who taught her how to quilt herself. She stood there with her scarred hands hidden in the folds of her skirt. She looked at her sister with something like fear but she wasn't mad at her. This was Maggie's portion. This was the way she knew God to work.

When I looked at her like that something hit me in the top of my head and ran down to the soles of my feet. Just like when I'm in church and the spirit of God touches me and I get happy and shout. I did something I never had done before: hugged Maggie to me, then dragged her on into the room, snatched the quilts out of Miss Wangero's hands and dumped them into Maggie's lap. Maggie just sat there on my bed with her mouth open.

"Take one or two of the others," I said to Dee.

But she turned without a word and went out to Hakim-a-barber.

"You just don't understand," she said, as Maggie and I came out to the car.

"What don't I understand?" I wanted to know.

"Your heritage," she said. And then she turned to Maggie, kissed her, and said, "You ought to try to make something of yourself, too, Maggie. It's really a new day for us. But from the way you and Mama still live you'd never know it."

She put on some sunglasses that hid everything above the tip of her nose and her chin.

Maggie smiled; maybe at the sunglasses. But a real smile, not scared. After we watched the car dust settle I asked Maggie to bring me a dip of snuff. And then the two of us sat there just enjoying, until it was time to go in the house and go to bed.

In Walker's story, you may have noticed that Dee seeks to remove the cultural artifacts from the site as she leaves her culture behind. Reema's boy saw himself as a fieldworker in training, and Dee considers herself a sophisticated collector of valuable folk art. Neither is successful at listening or looking at the language, the rituals, or the artifacts of their home culture.

Dee and Reema's boy serve as both insiders and outsiders. Their histories and kinships mark them as insiders. Yet they have each left their home cultures and returned, no longer able to read the culture or its artifacts in the same way as the people who continue to live there.

Both Gloria Naylor and Alice Walker illustrate culture as everyday lived experience that is not easily understood by outsiders. They show culture as more than kinship, geography, language, or ways of behaving and instead as a combination of all of these. And with these pieces of fiction, we've drawn on your strengths as a reader, the same kinds of strengths you will need while you are reading and researching in the field.

Responding to Reading

Reading is the essence of almost all college work. In this chapter, we've encouraged you to read cultures and artifacts, but we can't forget the importance of knowing and understanding what kinds of readers we are of texts. Fast readers are not necessarily good readers. Good reading means personal interaction with the text: taking notes, underlining, scribbling thoughts in margins, highlighting with purpose and discrimination. Good reading also means rereading, since each subsequent reading offers new insights and information that you may not have noticed at first. Just as we revisit our favorite movies to see new things and to remember lines and scenes, rereading gives us deeper access to texts.

Louise Rosenblatt, a teacher and scholar whose words open this chapter, suggests that we read across a spectrum that spans what she calls aesthetic and efferent responses. Aesthetic reading, for example, involves paying attention to the ways an author puts words together. It means envisioning sensory details, such as the image of a logging camp in a John Irving novel. It also means noticing the rhythm of words in a rap song or the play of puns in a Shakespeare play. In its extreme, a student focuses so much on metaphor, description, and language use that she misses the information necessary to answer a test question.

Efferent, meaning "to carry away," refers to a reader's ability to carry meaning away from a text. In an effective efferent reading, then, you are interpreting directions on an aspirin bottle, navigating a trip using Google Maps, or underlining important points in your biology textbook. In its extreme, a student focuses so much on the information at hand that she misses the way the item looks, feels, and sounds.

When you're a student, it's important to determine how much aesthetic reading and how much efferent reading each text requires. They are all different, as are our readings of them. We think the same is true of reading cultures. In any cultural moment, material artifact, community conversation, or ritual or language behavior, we need to notice how we slide along this spectrum of reading between efferent and aesthetic.

AESTHETIC VS. EFFERENT READING

- To read *aesthetically* means to read for language use.
- To read *efferently* means to read for practical information.

One way to understand how to write fieldwork is to read it. The essays in this book, ethnographic in nature and method, were done over a semester or a year but are not full ethnographies. Most studies that can claim themselves as "ethnographies" are done over long periods of time. We realize, however, that it can be difficult to read more than one study during a semester in which you're conducting your own fieldwork. One way to sample many approaches to doing fieldwork is to form book clubs within a class and have each small group read an ethnographic study or an ethnographic novel. In **Box 5**, our colleague Katie Ryan shares her process for forming book clubs in a first-year writing course devoted to fieldwork.

BOX 5

FIELDWORKING BOOK CLUBS

Kathleen Ryan, University Of Montana, Missoula, Montana

Purpose

The point of fieldwork is to tell the story of your reading of a culture, and the point of a fieldworking book club is to figure out the story of the book you are reading. This project shows you how doing fieldwork, like reading, is about acts of interpretation. In other words, the abilities you use for fieldworking translate into the abilities you use for reading, and, of course, the opposite is also true.

In a fieldworking book club, you will read an ethnography, an oral history, or an ethnographic fiction work with four or five of your classmates. The point of this book club is to collectively figure out what your book can teach you about being a fieldworker and what being a fieldworker can teach you about your book. The five phases of the project include choosing a book, writing in a reading journal, meeting regularly in class for book club discussions, presenting your book to the class with your book club at the end of the semester or year, and finally, individually reflecting on the entire project.

Action

1. Choose a Book

   When my students did fieldworking book clubs, each club chose one of these three books: *The Mole People*, an ethnography by Jennifer Toth about the homeless communities who live beneath the streets in New York City; *Mules and Men*, a historical study by Zora Neale Hurston of African American stories from Florida and hoodoo practices in Louisiana; and *The Handmaid's Tale*, novelist Margaret Atwood's futuristic fiction written from the viewpoint of Offred, a vital participant and outsider in a post–nuclear war society. I call this book ethnographic fiction because Offred writes from the perspective of a participant-observer in her culture and the text asks readers to read as fieldworkers. My students grouped themselves according to the book they chose.

2. Keep a Reading Journal

   Once you have a book and a club, you are ready to begin writing and talking together. You'll write regularly in a reading journal as you read. Bring at least a two-page journal entry and your book to each book club meeting. The reading journal serves as a place that documents your process of reading, a starting point for your club discussions, and a place for you to write about the text on your own. Here are some sample questions to ask of your reading:

   - What's the book about? How do I know?
   - How does the field researcher/narrator position himself or herself?
   - What choices do you imagine the author made in writing the book?
   - How do authorial choices in detail and style affect your reading?
   - How does reading with a club affect your reading?
   - How does the organization of the book help you think about the arrangement of your own research?
   - What do you bring to your book as a fieldworker? What do you bring to your book as a reader?

   Here is an excerpt from my student Matt Furbish's reading journal on *The Mole People*: "If Toth had not positioned herself in the story, she could not have shown exactly how much underground life changes a person. At the beginning of the book, she's just a sweet, innocent graduate student from Columbia. At the end, however, she comes to find a part of herself she never knew existed: her animal side."

3. Have Regular Book Club Meetings

   In my class, fieldworking book clubs meet once every two weeks. Students bring their book and most recent journal entry to each meeting. As a book club, their assignment is to explore reading and fieldworking by talking about this book. Each group is responsible for determining a reading schedule and an agenda of discussions aimed at fulfilling the assignments and the general goals of the fieldworking book club. Since they know they will be writing evaluations of the books and offering them to the others, their readings and discussions need to move in that direction. Here are some tips to help book club meetings run smoothly:

   - Exchange e-mail addresses and phone numbers to reach other members.
   - Give clear book club assignments for each meeting.
   - Do long-range planning by creating a reading schedule and preparing for the group review and presentation.
   - Be sure someone takes notes during class discussions.
   - Plan discussions around recurring questions, interests, and ideas that come up in journals.
   - Plan ahead for assignments.

4. Write a Group Paper, and Give a Presentation

   Each fieldworking book club writes a collaborative review of the book according to its qualities as ethnography, oral history, or ethnographic fiction, answering the question "How did this work contribute to your understanding of fieldworking and reading?" This review also becomes the content material for a creative and informative 20-minute class presentation.

5. Write an Individual Reflection

   Each club member also writes a one- or two-page summary reflection on the entire book club project. Students reread their journals, reread their group notes, and answer these questions:

   - What did you notice about the way you made sense out of the book as you read?
   - How did reading and talking about the book with others shape or change your thinking? Your reading?
   - What did you learn about the process of fieldworking?
   - What did you learn about your own project?
   - How does this book relate to your life in this class as a fieldworker and your life beyond this class as a writer and reader of books and culture?

FieldWriting: Published and Unpublished Written Sources

Fieldwriting depends far more on oral source material than on written sources. Your informants, along with your fieldnotes, will contribute the most important data to your fieldprojects. When fieldworkers write up their research, they treat informants' words in the same way that library researchers cite textual references.

But you'll still need to refer to written texts from both published and unpublished library and archival sources, as well as documents you've collected at your fieldsite, to support your fieldwork's oral sources. As all research writers know, the basic role of documentation is to attribute ideas that are not your own to their original source. For example, when we use the phrase "stepping in and stepping out" in this book, we put quotation marks around it to indicate that it is not our original idea. We do this because we want to attribute this term to Hortense Powdermaker, whose idea has given us a new way to explain the insider-outsider researcher stance.

One exception to information that requires documentation is common knowledge. Common knowledge refers to information that everyone might be expected to know, such as the presidents or the population of the United States. Sometimes it's difficult to determine, however, what common knowledge particular readers will have. Writers who are unsure of their own readers' common knowledge should include contextual information, which itself often comes from published written sources.

When you use documentation (published or unpublished) to support your fieldwork, you should refer to a more complete handbook or research manual, such as the Modern Language Association's *MLA Handbook for Writers of Research Papers*, used in the humanities. In other subject areas, your instructors may guide you toward other research manuals, such as the *Publication Manual of the American Psychological Association*, used in psychology and education; The *Chicago Manual of Style*, used in history; or one of the many other manuals of style specific to other disciplines, such as law, mathematics, science, medicine, linguistics, or engineering.

Following these examples and consulting a handbook will help you avoid inadvertent plagiarism. **Plagiarism** means using the words and ideas of others without giving them credit. Whether you intend to plagiarize or not, you are committing a serious offense to the academic community. Using appropriate citation conventions helps you avoid plagiarism.

The current convention for documenting any source—informant or text, published or unpublished—is to give as much information about the source as possible within your actual written text. This is called *intertextual citation*. Intertextual (or in-text) citation might include the author or informant's name and the book or document title, depending on how you introduce the material into your writing. Your first citation must always refer to the original source. For published sources, this would be the page number (for example, "Naylor 7" or "*Mama Day* 7"). For unpublished written sources, how you cite depends on the type of material you have collected. When you cite a written source intertextually, you must provide information that allows a reader to find the complete citation in your "Works Cited" section—or "References," "Bibliography," or "Fieldreading"—at the end. Intertextual documentation provides helpful context without interrupting the flow of your text and cluttering it with information that readers can find elsewhere. Another way of including outside source material without interrupting the flow of the text is to use a system of endnotes and footnotes. For more information on incorporating published and unpublished sources into your text, consult a handbook or research manual.

The Research Portfolio: An Option for Rereading

We suggest that you reread and review your portfolio periodically as it develops during the course of your project. Our classes have shared their work in progress with many combinations of partnerships: students work together throughout a whole semester (or year), small collaborative groups of students report back to one another, and (what we like best of all) the "weekly research assistant" puts the research efforts of an entire class at the disposal of one student and her project. All of these support systems help you see your data from perspectives other than your own. In other words, even an informed "other" can help you reread and reorganize the data as it accumulates.

Rereading the Artifacts

Fieldworker Rick Zollo wrote several short reflections about his positioning as he researched Iowa 80. In them, he was able to explore how his own personal history linked with his research and affected his work in the fieldsite. His portfolio included artifacts from the truck stop as well as his related reading and writing: a menu, a few brochures about trucking regulations, photocopies of articles he'd read about truckers, a trucker magazine, photographs he had taken at the truck stop, five writing exercises describing his fieldsite, and a **transcript** of an interview with one of his informants. Each time he reviewed his portfolio, he wrote a short commentary about where he found himself in the research process.

Researching another culture can be both messy and confusing, but if you reflect on the process, you'll find yourself sorting out the mess and clarifying much of the confusion. We believe that the process of reflecting is just as important as the final end product of an ethnographic study. For this reason, we want you to take time to think and write about what you've actually learned from each exercise you do at different stages of your research process. Get together with your portfolio partner, and share your work. Have your partner ask questions about your project, and include those questions and responses in your portfolio as well:

- How does your own personal history affect what you've chosen?
- What does each artifact represent about a growing theme in your research?
- How do the artifacts connect to one another?

Rereading Your Reading

For your portfolio, you'll want to review each of the short readings you did and reflect on them: Gloria Naylor's introduction to her novel *Mama Day*, the excerpt from Laura Bohannan's essay "Shakespeare in the Bush," and Alice Walker's short story "Everyday Use."

Look through your portfolio for the books, pamphlets, articles, and other print materials you've collected from magazines, journals, and the Web. Review what you have, and try to explain it to a partner: describe which information relates directly to the questions you're asking about your topic, which information might take you in a different direction, which information gave you background material that you might now discard. Apply a stick-on note with a short summary to each written artifact, and take some time to show your partner—or your group—how you think it connects to the whole project. Our students find this a great way to begin organizing data thematically.

- What categories could you use to tell the story of your project so far?
- What written source offers a historical backdrop or an important understanding about the culture you're studying?
- Which written sources represent—or come directly from—the culture itself? If you don't have a piece of writing from or about your culture, where might you locate one?

Rereading Your Sources of Support

The multiple perspectives in your study can come from your classmates as well as your informants. One simple way to do this is bring a friend, relative, or classmate to your fieldsite to take notes, and then reciprocate by visiting that person's site.

As you work with the materials in your portfolio, you'll notice that you've had lots of assistance from others, and it's always useful to acknowledge your sources of support: who helped you gain access to the culture, who suggested key informants, who found an article about your topic. Who worked with you in organizing your data? Who asked an insightful question? Who went with you to your fieldsite? Of course, one strategy for enriching your data is to assign someone as your research partner for the whole course of your project.

Our favorite strategy is the "weekly research assistant." Everyone in the class becomes your research assistant for a week, including your teacher. You design their assignments (three people, for example, read articles and write reports for you, three people go with you to your fieldsite on one day, two people do Web searches on your topic, four people try out a cultural practice and report in writing about how it worked). A week later, you have accumulated much new data for your portfolio and lots of new insights on your project.

Rereading Your Writing

If you've worked on the boxes in this chapter, you may have already

- written about your positionality (the assumptions you carry into your fieldsite)
- written about an everyday object or event using the double-entry format
- kept notes for a book club
- considered the process of negotiating entry and worked with ethics statements
- selected and "read" a cultural artifact

READ YOUR FIELDSITE

Learning to read levels of explicit and implicit behaviors, rules, languages, and codes can take time. Use this exercise to practice how to read your fieldsite and to move from outsider to insider without disturbing the culture.

1. Try to identify the codes or behaviors you're unfamiliar with in your site. In what situations must you act with care? Learn new rules of politeness? Wait to be told what to do? What behaviors do you need to observe quietly to master? In what ways do the people in that culture expect you to behave like them? Excuse you for doing things your own way?
2. Make a list of questions you would like to ask an insider in this culture. For example, how do insiders know when a meal begins and ends, and what are the codes of behavior for eating? If you are studying abroad where English is not the primary spoken language, identify what you are unsure of: how to make a phone call, how to greet someone or ask directions, or how to locate a bathroom.
3. Choose a single code or behavior you've identified. Describe in a detailed paragraph the rules an outsider would need to know to fit into the culture. As Paulo Freire would say, what "words" do you have to "read" to understand the "world" in which you are participating?

CHAPTER 10

Researching People: The Collaborative Listener

Portraying people depends on careful listening and observing. In this chapter you will learn to:

- use details to describe people
- gather information from informants
- transcribe others' conversation
- borrow elements of fiction writing

Researching people means stepping in to the worldviews of others. When we talk with people in the field or study the stuff of their lives—their stories, artifacts, and surroundings—we enter their perspectives by partly stepping out of our own.

> Ethnography is interaction, collaboration. What it demands is not hypotheses, which may unnaturally close study down, obscuring the integrity of the other, but the ability to converse intimately.
>
> —Henry Glassie

In an informal way, you are always gathering data about people's backgrounds and perspectives—their worldviews. "So where are you from?" "How do you like it here?" "Did you know anyone when you first came here?" Not only do you ask questions about people's backgrounds, but you also notice their artifacts and adornments—the things with which they represent themselves: T-shirts, jewelry, particular kinds of shoes or hairstyles. The speculations and questions we form about others cause us to make hypotheses about the people we meet. We may ask questions, or we may just listen. But unless we listen closely, we'll never understand others from their perspectives. We need to know what it's like for *that* person in *this* place.

Even in an informal conversation, we conduct a kind of ethnographic interview. Good interviewing is collaboration between you and your informant, not very different from a friendly talk. Listening to your relatives share stories at a wedding, pouring over a photo album with your grandmother, and gossiping about old times at a school reunion

Chapter 10, "Researching People: The Collaborative Listener," from *FieldWorking: Reading and Writing Research*, Fourth Edition, by Bonnie Stone Sunstein and Elizabeth Chiseri-Strater, pp. 219–270 (Chapter 5).

are all instances in which you can gather data through collaborative listening. You've experienced your local media interviewing sports heroes and newsworthy citizens, and you know famous television and radio interviewers such as Oprah, Barbara Walters, and Charlie Rose. Your fieldworking interviews might employ the same skills: establishing rapport, letting your informant digress from your questions, as well as carefully listening and navigating the conversation process.

This chapter will help you strengthen the everyday skills of listening, questioning, and researching people who interest you. You'll experience interactive ways to conduct interviews and **oral histories**. You'll look for and discover meaning in your informants' everyday cultural artifacts. You'll gather, analyze, write, and reflect on **family stories**. And you'll read some examples of how other fieldworkers have researched and written about people's lives.

The Interview: Learning How to Ask

Fieldworkers listen to and record stories from the point of view of the informant—not their own. Letting people speak for themselves by telling about their lives seems an easy enough principle to follow. But in fact, there are some important strategies for both asking questions and listening to responses. Those strategies are part of interviewing—learning to ask and learning to listen.

Interviewing involves an ironic contradiction: you must be both structured and flexible at the same time. While it's critical to prepare for an interview with a list of planned questions to guide your talk, it is equally important to follow your informant's lead. Sometimes the best interviews come from a comment, a story, an artifact, or a phrase you couldn't have anticipated. The energy that drives a good interview—for both you and your informant—comes from expecting the unexpected.

Expecting the Unexpected

It's happened to both of us as interviewers. As part of a two-year project, Elizabeth conducted in-depth interviews with Anna, a college student who was a dancer. Anna identified with the modern dancers at the university and also was interested in animal rights, organic foods, and ecological causes. She wore a necklace that Elizabeth thought served as a spiritual talisman or represented a political affiliation. When she asked Anna about it, she learned that the necklace actually held the key to Anna's apartment—a much less dramatic answer than Elizabeth anticipated. Anna claimed that she didn't trust herself to keep her key anywhere but around her neck, and that information provided a clue to her temperament that Elizabeth wouldn't have known if she hadn't asked and had persisted in her own speculations.

In a shorter project, Bonnie interviewed Ken, a school superintendent, over a period of eight months. As Ken discussed his beliefs about education, Bonnie connected his ideas with the writings of progressivist philosopher John Dewey. At the time, she was reading educational philosophy herself and was greatly influenced by Dewey's ideas. To her, Ken seemed to be a contemporary incarnation of Dewey. Eventually, toward the end of their interviews, Bonnie asked Ken which of Dewey's works had been the most important to him. "Dewey?" he asked. "John Dewey? Never exactly got around to reading him."

No matter how hard we try to lay aside our assumptions when we interview others, we always carry them with us. Rather than ignore our hunches, we need to form questions around them, follow them through, and see where they will lead us. Asking Anna about her necklace, a personal artifact, led Elizabeth to new understandings about Anna's self-concept and habits that later became important in her analysis of Anna's literacy. Bonnie's admiration for Dewey had little to do directly with Ken's educational philosophy, but her follow-up questions centered on the scholars who did shape Ken's theories. It is our job to reveal our informant's perspectives and experiences rather than our own. And so our questions must allow us to learn something new, something that our informant knows and we don't. We must learn how to ask.

Asking

Asking involves collaborative listening. When we interview, we are not extracting information the way a dentist pulls a tooth, but we make meaning together like two dancers, one leading and one following. Interview questions range between closed and open.

Closed Questions

Closed questions are like those we answer on application forms or in magazines: How many years of schooling have you had? Do you rent your apartment? Do you own a car? Do you have any distinguishing birthmarks? Do you use bar or liquid soap? Do you drink sweetened or unsweetened tea, caffeinated or decaffeinated coffee? Some closed questions are essential for gathering background data: Where did you grow up? How many siblings did you have? What was your favorite subject in school? But these questions often yield single phrases as answers and can shut down further talk. Closed questions can start an awkward volley of single questions and abbreviated answers.

To avoid asking too many closed questions, you'll need to prepare ahead of time by doing informal research about your informants and the topics they represent. For example, if you are interviewing a woman in the air force, you may want to read something about the history of women in aviation. You might also consult an expert in the field or telephone government offices to request informational materials so that you avoid asking questions that you could answer for yourself, like "How many years have women been allowed to fly planes in the U.S. Air Force?" When you are able to do background research, your knowledge of the topic and the informant's background will demonstrate your level of interest, put the informant at ease, and create a more comfortable interview situation.

Open Questions

Open questions, by contrast, help elicit your informant's perspective and allow for a more conversational exchange. Because there is no single answer to open-ended questions, you will need to listen, respond, and follow the informant's lead. Because there is no single answer, you can allow yourself to engage in a lively, authentic response. In other words, simply being interested will make you a good field interviewer. Here are some very general open questions—sometimes called *experiential* and *descriptive*—that encourage the informant to share experiences or to describe them from his or her own point of view.

OPEN QUESTIONS FOR YOUR INFORMANT

- Tell me more about the time when...
- Describe the people who were most important to...
- Describe the first time you...
- Tell me about the person who taught you about...
- What stands out for you when you remember...
- Tell me the story behind that interesting item you have.
- Describe a typical day in your life.
- How would you describe yourself to yourself?
- How would you describe yourself to others?

When thinking of questions to ask an informant, make your informant your teacher. You want to learn about his or her expertise, knowledge, beliefs, and worldview.

BOX 6

USING A CULTURAL ARTIFACT IN AN INTERVIEW

Purpose

This exercise mirrors the process of conducting interviews over time with an informant. It emphasizes working with the informant's perspective, making extensive and accurate observations, speculating and theorizing, confirming and disconfirming ideas, writing up notes, listening well, sharing ideas collaboratively, and reflecting on your data.

To introduce interviewing in our courses, we use an artifact exchange. This exercise allows people to investigate the meaning of an object from another person's point of view.

Action

Choose a partner from among your colleagues. You will act as both interviewer and informant. Select an interesting artifact that your partner is either wearing or carrying: a key chain, a piece of jewelry, an item of clothing. Both partners should be sure the artifact is one the owner feels comfortable talking about. If, for example, the interviewer says, "Tell me about that pin you are wearing," but the informant knows that her watch has more meaning or her bookbag holds a story, the interviewer should follow her lead. Once you've each chosen an artifact, try the following process. Begin by writing observational and personal notes as a form of background research before interviewing:

1. *Take observational notes.* Take quiet time to inspect, describe, and take notes on your informant's artifact. Pay attention to its form and speculate about its function. Where do you think it comes from? What is it used for?
2. *Take personal notes.* What does it remind you of? What do you already know about things similar to it? How does it connect to your own experience? What are your hunches about the artifact? In other words, what assumptions do you have about it? (For example, you may be taking notes on someone's ring and find yourself speculating about how much it costs and whether the owner of the artifact is wealthy.) It is important here to identify your assumptions and not mask them.
3. *Interview the informant.* Ask questions and take notes on the story behind the artifact. What people are involved in it? Why is it important to them? How does the owner use it? Value it? What's the cultural background behind it? After recording your informant's responses, read your observational notes to each other to verify or clarify the information.

4. *Theorize.* Think of a metaphor that describes the object. How does the artifact reflect something you know about the informant? Could you find background material about the artifact? Where would you look? How does the artifact relate to history or culture? If, for example, your informant wears earrings made of spoons, you might research spoon making, spoon collecting, or the introduction of the spoon in polite society. Maybe this person had a famous cook in the family, played the spoons as a folk instrument, or used these as baby spoons in childhood.
5. *Write.* In several paragraphs about the observations, the interview, and your theories, create a written account of the artifact and its relationship to your informant. Give a draft to your informant for a response.
6. *Exchange.* The informant writes a response to your written account, detailing what was interesting and surprising. At this point, the informant can point out what you didn't notice, say, or ask that might be important to a further understanding of the artifact. You will want to exchange your responses again, explaining what you learned from the first exchange.
7. *Reflect.* Write about what you learned about yourself as an interviewer. What are your strengths? Your weaknesses? What assumptions or preconceptions did you find that you had that interfered with your interviewing skills? How might you change this?
8. *Change roles and repeat this process.*

In interviews, researchers sometimes use cultural artifacts to enter into the informant's perspective. We might start by talking about something in our informant's environment: a framed snapshot, a CD or DVD collection, an interesting or unusual object in the room—anything that will encourage comfortable conversation. When we invite informants to tell stories about their artifacts, we learn about the artifacts themselves and, indirectly, about other aspects of their world that they might not think to talk about. Artifacts, like stories, can mediate between individuals and their cultures.

Learning How to Listen

Although most people think that the key to a good interview is asking a set of good questions, we and our students have found that the real key to interviewing is being a good listener. Think about your favorite television or radio talk show personalities. What do they do to make their informants comfortable and keep conversation flowing? Think about someone you know whom you've always considered a good listener. Why does that person make you feel that way?

Good listeners guide the direction of thoughts; they don't interrupt or move conversation back to themselves. Good listeners use their body language to let informants understand that their informants' words are important to them, not allowing their eyes to wander, not fiddling, not checking their watches or their phones. They encourage response with verbal acknowledgments and follow-up questions, with embellishments and examples.

To be a good listener as a field interviewer, you must also have structured plans with focused questions. And you must be willing to change them as the conversation moves in different directions. With open questions, background research, and genuine interest in your informant, you'll find yourself holding a collaborative conversation from which you'll both learn. It is the process, not the preplanned information, that makes an interview successful.

ETIQUETTE FOR CONDUCTING AN INTERVIEW

In addition to preparing yourself with guiding questions and good listening habits, here are some basic rules of etiquette for conducting a successful interview. Always keep in mind that you are using someone's time.

- Arrange for the interview at your informant's convenience. Your interview should fit into that person's schedule, not vice versa. Put his or her needs first.
- Explain your project in plain language that your informant will understand. Don't bore or scare them with insider expressions such as "ethnographic" or "fieldsite research."
- Agree on a quiet place to talk. Avoid places like cafés that have a lot of ambient noise.
- Arrive on time and be prepared. Make sure your equipment works (pens, batteries, recording devices). Have your questions and notepad ready.
- Dress appropriately for the setting and for your informant. You'd wear something different to interview a lifeguard on the beach than your grandmother in her living room.
- Don't try to squeeze too much into a short time. Be sensitive to social cues and, if necessary, arrange for an additional interview.
- Thank your informant and follow up with a thank-you note, e-mail, or, if appropriate, a token of gratitude.

Recording and Transcribing

Interviews provide the bones of any fieldwork project. You need your informants' actual words to support your findings. Without informants' voices, you have no perspective to share except your own. When you record and transcribe your interviews, you bring to life the language of the people whose culture you study.

The process of recording and transcribing interviews has been advanced by computers, software, and audio recorders that are small, relatively inexpensive, and easily available. It's no coincidence that interviewing and collecting oral histories have become more popular in recent years with these accessible technologies. With a counting feature to keep track of slices of conversation and a pause button to slow down the transcription process, even the most basic recorder becomes a valuable tool for the interviewer.

Your choice of recording device will partially depend on whether you need a recorder that is lightweight and handheld, high resolution, and low noise, or one that records to a memory card. You may find that an inexpensive recorder will suit your purposes just fine if you want to record one-on-one in a quiet space and transcribe it yourself before integrating the interview into your own text. However, if you plan to record in a noisy setting and make both the audio and written transcription available, you will need a higher-quality recording device.

How you are going to share your work is another consideration. Will you transcribe it into print only, or will you also distribute it as an audio file, podcast, or part of a multimedia presentation? How you will use your interview material will affect what kind of equipment you purchase or rent.

Advances in recording devices and software have cut down the tedium of sorting, classifying, and organizing huge amounts of data. But transcribing is tedious business nonetheless. Three or more hours might be required to transcribe one hour of recording. And editing your audio files (if you choose to do that) will require even more time. However, you learn an enormous amount about your informants and yourself as you listen, replay, and select the sections for your study.

You don't want to record everything you hear, nor do you want to transcribe it all. That's why it's important to prepare ahead—with research, guiding questions, and adequate equipment as well as knowledge of how to use it. The following guidelines will help make your recording and transcribing go smoothly.

- ***Obtain your equipment*** Before borrowing or purchasing quality equipment, research what's available. A digital counter that helps keep track of time, multidirectional microphones that minimize ambient noise, and functions that record separate tracks are some key features that will facilitate your research. Investigate what's available and appropriate to your research.
- ***Prepare your equipment*** Dead batteries and full memory cards can ruin your data collection. Always carry extras. Test your recorder before using it by stating your name, the date, the place of the interview, and the full name

of your informant, and then playing this information back to yourself. If you use a microphone, check out its range before you begin. Most fieldworkers have stories of losing interviews because of equipment malfunction. Be prepared.

- ***Plan to take notes*** Consider how you will take fieldnotes during the interview so that you'll capture all the features of the experience and have a backup in case your recording equipment fails. You want to note the environment where the interview takes place, the facial and body language of your informant's responses, and any hesitations or interruptions that take place. Your fieldnotes will help supplement the actual recording. Also consider taking photos that you can use later to jog your memory.
- ***Organize your interview time*** Be considerate in setting up a time and place for the interview. Ask your informant what's convenient for him or her. Arrive a few minutes early and test your equipment as well as the space so that you don't have any extraneous noise or distractions. Remember to have a timepiece—be it a watch or a phone—so that you can keep track of interview time.
- ***Organize time to listen to your audio*** Begin the labeling process as soon as possible. Key the filename (date, place, and informant's name) into your audio device or download the file from your memory card and label it on your computer. Also write down the filename of each recording in your fieldnotes. After the interview, listen to the recording as soon as you can to keep it fresh in your mind. Take notes as you listen for topics covered, themes that emerge, and possible follow-up questions.
- ***Transcribe the interview*** As soon as you can, begin to transcribe your recording. Don't wait too long, as the initial listening process enhances your memory of the interview and your sense of purpose about the project. Remember that you do not need to transcribe all the material you record—only the sections that are useful to your study. To transcribe, listen directly from the recorder or upload your audio files to your computer. Check with your media lab to see if they have a device sometimes known as a footswitch. If they do, you can attach it to your audio device to stop and start the recording as needed. This can be immensely helpful. Whatever sections you decide to use, transcribe them word for word using parentheses or brackets to indicate pauses, laughing, interruptions, sections you want to leave out, or unintelligible words. For example: [Regina laughs nervously] or [phone rang, maybe match? Or march?—check with Regina] or [unintelligible word].
- ***Bring your informant's language to life*** As a transcriber, you must bring your informant's speech to life as accurately and appropriately as you can. Most researchers agree that a person's grammar should remain as spoken. If an informant says, "I done," for example, it's not appropriate to alter it

to "I did." But if when you share the transcript with your informant she chooses to alter it, respect those changes. As well, many characteristics of oral language have no equivalents in print. It is too difficult for either transcriber or reader to attempt to capture dialect in written form. "Pahk the cah in Hahvahd Yahd" is a respelling of a Boston accent, meant to show how it sounds. But to a reader who's never heard it—even to an insider Bostonian who isn't conscious of her accent—the written version of her oral dialect looks artificial and complicates the reading process. Anthropologists and folklorists have long debated how to record oral language and currently discourage the use of spelling as a way to approximate oral language.

- ***Share your transcript*** Offer the transcripts to your informant to read for accuracy, but realize that you won't get many takers. Most informants would rather wait for your finished, edited version of the interview. In any case, the informant needs the opportunity to read what you've written. In some instances, the informant may make corrections or ask for deletions. But most of the time, the written interview becomes a kind of gift in exchange for the time spent interviewing.
- ***Edit the audio files*** You may decide to go beyond the written transcript to include your raw audio recording in a Web-based media presentation that will add an extra dimension to your project. To create a usable audio clip, you will need to use software to edit or splice your recordings together. Talk to fellow students or researchers about what they use. If possible, test-drive the editing software in order to understand its full capacities before you purchase it.

You'll also want to consider what medium in which to share your audio clips, as this will affect their length and content. Blogs, multimedia presentations, and podcasts are some of the popular formats at the time of this writing. Be sure to include the URL for your blog, Web site, or podcast in your written work—especially if you plan to publish it—so that your readers can access it and enhance their understanding of your study.

REMINDERS FOR RECORDING AND TRANSCRIBING

- Set up your interview.
- Familiarize yourself with your recording device.
- Arrive early and evaluate your recording environment.
- Conduct the interview and take notes.
- Arrange sufficient time for listening to and transcribing the interview.
- Consider your final presentation format and its audience.

Fieldworkers must turn interview transcripts into writing, making a kind of verbal film. As interesting as interview transcripts are to the researcher, they are only partial representations of the actual interview process. Folklorist Elliott Oring observes, "Lives are not transcriptions of events. They are artful and enduring symbolic constitutions which demand our engagement and identification. They are to be perceived and understood as wholes" (258). To bring an informant's life to the page, you must use a transcript within your own text, sometimes describing the setting, the informant's physical appearances, particular mannerisms, and language patterns and intonations. The transcript by itself has little meaning until you bring it to life.

The Informant's Perspective: An Anthropologist on Mars

Most field interviews in their final form look smooth and polished and don't reveal any fumbling, false starts, missed appointments, muddled communication, and malfunctioning equipment. Because fieldworking takes a long time, once interviewers and informants establish rapport, the early messiness and hesitations of the relationship fade into the background. When they experience troubles with interviewing, most researchers decide not to highlight them. But they talk and write about them a lot. Our favorite interviewer's story comes from the *Foxfire* collection (edited by Eliot "Wig" Wigginton and others). In this excerpt, a high school student named Paul Gillespie (working alongside his teacher, Wigginton) interviews an elderly informant named Aunt Arie at her house in the Appalachian Mountains.

> [W]e walked in on her on Thanksgiving morning. She had her back to the door, and we startled her. There she was trying to carve the eyeballs out of a hog's head. I was almost sick to my stomach, so Wig helped operate on this hog's head while I turned my head and held the microphone of the tape recorder in the general vicinity of the action.
>
> They struggled for at least fifteen minutes, maybe more, and then I witnessed one of the most amazing events of my life. Aunt Arie took an eyeball, went to the back door, and flung it out. When she threw it, the eyeball went up on the tin roof of an adjoining outbuilding, rolled off, snagged on the clothesline, and hung there bobbing like a yo-yo. I had Wig's Pentax, so I took a picture of it, and it appeared in a subsequent issue of the magazine. It was very funny, remarkable. (56)

Oliver Sacks is a doctor who specializes in disorders of the nervous system and uses some fieldworking strategies to understand the perspectives of his patients. Rather than examining them in a hospital setting, Sacks visits his patients in their own contexts to explore their lives "as they live in the real world." In fact, in the preface to his bestselling collection of interviews, *An Anthropologist on Mars: Seven*

Paradoxical Tales, he describes his fieldwork as "house calls at the far borders of human experience" (xx).

In one interview, he visits Temple Grandin, a woman with autism who, as a professor of animal science at Colorado State University, studies animal behavior. Sacks wanted to find out about autism from an insider's perspective. After researching autism from a medical point of view, he realized that he needed a person to give it voice, to create a portrait of the autistic person. Grandin told him that in her daily life, she feels like an outsider, like a researcher from another planet who is constantly studying the culture in which she lives to understand it. She provided Sacks with a critical understanding of her autistic worldview—as well as the title for his study—with the comment, "Much of the time I feel like an anthropologist on Mars."

In this essay from *An Anthropologist on Mars,* Sacks makes use of all the interviewing skills we've introduced in this chapter. He presents his information about Temple Grandin, offering details of her home, her own words, and her body language, and giving us especially her squeeze machine—the artifact which makes her so unique. Rather than relying on a question/answer interview format, Sacks holds an ordinary conversation with her as they drive together. By making her comfortable and by being interested in her life, Sacks allows Grandin to tell stories about her past relationship with her "enriched" research pigs—which provides him (and later us, his readers) with important insights about Grandin's personality as well as her neurological disorder.

When he arrives at her house after the ride, he observes the artifacts there—buttons, badges, and the squeeze machine—which offer more information about her private and professional lives, about her worldview. Sacks focuses on his informant's unusual apparatus for receiving affection and even tries it out to feel her perspective.

Although Sacks's polished final essay reveals none of the bones of the interview (as we offered with Cindie Marshall's PDF on Canvas), it's a good guess that Sacks took piles of fieldnotes and probably even recorded his conversation. The overall effect is that Sacks allows Grandin's words, her stories, and even her artifacts to guide his account of her story. Because of his careful research and detailed writing, this essay remains her story and not his.

Notice that each of the details he offers is like a puzzle piece, fitting one item at a time into this description.

An Anthropologist on Mars

OLIVER SACKS

Early the next morning, a Saturday, Temple picked me up in her four-wheel-drive, a rugged vehicle she drives all over the West to visit farms, ranches, corrals, and meat plants. As we headed for her house, I quizzed her about the work she had done for her Ph.D.; her thesis on the effects of enriched and impoverished environments on the development of pigs' brains. She told me about the great differences that developed between the two groups—how sociable and delightful the "enriched" pigs became, how hyperexcitable and aggressive (and almost "autistic") the "impoverished" ones were by contrast. (She wondered whether impoverishment of experience was not a contributing factor in human autism.) "I got to love my enriched pigs," she said. "I was very attached. I was so attached I couldn't kill them." The animals had to be sacrificed at the end of the experiment so their brains could be examined. She described how the pigs, at the end, trusting her, let her lead them on their last walk, and how she had calmed them, by stroking them and talking to them, while they were killed. She was very distressed at their deaths—"I wept and wept."

Courtesy of Temple Grandin

FIGURE 10.1 Temple Grandin, Ph.D., a gifted animal scientist

She had just finished the story when we arrived at her home—a small two-story town house, some distance from the campus. Downstairs was comfortable, with the usual amenities—a sofa, armchairs, a television, pictures on the wall—but I had the sense that it was rarely used. There was an immense sepia print of her grandfather's farm in Grandin, North Dakota, in 1880; her other grandfather, she told me, had invented the automatic pilot for planes. These two were the progenitors, she feels, of her agricultural and engineering talents. Upstairs was her study, with her typewriter (but no word processor), absolutely bursting with manuscripts and books—books everywhere, spilling out of the study into every room in the house. (My own little house was once described as "a machine for working," and I had a somewhat similar impression of Temple's.) On one wall was a large cowhide with a huge collection of identity badges and caps, from the hundreds of conferences she has lectured at. I was amused to see, side by side, an I.D. from the American Meat Institute and one from the American Psychiatric Association. Temple has published more than a hundred papers, divided between those on animal behavior and facilities management and those on autism. The intimate blending of the two was epitomized by the medley of badges side by side.

Finally, without diffidence or embarrassment (emotions unknown to her), Temple showed me her bedroom, an austere room with whitewashed walls and a single bed and, next to the bed, a very large, strange-looking object. "What is that?" I asked.

"That's my squeeze machine," Temple replied. "Some people call it my hug machine."

The device had two heavy, slanting wooden sides, perhaps four by three feet each, pleasantly upholstered with a thick, soft padding. They were joined by hinges to a long, narrow bottom board to create a V-shaped, body-sized trough. There was a complex control box at one end, with heavy-duty tubes leading off to another device, in a closet. Temple showed me this as well. "It's an industrial compressor," she said, "the kind they use for filling tires."

"And what does this do?"

"It exerts a firm but comfortable pressure on the body, from the shoulders to the knees," Temple said. "Either a steady pressure or a variable one or a pulsating one, as you wish," she added. "You crawl into it—I'll show you—and turn the compressor on, and you have all the controls in your hand, here, right in front of you."

When I asked her why one should seek to submit oneself to such pressure, she told me. When she was a little girl, she said, she had longed to be hugged but had at the same time been terrified of all contact. When she was hugged, especially by a favorite (but vast) aunt, she felt overwhelmed, overcome by sensation; she had a sense of peacefulness and pleasure, but also of terror and engulfment. She started to have daydreams—she was just five at the time—of a magic machine that could squeeze her powerfully but gently, in a huglike way, and in a way entirely commanded and controlled by her. Years later, as an adolescent, she had seen a picture of a squeeze chute designed to hold or restrain calves and realized that that was it: a little modification to make it suitable for human use, and it could be her magic machine. She had considered other devices—inflatable suits, which could exert an even pressure all over the body—but the squeeze chute, in its simplicity, was quite irresistible.

Being of a practical turn of mind, she soon made her fantasy come true. The early models were crude, with some snags and glitches, but she eventually evolved a totally comfortable, predictable system, capable of administering a "hug" with whatever parameters she desired. Her squeeze machine had worked exactly as she hoped, yielding the very sense of calmness and pleasure she had dreamed of since childhood. She could not have gone through the stormy days of college without her squeeze machine, she said. She could not turn to human beings for solace and comfort, but she could always turn to it. The machine, which she neither exhibited nor concealed but kept openly in her room at college, excited derision and suspicion and was seen by psychiatrists as a "regression" or "fixation"—something that needed to be psychoanalyzed and resolved. With her characteristic stubbornness, tenacity, single-mindedness, and bravery—along with a complete absence of inhibition or hesitation—Temple ignored all these comments and reactions and determined to find a scientific "validation" of her feelings.

Both before and after writing her doctoral thesis, she made a systematic investigation of the effects of deep pressure in autistic people, college students, and animals, and recently a paper of hers on this was published in the *Journal of Child and Adolescent Psychopharmacology*. Today, her squeeze machine, variously modified, is receiving extensive clinical trials. She has also become the world's foremost designer of squeeze chutes for cattle and has published, in the meat-industry and veterinary literature, many articles on the theory and practice of humane restraint and gentle holding.

While telling me this, Temple knelt down, then eased herself, facedown and at full length, into the "V," turned on the compressor (it took a minute for the master cylinder to fill), and twisted the controls. The sides converged, clasping her firmly, and then, as she made a small adjustment, relaxed their grip slightly. It was the most bizarre thing I had ever seen, and yet, for all its oddness, it was moving and simple. Certainly there was no doubt of its effect. Temple's voice, often loud and hard, became softer and gentler as she lay in her machine. "I concentrate on how gently I can do it," she said, and then spoke of the necessity of "totally giving in to it. . . . I'm getting real relaxed now," she added quietly. "I guess others get this through relation with other people."

It is not just pleasure or relaxation that Temple gets from the machine but, she maintains, a feeling for others. As she lies in her machine, she says, her thoughts often turn to her mother, her favorite aunt, her teachers. She feels their love for her, and hers for them. She feels that the machine opens a door into an otherwise closed emotional world and allows her, almost teaches her, to feel empathy for others.

After twenty minutes or so, she emerged, visibly calmer, emotionally less rigid (she says that a cat can easily sense the difference in her at these times), and asked me if I would care to try the machine.

Indeed, I was curious and scrambled into it, feeling a little foolish and self-conscious—but less so than I might have been, because Temple herself was so wholly lacking in self-consciousness. She turned the compressor on again and filled the master cylinder, and I experimented gingerly with the controls. It was indeed a sweet, calming feeling—one that reminded me of my deep-diving days long ago, when I felt the pressure of the water on my diving suit as a whole-body embrace.

As you can tell from this essay on Temple Grandin, the process of asking and listening collaboratively allows us to gain the perspective of an "other." Examining our own assumptions and worldviews from the vantage points of others exposes us to our quirks and shortcomings and cultural biases. In the process of understanding others, we come to more fully understand ourselves.

Gathering Family Stories

Yet another way to gather data from an informant is to listen for stories. Temple Grandin's stories and Marshall's PDF on Canvas came directly out of answers to their interviewer's questions. But sometimes stories that are buried and unconscious offer important information about our lives.

Stories, like artifacts, serve to tell us about our informants' worldviews and function as data in our fieldwork. Informants have entire repertoires of stories based on their childhoods, their interests, their occupations. Our job as researchers is to elicit our informants' stories, record them, and carefully analyze what they mean. Researchers who study verbal art think about stories in these ways:

- Stories preserve a culture's values and beliefs.
- Stories help individuals endure, transform, or reject cultural values for themselves.
- Stories exist because of the interrelationship between tellers and audiences.

The most influential kinship structure is, of course, the family. And stories begin in our families. And to understand someone's culture, we often need to understand the person's family too. Family stories help us do that. Because we first hear them when we're young, family stories influence and shape us. In many cultures, family storytelling sessions are a deliberate way of passing along values. They are often expected events, almost ritualized performances. Judith Ortiz Cofer, in a memoir of her Puerto Rican childhood, writes about how the younger females in her extended family were encouraged to eavesdrop on the adult storytelling ritual:

> At three or four o'clock in the afternoon, the hour of the *café con leche*, the women of my family gathered in Mama's living room to speak of important things and retell family stories meant to be overheard by us young girls, their daughters....It was on these rockers that my mother, her sisters, and my grandmother sat these afternoons of my childhood to tell their stories, teaching each other, and my cousin and me, what it was like to be a woman, more specifically, a Puerto Rican woman. They talked about life on the island, and life in Los Nueva Yores, their way of referring to the United States from New York City to California: the other place, not home, all the same. They told real-life

> stories, though, as I later learned, always embellishing them with a little or a lot of dramatic detail. And they told *cuentos*, the morality and cautionary tales told by the women in our family for generations; stories that became part of my subconscious as I grew up in two worlds. (64–65)

These stories from Ortiz Cofer's childhood were not merely afternoon entertainment. Her family's stories recorded history and carried instructions about behaviors, rules, and beliefs. Like the legends, folk tales, and proverbs of specific cultures, family stories reflect the ways of acting and even of viewing the world sanctioned or approved by a family. Ortiz Cofer's relatives conserve cultural traditions of their old country, Puerto Rico, and translate them into the "Los Nueva Yores" culture.

In addition to preserving cultural values, many writers suggest that the act of storytelling is also an act of individual survival. To endure in our families and the culture at large, we must explain our lives to ourselves. First we share our stories, and then we reflect on what they mean. Our own storytelling memories teach us about our personal histories. When you think of a family story, try to decide why it survived, which tellers have different versions, what parts of the story remain the same no matter who tells it, and how you've refashioned it for your own purposes.

Family stories are often transformed in oral retellings, but they clearly change when they are written down. Although they belong to the oral narrative tradition, writing them down helps us analyze their meaning and potential relevance to our own lives.

BOX 7

WRITING A FAMILY STORY

Purpose

We're not always conscious of how our family stories serve us, nor are our informants. But they are worth exploring as a rich source of data when we want to better understand our own lives—and the lives of the people with whom we're working. As scholar Elizabeth Stone, in *Black Sheep and Kissing Cousins: How Our Family Stories Shape Us*, writes,

> What struck me about my own family stories was first, how much under my skin they were; second, once my childhood was over, how little deliberate attention I ever paid to them; and third, how thoroughly invisible they were to anyone else. Going about my daily life, I certainly never told them aloud and never even alluded to them.... Those who say that America is a land of rootless nomads who travel light, uninstructed by memory and family ties, have missed part of the evidence.

Action

Recall a family story you've heard many times. It may fall into one of these categories: fortunes gained and lost, heroes, "black sheep," eccentric or oddball relatives, acts of retribution and revenge, or family feuds. After writing the story, analyze its meaning. When is this story most often told, and why? What kinds of warnings or messages does this story convey? For the family? For an outsider? What kind of lesson does the story teach? How does your story reflect your family's values? How has it changed or altered through various retellings? Which family members would have different versions?

Family stories preserve family beliefs through morality lessons with subliminal messages and subconscious instructions. Some family stories act as cautionary tales, or what writer Judith Ortiz Cofer calls *cuentos*, to pass on warnings about behavior to the next generation. Through storytelling, family tales can be transformed and reshaped to make them fit the teller's needs and life circumstances. As they transform family stories, tellers can remain loyal to the family unit but be released from it as well. They can connect us with our families while allowing us our identities as we reshape them to fit our own lives and our own audiences.

One Family Story: The Core and Its Variants

When Donna Niday, a professor at Iowa State University, was a student in Bonnie's class, she decided to study one of her family's stories. It illustrates a significant idea: that different family members tell one story in very different ways, and each way reveals something about the teller. Donna was in her forties at the time, and she was lucky that her mother and sisters were all alive and accessible while she conducted her study. In researching "The Baby on the Roof," Donna expected to get different perspectives from the five Riggs sisters—her own mother and her four aunts who grew up on a farm in the rural Midwest of the 1920s. She began by interviewing her cousins to see what they remembered about the story, which would have been passed down to them by their mothers. Just as she suspected, each of Donna's cousins told the story with different details and points of emphasis. She confirmed the aunts' family reputations: "she was the daring one" or "she was always the chicken."

Donna was realistic enough to know that there would be no "true" version of the tale, but the story would have a stable core, a basic frame, shared among the sisters. She also anticipated that there would be many variants, differences in details according to the tellers. She interviewed each elderly sister in her home, allowing time to look through family photo albums together and to visit before recording the stories. As she listened and recorded, Donna gathered both the core story and its variants.

The oldest sister, Eleanor, who claimed responsibility for the secret family event, told the core story this way, emphasizing herself and the baby:

> I took Mary to the top of the house when Mom went out to work. You know, all four of us took the ladder—went down to the barn and got the big ladder. Mom just said to take care of Mary, and I did. I took her everywhere I went. Mary was six months old. Well, she was born in January. This would be June, I suppose, when we were doing hay. I knew she'd lay wherever you put her. And so there was a flat place there on the roof. There wasn't any danger—I don't think there was ever any danger of her getting away at all. Yeah, we could see them mowing. If Mom had ever looked toward the house, she would have had a heart attack to see her kids up on the roof. Especially when we were supposed to be looking after the baby. Yeah, well see, I was ten when Mary was born, so I was ten then, a little past ten. I should have known better, but it shows that you can't trust ten-year-olds. I never got punished for that because Mom never did find out.

And so, with Eleanor's version, Donna had the core family story: four sisters spent the day on the roof with their six-month-old baby sister while their mother and father mowed the fields. Each sister provided her own variation. One remembers that the parents were mowing hay; another insists they were cutting oats. Such details would also change the time of the story from June to late summer or early fall. The sisters debate other details. Donna's mother rejects the idea that they got a ladder from the barn, saying they climbed on a chair or rain barrel to reach the lower part of the farmhouse roof, which was accessible from their bedrooms. Another of the sisters tells the story as if she remained on the ground while the others climbed to the roof. When they challenge her version, this sister admits that she probably did follow the others. She confesses jealousy of the new baby: until then, she had been the baby of the family. "They weren't worried about me," she recalls. "They were only worried about Mary, the baby."

Mary's version of the story deviates the most. She claims that she fell off the roof and that her sisters climbed down and put her "right back on." Because Mary's variant has no support from the other sisters, she retreats by saying, "Maybe I just dreamed that, but it seems like I fell off when I was up there. Of course, I wasn't really old enough to remember."

FIGURE 10.2 The Riggs family farmhouse

After recording and transcribing all five versions of this story, Donna proposes that the "baby on the roof" story displays defiance of authority and rebellion against rules for these otherwise compliant farm girls. She also thinks that the story illustrates "pluck and adventure," as no harm was actually done. Donna admits that her mother and aunts would deny that these stories convey any meaning other than "pure entertainment" and confesses that any analysis of the meaning of these stories is her own. She recognizes that each sister embellished the story based on her family reputation, individual temperament, and storytelling ability. Donna's conclusions are consistent with what we know: that a story has a stable core of details but also many variants according to the tellers.

DISCOVER CORE DETAILS IN YOUR INFORMANTS' STORIES

Use the following questions to uncover the core details of your informants' stories:

- What facts are stable?
- What's the chronology of the story?
- What characters are key?
- What is the central conflict in the story?
- What is the theme?
- Does the story contain a cultural message or lesson?

Donna followed several important steps in gathering her family stories, steps that any fieldworker considers:

- She conducted preliminary research by interviewing the people involved—in this case, her mother and aunts. Had they all told the same story, the project would not have illustrated the core and variants inherent in family stories.
- She interviewed her informants in their own home settings, making all participants comfortable as she recorded and asked questions. She didn't rush her project; she allowed time for scheduling, visiting, interviewing, transcribing, sharing the transcripts, and writing her paper.
- She triangulated her data in two ways. First, by checking the five stories against one another, she could see how one story might verify another or disconfirm it. She shared her work with the sisters as she went along and afterward so that they might confirm, disconfirm, or add to each other's stories.
- She acknowledged the importance of her informants' participation. In this case, as they were her relatives, she presented her essay in a family album complete with photos of the old farmhouse as a gift in return for the time and energy they spent helping her learn how to listen to family stories. This kind of **reciprocity** is crucial to the ethics of fieldworking.

Stories that are passed down within a culture help to shape a culture's self-identity. But it's also true that the variants (each teller's version) of a story can explain even more. Knowing how the variants differ helps us find clues about informants, their worldviews, and how a culture has changed over time. If you are working in a fieldsite, you will want to find any important stories that have come out of a shared event, an important moment, or a special person whom everyone knows.

In your own work, it is important to record each teller's version as audio or video or by careful word-for-word notetaking. Whether you record several versions of one story or several stories about one event, you will need to look for the unchanging core elements as well as the variants' details. After gathering stories, analyze your data. Here are some things to look for.

DISCOVER THE VARIANTS IN YOUR INFORMANTS' STORIES

Use the following questions to uncover the variants in your informants' stories:

- What are the features that change?
- Why do those features change?
- What do the variants suggest about the tellers?
- What do the variants suggest about their audiences?

You may want to find some features that don't fit the other versions, and those will provide clues about the teller's positions and attitudes toward the story and the cultural themes that the story contains.

Gathering Oral Histories

In an oral history, the fieldworker gathers real-life stories about the past experiences of a particular person, family, region, occupation, craft, skill, or topic. The fieldworker records spoken recollections and personal reflections from living people about their past lives, creating a history.

Anthropological fieldworkers who record an entire life's history as well as speculate on the relationship between that life and the culture it represents are called **ethnohistorians**, and their studies span many years. Over ten years' time, folklorist Henry Glassie visited, interviewed, and wrote about one four-square-mile Irish community in *Passing the Time in Balleymenone*. Shirley Brice Heath, a linguist, researched literacy in the Piedmonts of the southeastern United States for her study *Ways with Words*, and spent 14 years gathering data from parents, teachers, and children there. Anthropologist Ruth Behar traveled back and forth between the United States and Mexico for over five years and wrote a life history of Esperanza, a Mexican street peddler, in her book *Translated Woman*.

However, not all oral histories need to be full-length ethnographic studies. There are many national oral history projects, including Save Our Sounds, Story Corps, and the Veterans' Oral History project, all sponsored by the American Folklife Center of the Library of Congress. A quick Internet search reveals a range of local, national, and global projects that all use forms of oral history collection.

Gathering oral history is not new. A successful traditional project in the United States comes from a group of high school students in 1970s rural Georgia. There, teenagers documented the stories, folk arts, and crafts of elderly people in their Appalachian community, writing about moonshine, faith-healing, building log cabins, dressing hogs, and farming practices. With their teacher Eliot Wigginton, they originally published their fieldwork in the high school's *Foxfire* magazine, and later collected these articles into the now classic *Foxfire* anthologies (12 books in total), one of which gives us the eyeball story on p. 202.

In this section, we introduce you to three different varieties of oral histories: one visual, one auditory, and one textual. Our first oral historian, Nancy Hauserman, is a professor of law and ethics in the College of Business at the University of Iowa and an amateur photographer. Nancy has always been interested in the lives of people who are often invisible and ignored. In one study, she spoke to workers at University of Iowa Hospitals and Clinics, a large hospital in Iowa City, recording their perspectives on the value of their work. She also photographed them on the job. As she writes, her project combined her "love of taking photos along with a deep appreciation for the myriad kindness people do for others every day." Nancy's collection, called "Taking Care: A Recognition of Good People Doing Things," is a permanent exhibit on the walls of the hospital and has also been published as a book. Its power, we believe, comes from the artful combination of photographs of ordinary people in their workplace supported by the words of each informant. Their words are ones you might not always have the chance to hear.

We present here two of her seventeen oral history portraits, this one of Allen Reed, a custodian, followed by one of Mona Ibrahim, a dietetic clerk, both of whom talk about how they feel about their jobs.

Taking Care

NANCY HAUSERMAN

Allen Reed, Custodian

I work second shift with the project crew. I pick up already bagged trash and make it disappear. I strip and wax hardwood floors, clean carpet, move furniture before and after meetings, burnish and wax floors. When I'm House Man, I do anything for anyone as needed.

Any requests I get from patients and visitors, if I can take care of it, it's with a positive attitude like "I'm gonna take care of this for ya." In fact I see somebody that's, well, you just know these people are lost. I will walk up and say, "Excuse me I'm Allen Reed. Can I give you some assistance?" They may say, "We're looking for Emergency." I never give directions to Emergency; I always walk them to the Emergency Room, because if you're asking for the Emergency Room, you have other things on your mind. And when some folks say, "Well, you're not going to get in trouble are you?" I tell them, "It's not a problem, anytime you folks need help that can be my top priority beside what I'm supposed to be doing." So I never take no for an answer; I never say I can't do it, I always look into it, and I'll work on a problem as long as it takes to get it done.

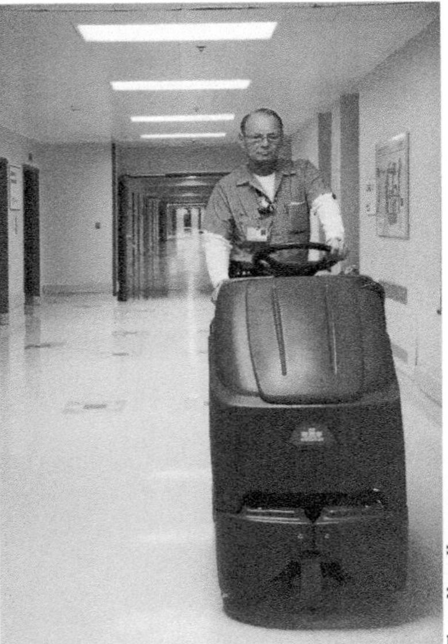

Photos: Nancy Hauserman

FIGURE 10.3 Allen Reed, custodian, University of Iowa Hospitals and Clinics

I'm here every day because I enjoy helping people. There's no time that I haven't been able to give directions or take someone where they needed to be or help a patient or a visitor out. It makes you feel like you've accomplished something at the end of the night, especially when I'm House Man and I get a lot of different calls during the night from patients or visitors. It makes a difference.

I always try to say, is this what I would want?

Mona Ibrahim, Dietetic Clerk

I take patient orders on the phone and check to make sure they are ordering according to their diets. If the food isn't on their diet, I try to suggest what they could have instead. I call patients if they don't call in for meals for a while. We use computers now, but for years it was all done by paper.

I think what I do makes it easier sometimes [for patients and families]. When patients are ordering, sometimes the family is not there. They call and ask how they should order…they don't know their diet sometimes so we try to tell them what they can have and what they can't. At the same time, sometimes they just like to talk to me on the phone. When speaking to someone for a while and they call you…the way they answer, you can tell that they feel there is someone there that they know.

You think about it as if you were in their place. They can be comforted by someone to speak to.

Photos: Nancy Hauserman

FIGURE 10.4 Mona Ibrahim, dietetic clerk

Recorded—rather than written—oral histories have their own strengths. In them, you can experience a range of linguistic features: people's actual voices, their accents, hesitations, intonations, laughter, and the overall rhythm of their speech. How many times do you wish you could bring back the voice of someone you've lost? An audio interview offers us the ability to do that. As the researcher, you choose among the recorded data about how much or how little of the informant's language you want to include. You also choose what form—electronic or print—you will present it in. No matter what technology you use or whether your recorded oral history ends up as an essay or an mp3 file, you will need to decide how to incorporate your informants' words with your own. Some oral histories present only the informants' words. But note that the editor of those words is usually the researcher. As with other data collections, most oral historians record far more words than they use, whether the final presentation is on paper or in an audio file. It may seem easy to simply record someone else's life story, but the responsibility for arranging, organizing, and editing it is still yours.

One of our favorite examples of auditory oral history is the StoryCorps project. It began in 2003, became associated with the American Folklife Center at the Library of Congress, and is now a regularly featured series on National Public Radio. Dave Isay, the founder of StoryCorps, began with a booth in Grand Central Station in New York. On the day it launched, Studs Terkel, a great oral historian of the twentieth century, proclaimed, "Today we shall begin celebrating the lives of the uncelebrated." Since then, the project has added many permanent and mobile recording studio-booths around the country. You could go to one with your boss or favorite teacher, for example, and spend 45 minutes talking with the assistance of a facilitator. You'd end up with a broadcast-quality CD for yourself—as well as contributing your story to the archive at the American Folklife Center. It is from these CDs that StoryCorps has edited three-minute oral histories and organized them into a range of topics. You can sample them at http://storycorps.org/listen.

We'd like to share one example from Isay's first collection, *Listening Is an Act of Love: A Celebration of American Life from the StoryCorps Project* (2007), recorded in Portland, Maine, between Joyce Butler, 73, and her daughter, Stephanie Butler, 47. In it, Joyce talks about her mother, who was a welder and single mom during World War II.

Listening Is an Act of Love

JOYCE BUTLER, 73, INTERVIEWED BY HER DAUGHTER, STEPHANIE BUTLER, 47

Joyce Butler: My parents divorced in 1941. In those days divorce was not as common as it is now. A divorced woman was called a "grass widow," and grass widows were scorned. There was a stigma attached, which is why it took such courage for my mother to ask for a divorce from my father. We moved to Maine Avenue in Portland.

Even though my father paid my mother money every month, it wasn't enough. She had to go to work, and she had not finished high school. So she worked in the laundry, and she finally got a job at Montgomery Ward department store on Congress Street. And we kids were more or less on our own. That was not a happy time for me—I missed my mother.

During the war, the shipyard had begun to function in South Portland, and these young women would come into the store, all dressed in these big boots and rough overalls. And they would have checks of six hundred dollars to cash for their shopping. She finally asked, "Where do you work that you make so much money?" They said, "In the shipyard." So my mother went over and tried to get a job. The man who interviewed asked if she wanted to be a welder or a burner, and my mother said, "Which pays the most?" And he said, "A welder." And she said, "That's what I want to do." And he said, "Oh, a mercenary, huh?" And she said, "No. I have four children to take care of."

Her shift was midnight to 6:00 a.m., so she could be home with us during the day. I remember her dressing in that heavy clothing and big boots—men's clothing. Once she fell and hurt her ankle, and they brought her home in the middle of the night, and she was weeping. It was awful.

It was bitter cold in the winter, going into the bowels of those steel ships. They had to wiggle into narrow crawl spaces and lay on their backs and weld overhead. She was very thin in those years, but I remember her neck and her chest, all spotted with burn marks from the sparks. They had to wear special goggles, but even so, sometimes they would have a flash condition in their eyes. She suffered from that, and they had to take her to the hospital once.

After the shipyard closed, she went back to Montgomery Ward and worked all day. And at five o'clock when she got out of Montgomery Ward, she got on a bus and worked in the S. D. Warren Paper Mill from six o'clock until midnight. Came home, got up in the morning, and went back to Montgomery Ward.

Stephanie Butler: Bless her heart.

Joyce: My mother wanted to keep us together as a family. She was determined.

Our final example is of a textually-rendered oral history and comes from the Great Depression. In the United States of the 1930s, writers were among the many unemployed. The government sponsored the Federal Writers' Project, which put writers to work as interviewers. Among them were Claude McKay, Richard Wright, Saul Bellow, Loren Eisley, and Ralph Ellison. This project's goal was to record the life histories of ordinary American people whose stories had never been told: carpenters, cigar makers, dairy people, seamstresses, peddlers, railroad men, textile workers, salesladies, and chicken farmers were among the informants.

One collection of these life histories, *These Are Our Lives* (1939), assembled by R. R. Humphries for the Federal Writers' Project, includes the life story of Lee Lincoln, a man who learns to read and write as an adult. The fieldworker, Jennette Edwards, inserts her own observations and description into the interview while quoting Lee's words directly as she collected them. As you read Edwards' piece "I Can Read and I Can Write" (available on Canvas), remember it was written in 1939, when black Americans were called Negroes, when jobs were difficult to get, and $65 a month was a decent living. You may want to think about other cultural assumptions, attitudes, and beliefs that have changed in the past decades.

BOX 8

STARTING AN ORAL HISTORY

Purpose

Many oral histories today are gathered from ordinary people who have lived through extraordinary times and experiences. Contemporary informants can share their life histories and experiences from, for example, the women's movement, the civil rights movement, the Holocaust in Europe, or the end of apartheid in South Africa. Other oral histories can record the everyday life during an occupation that no longer exists. Studs Terkel's collections of occupational stories, *Working*, and of Depression stories, *In Hard Times*, offer examples of short histories from real people whose voices are seldom heard or recorded.

Possible projects for an oral history are limited only by your imagination and access to the people you wish to interview. Many people begin an oral history by interviewing their relatives, friends, or teachers about living through a particular era or a time of personal struggle that resulted in dramatic life changes. Perhaps you know someone who's lived through a major catastrophe (such as an earthquake or a flood) or someone who's been caught personally in a political or social entanglement (like war, bankruptcy, or discrimination). Such people make good subjects for oral history.

Many local and compelling oral history projects can emerge in unexpected places and on unexpected topics. Think about someone you know who has a particular skill, such as cooking ethnic food, whittling wooden figures, weaving, or embroidering, or an unusual hobby such as clogging, playing the bagpipes, or raising llamas. Someone's lifelong passion can yield fascinating oral histories. Good subjects for oral histories also hide in places where people spend their time alone—for example, in garages tinkering with engines or in antique shops restoring items others have discarded.

Action

If you're interested in pursuing an oral history project, spend some time interviewing someone who fascinates you. As with any other interviewing project, all of the information you record in your fieldnotes may not be what you'll use in a final write-up, but you'll need to record it nonetheless. Your choices of details will help you feature your subject without distracting the reader from the informant's own words. An elaborate oral history takes a great deal of time. We hope that what you'll learn by reading and writing oral history is that it's important to foreground the informant and her words and to background the topic, yourself, and her surroundings.

FieldWriting: Using Character, Setting, and Theme to Create a Portrait

To bring their informants to the page from a pile of data, fieldwriters must pay close attention to informants' personal characteristics and surroundings and write about details that relate to the overall themes they want to highlight. Creating verbal portraits means studying your fieldnotes, selecting your most relevant details, and drafting sentences that portray each informant against a cultural backdrop. In this chapter, the fieldwriters who give us portraits write them on the basis of carefully gathered observations from their fieldnotes and other sources and their own interpretations confirmed by their data.

Details of Character

Choosing the details to describe an interview with an informant is hard work. Fieldwriters must gather and record far more information than they will ever use because during data collection they don't know the themes they'll eventually want to highlight. Written portraits of an informant require noting the same kinds of character details that fiction writers use: physical features, material artifacts, body language, oral language patterns, and personal history. But those details are borne in fieldnotes, interviews, artifacts, and documents.

- *Physical features* (vine-shaped tattoo around wrist; brown hair with gray, neatly pulled back)
- *Material artifacts* (new Lee jeans, pale yellow sweater)
- *Body language* (sitting alone drinking beer, shooting pool)
- *Oral language patterns* (Alice and Christie discuss the bikers' treatment of women)
- *Personal history* (goes to Ralph's every day, moved from Michigan three years ago)

Details of Setting

When fieldwriters paint verbal portraits, they also create a backdrop for their informants. We call these landscapes "verbal snapshots." Setting details must be organized from notes about time, place, weather, color, and other sensory impressions at the fieldsite.

To bring her reader into Ralph's, Cindie Marshall moves from exterior to interior. She selects details of texture and space to represent Ralph's Sports Bar outside, focusing first on the parking lot.

As she moves inside, she describes tastes and smells in an atmosphere of smoke, stale beer, cigarette ashes, and body odor. Cindie also listens to the sounds from the jukebox. Her selection of details to present an image of Ralph's, a so-called sports bar, defies her earlier assumptions about such places.

Details of Theme

Fieldwriters must choose details to support the themes they want to highlight. In fieldworking, themes don't emerge directly from lists in fieldnotes, words in transcripts, or library books and collected artifacts, but such sources suggest them. Themes *do come* from active interpretation of your data, as you study it, triangulate it, organize it, reflect on it, and write about it. Themes are bigger than the actual details you record, but those details, as they cluster into categories of data and images from your observations, generate larger interpretations.

For example, in her study of Ralph's Sports Bar, Cindie's themes (PDF on Canvas) work off of the contrasts she observed within the subculture in the biker bar. She arrives at Ralph's with a mental image of what a sports bar is like, and immediately that image contrasts with the reality of this biker sports bar. As she spends more time and takes more notes, Cindie sees other contrasting themes within this subculture.

Another set of contrasting themes is that of bikers as a community of independent people who "do their own thing," but Cindie sees that within this subculture, they come together only to be separated: "I also wanted to know why three groups in a bar would come together in a place just to be segregated." Cindie interprets still another contrast when she notices that the biking subculture includes many women. Her fieldnotes report 13 people at the bar, 8 men and 5 women. But this inclusion is deceptive when her informant Teardrop describes her life as a biker woman: "What Teardrop had described was sheer abuse, and she wore that abuse both on her face, in the shape of a teardrop, and in her smile, which was darkened by missing teeth."

Fieldwriting is a skill that requires close observation, careful documentation, and the rendering of data into thick descriptions of informants within their cultural spaces. To be an accurate and sensitive fieldwriter, you'll need to manipulate your multiple data sources, call on your informants' voices, examine your reflective writing, and craft a text so that it will give your reader a sense of participating in the fieldwork you've experienced. As we collect data about people, we must continually look over what we've gathered in terms of ourselves, our informants, and the information's meaning against the larger backdrop of our research. In addition to carefully retelling our informants' stories, we need to ensure that we present the narrative situation fairly, including our own roles in it. In his book *Writing the New Ethnography*, H. L. "Bud" Goodall offers some helpful questions for researchers to ask themselves as they write up interviews, oral histories, and storytelling situations (106–7):

1. What is the context, and where are you in this scene? What is the nature of the relationship between you and your informant?
2. What's the meaning behind the recorded words? What influences your informants' and your own fixed positions? Subjective positions? What power relationship exists between you and your informant?
3. What do you hear in the way the informant speaks? What are the gaps? The tones? The rhythms? The emphases (of both you and your informant)?

In the process of collecting data about people, we must continually look over what we've gathered in terms of ourselves, our informants, and its meaning against the backdrop of our research. We bring to our narratives about our informants as much as they bring to the data we've collected about them. In addition to rendering careful verbal portraits, we need to break down the conversational context to ensure that we present it fairly.

BOX 9

WRITING A VERBAL PORTRAIT

Jennifer S. Cook, Rhode Island College

Purpose

Just as a verbal snapshot asks you to synthesize data from your fieldnotes, a verbal portrait asks you to synthesize data from your interviews. It is another way to make sense of your data.

A verbal portrait asks that you use data from your interview to paint a portrait of your participant in a brief piece of writing (500 words) that is rich with description, illustrative quotes (carefully selected), and thoughtful (but spare) commentary.

In crafting your portrait, you are making choices about what to include and exclude, about what to reveal and what to ignore. These kinds of editorial choices are a way for you to interpret your interview data. Additionally, you need to include some evaluation or assessment (analysis) of the person and his or her role in the subculture you are studying. In asking yourself, "What was the essence of this interview?" you also need to ask, "What is the essence of this person?" Both of these questions are central to the kinds of analysis you should include in your verbal portrait.

Action

To craft your verbal portrait, you need not only interview data and analysis (an interview transcript you have analyzed) but also a description of your participant. Your job here is to create an image in the minds of your readers. It also helps to have "supporting data"—that is, details about the time of day, the weather, the location of the interview, and a description of the space, as well as other significant details about context. Once you have these essential ingredients, you can begin to sketch a portrait of your participant. Remember that your overarching goal here is to capture the essence of the person, his words, and what he means to the fieldstudy.

Once you have sketched your portrait, share it with a colleague or classmate to see if you have successfully communicated the essence of this person and his role in the subculture. You may ask your reader to keep these questions in mind as she reads.

- What images or details from this piece create the most vivid impressions?
- What "clues" do you get from this piece about the essence of this subculture?
- What clutter can I omit to make this piece stronger or clearer?
- What would you like to know more about? Where can I provide more detail and information?

The Research Portfolio: Reflective Documentation

Whether you've chosen to learn to research people by continuing your major fieldwork project or by trying separate short studies, we hope you've seen that the researcher-informant relationship is a symbiotic one. It is full of interaction, collaboration, and mutual teaching and learning. In this chapter, we focus on how people are a dominant source of data in the field—through family stories, remembered histories, responses to questions, the personal artifacts they consider important, and your own observation of them.

The research portfolio is an important place to record, keep track of, and make sense of the skills you've learned, the routines and organization you've used, and your responses to readings that illustrate how other fieldworkers have written about their work. Listing and categorizing your research processes illustrate your progress as a fieldworker. We like to call this charting process "reflective documentation."

For your portfolio, try listing, mapping, outlining, or charting the skills you've learned and the variety and amounts of material you've gathered. You may want to document each of your projects from this chapter separately: family stories, oral histories, and interviews. Or if you are working on a large project, use the questions to document what is relevant to your project. Here is an outline framed around fieldworking strategies. You might choose a few questions under each category, try to work with them all, or document your work in a different way:

I. Prepare for the field.

   A. What did you read to prepare for your fieldwork? Where did you find it?

   B. What did you learn from reading the fieldwork of others?

   C. How did you select your informants? How did you prepare before meeting them?

   D. How did you gain access to your informants and your fieldsites? Were there any problems? What might you do differently next time?

   E. What assumptions did you have going into the field? How did you record them? What did you expect to see, and what did you actually find?

II. Use the researcher's tools.

   A. How did you record your fieldnotes? Did you separate observational notes from personal notes? Did you invent your own method for organizing your fieldnotes?

   B. What equipment did you use? What would you want at hand if you could do this work again?

   C. How did you transcribe your recordings?

D. What interviewing skills did you develop? What skills would you like to work on?

E. What different types of data did you gather? Print sources? Cultural artifacts? Stories and interviews?

III. Interpret your fieldwork.

A. Which initial impressions turned out to be part of your final piece? Which ideas did you discard?

B. What strategies did you develop to categorize your data? Did you use patterns that were linear? Thematic? Chronological? Abstract to concrete? Concrete to abstract?

C. What strategies did you develop to analyze your data? What didn't fit?

D. What is your favorite piece of data—or data source—and why?

IV. Present your findings.

A. What decisions did you make about writing up your fieldwork?

B. How much of your voice is in the final project? How much of your informants' voices?

C. What details did you select to illustrate key points to bring your informants to life?

D. Did you use subheadings to guide your reader in your final paper or some other way to organize your material?

You might decide to use these questions to help you write an essay or commentary about your process as a researcher.

Wherever people interact in the same space, you have an opportunity to look carefully at artifacts, personal histories, traditional stories, and ways of behaving together and alone. But simply describing people as you see them does not produce sufficient data for a fieldstudy. You must use many different ways to gather their perspectives on their experiences—and do so in their voices. As you gather information about others, you'll also need to record your own feelings, responses, and reactions as you learn about them and your understanding deepens and shifts. Eventually, your responsibility is to the informants' voices, perspectives, stories, and histories—as much as it is to your own.

REFLECT ON RESEARCHING PEOPLE

Try listing the people who are present at your fieldsite. Use the following questions to guide your exploration of how they interact:

1. How many people are there? Have you talked to each of them? What connections and disconnections exist between them? How do they help each other? How do they define their roles within that culture—for themselves and for others? Who defines the roles for them?
2. What artifacts or stories have more than one person discussed with you? How have those artifacts or stories helped explain the culture or those people's places in it? How did each person talk about the artifact or tell the story? How was each story different? What was the same about the stories?
3. Whose oral histories would you like to gather? If you had time for a much longer study about your fieldsite, who else would you interview? What stories or artifacts would you want to understand? Whose personal histories would probably yield interesting information for you?

Whether or not this is your first fieldstudy, the skills of asking and listening—of collaborating in conversation with others—are lifetime skills for personal interactions with family, with friends, with coworkers, and in new cultural contexts. Practicing these skills, reflecting on what you're learning, and writing from other people's perspectives will strengthen your ability to talk, analyze, evaluate, and become a more active and knowledgeable citizen.

part 3

Reading and Understanding Arguments

CHAPTER

11

Understanding Arguments and Reading Them Critically

LEFT TO RIGHT: Paul Archuleta/Getty Images; Daily Beast; Chelsea Guglielmino/Getty Images

On October 15, 2017, actor and activist Alyssa Milano took to Twitter to issue a call to action:

Alyssa Milano
@Alyssa_Milano

If you've been sexually harassed or assaulted write 'me too' as a reply to this tweet.

Me too.

Suggested by a friend: "If all the women who have been sexually harassed or assaulted wrote 'Me too.' as a status, we might give people a sense of the magnitude of the problem."

1:21 PM - 15 Oct 2017

Milano was joining the conversation surrounding a spate of revelations about very high-profile and powerful men accused of sexual harassment: Bill Cosby, Roger Ailes, Bill O'Reilly, and Harvey Weinstein. Milano's tweet argues for standing up and speaking out—in big numbers—and her message certainly hit a nerve: within 24 hours, 4.7 million people around the world had joined the "me too" conversation, with over 12 million posts and comments. Some of these comments pointed out that the "me too" movement is actually more than ten years old: it began with activist Tarana Burke, who was directing a Girls for Gender Equity program in Brooklyn, aimed at giving voice to young women of color. As Burke told CNN after Milano's tweet went viral: "It's not about a viral campaign for me. It's about a movement."

Burke's reaction to the 2017 meme makes an important point, one that was echoed in some of the responses Milano received and further elaborated by Jessi Hempel, the editorial director of Backchannel, in "The Problem with #metoo and Viral Outrage." Hempel says that "on its surface," #metoo has what looks to be the makings of an "earnest and effective social movement." But like Burke, Hempel wonders whether #metoo will actually have the power and longevity of a true social movement. She's concerned that while millions of people are weighing in, at last, on a long-ignored issue, the campaign may not culminate in real change:

> In truth, however, #MeToo is a too-perfect meme. It harnesses social media's mechanisms to drive users (that's you and me) into escalating states of outrage while exhausting us to the point where we cannot meaningfully act.

Hempel cites extensive research by Yale professor Molly Crockett that suggests that "digital technologies may be transforming the way we experience outrage, and limiting how much we can actually change social realities." In other words, expressing outrage online lets us talk the talk but not walk the walk of actual change.

In spite of these caveats, the work begun by Tarana Burke over a decade ago and given new urgency by Alyssa Milano has led to a series of high-profile firings, and some criminal convictions, in many sectors of society, from the Hollywood film industry (Weinstein's company had to declare bankruptcy) to New York's cultural scene (the Metropolitan Opera fired its conductor, James Levine) to Congress (Senator Al Franken was forced to resign his seat) to the world of sports (Olympics team doctor Larry Nassar was sentenced to 40 to 175 years in prison for assaulting as many as 160 women athletes). In short, it now looks as though #metoo does constitute a genuine movement that will continue to lead to actual, concrete changes in cultural attitudes and practices. Certainly, the argument over its effectiveness and reach will continue, much of it playing out on social media platforms.

As this example shows, arguments on social media occur on crowded, two-way channels, with claims and counterclaims whizzing by, fast and furious. Such tools reach audiences (like the 4.7 million who initially responded to #metoo) and they also create them, offering an innovative way to make and share arguments. Just as importantly, anyone, anywhere, with access to a phone, tablet, or other electronic device, can launch arguments that circle the globe in seconds. Social networking and digital tools are increasingly available to all—for better or for worse, as shown by the recent example of Facebook's allowing data from 50 million users to be used for political purposes.

Everything Is an Argument

As you know from your own experiences with social media, arguments are all around us, in every medium, in every genre, in everything we do. There may be an argument on the T-shirt you put on in the morning, in the sports column you read on the bus, in the prayers you utter before an exam, in the off-the-cuff political remarks of a teacher lecturing, on the bumper sticker on the car in front of you, in the assurances of a health center nurse that "This won't hurt one bit."

The clothes you wear, the foods you eat, and the groups you join make nuanced, sometimes unspoken assertions about who you are and what you value. So an argument can be any text—written, spoken, aural, or visual—that expresses a point of view. In fact, some theorists claim that language is inherently persuasive. When you say, "Hi, how's it going?" in one sense you're arguing that your hello deserves a response. Even humor makes an argument when it causes readers to recognize—through bursts of laughter or just a faint smile—how things are and how they might be different.

More obvious as arguments are those that make direct claims based on or drawn from evidence. Such writing often moves readers to recognize problems and to consider solutions. Persuasion of this kind is usually easy to recognize:

> The National Minimum Drinking Age Act, passed by Congress [in 1984], is a gross violation of civil liberties and must be repealed. It is absurd and unjust that young Americans can vote, marry, enter contracts, and serve in the military at 18 but cannot buy an alcoholic drink in a bar or restaurant.
>
> —Camille Paglia, "The Drinking Age Is Past Its Prime"

> We will become a society of a million pictures without much memory, a society that looks forward every second to an immediate replication of what it has just done, but one that does not sustain the difficult labor of transmitting culture from one generation to the next.
>
> —Christine Rosen, "The Image Culture"

RESPOND

Can an argument really be any text that expresses a point of view? What kinds of arguments—if any—might be made by the following items?

a Golden State Warriors cap

Nike Air Zoom Pegasus 34

the "explicit lyrics" label on a best-selling rap CD

the health warnings on a package of cigarettes

a Tesla Model 3 electric car

a pair of Ray-Ban sunglasses

Why Read Arguments Critically and Rhetorically?

More than two millennia ago, Aristotle told students that they needed to know and understand and use the arts of rhetoric for two major reasons: to be able to get their ideas across effectively and persuasively and to protect themselves from being manipulated by others. Today, we need these abilities more than ever before: as we are inundated with "alternative facts," "fake news," mis- and disinformation, and often even outright lies, the ability to read between the lines, to become fact-checkers, to practice what media critic Howard Rheingold calls "crap detection" (see p. 448), and to read with careful attention are now survival skills.

Steve Nease

This need is so acute that new courses are springing up on college campuses, such as one at the University of Washington named (provocatively) "Calling Bullshit," which Professors Carl Bergstrom and Jevin West define as "language, statistical figures, graphics, and other forms of presentation intended to persuade by impressing and overwhelming a reader or listener with a blatant disregard for truth and logical coherence." (Search for "The Fine Art of Sniffing Out Crappy Science" on the Web.) These professors are particularly interested in the use of statistics and visual representation of data to misinform or confuse, and in showing how "big data" especially can often obscure rather than reveal valid claims, although they acknowledge the power of verbal misinformation as well.

You can practice self-defense against such misrepresentation by following some sound advice:

- Pay attention, *close* attention, to what you are reading or viewing. While it's tempting to skim, avoid the temptation, especially when the stakes are high. Keep focused on the text at hand, with your critical antenna up!
- Keep an eye out for "click bait," those subject lines or headings that scream "read me, read me" but usually lead to little information.
- Be skeptical. Check the author, publisher, sources: how reliable are they?
- Look for unstated assumptions behind claims—and question them.
- Distinguish between facts that have verifiable support and claims and those which may or may not be completely empty.
- Learn to triangulate: don't take the word of a single source but look for corroboration from other reliable sources.
- Become a fact checker! Get familiar with nonpartisan fact-checkers like Politifact, FactCheck.org, the Sunlight Foundation, and Snopes.com.

You will find additional information about reading attentively and critically throughout this book, especially in **Chapters 12 and 21**.

Why Listen to Arguments Rhetorically and Respectfully?

Rhetorician Krista Ratcliffe recommends that we all learn to listen rhetorically, which she defines as "a stance of openness" you can take in relation to any person, text, or culture. Taking such a stance is not easy, especially when emotions and disagreements run high, but doing so is a necessary step in understanding where other people are coming from and in acknowledging that our own stances are deeply influenced by forces we may not even be aware of. Even when we stand on the shoulders of giants, our view is limited and partial, and it's good to remember that this maxim is true for everyone.

Amid the extreme divisions in the United States today, amid the charges and countercharges, the ongoing attacks of one group on another, it's especially important to learn to listen to others, even others with whom we drastically disagree. Scholars and pundits alike have written about the "echo chambers" we often inhabit, especially online, where we hear only from people who think as we do, act as we act, believe as we believe. Such echo chambers are dangerous to a democracy. As a result, some are advocating for rhetorical listening. Oprah Winfrey, for example, brought together a group of women, half of whom supported Trump and half of whom supported Clinton, over "croissants and great jam." At first no one wanted to participate, but once Winfrey got them together and they started listening to one another's stories, the women began to find small patches of common ground. Listening openly and respectfully was the key. So it is with the website and app "Hi from the Other Side," where people can sign up to be paired with someone on another side of an issue, get guidance on how to begin a conversation, and eventually meet to pursue common ground and common interests (see https://www.hifromtheotherside.com for more information).

You can begin to practice rhetorical listening as you get to know people who differ from you on major issues, listening to their views carefully and respectfully, asking them for that same respect, and beginning to search for some common ground, no matter how small. Arguments are never won by going nowhere except "Yes I can"/"No you can't" over and over again, yet that's the way many arguments are conducted today. Learning to listen rhetorically and beginning to find some small commonality is usually a better way to argue constructively than plunging right in with accusations or dramatic claims.

Why We Make Arguments

As this discussion suggests, in the politically divided and entertainment-driven culture of the United States today, the word *argument* may well call up negative images: the hostile scowl, belligerent tweet, or shaking fist of a politician or news pundit who wants to drown out other voices and prevail at all costs. This winner-take-all view has a long history, but it often turns people off to the whole process of using reasoned conversation to identify, explore, and solve problems. Hoping to avoid perpetual standoffs with people on "the other side," many people now sidestep opportunities to speak their minds on issues shaping their lives and work. We want to counter this attitude throughout this book: we urge you to examine your values and beliefs, to understand where they come from, and to voice them clearly and cogently in arguments you make, all the while respecting the values and beliefs of others.

Some arguments, of course, *are* aimed at winning, especially those related to politics, business, and law. Two candidates for office, for example, vie for a majority of votes; the makers of one smartphone try to outsell their competitors by offering more features at a lower price; and two lawyers try to outwit each other in pleading to a judge and jury. In your college writing, you may also be called on to make arguments that appeal to a "judge" and "jury" (perhaps your instructor and classmates). You might, for instance, argue that students in every field should be required to engage in service learning projects. In doing so, you will need to offer better arguments or more convincing evidence than those with other perspectives—such as those who might regard service learning as a politicized or coercive form of education. You can do so reasonably and responsibly, no name-calling required.

There are many reasons to argue and principled ways to do so. We explore some of them in this section.

Arguments to Convince and Inform

We're stepping into an argument ourselves in drawing what we hope is a useful distinction between *convincing* and—in the next section—*persuading*. (Feel free to disagree with us!) Arguments to convince lead audiences to accept a claim as true or reasonable—based on information or evidence that seems factual and reliable; arguments to persuade then seek to move people beyond conviction to *action*. Academic arguments often combine both elements.

Many news reports and analyses, white papers, and academic articles aim to convince audiences by broadening what they know about a subject. Such fact-based arguments might have no motives beyond laying out what the facts are. Here's an opening paragraph from a 2014 news story by Anahad O'Connor in the *New York Times* that itself launched a thousand arguments (and lots of huzzahs) simply by reporting the results of a recent scientific study:

> Many of us have long been told that saturated fat, the type found in meat, butter and cheese, causes heart disease. But a large and exhaustive new analysis by a team of international scientists found no evidence that eating saturated fat increased heart attacks and other cardiac events.
>
> —Anahad O'Connor, "Study Questions Fat and Heart Disease Link"

Wow. You can imagine how carefully the reporter walked through the scientific data, knowing how this new information might be understood and repurposed by his readers.

Similarly, in a college paper on the viability of nuclear power as an alternative source of energy, you might compare the health and safety record of a nuclear plant to that of other forms of energy. Depending upon your findings and your interpretation of the data, the result of your fact-based presentation might be to raise or alleviate concerns readers have about nuclear energy. Of course, your decision to write the argument might be driven by your conviction that nuclear power is much safer than most people believe.

Today, images offer especially powerful arguments designed both to inform and to convince. For example, David Plunkert's cover art for the August 28, 2017, issue of the *New Yorker* is simple yet very striking. Plunkert, who doesn't often involve himself with political subjects, said he was prompted to do so in response to what he saw as President Trump's "weak pushback" against the hateful violence on exhibit in Charlottesville, Virginia, on August 11, 2017: "A picture does a better job showing my thoughts than words do; it can have a light touch on a subject that's extremely scary."

David Plunkert/The New Yorker © Condé Nast

Arguments to Persuade

Today, climate change may be the public issue that best illustrates the chasm that sometimes separates conviction from persuasion. Although the weight of scientific research attests to the fact that the earth is warming and that humans are responsible for a good bit of that warming, convincing people to accept this evidence and persuading them to act on it still doesn't follow easily. How then does change occur? Some theorists suggest that persuasion—understood as moving people to do more than nod in agreement—is best achieved via appeals to emotions such as fear, anger, envy, pride, sympathy, or hope. We think that's an oversimplification. The fact is that persuasive arguments, whether in advertisements, political blogs, YouTube videos, tweets, or newspaper editorials, draw upon *all* the appeals of rhetoric (see p. 250) to motivate people to act—whether it be to buy a product, pull a lever for a candidate, or volunteer for a civic organization. Here, once again, is Camille Paglia driving home her argument that the 1984 federal law raising the drinking age in the United States to 21 was a catastrophic decision in need of reversal:

> What this cruel 1984 law did is deprive young people of safe spaces where they could happily drink cheap beer, socialize, chat, and flirt in a free but controlled public environment. Hence in the 1980s we immediately got the scourge of crude binge drinking at campus fraternity keg parties, cut off from the adult world. Women in that boorish free-for-all were suddenly fighting off date rape. Club drugs—Ecstasy, methamphetamine, ketamine (a veterinary tranquilizer)—surged at raves for teenagers and on the gay male circuit scene.

Paglia chooses to dramatize her argument by sharply contrasting a safer, more supportive past with a vastly more dangerous present when drinking was forced underground and young people turned to highly risky behaviors. She doesn't hesitate to name them either: binge drinking, club drugs, raves, and, most seriously, date rape. This highly rhetorical, one might say *emotional*, argument pushes readers hard to endorse a call for serious action—the repeal of the current drinking age law.

WPA Pool/Getty Images

Admit it, Duchess of Cornwall. You *knew* abandoned dogs need homes, but it was heartrending photos on the Battersea Dogs & Cats Home Web site that *persuaded* you to visit the shelter.

RESPOND

Apply the distinction made here between convincing and persuading to the way people respond to two or three current political or social issues. Is there a useful distinction between being convinced and being persuaded? Explain your position.

Arguments to Make Decisions

Closely allied to arguments to convince and persuade are arguments to examine the options in important matters, both civil and personal—from managing out-of-control deficits to choosing careers. Arguments to make decisions occur all the time in the public arena, where they are often slow to evolve, caught up in electoral or legal squabbles, and yet driven by a genuine desire to find consensus. In recent years, for instance, Americans have argued hard to make decisions about health care, the civil rights of same-sex couples, and the status of more than 11 million undocumented immigrants in the country. Subjects so complex aren't debated in straight lines. They get haggled over in every imaginable medium by thousands of writers, politicians, and ordinary citizens working alone or via political organizations to have their ideas considered.

For college students, choosing a major can be an especially momentous personal decision, and one way to go about making that decision is to argue your way through several alternatives. By the time you've explored the pros and cons of each alternative, you should be a little closer to a reasonable and defensible decision.

Sometimes decisions, however, are not so easy to make.

Ed Fischer/CartoonStock.com

Arguments to Understand and Explore

Arguments to make decisions often begin as choices between opposing positions already set in stone. But is it possible to examine important issues in more open-ended ways? Many situations, again in civil or personal arenas, seem to call for arguments that genuinely explore possibilities without constraints or prejudices. If there's an "opponent" in such situations at all (often there is not), it's likely to be the status quo or a current trend which, for one reason or another, puzzles just about everyone. For example, in trying to sort through the extraordinary complexities of the 2011 budget debate, philosophy professor Gary Gutting was able to show how two distinguished economists—John Taylor and Paul Krugman—drew completely different conclusions from the exact same sets of facts. Exploring how such a thing could occur led Gutting to conclude that the two economists were arguing from the same facts, all right, but that they did not have *all* the facts possible. Those missing or unknown facts allowed them to fill in the blanks as they could, thus leading them to different conclusions. By discovering the source of a paradox, Gutting potentially opened new avenues for understanding.

Exploratory arguments can also be personal, such as Zora Neale Hurston's ironic exploration of racism and of her own identity in the essay "How It Feels to Be Colored Me." If you keep a journal or blog, you have no doubt found yourself making arguments to explore issues near and dear to you. Perhaps the essential argument in any such piece is the writer's realization that a problem exists—and that the writer or reader needs to understand it and respond constructively to it if possible.

Explorations of ideas that begin by trying to understand another's perspective have been described as **invitational arguments** by researchers Sonja Foss, Cindy Griffin, and Josina Makau. Such arguments are interested in inviting others to join in mutual explorations of ideas based on discovery and respect. Another kind of argument, called **Rogerian argument** (after psychotherapist Carl Rogers), approaches audiences in similarly nonthreatening ways, finding common ground and establishing trust among those who disagree about issues. Writers who take a Rogerian approach try to see where the other person is coming from, looking for "both/and" or "win/win" solutions whenever possible.

"You say it's a win-win, but what if you're wrong-wrong and it all goes bad-bad?"

FIGURE 11.1 The risks of Rogerian argument

RESPOND

What are your reasons for making arguments? Keep notes for two days about every single argument you make, using our broad definition to guide you. Then identify your reasons: How many times did you aim to convince? To inform? To persuade? To explore? To understand?

Occasions for Argument

In a fifth-century BCE textbook of **rhetoric** (the art of persuasion), the philosopher Aristotle provides an ingenious strategy for classifying arguments based on their perspective on time—past, future, and present. His ideas still help us to appreciate the role arguments play in society in the twenty-first century. As you consider Aristotle's occasions for argument, remember that all such classifications overlap (to a certain extent) and that we live in a world much different than his.

Arguments about the Past

Debates about what has happened in the past, what Aristotle called **forensic arguments**, are the red meat of government, courts, businesses, and academia. People want to know who did what in the past, for what reasons, and with what liability. When you argue a speeding ticket in court, you are making a forensic argument, claiming perhaps that you weren't over the limit or that the officer's radar was faulty. A judge will have to decide what exactly happened in the past in the unlikely case you push the issue that far.

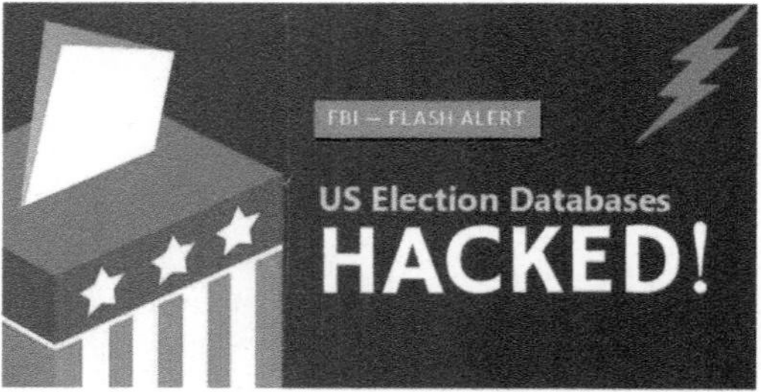

In the aftermath of the 2016 election, many researchers both in and outside the government devoted themselves to trying to understand the effects of hacking on the election and, more specifically, the extent to which Russia was involved in such activities. Cybersecurity experts from agencies such as the CIA, FBI, and Homeland Security argued that they had extensive evidence to show that Russia had conducted a number of hacking expeditions and had manipulated messages on social media to try to disrupt the American elections. Others inside the Trump administration argued that the evidence wasn't convincing; the president even declared that it had been "made up." As this book goes to press, the argument over what happened is still raging. What hacks actually occurred in the run-up to the election? Which state voting procedures, if any, were violated? What part did the Russian government play? These are all forensic questions to be carefully investigated, argued, and answered by agencies and special counsels currently at work.

Some forensic arguments go on...and on and on. Consider, for example, the lingering arguments over Christopher Columbus's "discovery" of America. Are his expeditions cause for celebration or notably unhappy chapters in human history? Or some of both? Such arguments about past actions—heated enough to spill over into the public realm—are common in disciplines such as history, philosophy, and ethics.

Chip Somodevilla/Getty Images

FIGURE 11.2 James B. Comey, former director of the FBI who was fired by President Trump, testifies before the Senate Intelligence Committee on June 8, 2017.

Arguments about the Future

Debates about what will or should happen in the future—**deliberative arguments**—often influence policies or legislation for the future. *Should local or state governments allow or even encourage the use of self-driving cars on public roads? Should colleges and universities lend support to more dual-credit programs so that students can earn college credits while still in high school? Should coal-fired power plants be phased out of our energy grid?* These are the sorts of deliberative questions that legislatures, committees, or school boards routinely address when making laws or establishing policies.

But arguments about the future can also be speculative, advancing by means of projections and reasoned guesses, as shown in the following passage from an essay by media analyst Marc Prensky. He argues that while professors and colleges will always be responsible for teaching students to learn from the knowledge provided by print texts, it's about time for some college or university to be the first to ban physical, that is to say *paper*, books on its campus, a controversial proposal to say the least:

> So, as counterintuitive as it may sound, eliminating physical books from college campuses would be a positive step for our 21st-century students, and, I believe, for 21st-century scholarship as well. Academics, researchers, and particularly teachers need to move to the tools of the future. Artifacts belong in museums, not in our institutions of higher learning.
>
> —Marc Prensky, "In the 21st-Century University, Let's Ban Books"

Arguments about the Present

Arguments about the present—what Aristotle terms **epideictic** or **ceremonial arguments**—explore the current values of a society, affirming or challenging its widely shared beliefs and core assumptions. Epideictic arguments are often made at public and formal events such as inaugural addresses, sermons, eulogies, memorials, and graduation speeches. Members of the audience listen carefully as credible speakers share their wisdom. For example, as the selection of college commencement speakers has grown increasingly contentious, Ruth J. Simmons, the first African American woman to head an Ivy League college, used the opportunity of such an address (herself standing in for a rejected speaker) to offer a timely and ringing endorsement of free speech. Her words perfectly illustrate epideictic rhetoric:

> Universities have a special obligation to protect free speech, open discourse and the value of protest. The collision of views and ideologies is in the DNA of the academic enterprise. No collision avoidance technology is needed here. The noise from this discord may cause others to criticize the legitimacy of the academic enterprise, but how can knowledge advance without the questions that overturn misconceptions, push further into previously impenetrable areas of inquiry and assure us stunning breakthroughs in human knowledge? If there is anything that colleges must encourage and protect it is the persistent questioning of the status quo. Our health as a nation, our health as women, our health as an industry requires it.
>
> —Ruth J. Simmons, Smith College, 2014

Perhaps more common than Simmons's impassioned address are values arguments that examine contemporary culture, praising what's admirable and blaming what's not. In the following argument, student Latisha Chisholm looks at the state of rap music after Tupac Shakur:

> With the death of Tupac, not only did one of the most intriguing rap rivalries of all time die, but the motivation for rapping seems to have changed. Where money had always been a plus, now it is obviously more important than wanting to express the hardships of Black communities. With current rappers, the positive power that came from the desire to represent Black people is lost. One of the biggest rappers now got his big break while talking about sneakers. Others announce retirement without really having done much for the soul or for Black people's morale. I equate new rappers to NFL players that don't love the game anymore. They're only in it for the money.…It looks like the voice of a people has lost its heart.
>
> —Latisha Chisholm, "Has Rap Lost Its Soul?"

As in many ceremonial arguments, Chisholm here reinforces common values such as representing one's community honorably and fairly.

Michael N. Todaro/Getty Images

FIGURE 11.3 Are rappers since Tupac—like Jay Z—only in it for the money? Many epideictic arguments either praise or blame contemporary culture in this way.

RESPOND

In a recent magazine, newspaper, or blog, find three editorials—one that makes a forensic argument, one a deliberative argument, and one a ceremonial argument. Analyze the arguments by asking these questions: Who is arguing? What purposes are the writers trying to achieve? To whom are they directing their arguments? Then decide whether the arguments' purposes have been achieved and how you know.

Occasions for Argument

	PAST	FUTURE	PRESENT
What is it called?	Forensic	Deliberative	Epideictic
What are its concerns?	What happened in the past?	What should be done in the future?	Who or what deserves praise or blame?
What does it look like?	Court decisions, legal briefs, legislative hearings, investigative reports, academic studies	White papers, proposals, bills, regulations, mandates	Eulogies, graduation speeches, inaugural addresses, roasts

Kinds of Argument

Yet another way of categorizing arguments is to consider their status or stasis—that is, the specific *kinds of issues they address*. This approach, called **stasis theory**, was used in ancient Greek and Roman civilizations to provide questions designed to help citizens and lawyers work their way through legal cases. The status questions were posed in sequence because each depended on answers from the preceding ones. Together, the queries helped determine the point of contention in an argument—where the parties disagreed or what exactly had to be proven. A modern version of those questions might look like the following:

- Did something happen?
- What is its nature?
- What is its quality or cause?
- What actions should be taken?

Each stasis question explores a different aspect of a problem and uses different evidence or techniques to reach conclusions. You can use these questions to explore the aspects of any topic you're considering. You'll discover that we use stasis theory to define key types of argument in **Part 4**.

Did Something Happen? Arguments of Fact

There's no point in arguing a case until its basic facts are established. So an **argument of fact** usually involves a statement that can be proved or disproved with specific evidence or testimony. For example, the question of pollution of the oceans—is it really occurring?—might seem relatively easy to settle. Either scientific data prove that the oceans are being dirtied as a result of human activity, or they don't. But to settle the matter, writers and readers need to ask a number of other questions about the "facts":

- Where did the facts come from?
- Are they reliable?
- Is there a problem with the facts?
- Where did the problem begin and what caused it?

For more on arguments based on facts, see **Chapters 15 and 27**.

What Is the Nature of the Thing? Arguments of Definition

Some of the most hotly debated issues in American life today involve questions of definition: we argue over the nature of the human fetus, the meaning of "amnesty" for immigrants, the boundaries of sexual assault. As you might guess, issues of definition have mighty consequences, and decades of debate may nonetheless leave the matter unresolved. Here, for example, is how one type of sexual assault is defined in an important 2007 report submitted to the U.S. Department of Justice by the National Institute of Justice:

> We consider as incapacitated sexual assault any unwanted sexual contact occurring when a victim is unable to provide consent or stop what is happening because she is passed out, drugged, drunk, incapacitated, or asleep, regardless of whether the perpetrator was responsible for her substance use or whether substances were administered without her knowledge. We break down incapacitated sexual assault into four subtypes....
>
> —"The Campus Sexual Assault (CSA) Study: Final Report"

The specifications of the definition go on for another two hundred words, each of consequence in determining how sexual assault on college campuses might be understood, measured, and addressed.

Of course many **arguments of definition** are less weighty than this, though still hotly contested: Is playing video games a sport? Can Batman be a tragic figure? Is LeBron James a hero for our age? (For more about arguments of definition, see **Chapter 16**.)

What Is the Quality or Cause of the Thing? Arguments of Evaluation

Arguments of evaluation present criteria and then measure individual people, ideas, or things against those standards. For instance, a 2017 article in the *Atlantic* examined "How Pixar Lost Its Way," arguing that "The golden age of Pixar is over." Chronicling the company's success from the first *Toy Story* (1995), the writer identifies what Pixar accomplished so well:

> The theme that the studio mined with greatest success during its first decade and a half was parenthood, whether real (Finding Nemo, The Incredibles) or implicit (Monsters, Inc., Up). Pixar's distinctive insight into parent-child relations stood out from the start, in Toy Story, and lost none of its power in two innovative and unified sequels.
>
> —Christopher Orr, "How Pixar Lost Its Way"

As we read this article, we are bound to ask what happened: why and how did Pixar lose its way? And Christopher Orr probes further, suggesting that the sale of Pixar to Disney and the dependence on sequel after sequel led to the downturn. As he concludes his analysis of Pixar's evolution, Orr distressingly notes the announcement of plans for *Toy Story 4*, which unravels the trilogy's neat arc.

Zohar Lazar

For much more about arguments of evaluation, see **Chapter 17**.

What Actions Should Be Taken? Proposal Arguments

After facts in a controversy have been confirmed, definitions agreed on, evaluations made, and causes traced, it may be time for a **proposal argument** answering the question *Now, what do we do about all this?* For example, in developing an argument about out-of-control student fees at your college, you might use all the prior stasis questions to study the issue and determine exactly how much and for what reasons these costs are escalating. Only then will you be prepared to offer knowledgeable suggestions for action. In examining a nationwide move to eliminate remedial education in four-year colleges, John Cloud offers a notably moderate proposal to address the problem:

> Students age twenty-two and over account for 43 percent of those in remedial classrooms, according to the National Center for Developmental Education.... [But] 55 percent of those needing remediation must take just one course. Is it too much to ask them to pay extra for that class or take it at a community college?
>
> —John Cloud, "Who's Ready for College?"

For more about proposal arguments, see **Chapter 18**.

FIGURE 11.4 The No Child Left Behind Act was signed in 2002 with great hopes and bipartisan support, but it did not lead to the successes those proposing it had hoped for.

STASIS QUESTIONS AT WORK

Suppose you have an opportunity to speak at a student conference on the impact of climate change. You are tentatively in favor of strengthening industrial pollution standards aimed at reducing global warming trends. But to learn more about the issue, you use the stasis questions to get started.

- **Did something happen?** Does global warming exist? *Maybe not*, say many in the oil and gas industry; at best, evidence for global warming is inconclusive. *Yes*, say most scientists and governments; climate change is real and even seems to be accelerating. To come to your conclusion, you'll weigh the facts carefully and identify problems with opposing arguments.
- **What is the nature of the thing?** Skeptics define climate change as a naturally occurring event; most scientists base their definitions on change due to human causes. You look at each definition carefully: *How do the definitions foster the goals of each group? What's at stake for each group in defining it that way?*
- **What is the quality or cause of the thing?** Exploring the differing assessments of damage done by climate change leads you to ask who will gain from such analysis: *Do oil executives want to protect their investments? Do scientists want government money for grants? Where does evidence for the dangers of global warming come from? Who benefits if the dangers are accepted as real and present, and who loses?*
- **What actions should be taken?** If climate change is occurring naturally or causing little harm, then arguably *nothing* needs to be or can be done. But if it is caused mainly by human activity and dangers, action is definitely called for (although not everyone may agree on what such action should be). As you investigate the proposals being made and the reasons behind them, you come closer to developing your own argument.

Appealing to Audiences

Exploring all the occasions and kinds of arguments available will lead you to think about the audience(s) you are addressing and the specific ways you can appeal to them. Audiences for arguments today are amazingly diverse, from the flesh-and-blood person sitting across a desk when you negotiate a student loan to your "friends" on social media, to the "ideal" reader you imagine for whatever you are writing, to the unknown people around the world who may read a blog you have posted. The figure on the following page suggests just how many dimensions an audience can have as writers and readers negotiate their relationships with a text, whether it be oral, written, or digital.

As you see there, texts usually have **intended readers**, the people writers hope and expect to address—let's say, routine browsers of a newspaper's op-ed page. But writers also shape the responses of these actual readers in ways they imagine as appropriate or desirable—for example, maneuvering readers of editorials into making focused and knowledgeable judgments about politics and culture. Such audiences, as imagined and fashioned by writers within their texts, are called **invoked readers**.

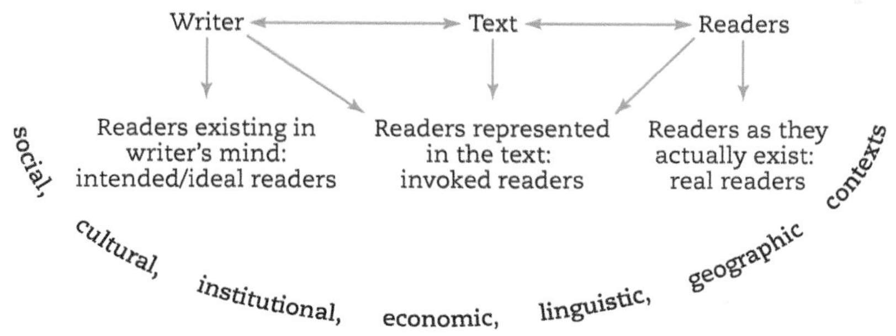

FIGURE 11.5 Readers and writers in context

Making matters even more complicated, readers can respond to writers' maneuvers by choosing to join the invoked audiences, to resist them, or maybe even to ignore them. Arguments may also attract "real" readers from groups not among those that writers originally imagined or expected to reach. You may post something on the Web, for instance, and discover that people you did not intend to address are commenting on it. (For them, the experience may be like reading private email intended for someone else: they find themselves drawn to and fascinated by your ideas!) As authors of this book, we think about students like you whenever we write: you are our intended readers. But notice how in dozens of ways, from the images we choose to the tone of our language, we also invoke an audience of people who take writing arguments seriously. We want you to become that kind of reader.

So audiences are *very* complicated and subtle and challenging, and yet you somehow have to attract and even persuade them. As always, Aristotle offers an answer. He identified three time-tested appeals that speakers and writers can use to reach almost any audience, labeling them *pathos*, *ethos*, and *logos*—strategies as effective today as they were in ancient times, though we usually think of them in slightly different terms. Used in the right way and deployed at the right moment, emotional, ethical, and logical appeals have enormous power, as we'll see in subsequent chapters.

RESPOND

You can probably provide concise descriptions of the intended audience for most textbooks you have encountered. But can you detect their invoked audiences—that is, the way their authors are imagining (and perhaps shaping) the readers they would like to have? Carefully review this entire chapter, looking for signals and strategies that might identify the audience and readers invoked by the authors of *Everything's an Argument*.

Emotional Appeals: Pathos

Emotional appeals, or **pathos**, generate emotions (fear, pity, love, anger, jealousy) that the writer hopes will lead the audience to accept a claim. Here is an alarming sentence from a book by Barry B. LePatner arguing that Americans need to make hard decisions about repairing the country's failing infrastructure:

> When the I-35W Bridge in Minneapolis shuddered, buckled, and collapsed during the evening rush hour on Wednesday, August 1, 2007, plunging 111 vehicles into the Mississippi River and sending thirteen people to their deaths, the sudden, apparently inexplicable nature of the event at first gave the appearance of an act of God.
>
> —*Too Big to Fall: America's Failing Infrastructure and the Way Forward*

If you ever drive across a bridge, LePatner has probably gotten your attention. His sober and yet descriptive language helps readers imagine the dire consequence of neglected road maintenance and bad design decisions. Making an emotional appeal like this can dramatize an issue and sometimes even create a bond between writer and readers. (For more about emotional appeals, see Chapter 25.)

Ethical Appeals: Ethos

When writers or speakers come across as trustworthy, audiences are likely to listen to and accept their arguments. That trustworthiness (along with fairness and respect) is a mark of **ethos**, or credibility. Showing that you know what you are talking about exerts an ethical appeal, as does emphasizing that you share values with and respect your audience. Once again, here's Barry LePatner from *Too Big to Fall*, shoring up his authority for writing about problems with America's roads and bridges by invoking the ethos of people even more credible:

> For those who would seek to dismiss the facts that support the thesis of this book, I ask them to consult the many professional engineers in state transportation departments who face these problems on a daily basis. These professionals understand the physics of bridge and road design, and the real problems of ignoring what happens to steel and concrete when they are exposed to the elements without a strict regimen of ongoing maintenance.

It's a sound rhetorical move to enhance credibility this way. For more about ethical appeals, see Chapter 26.

Logical Appeals: Logos

Appeals to logic, or **logos**, are often given prominence and authority in U.S. culture: "Just the facts, ma'am," a famous early TV detective on *Dragnet* used to say. Indeed, audiences respond well to the use of reasons and evidence—to the presentation of facts, statistics, credible testimony, cogent examples, or even a narrative or story that embodies a sound reason in support of an argument. Following almost two hundred pages of facts, statistics, case studies, and arguments about the sad state of American bridges, LePatner can offer this sober, logical, and inevitable conclusion:

> We can no longer afford to ignore the fact that we are in the midst of a transportation funding crisis, which has been exacerbated by an even larger and longer-term problem: how we choose to invest in our infrastructure. It is not difficult to imagine the serious consequences that will unfold if we fail to address the deplorable conditions of our bridges and roads, including the increasingly higher costs we will pay for goods and services that rely on that transportation network, and a concomitant reduction in our standard of living.

For more about logical appeals, see **Chapter 27**.

Bringing It Home: *Kairos* and the Rhetorical Situation

In Greek mythology, Kairos—the youngest son of Zeus—was the god of opportunity. He is most often depicted as running, and his most unusual characteristic is a shock of hair on his forehead. As Kairos dashes by, you have a chance to seize that lock of hair, thereby seizing the opportune moment; once he passes you by, however, you've missed your chance.

Heritage Images/Getty Images

FIGURE 11.6 *Time as Occasion (Kairos)* by Italian Renaissance painter Francesco de' Rossi

Kairos is also a term used to describe the most suitable time and place for making an argument and the most opportune ways of expressing it. It is easy to point to rhetorical moments, when speakers find exactly the right words to stir—and stir up—an audience: Franklin Roosevelt's "We have nothing to fear but fear itself," Ronald Reagan's "Mr. Gorbachev, tear down this wall," and of course Martin Luther King Jr.'s majestic "I have a dream. . . ." But *kairos* matters just as much in less dramatic situations, whenever speakers or writers must size up the core elements of a rhetorical situation to decide how best to make their expertise and ethos work for a particular message aimed at a specific audience. The diagram below hints at the dynamic complexity of the rhetorical situation.

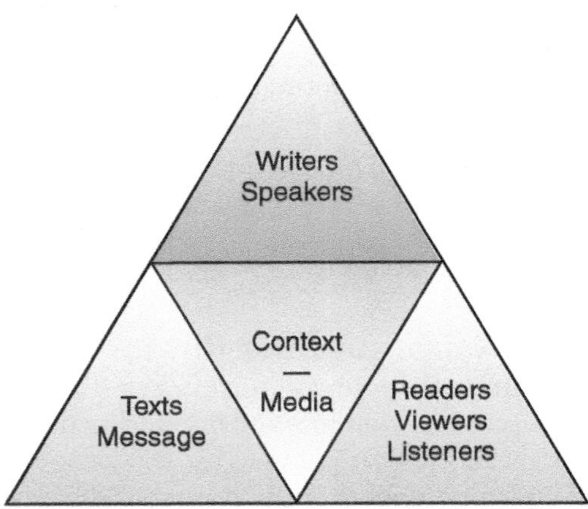

FIGURE 11.7 The rhetorical situation

But rhetorical situations are embedded in contexts of enormous social complexity. The moment you find a subject, you inherit all the knowledge, history, culture, and technological significations that surround it. To lesser and greater degrees (depending on the subject), you also bring personal circumstances into the field—perhaps your gender, your race, your religion, your economic class, your habits of language. And all those issues weigh also upon the people you write to and for.

So considering your rhetorical situation calls on you to think hard about the notion of *kairos*. Being aware of your rhetorical moment means being able to understand and take advantage of dynamic, shifting circumstances and to choose the best (most timely) proofs and evidence for a particular place, situation, and audience. It means seizing moments and enjoying opportunities, not being overwhelmed by them. Doing so might even lead you to challenge the title of this text: *is* everything an argument?

That's what makes writing arguments exciting.

RESPOND

Take a look at the bumper sticker below, and then analyze it. What is its purpose? What kind of argument is it? Which of the stasis questions does it most appropriately respond to? To what audiences does it appeal? What appeals does it make and how?

filo/Getty Images

CULTURAL CONTEXTS FOR ARGUMENT

Considering What's "Normal"

If you want to communicate effectively with people across cultures, then learn about the traditions in those cultures and examine the norms guiding your own behavior:

- Explore your assumptions! Most of us regard our ways of thinking as "normal" or "right." Such assumptions guide our judgments about what works in persuasive situations. But just because it may seem natural to speak bluntly in arguments, consider that others may find such aggression startling or even alarming.
- Remember: ways of arguing differ widely across cultures. Pay attention to how people from groups or cultures other than your own argue, and be sensitive to different paths of thinking you'll encounter as well as to differences in language.
- Don't assume that all people share your cultural values, ethical principles, or political assumptions. People across the world have different ways of defining *family*, *work*, or *happiness*. As you present arguments to them, consider that they may be content with their different ways of organizing their lives and societies.
- Respect the differences among individuals *within* a given group. Don't expect that every member of a community behaves—or argues—in the same way or shares the same beliefs. Avoid thinking, for instance, that there is a single Asian, African, or Hispanic culture or that Europeans are any less diverse or more predictable than Americans or Canadians in their thinking. In other words, be skeptical of stereotypes.

CHAPTER 12

Rhetorical Analysis

Left to right: Alfred Eisenstaedt/The LIFE Picture Collection/Getty Images; Steve Debenport/Getty Images

If you watched the 2016 Super Bowl between the Carolina Panthers and the Denver Broncos, you may remember the commercial in which the images above appeared. For a full 60 seconds, "Portraits"—which celebrates the seventy-fifth birthday of Jeep—shows still photographs of the faces of a wide range of people, all of whom have had some connection with the iconic Jeep. B. B. King, one of the most influential blues musicians of all time, recorded a cover of the famous Duke Ellington song, "Jeep's Blues," and Marilyn Monroe rode in a Jeep when she visited troops in 1954. One of the noncelebrities in the commercial is a young woman holding her hands in front of her face; who knows what her connection might be? This advertisement, which won the Super Clio for the best ad of the 2016 Super Bowl, plays in black and white, flashing from one memorable face to another, as a voice speaks to viewers:

> I've seen things no man should bear and those that every man should dare, from the beaches of Normandy to the farthest reaches of the earth. In my life, I've lived millions of lives. I've outrun robots and danced with dinosaurs. I've faced the faces of fear, and of fortitude, and witnessed great beauty in the making. I've kept the company of kings—and queens. But I'm no royalty or saint. I've traveled, trekked, wandered, and roamed only to find myself right where I belong.

As the portraits are shown, they are occasionally joined by an image of a Jeep, and the ad closes with these lines:

Within seconds of its showing, the ad had been viewed on YouTube over 15,000 times. So how do we account for the power of such advertisements? That would be the work of a **rhetorical analysis**, the close, critical reading of a text or, in this case, a video commercial, to figure out exactly how it functions. Certainly, Iris, the ad agency that created "Portraits," counted on the strong emotional appeal of the photographs, assuming that the faces represented would stir strong sentiments, along with the lyrical words of the voiceover.

The ad's creators pushed the envelope of convention, too, by rejecting the over-the-top, schmaltzy, or super-cute techniques of other advertisements and by the muted product connection. As Super Clio commissioner Rob Reilly put it, "I liked the restraint it showed for the Super Bowl, to not use the typical tricks. Jeep could have easily shown driving footage...but they chose to show very little product and tell a great story." Another Clio juror found that the ad "credits people with intelligence and asks you to decode it." (For more information on analyzing images, see Chapter 29.)

Rhetorical analysis and critical reading also probe the contexts that surround any argument or text—its impact on a society, its deeper implications, or even what it lacks or whom it excludes. Predictably, the widely admired Jeep commercial found its share of critics. In a review of the ad for *Wired*, Jenna Garrett helps viewers understand some of the choices made by the advertisers, such as the decision to show the ad in portrait format (and thus using only a third of the TV screen) in recognition that many would be watching on cell phones and tablets (indeed, she reports, the ad looks very fine on those devices). But she then turns to faults she finds with the ad:

> Some of the photos are legitimately great, taken by the likes of celebrity photographer Martin Schoeller. But others look like vacation snapshots, and many of the Jeep images were "fan photos" taken by people doing, well, whatever. Although the photos make the point that Jeep has been everywhere and loved by everyone, the ad doesn't feel cohesive. The pictures of Terminator and T-rex, for example, were jarring, particularly the Terminator's red eyes (the only splash of color in the entire ad). And speaking from a strictly technical perspective, the photos are all over the map in terms of contrast, and some of the crops are entirely too tight.
>
> —Jenna Garrett, "Why Jeep's $10M Super Bowl Ad Only Used a Third of the Screen"

Other reviewers found the advertisement over-sentimental, even saccharine; still others noted some lack of diversity.

Whenever you undertake a rhetorical analysis, do what these reviewers did: read (and view) critically, noting every detail and asking yourself how those details affect the audience, how they build agreement or adherence to the argument—or how they do not do so. And ask plenty of questions: Why does an ad for a cell phone or breakfast sandwich make people want one immediately? How does an op-ed piece in the *Washington Post* suddenly change your long-held position on immigration? Critical reading and rhetorical analysis can help you understand and answer these questions. Dig as deep as you can into the context of the item you are analyzing, especially when you encounter puzzling, troubling, or unusually successful appeals—ethical, emotional, or logical. Ask yourself what strategies a speech, editorial, opinion column, film, or ad uses to move your heart, win your trust, and change your mind—or why, maybe, it fails to do so.

Composing a Rhetorical Analysis: Reading and Viewing Critically

You perform a rhetorical analysis by analyzing how well the components of an argument work together to persuade or move an audience. You can study arguments of any kind—advertisements (as we've seen), Web sites, editorials, political cartoons, and even songs, movies, photographs, buildings, or shopping malls. In every case, you'll need to focus your rhetorical analysis on elements that stand out or make the piece intriguing or problematic. You could begin by exploring *some* of the following issues:

- What is the purpose of this argument? What does it hope to achieve?
- Who is the audience for this argument? Who is ignored or excluded?
- What appeals or techniques does the argument use—emotional, logical, ethical?

- What type of argument is it, and how does the genre affect the argument? (You might challenge the lack of evidence in editorials, but you wouldn't make the same complaint about bumper stickers.)
- Who is making the argument? What ethos does it create, and how does it do so? What values does the ethos evoke? How does it make the writer or creator seem trustworthy?
- What authorities does the argument rely on or appeal to?
- What facts, reasoning, and evidence are used in the argument? How are they presented?
- Can you detect the use of misinformation, disinformation, "fake" news, or outright lies?
- What claims does the argument make? What issues are raised—or ignored or evaded?
- What are the contexts—social, political, historical, cultural—for this argument? Whose interests does it serve? Who gains or loses by it?
- Can you identify fallacies in the argument—emotional, ethical, or logical? (See **Chapter 13**.)
- How is the argument organized or arranged? What media does the argument use and how effectively?
- How does the language and style of the argument work to persuade an audience?

In answering questions like these, try to show *how* the key devices in an argument actually make it succeed or fail. Quote freely from a written piece, or describe the elements in a visual argument. (Annotating a visual text is one option.) Let readers know where and why an argument makes sense and where it falls apart. If you believe that an argument startles, challenges, insults, or lulls audiences, explain why that is the case and provide evidence. Don't be surprised when your rhetorical analysis itself becomes an argument. That's what it should be.

Understanding the Purpose of Arguments You Are Analyzing

To understand how well any argument works, begin with its purpose: Is it to sell running shoes? To advocate for limits to college tuition? To push a political agenda? In many cases, that purpose may be obvious. A conservative blog will likely advance right-wing causes; ads from a baby food company will likely show happy infants delighted with stewed prunes.

But some projects may hide their persuasive intentions. Perhaps you've responded to a mail survey or telephone poll only to discover that the questions are leading you to switch your cable service or buy apartment insurance. Do such stealthy arguments succeed? Do consumers resent the intrusion? Answering questions like these provides material for useful rhetorical analyses that assess the strengths, risks, and ethics of such strategies.

Understanding Who Makes an Argument

Knowing *who* is claiming *what* is key to any rhetorical analysis. That's why persuasive appeals usually have a name attached to them. Remember the statements included in TV ads during the last federal election: "Hello, I'm X—and I approve this ad"? Federal law requires such statements so we can tell the difference between ads a candidate endorses and ones sponsored by groups not even affiliated with the campaigns. Their interests and motives might be very different.

FIGURE 12.1 Senator Elizabeth Warren endorsing Kamala Harris, who won the 2016 race to replace long-time California senator Barbara Boxer

But knowing a name is just a starting place for analysis. You need to dig deeper, and you could do worse than to Google such people or groups to discover more about them. What else have they produced? Who publishes them: the *Wall Street Journal*, the blog *The Daily Kos*, or even a LiveJournal celebrity gossip site such as *Oh No They Didn't*? Check out related Web sites for information about goals, policies, contributors, and funding.

RESPOND

Describe a persuasive moment that you can recall from a speech, an editorial, an advertisement, a YouTube clip, or a blog posting. Or research one of the following famous persuasive moments and describe the circumstances—the historical situation, the issues at stake, the purpose of the argument—that make it so memorable.

Abraham Lincoln's Gettysburg Address (1863)

Elizabeth Cady Stanton's Declaration of Sentiments at the Seneca Falls Convention (1848)

Chief Tecumseh's address to General William Henry Harrison (1810)

Winston Churchill's radio addresses to the British people during World War II (1940)

Martin Luther King Jr.'s "Letter from Birmingham Jail" (1963)

Ronald Reagan's tribute to the *Challenger* astronauts (1986)

Toni Morrison's speech accepting the Nobel Prize (1993)

Former President Obama's eulogy in memory of the worshippers killed at the Emmanuel AME Church in Charleston (2015)

Identifying and Appealing to Audiences

Most arguments are composed with specific audiences in mind, and their success depends, in part, on how well their strategies, content, tone, and language meet the expectations of that audience. So your rhetorical analysis of an argumentative piece should identify its target readers or viewers (see "Appealing to Audiences," p. 250) if possible, or make an educated guess about the audience, since most arguments suggest whom they intend to reach and in what ways.

Both a flyer stapled to a bulletin board in a college dorm ("Why you shouldn't drink and drive") and a forty-foot billboard for Bud Light might be aimed at the same general population—college students. But each will adjust its appeals for the different moods of that group in different moments. For starters, the flyer will appeal to students in a serious vein, while the beer ad will probably be visually stunning and virtually text-free.

You might also examine how a writer or an argument establishes credibility with an audience. One effective means of building credibility is to show respect for your readers or viewers, especially if they may not agree with you. In introducing an article on problems facing African American women in the workplace, editor-in-chief of *Essence* Diane Weathers considers the problems that she faced with respecting all her potential readers:

> We spent more than a minute agonizing over the provocative cover line for our feature "White Women at Work." The countless stories we had heard from women across the country told us that this was a workplace issue we had to address. From my own experience at several major magazines, it was painfully obvious to me that Black and White women are not on the same track. Sure, we might all start out in the same place. But early in the game, most sisters I know become stuck—and the reasons have little to do with intelligence or drive. At some point we bump our heads against that ceiling. And while White women may complain of a glass ceiling, for us, the ceiling is concrete.
>
> So how do we tell this story without sounding whiny and paranoid, or turning off our White-female readers, staff members, advertisers and girlfriends? Our solution: Bring together real women (several of them highly successful senior corporate executives), put them in a room, promise them anonymity and let them speak their truth.
>
> —Diane Weathers, "Speaking Our Truth"

FIGURE 12.2 Retailers like Walmart build their credibility by simple "straight talk" to shoppers: we *always* have low prices. Here the use of red, white, and blue says "we're all-American," while the simple layout and direct statement (a promise, really) say they are talking the talk as well as walking the walk.

Both paragraphs affirm Weathers's determination to treat audiences fairly *and* to deal honestly with a difficult subject. The strategy would merit attention in any rhetorical analysis.

Look, too, for signals that writers share values with readers or at least understand an audience. In the following passage, writer Jack Solomon is clear about one value that he hopes readers have in common—a preference for "straight talk":

> There are some signs in the advertising world that Americans are getting fed up with fantasy advertisements and want to hear some straight talk. Weary of extravagant product claims..., consumers trained by years of advertising to distrust what they hear seem to be developing an immunity to commercials.
>
> —Jack Solomon, "Masters of Desire: The Culture of American Advertising"

But straight talk still requires common sense. If ever a major television ad seriously misread its audience, it may have been a spot that ran during the 2014 Winter Olympics for Cadillac's pricey new plug-in hybrid, the ELR. The company seemed to go out of its way to offend a great many people, foreign and domestic. As is typical strategy in rhetorical analyses, *Huffington Post*'s Carolyn Gregoire takes care to describe in detail the item she finds offensive—a shot of a man overlooking the pool in his backyard and asking why we work so hard, "For this? For stuff?":

> [I]t becomes clear that the answer to this rhetorical question is actually a big fat YES. And it gets worse. "Other countries, they work," he says. "They stroll home. They stop by the cafe. They take August off. Off."
>
> Then he reveals just what it is that makes Americans better than all those lazy, espresso-sipping foreigners.
>
> "Why aren't you like that?" he says. "Why aren't we like that? Because we're crazy, driven, hard-working believers, that's why."
>
> —Carolyn Gregoire, "Cadillac Made a Commercial about the American Dream, and It's a Nightmare"

Her conclusion then is blistering, showing how readily a rhetorical analysis becomes an argument—and subject to criticism itself:

> Cadillacs have long been a quintessentially American symbol of wealth and status. But as this commercial proves, no amount of wealth or status is a guarantee of good taste. Now, the luxury car company is selling a vision of the American Dream at its worst: Work yourself into the ground, take as little time off as possible, and buy expensive sh*t (specifically, a 2014 Cadillac ELR).

Examining Arguments Based on Emotion: Pathos

Some emotional appeals are just ploys to win over readers with a pretty face, figurative or real. You've seen ads promising an exciting life and attractive friends if only you drink the right soda or wear a particular brand of clothes. Are you fooled by such claims? Probably not, if you pause to think about them. But that's the strategy—to distract you from thought just long enough to make a bad choice. It's a move worth commenting on in a rhetorical analysis.

Yet emotions can add real muscle to arguments, too, and that's worth noting. For example, persuading people not to drink and drive by making them fear death, injury, or arrest seems like a fair use of an emotional appeal. Public service announcements often use emotion-laden images to remind drivers to think of the consequences.

In analyzing emotional appeals, judge whether the emotions raised—anger, sympathy, fear, envy, joy, love, lust—advance the claims offered. Look, for example, at these photographs of protests in Charlottesville, Virginia, over the possible removal of a statue of General Robert E. Lee.

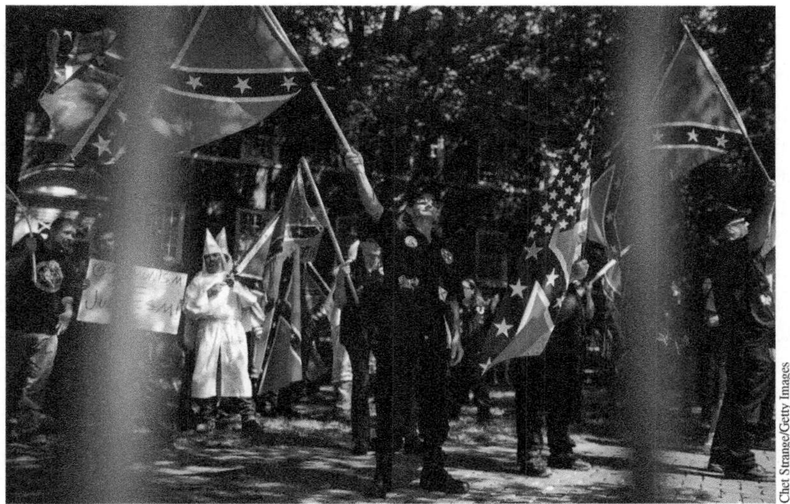

FIGURE 12.3 This photo shows proud members of the Loyal White Knights of the Ku Klux Klan, some carrying Confederate flags. What emotions do you think these protesters wanted to appeal to? What emotions does the photo stir in you?

FIGURE 12.4 Or how about this photo, from the same rally, showing counterprotesters: again, what emotions are being appealed to? How effective do you find either of these photos in appealing to your emotions?

The August 2017 rally in Charlottesville stirred emotions across the country, as ordinary people, commentators, and politicians weighed in on issues of white supremacy, neo-Nazism, fascism, race-based hatred, and bigotry. President Trump at first suggested that there was plenty of blame on "all sides," but later adjusted that statement when many accused him of drawing a false equivalency between those advocating for Nazism and those who were protesting against it.

But arguments that appeal to emotions don't have to be as highly charged—and dangerous—as the Charlottesville event was. Consider, for example, how columnist Ron Rosenbaum makes the reasonable argument he offers for fatty foods all the more attractive by loading it with emotional language:

> The foods that best hit that sweet spot and "overwhelm the brain" with pleasure are high-quality fatty foods. They discourage us from overeating. A modest serving of short ribs or Peking duck will be both deeply pleasurable and self-limiting. As the brain swoons into insensate delight, you won't have to gorge a still-craving cortex with mediocre sensations. "Sensory-specific satiety" makes a slam-dunk case (it's science!) for eating reasonable servings of superbly satisfying fatty foods.
>
> —Ron Rosenbaum, "Let Them Eat Fat"

Does the use of evocative language ("swoons," "insensate delight," "superbly satisfying," "slam-dunk") convince you, or does it distract from considering the scientific case for "sensory-specific satiety"? Your task in a rhetorical analysis is to study an author's words, the emotions they evoke, and the claims they support and then to make this kind of judgment.

Chicago Tribune/Getty Images

FIGURE 12.5 Short ribs: health food? Who does this photo appeal to—and who might it turn off?

RESPOND

Browse YouTube or another Web site to find an example of a powerful emotional argument that's made visually, either alone or using words as well. In a paragraph, defend a claim about how the argument works. For example, does an image itself make a claim, or does it draw you in to consider a verbal claim? What emotion does the argument generate? How does that emotion work to persuade you?

Examining Arguments Based on Character: Ethos

It should come as no surprise: readers believe writers who seem honest, wise, and trustworthy. So in analyzing the effectiveness of an argument, look for evidence of these traits. Does the writer have the experience or authority to write on this subject? Are all claims qualified reasonably? Is evidence presented in full, not tailored to the writer's agenda? Are important objections to the author's position acknowledged and addressed? Are sources documented? Above all, does the writer sound trustworthy?

When a Norwegian anti-immigration extremist killed seventy-six innocent people in July 2011, Prime Minister Jens Stoltenberg addressed the citizens of Norway (and the world), and in doing so evoked the character or ethos of the entire nation:

> We will not let fear break us! The warmth of response from people in Norway and from the whole world makes me sure of this one thing: evil can kill a single person, but never defeat a whole people. The strongest weapon in the world—that is freedom of expression and democracy.

In analyzing this speech, you would do well to look at the way this passage deploys the deepest values of Norway—freedom of expression and democracy—to serve as a response to fear of terrorism. In doing so, Stoltenberg evokes ethical ideals to hold onto in a time of tragedy.

Or take a look at the following paragraph from a blog posting by Timothy Burke, a teacher at Swarthmore College and parent of a preschool child who is trying to think through the issue of homework for elementary school kids:

Burke establishes his ethos by citing his reading and his talks with other parents.

He underscores his right to address the matter.

He expresses concern about immoderate arguments and implies that he will demonstrate an opposite approach.

> So I've been reading a bit about homework and comparing notes with parents. There is a lot of variation across districts, not just in the amount of homework that kids are being asked to do, but in the kind of homework. Some districts give kids a lot of time-consuming busywork; other districts try to concentrate on having homework assignments be substantive work that is best accomplished independently. Some give a lot from a very early point in K-12 education; some give relatively little. As both a professional educator and an individual with personal convictions, I'd tend to argue against excessive amounts of homework and against assigning busywork. But what has ultimately interested me more about reading various discussions of homework is how intense the feelings are swirling around the topic and how much that intensity strikes me as a problem in and of itself. Not just as a symptom of a kind of civic illness, an inability to collectively and democratically work through complex issues, but also in some cases as evidence of an educational failure in its own right.

In considering the role of ethos in rhetorical analyses, pay attention to the details right down to the choice of words or, in an image, the shapes and colors. The modest, tentative tone that Burke uses in his blog is an example of the kind of choice that can shape an audience's perception of ethos. But these details need your interpretation. Language that's hot and extreme can mark a writer as either passionate or loony. Work that's sober and carefully organized can paint an institution as competent or overly cautious. Technical terms and abstract phrases can make a writer seem either knowledgeable or pompous.

Examining Arguments Based on Facts and Reason: Logos

In analyzing most arguments, you'll have to decide whether an argument makes a plausible claim and offers good reasons for you to believe it. Not all arguments will package such claims in a single neat sentence, or **thesis**—nor should they. A writer may tell a story from which you have to infer the claim. Visual arguments may work the same way: viewers have to assemble the parts and draw inferences in order to get the point. Take a look, for instance, at this advertisement for GEICO insurance:

This ad draws attention with a snappy photo of a large silver watch and a headline: "That watch won't pay for itself." The smaller text below mentions other luxury items consumers may covet: designer aviators, for example, that don't "come cheap." Then the logical shift: if you want luxury things you would do well to save money. And how to save money? "So switch to GEICO and save money for the things you love." There's an implied syllogism here:

> You need to save money so you can afford the things you love.
>
> GEICO will help you save money.
>
> GEICO will help you afford the things you love.

But a little critical thinking can lead you to question each of these implied premises. Is the reason to save money really to buy luxury items? Just exactly how will GEICO help you save money? How much is your current insurance and how does that compare to the cost of GEICO? Maybe GEICO does offer a very good deal on insurance, but you'll need to do some more research to assure yourself of that fact. (For more on analyzing visual images, see **Chapter 29**.)

Some print arguments (like those on an editorial page) may be perfectly obvious: writers stake out a claim and then present reasons that you should consider, or they may first present reasons and lay out a case that leads you to accept a claim in the conclusion. Consider the following example. In a tough opinion piece in *Time*, political commentator John McWhorter argues that filmmaker Spike Lee is being racist when he rails against hipsters moving into Fort Greene, a formerly all-black neighborhood in Brooklyn, New York. Lee fears that the whites are raising housing prices, pushing out old-time residents and diminishing the African American character of Fort Greene. McWhorter, an African American like Lee, sees matters differently:

> Basically, black people are getting paid more money than they've ever seen in their lives for their houses, and a once sketchy neighborhood is now quiet and pleasant. And this is a bad thing...why?
>
> Lee seems to think it's somehow an injustice whenever black people pick up stakes. But I doubt many of the blacks now set to pass fat inheritances on to their kids feel that way. This is not the old story of poor blacks being pushed out of neighborhoods razed down for highway construction. Lee isn't making sense.
>
> —John McWhorter, "Spike Lee's Racism Isn't Cute"

When you encounter explicit charges like these, you analyze whether and how the claims are supported by good reasons and reliable evidence. A lengthy essay may, in fact, contain a series of claims, each developed to support an even larger point. Here's McWhorter, for instance, expanding his argument by suggesting that Lee's attitudes toward whites are irreconcilable.

> "Respect the culture" when you move in, Lee growls. But again, he isn't making sense. We can be quite sure that if whites "respected" the culture by trying to participate in it, Lee would be one of the first in line to call it "appropriation." So, no whites better open up barbecue joints or spoken word cafes or try to be rappers. Yet if whites walk on by the culture in "respectful" silence, then the word on the street becomes that they want to keep blacks at a distance.

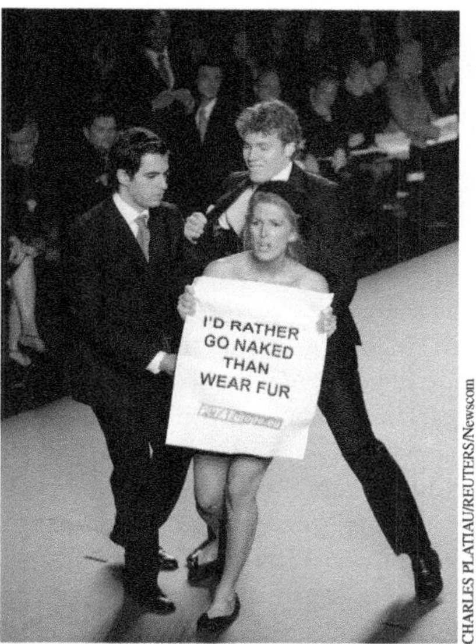

FIGURE 12.6 An anti-fur protestor in London makes a rather specific claim.

Indeed, every paragraph in an argument may develop a specific and related idea. In a rhetorical analysis, you need to identify all these separate propositions and examine the relationships among them: Are they solidly linked? Are there inconsistencies that the writer should acknowledge? Does the end of the piece support what the writer said (and promised) at the beginning?

You'll also need to examine the quality of the information presented in an argument, assessing how accurately such information is reported, how conveniently it's displayed (in charts or graphs, for example), and how well the sources cited represent a range of *respected* opinions on a topic. (For more information on the use of evidence, see **Chapter 27**.)

Knowing how to judge the quality of sources is more important now than ever before because the digital universe is full of junk. In some ways, the computer terminal has become the equivalent of a library reference room, but the sources available online vary widely in quality and have not been evaluated by a library professional. As a consequence, you must know the difference between reliable, firsthand, or fully documented sources and those that don't meet such standards. (For using and documenting sources, see **Chapters 21, 22, and 24**.)

Examining the Arrangement and Media of Arguments

Aristotle carved the structure of logical argument to its bare bones when he observed that it had only two parts:

- statement
- proof

You could do worse, in examining an argument, than to make sure that every claim a writer makes is backed by sufficient evidence. Some arguments are written on the fly in the heat of the moment. Most arguments that you read and write, however, will be more than mere statements followed by proofs. Some writers will lay their cards on the table immediately; others may lead you carefully through a chain of claims toward a conclusion. Writers may even interrupt their arguments to offer background information or cultural contexts for readers. Sometimes they'll tell stories or provide anecdotes that make an argumentative point. They'll qualify the arguments they make, too, and often pause to admit that other points of view are plausible.

In other words, there are no set formulas or acceptable patterns that fit all successful arguments. In writing a rhetorical analysis, you'll have to assess the organization of a persuasive text on its own merits.

It's fair, however, to complain about what may be *absent* from an argument. Most arguments of proposal (see **Chapter 18**), for example, include a section that defends the feasibility of a new idea, explaining how it might be funded or managed. In a rhetorical analysis, you might fault an editorial that supports a new stadium for a city without addressing feasibility issues. Similarly, analyzing a movie review that reads like an off-the-top-of-the-head opinion, you might legitimately ask what criteria of evaluation are in play (see **Chapter 17**).

Rhetorical analysis also calls for you to look carefully at an argument's transitions, headings and subheadings, documentation of sources, and overall tone or voice. Don't take such details for granted, since all of them contribute to the strength—or weakness—of an argument.

Nor should you ignore the way a writer or an institution uses media. Would an argument originally made in a print editorial, for instance, work better as a digital presentation (or vice versa)? Would a lengthy essay have more power if it included more illustrations—graphs, maps, photographs, and so on? Or do these images distract from a written argument's substance?

Finally, be open to the possibility of new or nontraditional structures of arguments. The visual arguments that you analyze may defy conventional principles of logic or arrangement—for example, making juxtapositions rather than logical transitions between elements or using quick cuts, fades, or other devices to link ideas. Quite often, these nontraditional structures will also resist the neatness of a thesis, leaving readers to construct at least a part of the argument in their heads. As we saw with the "Portraits" Jeep spot at the beginning of this chapter, advertisers are growing fond of soft-sell multimedia productions that can seem like something other than what they really are—product pitches. We may be asked not just to buy a product but also to live its lifestyle or embrace its ethos. Is that a reasonable or workable strategy for an argument? Your analysis might entertain such possibilities.

Looking at Style

Even a coherent argument full of sound evidence may not connect with readers if it's dull, off-key, or offensive. Readers naturally judge the credibility of arguments in part by how stylishly the case is made—even when they don't know exactly what style is (for more on style, see **Chapter 28**). In fact, today rhetoricians and media critics alike point out the crucial importance of style in getting and holding attention in a time when readers are drowning in an overload of information.

Consider how these simple, blunt sentences from the opening of an argument for gun control shape your image of the author and probably determine whether you're willing to continue to read the whole piece:

> Six minutes and about twenty seconds. In a little over six minutes, seventeen of our friends were taken from us. Fifteen were injured, and everyone—absolutely everyone—in [our] community was forever altered. Everyone who was there understands. Everyone who has been touched by the cold grip of gun violence understands.
>
> —Emma Gonzalez, speech delivered
> at March for Our Lives on March 24, 2018

The strong, straightforward tone, the drum-beat use of repetition, and the stark evocation of just how little time it took to take the lives of seventeen high school students and staff set the style for this speech, which led to six minutes of silence and then to prolonged, and loud, applause and cheers.

Now consider the brutally sarcastic tone of Nathaniel Stein's hilarious parody of the Harvard grading policy, a piece he wrote following up on a professor's complaint of out-of-control grade inflation at the school. Stein borrows the formal language of a typical "grading standards" sheet to mock the decline in rigor that the professor has lamented:

> The A+ grade is used only in very rare instances for the recognition of truly exceptional achievement.
>
> For example: A term paper receiving the A+ is virtually indistinguishable from the work of a professional, both in its choice of paper stock and its font. The student's command of the topic is expert, or at the very least intermediate, or beginner. Nearly every single word in the paper is spelled correctly; those that are not can be reasoned out phonetically within minutes. Content from Wikipedia is integrated with precision. The paper contains few, if any, death threats. . . .

> An overall course grade of A+ is reserved for those students who have not only demonstrated outstanding achievement in coursework but have also asked very nicely.
>
> Finally, the A+ grade is awarded to all collages, dioramas and other art projects.
>
> —Nathaniel Stein, "Leaked! Harvard's Grading Rubric"

Both styles probably work, but they signal that the writers are about to make very different kinds of cases. Here, style alone tells readers what to expect.

Manipulating style also enables writers to shape readers' responses to their ideas. Devices as simple as repetition, parallelism, or even paragraph length can give sentences remarkable power. Consider this brief announcement by Jason Collins, who played for the Washington Wizards:

> I'm a 34-year-old NBA center. I'm black. And I'm gay.
>
> I didn't set out to be the first openly gay athlete playing in a major American team sport. But since I am, I'm happy to start the conversation. I wish I wasn't the kid in the classroom raising his hand and saying, "I'm different." If I had my way, someone else would have already done this. Nobody has, which is why I'm raising my hand.
>
> —Jason Collins, *Sports Illustrated*, May 6, 2013

In this passage, Collins opens with three very short, very direct, and roughly parallel sentences. He also uses repetition of first-person pronouns to hammer home that he is claiming his own identity with this statement. Doing so invites readers and listeners to listen to his experience and to walk in his shoes, even for a brief time.

© Gary A. Vasquez/USA Today Sports Images

FIGURE 12.7 Jason Collins

In a rhetorical analysis, you can explore such stylistic choices. Why does a formal style work for discussing one type of subject matter but not another? How does a writer use humor or irony to underscore an important point or to manage a difficult concession? Do stylistic choices, even something as simple as the use of contractions or personal pronouns, bring readers close to a writer, or do technical words and an impersonal voice signal that an argument is for experts only?

To describe the stylistic effects of visual arguments, you may use a different vocabulary and talk about colors, camera angles, editing, balance, proportion, fonts, perspective, and so on. But the basic principle is this: the look of an item—whether a poster, an editorial cartoon, or a film documentary—can support the message that it carries, undermine it, or muddle it. In some cases, the look will *be* the message. In a rhetorical analysis, you can't ignore style.

FIGURE 12.8 Here's an award-winning poster for *Beauty and the Beast,* praised by critics for its stylistic elegance. As a commentator for DigitalSpy put it, "So chic. So stylish. So yellow."

A rhetorical analysis would note that the bright yellow dress and title evoke the sun as the image of Beauty dominates the middle of the image, while the beast's profile is superimposed on a full moon. Here the simplicity, vivid color, and careful juxtaposition suggest that these two are made for each other. (For more on analyzing visual images, see **Chapter 29**.)

RESPOND

Find a recent example of a visual argument, either in print or on the Internet. Even though you may have a copy of the image, describe it carefully in your paper on the assumption that your description is all readers may have to go on. Then make a judgment about its effectiveness, supporting your claim with clear evidence from the "text."

Examining a Rhetorical Analysis

On the following pages, well-known *New York Times* columnist Nicholas Kristof reports on his family's annual vacation, when they "run away to the mountains." He argues that we are plagued by "nature deficit disorder," that we have lost our connection with the wilderness, with the land that supports us, and that we must do our best to preserve and protect the "natural splendor that no billionaire is allowed to fence off." Responding to Kristof's argument with a careful critical reading and detailed rhetorical analysis is Cameron Hauer, a student at Portland State University.

Fleeing to the Mountains

NICHOLAS KRISTOF

Brent N. Clarke/Getty Images

ON THE PACIFIC CREST TRAIL, NORTHWEST OF TRUCKEE, Calif. —

This will make me sound grouchy and misanthropic, but I sometimes wonder if what makes America great isn't so much its people as its trees and mountains.

In contrast to many advanced countries, we have a vast and spectacular publicly owned wilderness, mostly free and available to all. In an age of inequality, the affluent have gated neighborhoods, private schools, backup generators and greater influence on elected officials. But our most awe-inspiring wild places have remained largely a public good to be shared by all, a bastion of equality.

My family and I have been backpacking on the Pacific Crest Trail through the Sierras north of Donner Pass, enjoying magnificent splendor that no billionaire is allowed to fence off. We all have equal access, at no charge: If you can hold your own against mosquitoes and bears, the spot is yours for the night.

Yet these public lands are at risk today. More on that in a moment, but first let me tell you about the Kristofs' grand vacation. As we do each summer, we ran away from home to the mountains. We escaped the tether of email and cellphones, the tyranny of the inbox, and fled with everything we needed on our backs.

We're yanked back to a simple life. We sleep under the stars rather than in a tent; if it rains we pull out a tarp to keep dry. Dawn wakes us up, we roll up our sleeping bags and plastic ground sheet, wolf down trail mix or granola bars and start down the path. We fill our water bottles at passing streams, stop for rest and meals wherever we fancy, chat as we walk, and when dusk comes we look for a flat spot, kick aside any rocks and branches and unroll our ground sheet and sleeping bags again.

Granted, we also moan about blisters. And marauding mosquitoes. And the heat—or, sometimes, the cold. We whine a lot, but that builds family solidarity.

This is also a spiritual experience: It's a chance to share a reverence for the ethereal scenery of America's wild places. The wilderness is nature's cathedral, and it's a thrill to worship here.

Caroline Kristof

The march of civilization has been about distancing ourselves from the raw power of nature. At home, we move the thermostat up or down by a degree, and we absorb the idea that we are lords of the universe. On the trail, we are either sweating or freezing, and it always feels as if the path is mainly uphill. Nature mocks us, usefully reminding us who's boss.

If your kids are suffering from what the writer Richard Louv calls nature-deficit disorder, I recommend that you all run away from home together. Flee to the mountains. It's heaven with blisters.

There are often charges to enter much-trafficked spots like Yellowstone or Yosemite, but the wilderness is mostly free to hikers.

This is our collective patrimony, a tribute to the wisdom of Theodore Roosevelt, Gifford Pinchot and other visionaries who preserved our wild places for the future. Thank God for them. Otherwise, these lands might have been carved up and sold off as ranches for the rich.

Because of the foresight of past generations, the federal government owns one million square miles, an area three times the size of California, Oregon and Washington combined. Much of this is unspoiled, our inheritance and our shared playground.

Yet today, President Trump sees this heritage as an opportunity for development. More aggressively than past administrations, Trump's is systematically handing over America's public lands for private exploitation in ways that will scar the land forever.

The Trump administration lifted a moratorium on new coal mining leases on public land, it is drawing up plans to reduce wilderness protected as national monuments and it is rapidly opening up additional public lands to coal mining and oil and gas drilling.

A second challenge comes from our paralysis in the face of climate change, compounded by the Trump administration, and the risks this creates to our wilderness. A warmer climate has led to droughts and to the 20-year spread of the mountain pine beetle, and a result is the death of vast swaths of Western forests. Last year, 62 million trees died in California alone, the Forest Service says, and in Oregon and Washington I've watched forests turn brown and sickly. In parts of Wyoming and Colorado, the pine beetle has killed almost all the mature lodgepole pine trees, and it's arguably even worse in British Columbia.

The third risk is from gradual degradation and chronic underfunding. Even before Trump took office, wilderness trails and campgrounds were in embarrassing disrepair. How is it that we could afford to construct these trails 80 years ago in the Great Depression but cannot manage even to maintain them today?

When public lands are lost—or mined in ways that scar the landscape—something has been lost forever on our watch. A public good has been privatized, and our descendants have been robbed.

To promote an understanding of what is being lost, I encourage everyone to run away from home as well. Flee to the mountains, deserts and babbling brooks to get in touch with wild spaces, to find perspective and humility. The wilderness nourishes our souls, if we let it.

Appeal, Audience, and Narrative in Kristof's Wilderness

CAMERON HAUER*

Courtesy of Cameron Hauer

Connects article to personal experience to create an ethical appeal

Growing up in an outdoorsy middle class family instilled a love of the outdoors in me from an early age. I joined a local Boy Scouts chapter as a pre-adolescent and spent practically every other weekend in the pristine wilderness of Washington, Idaho, and Montana. From alpine skiing in the Canadian Rockies to 50-mile backpacking treks, the wilderness was a big part of my life. I owe a lot of personal development and fond memories to America's vast and mostly public wilderness, the value of which Nicholas Kristof captures stirringly in his *New York Times* op-ed column, "Fleeing to the Mountains."

Provides brief overview of Kristof's argument and major claim

Kristof's article is principally a piece of epideictic rhetoric, extolling the virtues of America's publicly owned wilderness areas and those who created them while casting blame on those who try to undermine them. Early in the piece, Kristof connects public ownership of wild lands to a core set of American values, regarding the country's public lands as "a bastion of equality." In the wilderness, he says, "we all have equal access, no charge." Kristof warns, however, that America's wilderness is under attack.

Identifies appeals used and provides examples

To bolster his case for the specialness of America's wildlands, Kristof relies heavily on ethical and emotional appeals: a lively account of his family's backpacking trips and the ways they free them from the technologically structured rigidity of modern city life. In these sections, Kristof's style ranges from breezy and playful (the wilderness is "heaven with blisters") to awestruck and reverent (it is "our inheritance and shared playground"). This section also offers personal testimony; Kristof has spent a lot of time in wild places, and he is well positioned to describe their virtues. He invites readers to share this ethic, to revel in the joy provided by open spaces, but also to regard them as an almost sacred inheritance.

Transition sentence signals a shift in the argument

About halfway through the column, Kristof makes a shift to address threats facing our wilderness. He lays blame on those in power, like President Trump, who "sees this heritage as an

*Cameron Hauer is a student at Portland State University, where he is majoring in Applied Linguistics, having returned to school after a decade spent cooking in fine dining establishments in the Pacific Northwest.

opportunity for development" and is "systematically handing over America's public lands for private exploitation in ways that will scar the land forever." Kristof's style here becomes more somber and more reliant on verifiable facts. The primary appeal shifts to logos rather than the ethos and pathos of the earlier sections. Whereas before he was trying to evoke a particular feeling and ethic, his present goal is to convince readers that public lands in the U.S. are under threat by marshaling a series of facts about actions of the Trump Administration that Kristof believes undermine the U.S. public wilderness system. These facts include lifting a moratorium on new mining leases and opening up new lands to fossil fuel extraction. He also describes the effects of climate change, which he argues the Trump Administration ignores, and chronic underfunding, which he notes predates Trump. In the online version of the column, Kristof includes hyperlinks so readers can fact-check his evidence. This is the only section in which hyperlinks appear, underscoring again the shift to logical appeals. Note, however, that Kristof lessens the effect of what could be an abrupt shift in appeal by maintaining his established narrative, of wilderness as an inheritance.

Discusses style and use of evidence

Several elements of Kristof's argument give special insight into the particular moment in which Kristof offers his argument as well as into the audience he is addressing. The place of Trump in Kristof's narrative is particularly significant, because what Kristof describes as a unique threat to American public lands is simply the implementation of long-standing Republican Party policy. If he had wanted to, Kristof could fairly ascribe the policies of privatization and fossil fuel extraction to the GOP as a whole. But in the rhetorical context Kristof occupies—a left-of-center newspaper in 2017—choosing Trump as the avatar of anti-environmental policies is a strong, if obvious, rhetorical move. To a liberal readership still reeling from the shock of the 2016 election, the invocation of Trump is an invitation for the audience to adopt Kristof's pro-wilderness platform as a plank of a broader anti-Trump agenda.

Puts Kristof's article in rhetorical context

Analyzes author's intended audience

It is also worth noting some telling elisions in Kristof's argument. In the narrative Kristof provides, wild lands are either public and devoted to use by the people, or privatized and devoted to resource extraction and "ranches for the rich." To Kristof's invoked audience, which bristles at the rapacity of unrestrained free enterprise and its attendant inequality, this framework may be convincing, but a rural conservative who believes strongly in the primacy of property rights will probably be unmoved. While it may seem natural to progressives to regard public ownership as an unmitigated good, conservatives often view such ownership with extreme suspicion. Whereas Kristof views public ownership as a means of providing equal access for all Americans, rural conservatives may view it as a means by which potentially valuable resources are turned into playgrounds for yuppies. And whereas Kristof views private ownership as facilitating degradation and waste, conservatives may view it as a means by which hardworking people can make a decent living off the land.

Offers a critique of Kristof's position

Such considerations bring up another important evasion in Kristof's argument, one that may stand out sharply to both left and right. Kristof's characterization of public lands as "a bastion of equality" may be true in a narrow, legal sense: most of these places are open to the public, free of charge. But to get access to wilderness requires a decent salary and paid time off, among other things. In an economic system where millions struggle to afford basic food and housing, unfettered use of America's wildlands remains out of reach.

Points out another flaw in Kristof's argument

These evasions and omissions may point to Kristof's biases and his own rhetorical stance, but they should not be regarded as damning. Even if Kristof has rejoinders to these objections—and it's likely he does—it would be hard to give them their due in the restricted format of a newspaper column. This op-ed article is, after all, crafted for a particular audience. To address the concerns of staunch conservatives would probably require Kristof to adopt very different rhetorical strategies. Kristof's readers are mostly a self-selecting group of liberals already sympathetic in some ways to his views. Thus the rhetorical goal is not to convince a group of hostile adversaries of his position but to persuade a group of amenable readers that this particular issue—and this particular ethic—is one that they should adopt as their own.

Analyzes the genre of Kristof's piece (and its limitations)

Work Cited

Kristof, Nicholas. "Fleeing to the Mountains." *Everything's an Argument*, 8th ed., by Andrea A. Lunsford and John J. Ruszkiewicz, Bedford/St. Martin's, 2018, pp. 118–20. Reprint of "Fleeing to the Mountains," *The New York Times*, 12 August 2017.

GUIDE TO WRITING A RHETORICAL ANALYSIS

Finding a Topic

A rhetorical analysis is usually assigned: you're asked to show how an argument works and to assess its effectiveness. When you can choose your own subject for analysis, look for one or more of the following qualities:

- a complex verbal or visual argument that challenges you—or disturbs or pleases you
- a text that raises current or enduring issues of substance
- a text that you believe should be taken more seriously

Look for arguments to analyze in the editorial and op-ed pages of any newspaper, political magazines such as the *Nation* or *National Review*, Web sites of organizations and interest groups, political blogs such as *Huffington Post* or *Power Line*, corporate Web sites that post their TV ad spots, videos and statements posted to YouTube, and so on.

Researching Your Topic

Once you've got a text to analyze, find out all you can about it. Use library or Web resources to explore:

- who the author is and what his or her credentials are
- if the author is an institution, what it does, what its sources of funding are, who its members are, and so on
- who is publishing or sponsoring the piece and what the organization typically publishes
- what the leanings or biases of the author and publisher might be, where they are coming from in the argument, and what influences may have led them to make the argument
- what the context of the argument is—what preceded or provoked it and how others have responded to it

Formulating a Claim

Begin with a hypothesis. A full thesis might not become evident until you're well into your analysis, but your final thesis should reflect the complexity of the piece that you're studying. In developing a thesis, consider questions such as the following:

- What is the major claim of the argument? What evidence is presented in support of it?
- How can I describe what this argument achieves?

- What is the purpose, and is it accomplished?
- What audiences does the argument address and what audiences does it ignore, and why?
- Which rhetorical appeals does the argument make use of and which will likely influence readers most: ethos of the author? emotional appeals? logical progression? style, use of images or other illustrations? What aspects of the argument work better than others?
- How do the rhetorical elements of ethos, pathos, and logos interact?

Here's the hardest part for most writers of rhetorical analyses: whether you agree or disagree with an argument should not keep you from careful, meticulous analysis: you need to stay out of the fray and pay attention only to how—and to how well—the argument works.

Examples of Possible Claims for a Rhetorical Analysis

- Some people admire the directness and plain talking of Donald Trump; others are put off by his lack of information, his tendency to stretch or ignore the truth, and his noisy bluster. A close look at several of his tweets and public appearances will illuminate both sides of this debate.
- Today's editorial in the *Daily Collegian* about campus crimes may scare first-year students, but its anecdotal reporting doesn't get down to hard numbers—and for a good reason. Those statistics don't back the position taken by the editors.
- The imageboard 4chan has been called an "Internet hate machine," yet others claim it as a great boon to creativity. A close analysis of its home-page can help to settle this debate.
- The original design of New York's Freedom Tower, with its torqued surfaces and evocative spire, made a stronger argument about American values than its replacement, a fortress-like skyscraper stripped of imagination and unable to make any statement except "I'm 1,776 feet tall."
- The controversy over speech on campuses has reached a fever pitch, with some arguing that those who spout hate and bigotry and prejudice should be barred from speaking.

Preparing a Proposal

If your instructor asks you to prepare a proposal for your rhetorical analysis, here's a format you might use:

- Provide a copy of the work you're analyzing, whether it's a print text, a photograph, a digital image, or a URL, for instance.

- Offer a working hypothesis or tentative thesis.
- Indicate which rhetorical components seem especially compelling and worthy of detailed study and any connections between elements. For example, does the piece seem to emphasize facts and logic so much that it becomes disconnected from potential audiences? If so, hint at that possibility in your proposal.
- Indicate background information you intend to research about the author, institution, and contexts (political, economic, social, and religious) of the argument.
- Define the audience you'd like to reach. If you're responding to an assignment, you may be writing primarily for a teacher and classmates. But they make up a complex audience in themselves. If you can do so within the spirit of the assignment, imagine that your analysis will be published in a local newspaper, Web site, or blog.
- Conclude by briefly discussing the key challenges you anticipate in preparing a rhetorical analysis.

Considering Genre and Media

Your instructor may specify that you use a particular genre and/or medium. If not, ask yourself these questions to help you make a good choice:

- What genre is most appropriate for your rhetorical analysis? Does it call for an academic essay, a report, an infographic, a poster, brochure, or something else?
- What medium is most appropriate for your analysis? Would it be best delivered orally to a live audience? Presented as an audio essay or podcast? Presented in print only or in print with illustrations?
- Will you need visuals, such as moving or still images, maps, graphs, charts—and what function will they play in your analysis? Make sure they are not just "added on" but are necessary components of the analysis.

Thinking about Organization

Your rhetorical analysis is likely to include the following:

- Facts about the text you're analyzing: provide the author's name; the title or name of the work; its place of publication or its location; the date it was published or viewed.
- Evidence that you have read the argument carefully and critically, that you have listened closely to and understand the points it is making, and that you have been open and fair in your assessment.
- Contexts for the argument: readers need to know where the text is coming from, to what it may be responding, in what controversies it might be embroiled, and so on. Don't assume that they can infer the important contextual elements.

- A synopsis of the text that you're analyzing: if you can't attach the original argument, you must summarize it in enough detail so that a reader can imagine it. Even if you attach a copy of the piece, the analysis should include a summary.
- Some claim about the work's rhetorical effectiveness: it might be a simple evaluative claim or something more complex. The claim can come early in the paper, or you might build up to it, providing the evidence that leads toward the conclusion you've reached.
- A detailed analysis of how the argument works: although you'll probably analyze rhetorical components separately, don't let your analysis become a dull roster of emotional, ethical, and logical appeals. Your rhetorical analysis should be an argument itself that supports a claim; a simple list of rhetorical appeals won't make much of a point.
- Evidence for every point made in your analysis.
- An assessment of alternative views and counterarguments to your own analysis.

Getting and Giving Response: Questions for Peer Response

If you have access to a writing center, discuss the text that you intend to analyze with a writing consultant before you write the analysis. Try to find people who agree with the argument and others who disagree, and take notes on their observations. Your instructor may assign you to a peer group for the purpose of reading and responding to one another's drafts; if not, share your draft with someone on your own. You can use the following questions to evaluate a draft. If you're evaluating someone else's draft, be sure to illustrate your points with examples. Specific comments are always more helpful than general observations.

The Claim

- Does the claim address the rhetorical effectiveness of the argument itself rather than the opinion or position that it takes?
- Is the claim significant enough to interest readers?
- Does the claim indicate important relationships between various rhetorical components?
- Would the claim be one that the creator of the piece would regard as serious criticism?

Evidence for the Claim

- Is enough evidence given to support all your claims? What evidence do you still need?
- Is the evidence in support of the claim simply announced, or are its significance and appropriateness analyzed? Is a more detailed discussion needed?

- Do you use appropriate evidence, drawn from the argument itself or from other materials?
- Do you address objections readers might have to the claim, criteria, or evidence?
- What kinds of sources might you use to explain the context of the argument? Do you need to use sources to check factual claims made in the argument?
- Are all quotations introduced with appropriate signal phrases (for instance, "As Áida Álvarez points out"), and do they merge smoothly into your sentences?

Organization and Style

- How are the parts of the argument organized? How effective is this organization? Would some other structure work better?
- Will readers understand the relationships among the original text, your claims, your supporting reasons, and the evidence you've gathered (from the original text and any other sources you've used)? If not, what could be done to make those connections clearer? Are more transitional words and phrases needed? Would headings or graphic devices help?
- Are the transitions or links from point to point, sentence to sentence, and paragraph to paragraph clear and effective? If not, how could they be improved?
- Is the style suited to the subject and appropriate to your audience? Is it too formal? Too casual? Too technical? Too bland or boring?
- Which sentences seem particularly effective? Which ones seem weakest, and how could they be improved? Should some short sentences be combined, or should any long ones be separated into two or more sentences?
- How effective are the paragraphs? Do any seem too skimpy or too long? Do they break the analysis at strategic points?
- Which words or phrases seem particularly effective, accurate, and powerful? Do any seem dull, vague, unclear, or inappropriate for the audience or your purpose? Are definitions provided for technical or other terms that readers might not know?

Spelling, Punctuation, Mechanics, Documentation, and Format

- Check the spelling of the author's name, and make sure that the name of any institution involved with the work is correct. Note that the names of many corporations and institutions use distinctive spelling and punctuation.
- Check the title of the text you're analyzing so you're sure to get it right.
- Look for any errors in spelling, punctuation, capitalization, and the like.
- Check the format of your assignment and make sure it matches instructions given on your original assignment.

RESPOND

Find an argument on the editorial page or op-ed page in a recent newspaper. Read it carefully and critically, taking time to make sure you understand the claims it is making and the evidence that backs up the claim. Then analyze it rhetorically, using principles discussed in this chapter. Show how it succeeds, fails, or does something else entirely. Perhaps you can show that the author is unusually successful in connecting with readers but then has nothing to say. Or perhaps you discover that the strong logical appeal is undercut by a contradictory emotional argument. Be sure that the analysis includes a summary of the original essay and basic publication information about it (its author, place of publication, and publisher).

Analyzing Multimodal Arguments

A multimodal argument can be complex. But you can figure it out by giving careful attention to its key components: the creators and distributors; the medium it uses; the viewers and readers it hopes to reach; its content and purpose; its design. Following are some questions to ask when you want to understand the rhetorical strategies in arguments and interactions you encounter in social media or on blogs, vlogs, Web sites, podcasts, or other nontraditional media. It's worth noting that the questions here don't differ entirely from those you might ask about books, journal articles, news stories, or print ads when composing a rhetorical analysis.

Questions about Creators and Distributors

- Who is responsible for this multimodal text? Experts? Bots? Trolls? Did someone else distribute, repurpose, or retweet the item?
- What can you find out about these people and any other work they might have done?
- What does the creator's attitude seem to be toward the content: serious, ironic, emotionally charged, satiric, comic? What is the attitude of the distributor, if different from the creator?
- What do the creator and the distributor expect the effects of the text or posting to be? Do they share the same intentions? (Consider, for example, that someone might post an item in order to mock or criticize it.)

Questions about the Medium

- Which media are used by this text? Images only? Words and images? Sound, video, animation, graphs, charts? Does the site or environment where the text appears suggest a metaphor: photo album, pin-up board, message board, chat room?

- In what ways is this text or its online environment interactive? Who can contribute to or comment on it? Where can an item be sent or redirected? How did it get to where you encountered it?
- How do various texts work together on the site? Do they make arguments? Accumulate evidence? Provide readers with examples and illustrations?
- What effect does the medium have on messages or items within it? How would a message, text, or item be altered if different media were used?
- Do claims or arguments play an explicit role in the medium? How are they presented, clarified, reinforced, connected, constrained, or commented upon?

Questions about Audience and Viewers

- What are the likely audiences for the text or medium? How are people invited into the text or site? Who might avoid the experience?
- How does the audience participate in the site or platform? Does the audience respond to content, create it, or something else? What audience interactions or connections occur there? Can participants interact with each other?
- How does the text or media site evoke or reward participation? Are audience members texted or emailed about events or interactions in the site?

Questions about Content and Purpose

- What purpose does the multimodal text achieve? What is it designed to convey?
- What social, cultural, or political values does the text or site support? Cultural interaction? Power? Resistance? Freedom?
- Does the text, alone or in reaction to others, reinforce these values or question them? Does the text constitute an argument in itself or contribute to another claim in some way—as an illustration, example, exception, metaphor, analogy?
- What emotions does the multimodal site or text evoke? Are these the emotions that it intends to raise? How does it do it?

Questions about Design

- How does the site present itself? What draws you to it? How easy is the environment to learn, use, or subscribe to?
- How is the multimodal text or environment structured? Does the structure enhance its purpose or functionality? If it presents data, is the information easy to understand? (See also **Chapter 29**, "Visual Rhetoric.")
- How are arguments, concepts, or ideas presented or framed within the multimodal text or environment? How are ideas identified? How are these ideas amplified or connected to other supporting texts and ideas?

- What details are emphasized in the text or media environment? What details are omitted or de-emphasized? To what effect? Is anything downplayed, ambiguous, confusing, distracting, or obviously omitted? Why?
- What, if anything, is surprising about the design of the text or environment? What do you think is the purpose of that surprise?
- How are you directed to move within the text or site? Are you encouraged to read further? Click on links? Contribute links and information?

RESPOND

Using the discussion of multimodal arguments in this chapter and the questions about multimodal texts and platforms above, find a multimodal text that makes an intriguing argument *or* a social media platform where you sometimes encounter debates about political and social issues. Then read carefully and critically in order to write a brief rhetorical analysis of the text or the site, focusing more on the way the messages are conveyed than on the messages that are in play.

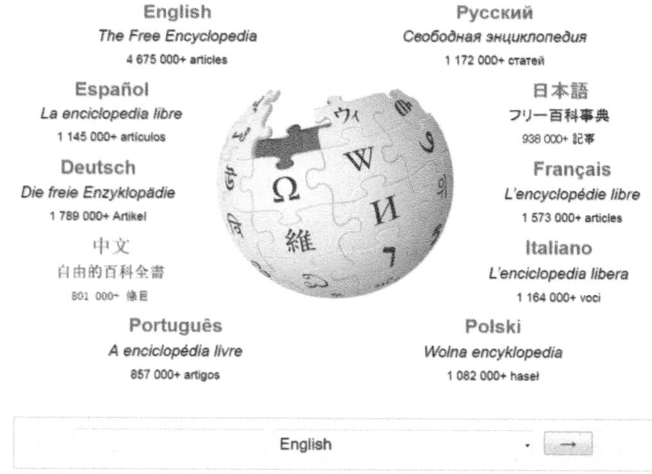

FIGURE 12.9 This is the central image on the homepage of Wikipedia, a collaborative nonprofit encyclopedia project. Since its launch (as Nupedia) in 2000, Wikipedia has grown to include 42 million articles in 295 languages (5.5 million articles in English), all of them authored by volunteers around the world. This central image acts as a logo, a portal to access the site's content, and, in a way, a mission statement for the organization. How does your eye construct this logo? What do you notice first, and how do your eyes move around the page? Do the parts make sense when you put them together?

CHAPTER

13

Fallacies of Argument

Left to right: Nate Beeler, The Columbus Dispatch/Cagle Cartoons, Inc.; The Upturned Microscope

Do these cartoons ring a bell with you? The first panel skewers slippery slope arguments, which aim to thwart action by predicting dire consequences: "occupy" enough spaces and the Occupy movement looks just like the Tea Party. In the second item, an example of a straw man argument, the first author of an academic paper puts down his coauthor by shifting the subject, saying that the coauthor is an egotist who cares only for fame, not what the coauthor had said at all. And the third image provides an example of a very common fallacy, the *ad hominem* argument, in which a speaker impugns the character of an opponent rather than addressing the arguments that person raises. Rather than argue the point that human cloning is wrong, the bird says, simply, "you're an idiot."

Candidate Donald Trump made something of a specialty of the *ad hominem* argument. Rather than address their arguments directly, he attacked the characters of his opponents: Marco Rubio was always "little Marco," Hillary Clinton was always "crooked," Elizabeth Warren was "goofy," and Cruz was always "Lyin' Ted." Early on in the campaign, when asked about rival candidate Carly Fiorina's plans, he said, "Can you imagine that, the face of our next president? I mean, she's a woman and I'm not supposed to say bad things, but really, folks, come on." Classic *ad hominem*, and oftentimes such tactics work all too well!

Fallacies are argumentative moves flawed by their nature or structure. Because such tactics can make principled argument more difficult, they potentially hurt everyone involved, including the people responsible for them. The worst sorts of fallacies muck up the frank but civil conversations that people should be able to have, regardless of their differences.

Yet it's hard to deny the power in offering audiences a compelling either/or choice or a vulnerable straw man in an argument: these fallacies can have great persuasive power. For exactly that reason, it's important that you can recognize and point out fallacies in the work of others—and avoid them in your own writing. This chapter aims to help you meet these goals: here we'll introduce you to fallacies of argument classified according to the emotional, ethical, and logical appeals we'll discuss later (see **Chapters 25, 26, and 27**).

Fallacies of Emotional Argument

Emotional arguments can be powerful and suitable in many circumstances, and most writers use them frequently. However, writers who pull on their readers' heartstrings or raise their blood pressure too often—or who oversentimentalize—can violate the good faith on which legitimate argument depends.

Scare Tactics

Politicians, advertisers, and public figures sometimes peddle their ideas by frightening people and exaggerating possible dangers well beyond their statistical likelihood. Such ploys work because it's easier to imagine something terrible happening than to appreciate its rarity.

Scare tactics can also be used to stampede legitimate fears into panic or prejudice. Laborers who genuinely worry about losing their jobs can be persuaded to fear immigrants who might work for less money. Seniors living on fixed incomes can be convinced that minor changes to entitlement programs represent dire threats to their well-being. Such tactics have the effect of closing off thinking because people who are scared often act irrationally. Even well-intended fear campaigns—like those directed against smoking, unprotected sex, or the use of illegal drugs—can misfire if their warnings prove too shrill or seem hysterical. People just stop listening.

Either/Or Choices

Either/or choices can be well-intentioned strategies to get something accomplished. Parents use them all the time ("Eat your broccoli, or you won't get dessert"). But they become fallacious arguments when they reduce a complicated issue to excessively simple terms (e.g., "You're either for me or against me") or when they're designed to obscure legitimate alternatives. Here, for example, is Riyad

Mansour, the Palestinian representative to the United Nations, offering the nation of Israel just such a choice in an interview on PBS in January 2014:

> It is up to them [the Israelis] to decide what kind of a state they want to be. Do they want to be a democratic state where Israel will be the state for all of its citizens? Or do they want to be a state for the Jewish people, therefore excluding 1.6 million Palestinian Arabs who are Israelis from their society? That debate is not our debate. That debate is their debate.

But Joel B. Pollak, writing for Breitbart News Network, describes Mansour's claim as a "false choice" since Israel already is a Jewish state that nonetheless allows Muslims to be full citizens. The either/or argument Mansour presents, according to Pollak, does not describe the realities of this complex political situation.

FIGURE 13.1 A false choice?

Slippery Slope

The **slippery slope** fallacy portrays today's tiny misstep as tomorrow's slide into disaster. Some arguments that aim at preventing dire consequences do not take the slippery slope approach (for example, the parent who corrects a child for misbehavior now is acting sensibly to prevent more serious problems as the child grows older). A slippery slope argument becomes wrongheaded when a writer exaggerates the likely consequences of an action, usually to frighten readers. As such, slippery slope arguments are also scare tactics. In recent years, the issue of gun ownership in America has evoked many slippery slope arguments. Here are two examples:

> "Universal background checks will inevitably be followed by a national registry of gun-owners which will inevitably be followed by confiscation of all their guns." Or, "A ban on assault-style weapons and thirty+ round magazines will inevitably be followed by a ban on hand guns with ten-round magazines...."
>
> —Michael Wolkowitz, "Slippery Slopes, Imagined and Real"

Social and political ideas and proposals do have consequences, but they aren't always as dire as writers fond of slippery slope tactics would have you believe.

Overly Sentimental Appeals

Overly **sentimental appeals** use tender emotions excessively to distract readers from facts. Often, such appeals are highly personal and individual and focus attention on heartwarming or heartrending situations that make readers feel guilty if they challenge an idea, a policy, or a proposal. Emotions can become an impediment to civil discourse when they keep people from thinking clearly.

Such sentimental appeals are a major vehicle of television news, where tugging at viewers' heartstrings can mean high ratings. For example, when a camera documents the day-to-day sacrifices of a single parent trying to meet mortgage payments and keep her kids in college, the woman's on-screen struggles can seem to represent the plight of an entire class of people threatened by callous bankers and college administrators. But while such human interest stories stir genuine emotions, they seldom give a complete picture of complex social or economic issues.

Tim Boyle/Getty Images

Spencer Platt/Getty Images

FIGURE 13.2 The first image, taken from a gun control protest, is designed to elicit sympathy by causing the viewer to think about the dangers guns pose to innocent children and, thus, support the cause. The second image supports the other side of the debate.

Bandwagon Appeals

Bandwagon appeals urge people to follow the same path everyone else is taking. Such arguments can be relatively benign and seem harmless. But they do push people to take the easier path rather than think independently about what choices to make or where to go.

Many American parents seem to have an innate ability to refute bandwagon appeals. When their kids whine, *Everyone else is going camping without chaperones*, the parents reply, *And if everyone else jumps off a cliff (or a railroad bridge or the Empire State Building), you will too?* The children groan—and then try a different line of argument.

Advertisers use bandwagon appeals frequently, as this example of a cellphone ad demonstrates:

Unfortunately, not all bandwagon approaches are so transparent. In recent decades, bandwagon issues have included a war on drugs, the nuclear freeze movement, campaigns against drunk driving—and for freedom of speech, campaigns for immigration reform, bailouts for banks and businesses, and *many* fads in education. All these issues are too complex to permit the suspension of judgment that bandwagon tactics require.

Fallacies of Ethical Argument

Because readers give their closest attention to authors they respect or trust, writers usually want to present themselves as honest, well-informed, likable, or sympathetic. But not all the devices that writers use to gain the attention and confidence of readers are admirable. (For more on appeals based on character, see Chapter 26.)

Appeals to False Authority

Many academic research papers find and reflect on the work of reputable authorities and introduce these authorities through direct quotations or citations as credible evidence. (For more on assessing the reliability of sources, see Chapter 21.) **False authority**, however, occurs when writers offer themselves or other authorities as sufficient assumption for believing a claim:

Claim	X is true because I say so.
Assumption	What I say must be true.

Claim	X is true because Y says so.
Assumption	What Y says must be true.

Though they are seldom stated so baldly, claims of authority drive many political campaigns. American pundits and politicians are fond of citing the U.S. Constitution and its Bill of Rights (Canadians have their Charter of Rights and Freedoms, and Britain has had its Bill of Rights since the seventeenth century) as ultimate authorities, a reasonable practice when the documents are interpreted respectfully. However, the rights claimed sometimes aren't in the texts themselves or don't mean what the speakers think they do. And most constitutional matters are debatable—as volumes of court records prove. Likewise, religious believers often base arguments on books or traditions that wield great authority in a particular religious community. But the power of such texts is often limited to that group and less capable of persuading others solely on the grounds of authority.

In short, you should pay serious attention to claims supported by respected authorities, such as the Centers for Disease Control, the National Science Foundation, or the *Globe and Mail*. But don't accept information simply because it is put forth by such offices and agencies. To quote a Russian proverb made famous by Ronald Reagan, "Trust, but verify."

Dogmatism

A writer who asserts or assumes that a particular position is the *only one* that is conceivably acceptable is expressing **dogmatism**, a fallacy of character that undermines the trust that must exist between those who make and listen to arguments. When people or organizations write dogmatically, they imply that no arguments are necessary: the truth is self-evident and needs no support. Here is an extreme example of such an appeal, quoted in an *Atlantic* story by Tracy Brown Hamilton and describing an anti-smoking appeal made by the Third Reich:

> "Brother national socialist, do you know that your Fuhrer is against smoking and thinks that every German is responsible to the whole people for all his deeds and omissions, and does not have the right to damage his body with drugs?"
>
> —Tracy Brown Hamilton, "The Nazis' Forgotten Anti-Smoking Campaign"

Subjects or ideas that can be defended with facts, testimony, and good reasons ought not to be off the table in a free society. In general, whenever someone suggests that even raising an issue for debate is totally unacceptable—whether on the grounds that it's racist, sexist, unpatriotic, blasphemous, insensitive, or offensive in some other way—you should be suspicious.

Ad Hominem Arguments

Ad hominem (Latin for "to the man") **arguments** attack the character of a person rather than the claims he or she makes: when you destroy the credibility of your opponents, you either destroy their ability to present reasonable appeals or distract from the successful arguments they may be offering. During the 2016 presidential primary, Marco Rubio criticized rival candidate Ted Cruz for not speaking Spanish: was that a valid argument for why Cruz would not make a good president? Such attacks, of course, aren't aimed at men only, as columnist Jamie Stiehm proved when she criticized Supreme Court Justice Sonia Sotomayor for delaying an Affordable Care Act mandate objected to by the Little Sisters of the Poor, a Catholic religious order. Stiehm directly targets Sotomayor's religious beliefs:

> Et tu, Justice Sonia Sotomayor? Really, we can't trust you on women's health and human rights? The lady from the Bronx just dropped the ball on American women and girls as surely as she did the sparkling ball at midnight on New Year's Eve in Times Square. Or maybe she's just a good Catholic girl.
>
> —Jamie Stiehm, "The Catholic Supreme Court's War on Women"

Stiehm then widens her *ad hominem* assault to include Catholics in general:

> Sotomayor's blow brings us to confront an uncomfortable reality. More than WASPs, Methodists, Jews, Quakers or Baptists, Catholics often try to impose their beliefs on you, me, public discourse and institutions. Especially if "you" are female.

Arguably, *ad hominem* tactics like this turn arguments into two-sided affairs with good guys and bad guys (or gals), and that's unfortunate, since character often really *does* matter in argument. Even though the norms of civic discourse were strained to the limit during and after the 2016 presidential election, most people still expect the proponent of peace to be civil, a secretary of the treasury to pay his or her taxes, the champion of family values to be a faithful spouse, and the head of the Environmental Protection Agency to advocate for protecting the environment. But it's fallacious to attack any of these people for their traits, backgrounds, looks, or other irrelevant information.

Stacking the Deck

Just as gamblers try to stack the deck by arranging cards so they are sure to win, writers **stack the deck** when they show only one side of the story—the one in their favor. In a 2016 *New Yorker* article, writer Kathryn Schulz discusses the Netflix series *Making a Murderer*. Schulz notes that the filmmakers have been accused of limiting their evidence in order to convince viewers that the accused, Steven Avery, had been framed for the crime:

> Ricciardi and Demos have dismissed the idea, claiming that they simply set out to investigate Avery's case and didn't have a position on his guilt or innocence. Yet...the filmmakers minimize or leave out many aspects of Avery's less than savory past, including multiple alleged incidents of physical and sexual violence. They also omit important evidence against him,...evidence that would be nearly impossible to plant....Ricciardi and Demos instead stack the deck to support their case for Avery, and, as a result, wind up mirroring the entity that they are trying to discredit.
>
> —Kathryn Schulz, "Dead Certainty: How *Making a Murderer* Goes Wrong"

In the same way, reviewers have been critical of documentaries by Michael Moore and Dinesh D'Souza that resolutely show only one side of a story or prove highly selective in their coverage. When you stack the deck, you take a big chance that your readers will react like Schulz and decide not to trust you: that's one reason it's so important to show that you have considered alternatives in making any argument.

Fallacies of Logical Argument

You'll encounter a problem in any argument when the claims, assumptions, or proofs in it are invalid, insufficient, or disconnected. In theory, such problems seem easy enough to spot, but in practice, they can be camouflaged by a skillful use of words or images. Indeed, logical fallacies pose a challenge to civil argument because they often seem reasonable and natural, especially when they appeal to people's self-interests.

Hasty Generalization

A **hasty generalization** is an inference drawn from insufficient evidence: because *my* Fiat broke down, then *all* Fiats must be junk. It also forms the basis for most stereotypes about people or institutions: because *a few* people in a large group are observed to act in a certain way, *all* members of that group are inferred to behave similarly. The resulting conclusions are usually sweeping claims of little merit: *women are bad drivers*; *men are slobs*; *English teachers are nitpicky*; *computer jocks are*...; and on and on.

To draw valid inferences, you must always have sufficient evidence (see Chapter 20) and you must qualify your claims appropriately. After all, people do need generalizations to make reasonable decisions in life. Such claims can be offered legitimately if placed in context and tagged with sensible qualifiers—*some, a few, many, most, occasionally, rarely, possibly, in some cases, under certain circumstances, in my limited experience.*

Faulty Causality

In Latin, **faulty causality** is known as *post hoc, ergo propter hoc,* which translates as "after this, therefore because of this"—the faulty assumption that because one event or action follows another, the first causes the second. Consider a lawsuit commented on in the *Wall Street Journal* in which a writer sued Coors (unsuccessfully), claiming that drinking copious amounts of the company's beer had kept him from writing a novel. This argument is sometimes referred to as the "Twinkie defense," referring to a claim that the person who shot and killed San Francisco Supervisor Harvey Milk had eaten so many Twinkies and other sugary foods that his reasoning had been impaired. The phrase is now sometimes used to label the claims of criminals that their acts were caused by something beyond their control.

Of course, some actions do produce reactions. Step on the brake pedal in your car, and you move hydraulic fluid that pushes calipers against disks to create friction that stops the vehicle. In other cases, however, a supposed connection between cause and effect turns out to be completely wrong. For example, doctors now believe that when an elderly person falls and breaks a hip or leg, the injury usually caused the fall rather than the other way around.

That's why overly simple causal claims should always be subject to scrutiny. In summer 2008, writer Nicholas Carr posed a simple causal question in a cover story for the *Atlantic*: "Is Google Making Us Stupid?" Carr essentially answered yes, arguing that "as we come to rely on computers to mediate our understanding of the world, it is our own intelligence that flattens" and that the more one is online the less he or she is able to concentrate or read deeply.

But others, like Jamais Cascio (senior fellow at the Institute for Ethics and Emerging Technologies), soon challenged that causal connection: rather than making us stupid, Cascio argues, Internet tools like Google will lead to the development of "'fluid intelligence'—the ability to find meaning in confusion and to solve new problems, independent of acquired knowledge." The final word on this contentious causal relationship—the effects on the human brain caused by new technology—has yet to be written, and will probably be available only after decades of complicated research.

Begging the Question

Most teachers have heard some version of the following argument: *You can't give me a C in this course; I'm an A student.* A member of Congress accused of taking kickbacks can make much the same argument: *I can't be guilty of accepting such bribes; I'm an honest person.* In both cases, the claim is made on grounds that can't be accepted as true because those grounds themselves are in question. How can the accused bribe-taker defend herself on grounds of honesty when that honesty is in doubt? Looking closely at the arguments below helps to see the fallacy:

Claim	You can't give me a C in this course...
Reason	...because I'm an A student.
Assumption	An A student is someone who can't receive Cs.

Claim	Representative X can't be guilty of accepting bribes...
Reason	...because she's an honest person.
Assumption	An honest person cannot be guilty of accepting bribes.

With the assumptions stated, you can see why **begging the question**—assuming as true the very claim that's disputed—is a form of circular argument that goes nowhere.

Equivocation

Equivocations—half truths or arguments that give lies an honest appearance—are usually based on tricks of language. Consider the plagiarist who copies a paper word for word from a source and then declares that "I wrote the entire paper myself"—meaning that she physically copied the piece on her own. But the plagiarist is using *wrote* equivocally and knows that most people understand the word to mean composing and not merely copying words.

Parsing words carefully can sometimes look like equivocation or be the thing itself. For example, during the 2016 presidential campaign, Hillary Clinton was asked regularly (some would say she was hounded) about her use of a private email server and about whether any of the emails contained classified information. Here's what she said on February 1, 2016:

> The emails that I was received were not marked classified. Now, there are disagreements among agencies on what should have been perhaps classified retroactively, but at the time that doesn't change the fact that they were not marked classified.
>
> —*NPR Morning Edition*, February 1, 2016

Many commentators at the time felt that this statement was a clear equivocation, and this controversy continued to haunt Clinton throughout her campaign.

Non Sequitur

A **non sequitur** is an argument whose claims, reasons, or assumptions don't connect logically. You've probably detected a non sequitur when you react to an argument with a puzzled, "Wait, that doesn't follow." Children are adept at framing non sequiturs like this one: *You don't love me or you'd buy me a new bike.* It doesn't take a parental genius to realize that love has little connection with buying children toys.

Non sequiturs often occur when writers omit steps in an otherwise logical chain of reasoning. For example, it might be a non sequitur to argue that since postsecondary education now costs so much, it's time to move colleges and university instruction online. Such a suggestion *may* have merit, but a leap from brick-and-mortar schools to virtual ones is extreme. Numerous issues and questions must be addressed step-by-step before the proposal can be taken seriously.

Politicians sometimes resort to non sequiturs to evade thorny issues or questions. Here, for example, is Donald Trump replying to questions in a 2017 interview with Michael Scherer of *Time Magazine:*

> *Scherer:* Mitch McConnell has said he'd rather you stop tweeting, that he sees it as a distraction.
>
> *Trump:* Mitch will speak for himself. Mitch is a wonderful man. Mitch should speak for himself.

Here Trump does not respond to the claim the interviewer says Senate Majority Leader Mitch McConnell has made, but instead abruptly changes the subject, commenting instead on McConnell, saying he is a "wonderful man."

Straw Man

Those who resort to the **straw man** fallacy attack arguments that no one is really making or portray opponents' positions as more extreme or far less coherent than they actually are. The speaker or writer thus sets up an argument that is conveniently easy to knock down (like a man of straw), proceeds to do so, and then claims victory over an opponent who may not even exist.

Straw men are especially convenient devices for politicians who want to characterize the positions of their opponents as more extreme than they actually are: consider obvious memes such as "war on women" and "war on Christmas." But straw man arguments are often more subtle. For instance, Steven Novella of Yale University argues that political commentator Charles Krauthammer slips into the fallacy when he misconstrues the meaning of "settled science" in a column on climate change. Novella rebuts Krauthammer's assertion that "There is nothing more anti-scientific than the very idea that science is settled, static, impervious to challenge" by explaining why such a claim is deceptive:

> Calling something an established scientific fact means that it is reasonable to proceed with that fact as a premise, for further research or for policy. It does not mean "static, impervious to challenge." That is the straw man. Both evolution deniers and climate change deniers use this tactic to misinterpret scientific confidence as an anti-scientific resistance to new evidence or arguments. It isn't.
>
> —Steven Novella, *NeuroLogica Blog*, February 25, 2014

In other words, Krauthammer's definition of *science* is not one that most scientists use.

Red Herring

This fallacy gets its name from the old British hunting practice of dragging a dried herring across the path of the fox in order to throw the hounds off the trail. A **red herring** fallacy does just that: it changes the subject abruptly or introduces an irrelevant claim or fact to throw readers or listeners off the trail. For example, people skeptical about climate change will routinely note that weather is always changing and point to the fact that Vikings settled in Greenland one thousand years ago before harsher conditions drove them away. True, scientists will say, but the point is irrelevant to arguments about worldwide global warming caused by human activity.

The red herring is not only a device writers and speakers use in the arguments they create, but it's also a charge used frequently to undermine someone else's arguments. Couple the term "red herring" in a Web search to just about any political or social cause and you'll come up with numerous articles complaining of someone's use of the device.

> climate change + red herring
>
> white supremacy + red herring
>
> immigration reform + red herring

"Red herring" has become a convenient way of saying "I disagree with your argument" or "your point is irrelevant." And perhaps making a too-easy rebuttal like that can itself be a fallacy?

Faulty Analogy

Comparisons can help to clarify one concept by measuring it against another that is more familiar. Consider the power and humor of this comparison attributed to Mark Twain, an implicit argument for term limits in politics:

> Politicians and diapers must be changed often, and for the same reason.

When comparisons such as this one are extended, they become *analogies*—ways of understanding unfamiliar ideas by comparing them with something that's better known (see p. 539). But useful as such comparisons are, they may prove false if either taken on their own and pushed too far, or taken too seriously. At this point, they turn into **faulty analogies**—inaccurate or inconsequential comparisons between objects or concepts. Secretary of Education Betsy DeVos found herself in a national controversy following a statement she made after meeting with Historically Black Colleges and Universities presidents in Washington, when she made an analogy between HCBUs and her advocacy of "school choice" today:

> They [African Americans] saw that the system wasn't working, that there was an absence of opportunity, so they took it upon themselves to provide the solution. HBCUs are real pioneers when it comes to school choice. They are living proof that when more options are provided to students, they are afforded greater access and greater quality. Their success has shown that more options help students flourish.

What commentators immediately pointed out was that this statement included a false analogy. HBCUs were not created to provide more choice for African American students (and thus be analogous to DeVos's push for charter schools and school "choice") but rather because these students had little to no choice; after the Civil War, African American students were barred from most white public institutions.

Paralipsis

This fallacy (sometimes spelled *paralepsis* and often compared with occultatio) has been so predominant in the last two years that we think it's worthy of inclusion here. Basically, this fallacy occurs when speakers or writers say they will NOT talk about something, thus doing the very thing they say they're not going to do. It's a way of getting a point into an argument obliquely, of sneaking it in while saying that you are not doing so. Although paralipsis is rampant today, it is not new: Socrates famously used it in his trial when he said he would not mention his grieving wife and children who would suffer so mightily at his death. In the 2016 presidential campaign and in the first years of his presidency, Donald Trump used paralipsis repeatedly. Here, for instance, he is at a campaign rally in Fort Dodge, Iowa, speaking about rival candidate Marco Rubio:

> I will not call him a lightweight, because I think that's a derogatory term, so I will not call him a lightweight. Is that OK with you people? I refuse to say that he's a lightweight.

Martin Shovel/Creativity Works

Although he is the most conspicuous user of paralipsis today, Trump is by no means the only politician to use this fallacy. Here's a commentator reporting on presidential candidate Bernie Sanders at a 2016 town hall meeting in Iowa:

> Sen. Bernie Sanders (I-Vt.) on Friday called Bill Clinton's sexual scandals "totally disgraceful and unacceptable" but said he would not use the former president's infidelities against Hillary Clinton. "Hillary Clinton is not Bill Clinton. What Bill Clinton did, I think we can all acknowledge was totally, totally, totally disgraceful and unacceptable."
>
> —Reporter Lisa Hagen, *The Hill*

In saying he would not use the former president's scandalous behavior against Hillary Clinton, he in fact does just the opposite.

Finally, you may run across the use of paralipsis anywhere, even at the movies, as spoken here by Robert Downey Jr.'s character Tony Stark:

> I'm not saying I'm responsible for this country's longest run of uninterrupted peace in 35 years! I'm not saying that from the ashes of captivity, never has a phoenix metaphor been more personified! I'm not saying Uncle Sam can kick back on a lawn chair, sipping on an iced tea, because I haven't come across anyone man enough to go toe to toe with me on my best day. It's not about me!
>
> —Robert Downey Jr., *Iron Man 2* (2010)

You may be tempted to use this fallacy in your own writing, but beware: it is pretty transparent and may well backfire on you. Better to say what you believe to be the truth—and stick to it.

RESPOND

1. Examine each of the following political slogans or phrases for logical fallacies.

   "Resistance is futile." (Borg message on *Star Trek: The Next Generation*)

   "It's the economy, stupid." (sign on the wall at Bill Clinton's campaign headquarters)

   "Make love, not war." (antiwar slogan popularized during the Vietnam War)

   "Build bridges, not walls." (attributed to Martin Luther King Jr.)

   "Stronger Together" (campaign slogan)

   "Guns don't kill, people do." (NRA slogan)

   "Dog Fighters Are Cowardly Scum." (PETA T-shirt)

   "If you can't stand the heat, get out of the kitchen." (attributed to Harry S Truman)

2. Hone your critical reading skills by choosing a paper you've written for a college class and analyze it for signs of fallacious reasoning. Then find an editorial, a syndicated column, and a news report on the same topic and look for fallacies in them. Which has the most fallacies—and what kind? What may be the role of the audience in determining when a statement is fallacious? How effective do you think the fallacies were in speaking to their intended audience?

3. Find a Web site that is sponsored by an organization (the Future of Music Coalition, perhaps), a business (Coca-Cola, Pepsi), or another group (the Democratic or Republican National Committee), and analyze the site for fallacious reasoning. Among other considerations, look at the relationship between text and graphics and between individual pages and the pages that surround or are linked to them.

4. Political blogs such as *Mother Jones* and *InstaPundit* typically provide quick responses to daily events and detailed critiques of material in other media sites, including national newspapers. Study one such blog for a few days to see whether and how the site critiques the articles, political commentary, or writers it links to. Does the blog ever point out fallacies of argument? If so, does it explain the problems with such reasoning or just assume readers will understand the fallacies? Summarize your findings in a brief oral report to your class.

part 4

Categories of Stasis

CHAPTER

14

Stasis Theory: An Introduction

Do you ever wonder why so many public issues never seem to get resolved? Hotly debated problems seem to be dominated by the loudest, most quarrelsome voices, hopelessly circling the issue rather than making progress in addressing it. Let's take the example of climate change. Some people argue for specific solutions to the problem of global climate change, like funding alternative energy or passing laws that will reduce carbon emissions; others insist that dramatic change in the environment is a natural occurrence we need not worry about. Because these arguments respond to different questions about climate change, neither group can make any headway. The first argument is made in response to the question, "What should be done about global climate change?" The second answers the question, "What is happening with the climate?" If these two parties were to speak with each other, they would be at cross-purposes, unable to agree on what aspect of climate change to discuss, and the pressing issue of climate change would fall by the wayside.

The good news is that we can avoid these impasses in productive deliberation by using ***stasis theory***, a rhetorical tool that has proven useful for more than 2000 years in locating the "heart" of a disagreement. This chapter introduces stasis theory as a method to analyze and intervene in issues of public importance. Originally developed by the ancient Greeks and Romans for use in the courtroom, the word *stasis* comes from a Greek word meaning "stand still," or a location in a debate at which parties deliberate over the same question before proceeding to the next in their quest to solve a problem. There are four stases—*fact* or *conjecture*, *definition*, *quality*, and *policy*—organized in a sequence that naturally emerges as an issue is first brought to our attention and, later, solutions to the issue are found. When parties are "in stasis," they are in agreement over where the heart of their dispute lies, positioning them to engage in healthy deliberation on the same question. When parties are arguing about two different aspects of an issue, as in the case with our example of climate change above, they are "out of stasis." Stasis theory helps uncover the nature of a disagreement so that participants can develop arguments that will move the debate forward.

Using stasis theory helps us analyze and categorize different ***stakeholder*** perspectives and consider aspects of an issue that may otherwise be forgotten or overlooked. *Stakeholders* are the individuals and groups most affected by and/or invested in an issue. For example, in the issue of climate change, lawmakers, coal miners, and coastal residents are all stakeholders because they have clear interests in and concerns over how climate change is defined and addressed. You'll find that most public issues have many kinds of stakeholders with a variety of different positions on and "stakes" in the issue. The kinds of claims they make can be analyzed to see how those claims intersect with the four stases. These intersections are the object of analysis when you use stasis theory. Because the stasis questions are sequential—each depends on answers from the questions that precede it—they provide a framework to compare arguments and determine why certain stakeholders remain in disagreement.

The Four Stases

Each stasis indicates a stage in the argument that stakeholders are making and the questions they are answering with their particular claim. The four stases are as follows:

Fact or Conjecture

This stasis concerns whether a problem exists or not. Arguments of fact, also called arguments of "conjecture," speculate over the "facts" of the issue at hand. While facts may seem easy to agree upon because they initially appear like incontrovertible hard evidence, we witness different groups disagreeing over how to interpret hard evidence frequently. Questions of fact may seek to correct errors of fact or challenge widely held societal myths: Does consuming sugary beverages increase the risk of health issues? Are animals being harmed in cosmetic testing? Does stem cell research help create cures for diseases?

In the debate surrounding mandatory vaccinations for children attending public schools, stakeholders disagree over the existence of a controversy surrounding the safety of immunizations for diseases like measles and whooping cough. Many pediatricians claim that vaccinations for children are researched and well-tested and, in the vast majority of patients, do not cause significant side effects or health problems. Some parents, on the other hand, believe that there isn't enough evidence to prove that vaccinations will not cause health problems in all children. Both stakeholder communities are debating the existence of a problem; they are questioning a fact that is central to the larger social issue surrounding mandatory vaccinations for public school children.

Questions of Fact/Conjecture

- Did something happen? Is something happening?
- Does something exist?
- Is this an established fact?
- What caused this to happen?

Definition

Once the existence and facts of an issue have been agreed upon, the next stasis is definition. The specific ways that a stakeholder defines an issue reveal how they conceptualize that problem and how they would categorize it. Questions of definition might seek to challenge or broaden an existing definition or determine whether something fits an existing definition. Is assisting in suicide a crime? Should marijuana be considered a medical treatment for degenerative diseases? Are certain voter laws examples of voter suppression? People often fail to provide a clear-cut definition of the issue they are debating, but the way they conceptualize or categorize a problem will often indicate that a definition is at the heart of their argument.

One hotly debated argument of definition involves how to categorize NFL players kneeling during the national anthem. Owners, fans, players, and coaches disagree over whether or not the act of kneeling should be defined as patriotic. Some military veterans and politicians have claimed that taking a knee during the performance of the national anthem is unpatriotic because it disrespects the nation and those who fought for its freedoms. Others, such as politician Beto O'Rourke, argue that protesting systemic racism in the country through kneeling *is* patriotic, because non-violent protests also fight for the freedoms of American citizens. Because both of these arguments are concerned with defining and categorizing kneeling during the national anthem (either as a patriotic act or an unpatriotic act), these two parties are in stasis at the point of definition.

Questions of Definition

- Since something exists, what should we call it?
- How should we define this thing?
- How should we categorize this thing?

Quality or Evaluation

After parties are able to agree on how an issue is defined, the subsequent stasis to consider is quality. The stasis of quality is concerned with how we judge a problem's worth or level of importance. Are standardized test scores the best way to judge a student's academic success? Are genetically modified fruits and vegetables less healthy than traditionally grown produce? Is privatized healthcare the best way to ensure that Americans stay healthy? This stasis is also referred to as "evaluation," highlighting the role that values play in deliberation. What an individual or group cares about will help them to decide whether something is good or bad, relevant or irrelevant.

Discussions about the affordability of attending college often proceed from the point of quality. While most agree on the facts of what college costs and define the issue as one that impacts the lives of college students and their families, they may disagree about whether or not a high cost of a college education is a significant problem. Stakeholders such as the National Education Association consider the cost of attending college to be a serious problem in need of addressing because they value nation-wide accessibility to formal education. Another stakeholder, current Secretary of Education Betsy DeVos, does not consider the issue to be as pertinent because there are several alternative options, such as vocational programs, that keep the affordability of college from becoming a pressing issue. Both arguments contain value judgments on the issue of college affordability and are therefore taking up the stasis of quality.

Questions of Quality/Evaluation

- Is this thing good or bad? Better or worse?
- Is this thing relevant or not?
- Is this thing justified or not?

Policy or Proposal

Finally, arguments over policies or proposed solutions are concerned with what should be done about a problem. How should college athletes be rewarded for their service to their universities? What percentage of tax funds should be used to pay for abortions at government funded clinics? What should the local government do to ensure Norman residents have access to clean drinking water? Proposals can prescribe or reject changes to existing practices, rules, and policies, or explore new options for addressing a problem. It is common for stakeholders who care deeply about the issue at hand to enter a debate by immediately making an argument of policy without considering the previous three stases. Because the stases are sequential, it will be difficult for parties to achieve consensus about the best course of action, if they disagree, first, about the facts, definitions, or quality of the issue.

On the subject of animal testing, let's consider two animal rights groups: People for the Ethical Treatment of Animals (PETA) and the Humane Society of the United States (HSUS). If they agree about the existence and definition of the problem of testing cosmetics on animals and both judge the problem as severe and urgent, they may find that they only disagree about what specific procedure should be set in place in order to address the problem. PETA asserts that large corporations should fund research into testing alternatives like advanced computer modeling techniques. HSUS argues that individual consumers must adjust their spending patterns to only purchase animal-friendly products. These stakeholders are in stasis at the point of policy because they are prepared, after agreeing at the three preceding points of stasis, to discuss differing approaches to solving the problem.

Questions of Policy/Proposal

- What should be done about this thing?
- What actions should be taken?
- How should we solve this problem?

Using Stasis Theory

In your Composition courses at the University of Oklahoma, you will use stasis theory in two different ways: as a form of *analysis* to help you categorize and deeply understand others' arguments regarding a public issue, and as a framework for *invention* to determine ethical and effective ways to intervene in the conversation surrounding that issue.

Using Stasis Theory for Analysis

It can be all too easy to oversimplify public issues as black-and-white, right-and-wrong, or red-or-blue. Yet, no issue is simply two-sided, and using stasis theory for analysis helps us to understand, with more clarity, the full complexity of issues and why they don't immediately get resolved. As a tool for rhetorical analysis, stasis theory is more than just a means of categorizing and labeling arguments. Using the stasis questions to determine the crucial point of disagreement in an issue requires extensive research into the values, beliefs, claims, and concerns that motivate and shape the stakeholder's perspective on an issue. This research, first, helps us categorize the arguments made by the various stakeholders. In other words, you can determine whether and where those stakeholders are in stasis in order to locate the most pressing point of disagreement.

For example, stasis theory can help us understand the current state of deliberations surrounding "bathroom bills"—legislation defining how transgender individuals may use public restrooms—with more clarity. Some members of the transgender community have argued that being denied access to certain bathrooms is a matter of safety because they fear being physically harmed when entering a restroom assigned to a gender that does not visually appear to coincide with their own. Using stasis theory, you can identify their argument at the point of definition—asserting that the problem should be defined as an issue of safety—and the point of quality—asserting that the issue is significant and relevant in their lives. Another stakeholder, the American Civil Liberties Union, levies an argument that many bathroom bills violate the rights and freedoms of a group of citizens. Because they perceive that rights are being violated, the ACLU also considers, at the point of quality, that the denial of access to a particular bathroom is an urgent and exigent problem that should be resolved. Both of these stakeholders would be able to converse with each other at the point of policy because they have not agreed on what specifically should be done in order to correct the problem.

However, other stakeholders, like the Republican legislators in Texas, would not be able to enter into a conversation about policy with these two groups. In 2015, they proposed a bill that would require individuals to use the restroom that corresponded with the gender listed on their driver's license. This proposal, because it seems in conflict with the values and concerns expressed by both the transgender community and the ACLU, suggests that the Texas Legislature also understands the facts and definitions of this issue differently from these other stakeholders. While the legislators may also value the safety of the general public, their understanding of the facts surrounding transgender identity or the competing definitions of how to conceptualize the public problem differs substantially from the other two stakeholder groups. Therefore, you could locate the most pressing point of disagreement in this conversation back to a stasis of fact. For the sake of this example, these stakeholder positions have been greatly simplified. To fully understand the complexity of stakeholders' arguments and, of the current state of the larger issue, you will need to do a lot of research to find out what motivates these positions and to determine if stakeholders who are consolidated into one general community—such as *all* members of the transgender community—can be further categorized into smaller stakeholder groups based on their particular perspectives on an issue. Your research, categorization, and analysis of the stakeholders in an issue should lead you to better understand the current state of that issue as well as the different arguments that are actually being made and what motivates those arguments.

Using stasis theory to analyze stakeholder arguments isn't an exact science. Extensive research into a stakeholder's perspective on an issue might make it *more* difficult to identify their stasis. Don't worry if the arguments you are analyzing don't seem to fit clearly into any one stasis. Instead, pay attention to the important details of the argument and how it is motivated by the stakeholder's values, interests, and concerns. For example, you might find it extremely challenging to neatly categorize the arguments of stakeholders in the troubling issue of sexual assault on university campuses. Two stakeholders—victims of sexual assault and assailants who claim innocence—immediately appear to be arguing over the existence of a problem; they both seem to be making claims of fact over whether or not the assault occurred. However, after analyzing the arguments, interests, and concerns of the accused more closely, it might become apparent that what is really being called into question is the definition of assault; this definition impacts how the facts are considered *and* evaluated. For example, assailants who define consent as permission that can be granted by an intoxicated individual have a different factual understanding and evaluation of sexual encounters than do the victims who might believe that consent cannot be given by intoxicated people. Because facts and definitions cannot be separated in this case, it is difficult to determine, conclusively, where these stakeholders are in stasis. Regardless, using stasis theory to analyze these two arguments allows us to understand that differing definitions of sexual assault are a critical factor in determining why the problem has long gone unresolved on college campuses across the country.

As you can see, stasis theory is a framework that helps you understand and synthesize the abundance of arguments in any given issue in order to isolate and analyze the heart of the disagreement, and, eventually, to locate the most effective points of intervention in the larger conversation.

Using Stasis Theory for Invention

If, as Kenneth Burke suggests, we think about public deliberation as a never-ending and long-standing conversation in a crowded "parlor," we must listen to get a sense for the "tenor" of the conversation before interjecting with our own arguments. As a tool for invention, stasis theory can help you locate that core in order to make deliberate and well-reasoned decisions about the types of arguments we compose. In this way, stasis theory can generate new ideas *in addition to* describing ideas that already exist in the public sphere. When we intervene in discussions of public problems, we don't want to just make *winning* arguments; we want to make effective *and ethical* arguments that respond to the needs and concerns of other stakeholders and invite productive conversation in the future. Your efforts to argue will not always result in changed minds or actions, but using stasis theory as a prewriting technique will aid you in deciding *whom* you need to convince, *what* you need to convince them of, and *how* you can do so most effectively. It prepares you, in other words, to tailor your arguments to particular stakeholder audiences.

Part of crafting your argument for a specific stakeholder is determining which of the stases you should address in order to move the conversation forward productively. Your argument may be multifaceted. To respond to your stakeholder audience's argument of policy, for example, you may have to address a preceding point first, before you levy your own proposal. When making an argument about the issue of mass incarceration to the President, you may realize that, though you want to offer a proposal to solve the problem—increased funding for rehabilitation programs instead of prison maintenance—your stakeholder audience may still be questioning the quality of the problem. In fact, Donald Trump had previously expressed a judgment that putting more criminals in prison would result in safer communities. Therefore, you may first choose to thoroughly evaluate our current prison system, indicating that time in prison does not lead to a decrease in recidivism rates, thereby arguing that the current prison system is not effectively deterring crime. In choosing to make an initial argument of quality, you meet your stakeholder audience in stasis.

If President Trump is persuaded by your argument of quality, you can then move on to persuade him to accept your proposal for rehabilitation programs.

Similarly, when you try to make an effective and respectful argument to a stakeholder audience, it can feel like you need to address *all* four stases in order to be convincing. When attempting to intervene in the issue of using spanking as a disciplinary technique, you might initially feel that you need to convince your stakeholder audience—parents of young children in Norman—of the facts that demonstrate the myriad lasting effects of the use of corporal punishment on children, challenge definitions of spanking as a viable form of discipline, and establish the negative quality of the technique, all before suggesting a particular course of action to remedy the problem. However, stasis theory helps you not only avoid arguing at cross-purposes, but also avoid making arguments with which your audience already agrees, allowing you to locate the specific difference of viewpoint that you need to address. Research into the values and concerns of this particular stakeholder community might reveal that, because they already agree at the points of fact, definition, and quality, you should focus the majority of your efforts on engaging with this audience on what to do to solve the problem (stasis of policy). Your work should be to detail how they might proceed to solve the problem by, for example, implementing certain types of behavioral therapy in their parenting strategies. Using stasis as a pre-writing technique should steer your decisions when you compose an argument so you can make more precise and focused arguments.

In this way, the four stases also serve as argumentative "forms." Writing an argument of definition requires a different set of choices regarding the structure and organization of the argument and the types of evidence used to support it than does an argument of quality. The next four chapters will give you a framework for how to write arguments of fact, definition, evaluation or quality, and policy or proposal. These chapters will come in handy after you've used stasis theory for analysis and are ready to begin crafting an argument for a particular stakeholder.

CHAPTER

15

Arguments of Fact

Left to right: Richard Baker/Getty Images;Alfred Eisenstaedt/Getty Images;David R. Frazier Photolibrary, Inc./Alamy Stock Photo

Some people believe that extensive use of smartphones and social media is especially harmful to children and young adults, and recent research provides disturbing evidence that they may be right.

In the past, female screen stars like Marilyn Monroe could be buxom and curvy, less concerned about their weight than actresses today. Or so the legend goes. But measuring the costumes worn by Monroe and other actresses reveals a different story.

When an instructor announces a tough new attendance policy for her course, a student objects that there is no evidence that students who regularly attend classes perform any better than those who do not. The instructor begs to differ.

Understanding Arguments of Fact

Factual arguments come in many varieties, but they all try to establish whether something is or is not so, answering questions such as *Is a historical legend true? Has a crime occurred?* or *Are the claims of a scientific study replicable?* At first glance, you might object that these aren't arguments at all but just a matter of looking things up and then writing reports. And you'd be correct to an extent: people don't usually argue factual matters that are settled or undisputed (*The earth revolves around the sun*), that might be decided with simple research (*The Mendenhall Glacier has receded 1.75 miles since 1958*), or that are the equivalent of a rule (*One mile measures 5,280 feet*). Reporting facts, you might think, should be free of the friction of argument.

But the authority of "facts" has been routinely challenged. With a full generation of contemporary philosophers insisting that reality is just a creation of language, perhaps it's not surprising that politicians and pundits now find themselves arguing over "fake news," "known facts," and "alternative facts."

Yet facts do still become arguments whenever they're controversial on their own or challenge people's conventional beliefs and lifestyles. Disagreements about childhood obesity, endangered species, or energy production ought to have a kind of clean, scientific logic to them. But that's rarely the case because the facts surrounding them must be interpreted. Those interpretations then determine what we feed children, where we can build a dam, or how we heat our homes. In other words, serious factual arguments almost always have consequences. *Can we rely on wind and solar power to solve our energy needs? Will the Social Security trust fund really go broke? Is it healthy to eat fatty foods?* People need well-reasoned factual arguments on subjects of this kind to make informed decisions. Such arguments educate the public.

For the same reason, we need arguments to challenge beliefs that are common in a society but held on the basis of inadequate or faulty information. We sometimes need help, too, noticing change that is occurring all around us. So corrective arguments appear daily in the media, often based on studies written by scientists or researchers that the public would not encounter on their own. Many people, for example, still believe that talking on a cell phone while driving is just like listening to the radio. But their intuition is not based on hard data: scientific studies show that using a cell phone in a car is comparable to driving under the influence of alcohol. That's a fact. As a result, fifteen states (and counting) have banned the use of handheld phones while driving—and almost all now ban texting while driving.

Factual arguments also routinely address broad questions about how we understand the past. For example, are the accounts that we have of the American founding—or the Civil War, Reconstruction, or the heroics of the "Greatest Generation" in World War II—accurate? Or do the "facts" that we teach today sometimes reflect the perspectives and prejudices of earlier times or ideologies? The telling of history is almost always controversial and rarely settled: the British and Americans will always tell different versions of what happened in North America in 1776.

The Internet puts mountains of information at our fingertips, but we need to be sure to confirm whether or not that information is fact, using what Howard Rheingold calls "crap detection," the ability to distinguish between accurate information and inaccurate information, misinformation, or disinformation. (For more on "crap detection," see **Chapter 21**, "Evaluating Sources.")

As you can see, arguments of fact do much of the heavy lifting in our world. They report on what has been recently discovered or explore the implications of that new information. They also add interest and complexity to our lives, taking what might seem simple and adding new dimensions to it. In many situations, they're the precursors to other forms of analysis, especially causal and proposal arguments. Before we can explore why things happen as they do or solve problems, we need to do our best to determine the facts.

Jeff Stahler/Andrews McMeel Syndication

RESPOND

For each topic in the following list, decide whether the claim is worth arguing to a college audience, and explain why or why not.

Earthquakes at Yellowstone National Park are increasing in number and intensity.

Many people die annually of heart disease.

The planet would benefit enormously if more people learned to eat insects.

Japan might have come to terms more readily in 1945 if the Allies in World War II hadn't demanded unconditional surrender.

Boys would do better in school if there were more men teaching in elementary and secondary classrooms.

The benefits of increasing oil and natural gas production via fracking more than outweigh the environmental downsides of the process.

There aren't enough high-paying jobs for college graduates these days.

Hydrogen may never be a viable alternative to fossil fuels because it takes too much energy to change hydrogen into a usable form.

Characterizing Factual Arguments

Factual arguments are often motivated by simple human curiosity or suspicion: *Are people who earn college degrees happier than those who don't? If being fat is so unhealthy, why aren't mortality rates rising? Does it matter economically that so many young people today think of themselves as foodies?* Researchers may notice a pattern that leads them to look more closely at some phenomenon or behavior, exploring questions such as *What if?* or *How come?* Or maybe a writer first notes something new or different or unexpected and wants to draw attention to that fact: *Contrary to expectations, suicide rates are much higher in rural areas than in urban ones.*

Such observations can lead quickly to **hypotheses**—that is, toward tentative and plausible statements of fact whose merits need to be examined more closely. *Perhaps people at different educational levels define happiness differently? Maybe being a little overweight isn't as bad for people as we've been told? Maybe self-identifying as a "foodie" is really a marker of class and social aspirations?* To support such hypotheses, writers then have to uncover evidence that reaches well beyond the casual observations that triggered an initial interest—like a news reporter motivated to see whether there's a verifiable story behind a source's tip.

For instance, the authors of *Freakonomics*, Stephen J. Dubner and Steven D. Levitt, were intrigued by the National Highway Traffic Safety Administration's claim that car seats for children were 54 percent effective in preventing deaths in auto crashes for children below the age of four. In a *New York Times* op-ed column entitled "The Seat-Belt Solution," they posed an important question about that factual claim:

> But 54 percent effective compared with what? The answer, it turns out, is this: Compared with a child's riding completely unrestrained.

Their initial question about that claim led them to a more focused inquiry, then to a database on auto crashes, and then to a surprising conclusion: for kids above age twenty-four months, those in car seats were statistically safer than those without any protection but weren't safer than those confined by ordinary seat belts (which are much simpler, cheaper, and more readily available devices). Looking at the statistics every which way, the authors wonder if children older than two years would be just as well off physically—and their parents less stressed and better off financially—if the government mandated seat belts rather than car seats for them.

What kinds of evidence typically appear in sound factual arguments? The simple answer might be "all sorts," but a case can be made that factual arguments try to rely more on "hard evidence" than do "constructed" arguments based on logic and reason (see **Chapter 27**). Even so, some pieces of evidence are harder than others!

Developing a Factual Argument

Entire Web sites are dedicated to finding and posting errors from news and political sources. Some, like Media Matters for America and Accuracy in Media, take overtly partisan stands. Here's a one-day sampling of headlines from Media Matters:

> After NASA Announces It Found Water on Mars, Rush Limbaugh Says It's Part of a Climate Change Conspiracy
>
> Trump administration met with a GOP donor and a Fox contributor about a fake story meant to distract from Russia probe
>
> Fox hosts can't keep their facts straight while praising Trump's immigration cuts

And here's a listing from Accuracy in Media from the same day:

> Major Newspapers Just Pretend to Have Conservative Columnists
>
> Left Claims Hitler-Style "Indoctrination" in Trump's Boy Scouts Speech
>
> *Washington Post* Reluctantly Admits Stock Market Gains Linked to Trump

It would be hard to miss the blatant political agendas at work on these sites.

Other fact-checking organizations have better reputations when it comes to assessing the truths behind political claims and media presentations. Although both are also routinely charged with bias, Pulitzer Prize–winning PolitiFact.com and FactCheck.org at least make an effort to seem fair-minded across a broader political spectrum. FactCheck.org, for example, provides a detailed analysis of the claims it investigates in relatively neutral and denotative language, and lists the sources its researchers used—just as if its writers were doing a research paper. At its best, FactCheck.org demonstrates what one valuable kind of factual argument can accomplish.

Any factual argument that you might compose—from how you state your claim to how you present evidence and the language you use—should be similarly shaped by the occasion for the argument and a desire to serve the audiences that you hope to reach. We can offer some general advice to help you get started.

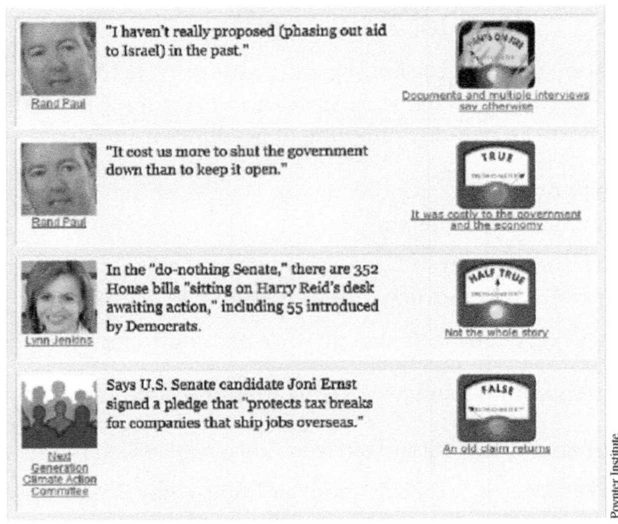

FIGURE 15.1 PolitiFact uses a meter to rate political claims from "True" to "Pants on Fire."

RESPOND

The Annenberg Public Policy Center at the University of Pennsylvania hosts FactCheck.org, a Web site dedicated to separating facts from opinion or falsehood in the area of politics. It claims to be politically neutral. Find a case that interests you, either a recent controversial item listed on its homepage or another from its archives. Carefully study the item. Pay attention to the devices that FactCheck.org uses to suggest or ensure objectivity and the way that it handles facts and statistics. Then offer your own brief *factual* argument about the site's objectivity.

Researching Your Hypothesis

How and where you research your subject will depend, naturally, on your subject. You'll certainly want to review Chapter 20, "Finding Evidence," Chapter 21, "Evaluating Sources," and Chapter 22, "Using Sources," before constructing an argument of fact. Libraries and the Web will provide you with deep resources on almost every subject. Your task will typically be to separate the best sources from all the rest. The word *best* here has many connotations: some reputable sources may be too technical for your audiences; some accessible sources may be pitched too low or be too far removed from the actual facts.

You'll be making judgment calls like this routinely. But do use primary sources whenever you can. For example, when gathering a comment from a source on the Web, trace it whenever possible to its original site, and read the comment in its full context. When statistics are quoted, follow them back to the source that offered them first to be sure that they're recent and reputable. Instructors and librarians can help you appreciate the differences. Understand that even sources with pronounced biases can furnish useful information, provided that you know how to use them, take their limitations into account, and then share what you know about the sources with your readers.

Sometimes, you'll be able to do primary research on your own, especially when your subject is local and you have the resources to do it. Consider conducting a competent survey of campus opinions and attitudes, for example, or study budget documents (often public) to determine trends in faculty salaries, tuition, student fees, and so on. Primary research of this sort can be challenging because even the simplest surveys or polls have to be intelligently designed and executed in a way that samples a representative population (see **Chapter 27**). But the work could pay off in an argument that brings new information to readers.

Refining Your Claim

As you learn more about your subject, you might revise your hypothesis to reflect what you've discovered. In most cases, these revised hypotheses will grow increasingly complex and specific. Following are three versions of essentially the same claim, with each version offering more information to help readers judge its merit:

- Americans really did land on the moon, despite what some people think!
- Since 1969, when the *Eagle* supposedly landed on the moon, some people have been unjustifiably skeptical about the success of the United States' *Apollo* program.
- Despite plentiful hard evidence to the contrary—from *Saturn V* launches witnessed by thousands to actual moon rocks tested by independent labs worldwide—some people persist in believing falsely that NASA's moon landings were filmed on deserts in the American Southwest as part of a massive propaganda fraud.

'...And, of course, there are the conspiracy theorists who say that it was all a big hoax and I didn't jump over it at all.'

KES/CartoonStock.com

The additional details about the subject might also suggest new ways to develop and support it. For example, conspiracy theorists claim that the absence of visible stars in photographs of the moon landing is evidence that it was staged, but photographers know that the camera exposure needed to capture the foreground—astronauts in their bright space suits—would have made the stars in the background too dim to see. That's a key bit of evidence for this argument.

As you advance in your research, your thesis will likely pick up even more qualifying words and expressions, which help you to make reasonable claims. Qualifiers—words and phrases such as *some, most, few, for most people, for a few users, under specific conditions, usually, occasionally, seldom,* and so on—will be among your most valuable tools in a factual argument.

Sometimes it will be important to contextualize a factual claim for others who may find it hard to accept. Of course, you could just present the hard numbers, but research suggests that many people double down on their positions when offered contrary facts. What to do? Michael Shermer, writing in *Scientific American*, suggests these common sense strategies:

> [W]hat can we do to convince people of the error of their beliefs? From my experience, 1. keep emotions out of the exchange, 2. discuss, don't attack (no *ad hominem* and no *ad Hitlerum*), 3. listen carefully and try to articulate the other position accurately, 4. show respect, 5. acknowledge that you understand why someone might hold that opinion, and 6. try to show how changing facts does not necessarily mean changing worldviews. These strategies may not always work to change people's minds, but now that the nation has just been put through a political fact-check wringer, they may help reduce unnecessary divisiveness.
>
> —Michael Shermer, "How to Convince Someone When Facts Fail"

Deciding Which Evidence to Use

In this chapter, we've blurred the distinction between factual arguments for scientific and technical audiences and those for the general public (in magazines, blogs, social media sites, television documentaries, and so on). In the former kind of arguments, readers will expect specific types of evidence arranged in a formulaic way. Such reports may include a hypothesis, a review of existing research on the subject, a description of methods, a presentation of results, and finally a formal discussion of the findings. If you are thinking "lab report," you are already familiar with an academic form of a factual argument with precise standards for evidence.

Less scientific factual arguments—claims about our society, institutions, behaviors, habits, and so on—are seldom so systematic, and they may draw on evidence from a great many different media. For instance, you might need to review old newspapers, scan videos, study statistics on government Web sites, read transcripts of congressional hearings, record the words of eyewitnesses to an event, glean information by following experts on Twitter, and so on. Very often, you will assemble your arguments from material found in credible, though not always concurring, authorities and resources—drawing upon the factual findings of scientists and scholars, but perhaps using their original insights in novel ways.

For example, you might be intrigued by a much cited article from the *Atlantic* (August 5, 2017) in which author Jean M. Twenge reviews evidence that suggests that adolescents who spend more and more time on their cellphones are increasingly unhappy—to the detriment of their emotional health. Here's an important moment in her lengthy argument:

> You might expect that teens spend so much time in these new spaces because it makes them happy, but most data suggest that it does not. The Monitoring the Future survey, funded by the National Institute on Drug Abuse and designed to be nationally representative, has asked 12th-graders more than

> 1,000 questions every year since 1975 and queried eighth- and 10th-graders since 1991. The survey asks teens how happy they are and also how much of their leisure time they spend on various activities, including nonscreen activities such as in-person social interaction and exercise, and, in recent years, screen activities such as using social media, texting, and browsing the web. The results could not be clearer: Teens who spend more time than average on screen activities are more likely to be unhappy, and those who spend more time than average on nonscreen activities are more likely to be happy.
>
> There's not a single exception. All screen activities are linked to less happiness, and all nonscreen activities are linked to more happiness.
>
> —Jean M. Twenge, "Have Smartphones Destroyed a Generation?"

Reading such dire news (and the article reports even more frightening increases in suicide), may raise new questions for you: Are there contrary studies? Is it conceivable that time spent online has benefits? Twenge herself notes, for example, that teen pregnancies have dropped dramatically in recent years. Perhaps, too, adolescents so inwardly directed by screen use might develop into more sensitive and less violent adults? Such considerations might lead you to look for research that complicates the earlier work by bringing fresh facts or perspectives to the table.

Often, though, you may have only a limited number of words or pages in which to make an academic argument. What do you do then? You present your best evidence as powerfully as possible: you *can* make a persuasive factual case with just a few examples—three or four often suffice to make a point. Indeed, going on too long or presenting even good data in uninteresting ways can undermine a claim.

Presenting Your Evidence

In *Hard Times* (1854), British author Charles Dickens poked fun at a pedagogue he named Thomas Gradgrind, who preferred hard facts before all things human or humane. When poor Sissy Jupe (called "girl number twenty" in his awful classroom) is unable at his command to define *horse*, Gradgrind turns to his star pupil, Bitzer:

> "Bitzer," said Thomas Gradgrind. "Your definition of a horse."
>
> "Quadruped. Graminivorous. Forty teeth, namely twenty-four grinders, four eyeteeth, and twelve incisive. Sheds coat in the spring; in marshy countries, sheds hoofs, too. Hoofs hard, but requiring to be shod with iron. Age known by marks in mouth." Thus (and much more) Bitzer.
>
> "Now girl number twenty," said Mr. Gradgrind. "You know what a horse is."
>
> —Charles Dickens, *Hard Times*

But does Bitzer? Rattling off facts about a subject isn't quite the same thing as knowing it, especially when your goal is, as it is in an argument of fact, to educate and persuade audiences. So you must take care how you present your evidence.

Factual arguments, like any others, take many forms. They can be as simple and pithy as a letter to the editor (or Bitzer's definition of a horse) or as comprehensive and formal as a senior thesis or even a dissertation, meant for just two or three readers evaluating the competence of your work. But to earn the attention of readers in more public forums, you may need to work harder, affirming your expertise by offering engaging and authoritative sources, presenting your argument with grace and clarity, including tables, graphs, photographs and other visual evidence when appropriate, and documenting all your claims. Such moves will establish the ethos of your work, making it seem serious, credible, well-conceived, and worth reading.

Considering Design and Visuals

When you prepare a factual argument, consider how you can present your evidence most effectively. Precisely because factual arguments often rely on evidence that can be measured, computed, or illustrated, they benefit from thoughtful, even artful presentation of data. If you have lots of examples, you might arrange them in a list (bulleted or otherwise) and keep the language in each item roughly parallel. If you have an argument that can be translated into a table, chart, or graph (see Chapter 29), try it. On page 328, for example, are three of the six tables that accompanied Jean M. Twenge's essay on smartphones, all dramatically illustrating a decline in various adolescent behaviors following the introduction of the iPhone in 2007. And if there's a more dramatic medium for your factual argument—a Prezi slide show, a multimedia mashup, a documentary video posted via a social network—experiment with it, checking to be sure it would satisfy the assignment.

Images and photos—from technical illustrations to imaginative re-creations—have the power to document what readers might otherwise have to imagine, whether actual conditions of drought, poverty, or a disaster like Hurricane Harvey that dropped 27 trillion gallons of water on Texas and Louisiana in 2017, or the dimensions of the Roman forum as it existed in the time of Julius Caesar. Readers today expect the arguments they read to include visual elements, and there's little reason not to offer this assistance if you have the technical skills to create them.

Consider also the rapid development of the genre known as infographics—basically data presented in bold visual form. These items can be humorous and creative, but many, such as "Learning Out of Poverty" on p. 329, make powerful factual arguments even when they leave it to viewers to draw their own conclusions. Just search "infographics" on the Web to find many examples.

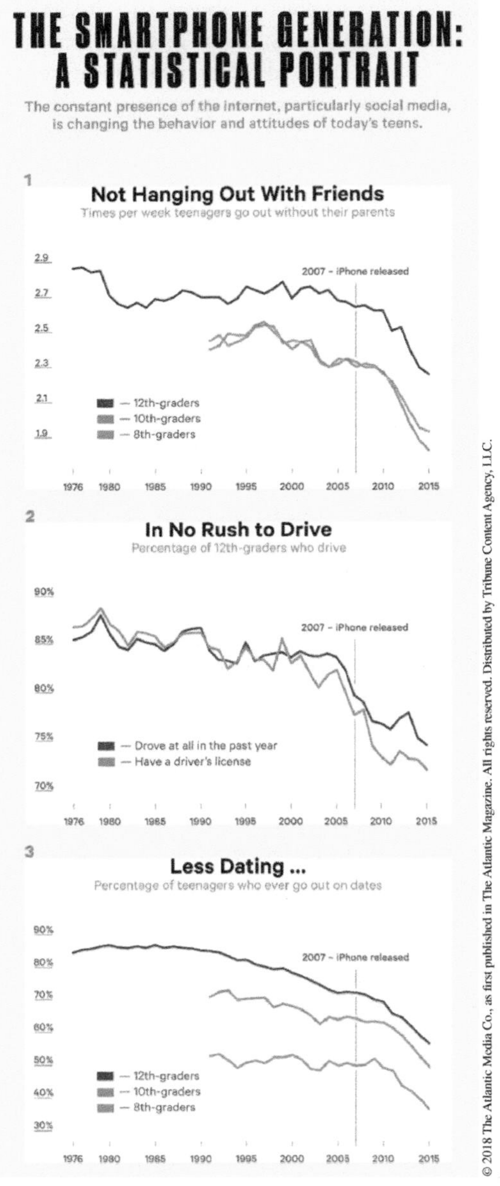

FIGURE 15.2 Jean M. Twenge uses graphs to support her claims about the impact of smartphones on teenagers.

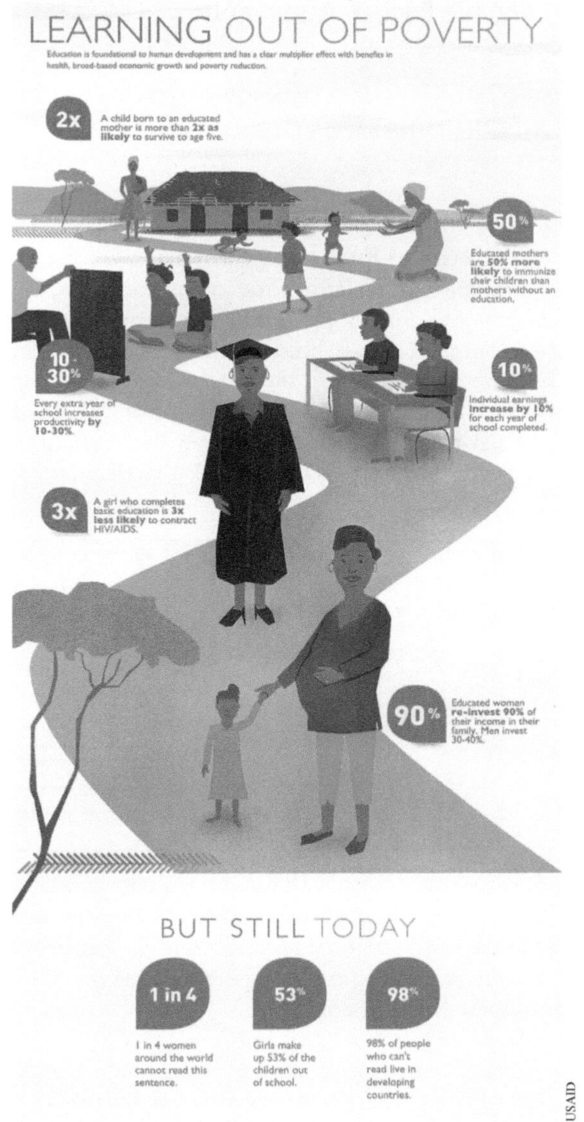

FIGURE 15.3 "Learning Out of Poverty." Infographics like this one turn facts and data into arguments.

Two Sample Factual Arguments

The Snacktivities and Musings of a Millennial Foodie

KATE BEISPEL*

Beispel draws readers in with a first-person point of view.

It's 80 degrees and I'm breaking a sweat as I hoist my just-bought lobster roll into the air, struggling to position it in a way that focuses on the mountain of chopped lobster baking in butter, while subtly blurring out the ocean behind it. I have one goal for this picture—to make it on to the *Food in the Air* Instagram account. I've spent months of my life positioning meals in front of breathtaking backdrops and sending them in to the anonymous geniuses that run this account, with no success. This meal, I've decided, will be my big break.

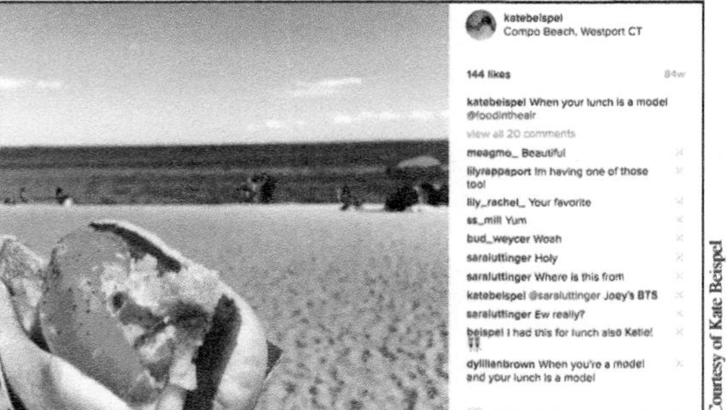

Courtesy of Kate Beispel

It turns out it wasn't. But that hasn't stopped me. I've continued to seek out amazing meals and yell "wait, wait, wait" if someone dares to take a bite before I take a picture. Trying new foods, finding something amazing, and sharing it with all of my followers is one of my hobbies. And I'm not alone.

---

*Kate Beispel wrote "The Snacktivities and Musings of a Millennial Foodie" for a writing class when she was a senior at the University of Texas at Austin. Drawing on both personal experience and a number of sources, this communications/journalism major argues that her generation, so uniquely and oddly focused on food and technology, is changing both business and culture. To prove her case, she draws on plentiful lifestyle evidence that members of her generation will almost certainly recognize. Beispel is pursuing a career in technology and media.

The word *love* doesn't do justice to the relationship between Millennials and food. It's no secret—we're obsessed. It's a strange dichotomy—that a generation often perceived as unwilling to work hard in a job market with little prospects would be so invested in a gourmet lifestyle at a relatively young age. According to *Bon Appetit*, a monthly food magazine owned by Condé Nast, Millennials spend over $96 billion a year on food. Forty-four percent of the money they spend on food goes towards eating out (Peele). The numbers don't lie: this is a generation that values food and the experience that comes with dining. And of course, there's a name for them. Foodies.

Factual evidence from a reputable magazine supports Beispel's claim about millennials' obsession with food.

"Foodies" are self-proclaimed food critics who understand the industry and all it has to offer. Or at least they think they do. They may *even* have a food blog. Foodies need neither a formal background in culinary education nor the ability to cook. Last week my friends and I decided to try poke, a Hawaiian fish salad dish that's very in right now. With no prior experience trying poke and no knowledge of what it's supposed to taste like, we critiqued our bowls as if we were Hawaiian natives. "The chunks of fish are too large," remarked my friend. "They should be about 50% smaller," someone else agreed. I couldn't help but roll my eyes and laugh at the way foodies of this generation speak of food with the confidence of seasoned chefs.

Poking fun at herself and her friends, Beispel supports her claim with an example and gains the trust of her readers.

While Millennials are not the only age group who loves food, the aspects they value differ from those of other generations. Cherishing the quality of food has been a characteristic important to many diners over the years. The term "gourmet" has long been used to describe these food connoisseurs. Michelin star restaurants, *New York Times* restaurant reviews, and celebrities who write cookbooks aren't new to the scene either—these things have been present in food culture for decades. Yet it is hard to pin down exactly when "foodie" began to replace "gourmet" as a term to describe those with educated palettes.

Defining the term *gourmet*, Beispel analyzes how millennials differ from previous generations.

Many still link an obsession with food to affluence and class, but the term foodie clearly lacks upper-class connotations. The Millennial foodie doesn't need or expect tablecloths and silver spoons, and some extremely popular restaurants today even arrive in the form of food trucks. Today, fifty percent of Millennials refer to themselves as foodies, according to a recent study conducted by advertising agency BBDO, further indicating that the food obsession

This paragraph builds on the previous one by expanding the analysis of millennial foodies.

and appreciation isn't just for the wealthy ("How Millennials"). Where there's a food line, there's a Millennial waiting: foodie culture is accessible to anyone who wants to be a part of it.

The importance of technology is emphasized via survey data.

Unsurprisingly, technology has signaled the difference between gourmet cultures of the past and the foodies of the present and future. In a 2014 Nielsen survey, Millennials cited technology as *the* defining characteristic of their generation ("Millennials: Technology"). For a generation obsessed with food, having the ability to share and tell stories about their meals is key. And they don't hold back. They believe that the aesthetics and presentation of a plate can't be enjoyed without photographic evidence of it first.

Walk into a restaurant and look around—people are photographing their food before they eat. What they plan to do with this picture is anybody's guess. But there's no shortage of platforms available for Millennials to share their culinary experiences and combine their two favorite obsessions—food and technology. A Tumblr account entitled "Pictures of Hipsters Taking Pictures of Food" even exists solely to document people photographing food that they didn't cook and simply ordered (a skill in itself).

Pictures of Hipsters Taking Pictures of Food Tumblr

A photograph provides visual evidence of Beispel's point.

Clearly, food has gone viral. Instagram is a foodie haven. Accounts like @igbrunchclub and @infatuation have upwards of 700,000 followers who tune in to see what these often non-certified and not-formally educated Instagram users have to say about food. For more specialized food experiences, Instagram users can check out accounts such as @spoonuniversity or @newforkcity that tailor their accounts to college students or specific cities. Even though @ tinyfoods posts only pictures of miniature food, the site still has thousands of followers. There is a luscious culinary experience for any range of tastes and interests on the 'Gram. It's hard to exit the app without feeling hungry.

Snapchat and Facebook have also jumped on the bandwagon. The food phenomenon is now global and at the tip of a foodie's fingers. Open up Snapchat and the *Food Network* Snapchat channel boasts endless recipes, hacks, and pictures. Users can even subscribe to the network so they never miss the carefully selected and curated content. Buzzfeed's "Tasty" videos reach tens of millions of viewers and create quick recipes on camera for users to mimic at home. The comments are full of thousands of Facebook users tagging their friends so they tune into the content as well.

Beispel offers more evidence from social media platforms.

And, of course, there's Yelp. I don't remember the last time I picked a restaurant or ordered a dish without Yelping it first. For those who aren't familiar, Yelp is the Wikipedia of food. Users can rate and review restaurants (among other establishments), post pictures of dishes, and provide other information and tips about dining out. Yelp enables food lovers to have additional control of their dining experience. It eliminates the questioning over whether you'll like a new restaurant or dish. You can visualize your food before you eat it and see what other people thought of it. You know the best dishes on the restaurant menu before you arrive. That's not to discount the untrustworthiness of Yelp and the type of person who would be inclined to post a review: usually someone who had a one-star or five-star experience. Generally, though, thanks to technology, there's less risk for foodies when dining out.

More important, the bizarre, distinctive, and often laughable behavior of Millennial foodies is more than a social phenomenon—this food-obsessed species has the ability to drive society in powerful directions. Food giants are now changing their core values to align with those of Millennials. For a generation that isn't particularly brand loyal and values health, convenience, and low prices, companies are launching new products and remarketing old ones. Due to poor sales, PepsiCo, for example, has dropped ingredients perceived as unhealthy. Whole Foods plans to open a chain of grocery stores directed at a 30 and under crowd, with lower prices for healthy, high-quality food. These stores will also feature smaller packaging, catering to an age group that has yet to start a family.

The effects of millennials' purchasing habits are explored.

So look around: the power of the Millennial foodies is real. They have become unpaid brand ambassadors for restaurants they prefer. They're marketers and promoters, too, for their favorite foods—just add a geotag to say whatever restaurant you're at and anyone can access your photo and opinions. Non-foodies may love to hate them, but foodies are devoted to anything and anybody who stylishly satisfies their hunger. And they've probably taken a picture of your meal while you weren't looking. The phrase "you are what you eat" has been completely redefined.

Beispel concludes her argument with a new spin on an old adage.

Works Cited

"How Millennials Are Changing the Foodie Game." *RDP Food Service*, rdpfoodservice.com/blog/millennials-changing-foodie-game/. Accessed 8 Mar. 2017.

"Millennials: Technology = Social Connection." *Nielsen*, 26 Feb. 2014, www.nielsen.com/us/en/insights/news/2014/millennials-technology-social-connection.html.

Peele, Anna. "Just How Food-Obsessed Is the Typical Millennial?" *Bon Appetit*, 16 Feb. 2016, www.bonappetit.com/entertaining-style/pop-culture/article/millennials-and-food.

Pictures of Hipsters Taking Pictures of Food, Tumblr, pohtpof.tumblr.com/. Accessed 8 Mar. 2017.

Don't Believe Facebook: The Demise of the Written Word Is Very Far Off

MICHAEL HILTZIK**

June 17, 2016

Facebook executive Nicola Mendelsohn shook up the online-o-sphere earlier this week with one of those offhand declarations that sound superficially profound for a moment or two but are vacuous at their core. In five years, she told a *Fortune* conference in London, her platform will probably be "all video," and the written word will be essentially dead.

"I just think if we look already, we're seeing a year-on-year decline on text," she said. "If I was having a bet, I would say: video, video, video." That's because "the best way to tell stories in this world, where so much information is coming at us, actually is video. It conveys so much more information in a much quicker period. So actually the trend helps us to digest much more information."

This is, of course, exactly wrong. We don't mean her prediction about Facebook; in that respect she's talking her own book, since Facebook has made a big commercial bet on video. It's her assertion that video conveys more information—and faster—than text that's upside-down.

We'll outsource the initial pushback to Kevin Drum of *Mother Jones*, who observes, "Video has many benefits, but information density generally isn't one of them....I can read the transcript of a one-hour speech in about five or 10 minutes and easily pick out precisely what's interesting and what's not. With video, I have to slog through the full hour." That's why his policy is never to click a link that goes to video.

Drum's most salient point applies to the definition of the "information" people are seeking when they're accessing video or text. "I read/view stuff on the Web in order to gather actual information that I can comment on," he writes. Plainly, video is hopelessly overmatched by text in conveying hard information—facts, figures, data. A given video may arguably convey more "information" in bulk, but most of that is self-reinforcing context—color, motion, sound. The underlying factual information is relatively meager, in the same sense that the energy capacity of an electric-car battery can't match that of an average gasoline fuel tank (the range of a fully charged Tesla Model S is about 250 miles, while that of a typical gasoline-fueled sedan can exceed 400).

**Michael Hiltzik's argument originally appeared in the *Los Angeles Times*, where he is a columnist who ordinarily writes about financial issues. You'll see that orientation in his reflections on why the written word will likely thrive in the digital era. The piece includes no endnotes, but we've underlined where the online text provides links to source materials.

Then there's the challenge of extracting usable information from video vs. text. Video is a linear medium: You have to allow it to unspool frame by frame to glean what it's saying. Text can be absorbed in blocks; the eye searches for keywords or names or other pointers such as quotation marks. Text is generally searchable online. Some programs can convert some videos to searchable form, but more often, the search is done via a transcript keyed to points in the video. Here, for example, is the full transcript of "Meet the Press" for May 29. Below is the video of the entire show. If your task was to find the moment when Chuck Todd first mentioned Trump University, which would you use to find it? (We're not even counting the five commercial breaks.) [*A video appears here in Hiltzik's original text.*]

Give up? It's at about the 24:43 mark.

The demise of text is often predicted, but the horizon seems to perpetually recede. Tech writer Tim Carmody puts his finger on the reasons why "text is surprisingly resilient" in an essay at Kottket.org: "It's cheap, it's flexible, it's discreet. Human brains process it absurdly well considering there's nothing really built-in for it. Plenty of people can deal with text better than they can spoken language, whether as a matter of preference or necessity. And it's endlessly computable—you can search it, code it....In short, all of the same technological advances that enable more and more video, audio, and immersive VR entertainment also enable more and more text. We will see more of all of them as the technological bottlenecks open up."

He concludes that "nothing has proved as invincible as writing and literacy. Because text is just so malleable. Because it fits into any container we put it in. Because our world is supersaturated in it, indoors and out. Because we have so much invested in it....Unless our civilization fundamentally collapses, we will never give up writing and reading."

In predicting a world overtaken by video, Mendelsohn seems to be making a category error; she's conflating visual with video. Facebook and other online platforms understand that their users are accessing their sites for their visual offerings, but that's not the same as saying they're doing nothing but watching clips.

That notion is contradicted by the findings of Oxford University's Reuters Institute for the Study of Journalism in its just-released Digital News Report for 2016.

The study found that most consumers of online news (59%) still gravitate to news articles—that is, text; only 24% said they accessed news video in the week before they were polled. "One surprise in this year's data," the report's authors found, "is that online news video appears to be growing more slowly than might be expected." The 24% figure "represents surprisingly weak growth given the explosive growth and prominence on the supply side." In other words, there's more video than ever before, but it's not attracting a commensurately large audience.

Why not? For the same reasons Drum mentioned:

They take too long to load and unspool, and extracting the sought-after information is slower and more inconvenient than reading the written word. The number-two complaint—"Pre-roll ads put me off"—is another artifact of the linear nature of video, compounded by the cleverness of video providers in forcing you to watch through an entire ad, or three, before the clip even starts.

The secret underlying Mendelsohn's claim is that there is something at which video is better than text: marketing.

The goal of advertising is not to impart information, but to keep it from the audience—to distract viewers from thinking too hard or asking questions. Video is ideal for that because that color, movement, noise, and light is all distraction. Video is entertainment, often of the empty-calorie variety. People love circuses, but they don't normally go there to study zoology.

Indeed, it seems that most of the articles (yes, articles) written about the coming dominance of video look at the phenomenon from the marketer's standpoint: "A recent campaign from Volkswagen," the Guardian reported last year, "saw a trio of its videos viewed a combined 155 million times." Here's a safe bet: those videos weren't produced to explain why the car company had been faking emissions data, but to entice viewers to buy their cars. Mendelsohn, by the way, came to Facebook from the advertising industry.

Certainly text and the written word will change to meet the demands of the new technologies through which we do our reading. That's always been the case. Novels tended to be structured as a series of cliffhangers when they were read in monthly installments in a popular magazine; and in a different narrative form when they began to be printed in books sized to fit conveniently in a saddlebag, or valise, or before the fireplace. The length of news articles began to shrink when the reading audience began to migrate from newspapers that arrived on the stoop in the morning and were kept around to be perused at leisure, and toward smartphones and pads to be read between elevator stops.

That's a testament to the infinite malleability of text. Text can conform to the relentless shrinkage of people's attention spans; video can't. Who will have time in the future to watch even a five-minute video, when they can learn so much more by scanning five paragraphs of text? "Bet for better video, bet for better speech, bet for better things we can't imagine," Carmody writes, "but if you bet against text, you will lose."

CHAPTER

16

Arguments of Definition

Left to right: Bill Wight/Getty Images; T3 Magazine/Getty Images; Bastiaan Slabbers/iStock/Getty Images

A panel of judges must decide whether computer-enhanced images must be identified as such in a contest for landscape photography. At what point is an electronically manipulated image no longer a *photograph*—or does it even matter?

Everyone seems convinced that products like Amazon's Alexa and Apple's Homekit are redefining the way people live in and control their homes. But what exactly do these products do? What defines *them*?

A conservative student group accuses the student government on campus of sponsoring a lecture series featuring a disproportionate number of "social justice warrior types." A spokesperson for the student government defends its program by questioning whether the term actually means anything.

Understanding Arguments of Definition

Definitions matter. Just ask scientists, mathematicians, engineers, judges—or people who want to use restrooms consistent with their gender identification. Looking back, in 1996 the Congress passed, and President Clinton signed, the Defense of Marriage Act (DOMA), which defined marriage in federal law this way:

> In determining the meaning of any Act of Congress, or of any ruling, regulation, or interpretation of the various administrative bureaus and agencies of the United States, the word "marriage" means only a legal union between one man and one woman as husband and wife, and the word "spouse" refers only to a person of the opposite sex who is a husband or a wife. 1 U.S.C. 7.

This decision and its definitions of *marriage* and *spouse* have been challenged over and over again in the ensuing decades, leading eventually to another Supreme Court decision, in the summer of 2013, that declared DOMA unconstitutional. The majority opinion, written by Justice Kennedy, found that the earlier law was discriminatory and that it labeled same-sex unions as "less worthy than the marriage of others." In so ruling, the court affirmed that the federal government cannot differentiate between a "marriage" of heterosexuals and one of homosexuals. Debates over laws that involve definitions of marriage and, more recently, gender are still ongoing, and you might want to check the status of such controversies in your own state.

Cases like these demonstrate that arguments of definition aren't abstract academic exercises: they often have important consequences for ordinary people—that's why farmers, landowners, Congress, and the Environmental Protection Agency have battled for decades over how that agency defines "wetlands," which Congress long ago gave it power to regulate. And why it was so controversial when in *Citizens United v. Federal Election Commission* (2010) the Supreme Court decided that individuals in association—such as unions or corporations—are equivalent to individual citizens when it comes to the exercise of free speech rights and thus have no limit on their spending in election campaigns. Opponents of the decision argue that it enhances the power of monied interests in American politics; others see it as affirming free speech in the face of increasing government censorship.

Arguments about definition even sometimes decide what someone or something is or can be. Such arguments can both include or exclude: A wolf in Montana either is an endangered species or it isn't. An unsolicited kiss is or is not sexual harassment. A person merits official political refugee status in the United States or doesn't. Another way of approaching definitional arguments, however, is to think of what falls between *is* and *is not* in a definitional claim. In fact, many definitional disputes occur in that murky realm.

Consider the controversy over how to define *human intelligence*. Some argue that human intelligence is a capacity that is measured by tests of verbal and mathematical reasoning. In other words, it's defined by IQ and SAT scores. Others define *intelligence* as the ability to perform specific practical tasks. Still others interpret *intelligence* in emotional terms as a competence in relating to other people. Any of these positions could be defended reasonably, but perhaps the wisest approach would be to construct a definition of *intelligence* that is rich enough to incorporate all these perspectives—and maybe more.

The fact is that crucial political, social, and scientific terms—such as *intelligence, justice, free speech,* or *gender*—are reargued, reshaped, and updated for the times.

Why not just consult a dictionary when the meanings of terms are disputed? It doesn't work that way, no matter how up to date or authoritative a dictionary might be. In fact, dictionaries (almost by definition!) inevitably reflect the way individual groups of people use words at a specified time and place. And like any form of writing, these reference books mirror the interests and prejudices of their makers—as shown, perhaps most famously, in the entries of lexicographer Samuel Johnson (1709–1784), who gave the English language its first great dictionary. No friend of the Scots, Johnson defined *oats* as "a grain which in England is generally given to horses, but in Scotland supports the people." (To be fair, he also defined *lexicographer* as "a writer of dictionaries, a harmless drudge.") Thus, it's possible to disagree with dictionary definitions or to regard them merely as starting points for arguments.

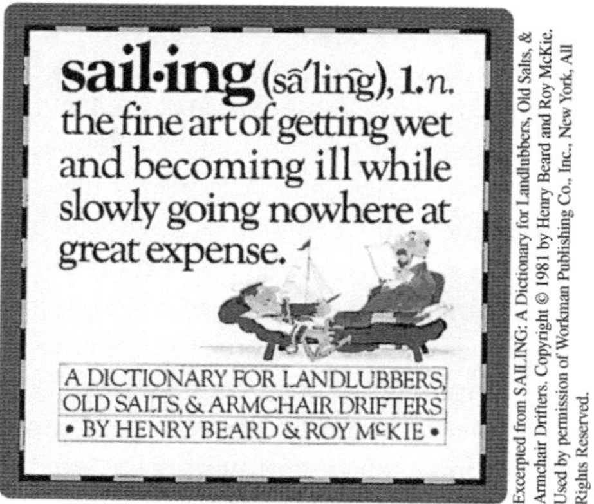

FIGURE 16.1 The *Dictionary for Landlubbers* defines words according to their point of view!

RESPOND

Briefly discuss how you might define the italicized terms in the following controversial claims of definition. Compare your definitions of the terms with those of your classmates.

Graphic novels can be *serious literature.*

Burning a nation's flag is a *hate crime.*

Neither Matt Drudge nor Rachel Maddow is a *journalist.*

College sports programs have become *big businesses.*

Plagiarism can be an act of *civil disobedience.*

The menus at Taco Bell and Panda Express illustrate *cultural appropriation.*

Satanism is a *religion* properly protected by the First Amendment.

The District of Columbia should not have all the privileges of an American *state.*

Polyamorists should have the option of *marriage.*

Kinds of Definition

Because there are various kinds of definitions, there are also different ways to make a definition argument. Fortunately, identifying a particular type of definition is less important than appreciating when an issue of meaning is at stake. Let's explore some common definitional issues.

Formal Definitions

Formal definitions are what you find in dictionaries. Such definitions place a term in its proper **genus** and **species**—first determining its class and then identifying the features or criteria that distinguish it from other members of that class. That sounds complicated, but an example will help you see the principle. To define *electric car*, for example, you might first place it in a general class—*passenger vehicles*. Then you define its species. Here's how the U.S. Department of Energy does that, explaining specific differences between cars powered by electricity (EVs):

> Just as there are a variety of technologies available in conventional vehicles, plug-in electric vehicles (also known as electric cars or EVs) have different capabilities that can accommodate different drivers' needs. A major feature of EVs is that drivers can plug them in to charge from an off-board electric power source. This distinguishes them from hybrid electric vehicles, which supplement an internal combustion engine with battery power but cannot be plugged in.

Got that? It gets even more complicated (or precise) as the government goes on to distinguish among plug-in hybrid electric vehicles (PHEVs), all-electric vehicles (AEVs), battery electric vehicles (BEVs), and even fuel cell electric vehicles (FCEVs).

But all these definitional distinctions can actually make matters clearer. For instance, suppose that you are considering a new car and prefer an electric one this time. Quickly, the definitional question becomes—*what kind?* A Toyota Prius, or maybe a Tesla Model 3? How do they differ? Both are clearly passenger cars—one might even add four-door sedans, so the *genus* raises no question. But the Prius is an electrically *assisted* version of a regular gasoline car while the Tesla is fully electric—just battery and motor, no engine. That's the *species* difference, which obviously has consequences for consumers concerned, let's say, either about range or about CO_2 emissions. (Or maybe it just comes down to good looks?)

dpa picture alliance/Alamy

FIGURE 16.2 Tesla Model 3

Operational Definitions

Operational definitions identify an object or idea by what it does or by what conditions create it. For example, someone's offensive sexual imposition on another person may not meet the technical definition of *harassment* unless it is considered *unwanted*, *unsolicited*, and *repeated*. These three conditions then define what makes an act that might be acceptable in some situations turn into harassment. But they might also then become part of a highly contentious debate: were the conditions actually present in a given case? For example, could an offensive act be harassment if the accused believed sexual interest was mutual and therefore solicited?

As you might imagine, arguments arise from operational definitions whenever people disagree about what the conditions define or whether these conditions have been fulfilled. Here are some examples of those types of questions:

Questions Related to Conditions

- Can institutional racism occur in the absence of specific and individual acts of racism?
- Can people paid for their community service still be called volunteers?
- Does academic dishonesty occur if a student accepts wording suggested by a writing center tutor?

Questions Related to Fulfillment of Conditions

- Has an institution supported traditions or policies that have led to widespread racial inequities?
- Was the compensation given to volunteers really "pay" or simply "reimbursement" for expenses?
- Did the student actually copy down what the tutor said with the intention of using it?

THE PRINCE RECONSIDERS:
IS WAKING SLEEPING BEAUTY WITH A KISS SEXUAL HARASSMENT?
Cartoonstock Ltd./CartoonStock.com

FIGURE 16.3 Prince Charming considers whether an action would fulfill the conditions for an operational definition.

RESPOND

This chapter opens with three rhetorical situations that center on definitional issues: What is Alexa? What is a photograph? What defines a social justice warrior (SJW)? Select one of these situations, and then address it, using the strategies either of formal definitions or of operational ones. For example, might a formal definition help to explain what products like Alexa or Homekit are? (You may have to do some quick research.) Would an operational definition work to explain or defend what SJWs allegedly do or don't do?

Definitions by Example

Resembling operational definitions are **definitions by example**, which define a class by listing its individual members. Such definitions can be helpful when it is easier to illustrate or show what related people or things have in common than to explain each one in precise detail. For example, one might define the broad category of *virtual reality products* by listing the major examples of these items or define *Libertarian Democrat* by naming politicians or thinkers associated with that title.

David McKinney

FIGURE 16.4 An app like Discovr Music defines musical styles by example when it connects specific artists or groups to others who make similar sounds.

Arguments of this sort may focus on who or what may be included in a list that defines a category—*classic movies, worst natural disasters, groundbreaking painters, acts of terror*. Such arguments often involve comparisons and contrasts with the items that most readers would agree belong in this list. One could ask why Washington, D.C., is denied the status of a state: how does it differ from the fifty recognized American states? Or one might wonder why the status of planet is denied to asteroids, when both planets and asteroids are bodies that orbit the sun. A comparison between planets and asteroids might suggest that size is one essential feature of the eight recognized planets that asteroids don't meet. (In 2006, in a famous exercise in definitional argument, astronomers decided to deny poor Pluto its planetary classification.)

Negative Definitions

Definitional arguments sometimes involve explaining what a person, thing, or concept is by defining what it is *not* or explaining with what it should be contrasted. Such strategies of definition play a substantial role in politics today, as individuals or political groups craft public images that show them in the best light—as *not* radicals, *not* fascists, *not* Alt-Right, *not* Antifa, *not* coastal elitists, *not* one-percenters, and so on. But this strategy of argument has other uses as well, especially when a writer wants to counter stereotypes or change expectations. For a thoughtful—and particularly apropos—example, see Rob Jenkins's "Defining the Relationship" at the end of this chapter.

Developing a Definitional Argument

Definitional arguments don't just appear out of the blue; they often evolve from daily life. You might get into an argument over the definition of *ordinary wear and tear* when you return a rental car with some soiled upholstery. Or you might be asked to write a job description for a new position to be created in your workplace: you have to define the job position in a way that doesn't step on anyone else's turf. Or maybe employees at your school object to being defined as *temporary workers* when they've held their same jobs for years. Or someone derides one of your best friends as *fake woke* and you're unsure how to read the term. In a dozen ways every day, you encounter situations that are questions of definition. They're so inevitable that you barely notice them for what they are.

Formulating Claims

In addressing a question of definition, you'll likely formulate a *tentative claim*—a declarative statement that represents your first response to such situations. Note that such initial claims usually don't follow a single definitional formula.

Claims of Definition

A person paid to do public service is not a *volunteer.*

Institutional racism can exist—maybe even thrive—in the absence of overt civil rights violations.

Climate change is not the same thing as *global warming.*

Political bias has been routinely practiced by some media outlets.

Theatergoers shouldn't confuse *musicals* with *operas.*

None of the statements listed here could stand on its own because it likely reflects a first impression and gut reaction. But that's fine because making a claim of definition is typically a starting point, a cocky moment that doesn't last much beyond the first serious rebuttal or challenge. Statements like these aren't arguments until they're attached to reasons, data, assumptions, and evidence.

Finding good reasons to support a claim of definition usually requires formulating a general definition by which to explore the subject. To be persuasive, the definition must be broad and not tailored to the specific controversy:

A volunteer is...

Institutional racism is...

Climate change is...but global warming is...

Political bias is...

A musical is...but an opera is...

Now consider how the following claims might be expanded with a general definition to become full-fledged definitional arguments:

Arguments of Definition

Someone paid to do public service is not a volunteer because volunteers are people who...

Institutional racism can exist even in the absence of overt violations of civil rights because, by definition, institutional racism is...

Climate change differs from global warming because...

Political bias in media outlets is evident whenever...

Musicals focus on words first while operas...

Notice, too, that some of the issues can involve comparisons between things—such as operas and musicals.

Crafting Definitions

Imagine that you decide to tackle the concept of *paid volunteer* in the following way:

> Participants in the federal AmeriCorps program are not really volunteers because they receive "education awards" for their public service. Volunteers are people who work for a cause without receiving compensation.

The definition of *volunteers* will be crucial to the shape of the argument. In fact, you might think you've settled the matter with this tight little formulation. But now it's time to listen to the readers over your shoulder, who are pushing you further. Do the terms of your definition account for all pertinent cases of volunteerism—in particular, any related to the types of public service AmeriCorps members might be involved in? What do you do with unpaid interns: how do they affect your definition of *volunteers*? Consider, too, the word *cause* in your original claim of the definition:

> Volunteers are people who work for a cause without receiving compensation.

Cause has political connotations that you may or may not intend. You'd better clarify what you mean by *cause* when you discuss its definition in your paper. Might a phrase such as *the public good* be a more comprehensive or appropriate substitute for *a cause*? And then there's the matter of *compensation* in the second half of your definition:

> Volunteers are people who work for a cause without receiving compensation.

Aren't people who volunteer to serve on boards, committees, and commissions sometimes paid, especially for their expenses? What about members of the so-called all-volunteer military? They're financially compensated during their years of service, and they enjoy benefits after they complete their tours of duty.

As you can see, you can't just offer up a definition as part of an argument and expect that readers will accept it. Every part of a definition has to be interrogated, critiqued, and defended. So investigate your subject in the library, on the Internet, and in conversation with others, especially *genuine* experts if you can. You might then be able to present your definition in a single paragraph, or you may have to spend several pages coming to terms with the complexity of the core issue.

After conducting research of this kind, you'll be in a better position to write an extended definition that explains to your readers what you believe makes a volunteer a volunteer, how to identify institutional racism, or how to distinguish between a musical and an opera.

Matching Claims to Definitions

Once you've formulated a definition that readers will accept—a demanding task in itself—you might need to look at your particular subject to see if it fits your general definition. It should provide evidence of one of the following:

- It is a clear example of the class defined.
- It clearly falls outside the defined class.
- It falls between two closely related classes or fulfills some conditions of the defined class but not others.
- It defies existing classes and categories and requires an entirely new definition.

How do you make this key move in an argument? Here's an example from an article by Anthony Tommasini entitled "Opera? Musical? Please Respect the Difference." Early in the piece, Tommasini argues that a key element separates the two musical forms:

> Both genres seek to combine words and music in dynamic, felicitous and, to invoke that all-purpose term, artistic ways. But in opera, music is the driving force; in musical theater, words come first.
>
> This explains why for centuries opera-goers have revered works written in languages they do not speak.

Tommasini's claim of definition (or of difference) makes sense because it clarifies aspects of the two genres.

If evidence you've gathered while developing an argument of definition suggests that similar limitations may be necessary, don't hesitate to modify your claim. It's amazing how often seemingly cut-and-dried matters of definition become blurry—and open to compromise and accommodation—as you learn more about them. That has proved to be the case as various campuses across the country have tried to define *hate speech* or *internship*—tricky matters indeed. And even the Supreme Court has never said exactly what *pornography* is. Just when matters seem to be settled, new legal twists develop. Should virtual child pornography created with software be illegal, as is the real thing? Or is a virtual image—even a lewd one—an artistic expression that is protected (as other works of art are) by the First Amendment?

Considering Design and Visuals

In thinking about how to present your argument of definition, you may find a simple visual helpful, such as the Venn diagram below from Wikimedia Commons that defines *sustainability* as the place where our society and its economy intersect with the environment. Such a visual might even suggest a structure for an oral presentation.

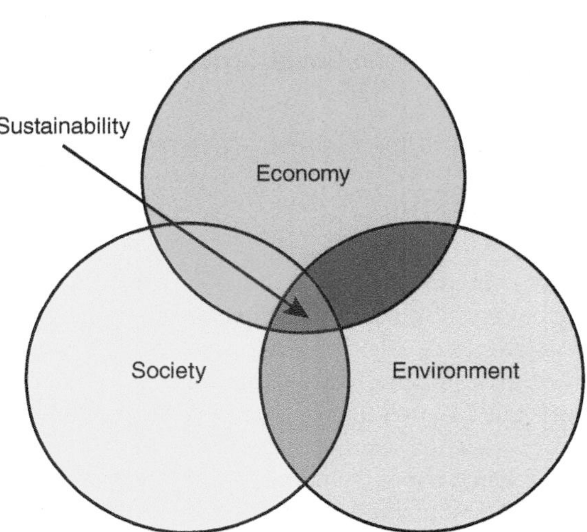

Remember too that visuals like photographs, charts, and graphs can also help you make your case. Such items could demonstrate that the conditions for a definition have been met—for example, a widely circulated photograph of children in Flint, Michigan, carrying bottled water (see below) might define *crisis* or *civic collapse*. Or you might create a graphic yourself to illustrate a concept you are defining, perhaps through comparison and contrast.

Wayne Lawrence

Finally, don't forget that basic design elements—such as boldface and italics, headings, or links in online text—can contribute to (or detract from) the credibility and persuasiveness of your argument of definition. (See **Chapter 29** for more on "Visual Rhetoric.")

Two Sample Definitional Arguments

Who Are You Calling Underprivileged?

NATASHA RODRIGUEZ*

I have come to loathe the word "underprivileged." When I filled out my college applications, I checked off the Latino/Hispanic box whenever I was asked to give my ethnicity. My parents in turn indicated their income, hoping that we would qualify for financial aid. But while I waited for acceptances and rejections, several colleges I was considering sent me material that made me feel worthless rather than excited about attending those institutions.

The first mailing I received was a brochure that featured a photograph of African-American, Asian, and Latino teens standing around in a cluster, their faces full of laughter and joy. The title of the brochure was "Help for Underprivileged Students." At first I was confused: "Underprivileged" was not a word that I associated with myself. But there was the handout, with my name printed boldly on the surface.

The author questions the connotations of *underprivileged*.

The text went on to inform me that, since I was a student who had experienced an underprivileged life, I could qualify for several kinds of financial aid and scholarships. While I appreciated the intent, I was turned off by that one word—"underprivileged."

I had never been called that before. The word made me question how I saw myself in the world. Yes, I needed financial aid, and I had received generous scholarships to help me attend a private high school on the Upper East Side of New York. Surely that didn't mean that I had lived a less-privileged life than others. My upbringing had been very happy.

What does "underprivileged" actually mean? According to most dictionaries, the word refers to a person who does not enjoy the same standard of living or rights as a majority of people in a society. I don't fit that definition. Even though my family does not have a lot of money, we have always had enough to get by, and I have received an excellent education.

The author then gives a standard definition for *underprivileged* and explains why she refuses the label.

*Natasha Rodriguez wrote this argument while a student at Sarah Lawrence College. She went on to do graduate work in journalism at Columbia University.

What angered me most about the label was why colleges would ever use such a term. Who wants to be called underprivileged? I'm sure that even those who have had no opportunities would not want their social status rubbed in their faces so blatantly. People should be referred to as underprivileged only if they're the ones who are calling themselves that.

Misfortune, like beauty, is in the eye of the beholder. It's not appropriate to slap labels on people that they might not like or even agree with. Social research has found that those who are negatively labeled usually have lower self-esteem than others who are not labeled in that way. So why does the label of "underprivileged" persist?

Most colleges brag about the diversity of their students. But I don't want to be bragged about if my ethnicity is automatically associated with "underprivileged." Several colleges that had not even received information on my parents' finances just assumed that I was underprivileged because I had checked "Latino/Hispanic" on their applications.

The author examines the assumptions colleges make based on ethnicity and income.

That kind of labeling has to stop. Brochures and handouts could be titled "Help for Students in Need" rather than "Help for Underprivileged Students." I am sure that many people, myself included, are more than willing to admit that they require financial aid, and would feel fine about a college that referred to them as a student in need.

That's a definition I can agree with. I am a student in need; I'm just not an underprivileged one.

The essay concludes with the author's own self-definition.

Defining the Relationship

ROB JENKINS**

August 9, 2016

Dear Students: I think it's time we had the talk. You know, the one couples who've been together for a while sometimes have to review boundaries and expectations? Your generation calls this "DTR"—short for "defining the relationship."

We definitely need to define our relationship because, first of all, it is a long-term relationship—maybe not between you and me, specifically, but between people like you (students) and people like me (professors). And, second, it appears to need some defining, or redefining. I used to think the boundaries and expectations were clear on both sides, but that no longer seems to be the case.

The truth is, I wonder if college students today truly understand the nature of their relationship to professors. Perhaps their experiences with other authority figures—high-school teachers, parents, and bosses—have led them to make assumptions that aren't quite accurate. Or perhaps students are just not too thrilled with authority figures in general. That's always been the case, to some extent. But it seems to me, after 31 years of college teaching, that the lines have grown blurrier, the misconceptions more profound.

So I'd like to take a few moments to define the professor-student relationship. And if no one has ever put it to you quite this way before—well, that just highlights the need for a DTR.

And by the way, please keep in mind that I'm not trying to offend you or tick you off. I actually like you quite a bit, or I wouldn't even bother having this discussion.

I don't work for you. Students (or their parents), when they're unhappy with something I've said or done, occasionally try throwing this line in my face: "You work for me." They mean that by paying tuition and taxes, they pay my salary and I should, therefore, be responsive in the way they desire.

Let's dismiss that old canard right off the bat. Yes, as a professor at a state institution, I am a public employee. But that's precisely the point: I'm employed by the college and by the public, not by any particular member of the public. My duty—to the institution and to the people of this state—is to ensure that students in my courses meet the standards set by the college's faculty and are well-prepared for further study and for life.

**Rob Jenkins is an associate professor of English at Georgia State University–Perimeter College and a regular contributor to the *Chronicle of Higher Education*, where this argument was published.

You're not a customer, and I'm not a clerk. Unfortunately, too many students have been told for too long that they are "customers" of the institution—which means, of course, that they're always right. Right?

Wrong. This is not Wal-Mart. You are not a customer, and I don't even own a blue smock. Our relationship is much more like that of doctor and patient. My only obligation: to tell you what you need to hear (not what you want to hear) and to do what I think is best (not what you think is best).

I'm not a cable network or streaming site. What you get out of this relationship is that you'll be better equipped to succeed in this and other college courses, and life in general. What I get is a great deal of professional and personal satisfaction.

Natives of today's social-media-fueled digital universe have come to expect that everything they want will be available whenever they want it, on demand. That includes, or ought to include, their professors. I mean, we have email, don't we? And cellphones?

Consider this official notice that I have opted out of the on-demand world. My office hours are listed on my syllabus. If for some reason I can't be in my office during those hours, I'll let you know beforehand if possible or post a note on my door. But I'm usually there.

As for email, yes, I have it and I check it often, but not constantly. I do have a life outside this classroom—a wife, kids, hobbies, other professional obligations. That's why I don't give out my private cell number. If you need me after hours, email me and I'll probably see it and respond within 24 to 48 hours.

I'm not a high-school teacher. A common refrain among first-year college students is, "But my high-school teacher said. . . ."

Those teachers did their best to prepare you for college and tell you what to expect. Unfortunately, some of their information was outdated or just plain wrong. For example, not every essay has exactly five paragraphs, and it's OK, in certain situations, to begin a sentence with "because." One of the main differences between them and me is that I'm not telling you how you're going to do things "once you get to college." This is college, and this is how we do things.

Plus, because of something called "academic freedom," which most college professors enjoy but most high-school teachers don't, I'm not nearly as easy to intimidate when you think you deserved an A. I'm sure you (or your parents) would never dream of trying anything like that, but I thought I'd go ahead and mention it, just in case.

I'm not your boss. Please don't misunderstand: I don't take a "my way or the highway" approach to teaching. In my view, that's not what education, and certainly not higher education, is all about. I'm here to help you learn. Whether you choose to accept that help—ultimately, whether you choose to learn anything—is up to you.

My role is not to tell you what to do, like your shift manager at the fast-food restaurant. Rather, I will provide information, explain how to do certain things, and give you regular assignments and assessments designed to help you internalize that knowledge and master those skills. Internalizing and mastering are your responsibility. I can't "fire" you, any more than you can get me fired. But I can and will evaluate the quality and timeliness of your work, and that evaluation will be reflected in your final grade.

I'm not your parent. Some of my colleagues (especially among the administration) believe the institution should act "in loco parentis," which means "in the place of a parent." In other words, when you're away from your parents, we become your parents.

I've never really subscribed to that theory, at least not in the classroom. I suppose there are certain areas of the college, like student services, that have some parental-like obligation to students. But as a professor, I don't. And what that means, more than anything else, is that I'm not going to treat you like a child.

I'm not your BFF. When I first started teaching, I was only a few years older than many of my students. It was tempting, at times, to want to be friends with some of them. I occasionally struggled to maintain an appropriate professional distance.

Not anymore. I've been doing this for a while now—over 30 years—and I'm no longer young. (Sadly, I'm no longer mistaken for a student, either.) I try to be friendly and approachable, but if by "friendly" you think I mean "someone to hang out with," I don't. I regret that we cannot actually be friends.

That applies to virtual friendship, too. Even if you happen to track me down on Facebook, I will not accept your friend request. You're welcome to follow me on Twitter, if you like, but I won't follow you back. And I don't do Instagram or Snapchat or, um, whatever else there is.

I'm not your adversary. Just because we're not best buds, please don't think I'm your enemy. Nothing could be further from the truth. In fact, if by "friend" you mean someone who cares about your well-being and success, then I guess I am a friend after all.

Yet there is always a degree of tension in the student-professor relationship. You may at times feel that I am behaving in an adversarial manner—questioning the quality and relevance of your work, making judgments that you perceive as negative. Understand that is only because I do want you to succeed. It's not personal, on my end, and you must learn not to take it personally.

I'd like to be your partner. More than anything, I'd like for us to form a mutually beneficial alliance in this endeavor we call education.

I pledge to do my part. I will:

- Stay abreast of the latest ideas in my field.
- Teach you what I believe you need to know, with all the enthusiasm I possess.
- Invite your comments and questions and respond constructively.
- Make myself available to you outside of class (within reason).
- Evaluate your work carefully and return it promptly with feedback.
- Be as fair, respectful, and understanding as I can humanly be.
- If you need help beyond the scope of this course, I will do my best to provide it or see that you get it.

In return, I expect you to:

- Show up for class each day or let me know (preferably in advance) if you have some good reason to be absent.
- Do your reading and other assignments outside of class and be prepared for each class meeting.
- Focus during class on the work we're doing and not on extraneous matters (like whoever or whatever is on your phone at the moment).
- Participate in class discussions.
- Be respectful of your fellow students and their points of view.
- In short, I expect you to devote as much effort to learning as I devote to teaching.

What you get out of this relationship is that you'll be better equipped to succeed in this and other college courses, work-related assignments, and life in general. What I get is a great deal of professional and personal satisfaction. Because I do really like you guys and want the best for you.

All in all, that's not a bad deal. It's a shame more relationships aren't like ours.

CHAPTER

17

Evaluations

Left to right: Mario Tama/Getty Images;© Jonah Willihnganz, The Stanford Storytelling Project;Anton_Ivanov/Shutterstock

"We don't want to go there for coffee. Their beans aren't fair trade, the drinks are high in calories, and the stuff is *way* overpriced."

The campus storytelling project has just won a competition sponsored by NPR, and everyone involved is thrilled. Then they realize that this year all but one of the leaders of this project will graduate and that they have very few new recruits. So they put their heads together to figure out what qualities they need in new recruits that will help maintain the excellence of their project.

Orson Welles's masterpiece *Citizen Kane* is playing at the Student Union for only one more night, but the new Marvel Avengers epic is featured across the street in 3-D. Guess which movie your roomie wants to see? You intend to set her straight.

Understanding Evaluations

Evaluations are everyday arguments. By the time you leave home in the morning, you've likely made a dozen informal evaluations: You've selected neat but informal clothes because you have a job interview with a manufacturing company looking for machinists. You've chosen low-fat yogurt and fruit over the pancakes you really love. You've queued up the perfect playlist on your iPhone for your hike to campus. In each case, you've applied criteria to a particular problem and then made a decision. That's evaluating on the fly.

Some professional evaluations require more elaborate standards, evidence, and paperwork (imagine an aircraft manufacturer certifying a new jet for passenger service), but they don't differ structurally from the simpler choices that people make all the time. People love to voice their opinions, and they always have. In fact, a mode of ancient rhetoric—called the *ceremonial* or *epideictic* (see **Chapter 11**)—was devoted entirely to speeches of praise and blame.

Today, rituals of praise and (mostly) blame are a significant part of American life. Adults who would choke at the notion of debating causal or definitional claims will happily spend hours appraising the Oakland Raiders, Boston Red Sox, or Pittsburgh Penguins. Other evaluative spectacles in our culture include awards shows, late-night comedy shows, most-valuable-player presentations, lists of best-dressed or worst-dressed celebrities, literary prizes, consumer product magazines, and—the ultimate formal public gesture of evaluation—elections. Indeed, making evaluations is a form of entertainment in America and generates big audiences (think of *The Voice*) and revenues.

Erik Williams/AP Images

FIGURE 17.1 Arguments about sports are usually evaluations of some kind.

RESPOND

The last ten years have seen a proliferation of "reality" talent shows around the world—*Dancing with the Stars, So You Think You Can Dance, American* (or *Canadian* or *Australian* or many other) *Idol, America's Got Talent, The Voice*, and so on. Write a short opinion piece assessing the merits of a particular "talent" show. What should a proper event of this kind accomplish? Does the event you're reviewing do so?

Criteria of Evaluation

Arguments of evaluation can produce simple rankings and winners or can lead to profound decisions about our lives, but they always involve standards. The particular standards we establish for judging anything—whether a political candidate, consumer product, work of art, or career strategy—are called **criteria of evaluation**. Sometimes criteria are self-evident: a truck that gets nine miles per gallon is a gas hog, and a piece of fish that smells even a little off shouldn't be eaten. But criteria get complicated when a subject is abstract: *What constitutes a fair wage? What are the qualities of a classic song? What makes an event worthy of news coverage?* Struggling to identify such amorphous criteria of evaluation can lead to important insights into your values, motives, and preferences.

Why make such a big deal about criteria when many acts of evaluation seem effortless? Because we should be suspicious of opinions we offer too casually. Spontaneous quips and snap judgments can't carry the same weight as well-informed and well-argued opinions. Serious evaluations require reflection, and when we look deeply into our judgments, we sometimes discover important questions that typically go unasked, many prefaced by *why*:

- You challenge the grade you received in a course, but you don't question the practice of grading.
- You argue passionately that a Democratic Congress is better for America than a Republican one, but you fail to consider why voters get only two choices.
- You argue that news coverage is biased, but it doesn't occur to you to ask what makes an event worthy of news coverage.

Push an argument of evaluation hard enough and even simple judgments become challenging and intriguing.

In fact, for many writers, grappling with criteria is the toughest step in producing an evaluation. When you offer an opinion about a topic you know well, readers ought to learn something from your argument. So you need to formulate and then justify the criteria for your opinions, whatever the subject.

Do you think, for instance, that you could explain what (if anything) makes a veggie burger good? Though many people have eaten veggie burgers, they probably haven't spent much time thinking about them. Moreover it wouldn't be enough merely to assert that a proper one should be juicy or tasty—such observations are trite, uninteresting, and obvious. The following criteria offered on the *Cook's Illustrated* Web site show what happens when experts give the matter their attention:

> We wanted to create veggie burgers that even meat eaters would love. We didn't want them to taste like hamburgers, but we did want them to act like hamburgers, *having a modicum of chew, a harmonious blend of savory ingredients, and the ability to go from grill to bun without falling apart.* [emphasis added]
>
> —*Cook's Illustrated*

After a lot of experimenting, *Cook's Illustrated* came up with a recipe that met these criteria.

Ildi Papp/AGE Fotostock

FIGURE 17.2 What criteria of evaluation are embedded in this visual argument?

Criteria of evaluation aren't static, either. They may evolve over time depending upon audience. Much market research, for example, is designed to find out what particular consumers want now or may want in the future—what their criteria are for choosing a product or service. In good economic times, people may demand homes with soaring entryways, lots of space, and premium appliances. In tougher times, they may care more about quality insulation and energy-efficient stoves and dishwashers. Shifts in values, attitudes, and criteria happen all the time.

Criteria can also reveal biases we hardly notice. In a *Current Affairs* column (July 28, 2017), Nathan J. Robinson, citing a 2007 study featured on the Our World In Data Web site, argues that we are blind to an especially insidious omission in mainstream American news coverage—the unspoken and often racially motivated criteria networks use to decide what merits public attention at all. Robinson contends that only "the purest kind of subconscious prejudice" is at work in determining whose death is worth reporting. Looking closely at 700,000 major network news stories, the researchers found that

> the loss of 1 European life was equivalent to the loss of 45 African lives, in terms of the amount of coverage generated. Deaths in Europe and the Americas were given tens of times more weight than Asian, African, and Pacific lives.

Robinson is clearly asking news providers and consumers alike to reconsider how they evaluate newsworthiness.

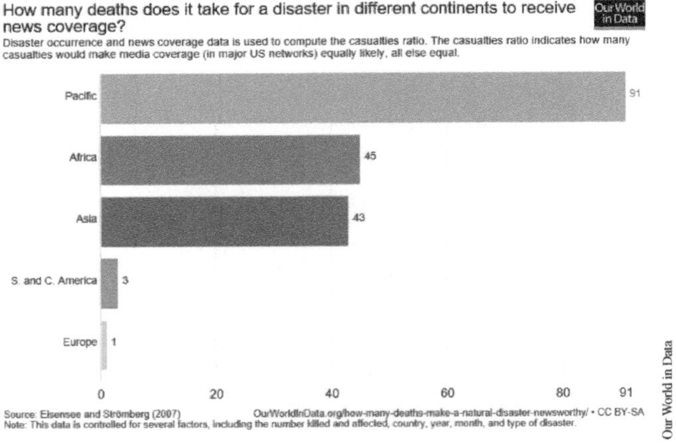

FIGURE 17.3 A graph from the Our World In Data Web site shows significant disparities in news coverage given to loss of life in different parts of the world.

RESPOND

Choose one item from the following list that you understand well enough to evaluate (or choose a category of your own). Develop several criteria of evaluation that you could defend to distinguish excellence from mediocrity in the area. Then choose an item that you don't know much about and explain the research you might do to discover reasonable criteria of evaluation for it.

- smartwatches
- NFL quarterbacks
- social media sites
- TV journalists
- video games
- virtual reality products
- Navajo rugs
- U.S. vice presidents
- organic vegetables
- electric cars
- spoken word poetry
- specialty coffee
- country music bands
- superhero films

Characterizing Evaluation

One way of understanding evaluative arguments is to consider the types of evidence they use. A distinction explored in Chapter 27 between hard evidence and constructed arguments based on reason is helpful here: we define **hard evidence** as facts, statistics, testimony, and other kinds of arguments that can be measured, recorded, or even found—the so-called smoking gun in a criminal investigation. We define constructed arguments based on reason as those that are shaped by language and various kinds of logic.

We can talk about arguments of evaluation the same way, looking at some as quantitative and others as qualitative. **Quantitative arguments** of evaluation employ criteria that can be measured, counted, or demonstrated in some mechanical fashion (something is taller, faster, smoother, quieter, or more powerful than something else). In contrast, **qualitative arguments** rely on criteria that must be explained through language and media, alluding to such matters as values, traditions, and emotions (something is more ethical, more beneficial, more handsome, or more noble than something else). A claim of evaluation might be supported by arguments of both sorts.

Quantitative Evaluations

At first glance, quantitative evaluations seem to hold all the cards, especially in a society as enamored of science and technology as our own is. Making judgments should be easy if all it involves is measuring and counting—and in some cases, that's the way things work out. *Who's the tallest or oldest or loudest person in your class?* If your classmates allow themselves to be measured, you could find out easily enough, using the right equipment and internationally sanctioned standards of measurement—the meter, the calendar, or the decibel.

But what if you were to ask, *Who's the smartest person in class?* You could answer this more complex question quantitatively, using IQ tests or college entrance examinations that report results numerically. In fact, almost all college-bound students in the United States submit to this kind of evaluation, taking either the SAT or the ACT to demonstrate their verbal and mathematical prowess. Such measures are widely accepted by educators and institutions, but they are also vigorously challenged. What do they actually measure? They predict likely academic success only in college, which is one kind of intelligence. As you might guess, quantitative measures of evaluation have limits. Devised to measure only certain criteria and ignore others, they have an inevitably limited perspective.

And yet quantitative evaluations may still be full of insight. For example, even if you are not concerned with finding a mate at this point, you might be interested to know what people are looking for in a potential partner. Good looks? Of course—according to a *Business Wire* story, 51 percent of the people on online dating services value attractiveness in a potential mate. Others look for modesty (39 percent), ambition (50 percent), and a sense of humor (67 percent). But what trumps all these qualities is something you might not have thought much about at this point: your credit rating. Fully 69 percent of those surveyed thought a good credit score was important or very important in considering whom they might date. An odd criterion? Not at all. Dr. Helen Fischer, chief scientific advisor for Match.com, explains why:

> When it comes to dating, a good credit score ups your mate value, helping you win a responsible, long-term partner, more so than some other qualities that online daters might highlight on their profile. Money talks, but your credit score can speak more about who you are as a person, and singles agree that those with good credit tend to be conscientious and reliable.
>
> —"Online Daters Say a Good Credit Score Is More Attractive Than a Fancy Car," *Business Wire*, August 21, 2017

Something to remember when your next credit card bill comes due?

Qualitative Evaluations

Many issues of evaluation that are closest to people's hearts aren't subject to quantification. *What makes a movie great or significant?* If you suggested a quantitative measure like length, your friends would probably hoot, "Get serious!" But what about box-office receipts, adjusted for inflation? Would films that made the most money—an easily quantifiable measure—be the "best pictures"? That select group would include movies such as *Star Wars*, *The Sound of Music*, *Gone with the Wind*, *Titanic*, *Avatar*, and *E.T.* An interesting group of films—but the best?

To define the criteria for "significant movie," you'd more likely look for the standards and evidence that serious critics explore in their arguments, abstract or complicated issues such as their societal impact, cinematic technique, dramatic structures, intelligent casting, and so on. Most of these markers of quality could be defined or identified with some precision but not actually measured or counted. You'd also have to make your case rhetorically, convincing the audience to accept the benchmarks of quality you are offering and yet appreciating that they might not.

Indeed, a movie reviewer (or anyone else) making strong qualitative judgments might spend as much time defending criteria of evaluation as providing evidence that these standards are present in a particular film. And putting those standards into action can be what makes a review attention getting or, even better, worth reading. Here's a paragraph from Mehera Bonner, an entertainment editor for *Marie Claire* who is not shy about applying a feminist perspective to Christopher Nolan's World War II epic *Dunkirk* (2017), depicting the evacuation of more than 300,000 allied soldiers trapped by German forces on the coast of France at the outset of the conflict:

[M]y main issue with *Dunkirk* is that it's so clearly designed for men to man-out over. And look, it's not like I need every movie to have "strong female leads." *Wonder Woman* can probably tide me over for at least a year, and I understand that this war was dominated by brave male soldiers. I get that. But the packaging of the film, the general vibe, and the tenor of the people applauding it just screams "men-only"—and specifically seems to cater to a certain type of very pretentious man who would love nothing more than to explain to me why I'm wrong about not liking it....[T]o me, *Dunkirk* felt like an excuse for men to celebrate maleness.

—Mehera Bonner, "I Think *Dunkirk* Was Mediocre at Best, and It's Not Because I'm Some Naïve Woman Who Doesn't Get It"

Kaspars Grinvalds/Shutterstock.com

FIGURE 17.4 Web sites such as Netflix and Rotten Tomatoes offer recommendations for films based on users' past selections and the ratings of other users and critics. Sometimes those judgments are at odds. Then whom do you trust?

RESPOND

For examples of powerful evaluation arguments, search the Web for eulogies or obituaries of famous, recently deceased individuals. Try to locate at least one such item, and then analyze the types of claims it makes about the accomplishments of the deceased. What types of criteria of evaluation hold the obituary or eulogy together? Why should we respect or admire the person?

Developing an Evaluative Argument

Developing an argument of evaluation can seem like a simple process, especially if you already know what your claim is likely to be. To continue the movie theme for one more example:

> *Citizen Kane* is likely the finest film ever made by an American director.

Having established a claim, you would then explore the implications of your belief, drawing out the reasons, assumptions, and evidence that might support it:

Claim	*Citizen Kane* is the finest film ever made by an American director...
Reason	...because it revolutionizes the way we see the world.
Assumption	Great films change viewers in fundamental ways.
Evidence	Shot after shot, *Citizen Kane* presents the life of its protagonist through cinematic images that viewers can never forget.

The assumption here is, in effect, an implied statement of criteria—in this case, the quality that defines "great film" for the writer. It may be important for the writer to share that assumption with readers and perhaps to identify other great films that similarly make viewers appreciate new perspectives.

As you can see, in developing an evaluative argument, you'll want to pay special attention to criteria, claims, and evidence.

Formulating Criteria

Although even casual evaluations (*This band sucks!*) might be traced to reasonable criteria, most people don't defend their positions until they are challenged (*Oh yeah?*). Writers who address readers with whom they share core values rarely discuss their criteria in great detail. Similarly, critics with established reputations in their fields aren't expected to restate all their principles every time they write reviews. They assume audiences will—over time—come to appreciate their standards. Indeed, the expertise they command becomes a part of their persuasive ethos (see **Chapter 26**). Still, criteria can make or break a piece.

So spend time developing your criteria of evaluation. What exactly makes a shortstop an all-star? What marks a standardized test as an unreliable measure of intelligence? What distinguishes an inspired rapper from a run-of-the-mill one? In cases like these, list the possibilities and then pare them down to the essential qualities. If you propose vague, dull, or unsupportable principles, expect to be challenged.

You're most likely to be vague about your beliefs when you haven't thought, read, or experienced enough about your subject. Push yourself at least as far as you imagine readers will. Anticipate readers looking over your shoulder, asking difficult questions. Say, for example, that you intend to argue that anyone who wants to stay on the cutting edge of personal technology will obviously want Microsoft's latest Surface Pro because it does so many amazing things. But what does that mean exactly? What makes the device "amazing"? Is it that it offers the flexibility of a touch screen, boasts an astonishing high-resolution screen, and gives artists the ability to draw with a stylus? These are particular features of the device. But can you identify a more fundamental quality to explain the product's appeal, such as a Surface user's experience, enjoyment, or productivity? You'll often want to raise your evaluation to a higher level of generality like this so that your appraisal of a product, book, performance, or political figure works as a coherent argument, and not just as a list of random observations.

Be certain, too, that your criteria of evaluation apply to more than just your topic of the moment. Your standards should make sense on their own merits and apply across the board. If you tailor your criteria to get the outcome you want, you are doing what is called "special pleading." You might be pleased when you prove that the home team is awesome, but it won't take skeptics long to figure out how you've cooked the books.

RESPOND

Local news and entertainment magazines often publish "best of" issues or articles that catalog their readers' and editors' favorites in such categories as "best place to go on a first date," "best ice cream sundae," and "best dentist." Sometimes the categories are specific: "best places to say 'I was retro before retro was cool'" or "best movie theater seats." Imagine that you're the editor of your own local magazine and that you want to put out a "best of" issue tailored to your hometown. Develop five categories for evaluation. For each category, list the evaluative criteria that you would use to make your judgment. Next, consider that because your criteria are assumptions, they're especially tied to audience. (The criteria for "best dentist," for example, might be tailored to people whose major concern is avoiding pain, to those whose children will be regular patients, or to those who want the cheapest possible dental care.) For several of the evaluative categories, imagine that you have to justify your judgments to a completely different audience. Write a new set of criteria for that audience.

Making Claims

In evaluations, claims can be stated directly or, more rarely, strongly implied. For most writers, strong and specific statements followed by reasonable qualifications work best. Consider the differences between the following three claims and how much greater the burden of proof is for the first claim:

> J. R. R. Tolkien is the best writer of fantasy ever.
>
> J. R. R. Tolkien's *The Lord of the Rings* is a better fantasy series than J. K. Rowling's *Harry Potter* series, even for children.
>
> For most readers, J. R. R. Tolkien's *The Return of the King* offers, arguably, a more profound examination of evil than J. K. Rowling's *Harry Potter and the Deathly Hallows*.

Here's a second set of examples demonstrating the same principle, that knowledgeable qualifications generally make a claim of evaluation easier to deal with and smarter:

> Chicago mayor Rahm Emanuel's recent suggestion for a new graduation requirement for high school seniors in his city sure is dumb!
>
> A proposal by Mayor Rahm Emanuel of Chicago that students in his city's schools not receive high school diplomas unless they've been admitted to college, joined the military, or are already employed, might do more harm than good.
>
> While praiseworthy in its goal to make high school seniors think about their futures, Mayor Emanuel's proposed graduation requirement might force many working-class students into making the wrong choices—going to trade school, joining the military, enrolling in second-rate online schools—just to claim a high school diploma they've already earned.

The point of qualifying theses like these isn't to make evaluative claims bland but to make them responsible and reasonable. Consider how Reagan Tankersley uses the criticisms of a musical genre he enjoys to frame an assertion he makes in its defense:

> Structurally, dubstep is a simple musical form, with formulaic progressions and beats, something that gives a musically tuned ear little to grasp or analyze. For this reason, a majority of traditionally trained musicians find the genre to be a waste of time. These people have a legitimate position.... However, I hold that it is the simplicity of dubstep that makes it special: the primal nature of the song is what digs so deeply into fans. It accesses the most primitive area in our brains that connects to the uniquely human love of music.
>
> —Reagan Tankersley, "Dubstep: Why People Dance"

Tankersley doesn't pretend that dubstep is a subtle or sophisticated musical form, nor does he expect his argument to win over traditionally minded critics. Yet he still makes a claim worth considering.

hurricanehank/Shutterstock.com

FIGURE 17.5 Dubstep band Dope D.O.D. performing live in Moscow in 2015

One tip: Nothing adds more depth to an opinion than letting others challenge it. When you can, use the resources of the Internet or local discussion boards to get responses to your opinions or topic proposals. It can be eye-opening to realize how strongly people react to ideas or points of view that you regard as perfectly normal. Share your claim and then, when you're ready, your first draft with friends, classmates, or tutors at the writing center, asking them to identify places where your ideas need additional support, either in the discussion of criteria or in the presentation of evidence.

Presenting Evidence

Generally, the more evidence in an evaluation the better, provided that the evidence is relevant. For example, in evaluating the performance of two laptops, the speed of their processors would be essential; the quality of their keyboards or the availability of service might be less crucial yet still worth mentioning. But you have to decide how much detail your readers want in your argument. For technical subjects, you might make your basic case briefly and then attach additional supporting documents at the end—tables, graphs, charts—for those who want more data.

Just as important as relevance in selecting evidence is presentation. Not all pieces of evidence are equally convincing, nor should they be treated as such. Select evidence that is most likely to influence your readers, and then arrange the argument to build toward your strongest points. In most cases, that best material will be evidence that's specific, detailed, memorable, and derived from credible sources. The following example comes from a celebratory defense of art and artists by musician, songwriter, and producer T Bone Burnett, delivered at the 2016 AmericanaFest music festival in Nashville. The energy of his language and the memorable examples likely solidify the case that music is foundational to the American mythology:

> This is the story of the United States: a kid walks out of his home with a song and nothing else, and conquers the world. We have replicated that phenomenon over and over: Elvis Presley, ... Rosetta Tharpe, Johnny Cash, Howlin Wolf, Mahalia Jackson, Bob Dylan, John Coltrane, Billie Holiday.
>
> —T Bone Burnett, Nashville, TN, September 22, 2016

Anna Webber/Getty Images

FIGURE 17.6 T Bone Burnett gave the keynote speech at the AmericanaFest (Americana Music Festival & Conference) in Nashville.

In evaluation arguments, don't be afraid to concede a point when evidence goes contrary to the overall claim you wish to make. If you're really skillful, you can even turn a problem into an argumentative asset, as Bob Costas does in acknowledging the flaws of baseball great Mickey Mantle in the process of praising him:

> None of us, Mickey included, would want to be held to account for every moment of our lives. But how many of us could say that our best moments were as magnificent as his?
>
> —Bob Costas, "Eulogy for Mickey Mantle"

Considering Design and Visuals

Visual components play a significant role in many kinds of evaluation arguments, especially during political campaigns—as the image below suggests. But they can also be important in more technical arguments as well (see for instance the Our World In Data graph on p. 360). As soon as numbers are involved in supporting your claim, think about ways to arrange quantitative information in tables, charts, graphs, or infographics to make the information more accessible to readers. Visual elements are especially helpful when comparing items. The facts can seem to speak for themselves if they are presented with care and deliberation.

But don't ignore other basic design features of a text—such as headings for the different criteria you're using or, in online evaluations, links to material related to your subject.

RESPOND

Take a close look at what artist Deborah Kass described in July 2016 as her "official fundraising screen print" for the presidential campaign of Hillary Clinton. In what ways did it make an argument of evaluation designed to make Americans consider voting for the Democratic candidate rather than for Republican Donald Trump? Would any elements in it make some voters perhaps less likely to support Clinton? Explain your assessment of the image.

Vote Hillary by Deborah Kass

Two Sample Evaluations

The Toxicity in Learning

JENNY KIM*

Sang Young Kim

Opening paragraphs focus on the emotional trauma of anticipating the MCAT—the Medical College Admission Test.

My eyes burst open. My body is shaking and my palms are sweaty. 528—perfect score; 521—the start of the 99th percentile; 516—minimum score needed for top tier medical schools, that is, 129 on all four sections. How do I compare to my peers? To those Ivy League applicants? Everything is a competition, and I need to be perfect. I must be crazy. Two weeks away from the most important test of my life to date, I'm suffering from insomnia.

In fact, I was convinced that I was crazy until I talked to my fellow peers who'd also fallen prey to one of the most demoralizing tests created: the MCAT. Of the fourteen people I talked to, thirteen of them had experienced nightmares and insomnia as the test drew near, and two of them continued to have trouble sleeping weeks after their exam! MCAT PTSD? Surely, that doesn't exist.

Perhaps MCAT PTSD isn't a real disease, but there has been a rise in an obsession with academic perfection that has led to increased suicide rates among students and the development of mental disorders (Duriez). To make matters worse, this preoccupation with scores and perfection is not limited to pre-med candidates. Across all disciplines, there is an unhealthy infatuation with a 4.0 GPA that detracts from true learning.

A thesis contrasts two modes of experiencing college: studying for the test and genuine learning for professional life.

Many of the skills and materials picked up in school *can* be integrated in innovative ways to tackle world problems, and it is a student's duty to acquire such skills and eventually advance their professions. But that is an impossible feat if students are immersed in a culture that emphasizes short-term memorization and immediate forgetfulness rather than careful analysis and the steady accumulation of knowledge. Unfortunately much of academia has adopted the habit of regurgitation. Despite the ubiquity of this toxic

*Jenny Kim, a biochemistry/pre-med major at the University of Texas at Austin, wrote "The Toxicity of Learning" for an Advanced Writing class when she was a junior—contrasting two styles of learning. In a topic proposal, she wrote, "I want to argue the importance of learning as opposed to getting 'good grades.' Although there is an overlap between the two, I do believe there is a fine line between going to school to learn and going to school to get a 4.0."

culture, college students should strive to escape it and yearn for something more: an insatiable curiosity and profound understanding of a field they're passionate about.

Recalling high school, I can see why many students are inclined to memorize and forget. Back then, I took all the advanced placement courses and excelled in them. But it was often enough just to memorize definitions and plug numbers into equations. Fast forward a few years. It is my second semester in college and my first in a research lab. I am standing beside four fellow freshmen on our first day. Before this, I'd never been given the opportunity to perform "actual research." The entirety of my lab experiences prior to college were disorganized AP Chemistry labs taught by a clueless but kind microbiology teacher. But that day, the professor running the lab, a researcher/educator, asked us a question regarding the biotechnology used to express antibiotics. My chest tightened. I had no idea what he was talking about, but the terms sounded familiar. True to our high school roots, the four other freshmen and I began blurting out definitions and random facts regarding PCR, bacteria, and selectivity. I had no idea what these concepts meant, much less how they related to one another, but assumed that if I included "buzz words" and science jargon in my answer, I would at least appear smart. I have never been so wrong. All five of us received a long, well-deserved lecture that day, and it was not pleasant.

Still in high-school mode, the author learns a painful lesson in her first college lab.

My desire to appear intelligent would be a classical example of surface motive. According to Dr. Bernardo Lopez, a professor and the vice dean faculty of philosophy and science at the University of Valencia, two questions arise when a student begins an academic task: "What do I want to accomplish with this? What can I do to accomplish it?" (Lopez). The answers to these questions are divided into two categories: surface and deep. Surface motive and learning are marked by short-term gratification and a lack of scholarly drive, such as my fruitless attempt to impress the professor. Deep motive and learning are characterized by a desire to apply oneself meaningfully at a higher conceptual level, with genuine curiosity for the subject at hand. In other words, it's the difference between memorizing to get a 4.0 as opposed to learning to build upon a pre-existing knowledge base.

Kim introduces technical terms to evaluate two contrasting styles of learning: surface motive and deep motive.

The research of Dr. Lopez comparing deep and surface learning revealed a correlation between deep learning motives/strategies and academic success. In his study, a greater portion of excellent

Almost by definition, students with deep learning motives succeed in their courses.

students—defined as those scoring in the 90th percentile on a university-wide exam—were found to use deep strategy and have deep motive when compared to average students. On the other hand, average students were found to use more surface strategy and have more surface motive than their more academically accomplished peers (Lopez).

Now, earning a 4.0 isn't necessarily bad. However, taking easy college classes just to "boost GPA" is a grand waste of time. The purpose of an education is to become more knowledgeable in an area of interest and develop practical skills to excel in said field. When tempted to take a pointless GPA booster or memorize their way into an A, college students should remind themselves why they're paying thousands of dollars and spending hundreds of sleepless nights to get an "education."

Merely going through the motions can earn high grades, but doesn't produce actual learning.

That being said, the first steps to escaping the regurgitation culture is for students to pursue a field *they're* drawn to and develop a desire to push that field forward. When asked by adults to justify their choice of major, most students mention passion, talent, or interest. But how can that be the case when many students lack a fundamental understanding of their area of study? What makes a good writer, a good biologist, or a good musician? Memorizing procedures and facts surely doesn't. Anyone can learn to read music, given a few days and a book, so what is it that distinguishes a true musician from a biology, English, or even a music major?

Mere knowledge does not translate into passion for a subject.

As an experienced tutor myself, I know that one of the most frustrating moments of teaching occurs when you realize your student has not learned anything from the past few lessons. There is a fine line between memorizing disconnected fragments and constructing a full roadmap in one's head. This is exactly the problem Dr. Eric Mazur, a physics professor at Harvard University, ran into when he decided to give a conceptual problem to test his students' understanding. When asked about Newton's third law of motion, the students could recite it word for word. However, when it came time to apply the concept, Newton's third law had conveniently transformed into a novel and bewildering idea. He found that very few of his students could even set up a simple quantitative problem based on the principles of the law (Weimer).

What differentiates a musician from a biology or English major, and even a "surface-driven" music major is not the capacity to read music, or the knowledge of when to use a détatché as opposed to a legato bow stroke. The difference lies in the musician's ability to express the distinct personas of different composers, or illustrate the variation within a single composer's work: charming the audience with celebratory birds in Spring then making the audience tremble from the harsh extreme of Winter while maintaining Vivaldi's sprightly sense of style throughout the entirety of *The Four Seasons*. It's only through motivated practice and careful analyses that a music major can consolidate fragments of knowledge into a whole and become an actual musician. Being able to play violin means nothing if the intonation, style, tone, volume, rhythm, and phrasing, among other things, aren't present.

An elaborate comparison explains the difference between rote learning and the real thing.

There are many college courses in which students can earn an A through sheer memorization or repetition. There are other college courses that will guarantee them an A on their transcript. But, students should remind themselves that they're acquiring an education. Surface motives and strategy may earn them gold stars and a 4.0 on their transcripts, but how will they memorize their way through an open heart surgery, their first novel, or a concert with the New York Symphony? And if that isn't enough to deter students from a toxic obsession with a 4.0, is a perfect GPA worth all those nervous breakdowns and panic attacks? Surely not. Passion for a field is one thing, obsession over scores and competition is another. Weimer offers this advice: "Don't aim for success if you want it; just do what you love and believe in, and it will come naturally." Now, excuse me while I check the average MCAT scores for my top medical schools.

Works Cited

Duriez, Kara. "Grade Obsession and Why It's a Serious Problem." sites.psu.edu/siowfa15/2015/09/17/grade-obsession-and-why-its-a-serious-problem/.

Lopez, Bernardo, et al. "Learning Styles and Approaches to Learning in Excellent and Average First-Year University Students." *European Journal of Psychology of Education*, vol. 28, no. 4, pp. 1361–79.

Weimer, Maryellen. "Do Your Students Understand the Material, or Just Memorize and Forget?" *Faculty Focus*, www.facultyfocus.com/articles/teaching-professor-blog/do-your-students-understand-the-material-or-just-memorize-and-forget/.

I took vitamins every day for a decade. Then I found out they're useless.

BECCA STANEK**

March 22, 2017

Save for a few lapses in my irresponsible college days, I've popped a multivitamin every single day since middle school.

First it was the chalky multivitamins that left a lump in my throat for minutes after I'd gulped one down. Then it was the slightly grainy, massive pills that my mom bought in bulk at Costco. (They were technically for post-menopausal women, but my mother assured me they would be just fine for my 17-year-old self.) Then last year, tired of big, bad-tasting pills, I bought gummy vitamins. Who doesn't like noshing on some candy that holds the promise of great health?

Well, last week I threw my vitamins away. I'll miss that sugary, fruity taste—but, according to my doctor, that's about all I'll be missing.

At my appointment last Wednesday, my doctor bluntly informed me that my multivitamins weren't doing a darn thing for me. Though the idea of getting just a little bit more of all the most important vitamins may seem like a foolproof idea, she informed me that more isn't necessarily better. Few people have vitamin deficiencies. Moreover, for those who do have a deficiency in, say, Vitamin D or Vitamin B12, those little grape-shaped gummies—or any multivitamin, for that matter—don't pack anywhere near enough of any one vitamin to correct that deficiency, she explained.

That could be passed off as just one doctor's opinion...except there are a plethora of studies out there that back up her argument. A much buzzed-about study published in *Annals of Internal Medicine* in 2013, for instance, came to this clear-cut conclusion after reviewing three trials of multivitamin supplements and 24 trials of "single or paired vitamins that randomly assigned more than 40,000 participants":

> Evidence is sufficient to advise against routine supplementation, and we should translate null and negative findings into action. The message is simple: Most supplements do not prevent chronic disease or death, their use is not justified,

**Becca Stanek, a writer for *TheWeek.com*, explains exactly why she gave up a habit common to many Americans—taking multivitamins. Citing ample research, she argues that most people don't need them and people with genuine vitamin deficiencies need something more potent than an over-the-counter pill. We've underlined the hyperlinked words and phrases to give you an idea of how a professional writer backs up important claims in an evaluative argument. You can find the piece online.

> and they should be avoided. This message is especially true for the general population with no clear evidence of micronutrient deficiencies, who represent most supplement users in the United States and in other countries. [Annals of Internal Medicine]

Specifically, the study found vitamins to be ineffective when it comes to reducing the risk of heart disease, cancer, declines in cognitive ability, and premature death. And, Quartz noted, some vitamins can even be "harmful in high enough quantities":

> Our bodies can easily get rid of excess vitamins that dissolve in water, like vitamin C, all the B vitamins, and folate, but they hold onto the ones that are fat soluble. Buildup of vitamin A, K, E, or D—all of which are necessary in low levels—can cause problems with your heart and kidneys, and can even be fatal in some cases. [Quartz]

Though the FDA says on its vitamins information page that there "are many good reasons to consider taking supplements," it indicates vitamins only "may be useful when they fill a specific identified nutrient gap that cannot or is not otherwise being met by the individuals' intake of food." The CDC estimated in 2014 that "nine out of 10 people in the U.S. are indeed getting enough of some important vitamins and nutrients."

So why are so many Americans still taking multivitamins? Steven Salzberg, a medicine professor at Johns Hopkins, told NPR multivitamins are "a great example of how our intuition leads us astray." "It seems reasonable that if a little bit of something is good for you, then more should be better for you. It's not true," Salzberg said. "Supplementation with extra vitamins or micronutrients doesn't really benefit you if you don't have a deficiency."

Americans' abysmally bad diets also give vitamin companies some marketing ammunition. When the average American is eating just one or two servings of fruits and veggies a day (experts recommend as many as 10 servings of fruits and veggies a day for maximum benefits), a little boost of vitamins might seem like a good idea. But popping a pill isn't going to make up for all those lost servings. "Food contains thousands of phyto-chemicals, fiber, and more that work together to promote good health that cannot be duplicated with a pill," said nutritionist Karen Ansel.

And if it's those tasty gummy vitamins we're falling back on, there's an even better chance we're not offsetting our sugar- and fat-laden diets. The women's gummy multivitamins I was taking pack three grams of sugar per gummy. A serving size is two gummies. Even before breakfast, I was consuming six grams of sugar—almost a quarter of the American Heart Association's recommended maximum sugar intake for women.

So why, if there are so many signs pointing to no on multivitamins, had I never really heard any of them until that fateful visit to the doctor? Pediatrician Paul Offit explained in a 2013 *New York Times* opinion article that it might have something to do with a bill introduced in the 1970s:

> In December 1972, concerned that people were consuming larger and larger quantities of vitamins, the FDA announced a plan to regulate vitamin supplements containing more than 150 percent of the recommended daily allowance. Vitamin makers would now have to prove that these "megavitamins" were safe before selling them. Not surprisingly, the vitamin industry saw this as a threat, and set out to destroy the bill. In the end, it did far more than that.
>
> Industry executives recruited William Proxmire, a Democratic senator from Wisconsin, to introduce a bill preventing the FDA from regulating megavitamins. [Paul Offit, via the *New York Times*]

That bill became law in 1976. Some 30 years later, almost a third of Americans were still taking a daily multivitamin. But count this gal out.

CHAPTER 18

Proposals

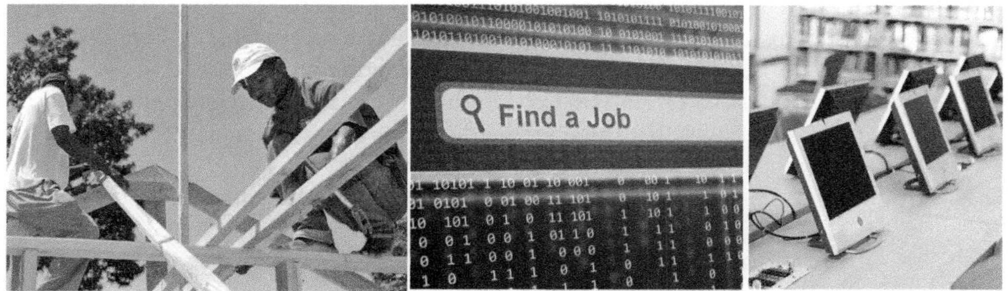

Left to right: Florian Kopp/imageBROKER/AGE Fotostock; spaxiax/Shutterstock; ESB Professional/Shutterstock

A student looking forward to spring break proposes to two friends that they join a group that will spend the vacation helping to build a school in a Haitian village.

Members of a business club at a community college talk about their common need to create informative, appealing, interactive résumés. After much discussion, three members suggest that the club develop a résumé app designed especially for students looking for a first job.

A project team at a large architectural firm works for three months developing a response to an RFP (request for proposal) to convert a university library into a digital learning center.

Understanding and Categorizing Proposals

We live in an era of big proposals—complex schemes for reforming health care, bold dreams to privatize space exploration, multibillion-dollar prototypes for hyperloop transport systems, serious calls for free post-secondary education, and so many other such ideas usually shot down to earth by budget realities. As a result, there's often more talk than action because persuading people (or legislatures) to do something—or *anything*!—is always hard. But that's what *proposal arguments* do: they provide compelling reasons for supporting or sometimes resisting change.

Such arguments, whether national or local, formal or casual, are important not only on the national scene but also in all of our lives. How many proposals do you make or respond to in one day to address problems and offer solutions? A neighbor might suggest that you volunteer to help revitalize a neglected city park; a campus group might demand more reasonably priced student/staff parking; a supervisor might ask for employee suggestions to improve customer satisfaction at a restaurant; or you might propose to a friend that you both invest in a vinyl record outlet. In each case, the proposal implies that there are good reasons for new action or that you've found a solution to a problem.

In their simplest form, proposal arguments look something like this:

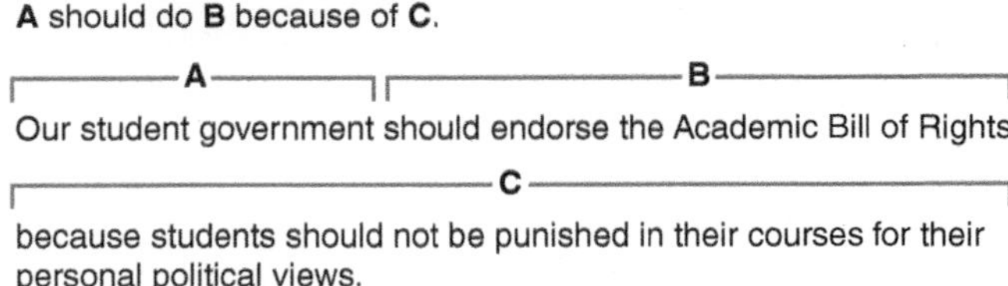

A should do B because of C.
A
B
Our student government should endorse the Academic Bill of Rights
C
because students should not be punished in their courses for their personal political views.

Proposals come at us so routinely that it's not surprising that they cover a dizzyingly wide range of possibilities. So it may help to think of proposal arguments as divided roughly into two kinds—those that focus on specific practices and those that focus on broad matters of policy. Here are several examples of each kind:

Proposals about Practices

- The college should allow students to pay tuition on a month-by-month basis.
- Conventional businesses should learn to compete with nontraditional competitors like Airbnb and Uber within the sharing economy.
- College athletes should be paid for the entertainment they provide.

Proposals about Policies

- The college should guarantee that in any disciplinary hearings students charged with serious misconduct be assured of regular due-process protections.
- The United Nations should make saving the oceans from pollution a global priority.
- Major Silicon Valley firms should routinely reveal the demographic makeup of their workforces.

RESPOND

People write proposal arguments to address problems and to change the way things are. But problems aren't always obvious: what troubles some people might be no big deal to others. To get an idea of the range of issues people face at your school (some of which you may not even have thought of as problems), divide into groups and brainstorm about things that annoy you about your institution, including things such as complex or restrictive registration procedures, poor scheduling of lab courses, and convoluted paperwork for student aid applications. Ask each group to aim for at least a half dozen gripes. Then choose three problems and, as a group, discuss how you'd prepare a proposal to deal with them.

Characterizing Proposals

1. They call for change, often in response to a problem.
2. They focus on the future.
3. They center on the audience.

Proposals always call for some kind of action. They aim at getting something done—or sometimes at *preventing* something from being done. Proposals marshal evidence and arguments to persuade people to choose a course of action: *Let's make the campus safer for people taking night courses. Let's create an organization for first-generation or working-class students. Let's ban drones from local airspace, especially at sporting and entertainment venues. Let's investigate incentives for supporting small business start-ups in our community*. But you know the old saying, "You can lead a horse to water, but you can't make it drink." It's usually easier to *convince* audiences what a good course of action is than to *persuade* them to take it (or pay for it). Even if you present a cogent proposal, you may still have work to do.

Proposal arguments must appeal to more than good sense. Ethos matters, too. It helps if a writer suggesting a change carries a certain *gravitas* earned by experience or supported by knowledge and research. If your word and credentials carry weight, then an audience is more likely to listen to your proposal. So when the commanders of three *Apollo* moon missions, Neil Armstrong, James Lovell, and Eugene Cernan, wrote an open letter to President Obama in 2010 expressing their dismay at his administration's decision to cancel NASA's plans for advanced spacecraft and new lunar missions, they won a wide audience:

> For the United States, the leading space faring nation for nearly half a century, to be without carriage to low Earth orbit and with no human exploration capability to go beyond Earth orbit for an indeterminate time into the future, destines our nation to become one of second or even third rate stature. While the President's plan envisages humans traveling away from Earth and perhaps toward Mars at some time in the future, the lack of developed rockets and spacecraft will assure that ability will not be available for many years.

But even their considerable ethos was not enough to carry the day with the space agency or the man who made the decision. Entrepreneurs like Elon Musk and Jeff Bezos have since acted on their own to privatize (at least partially) what had been a government monopoly, offering new proposals for innovative rockets and spacecraft.

NASA/Getty Images

FIGURE 18.1 Who thought *this* crazy idea could work? A fourteen-story tall SpaceX first-stage booster rocket successfully lands on a barge at sea after helping to launch a supply mission to the International Space Station (April 8, 2016).

Yet, as the photo demonstrates, proposal arguments inevitably focus on the future—what individuals, institutions, or entire governments should do over the upcoming weeks, months, or even decades. This orientation toward the future presents special challenges, since few of us have crystal balls. Proposal arguments must therefore offer the best evidence available to suggest that actions we recommend can achieve what they promise.

Proposals must also be tailored to reach and convince audiences to support, possibly approve, and quite often pay for them. Not surprisingly, politicians making public policy proposals not infrequently exaggerate the benefits and minimize the costs or disadvantages.

It makes sense that proposals aimed at general audiences make straightforward and relatively simple points, avoid technical language, and use visuals like charts, graphs, and tables to make supporting data comprehensible. You can find such arguments, for example, in newspaper editorials, letters to the editor, and actual proposal documents. Such appeals to broad groups make sense when a project—say, to finance new toll roads or build a sports arena—must surf on waves of community support.

But just as often, proposals need to win support from specific groups or individuals (such as bankers, developers, public officials, and legislators) who have power to make change actually happen. Arguments to them will usually be far more technical, detailed, and comprehensive than those aimed at the general public because such people likely know the subject already and they may be responsible eventually for implementing or financing the proposal. You can expect these experts or professionals—engineers, designers, administrators, bureaucrats—to have specific questions and, possibly, formidable objections.

So identifying your potential and most powerful audiences is critical to the success of any proposal. On your own campus, for example, a plan to alter admissions policies might be directed both to students in general and (perhaps in a different form) to the university president and provost, members of the faculty council, and admissions officers.

An effective proposal also has to be compatible with the values of the audience. Some ideas sound appealing, but cannot be enacted immediately—as California legislators discovered when in 2017 they first tried to implement single-payer, universal health care for that state. Citizens favored the idea, but legislators blanched at the considerable costs. Or consider a less complicated matter: many American towns and suburbs have a significant problem with expanding deer populations. Without natural predators, the deer are moving closer to homes, dining on gardens and shrubbery, and endangering traffic. Yet one obvious and feasible solution—culling the herds through hunting—is usually not saleable to communities (perhaps too many people remember *Bambi*).

Adrian Raeside

RESPOND

Work in a group to identify about half a dozen problems on your campus or in the local community, looking for a wide range of issues. (Don't focus on problems in individual academic classes.) Once you have settled on these issues, then use various resources—social media, the phone book (if you can find one), a campus directory—to locate specific people, groups, or offices whom you might address or influence to deal with the issues you have identified.

Developing Proposals

In developing a proposal, you will have to do some or all of the following:

- Define a problem that lacks a good solution or describe a need that is not currently addressed—and convince audiences the matter deserves attention.
- Make a strong claim that addresses the problem or need. Your solution should be an action directed at the future.
- Show why your proposal will fix the problem or address the need.
- Demonstrate that your proposal is feasible.

This might sound easy, but writing a proposal argument can be a process of discovery. At the outset, you think you know exactly what ought to be done, but by the end, you may see (and even recommend) other options.

Defining a Need or Problem

To make a proposal, first establish that a need or problem exists. You'll typically dramatize the problem that you intend to fix at the beginning of your project and then lead up to a specific claim that attempts to solve it. But in some cases, you could put the need or problem right after your claim as the major reason for adopting the proposal:

> Let's ban cell phones for students walking (or biking!) across college property. Why? Because we've become dangerous zombies. The few students not browsing the Web or chatting have to dodge their clueless and self-absorbed colleagues. Worse, no one speaks to or even acknowledges the people they pass on campus. We are no longer a functional community.

How can you make readers care about the problem you hope to address? Following are some strategies:

- Paint a vivid picture of the need or problem.
- Show how the need or problem affects people, both those in the immediate audience and the general public as well.
- Underscore why the need or problem is significant and pressing.
- Explain why previous attempts to address the issue may have failed.

For example, were you to propose that the military draft be restored in the United States or that all young men and women give two years to national service (a tough sell!), you might begin by drawing a picture of a younger generation that is self-absorbed, demands instant gratification, and doesn't understand what it means to participate as a full member of society. Or you might note how many young people today fail to develop the life skills they need to strike out on their own. Or you could define the issue as a matter of fairness, arguing that the current all-volunteer army shifts the burden of national service to a small and unrepresentative sample of the American population. Of course, you would want to cite authorities and statistics to prove that any problem you're diagnosing is real and that it touches your likely audience. Then readers *may* be willing to hear your proposal.

In describing a problem that your proposal argument intends to solve, be sure to review earlier attempts to fix it. Many issues have a long history that you can't afford to ignore (or be ignorant of). Understand too that some problems seem to grow worse every time someone tinkers with them. You might think twice before proposing any new attempt to change the current system of financing federal election campaigns when you discover that previous reforms have resulted in more bureaucracy, more restrictions on political expression, and more unregulated money flowing into the system. *"Enough is enough"* can be a potent argument when faced with such a mess.

RESPOND

If you review "My Free-Range Parenting Manifesto" at the end of this chapter (**p. 395**), a proposal by blogger and columnist Lenore Skenazy, you'll see that she spends quite a bit of time arguing that American children had more fun and learned more life skills in the past, when parents were (in general) less protective than she believes they are today. Chances are, you grew up in the highly protective environment she describes. If so, do you relate to the problem she defines in her manifesto? Or does the piece fail to engage your interest? If so, why?

Making a Strong and Clear Claim

After you've described and analyzed a problem, you're prepared to offer a fix. Begin with your claim (a proposal of what X or Y should do), followed by the reason(s) that X or Y should act and the effects of adopting the proposal:

Claim	Americans should encourage and support more scientists running for political office.
Reason	Scientists are trained to think more systematically and globally and may have greater respect for facts than the lifelong politicians who currently dominate American government.
Effects	Scientists will move our governments at all levels (local, state, federal) to make decisions based on facts and evidence rather than on emotions or the politics of the moment.

Having established a claim, you can explore its implications by drawing out the reasons, assumptions, and evidence that can support it most effectively:

Claim	In light of a recent U.S. Supreme Court decision that ruled that federal drug laws cannot be used to prosecute doctors who prescribe drugs for use in suicide, our state should immediately pass a bill legalizing physician-assisted suicide for patients who are terminally ill.
Reason	Physician-assisted suicide can relieve the suffering of those who are terminally ill and will die soon.
Assumption	The relief of suffering is desirable.
Evidence	Oregon voters have twice approved the state's Death with Dignity Act, which has been in effect since 1997, and to date the suicide rate has not risen sharply, nor have doctors given out a large number of prescriptions for death-inducing drugs. At least four other states, as well as the District of Columbia, have legalized physician-assisted suicide.

The *reason* sets up the need for the proposal, whereas the *assumption* and *evidence* demonstrate that the proposal is just and could meet its objective. Your actual argument would develop each point in detail.

RESPOND

For each problem and solution below, make a list of readers' likely objections to the solution offered. Then propose a solution of your own, and explain why you think it's more workable than the original.

Problem	Future deficits in the Social Security system
Solution	Raise the age of retirement to seventy-two.

Problem	Severe grade inflation in college courses
Solution	Require a prescribed distribution of grades in every class: 10% A; 20% B; 40% C; 20% D; 10% F.

Problem	Increasing rates of obesity in the general population
Solution	Ban the sale of high-fat sandwiches and entrees in fast-food restaurants.

Problem	Increase in sexual assaults on and around campus
Solution	Establish a 10:00 p.m. curfew on weekends.

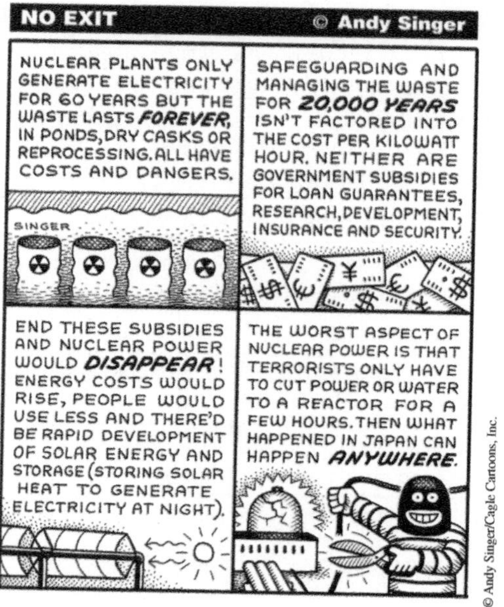

FIGURE 18.2 A proposal argument in four panels

Showing That the Proposal Addresses the Need or Problem

An important but tricky part of making a successful proposal lies in relating the claim to the need or problem that it addresses. Facts and probability are your best allies. Take the time to show precisely how your solution will fix a problem or at least improve upon the current situation. Sometimes an emotional appeal is fair play, too. Here, for example, is a paragraph from a group called YesCalifornia backing a referendum for that state to secede from the United States, a proposal that gained traction after the 2016 presidential election. The group explains what type of government California might expect after it leaves the United States:

> [O]ur referendum is a way to gauge the sense of the people on whether we Californians prefer the status quo of statehood, or if we want to see a change towards nationhood. Voting yes on the referendum is essentially voting yes to reform our system of government as well as our political and elections process to guarantee a more responsible and responsive government; move away from a two-party system; reduce the influence of big money in elections; restore the principle of one person, one vote; establish a system of proportional representation; and, engage disenfranchised voters. These are goals Californians and others are currently fighting for, yet under the corrupt U.S. political system, they are unlikely to be achieved.

The advocacy group seems to be claiming that an independent California would guarantee a more responsive government and a more engaged citizenry no longer swayed by big-money elections and two-party politics. Wishful thinking perhaps, but powerful rationale for change?

Alternatively, when you oppose an idea, these strategies work just as well in reverse: if a proposal doesn't fix a problem, you have to show exactly why. Perhaps you are skeptical about a proposal mentioned earlier in this chapter to reinstate a military draft in the United States. You might ask for proof that forced military conscription would, in fact, improve the moral fiber of young Americans. Or you might raise doubts about whether any new draft could operate without loopholes for well-connected or favored groups. Or, like Doug Bandow writing for *Forbes*, you might focus on the monetary and social costs of a restored draft: "Better to make people do grunt work than to pay them to do it? Force poorer young people into uniform in order to save richer old people tax dollars.... It would be a bad bargain by any measure."

Finally, if your own experience backs up your claim or demonstrates the need or problem that your proposal aims to address, then consider using it to develop your proposal. Consider the following questions in deciding when to include your own experiences in showing that a proposal is needed or will in fact do what it claims:

- Is your experience directly related to the need or problem that you seek to address or to your proposal about it?
- Will your experience be appropriate and speak convincingly to the audience? Will the audience immediately understand its significance, or will it require explanation?
- Does your personal experience fit logically with the other reasons that you're using to support your claim?

Be careful. If a proposal seems crafted to serve mainly your own interests, you won't get far.

Showing That the Proposal Is Feasible

To be effective, proposals must be *feasible*—that is, the action proposed can be carried out in a reasonable way. Demonstrating feasibility calls on you to present evidence—from similar cases, from personal experience, from observational data, from interview or survey data, from Internet research, or from any other sources—showing that what you propose can indeed be done with the resources available. "Resources available" is key: if the proposal calls for funds, personnel, or skills beyond reach or reason, your audience is unlikely to accept it. When that's the case, it's time to reassess your proposal, modify it, and test any new ideas against these revised criteria. This is also when you can reconsider proposals that others might suggest are better, more effective, or more workable than yours. There's no shame in admitting that you may have been wrong. When drafting a proposal, ask friends to think of counterproposals. If your own proposal can stand up to such challenges, it's likely a strong one.

Considering Design and Visuals

Because proposals often address specific audiences, they can take a number of forms—a letter, a memo, a Web page, a feasibility report, an infographic, a video, a prospectus, or even an editorial cartoon (see Andy Singer's "No Exit" item on p. 386). Each form has different design requirements. Indeed, the form of a proposal may determine its effectiveness.

For example, formal reports on paper or slides typically use straightforward headings to identify the stages of the presentation, terms such as Introduction, Nature of the Problem, Current Approaches or Previous Solutions, Proposal/ Recommendations, Advantages, Counterarguments, Feasibility, Implementation, and so on. Important data may be arrayed in tables and charts, all of them clearly labeled. Infographics making proposals will be more visually intense, with their claims and data presented in ways designed to grab readers and then hold their attention as they move through panels or pages. So before you produce a final copy of any proposal, be sure its overall design complements and enhances its messages.

Proposal arguments, especially those aimed at wide audiences, may rely on a wide range of graphic materials that to convey information—photographs, pie charts, scatter charts, timelines, maps, artist's renderings, and so on. Such items help readers visualize problems and then (if need be) imagine solutions. Any such items you find or create should be carefully designed, incorporated, and credited when you borrow them: they will contribute to your ethos.

Images also make proposals more interesting. Architects, engineers, and government agencies know this. For example, the rendering below helped viewers imagine what a future National Museum of African American History & Culture might look like on the Mall in Washington, D.C.—its structure suggesting the shape of African baskets. This winning proposal was offered in 2009 by designer David Adjaye, architect Philip Freelon, and the Freelon Adjaye Bond/Smith Group.

Courtesy of NMAAHC and Freelon Adjaye Bond/SmithGroup

FIGURE 18.3 The proposed design of the National Museum of African American History & Culture

But the building did evolve, gaining a third terrace and a bronze color to suggest other themes. Here's how the Smithsonian Web site describes the ideas evoked by the finished structure, which opened on September 24, 2016:

> From one perspective, the building's architecture follows classical Greco-Roman form in its use of a base and shaft, topped by a capital or corona. For our Museum, the corona is inspired by the three-tiered crowns used in Yoruban art from West Africa. Moreover, the building's main entrance is a welcoming porch, which has architectural roots in Africa and throughout the African Diaspora, especially the American South and Caribbean. Finally, by wrapping the entire building in an ornamental bronze-colored metal lattice, Adjaye pays homage to the intricate ironwork crafted by enslaved African Americans in Louisiana, South Carolina, and elsewhere.

Ian Dagnall/Alamy Stock Photo

FIGURE 18.4 The completed version

Two Sample Proposals

Addiction to Social Media: How to Overcome It

CALEB WONG*

Sean McElligott

The paper opens with a personal anecdote describing an issue: social media addiction.

I was broken. I applied to become a member of a student society—unlike many others, it seemed like the right fit—and I got an interview. Then I didn't get in, so I hurt myself. Succumbing to my worst instincts, I spent several hours on Facebook and Twitter, looking though the society's accounts and those of its members. I saw the gleam of their uniforms and the casual perfection of their lives, the heads of state they greeted and the inspirational quotations they tweeted. Social media invited me to view, at a distance, worlds in which I didn't belong, worlds I had been rejected from. "A-Plus human" read a comment on a post for students who were admitted into the organization. I went to bed feeling disappointed and terrible—basically, a D-minus human—and I decided to make a change that I had pondered and abandoned time and time again: deleting the social media apps from my phone. I realized I was addicted to a virtual life I wanted but couldn't have.

Evidence for social media addiction is offered from a variety of sources.

Apparently, I'm not alone in this predicament: struggling with an addiction to social media. Social media use is widespread; a Pew Research Center study found that nearly eight out of ten online American adults use Facebook, and 76 percent of those users use the site daily (Greenwood, Perrin, & Duggan, 2016). Smaller but still significant percentages also use Twitter and Instagram. Misery loves virtual company; another report by Mixpanel, a mobile analytics company, says that 50 percent of people who use social apps are on them for more than five hours a day—and the top 20 percent of users spent more than eight hours on these social apps (Mixpanel Trends, 2017). Social media has come to define my generation not only through selfies, posts, tweets, likes, and other online social activity, but also in terms of what a sinkhole it has become. The distractions never end—bottomless Facebook, Twitter, and Instagram are eerily and endlessly personalized—for our own lives. Much can be said about the shallowness and corrosive effect of social media

*Caleb Wong wrote this proposal paper for an Advanced Writing class while a junior at the University of Texas at Austin.

on civic life, but the most compelling argument against social media may be that it significantly hurts productivity. The computer science professor and productivity expert Cal Newport wrote in a *New York Times* column that the "ability to concentrate without distractions on hard tasks is becoming increasingly important in an increasingly complicated society" (Newport, 2016).

Sources are cited according to APA style.

The network effect—the digital web of contacts, pictures, videos, and posts—characterizes our connections to each other in the digital sphere. In terms of social media, it has created a powerful cue—a desire for a distraction—that draws us into an endless vortex of content. We see successful people posting pictures of the camaraderie they share on service projects or the fun times they have on the weekend at a party. When overdone, the network effect is not benign: a 2011 literature review found that it incorporates "classic" addiction symptoms such as mood modification, emotional preoccupation, tolerance as usage increases, withdrawal symptoms, and relapse (Kuss & Griffiths, 2011). In the most addicted people, this desire to use social media is so ingrained that they feel the euphoric high that comes from the anticipation of sharing a "buzzy" message before it's even sent.

The "network effect" is described and explained.

The author describes symptoms of social media addiction that many readers will recognize.

So how do we understand this addiction? Like tooth-brushing and nail-biting, using social media regularly is a habit. There are three parts to a habit: a cue, a routine, and a reward (Duhigg, 2016, p. 58). A cue is an automatic impulse that directs us to perform some action; that impulse could be a twitch to talk to someone or a desire to see the latest gossip. And then there's the routine: an action you take, whether it be physical, mental, or emotional. Swiping left or right on Tinder, scrolling through an Instagram or Facebook feed, obsessively checking mentions on Twitter—these are all examples of actions that might follow up on a social media cue. And then there's the reward, the pleasure we gain from performing the routine. Perhaps we forget our troubles for a moment or learn something new about our friends' lives.

So what's the solution? To change an addiction routine, you have to find out what your cue is and figure out how to get the same reward through a different response. For example, my desire for a momentary distraction from the humdrum of everyday life makes me wander into the voyeurism of social media for the reward of relaxation. But recognizing that cue, I realize that calling a friend or reading a print book, for example, would also help me relax, avoiding the addiction of social media. It's not easy; a recent study by

The paper offers specific solutions to the problem of social media addiction.

Duke University researchers suggests that habits prime us to feed our cravings by leaving specific marks in our brain (Chi, 2016). But it's certainly possible to change a habit—and hence your life—through this step.

Another key means of breaking the social media habit is to find a community to help you stick with new routines. Scientists from the Alcohol Research Group found that Alcoholics Anonymous attendance was "significantly associated with increased abstinence and reductions in drinking intensity," suggesting in particular that relationships with others can reinforce good habits (Tonigan, Miller & Schermer, 2002). As Lee Ann Kaskutas, a psychological scientist from AA, explains in an interview with Duhigg,

> At some point, people in AA look around the room and think, *if it worked for that guy, I guess it can work for me*. There's something really powerful about groups and shared experiences. People might be skeptical about their ability to change if they're by themselves, but a group will convince them to suspend disbelief. A community creates belief. (p. 85)

In scale and approach, some social addiction therapy resembles drug recovery programs.

Sound like rehab? It should. There are now Internet addiction camps which claim to foster self-efficacy in their clients through close, one-on-one therapy and recreational activities and group exercises. At a cost of about $20,000 for a 45-day program at reSTART, an Internet recovery retreat in Seattle, participants in the program attend individual and group therapy sessions, as well as go on group outings together such as feeding the homeless or hiking in a national park (Hepburn, 2013). Independent data is sparse on how well these recovery programs work, but according to a self-conducted 2015 Treatment Outcomes survey, the retreat found that more than 93 percent of participants in the program were unable to control their Internet usage before they came to camp; three to four years after completing the program, though, 57.14 percent of them were "extremely, likely or slightly likely" to control their social media use (reSTART, 2015). Clearly, the emphasis on connections with counselors and peers helps the participants respond in a healthier way to their cues. Instead of turning to social media or the other addictive properties of the Internet, they learn to get the same reward through a different routine, such as talking to real-life people or reading books or picking up other hobbies.

App designers, too, can play a role in making their social media apps less addicting. Tristan Harris, a design ethicist and a former "product philosopher" at Google, argues in a blog post that designers should stop exploiting the psychological vulnerabilities of users by helping them set boundaries (Harris, 2016). For example, the Facebook app might send reminders to people in the top percentile of its users to perhaps dial back on their usage. Also, Harris argues that apps should stop auto-playing videos, one after other to create a natural stopping point for social media use. Comparing addiction to slot machines, he writes that these apps seduce users by offering them different rewards—like a Tinder match or seeing a nice picture on Facebook—every time they use the app, keeping them coming back for the novelty.

Author suggests that app designers can play a role in reducing social media abuse.

Of course, advertisers are incentivized to keep us addicted because their income is tied to time spent on these social media applications. On average, most Facebook users are on the app 50 minutes a day, which correlates with its record-breaking net income of $1.5 billion in the first financial quarter of 2016, according to a *New York Times* article (Stewart, 2016). (If this the average amount of time spent on Facebook, imagine how much time the most addicted users spend on the app.)

Author acknowledges that social media apps are deliberately addicting.

As individuals and a nation, we might support a congressional investigation or a citizen's commission to investigate the pernicious effects of social media addiction. We should also insist that businesses endorse the responsible use of their products. There may be a free market for our minds, but our national mental health must be preserved for the sake of productivity and sanity. We prosecute dealers who sell heroin or cocaine or prescription drugs on the street because of their dangerous potential for abuse; we need to rein in the power of social media for the same reason. As a society, we must not just focus on treating individuals, but also the whole system to adequately address this problem. Without fear or favor, our government must examine how we can take back our lives from social media so we use it in moderation, not in excess. In the meantime, the causes of social media addiction, the habit sequence—cues, routines, and rewards—and the process of forming good habits must be taught in the workplace, school, and the home. When addicts are finally freed from the soft tyranny of their virtual feeds, they will be empowered to engage once again with the hard reality of the world around them.

Final proposal is for civic action of the kind applied to other societal problems.

Sources are cited in a references list, per APA style.

References

Chi, K. R. (2016, January 21). Why are habits so hard to break? [Press release]. Retrieved from Duke University website: https://today.duke.edu/2016/01/habits

Duhigg, C. (2012). *The power of habit*. New York, NY: Random House.

Greenwood, S., Perrin, A., & Duggan, M. (2016). *Social media update 2016*. Retrieved from Pew Research Center website: http://www.pewinternet.org/2016/11/11/social-media-update-2016/

Harris, T. (2016, May). How technology hijacks people's minds [Blog post]. Retrieved from http://www.tristanharris.com/2016/05/how-technology-hijacks-peoples-minds%E2%80%8A-%E2%80%8Afrom-a-magician-and-googles-design-ethicist/

Hepburn, N. (2013, January 24). Life in the age of internet addiction. *The Week*. Retrieved from http://theweek.com/articles/468363/life-age-internet-addiction

Kuss, D. J., & Griffiths, M. D. (2011). Online social networking and addiction—a review of the psychological literature. *International Journal of Environmental Research and Public Health*, 8(9), 3528–3552. http://doi.org/10.3390/ijerph8093528

Mixpanel Trends. (2017, March 30). Addiction [Blog post]. Retrieved from https://mixpanel.com/blog/2014/03/06/addiction/

Newport, C. (2016, November 19). Quit social media. Your career may depend on it. [Editorial]. *The New York Times*. Retrieved from https://nyti.ms/2jAKBYj

reSTART (2015). *2015 treatment outcome results*. Retrieved from https://netaddictionrecovery.com/programs/outcome-research/where-are-they-now/640-2015-treatment-outcome-results.html

Stewart, J. B. (2016, May 5). Facebook has 50 minutes of your time each day. It wants more. *The New York Times*. Retrieved from https://nyti.ms/2kpxL0j

Tonigan, J. S., Miller, W. R., & Schermer, C. (2002). Atheists, agnostics and Alcoholics Anonymous. *Journal of Studies on Alcohol*, 63(5), 534–541. Retrieved from https://www.jsad.com/

My Free-Range Parenting Manifesto

LENORE SKENAZY**

July 22, 2015

Back in 2009, the parenting site Babble listed the top 50 "mom" blogs in America—funniest, most fashionable, etc., and "most controversial."

That would be my blog, Free-Range Kids. Then it was voted most controversial again, a year later.

What crazy idea was I pushing? Don't vaccinate your kids? Clobber them when they cry? Teach them to play piano by threatening to burn their stuffed animals? Actually, my message was—and is—this: Our kids are just as safe and smart as we were when we were young. There's no reason to suddenly be afraid of everything they do, see, eat, wear, hear, touch, read, watch, lick, play or hug.

That idea runs smack up against the big, basic belief of our era: That our kids are in constant danger. It's an erroneous idea that is crippling our children and enslaving us parents.

Luckily, there's new pushback in the Capitol. Last week, Sen. Mike Lee introduced the first federal legislation in support of free-range parenting.

* * *

You've heard of me. I'm the New York City mom who let her 9-year-old ride the subway alone back in 2008. I wrote a column about it and two days later ended up on *The Today Show*, MSNBC, Fox News and (for contrast) NPR, defending myself as NOT "America's Worst Mom." But if you search that phrase you'll find me there for 77 Google pages.

I started my blog the weekend after the column ran to explain that I love safety—helmets, carseats, seatbelts—I just don't believe kids need a security detail every time they leave the house. As people found the site, I started hearing just how little we let kids do at all.

For instance, thanks to a mistaken belief that "We can't let our kids play outside like we did because times have changed!" only 13 percent of kids walk to school. One study found that in a typical week, only 6 percent of kids 9–13 play outside unsupervised. And *Foreign Policy* recently ran a piece about how army recruits are showing up for basic training not knowing to skip or do a somersault. It's like they totally missed the physical, frolicking part of childhood—along with

**Lenore Skenazy offers a proposal argument with passion, humor, and what used to be called common sense. Blogger, writer, and columnist, Skenazy became famous in 2008 when she allowed her nine-year-old son to ride by himself in a New York City subway. He survived.

its lessons. How are they going to roll away from an explosion, or skip over a landmine? And then of course there's the rise in childhood obesity, diabetes and depression.

That rise does not strike me as a coincidence. But here's the killer irony: The crime rate today is actually lower than it was when we were growing up. (And it's not lower because of helicopter parenting. We don't helicopter adults and yet crimes against them—murder, rape, assault—are all down.) We're back to the crime rate of 1963. So if it wasn't crazy for our parents to let us play outside, it is even less crazy today. But gripped by the fear of extremely rare and random tragedies hammered home by a hyperventilating news cycle, we are actually putting our kids at risk for increasingly common health risks.

Beyond those, however, there is something even sadder happening to the kids we keep indoors, or in adult-run activities "for their safety." By having their every moment supervised, kids don't get a chance to play the way we did—free play, without a coach or trophy or parents screaming from the bleachers.

This is catastrophic. Free play turns out to be one of the most important things a kid can do to develop into the kind of adult who's resilient, entrepreneurial—and a pleasure to be around.

You see, when kids play on their own, they first of all have to come up with something to do. That's called problem solving: "We don't have a ball, so what can we play?" They take matters into their own hands. Then, if they don't all agree, they have to learn to compromise—another good skill to have.

If there are a bunch of kids, someone has to make the teams. Leadership! If there's a little kid, the big kids have to throw the ball more gently. Empathy! For their part, the little kids want to earn the big kids' respect. So they act more mature, which is how they become more mature. They rise to the occasion. Responsibility!

And here's the most important lesson that kids who are "just" playing learn. How to lose. Say a kid strikes out. Now he has a choice. He can throw a tantrum—and look like a baby. He can storm off—and not get to play anymore. Or he can hold it together, however hard that is, and go to the back of the line.

Because play is so fun, a kid will usually choose the latter. And in doing that difficult deed—taking his lumps—the child is learning to control himself even when things are not going his way. The term for this is "executive function."

It's the crucial skill all parents want their kids to learn, and the easiest way to learn it is through play. In fact, Penny Wilson, a thought leader on play in Britain, calls fun the "orgasm" of play. Kids play because it's fun—not realizing that really they are actually ensuring the success of the species by learning how to function as a society.

Unfortunately, thanks to the belief that kids are in danger any second we're not watching them, this kind of play has all but evaporated. Walk to your local park the next sunny Saturday and take a look: Is there any child there who isn't a toddler with a caregiver, or a kid in uniform with a team?

Instead of letting our kids make their own fun, we enroll them in programs (fearful they'd otherwise "waste" some teachable time), or we keep them inside (fearful they'd otherwise be kidnapped). And if we do boldly say, "Go out and play!" often there's no one else out there for them to play with.

Can you imagine a country full of people who have been listening to Mozart since they were in the womb, but have no idea how to organize a neighborhood ballgame? My friend was recently telling a high school-age cousin about how he used to play pick-up basketball in the park, and the cousin couldn't understand how this was possible without supervision. "What happened if someone decided to cheat and fouled all the time?" the kid asked. "We just wouldn't play with him anymore," my friend replied. Said the cousin: "That's exclusion!" and that, he added, was a "form of" bullying.

Agghh! We are crippling kids by convincing them they can't solve any issues on their own. And as depressing as all this is, now there's another barrier to free play: The government.

You've all heard the story of the Alexander and Danielle Meitiv, the parents investigated by child protective services not once but twice for letting their kids walk home from the playground in Silver Spring, Maryland. While they were eventually found not guilty on both accounts, it seemed to require massive public outrage before the authorities let them go. Maryland has since "clarified" its CPS policy, which now states, "It is not the department's role to pick and choose among child-rearing philosophies and practices."

It sure isn't. But the authorities have a habit of doing just that. A mom in Austin was visited by the cops for letting her 6-year-old play within sight of the house. A mom in Chicago is on the child abuse registry for letting her children 11, 9 and 5 play in the park literally across the street from her house—even though she peeked out at them every 10 minutes. And I've heard from parents investigated for letting their kids walk to the library, the post office and the pizza shop.

Want more tales from the annals of government overprotection? Last year, four Rhode Island legislators proposed a bill that would make it illegal for a school bus to let off any children under 7th grade—that's age 11—unless there was an adult waiting there to walk them home from the bus stop. Naturally this was presented as just another new measure to keep kids safe. Fortunately—and perhaps just a bit due to agitation by the "most controversial" blog in America—the bill ended up shelved.

Another triumph: A library in Boulder, Colorado, had actually prohibited anyone under age 12 to be there without a guardian, because, "Children may encounter hazards such as stairs, elevators, doors, furniture, electrical equipment, or, other library patrons." Ah, yes, kids and furniture. What a recipe for disaster!

But that library regulation was beaten back, too.

The biggest ray of hope to date? Republican Sen. Mike Lee from Utah just added a groundbreaking "Free-Range" provision to the Every Child Achieves Act. It would permit kids to walk or ride their bikes to school at an age their parents deem appropriate, without the threat of criminal or civil action—provided this doesn't pre-empt state or local laws. "'Helicopter parents' should be free to hover over their own kids, but more 'Free-Range' parents have the exact same rights," the senator told me. "And government at all levels should trust loving moms and dads to make those decisions for their own families."

The Act, including Lee's amendment, passed the Senate on Thursday (although in the end Lee could not support the final version of the bill) and now must be reconciled with the House version.

Support for Lee's provision was bi-partisan. So if Free-Range was once "controversial," now it is the people's will. We are sick of seeing childhood through the kaleidoscope of doom. Sick of thinking, "A stranger near the school? Abduction!" "A child waiting in the car while mom returns a book? Instant death!" "A non-organic grape? That kid's a goner!"

Enough! It is time to stop making ourselves crazy with fear. All we need to do is adopt a new skepticism whenever we hear the words "for the safety of our precious children."

Those words precede grandstanding and bad laws. They precede sanctimony and scapegoating. They turn rational parents into outlaws and exuberant children into gelatinous lumps on the couch.

The way to keep kids safe is not by forbidding them to go outside. It's by giving them the freedom we loved when we were kids, to play, explore, goof up, run around, take responsibility and get lost in every sense of the expression. Here, then, is The Free-Range Kids' and Parents' Bill of Rights:

"Our kids have the right to some unsupervised time (with our permission) and parents have the right to give it to them without getting arrested."

Take this bill to your local legislators, or Congress, or the president (or his "Let's Move!" wife), and remind them: This is how we grew up. Why are we denying our kids a healthy, all-American upbringing?

It's time to save childhood—and the country. How can we be the home of the brave when we're too scared to let our kids go out and become smart, successful, resilient, resourceful and independent by doing what we all did at their age?

Playing.

part 5

Tools of Argument

CHAPTER

19

Academic Arguments

ingly plural politics, or cosmovisi
tive interpretations of "citizenship
many as "Source of Light."

WORKS CITED

Alaimo, Stacy. "Trans-Corporeal Feminis
Feminisms. Eds. Stacy Alaimo and
2008. 237–64.
Avatar. Dir. James Cameron. Perf. Sam
Twentieth Century Fox Film Corpor
Barrionuevo, Alexei. "Tribes of Amazon
11 Apr. 2010: A1.
Crude: The Real Price of Oil. Dir. Joe Berli
De la Cadena, Marisol. "Indigenous Cosn
beyond 'Politics.'" Cultural Anthropo
Eshelman, Robert S. "World Peoples Co
Mother Earth Kicks Off in Bolivia.

Left to right: 06photo/Shutterstock; Rogelio V. Solis/AP Images; Macmillan Learning

Much of the writing you will do in college (and some of what you will no doubt do later in your professional work) is generally referred to as *academic discourse* or *academic argument*. Although this kind of writing has many distinctive features, in general it shares these characteristics:

- It is based on research and uses evidence that can be documented.
- It is written for a professional, academic, or school audience likely to know something about its topic.
- It makes a clear and compelling point in a fairly formal, clear, and sometimes technical style.
- It follows agreed-upon conventions of format, usage, and punctuation.
- It is documented, using some professional citation style.

Academic writing is serious work, the kind you are expected to do whenever you are assigned an essay, research paper, or capstone project. You will find two examples of such work at the end of this chapter.

Understanding What Academic Argument Is

Academic argument covers a wide range of writing, but its hallmarks are an appeal to reason and a reliance on research. As a consequence, such arguments cannot be composed quickly, casually, or off the top of one's head. They require careful reading, accurate reporting, and a conscientious commitment to truth. But academic pieces do not tune out all appeals to ethos or emotion: today, we know that these arguments often convey power and authority through their impressive lists of sources and their immediacy. But an academic argument crumbles if its facts are skewed or its content proves to be unreliable.

Look, for example, how systematically Susannah Fox and Lee Rainie, director and codirector of the Pew Internet Project, present facts and evidence in arguing (in 2014) that the Internet has been, overall, a big plus for society and individuals alike.

> [Today,] 87% of American adults now use the Internet, with near-saturation usage among those living in households earning $75,000 or more (99%), young adults ages 18–29 (97%), and those with college degrees (97%). Fully 68% of adults connect to the Internet with mobile devices like smartphones or tablet computers.
>
> The adoption of related technologies has also been extraordinary: Over the course of Pew Research Center polling, adult ownership of cell phones has risen from 53% in our first survey in 2000 to 90% now. Ownership of smartphones has grown from 35% when we first asked in 2011 to 58% now.
>
> Impact: Asked for their overall judgment about the impact of the Internet, toting up all the pluses and minuses of connected life, the public's verdict is overwhelmingly positive: 90% of Internet users say the Internet has been a good thing for them personally and only 6% say it has been a bad thing, while 3% volunteer that it has been some of both. 76% of Internet users say the Internet has been a good thing for society, while 15% say it has been a bad thing and 8% say it has been equally good and bad.
>
> —Susannah Fox and Lee Rainie, "The Web at 25 in the U.S."

Note, too, that these writers draw their material from research and polls conducted by the Pew Research Center, a well-known and respected organization. Chances are you immediately recognize that this paragraph is an example of a research-based academic argument.

You can also identify academic argument by the way it addresses its audiences. Some academic writing is clearly aimed at specialists in a field who are familiar with both the subject and the terminology that surrounds it. As a result, the researchers make few concessions to general readers unlikely to encounter or appreciate their work. You see that single-mindedness in this abstract of an article about migraine headaches in a scientific journal: it quickly becomes unreadable to nonspecialists.

> **Abstract**
>
> Migraine is a complex, disabling disorder of the brain that manifests itself as attacks of often severe, throbbing head pain with sensory sensitivity to light, sound and head movement. There is a clear familial tendency to migraine, which has been well defined in a rare autosomal dominant form of familial hemiplegic migraine (FHM). FHM mutations so far identified include those in CACNA1A (P/Q voltage-gated Ca(2+) channel), ATP1A2 (N(+)-K(+)-ATPase) and SCN1A (Na(+) channel) genes. Physiological studies in humans and studies of the experimental correlate—cortical spreading depression (CSD)—provide understanding of aura, and have explored in recent years the effect of migraine preventives in CSD....
>
> —Peter J. Goadsby, "Recent Advances in Understanding Migraine Mechanisms, Molecules, and Therapeutics," *Trends in Molecular Medicine* (January 2007)

Yet this very article might later provide data for a more accessible argument in a magazine such as *Scientific American*, which addresses a broader (though no less serious) readership. Here's a selection from an article on migraine headaches from that more widely read journal (see also the infographic on p. 404).

> At the moment, only a few drugs can prevent migraine. All of them were developed for other diseases, including hypertension, depression and epilepsy. Because they are not specific to migraine, it will come as no surprise that they work in only 50 percent of patients—and, in them, only 50 percent of the time—and induce a range of side effects, some potentially serious.
>
> Recent research on the mechanism of these antihypertensive, antiepileptic and antidepressant drugs has demonstrated that one of their effects is to inhibit cortical spreading depression. The drugs' ability to prevent migraine with and without aura therefore supports the school of thought that cortical spreading depression contributes to both kinds of attacks. Using this observation as a starting point, investigators have come up with novel drugs that specifically inhibit cortical spreading depression. Those drugs are now being tested in migraine sufferers with and without aura. They work by preventing gap junctions, a form of ion channel, from opening, thereby halting the flow of calcium between brain cells.
>
> —David W. Dodick and J. Jay Gargus, "Why Migraines Strike," *Scientific American* (August 2008)

Such writing still requires attention, but it delivers important and comprehensible information to any reader seriously interested in the subject and the latest research on it.

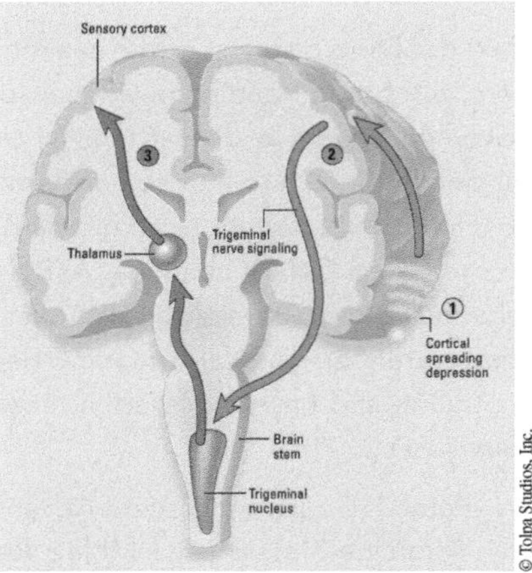

FIGURE 19.1 Infographic: The Root of Migraine Pain

Even when academic writing is less technical and demanding, its style will retain a degree of formality. In academic arguments, the focus is on the subject or topic rather than the authors, the tone is straightforward, the language is largely unadorned, and all the *i*'s are dotted and *t*'s crossed. Here's an abstract for an academic paper written by a scholar of communications on the Burning Man phenomenon, demonstrating those qualities:

> Every August for more than a decade, thousands of information technologists and other knowledge workers have trekked out into a barren stretch of alkali desert and built a temporary city devoted to art, technology, and communal living: Burning Man. Drawing on extensive archival research, participant observation, and interviews, this paper explores the ways that Burning Man's bohemian ethos supports new forms of production emerging in Silicon Valley and especially at Google. It shows how elements of the Burning Man world—including the building of a socio-technical commons, participation in project-based artistic labor, and the fusion of social and professional interaction—help shape and legitimate the collaborative manufacturing processes driving the growth of Google and other firms. The paper thus develops the notion that Burning Man serves as a key cultural infrastructure for the Bay Area's new media industries.
>
> —Fred Turner, "Burning Man at Google: A Cultural Infrastructure for New Media Production"

You might imagine a different and far livelier way to tell a story about the annual Burning Man gathering in Nevada, but this piece respects the conventions of its academic field.

MIKE NELSON/AFP/Getty Images

FIGURE 19.2 A scene from Burning Man

Another way you likely identify academic writing—especially in term papers or research projects—is by the way it draws upon sources and builds arguments from research done by experts and reported in journal articles and books. Using an even-handed tone and dealing with all points of view fairly, such writing brings together multiple voices and intriguing ideas. You can see these moves in just one paragraph from a heavily documented student essay examining the comedy of Chris Rock:

> The breadth of passionate debate that [Chris] Rock's comedy elicits from intellectuals is evidence enough that he is advancing discussion of the foibles of black America, but Rock continually insists that he has no political aims: "Really, really at the end of the day, the only important thing is being funny. I don't go out of my way to be political" (qtd. in Bogosian 58). His unwillingness to view himself as a black leader triggers Justin Driver to say, "[Rock] wants to be caustic and he wants to be loved" (32). Even supporters wistfully sigh, "One wishes Rock would own up to the fact that he's a damned astute social critic" (Kamp 7).
>
> —Jack Chung, "The Burden of Laughter: Chris Rock Fights Ignorance His Way"

Readers can quickly tell that author Jack Chung has read widely and thought carefully about how to support his argument.

As you can see even from these brief examples, academic arguments cover a broad range of topics and appear in a variety of media—as a brief note in a journal like *Nature*, for example, a poster session at a conference on linguistics, a short paper in *Physical Review Letters*, a full research report in microbiology, or an undergraduate honors thesis in history. What do all these projects have in common? One professor we know defines academic argument as "carefully structured research," and that seems to us to be a pretty good definition.

Conventions in Academic Argument Are Not Static

Far from it. In fact, the rise of new technologies and the role that blogs, wikis, social media, and other digital discourses play in all our lives are affecting academic writing as well. Thus, scholars today are pushing the envelope of traditional academic writing in some fields. Physicians, for example, are using narrative (rather than charts) more often in medicine to communicate effectively with other medical personnel. Professional journals now sometimes feature serious scholarly work in new formats—such as comics (as in legal scholar Jamie Boyle's work on intellectual property, or Nick Sousanis's Columbia University PhD dissertation, which is entirely in comic form). And student writers are increasingly producing serious academic arguments using a wide variety of modalities, including sound, still and moving images, and more. Obviously, the "research paper" need not be a paper at all: most academic research these days is available online—though, because of pay walls, not everyone can access it.

Developing an Academic Argument

In your first years of college, the academic arguments you make will probably include the features and qualities we've discussed above—and which you see demonstrated in the sample academic arguments at the end of this chapter. In addition, you can make a strong academic argument by following some time-tested techniques.

Choose a topic you want to explore in depth. Even if you are assigned a topic, look for an issue that intrigues you—one you *want* to learn more about. One of the hardest parts of producing an academic argument is finding a topic narrow enough to be manageable in the time you have to work on it but also rich enough to sustain your interest over the same period. Talk with friends about possible topics and explain to them why you'd like to pursue research on this issue. Look through your Twitter feeds and social media postings to identify themes or topics that leap out as compelling. Browse through books and articles that interest you, make a list of potential subjects, and then zero in on one or two top choices.

Get to know the conversation surrounding your topic. Once you've chosen a topic, expect to do even more reading and browsing—a lot more. Familiarize yourself with what's been said about your subject and especially with the controversies that currently surround it. Where do scholars agree, and where do they disagree? What key issues seem to be at stake? You can start by exploring online, using key terms that are associated with your topic. But you may be better off searching the more specialized databases at your library with the assistance of a librarian who can help you narrow your search and make it more efficient. Library databases will also give you access to materials not available via Google or other online search engines—including, for example, full-text versions of journal articles. For much more on identifying appropriate sources, see Chapter 20, "Finding Evidence."

Assess what you know and what you need to know. As you read about your topic and discuss it with others, take notes on what you have learned, including what you already know about it. Such notes should soon reveal where the gaps are in your knowledge. For instance, you may discover a need to learn about legal issues and thus end up doing research in a law school library. Or perhaps talking with experts about your topic might be helpful. Instructors on your campus may have the knowledge you need or be able to point you in the right direction, so explore your school's Web site to find faculty or staff to talk with. Make an appointment to visit them during office hours and bring the sorts of questions to your meeting that show you've done basic work on the subject. And remember that experts are now only a click away: a student we know, working on Internet privacy concerns, wrote a brief message to one of the top scholars in the field asking for help with two particular questions—and got a response within two days!

Come up with a claim about your topic. The chapters in Part 4, "Categories of Stasis," offer instruction in formulating thesis statements. Chapters 15–18, in particular, explain how to craft claims tailored to individual projects ranging from arguments of fact to proposals. Remember here, though, that good claims are controversial. After all, you don't want to debate something that everyone already agrees upon or accepts.

In addition, your claim needs to say something consequential about that important or controversial topic and be supported with strong evidence and good reasons (see Chapter 22). Here, for example, is the claim that student Charlotte Geaghan-Breiner makes after observing the alienation of today's children from the natural world and arguing for the redesign of schoolyards that invite children to interact with nature: "As a formative geography of childhood, the schoolyard serves as the perfect place to address nature deficit disorder." Charlotte develops her claim and supports it with evidence about the physical, psychological, academic, and social benefits of interacting with the natural world. She includes images illustrating the contrast between traditional schoolyards and "biophilic" (nature-oriented) schoolyards and establishes guidelines for creating natural play landscapes. (See Charlotte's complete essay, reprinted at the end of this chapter.)

Consider your rhetorical stance and purpose. Once you have a claim, ask yourself where you stand with respect to your topic and how you want to represent yourself to those reading your argument:

- You may take the stance of a reporter: you review what has been said about the topic; analyze and evaluate contributions to the conversation surrounding it; synthesize the most important strands of that conversation; and finally draw conclusions based on them.
- You may see yourself primarily as a critic: you intend to point out the problems and mistakes associated with some view of your topic.
- You may prefer the role of an advocate: you present research that strongly supports a particular view on your topic.

Whatever your perspective, remember that in academic arguments you want to come across as fair and evenhanded, especially when you play the advocate. For instance, in her essay about the effects of the phrase "thank you for your service" (or TYFYS) on veterans, sociology doctoral student Sidra Montgomery takes care to consider the feelings of both the civilians expressing gratitude and the veterans who receive it (see p. 424 later in this chapter). Your stance, of course, will always be closely tied to your purpose, which in most of your college writing will be at least twofold: to do the best job in fulfilling an assignment for a course and to support the claim you are making to the fullest extent possible. Luckily, these two purposes work well together.

Think about your audience(s). Here again, you will often find that you have at least two audiences—and maybe more. First, you will be writing to your instructor, so pay close attention to the assignment and, if possible, set up a conference to nail down your teacher's expectations: what will it take to convince this audience that you have done a terrific job of writing an academic argument? Beyond your instructor, you should also think of your classmates as an audience—informed, intelligent peers who will be interested in what you have to say. Again, what do you know about these readers, and what will they expect from your project?

Finally, consider yet another important audience—people who are already discussing your topic. These will include the authors whose work you have read and the larger academic community of which they are now a part. If your work appears online or in some other medium, you will reach more people than you initially expect, and most if not all of them will be unknown to you. As a result, you need to think carefully about the various ways your argument could be read—or misread—and plan accordingly.

Concentrate on the material you are gathering. Any academic argument is only as good as the evidence it presents to support its claims. Give each major piece of evidence (say, a lengthy article that addresses your subject directly) careful scrutiny:

- Summarize its main points.
- Analyze how those points are pertinent.
- Evaluate the quality of the supporting evidence.
- Synthesize the results of your analysis and evaluation.
- Summarize what you think about the article.

In other words, test each piece of evidence and then decide which to keep—and which to throw out. But do not gather only materials that favor your take on the topic. You want, instead, to look at all legitimate perspectives on your claim, and in doing so, you may even change your mind. That's what good research for an academic argument can do: remember the "conscientious commitment to truth" we mentioned earlier? Keep yourself open to discovery and change. (See **Chapter 21**, "Evaluating Sources," and **Chapter 22**, "Using Sources.")

Give visual materials and other media the same scrutiny you would to print sources, since you will likely be gathering or creating such materials in many academic disciplines. Remember that representing data visually always involves interpreting that material: numbers can lie and pictures distort. (For more information on evaluating and creating visuals, see **Chapter 29**.) In addition, infographics today often make complex academic arguments in a visual form. (See **p. 329** for one such example.)

Take special care with documentation. As you gather materials for your academic argument, record where you found each source so that you can cite it accurately. For all sources, whether print or digital, develop a working bibliography either on your computer or in a notebook you can carry with you. For each book, write the name of the author, the title of the book, the city of publication, the publisher, the date of publication, and the place that you found it (the section of the library, for example, and the call number for the book). For an e-book, note the format (Nook, Kindle, etc.) or the URL where you accessed it. For each newspaper, magazine, or journal article, write the name of the author, the title of the article, the title of the periodical, and the volume, issue, publication date, and exact page numbers. If you accessed the article online, include the name of the Web site or database where you found the source, the full URL, the date it was published on the Web or most recently updated, and the date you accessed and examined it. Include any other information you may later need in preparing a works cited list or references list. The simplest way to ensure that you have this information is to print a copy of the source, highlight source information, and write down any other pertinent information.

Remember, too, that different academic fields use different systems of documentation, so if your instructor has not recommended a style of documentation to you, ask in class about it. Scholars have developed these systems over long periods of time to make research in an area reliable and routine. Using documentation responsibly shows that you understand and respect the conventions of your field or major, thereby establishing your position as a member of the academic community. (For more detailed information, see **Chapter 24**, "Documenting Sources.")

Think about organization. As you review the research materials you have gathered, you are actually beginning the work of drafting and designing your project. Study the way those materials are organized, especially any from professional journals, whether print or digital. You may need to include in your own argument some of the sections or features you find in professional research:

- Does the article open with an abstract, summarizing its content?
- Does the article give any information about the author or authors and their credentials?
- Is there a formal introduction to the subject or a clear statement of a thesis or hypothesis?
- Does the article begin with a "review of literature," summarizing recent research on its topic?
- Does the piece describe its methods of research?
- How does the article report its results and findings?
- Does the article use charts and graphs or other visuals to report data?
- Does the piece use headings and subheadings?
- How does the work summarize its findings or how does it make recommendations?
- Does the essay offer a list of works cited or references?

Anticipate some variance in the way materials are presented from one academic field to another.

As you organize your own project, check with your instructor to see if there is a recommended pattern for you to follow. If not, create a scratch outline or storyboard to describe how your essay will proceed. In reviewing your evidence, decide which pieces support specific points in the argument. Then try to position your strongest pieces of evidence in key places—near the beginning of paragraphs, at the end of the introduction, or toward a powerful conclusion. In addition, strive to achieve a balance between, on the one hand, your own words and argument and, on the other hand, the sources that you use or quote in support of the argument. The sources of evidence are important supports, but they shouldn't overpower the structure of your argument itself. Finally, remember that your organization needs to take into account the placement of visuals—charts, tables, photographs, and so on. (For specific advice on structuring arguments, review the "Thinking about Organization" section in **Chapter 12**.)

Consider style and tone. Most academic argument adopts the voice of a reasonable, fair-minded, and careful thinker who is interested in coming as close to the truth about a topic as possible. An essay that achieves that tone may have some of the following features:

- It strives for clarity and directness, though it may use jargon appropriate to a particular field.
- It favors denotative rather than connotative language.
- It is usually impersonal, using first person (*I*) sparingly.
- In some fields, such as the sciences, it may use the passive voice routinely.
- It uses technical language, symbols, and abbreviations for efficiency.
- It avoids colloquialisms, slang, and sometimes even contractions.

The examples at the end of this chapter demonstrate traditional academic style, though there is, as always, a range of possibilities in its manner of expression.

Consider genre, design, and visuals. Most college academic arguments look more like articles in professional journals than like those one might find in a glossier periodical like *Scientific American*—that is, they are still usually black on white, use a traditional font size and type (like 12-point Times New Roman), and lack any conscious design other than inserted tables or figures. But such conventions are changing.

Indeed, student writers today can go well beyond print, creating digital documents that integrate a variety of media and array data in strikingly original ways. But always consider what genres best suit your topic, purpose, and audience and then act accordingly. As you think about the design possibilities for your academic argument, you may want to consult your instructor—and to test your ideas and innovations on friends or classmates.

In choosing visuals to include in your argument, be sure each one makes a strong contribution to your message and is appropriate and fair to your topic and your audience. Treat visuals as you would any other sources and integrate them into your text. Like quotations, paraphrases, and summaries, visuals need to be introduced and commented on in some way. In addition, label and number ("Figure 1," "Table 2," and so on) each visual, provide a caption that includes source information and describes the visual, and cite the source in your references page or works cited list. Even if you create a visual (such as a bar graph) by using information from a source (the results, say, of a Gallup poll), you must cite the source of the data. If you use a photograph you took yourself, cite it as a personal photograph.

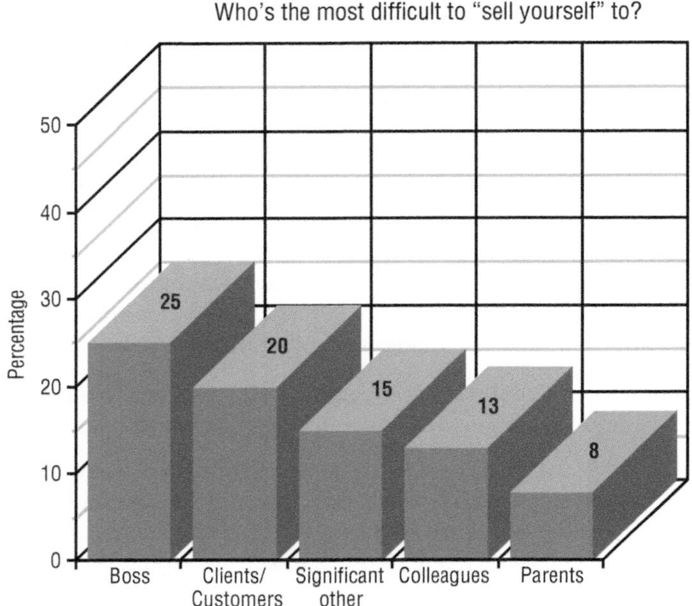

FIGURE 19.3 This bar chart, based on data from a Sandler Training survey of 1,053 adults, would be listed in your works cited or references under the authors' names.

Reflect on your draft and get responses. As with any important piece of writing, an academic argument calls for careful reflection on your draft. You may want to do a "reverse outline" to test whether a reader can pull a logical and consistent pattern out of the paragraphs or sections you have written. In addition, you can also judge the effectiveness of your overall argument, assessing what each paragraph contributes and what may be missing. Turning a critical eye to your own work at the draft stage can save much grief in the long run. Be sure to get some response from classmates and friends too: come up with a set of questions to ask them about your draft and push them for honest responses. Find out what in your draft is confusing or unclear to others, what needs further evidence, what feels unconvincing, and so on.

Edit and proofread your text. Proofread an academic argument at least three times. First review it for ideas, making sure that all your main points and supporting evidence make sense and fit nicely together. Give special attention to transitions and paragraph structure and the way you have arranged information, positioned headings, and captioned graphic items. Make sure the big picture is in focus.

Then read the text word by word to check spelling, punctuation, quotation marks, apostrophes, abbreviations—in short, all the details that can go wrong simply because of a slip in attention. To keep their focus at this level, some readers will even read an entire text backwards. Notice too where your computer's spelling and grammar checkers may be underlining particular words and phrases. Don't ignore these clear signals (and don't rely solely on them to spot errors, since such automated tools are not perfectly accurate).

Finally, check that every source mentioned in the academic argument appears in the works cited or references list and that every citation is correct. This is also the time to make any final touchups to your overall design. Remember that how the document looks is part of what establishes its credibility.

RESPOND

1. Look closely at the following five passages, each of which is from an opening of a published work, and decide which ones provide examples of academic argument. How would you describe each one, and what are its key features? Which is the most formal and academic? Which is the least? How might you revise them to make them more—or less—academic?

> During the Old Stone Age, between thirty-seven thousand and eleven thousand years ago, some of the most remarkable art ever conceived was etched or painted on the walls of caves in southern France and northern Spain. After a visit to Lascaux, in the Dordogne, which was discovered in 1940, Picasso reportedly said to his guide, "They've invented everything." What those first artists invented was a language of signs for which there will never be a Rosetta stone; perspective, a technique that was not rediscovered until the Athenian Golden Age; and a bestiary of such vitality and finesse that, by the flicker of torchlight, the animals seem to surge from the walls, and move across them like figures in a magic-lantern show (in that sense, the artists invented animation). They also thought up the grease lamp—a lump of fat, with a plant wick, placed in a hollow stone—to light their workplace; scaffolds to reach high places; the principles of stenciling and Pointillism; powdered colors, brushes, and stumping cloths; and, more to the point of Picasso's insight, the very concept of an image. A true artist reimagines that concept with every blank canvas—but not from a void.
>
> —Judith Thurman, "First Impressions," *New Yorker*

> I stepped over the curb and into the street to hitchhike. At the age of ten I'd put some pretty serious mileage on my thumb. And I knew how it was done. Hold your thumb up, not down by your hip as though you didn't much give a damn whether you got a ride or not. Always hitch at a place where a driver could pull out of traffic and give you time to get in without risking somebody tailgating him.
>
> —Harry Crews, "On Hitchhiking," *Harper's*

> Coral reef ecosystems are essential marine environments around the world. Host to thousands (and perhaps millions) of diverse organisms, they are also vital to the economic well-being of an estimated 0.5 billion people, or 8% of the world's population who live on tropical coasts (Hoegh-Guldberg 1999). Income from tourism and fishing industries, for instance, is essential to the economic prosperity of many countries, and the various plant and animal species present in reef ecosystems are sources for different natural products and medicines. The degradation of coral reefs can therefore have a devastating impact on coastal populations, and it is estimated that between 50% and 70% of all reefs around the world are currently threatened (Hoegh-Guldberg). Anthropogenic influences are cited as the major cause of this degradation, including sewage, sedimentation, direct trampling of reefs, over-fishing of herbivorous fish, and even global warming (Umezawa et al. 2002; Jones et al. 2001; Smith et al. 2001).
>
> —Elizabeth Derse, "Identifying the Sources of Nitrogen to Hanalei Bay, Kauai, Utilizing the Nitrogen Isotope Signature of Macroalgae," *Stanford Undergraduate Research Journal*

> While there's a good deal known about invertebrate neurobiology, these facts alone haven't settled questions of their sentience. On the one hand, invertebrates lack a cortex, amygdala, as well as many of the other major brain structures routinely implicated in human emotion. And unsurprisingly, their nervous systems are quite minimalist compared to ours: we have roughly a hundred thousand bee brains worth of neurons in our heads. On the other hand, some invertebrates, including insects, do possess the rudiments of our stress response system. So the question is still on the table: do they experience emotion in a way that we would recognize, or just react to the world with a set of glorified reflexes?
>
> —Jason Castro, "Do Bees Have Feelings?" *Scientific American*

> Bambi's mother, shot. Nemo's mother, eaten by a barracuda. Lilo's mother, killed in a car crash. Koda's mother in *Brother Bear*, speared. Po's mother in *Kung Fu Panda 2*, done in by a power-crazed peacock. Ariel's mother in the third *Little Mermaid*, crushed by a pirate ship. Human baby's mother in *Ice Age*, chased by a saber-toothed tiger over a waterfall....The mothers in these movies are either gone or useless. And the father figures? To die for!
>
> —Sarah Boxer, "Why Are All the Cartoon Mothers Dead?" *Atlantic*

2. Working with another student in your class, find examples from two or three different fields of academic arguments that strike you as being well written and effective. If possible, examine at least one from an online academic database so you can see what features periodical articles tend to offer. Then spend time looking at them closely. Do they exemplify the key features of academic arguments discussed in this chapter? What other features do they use? How are they organized? What kind of tone do the writers use? What use do they make of visuals? Draw up a brief report on your findings (a list will do), and bring it to class for discussion.

3. Read the following paragraphs about one writer's experience with anorexia, taken from a recent memoir, and then list changes that the writer might make to convert them into an argument for an academic journal, considering everything from tone and style to paragraphing and format.

> It began when I was at the start of my sophomore year in college, sleeping on my lofted bed and rising before dawn. Initially I was not focused on losing weight; I simply became...obsessed with asceticism and determined to get by on less. I mused on the phonetic similarity between "ascetic" and "aesthetic," believing that through self-denial I could achieve a sort of delicate beauty. Even words like "svelte" and "petite" began to assume, in my mind, a positive valence. Soon I would begin to think of anorexia in this way as well, conjuring a snow-white princess who glided along in a winter fairyland, leaving no footprints.
>
> Although I never stopped eating three meals a day, I severely restricted my diet and the range of foods I would eat. As the number of calories I consumed decreased with each passing week, food assumed more and more a central role in my life. I drove myself to extremes of hunger so that during class I'd be fantasizing about a green apple in my backpack, counting down the minutes until the lecture would end and I would savor that first juicy bite.
>
> —Ilana Kurshan, *If All the Seas Were Ink: A Memoir*

4. Choose two pieces of your college writing, and examine them closely. Are they examples of strong academic writing? How do they use the key features that this chapter identifies as characteristic of academic arguments? How do they use and document sources? What kind of tone do you establish in each? After studying the examples in this chapter, what might you change about these pieces of writing, and why?
5. Go to a blog that you follow, or check out one on the *Huffington Post* or *Ricochet*. Spend some time reading the articles or postings on the blog, and look for ones that you think are the best written and the most interesting. What features or characteristics of academic argument do they use, and which ones do they avoid?

Two Sample Academic Arguments

Title begins with a reference many readers will recognize (Sendak) and then points to the direction the argument will take.

Where the Wild Things Should Be: Healing Nature Deficit Disorder through the Schoolyard

CHARLOTTE GEAGHAN-BREINER*

Background information introduces a claim that states an effect and traces it back to its various causes.

Considerable evidence supports the claim.

The developed world deprives children of a basic and inalienable right: unstructured outdoor play. Children today have substantially less access to nature, less free range, and less time for independent play than previous generations had. Experts in a wide variety of fields cite the rise of technology, urbanization, parental over-scheduling, fears of stranger-danger, and increased traffic as culprits. In 2005 journalist Richard Louv articulated the causes and consequences of children's alienation from nature, dubbing it "nature deficit disorder." Louv is not alone in claiming that the widening divide between children and nature has distressing health repercussions, from obesity and attention disorders to depression and decreased cognitive functioning. The dialogue surrounding nature deficit disorder deserves the attention and action of educators, health professionals, parents, developers, environmentalists, and conservationists alike.

Presents a solution to the problem and foreshadows full thesis

The author identifies a weakness in the proposed solution.

The most practical solution to this staggering rift between children and nature involves the schoolyard. The schoolyard habitat movement, which promotes the "greening" of school grounds, is quickly gaining international recognition and legitimacy. A host of organizations, including the National Wildlife Federation, the American Forest Foundation, and the Council for Environmental Education, as well as their international counterparts, have committed themselves to this cause. However, while many recognize the need for "greened school grounds," not many describe such landscapes beyond using adjectives such as "lush," "green," and "natural." The literature thus lacks a coherent research-based proposal that both asserts the power of "natural" school grounds *and* delineates what such grounds might look like.

---

*Charlotte Geaghan-Breiner wrote this academic argument for her first-year writing class at Stanford University.

My research strives to fill in this gap. I advocate for the schoolyard as the perfect place to address nature deficit disorder, demonstrate the benefits of greened schoolyards, and establish the tenets of natural schoolyard design in order to further the movement and inspire future action.

Ending paragraph of the introduction presents the full thesis and outlines the entire essay.

Asphalt Deserts: The State of the Schoolyard Today

Author uses subheads to help guide readers through the argument.

As a formative geography of childhood, the schoolyard serves as the perfect place to address nature deficit disorder. Historian Peter Stearns argues that modern childhood was transformed when schooling replaced work as the child's main social function (1041). In this contemporary context, the schoolyard emerges as a critical setting for children's learning and play. Furthermore, as parental traffic and safety concerns increasingly constrain children's free range outside of school, the schoolyard remains a safe haven, a protected outdoor space just for children.

Explains why it's valuable to focus on the schoolyard

Despite the schoolyard's major significance in children's lives, the vast majority of schoolyards fail to meet children's needs. An outdated theoretical framework is partially to blame. In his 1890 *Principles of Psychology*, psychologist Herbert Spencer championed the "surplus energy theory": play's primary function, according to Spencer, was to burn off extra energy (White). Play, however, contributes to the social, cognitive, emotional, and physical growth of the child (Hart 136); "[l]etting off steam" is only one of play's myriad functions. Spencer's theory thus constitutes a serious oversimplification, but it still continues to inform the design of children's play areas.

Most U.S. playgrounds conform to an equipment-based model constructed implicitly on Spencer's surplus energy theory (Frost and Klein 2). The sports fields, asphalt courts, swing sets, and jungle gyms common to schoolyards relegate nature to the sidelines and prioritize gross motor play at the expense of dramatic play or exploration. An eight-year-old in England says it best: "The space outside feels boring. There's nothing to do. You get bored with just a square of tarmac" (Titman 42). Such an environment does not afford children the chance to graduate to new, more complex challenges as they develop. While play equipment still deserves a spot in the schoolyard, equipment-*dominated* playscapes leave the growing child bereft of stimulating interactions with the environment.

Quotations by children provide evidence to support the claim and bring in a personal touch.

Citations follow MLA style.

Also to blame for the failure of school grounds to meet children's needs are educators' and developers' adult-centric aims. Most urban schoolyards are sterile environments with low biodiversity (see fig. 1). While concrete, asphalt, and synthetic turf may be easier to maintain and supervise, they exacerbate the "extinction of experience," a term that Pyle has used to describe the disappearance of children's embodied, intuitive experiences in nature. Asphalt deserts are major instigators of this "cycle of impoverishment" (Pyle 312). Loss of biodiversity begets environmental apathy, which in turn allows the process of extinction to persist. Furthermore, adults' preference for manicured, landscaped grounds does little to enhance children's creative outdoor play. Instead of rich, stimulating play environments for children, such highly ordered schoolyards are constructed with adults' convenience in mind.

Presents reasons why schoolyards continue to be poorly designed

The figure is introduced in the text and has a caption.

Fig. 1: Addison Elementary in Palo Alto, CA, conforms to the traditional playground model, dominated by synthetic landcover and equipment.

The Greener, the Better: The Benefits of Greened School Grounds

A great body of research documents the physiological, cognitive, psychological, and social benefits of contact with nature. Health experts champion outdoor play as an antidote to two major trends in children of the developed world: the Attention Deficit Disorder and obesity epidemics. A 2001 study by Taylor, Kuo, and Sullivan indicates that green play settings decrease the severity of symptoms in children with ADD. They also combat inactivity in children by

Author cites research that discusses the health benefits of interacting with nature.

diversifying the "play repertoire" and providing for a wider range of physical activity than traditional playgrounds. In the war against childhood obesity, health advocates must add the natural schoolyard to their arsenal.

The schoolyard also has the ability to influence the way children play. Instead of being prescribed a play structure with a clear purpose (e.g., a swing set), children in natural schoolyards must discover the affordances of their environment—they must imagine what could be. In general, children exhibit more prosocial behavior and higher levels of inclusion in the natural schoolyard (Dyment 31). A 2006 questionnaire-based study of a greening initiative in Toronto found that the naturalization of the school grounds yielded a decrease in aggressive actions and disciplinary problems and a corresponding increase in civility and cooperation (Dyment 28). The greened schoolyard offers benefits beyond physical and mental health; it shapes the character and quality of children's play interactions.

Social benefits of interacting with nature

The schoolyard also has the potential to shape the relationship between children and the natural world. In the essay "Eden in a Vacant Lot," Pyle laments the loss of vacant lots and undeveloped spaces in which children can play and develop intimacy with the land. However, Pyle overlooks the geography of schoolyards, which can serve as enclaves of nature in an increasingly urbanized and developed world. Research has shown that school ground naturalization fosters nature literacy and intimacy just as Pyle's vacant lots do. For instance, a school ground greening program in Toronto dramatically enhanced children's environmental awareness, sense of stewardship, and curiosity about their local ecosystem (Dyment 37). When integrated with nature, the schoolyard can mitigate the effects of nature deficit disorder and reawaken children's innate biophilia, or love of nature.

Biophilic Design: Establishing the Tenets of Natural Schoolyard Design

The need for naturalized schoolyards is urgent. But how might theory actually translate into reality? Here I will propose four principles of biophilic schoolyard design, or landscaping that aims to integrate nature and natural systems into the man-made geography of the schoolyard.

The author establishes four guidelines for redesigning schoolyards.

The first is biodiversity. Schools should strive to incorporate a wide range of greenery and wildlife on their grounds (see fig. 2). Native plants should figure prominently so as to inspire children's interest in their local habitats. Inclusion of wildlife in school grounds can foster meaningful interactions with other species. Certain plants and flowers, for example, attract birds, butterflies, and other insects; aquatic areas can house fish, frogs, tadpoles, and pond bugs. School pets and small-scale farms also serve to teach children important lessons about responsibility, respect, and compassion for animals. Biodiversity, the most vital feature of biophilic design, transforms former "asphalt deserts" into realms teeming with life.

Photo by Charlotte Geaghan-Breiner

Fig. 2: A seating area at Ohlone School in Palo Alto, CA, features a healthy range of plant species.

The second principle that schoolyard designers should keep in mind is sensory stimulation. The greater the degree of sensory richness in an environment, the more opportunities it affords the child to imagine, learn, and discover. School grounds should feature a range of colors, textures, sounds, fragrances, and in the case of the garden, tastes. Such sensory diversity almost always accompanies natural environments, unlike concrete, which affords comparatively little sensory stimulation.

Diversity of topography constitutes another dimension of a greened schoolyard (Fjortoft and Sageie 83). The best school grounds afford children a range of places to climb, tunnel, frolic, and sit. Natural elements function as "play equipment": children can sit on stumps, jump over logs, swing on trees, roll down grassy mounds, and climb on boulders. The playscape should also offer nooks and crannies for children to seek shelter and refuge. While asphalt lots and play structures are still fun for children, they should not dominate the school grounds (see fig. 3).

A figure illustrates a specific point about play structures.

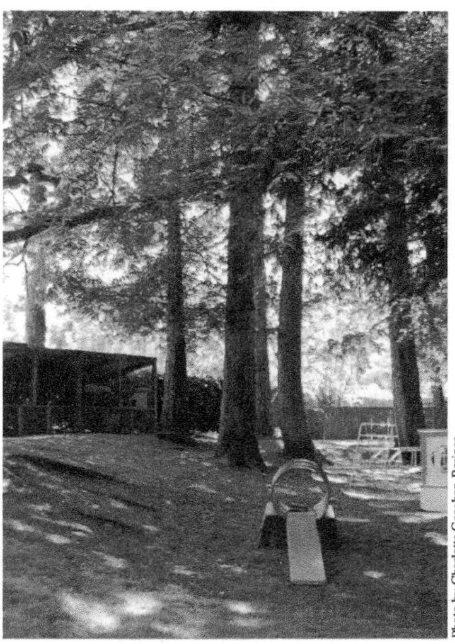
Photo by Charlotte Geaghan-Breiner

Fig. 3: Peninsula School in Menlo Park, CA, has integrated traditional equipment, such as a playhouse and slide, into the natural setting.

Last but not least, naturalized schoolyards must embody the theory of loose parts proposed by architect Simon Nicholson. "In any environment," he writes, "both the degree of inventiveness and the possibility of discovery are directly proportional to the number and kinds of variables in it" (qtd. in Louv 87). Loose parts—sand, water, leaves, nuts, seeds, rocks, and sticks—are abundant in the natural world. The detachability of loose parts makes them ideal for children's construction projects. While some might worry about the possible hazards of loose parts, conventional play equipment is far from safe: more than 200,000 of children's emergency room visits every year in the United States are linked to these built structures (Frost 217). When integrated into the schoolyard through naturalization, loose parts offer the child the chance to gain ever-increasing mastery of the environment.

The four tenets proposed provide a concrete basis for the application of biophilic design to the schoolyard. Such design also requires a frame-shift away from adult preferences for well-manicured grounds and towards children's needs for wilder spaces that can be constructed, manipulated, and changed through play (Lester and Maudsley 67; White and Stoecklin). Schoolyards designed according to the precepts of biodiversity, sensory stimulation, diversity of topography, and loose parts will go a long way in healing the rift between children and nature, a rift that adult-centric design only widens.

Grounds for Change

In conclusion, I have shown that natural schoolyard design can heal nature deficit disorder by restoring free outdoor play to children's lives in the developed world. Successful biophilic schoolyards challenge the conventional notion that natural and man-made landscapes are mutually exclusive. Human-designed environments, and especially those for children, should strive to integrate nature into the landscape. All schools should be designed with the four tenets of natural schoolyard design in mind.

Author restates her claim.

Though such sweeping change may seem impractical given limitations on school budgets, greening initiatives that use natural elements, minimal equipment, and volunteer work can be remarkably cost-effective. Peninsula School in Menlo Park, California, has minimized maintenance costs through the inclusion of hardy native species; it is essentially "designed for neglect" (Dyment 44). Gardens and small-scale school farms can also become their own source of funding, as they have for Ohlone Elementary School in Palo Alto, California. Ultimately, the cognitive, psychological, physiological, and social benefits of natural school grounds are priceless. In the words of author Richard Louv, "School isn't supposed to be a polite form of incarceration, but a portal to the wider world" (Louv 226). With this in mind, let the schoolyard restore to children their exquisite intimacy with nature: their inheritance, their right.

Offers examples of successful biophilic schoolyard design

Works Cited

The list of works cited follows MLA style.

Dyment, Janet. "Gaining Ground: The Power and Potential of School Ground Greening in the Toronto District School Board." *Evergreen*, 2006. www.evergreen.ca/downloads/pdfs/Gaining-Ground.pdf.

Fjortoft, Ingunn, and Jostein Sageie. "The Natural Environment as a Playground for Children." *Landscape and Urban Planning*, vol. 48, no. 2, Winter 2001, pp. 83-97.

Frost, Joe L. *Play and Playscapes*. Delmar, 1992.

Frost, Joe L., and Barry L. Klein. *Children's Play and Playgrounds*. Allyn and Bacon, 1979.

Hart, Roger. "Containing Children: Some Lessons on Planning for Play from New York City." *Environment and Urbanization*, vol. 14, no. 2, October 2002, pp. 135-48, doi.org/10.1177/0995624780201400211.

Lester, Stuart, and Martin Maudsley. *Play, Naturally: A Review of Children's Natural Play*. Play England, National Children's Bureau, 2007.

Louv, Richard. *Last Child in the Woods: Saving Our Children from Nature-Deficit Disorder*. Algonquin of Chapel Hill, 2005.

Nicholson, Simon. "How Not to Cheat Children: The Theory of Loose Parts." *Landscape Architecture*, vol. 62, October 1971, pp. 30-35.

Pyle, Robert M. "Eden in a Vacant Lot: Special Places, Species, and Kids in the Neighborhood of Life." *Children and Nature: Psychological, Sociocultural, and Evolutionary Investigations*, edited by Peter H. Kahn and Stephen R. Kellert, MIT Press, 2002, pp. 305-27.

Stearns, Peter N. "Conclusion: Change, Globalization, and Childhood." *Journal of Social History*, vol. 38, no. 4, 2005, pp. 1041-46.

Taylor, Andrea F., et al. "Coping with ADD: The Surprising Connection to Green Play Settings." *Environment and Behavior*, vol. 33, no. 1, 2001, pp. 54-77.

Titman, Wendy. *Special Places; Special People: The Hidden Curriculum of Schoolgrounds*. World Wide Fund for Nature, 1994, files.eric.ed.gov/fulltext/ED430384.pdf.

White, Randy. "Young Children's Relationship with Nature: Its Importance to Children's Development and the Earth's Future." *Taproot*, vol. 16, no. 2, 2006. *White Hutchinson Leisure and Learning Group*, www.whitehutchinson.com/children/articles/childrennature.shtml.

White, Randy, and Vicki Stoecklin. "Children's Outdoor Play and Learning Environments: Returning to Nature." *Early Childhood News*, Mar. 1998. *White Hutchinson Leisure and Learning Group*, https://www.whitehutchinson.com/children/articles/outdoor.shtml.

The Emotion Work of "Thank You for Your Service"

SIDRA MONTGOMERY**

In the post-9/11 era, "thank you for your service" (TYFYS) has become the new mantra of public support bestowed upon the veteran community. In the early 2000s, as the wars in Afghanistan and Iraq began escalating, "Support Our Troops" car magnets increasingly appeared on the trunks of cars across America. After well over 15 years of war, public gratitude is now most commonly expressed in small interactions between veterans and the public they've served—with strangers saying TYFYS or offering to pay for a coffee or meal. If you ask any recent servicemember or veteran how they feel when someone says TYFYS, you'll probably hear them express a strong opinion about the phrase. While some view it positively and enjoy these interactions, most find it awkward, uncomfortable or irritating. The message of support and gratitude that well-meaning Americans are attempting to express is often lost in translation with veterans.

A collection of op-ed pieces have addressed why servicemembers find TYFYS to be a point of disconnection rather than connection. James Kelly, an active-duty Marine, says that he hears the phrase so often it has become an "empty platitude," something people say only because it is "politically correct." Matt Richtel, a *New York Times* reporter, highlights how veterans feel the phrase can be self-serving; civilians get to pat themselves on the back because they are doing something for veterans, alleviating any sense of guilt in the era of an all-volunteer service. Another common complaint is that TYFYS doesn't start the conversation between veterans and civilians—it stunts it—leaving veterans feeling more isolated and less connected to the America they served. Veterans commonly remark that civilians don't even know what they are saying "thank you" for. Elizabeth Samet, a professor at West Point, argues that we've come to the other "unthinking extreme" with TYFYS as an attempt for atonement after the poor treatment of Vietnam veterans.

While many have tried to explain why veterans find TYFYS to be lacking, few have examined *how these interactions affect veterans.* Having interviewed servicemembers and veterans for the past 3 years in my professional life, and being a military spouse for the past 5 years, I have always been intrigued by how veterans handle these moments and interactions. I watch the discomfort when strangers approach my interview subjects or friends and say TYFYS—it becomes an

**Sidra Montgomery received her PhD in sociology in 2017 from the University of Maryland–College Park. Her work focuses specifically on the military and veterans. The piece appeared on March 21, 2017, on the Veterans Scholars Web site.

awkward stumble for the veteran to find a way to muster their appreciation for a gesture that doesn't necessarily square with its intent.

Emotion Work

As I analyzed the data I collected for my dissertation, a total of 39 interviews with wounded, injured, and ill post–9/11 veterans, I realized these interactions require veterans to engage in *emotion work*, a sociological concept defined by Arlie Hochschild. Emotion work is defined by Hochschild as "trying to change, in degree or quality, an emotion or feeling" (1979:561). It is an active attempt to shape and direct one's feelings to match the appropriate emotions for a given situation. For example, when someone thanks you for something you've done, you're supposed to feel good, right? Gratitude should give you that warm, fuzzy feeling inside. This is called "feeling rules"; it's how we know what we should be feeling in any given moment....

For veterans who genuinely appreciate and enjoy hearing TYFYS and other acts of gratitude, there is no "work" necessary because their feelings are appropriate given the situation. For Alex, a wounded Marine veteran, TYFYS makes him feel as though he is "seen" and that his service is validated:

> I like it. I really like it when people acknowledge my service. I'm not out there trying to get someone to do it, but when someone takes time out of their day to shake my hand and say, "Thank you for your service." It's like, "Wow. You know this country—it was worth it. You know it's—proud of your service to the country"...That's something special.

Alex's emotions are in line with what we expect to feel when someone says thank you and acknowledges something that we have done. He doesn't have to control or wrangle his emotions because they already align with the socially prescribed "feeling rules" and expectations.

My dissertation data suggests that 15 to 20% of veterans share Alex's feelings; they enjoy and appreciate when people thank them for their service or demonstrate their gratitude through other acts and gestures. Personally and anecdotally, I've found about the same split: 10–20% find TYFYS gratifying and associate it with positive feelings, and 80–90% of servicemembers and veterans feel uncomfortable or upset about the phrase.

For the majority of wounded veterans I interviewed, who don't have positive associations with TYFYS, these interactions necessitate emotion work. As they go about their day-to-day life, they are thrust into situations where they must acknowledge and negotiate the gratitude of total strangers through their own emotional response: emotions that do not match their true feelings in the situation. Luis, a young Marine Corps veteran with visible injuries, describes how he wrestles with having to do emotion work in these interactions:

> When people say thank you for your service, thank you for what you did...it's kind of lost its shock value or something. I've heard it so much that I'm embarrassed that I can't give them...like that first time when someone said thank you for your service...I feel like I don't give them enough sincerity, I feel bad...I feel embarrassed for myself because I can't do that, you know?...I just hear it sooooo much.

Luis wants to give others a genuine emotional reaction each time they thank him for his service, but he feels he can't because of the overwhelming number of times this happens to him. From this quote it's clear he is blaming himself for even having to perform emotion work in the first place. Connor, an Army veteran with invisible injuries, discusses how he handles TYFYS:

> I give the standard, thanks, appreciate it or happy to do it. Or I don't get into it. Even if I know it's totally fake I'm like, yeah, appreciate it. And I'll give just a fake answer. As fake as I got [from them], that's how much I'll give back...It'll be like..."oh, thanks" with the plastic smile. You know what I mean?

Connor attempts to mirror the level of sincerity in the interaction, aligning his own response with it. His comment about how he puts on a "plastic smile" describes how he engages in surface acting: a way to present the necessary emotion to others even though his own feelings haven't changed.

Another common strategy for veterans, especially wounded veterans who are frequently thanked for their service, is the use of predetermined responses. Having a rolodex of appropriate responses minimizes impromptu emotion work. Jackson, a Marine Corps veteran who has visible injuries, says that hearing TYFYS "*just gets old*" because he hears it so much. When I asked him how he usually responds, he said:

> [I will say] ". . . no, *thank you*." Another one is like some people [say] "thank *you guys* for what *you do*...you guys made coming home so much easier and so much more worth it." So make them feel just as adequate in a way.

Jackson reveals the set of responses that he (and others) normally give. These prepackaged responses increase the efficiency of Jackson's emotion work by creating sentiments that acknowledge and reciprocate the gratitude—an intentional move on Jackson's part.

Several years after her Marine Corps service, Susan, an invisibly injured veteran, has gained a new perspective on the TYFYS issue. She is now able to see it from another point of view:

> You get to finally a point—I finally went, you know, these people are very sincere, and you've got to let them just say the thing. Because they generally want to thank you. And this is so not your experience. You don't have to have it with them. And then it became okay going, you know what, they're really caring, lovely people most of the time...

Susan describes taking away her own investment in these interactions as a way to distance herself from constantly engaging in emotion work whenever someone says "thank you." She understands the moment to be more about the other person than herself. She also describes her engagement with deep acting: working to change the way she truly feels about these interactions; trying to bring her own emotions in line with what's expected.

The Cumulative Effect for Visibly Injured Veterans

For current servicemembers, veterans, and invisibly injured veterans, these moments of invited gratitude from strangers happen occasionally or in concentrated environments where they know they may be thanked or approached. For visibly injured veterans, these interactions happen every day. Visibly injured veterans are disproportionately burdened with doing the emotional work surrounding public gratitude because their status as wounded veterans can't be hidden or "taken off" like a uniform. And their visible injury only amplifies feelings of gratitude among the public, causing them to experience more of these moments and interactions.

Thomas, an Army veteran with visible injuries, describes:

> [Civilians]...they just all want to do the right things. And I mean, to that person they have one chance to make a difference to one person. But if it's you, they're the 100th person today to say "thank you for your service."

The cumulative effect of these interactions wears on Thomas and other visibly injured veterans:

> And what if everybody did that to me? Like, everywhere I went, what if every single person thought they were doing me a favor and said "thank you for your service." I would spend my whole life giving to other people. I could literally go every five feet and just be doling out good feelings to everybody. And I'm sorry, I'm an emotional bank account, we're all just emotional bank accounts.

Thomas's comments clearly reveal how visibly injured veterans can quickly become exhausted from the emotion work of receiving TYFYS and other gestures of gratitude. What seems like a small interaction in the moment is continually repeated for wounded veterans like Thomas.

The treatment of U.S. veterans has significantly changed over time, from the prosperous return of World War II veterans to the protests and mistreatment of Vietnam veterans to the new era of the all-volunteer force. It is important that as a nation, we engage in a constant reflection process of how we treat our veterans, from the largest of government programs to the smallest interpersonal interactions. The well-meaning intent behind TYFYS isn't always received by post–9/11 veterans in the same way.

Practical Suggestions: What Should We Be Doing to Show Our Gratitude and Appreciation?

Inevitably, after presenting these issues with TYFYS I get asked: *"well, what **should** we be doing?"* This is both a prudent and complicated question, and there is no one-size-fits-all answer. We all have our own personal preferences of what is meaningful to us based on our personality, life experiences, and our thoughts. I'm not here to say that I have *the* answer, but I have a couple suggestions based on my work with veterans:

1. **Judge whether the military member or veteran seems open to conversation with a stranger.** You know how you can tell whether the person next to you on a plane wants to talk or wants to be left alone? The same should go for your interactions with veterans, servicemembers, and wounded veterans. Do they appear willing to engage with others (i.e., making eye contact or already engaging in a friendly conversation with you), or do they look like they just want to grab their coffee and go about their day? If the latter—let them go about their day and reflect privately on your gratitude for their willingness to lay their life on the line for our freedom.
2. **If you want to show your support for veterans, find a local organization that helps veterans in your community.** Do your research, find out what organizations are doing to serve veterans and improve their lives. Give your financial support or your time (through volunteering).
3. **Go beyond "thank you for your service."** Ask them why they served, ask them when and where they served, ask them what they most enjoyed about their service. Dig deeper; cultivate gratitude for their service by learning more about it.

CHAPTER

20

Finding Evidence

Left to right: Wavebreakmedia Ltd/AGE Fotostock; Baloo-Rex May/CartoonStock.com; Zoonar/M KANG/AGE Fotostock

In making and supporting claims for academic arguments, writers use all kinds of evidence: data from journal articles; scholarly books; historical records from archives; blogs, wikis, social media sites, and other digital sources; personal observations and fieldwork; surveys; and even DNA. But such evidence doesn't exist in a vacuum. Instead, the quality of evidence—how and when it was collected, by whom, and for what purposes—may become part of the argument itself. Evidence may be persuasive in one time and place but not in another; it may convince one kind of audience but not another; it may work with one type of argument but not with the kind you are writing. The point is that finding "good" evidence for a research project is rarely a simple matter.

Considering the Rhetorical Situation

To be most persuasive, evidence should match the time and place in which you make your argument—that is to say, your rhetorical situation. For example, arguing that government officials in the twenty-first century should use the same policies to deal with economic troubles that were employed in the middle of the twentieth might not be convincing on its own. After all, almost every aspect of the world economy has changed in the past fifty years. In the same way, a writer may achieve excellent results by citing a detailed survey of local teenagers as evidence for education reform in her small rural hometown, but she may have less success using the same evidence to argue for similar reforms in a large urban community.

College writers also need to consider the fields that they're working in. In disciplines such as experimental psychology or economics, **quantitative data**—the sort that can be observed, collected and counted—may be the best evidence. In many historical, literary, or philosophical studies, however, the same kind of data may be less appropriate or persuasive, or even impossible to come by. As you become more familiar with a discipline, you'll gain a sense of what it takes to support a claim. The following questions will help you understand the rhetorical situation of a particular field:

- What kinds of data are preferred as evidence? How are such data gathered, tabulated, and verified?
- How are definitions, causal analyses, evaluations, analogies, and examples used as evidence?
- How are statistics or other numerical information used and presented as evidence? Are tables, charts, or graphs commonly used? How much weight do they carry?
- What or who counts as an authority in this field? How are the credentials of authorities established? How are research publications reviewed and research journals refereed?
- What weight do writers in the field give to **precedence**—that is, to examples of similar actions or decisions made in the past?
- Is personal experience allowed as evidence? When?
- How are quotations used as part of evidence?
- How are still or moving images or sound(s) used as part of evidence, and how closely are they related to the verbal parts of the argument being presented? Are other kinds of media commonly used to present evidence?

As these questions suggest, evidence may not always travel well from one field to another. Nor does it always travel easily from culture to culture. Differing notions of evidence can lead to arguments that go nowhere fast. For instance, when Italian journalist Oriana Fallaci interviewed Ayatollah Khomeini, Iran's supreme leader, in

1979, she argued in a way that's common in North American and Western European cultures: she presented claims that she considered to be adequately backed up with facts ("Iran denies freedom to people. . . . Many people have been put in prison and even executed, just for speaking out in opposition"). In response, Khomeini relied on very different kinds of evidence—analogies ("Just as a finger with gangrene should be cut off so that it will not destroy the whole body, so should people who corrupt others be pulled out like weeds so they will not infect the whole field") and, above all, the authority of the Qur'an. Partly because of these differing beliefs about what counts as evidence, the interview ended unsuccessfully.

FIGURE 20.1 The need for evidence depends a lot on the rhetorical situation.

CULTURAL CONTEXTS FOR ARGUMENT

The Rhetorical Situation

To take another example, a *Harvard Business Review* blog post from December 4, 2013, on "How to Argue across Cultures" recounts the story of a Western businessperson who was selling bicycles produced in China to a buyer in Germany. When the business owner went to pick up the bicycles, he noticed that they rattled. In considering how to bring up this defect with the Chinese supplier, the businessperson could have confronted him directly, relying on physical evidence to support his claim. He rejected this form of evidence, however, because he knew that such a confrontation would result in loss of face for the supplier and very likely lead to an undesirable outcome. So instead, he suggested that he and the Chinese supplier take a couple of bikes out for a ride, during which the bikes rattled away. At the end of the ride, the Western businessperson quietly mentioned that he "thought his bike had rattled" and then departed, leaving the Chinese supplier to consider his subtle presentation of evidence. And it worked: when the Germans received the bicycle delivery, the rattle had been repaired.

It's always good to remember, then, that when arguing across cultural divides, whether international or more local, you need to think carefully about how you're accustomed to using evidence—and about what counts as evidence to other people (without surrendering your own intellectual principles).

Searching Effectively

The evidence you will use in most academic arguments—books, articles, videos, documents, photographs and other images—will likely come from sources you locate in libraries, in databases, or online. How well you can navigate these complex territories will determine the success of many of your academic and professional projects. Research suggests that most students overestimate their ability to manage these tools and, perhaps more important, don't seek the help they need to find the best materials for their projects. In this chapter, we aim to point you in the right direction for successful academic research.

Explore library resources: printed works and databases. Your college library has printed materials (books, periodicals, reference works) as well as computers that provide access to its electronic catalogs, other libraries' catalogs, and numerous proprietary databases (such as Academic Search Complete, Academic OneFile, JSTOR) not available publicly on the Web. Crucially, libraries also have librarians whose job it is to guide you through these resources, help you identify reputable materials, and show you how to search for materials efficiently. The best way to begin a serious academic argument then is often with a trip to the library or a discussion with your professor or a research librarian.

Also be certain that you know your way around the library. If not, ask the staff there to help you locate the following tools: general and specialized encyclopedias; biographical resources; almanacs, yearbooks, and atlases; book and periodical indexes; specialized indexes and abstracts; the circulation computer or library catalog; special collections; audio, video, and art collections; and the interlibrary loan office, for requesting materials not available at your own library.

At the outset of a project, determine what kinds of sources you will need to support your project. (You might also review your assignment to see whether you're required to consult particular types or a specific number of sources.) If you'll use print sources, find out whether they're readily available in your library or whether you must make special arrangements (such as an interlibrary loan) to acquire them. For example, your argument for a senior thesis might benefit from material available mostly in old newspapers and magazines: access to them might require time and ingenuity. If you need to locate other nonprint sources (such as audiotapes, videotapes, artwork, or photos), find out where those are kept and whether you need special permission to examine them.

Most academic resources, however, will be on the shelves or available electronically through databases. Here's when it's important to understand the distinction between library databases and the Web. Your library's computers hold important resources that aren't on the Web or aren't available to you except through the library's system. The most important of these resources may be your library's catalog of its own holdings (mostly books). But college libraries also pay to subscribe to *scholarly databases* that you can use for free by logging in through your school library—for example, guides to journal and magazine articles, the Academic Search Complete database (which holds the largest collection of multidisciplinary journals), the LexisNexis database of news stories and legal cases, and various compilations of statistics.

Though many of these Web and database resources may be searchable through your own computer, consider exploring them initially at your college library. That's because these professional databases aren't always easy to use or intuitive: you may need to learn to focus and narrow your searches (by date, field, types of material, and so on) so that your results are manageable and full of relevant items. That's when librarians or your instructor can help, so ask them for assistance. They expect your questions.

Librarians may, for example, draw your attention to the distinction between subject headings and keywords. The Library of Congress Subject Headings (LCSH) are standardized words and phrases that are used to classify the subject matter of books and articles. Library catalogs and databases routinely use these subject headings to index their contents by author, title, publication date, and subject headings. When you do a subject search of the library's catalog, you need to use the exact wording of the subject headings. On the other hand, searches with *keywords* use the computer's ability to look for any term in any field of the electronic record. So keyword searching is less restrictive, but you'll still have to think hard about your search terms to get usable results and to learn how to limit or expand your search.

Determine, too, early on, how current your sources need to be. If you must investigate the latest findings about, say, a new treatment for malaria, check very recent periodicals, medical journals, and the Web. If you want broader coverage with more context and background information, look for reference materials or scholarly books. If your argument deals with a specific time period, newspapers, magazines, and books written during that period may be your best assets.

How many sources should you consult for an academic argument? Expect to examine many more sources than you'll end up using, and be sure to cover all major perspectives on your subject. Read enough sources to feel comfortable discussing it with someone with more knowledge than you. You don't have to be an expert, but your readers should sense that you are well informed.

Explore online resources. Chances are your first instinct when you need to find information is to do a quick keyword search on the Web, which in many instances will take you to a site such as Wikipedia, the free encyclopedia launched by Jimmy Wales in 2001. For years, many teachers and institutions argued that the information on Wikipedia was suspect and could not be used as a reliable source, particularly since anyone can edit and change the content on a Wikipedia page. Times have changed, however, and many serious research efforts now include a stop at Wikipedia. As always, however, let the buyer beware: you need to verify the credibility of all of your sources! If you intend to support a serious academic argument, remember to approach the Web carefully and professionally.

Web search engines such as Google or Bing make searching for material seem very easy—perhaps *too* easy. For an argument about the fate of the antihero in contemporary films, for example, typing in *film* and *antihero* produces far too many possible matches, or hits. Some of those hits might be generic and geared to current moviegoers rather than someone thinking about an analytical essay. You could further narrow the search by adding a third or fourth keyword—say, *French* or *current*—or you could simply type in a specific question. Google will always offer pages of links. But you need to be a critical user too, pushing yourself well beyond any initial items you turn up or using those sources to find more authoritative, diverse, or academic materials.

Google does have resources to help you refine your results or direct you to works better suited to academic research. When you search for any term, you can click "Help" at the bottom of the results page, which takes you to the Google Help Center. Click on "Filter and refine your results" and then "Advanced search," which will bring more options to narrow your focus in important ways.

But that's not the end of your choices. With an *academic* argument, you might want to explore your topic in either Google Books or Google Scholar. Both resources direct you to the type and quality of materials (scholarly journal articles, academic books) that you probably need for a term paper or professional project. And Google offers multimodal options as well: it can help you find images, photographs, videos, blogs, and so on. The lesson is simple. If your current Web searches typically don't go much beyond the first items a search engine offers, you aren't close to using all the power available to you. Explore the search tools you routinely use and learn what they can really do.

You should work just as deliberately with the academic databases you may have access to in a library or online—such as Academic Search Complete or Business Source Complete, among many others. As noted earlier, searching these professional tools often requires more deliberate choices and specific combinations of search terms and keywords. In doing such searches, you'll need to observe the search logic followed by the particular database—usually explained on a search page. For example, using Boolean operators such as *and* between keywords (*movies and heroes*) may indicate that both terms must appear in a file for it to be called up. Using *or* between keywords usually instructs the computer to locate every file in which either one word or the other shows up, and using *not* tells the computer to exclude files containing a particular word from the search results (*movies not heroes*).

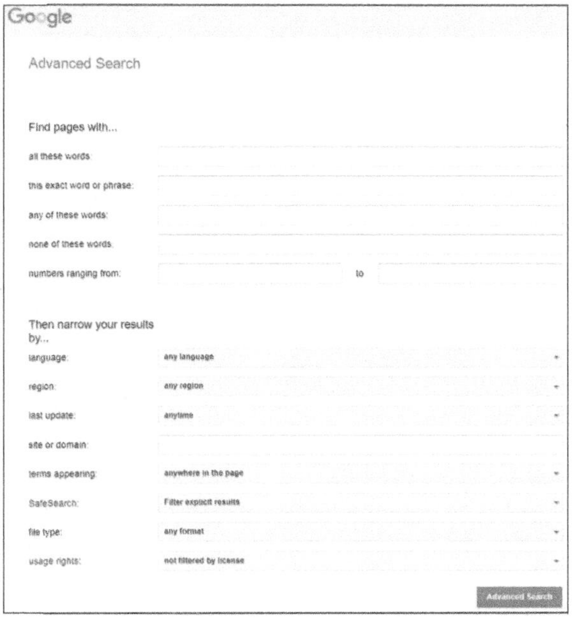

FIGURE 20.2 Most search engines offer many kinds of research tools like this "Advanced Search" page from Google.

SEARCHING ONLINE OR IN DATABASES

- Don't rely on simple Web searches only.
- Find library databases targeted to your subject.
- Use advanced search techniques to focus your search.
- Learn the difference between *subject heading* and *keyword* searches.
- Understand the differences between academic and popular sources.
- Admit when you don't know how to find material—you won't be alone!
- *Routinely* ask for help from librarians and instructors.

Collecting Data on Your Own

Not all your supporting materials for an academic argument must come from print or online sources. You can present research that you have carried out yourself or been closely involved with, often called *field research*; such research usually requires that you collect and examine data. Here, we discuss the kinds of firsthand research that student writers do most often.

Perform experiments. Academic arguments can be supported by evidence you gather through experiments. In the sciences, data from experiments conducted under rigorously controlled conditions is highly valued. In other fields, more informal experiments may be acceptable, especially if they're intended to provide only part of the support for an argument.

If you want to argue, for instance, that the recipes in *Bon Appétit* magazine are impossibly tedious to follow and take far more time than the average person wishes to spend preparing food, you might ask five or six people to conduct an experiment—following two recipes from a recent issue and recording and timing every step. The evidence that you gather from this informal experiment could provide some concrete support—by way of specific examples—for your contention.

But such experiments should be taken with a grain of salt (maybe organic in this case). They may not convince or impress certain audiences. And if your experiments can easily be attacked as skewed or sloppily done ("The people you asked to make these recipes couldn't cook a Pop-Tart"), then they may do more harm than good.

Make observations. "What," you may wonder, "could be easier than observing something?" You just choose a subject, look at it closely, and record what you see and hear. But trained observers say that recording an observation accurately requires intense concentration and mental agility. If observing were easy, all eyewitnesses would provide reliable stories. Yet experience shows that when several people observe the same phenomenon, they generally offer different, sometimes even contradictory, accounts of those observations.

Before you begin an observation yourself, decide exactly what you want to find out, and anticipate what you're likely to see. Do you want to observe an action that is repeated by many people—perhaps how people behave at the checkout line in a grocery store? Or maybe you want to study a sequence of actions—for instance, the stages involved in student registration, which you expect to argue is far too complicated. Or maybe you are motivated to examine the interactions of a notoriously contentious political group. Once you have a clear sense of what you'll analyze and what questions you'll try to answer through the observation, use the following guidelines to achieve the best results:

- Make sure that the observation relates directly to your claim.
- Brainstorm about what you're looking for, but don't be rigidly bound to your expectations.
- Develop an appropriate system for collecting data. Consider using a split notebook page or screen: on one side, record the minute details of your observations; on the other, record your thoughts or impressions.
- Be aware that how you record data will affect the outcome, if only in respect to what you decide to include in your observational notes and what you leave out.
- Record the precise date, time, and place of the observation(s).
- If the location you want to focus on is not a public one (for instance, an elementary school playground), ask for permission to conduct your observation.

You may be asked to prepare systematic observations in various science courses, including anthropology or psychology, where you would follow a methodology and receive precise directions. But observation can play a role in other kinds of arguments and use various media: a photo essay or audio/video clips, for example, might serve as academic arguments in some situations.

Conduct interviews. Some evidence is best obtained through direct interviews. If you can talk with an expert—in person, on the phone, or online—you might obtain information you couldn't have gotten through any other type of research. In addition to an expert opinion, you might ask for firsthand accounts, biographical information, or suggestions of other places to look or other people to consult. The following guidelines will help you conduct effective interviews:

- Determine the exact purpose of the interview, and be sure it's directly related to your claim.
- Set up the interview well in advance—preferably by a written communication. (An email is more polite than a text message.) Explain who you are, the purpose of the interview, and what you expect to cover. Specify, too, how much time it will take, and if you wish to record the session, ask permission to do so.

- Prepare a written list of both factual and open-ended questions. (Brainstorming with friends can help you come up with good questions.) Leave plenty of space for notes after each question. If the interview proceeds in a direction that you hadn't expected but that seems promising, don't feel that you have to cover every one of your questions.
- Record the subject's full name and title, as well as the date, time, and place of the interview.
- Be sure to thank those people whom you interview, either in person or with a follow-up letter or email message.

A serious interview can be eye-opening when the questions get a subject to reveal important experiences or demonstrate his or her knowledge or wisdom.

Use questionnaires to conduct surveys. Surveys usually require the use of questionnaires distributed to a number of people. Questions should be clear, easy to understand, and designed so that respondents' answers can be easily analyzed. Questions that ask respondents to say "yes" or "no" or to rank items on a scale (1 to 5, for example, or "most helpful" to "least helpful") are particularly easy to tabulate. Because tabulation can take time and effort, limit the number of questions you ask. Note also that people often resent being asked to answer more than about twenty questions, especially online.

Here are some other guidelines to help you prepare for and carry out a survey:

- Ask your instructor if your college or university requires that you get approval from the local Institutional Review Board (IRB) to conduct survey research. Many schools waive this requirement if students are doing such research as part of a required course, but you should check to make sure. Securing IRB permission usually requires filling out a series of online forms, submitting all of your questions for approval, and asking those you are surveying to sign a consent form saying they agree to participate in the research.
- Write out your purpose in conducting the survey, and make sure that its results will be directly related to your purpose.
- Brainstorm potential questions to include in the survey, and ask how each relates to your purpose and claim.
- Figure out how many people you want to contact, what the demographics of your sample should be (for example, men in their twenties or an equal number of men and women), and how you plan to reach these people.
- Draft questions that are as free of bias as possible, making sure that each calls for a short, specific answer. Avoid open-ended questions, whose responses will be harder to tabulate.
- Think about possible ways that respondents could misunderstand you or your questions, and revise with these points in mind.
- Test the questions in advance on several people, and revise those questions that are ambiguous, hard to answer, or too time-consuming to answer.

- If your questionnaire is to be sent by mail or email or posted on the Web, draft a cover letter explaining your purpose and giving a clear deadline. For mail, provide an addressed, stamped return envelope.
- On the final draft of the questionnaire, leave plenty of space for answers.
- Proofread the final draft carefully. Typos will make a bad impression on those whose help you're seeking.
- After you've done your tabulations, set out your findings in clear and easily readable form, using a chart or spreadsheet if possible.

"Next question: I believe that life is a constant striving for balance, requiring frequent tradeoffs between morality and necessity, within a cyclic pattern of joy and sadness, forging a trail of bittersweet memories until one slips, inevitably, into the jaws of death. Agree or disagree?"

FIGURE 20.3 A key requirement of survey questions is that they be easy to understand.

Draw upon personal experience. Personal experience can serve as powerful evidence when it's appropriate to the subject, to your purpose, and to the audience. If it's your only evidence, however, personal experience usually won't suffice to carry the argument. Your experiences may be regarded as merely "anecdotal," which is to say possibly exceptional, unrepresentative, or even unreliable. Nevertheless, personal experience can be effective for drawing in listeners or readers, as James Parker does in the following example. His full article goes on to argue that—in spite of his personal experience with it—the "Twee revolution" has some good things going for it, including an "actual moral application":

> Eight years ago or so, the alternative paper I was working for sent me out to review a couple of folk-noise-psych-indie-beardie-weirdie bands. I had a dreadful night. The bands were bad enough—"fumbling," I scratched in my notebook, "infantile"—but what really did me in was the audience. Instead of baying for the blood of these lightweights...the gathered young people—behatted, bebearded, besmiling—obliged them with patters of validating applause. I had seen it before, this fond curiosity, this acclamation of the undercooked, but never so much of it in one place: the whole event seemed to exult in its own half-bakedness. *Be as crap as you like* was the message to the performers. *The crapper, the better. We're here for you.* I tottered home, wrote a homicidally nasty nervous breakdown of a review, and decided I should take myself out of circulation for a while. No more live reviews until I calmed down. A wave of Twee—as I now realize—had just broken over my head.
>
> —James Parker, *Atlantic,* July/August 2014, p. 36

Indian Paintbrush/Kobal/REX/Shutterstock.com

FIGURE 20.4 *Moonrise Kingdom, directed by* Wes Anderson, film's primary advocate of Twee

RESPOND

1. The following general topic ideas once appeared on Yahoo! Groups's "Issues and Causes" page. Narrow one or two of the items down to a more specific subject by using research tools in the library or online such as scholarly books, journal articles, encyclopedias, magazine pieces, and/or informational Web sites. Be prepared to explain how the particular research resources influenced your choice of a more specific subject within the general subject area. Also consider what you might have to do to turn your specific subject into a full-blown topic proposal for a research paper assignment.

   Abortion debate
   Affirmative action
   Civil rights
   Community service and volunteerism
   Confederate flag debate
   Current events
   Drunk driving
   Environment
   Food safety
   Gender wars
   Housing
   Human rights
   Immigration reform
   Media ethics and accountability
   Multiculturalism
   Overpopulation
   Peace and nonviolence
   Poverty
   Race relations
   Ranting
   Road rage
   Voluntary simplicity

2. Go to your school or local library's online catalog page and locate its list of research databases. You may find them presented in various ways: by subject, by field, by academic major, by type—even alphabetically. Try to identify three or four databases that might be helpful to you either generally in college or when working on a specific project, perhaps one you identified in the previous exercise. Then explore the library catalog to see how much you can learn about each of these resources: What fields do they report on? What kinds of data do they offer (newspaper articles, journal articles, historical records)? How do they present the content of their materials (by abstract, by full text)? What years do they cover? What search strategies do they support (keyword, advanced search)? To find such information, you might look for a help menu or an "About" link on the catalog or database homepages. Write a one-paragraph description of each database you explore and, if possible, share your findings via a class discussion board or wiki.

3. What counts as evidence depends in large part on the rhetorical situation. One audience might find personal testimony compelling in a given case, whereas another might require data that only experimental studies can provide. Imagine that you want to argue that advertisements should not include demeaning representations of chimpanzees and that the use of primates in advertising should be banned. You're encouraged to find out that a number of companies such as Honda and Puma have already agreed to such a ban, so you decide to present your argument to other companies' CEOs and advertising officials. What kind of evidence would be most compelling to this group? How would you rethink your use of evidence if you were writing for the campus newspaper, for middle-schoolers, or for animal-rights group members? What can you learn about what sort of evidence each of these groups might value—and why?

4. Finding evidence for an argument is often a discovery process. Sometimes you're concerned not only with digging up support for an already established claim but also with creating and revising tentative claims. Surveys and interviews can help you figure out what to argue, as well as provide evidence for a claim.

   Interview a classmate with the goal of writing a brief proposal argument about the career that he/she should pursue. The claim should be something like *My classmate should be doing X five years from now.* Limit yourself to ten questions. Write them ahead of time, and don't deviate from them. Record the results of the interview (written notes are fine; you don't need to tape the interview). Then interview another classmate with the same goal in mind. Ask the same first question, but this time let the answer dictate the next nine questions. You still get only ten questions.

   Which interview gave you more information? Which one helped you learn more about your classmate's goals? Which one better helped you develop claims about his/her future?

CHAPTER 21

Evaluating Sources

Googleft

GOOGLE'S BIAS

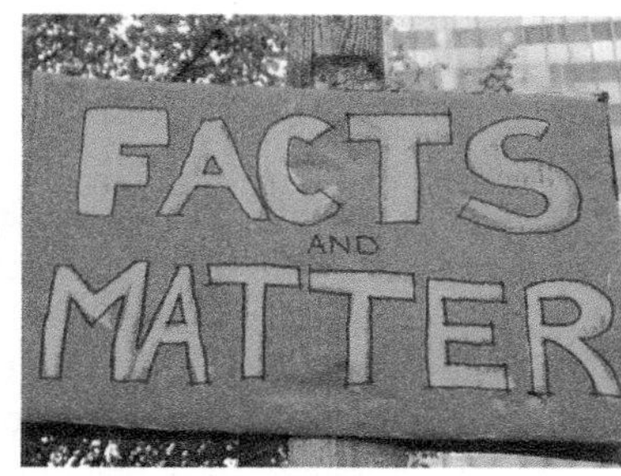

Left to right: Bartomeu Amengual/AGE Fotostock; Michael P. Ramirez/Creators Syndicate, Inc.; J. Bicking/Shutterstock.com

All the attention paid to "fake news" in our current political culture only underscores the point of this chapter: the effectiveness of an argument often depends on the quality of the sources that support or prove it. It goes without saying then, that you'll need to carefully evaluate and assess all the sources you use in your academic or professional work, including those that you gather in libraries, from other print sources, in online searches, or in your own field research.

Remember that different sources can contribute in different ways to your work. In most cases, you'll be looking for reliable sources that provide accurate information or that clearly and persuasively express opinions that might serve as evidence for a case you're making. At other times, you may be seeking material that expresses ideas or attitudes—how people are thinking and feeling at a given time. You might need to use a graphic image, a sample of avant-garde music, or a controversial YouTube clip that doesn't fit neatly into categories such as "reliable" or "accurate" yet is central to your argument. With any and all such sources and evidence, your goals are to be as knowledgeable about them and as responsible in their use as you can be and to share honestly what you learn about them with readers.

Jeff Stahler/Andrews McMeel Syndication

No writer wants to be naïve in the use of source material, especially since most of the evidence that is used in arguments on public issues—even material from influential and well-known sources—comes with considerable baggage. Scientists and humanists alike have axes to grind, corporations have products to sell, politicians have issues to promote, journalists have reputations to make, publishers and media companies have readers, listeners, viewers, and advertisers to attract and to avoid offending. All of these groups produce and use information to their own benefit, and it's not (usually) a bad thing that they do so. You just have to be aware that when you take information from a given source, it will almost inevitably carry with it at least some of the preferences, assumptions, and biases—conscious or not—of the people who produce and disseminate it. Teachers and librarians are not exempted from this caution: even when we make every effort to be clear and comprehensive in reporting information, we cannot possibly see that information from every angle. So even the most honest and open observer can deliver only a partial account of an event.

It's worth noting, however, that some sources—especially those you might encounter on social media—have no other motive but to deceive readers or to garner clicks that generate revenue. Material this deliberately deceptive has no place in academic work, unless you are looking for examples of manipulation, deception, or exploitation. If you cite such materials, even unwittingly, your research will be undermined and may be discredited. (See the section on "crap detection" later in this chapter.)

To correct for biases, draw on as many reliable sources as you can handle when you're preparing to write. Don't assume that all arguments are equally good or that all the sides in a controversy can be supported by the same weight of evidence and good reasons. But you want to avoid choosing sources so selectively that you miss essential issues and perspectives. That's easy to do when you read only sources that agree with you or when the sources that you read all seem to carry the same message. In addition, make sure that you read each source thoroughly enough that you understand its overall points: national research conducted for the Citation Project indicates that student writers often draw from the first paragraph or page of a source and then simply drop it, without seeing what the rest of the source has to say about the topic at hand. Doing so could leave you with an incomplete or inaccurate sense of what the source is saying.

John Cole/Cagle Cartoons, Inc.

FIGURE 21.1 Consider that sources may sometimes have motives for slanting or selecting the news.

Assessing Print Sources

Since you want information to be reliable and persuasive, it pays to evaluate each potential source thoroughly. The following principles can help you evaluate print materials:

- **Relevance.** Begin by asking what a particular source will add to your argument and how closely the source is related to your argumentative claim. For a book, the table of contents and the index may help you decide. For an article, look for an abstract that summarizes its content. If you can't identify what the source will add to your research, set it aside. You can almost certainly find something better.

- **Credentials of the author.** Sometimes the author's credentials are set forth in an article, in a book, or on a Web site, so be sure to look for them. Is the author an expert on the topic? To find out, you can gather information about the person on the Web easily enough—although you should check and cross-check what you discover. Another way to learn about the credibility of an author is to search Google Groups for postings that mention the author or to check a Citation Index to find out how other writers refer to this author. (If necessary, ask a librarian for assistance.) If you see your source mentioned by other sources you're using, look at how they cite it and what they say about it, which could provide clues to the author's credibility.
- **Stance of the author.** What's the author's position on the issue(s) involved, and how does this stance influence the information in the source? Does the author's stance support or challenge your own views?
- **Credentials of the publisher or sponsor.** If your source is from a newspaper, is it a major one (such as the *Wall Street Journal* or the *Washington Post*) that has historical credentials in reporting, or is it a tabloid? Is it a popular magazine like *O: The Oprah Magazine* or a journal sponsored by a professional group, such as the *Journal of the American Medical Association*? If your source is a book, is the publisher one you recognize or that has its own Web site? When you don't know the reputation of a source, ask several people with more expertise: a librarian, an instructor, or a professional in the field.
- **Stance of the publisher or sponsor.** Sometimes this stance will be obvious: a magazine called *Save the Planet!* will take a pro-environmental position, whereas one called *America First!* will probably take a populist stance. But other times, you need to read carefully between the lines to identify particular positions and see how the stance affects the message the source presents. Start by asking what the source's goals are: what does the publisher or sponsoring group want to make happen?
- **Currency.** Check the date of publication of every book and article. Recent sources are often more useful than older ones, particularly in the sciences. However, in some fields (such as history and literature), the most authoritative works may well be the older ones.
- **Accuracy.** Check to see whether the author cites any sources for the information or opinions in the article and, if so, how credible and current they are.
- **Level of specialization.** General sources can be helpful as you begin your research, but later in the project you may need the authority or currency of more focused sources. Keep in mind that highly specialized works on your topic may be difficult for your audience to understand.

- **Documentation.** Purely academic sources, such as scholarly journal articles, will contain thorough citations, but you should also check that more popular sources you use routinely identify their sources or provide verifiable evidence for claims they make. In many Web sources, documentation takes the form of links to the evidence cited.
- **Audience.** Was the source written for a general readership? For specialists? For advocates or opponents?
- **Length.** Is the source long enough to provide adequate details in support of your claim?
- **Availability.** Do you have access to the source? If it isn't readily accessible, your time might be better spent looking elsewhere.
- **Omissions.** What's missing or omitted from the source? Might such exclusions affect whether or how you can use the source as evidence?

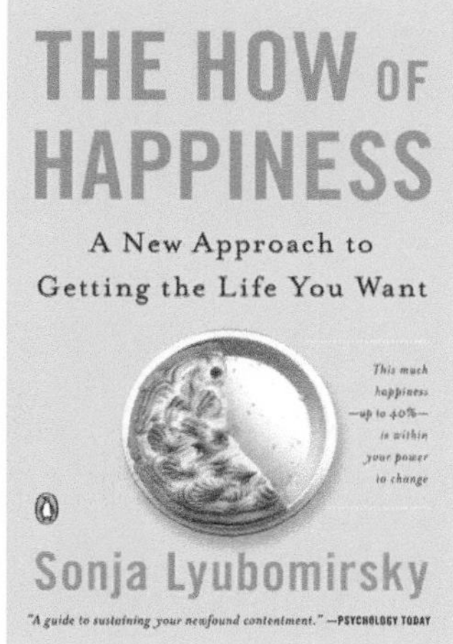

FIGURE 21.2 Note the differences between the covers of the *Journal of Abnormal Psychology*, an academic journal, and *The How of Happiness*, a book about psychology.

Assessing Electronic Sources

You'll probably find working with digital sources both exciting and frustrating, for even though these tools (the Web, social networks, Twitter, and so on) are enormously useful, they offer information of widely varying quality—and mountains and mountains of it. Yet there is no question that, for example, Twitter feeds from our era will be the subject of future scholarly analysis. Because Web sources are mostly open and unregulated, careful researchers look for corroboration before accepting factual claims they find online, especially if it comes from a site whose sponsor's identity is unclear.

© John Atkinson/Wrong Hands

Practicing Crap Detection

In online environments, you must be the judge of the accuracy and trustworthiness of the electronic sources you encounter. This is a problem all researchers face, and one that led media critic Howard Rheingold to develop a system for detecting "crap," that is, "information tainted by ignorance, inept communication, or deliberate deception." To avoid such "crap," Rheingold recommends a method of triangulation, which means finding three separate credible online sources that corroborate the point you want to make. But how do you ensure that these sources are credible? One tip Rheingold gives is to use sites like FactCheck.org to verify information, or to use the search term "whois" to find out about the author or sponsor of a site.

Alfred Eisenstadt/The Life Picture Collection/Getty Images

FIGURE 21.3 *Every man [and woman] should have a built-in automatic crap detector operating inside him.* —Ernest Hemingway, during a 1954 interview with Robert Manning

In making judgments about online sources, then, you need to be especially mindful and to rely on the same criteria and careful thinking that you use to assess print sources. You may find the following additional questions helpful in evaluating online sources:

- Who has posted the document or message or created the site/medium? An individual? An interest group? A company? A government agency? For Web sites, does the URL offer any clues? Note especially the final suffix in a domain name—*.com* (commercial), *.org* (nonprofit organization), *.edu* (educational institution), *.gov* (government agency), *.mil* (military), or *.net* (network). Also note the geographical domains that indicate country of origin—as in *.ca* (Canada), *.ar* (Argentina), or *.ru* (Russia). Click on some links of a Web site to see if they lead to legitimate and helpful sources or organizations.
- What can you determine about the credibility of the author or sponsor? Can the information in the document or site be verified in other sources? How accurate and complete is it? On a blog, for example, look for a link that identifies the creator of the site (some blogs are managed by multiple authors).
- Who is accountable for the information in the document or site? How thoroughly does it credit its sources? On a wiki, for example, check its editorial policies: who can add to or edit its materials?

- How current is the document or site? Be especially cautious of undated materials. Most reliable sites are refreshed or edited regularly and should list the date.
- What perspectives are represented? If only one perspective is represented, how can you balance or expand this point of view? Is it a straightforward presentation, or could it be a parody or satire?

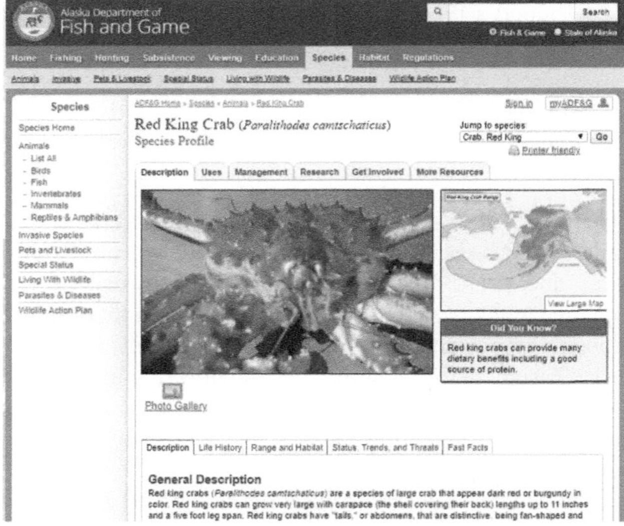

FIGURE 21.4 What are the kinds and levels of information available on these Web sites—a commercial site about the TV show *The Deadliest Catch* (top) and an Alaska Department of Fish and Game site on king crab (bottom)?

Assessing Field Research

If you've conducted experiments, surveys, interviews, observations, or any other field research in developing and supporting an argument, make sure to review your results with a critical eye. The following questions can help you evaluate your own field research:

- Have you rechecked all data and all conclusions to make sure they're accurate and warranted?
- Have you identified the exact time, place, and participants in all your field research?
- Have you made clear what part you played in the research and how, if at all, your role could have influenced the results or findings?
- If your research involved other people, have you gotten their permission to use their words or other materials in your argument? Have you asked whether you can use their names or whether the names should be kept confidential?
- If your research involved interviews, have you thanked the person or persons you interviewed and asked them to verify the words you have attributed to them?

RESPOND

1. The chapter claims that "most of the evidence that is used in arguments on public issues...comes with considerable baggage" (**p. 444**). Find an article in a journal, newspaper, or magazine that uses evidence to support a claim of some public interest. It might be a piece about new treatments for malaria, Internet privacy, dietary recommendations for schoolchildren, proposals for air-quality regulation, the rise in numbers of campus sexual assaults, and so on. Identify several specific pieces of evidence, information, or data presented in the article and then evaluate the degree to which you would accept, trust, or believe those statements. Be prepared to explain specifically why you would be inclined to trust or mistrust any claims based on the data.
2. Check out Goodreads (you can set up an account for free) and see what people there are recommending—or search for "common reading programs" or "common reading lists." Then choose one of the recommended books, preferably a work of nonfiction, and analyze it by using as many of the principles of evaluation for printed books listed in this chapter as you can without actually reading the book: Who is the author, and what are his/her credentials? Who is the publisher, and what is its reputation? What can you find out about the book's relevance and popularity: Why might the book be on the list? Who is the primary audience for the book? How lengthy is it? How difficult? Finally, consider how likely it is that the book you have selected would be used in an academic paper. If you do choose a work of fiction, might the work be studied in a literature course?
3. Choose a news or information Web site that you visit routinely. Then, using the guidelines discussed in this chapter, spend some time evaluating its credibility. You might begin by comparing it with Google News or Arts & Letters Daily, two sites that have a reputation for being reliable—though not necessarily unbiased.
4. On Web sites or social media, find several items that purport to offer information or news, but lead readers into a tangle of ads, photos, commentary, and other clickbait. You've seen the teases: Most Unfriendly Cities in the US! The video Hillary Clinton doesn't want you to watch! Is this the smartest kitten ever? Analyze the strategies items like these use to attract readers and the quality of information they offer. Are such items merely irksome or do they seriously diminish online communication and social media?

CHAPTER 22

Using Sources

Left to right: pixal/imageBROKER/AGE Fotostock; kstudija/Shutterstock; Paul Faith/PA Wire URN:9724483 (Press Association via AP Images)

You may gather an impressive amount of evidence on your topic—from firsthand interviews, from careful observations, and from intensive library and online research. But until that evidence is thoroughly understood and then woven into the fabric of your own argument, it's just a stack of details. You still have to turn that data into credible information that will be persuasive to your intended audiences.

Practicing Infotention

Today it's a truism to say that we are all drowning in information, that it is dousing us like water from a fire hose. Such a situation has advantages: it's never been easier to locate information on any imaginable topic. But it also has distinct disadvantages: how do you identify useful and credible sources among the millions available to you, and how do you use them well once you've found them? We addressed the first of these questions in **Chapter 20**, "Finding Evidence." But finding trustworthy sources is only the first step. Experts on technology and information like professors Richard Lanham and Howard Rheingold point to the next challenge: managing *attention*. Lanham points out that our age of information calls on us to resist the allure of every single thing vying for our attention and to discriminate among what deserves notice and what doesn't. Building on this insight, Rheingold has coined the term "**infotention**," which he says "is a word I came up with to describe a mind-machine combination of brain-powered attention skills and computer-powered information filters" (Howard Rheingold, "Infotention," http://www.rheingold.com).

Practicing infotention calls for synthesizing and thinking critically about the enormous amount of information available to us from the "collective intelligence" of the Web. And while some of us can learn to be mindful while multitasking (a fighter pilot is an example Rheingold gives of those who must learn to do so), most of us are not good at it and need to train ourselves, literally, to pay attention to attention (and intention as well), to be aware of what we are doing and thinking, to take a deep breath and notice where we are directing our focus. In short, writers today need to learn to focus their attention, especially online, and learn to avoid distractions. So just how do you put all these skills together to practice infotention?

Building a Critical Mass

Throughout the chapters in Part 5, "Tools of Argument," we've stressed the need to discover as much evidence as possible in support of your claim and to read and understand it as thoroughly as you can. If you can find only one or two pieces of evidence—only one or two reasons or illustrations to back up your thesis—then you may be on unsteady ground. Although there's no definite way of saying just how much evidence is enough, you should build toward a critical mass by having several pieces of evidence all pulling in the direction of your claim. Begin by putting Rheingold's triangulation into practice: find at least three credible sources that support your point.

And remember that **circumstantial evidence** (that is, indirect evidence that *suggests* that something occurred but doesn't prove it directly) may not be enough if it is the only evidence that you have. In the infamous case of Jack the Ripper, the murderer who plagued London's East End in 1888, nothing but circumstantial evidence ever surfaced and hence no one was charged with or convicted of the crimes. In 2007, however, amateur detective Russell Edwards bought a shawl at auction—a shawl found at one of the murder sites. After consulting with a number of scientific experts and using DNA evidence, Edwards identified Jack the Ripper as Aaron Kosminski, who eventually died in an asylum.

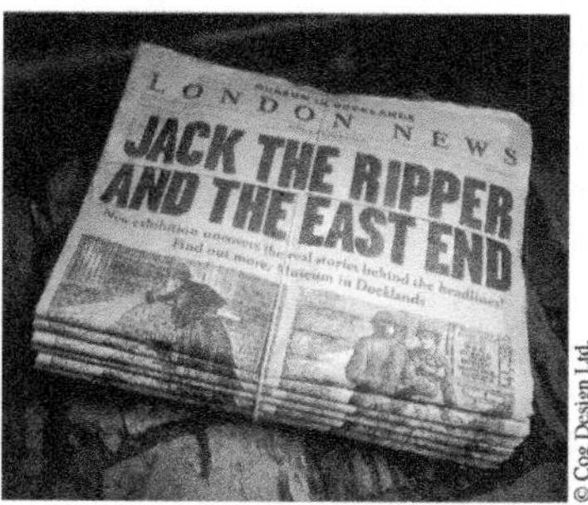

© Cog Design Ltd.

If your support for a claim relies solely on circumstantial evidence, on personal experience, or on one major example, you should extend your search for additional sources and good reasons to back up your claim—or modify the argument. Your initial position may simply have been wrong.

Synthesizing Information

As you gather information, you must find a way to make all the facts, ideas, points of view, and quotations you have encountered work with and for you. The process involves not only reading information and recording data carefully (paying "info-tention"), but also pondering and synthesizing it—that is, figuring out how the sources you've examined come together to support your specific claims. **Synthesis**, a form of critical thinking highly valued by academia, business, industry, and other institutions—especially those that reward innovation and creative thinking—is hard work. It almost always involves immersing yourself in your information or data until it feels familiar and natural to you.

At that point, you can begin to look for patterns, themes, and commonalities or striking differences among your sources. Many students use highlighters to help with this process: mark in blue all the parts of sources that mention point A; mark in green those that have to do with issue B; and so on. You are looking for connections among your sources, bringing together what they have to say about your topic in ways you can organize to help support the claim you are making.

You typically begin this process by paraphrasing or summarizing sources so that you understand exactly what they offer and which ideas are essential to your project. You also decide which, if any, sources offer materials you want to quote directly or reproduce (such as an important graph or table). Then you work to introduce such borrowed materials so that readers grasp their significance, and organize them to highlight important relationships. Throughout this review process, use "infotention" strategies by asking questions such as the following:

- Which sources help to set the context for your argument? In particular, which items present new information or give audiences an incentive for reading your work?
- Which items provide background information that is essential for anyone trying to understand your argument?
- Which items help to define, clarify, or explain key concepts of your case? How can these sources be presented or sequenced so that readers appreciate your claims as valid or, at a minimum, reasonable?
- Which of your sources might be used to illustrate technical or difficult aspects of your subject? Would it be best to summarize such technical information to make it more accessible, or would direct quotations be more authoritative and convincing?
- Which sources (or passages within sources) furnish the best support or evidence for each claim or sub-claim within your argument? Now is the time to group these together so you can decide how to arrange them most effectively.
- Which materials do the best job outlining conflicts or offering counterarguments to claims within a project? Which sources might help you address any important objections or rebuttals?

Remember that *yours* should be the dominant and controlling voice in an argument. You are like the conductor of an orchestra, calling upon separate instruments to work together to create a rich and coherent sound. The least effective academic papers are those that mechanically walk through a string of sources—often just one item per paragraph—without ever getting all these authorities to talk to each other or with the author. Such papers go through the motions but don't get anywhere. You can do better.

Paraphrasing Sources You Will Use Extensively

In a **paraphrase**, you put an author's ideas—including major and minor points—into your own words and sentence structures, following the order the author has given them in the original piece. You usually paraphrase sources that you expect to use heavily in a project. But if you compose your notes well, you may be able to use much of the paraphrased material directly in your paper (with proper citation) because all of the language is your own. A competent paraphrase proves you have read material or data carefully: you demonstrate not only that you know what a source contains but also that you appreciate what it means. There's an important difference.

"Who is the fairest one of all, and state your sources!"

Ed Fisher/The New Yorker Collection/The Cartoon Bank

FIGURE 22.1 Backing up your claims with well-chosen sources makes almost any argument more credible.

Here are guidelines to help you paraphrase accurately and effectively in an academic argument:

- Identify the source of the paraphrase, and comment on its significance or the authority of its author.
- Respect your sources. When paraphrasing an entire work or any lengthy section of it, cover all its main points and any essential details, following the same order the author uses. If you distort the shape of the material, your notes will be less valuable, especially if you return to them later, and you may end up misconstruing what the source is saying.
- If you're paraphrasing material that extends over more than one page in the original source, note the placement of page breaks since it is highly likely that you will use only part of the paraphrase in your argument. For a print source, you will need the page number to cite the specific page of material you want to use.
- Make sure that the paraphrase is in your own words and sentence structures. If you want to include especially memorable or powerful language from the original source, enclose it in quotation marks. (See "Using Quotations Selectively and Strategically" on p. 460.)

- Keep your own comments, elaborations, or reactions separate from the paraphrase itself. Your report on the source should be clear, objective, and free of connotative language.
- Collect all the information necessary to create an in-text citation as well as an item in your works cited list or references list. For online materials, be sure to record the URL so you know how to recover the source later.
- Label the paraphrase with a note suggesting where and how you intend to use it in your argument.
- Recheck to make sure that the words and sentence structures are your own and that they express the author's meaning accurately.

Here is a passage from linguist David Crystal's book *Language Play*, followed by a student's paraphrase of the passage.

> Language play, the arguments suggest, will help the development of pronunciation ability through its focus on the properties of sounds and sound contrasts, such as rhyming. Playing with word endings and decoding the syntax of riddles will help the acquisition of grammar. Readiness to play with words and names, to exchange puns and to engage in nonsense talk, promotes links with semantic development. The kinds of dialogue interaction illustrated above are likely to have consequences for the development of conversational skills. And language play, by its nature, also contributes greatly to what in recent years has been called metalinguistic awareness, which is turning out to be of critical importance to the development of language skills in general and literacy skills in particular (180).

Paraphrase of the Passage from Crystal's Book

> In *Language Play*, David Crystal argues that playing with language—creating rhymes, figuring out riddles, making puns, playing with names, using inverted words, and so on—helps children figure out a great deal, from the basics of pronunciation and grammar to how to carry on a conversation. This kind of play allows children to understand the overall concept of how language works, a concept that is key to learning to use—and read—language effectively (180).

Note how the student clearly identifies the title and author of the source in the opening line of her paraphrase, and how she restates the passage's main ideas without copying the exact words or phrasing of the original passage.

Summarizing Sources

Unlike a paraphrase, a **summary** records just the gist of a source or a key idea—that is, only enough information to identify a point you want to emphasize. Once again, this much-shortened version of a source puts any borrowed ideas into your own words. At the research stage, summaries help you identify key points you want to make or key points your sources are making that you want to refute and, just as important, provide a record of what you have read. In a project itself, a summary helps readers understand the sources you are using.

Here are some guidelines to help you prepare accurate and helpful summaries:

- Identify the thesis or main point in a source and make it the heart of your summary. In a few detailed phrases or sentences, explain to yourself (and readers) what the source accomplishes.
- When using a summary in an argument, identify the source, state its point, and add your own comments about why the material is significant for the argument that you're making.
- Include just enough information to recount the main points you want to cite. A summary is usually much shorter than the original. When you need more information or specific details, you can return to the source itself or prepare a paraphrase.
- Use your own words in a summary and keep the language objective and denotative. If you include any language from the original source, enclose it in quotation marks.
- Collect all the information necessary to create an in-text citation as well as an item in your works cited list or references list. For online sources without page numbers, record the paragraph, screen, or section number(s) if available.
- Label the summary with a note that suggests where and how you intend to use it in your argument. If your summary includes a comment on the source (as it might in the summaries used for annotated bibliographies), be sure that you won't later confuse your comments with what the source itself asserts.
- Recheck the summary to make sure that you've captured the author's meaning accurately and that the wording is entirely your own.

Following is a summary of the David Crystal passage on page 458:

> In *Language Play*, David Crystal argues that playing with language helps children figure out how language works, a concept that is key to learning to use—and read—language effectively (180).

Notice that the summary is shorter and—relatedly—less detailed than the paraphrase shown on page 458. The paraphrase gives several examples to explain what "language play" is, while the summary sticks to the main point of the passage.

Using Quotations Selectively and Strategically

To support your argumentative claims, you'll want to quote (that is, to reproduce an author's precise words) in at least three kinds of situations:

1. when the wording expresses a point so well that you cannot improve it or shorten it without weakening it,
2. when the author is a respected authority whose opinion supports your own ideas powerfully, and/or
3. when an author or authority challenges or seriously disagrees with others in the field.

Consider, too, that charts, graphs, and images may also function like direct quotations, providing convincing visual evidence for your academic argument.

AFP/Getty Images

FIGURE 22.2 A tragedy, not a sport?

In an argument, quotations from respected authorities will establish your ethos as someone who has sought out experts in the field. Just as important sometimes, direct quotations (such as a memorable phrase in your introduction or a detailed eyewitness account) may capture your readers' attention. Finally, carefully chosen quotations can broaden the appeal of your argument by drawing on emotion as well as logic, appealing to the reader's mind and heart. A student who is writing on the ethical issues of bullfighting, for example, might introduce an argument that bullfighting is not a sport by quoting Ernest Hemingway's comment that "the formal bull-fight is a tragedy, not a sport, and the bull is certain to be killed" and then accompany the quotation with an image such as the one on the previous page.

The following guidelines can help you quote sources accurately and effectively:

- Quote or reproduce materials that readers will find especially convincing, purposeful, and interesting. You should have a specific reason for every quotation.
- Don't forget the double quotation marks [" "] that must surround a direct quotation in American usage. If there's a quote within a quote, it is surrounded by a pair of single quotation marks [' ']. British usage does just the opposite, and foreign languages often handle direct quotations much differently.
- When using a quotation in your argument, introduce its author(s) and follow the quotation with commentary of your own that points out its significance.
- Keep quoted material relatively brief. Quote only as much of a passage as is necessary to make your point while still accurately representing what the source actually said.
- If the quotation extends over more than one page in the original source, note the placement of page breaks in case you decide to use only part of the quotation in your argument.
- In your notes, label a quotation you intend to use with a note that tells you where you think you'll use it.
- Make sure you have all the information necessary to create an in-text citation as well as an item in your works cited list or references list.
- Copy quotations carefully, reproducing the punctuation, capitalization, and spelling exactly as they are in the original. If possible, copy the quotation from a reliable text and paste it directly into your project.
- Make sure that quoted phrases, sentences, or passages fit smoothly into your own language. Consider where to begin the quotation to make it work effectively within its surroundings or modify the words you write to work with the quoted material.
- Use square brackets if you introduce words of your own into the quotation or make changes to it ("And [more] brain research isn't going to define further the matter of 'mind'").
- Use ellipsis marks if you omit material ("And brain research isn't going to define...the matter of 'mind'").

- If you're quoting a short passage (four lines or fewer in MLA style), it should be worked into your text, enclosed by quotation marks. Longer quotations should be set off from the regular text. Begin such a quotation on a new line, indenting every line a half inch or five to seven spaces. Set-off quotations do not need to be enclosed in quotation marks.
- Never distort your sources or present them out of context when you quote from them. Misusing sources is a major offense in academic arguments.

"Some irresponsible gossip mongers around the office have misquoted me as calling you a 'silly goose'."

Cartoon Resource/Shutterstock.com

Framing Materials You Borrow with Signal Words and Introductions

Because source materials are crucial to the success of arguments, you need to introduce borrowed words and ideas carefully to your readers. Doing so usually calls for using a signal phrase of some kind in the sentence to introduce or frame the source. Often, a signal phrase will precede a quotation. But you need such a marker whenever you introduce borrowed material, as in the following examples:

> According to noted primatologist Jane Goodall, the more we learn about the nature of nonhuman animals, the more ethical questions we face about their use in the service of humans.
>
> The more we learn about the nature of nonhuman animals, the more ethical questions we face about their use in the service of humans, according to noted primatologist Jane Goodall.
>
> The more we learn about the nature of nonhuman animals, according to noted primatologist Jane Goodall, the more ethical questions we face about their use in the service of humans.

In each of these sentences, the signal phrase tells readers that you're drawing on the work of a person named Jane Goodall and that this person is a "noted primatologist."

Now look at an example that uses a quotation from a source in more than one sentence:

> In *Job Shift*, consultant William Bridges worries about "dejobbing and about what a future shaped by it is going to be like." Even more worrisome, Bridges argues, is the possibility that "the sense of craft and of professional vocation...will break down under the need to earn a fee" (228).

The signal verbs *worries* and *argues* add a sense of urgency to the message Bridges offers. They also suggest that the writer either agrees with—or is neutral about—Bridges's points. Other signal verbs can have a more negative slant, indicating that the point being introduced by the quotation is open to debate and that others (including the writer) might disagree with it. If the writer of the passage above had said, for instance, that Bridges *unreasonably contends* or that he *fantasizes,* these signal verbs would carry quite different connotations from those associated with *argues*.

In some cases, a signal verb may require more complex phrasing to get the writer's full meaning across:

> Bridges recognizes the dangers of changes in work yet refuses to be overcome by them: "The real issue is not how to stop the change but how to provide the necessary knowledge and skills to equip people to operate successfully in this New World" (229).

As these examples illustrate, the signal verb is important because it allows you to characterize the author's or source's viewpoint as well as your own—so choose these verbs with care.

Some Frequently Used Signal Verbs

acknowledges	claims	emphasizes	remarks
admits	concludes	expresses	replies
advises	concurs	hypothesizes	reports
agrees	confirms	interprets	responds
allows	criticizes	lists	reveals
argues	declares	objects	states
asserts	disagrees	observes	suggests
believes	discusses	offers	thinks
charges	disputes	opposes	writes

Using Sources to Clarify and Support Your Own Argument

The best academic arguments often have the flavor of a hearty but focused intellectual conversation. Scholars and scientists create this impression by handling research materials strategically and selectively. Here's how some college writers use sources to achieve their own specific goals within an academic argument.

Establish context. Michael Hiltzik, whose article "Don't Believe Facebook: The Demise of the Written Word Is Very Far Off" appears in **Chapter 15**, sets the context for his argument when, at the end of his first paragraph, he paraphrases the claim of Facebook executive Nicola Mendelsohn: "In five years, she told a Fortune conference in London, her platform will probably be 'all video,' and the written word will be essentially dead." Then he uses a second paragraph to go into greater detail because Mendelsohn's view represents precisely the notion he intends to contest:

> "I just think if we look already, we're seeing a year-on-year decline on text," she said. "If I was having a bet, I would say: video, video, video." That's because "the best way to tell stories in this world, where so much information is coming at us, actually is video. It conveys so much more information in a much quicker period. So actually the trend helps us to digest much more information."

Only then does Hiltzik present his thesis—and it is short and sweet: "This is, of course, exactly wrong." As they say, *game on*. Readers clearly know what's at stake in the article and perhaps what evidence to expect from the paragraphs to follow (see **pp. 335–337**).

FIGURE 22.3 When using Web sources such as blogs, take special care to check authors' backgrounds and credentials.

Review the literature on a subject. You will often need to tell readers what authorities have already written about your topic, thus connecting them to your own argument. So, in a paper on the effectiveness of peer editing, Susan Wilcox does a very brief "review of the literature" on her subject, pointing to three authorities who support using the method in writing courses. She quotes from the authors and also puts some of their ideas in her own words:

> Bostock cites one advantage of peer review as "giving a sense of ownership of the assessment process" (1). Topping expands this view, stating that "peer assessment also involves increased time on task: thinking, comparing, contrasting, and communicating" (254). The extra time spent thinking over the assignment, especially in terms of helping someone else, can draw in the reviewer and lend greater importance to taking the process seriously, especially since the reviewer knows that the classmate is relying on his advice. This also adds an extra layer of accountability for the student; his hard work—or lack thereof—will be seen by peers, not just the instructor. Cassidy notes, "[S]tudents work harder with the knowledge that they will be assessed by their peers" (509): perhaps the knowledge that peer review is coming leads to a better-quality draft to begin with.

The paragraph is straightforward and useful, giving readers an efficient overview of the subject. If they want more information, they can find it by consulting Wilcox's works cited page.

Introduce a term or define a concept. Quite often in an academic argument, you may need to define a term or explain a concept. Relying on a source may make your job easier *and* enhance your credibility. That is what Laura Pena achieves in the following paragraph, drawing upon two authorities to explain what teachers mean by a "rubric" when it comes to grading student work:

> To understand the controversy surrounding rubrics, it is best to know what a rubric is. According to Heidi Andrade, a professor at SUNY-Albany, a rubric can be defined as "a document that lists criteria and describes varying levels of quality, from excellent to poor, for a specific assignment" ("Self-Assessment" 61). Traditionally, rubrics have been used primarily as grading and evaluation tools (Kohn 12), meaning that a rubric was not used until after students handed their papers in to their teacher. The teacher would then use a rubric to evaluate the students' papers according to the criteria listed on the rubric.

Note that the first source provides the core definition while information from the second offers a detail important to understanding when and how rubrics are used—a major issue in Pena's paper. Her selection of sources here serves her thesis while also providing readers with necessary information.

Present technical material. Sources can be especially helpful, too, when material becomes technical or difficult to understand. Writing on your own, you might lack the confidence to handle the complexities of some subjects. While you should challenge yourself to learn a subject well enough to explain it in your own words, there will be times when a quotation from an expert serves both you and your readers. Here is Natalie San Luis dealing with some of the technical differences between mainstream and Black English:

> The grammatical rules of mainstream English are more concrete than those of Black English; high school students can't check out an MLA handbook on Ebonics from their school library. As with all dialects, though, there are certain characteristics of the language that most Black English scholars agree upon. According to Samy Alim, author of *Roc the Mic Right,* these characteristics are the "[h]abitual *be* [which] indicates actions that are continuing or ongoing.... Copula absence.... Stressed *been*.... *Gon* [indicating] the future tense.... *They* for possessive.... Postvocalic *r*.... [and] *Ank* and *ang* for 'ink' and 'ing'" (115). Other scholars have identified "[a] bsence of third-person singular present-tense *s*.... Absence of possessive *'s*," repetition of pronouns, and double negatives (Rickford 111-24).

Note that using ellipses enables San Luis to cover a great deal of ground. Readers not familiar with linguistic terms may have trouble following the quotation, but remember that academic arguments often address audiences comfortable with some degree of complexity.

Develop or support a claim. Even academic audiences expect to be convinced, and one of the most important strategies for a writer is to use sources to amplify or support a claim.

Here is Manasi Deshpande in a student essay making a specific claim about disability accommodations on her campus: "Although the University has made a concerted and continuing effort to improve access, students and faculty with physical disabilities still suffer from discriminatory hardship, unequal opportunity to succeed, and lack of independence." Now watch how she weaves sources together in the following paragraph to help support that claim:

> The current state of campus accessibility leaves substantial room for improvement. There are approximately 150 academic and administrative buildings on campus (Grant). Eduardo Gardea, intern architect at the Physical Plant, estimates that only about nineteen buildings comply fully with the Americans with Disabilities Act (ADA). According to Penny Seay, PhD, director of the Center for Disability Studies at UT Austin, the ADA in theory "requires every building on campus to be accessible."

Highlight differences or counterarguments. The sources you encounter in developing a project won't always agree with each other or you. In academic arguments, you don't want to hide such differences, but instead point them out honestly and let readers make judgments based upon actual claims. Here is a paragraph in which Laura Pena again presents two views on the use of rubrics as grading tools:

> Some naysayers, such as Alfie Kohn, assert that "any form of assessment that encourages students to keep asking, 'How am I doing?' is likely to change how they look at themselves and what they're learning, usually for the worse." Kohn cites a study that found that students who pay too much attention to the quality of their performance are more likely to chalk up the outcome of an assignment to factors beyond their control, such as innate ability, and are also more likely to give up quickly in the face of a difficult task (14). However, Ross and Rolheiser have found that when students are taught how to properly implement self-assessment tools in the writing process, they are more likely to put more effort and persistence into completing a difficult assignment and may develop higher self-confidence in their writing ability (sec. 2). Building self-confidence in elementary-age writers can be extremely helpful when they tackle more complicated writing endeavors in the future.

In describing Kohn as a "naysayer," Pena may tip her hand and lose some degree of objectivity. But her thesis has already signaled her support for rubrics as a grading tool, so academic readers will probably not find the connotations of the term inappropriate.

These examples suggest only a few of the ways that sources, either summarized or quoted directly, can be incorporated into an academic argument to support or enhance a writer's goals. Like these writers, you should think of sources as your partners in developing and expressing ideas. But you are still in charge.

Avoiding "Patchwriting"

When using sources in an argument, writers—and especially those new to research-based writing—may be tempted to do what Professor Rebecca Moore Howard terms "**patchwriting**": stitching together material from Web or other sources without properly paraphrasing or summarizing and with little or no documentation. Here, for example, is a patchwork paragraph about the dangers wind turbines pose to wildlife:

> Scientists are discovering that technology with low carbon impact does not mean low environmental or social impacts. That is the case especially with wind turbines, whose long, massive fiberglass blades have been chopping up tens of thousands of birds that fly into them, including golden eagles, red-tailed hawks, burrowing owls, and other raptors in California. Turbines

> are also killing bats in great numbers. The 420 wind turbines now in use across Pennsylvania killed more than 10,000 bats last year—mostly in the late summer months, according to the State Game Commission. That's an average of 25 bats per turbine per year, and the Nature Conservancy predicts as many as 2,900 turbines will be set up across the state by 2030. It's not the spinning blades that kill the bats; instead, their lungs effectively blow up from the rapid pressure drop that occurs as air flows over the turbine blades. But there's hope we may figure out solutions to these problems because, since we haven't had too many wind turbines heretofore in the country, we are learning how to manage this new technology as we go.

The paragraph reads well and is full of details. But it would be considered plagiarized (see **Chapter 23**) because it fails to identify its sources and because most of the material has simply been lifted directly from the Web. How much is actually copied? We've highlighted the borrowed material:

> Scientists are discovering that technology with low carbon impact does not mean low environmental or social impacts. That is the case especially with wind turbines, whose long, massive fiberglass blades have been chopping up tens of thousands of birds that fly into them, including golden eagles, red-tailed hawks, burrowing owls, and other raptors in California. Turbines are also killing bats in great numbers. The 420 wind turbines now in use across Pennsylvania killed more than 10,000 bats last year—mostly in the late summer months, according to the State Game Commission. That's an average of 25 bats per turbine per year, and the Nature Conservancy predicts as many as 2,900 turbines will be set up across the state by 2030. It's not the spinning blades that kill the bats; instead, their lungs effectively blow up from the rapid pressure drop that occurs as air flows over the turbine blades. But there's hope we may figure out solutions to these problems because, since we haven't had too many wind turbines heretofore in the country, we are learning how to manage this new technology as we go.

But here's the point: an academic writer who has gone to the trouble of finding so much information will gain more credit and credibility just by properly identifying, paraphrasing, and quoting the sources used. The resulting paragraph is actually more impressive because it demonstrates how much reading and synthesizing the writer has actually done:

> Scientists like George Ledec of the World Bank are discovering that technology with low carbon impact "does not mean low environmental or social impacts" (Tracy). That is the case especially with wind turbines. Their massive blades spinning to create pollution-free electricity are also killing thousands of valuable birds of prey, including eagles, hawks, and

owls in California (Rittier). Turbines are also killing bats in great numbers (Thibodeaux). The *Pittsburgh Post-Gazette* reports that 10,000 bats a year are killed by the 420 turbines currently in Pennsylvania. According to the state game commissioner, "That's an average of 25 bats per turbine per year, and the Nature Conservancy predicts as many as 2,900 turbines will be set up across the state by 2030" (Schwartzel). It's not the spinning blades that kill the animals; instead, *Discovery News* explains, "the bats' lungs effectively blow up from the rapid pressure drop that occurs as air flows over the turbine blades" (Marshall). But there's hope that scientists can develop turbines less dangerous to animals of all kinds. "We haven't had too many wind turbines heretofore in the country," David Cottingham of the Fish and Wildlife Service points out, "so we are learning about it as we go" (Tracy).

Works Cited

Marshall, Jessica. "Wind Turbines Kill Bats without Impact." *Discovery News,* 25 Aug. 2008, dsc.discovery.com/news/2008/08/25/wind-turbine-bats.html.

Rittier, John. "Wind Turbines Taking Toll on Birds of Prey." *USA Today,* 4 Jan. 2005, usatoday30.usatoday.com/news/nation/2005-01-04-windmills-usat_x.htm.

Schwartzel, Erich. "Pa. Wind Turbines Deadly to Bats, Costly to Farmers." *Pittsburgh Post-Gazette,* 17 July 2011, www.post-gazette.com/business/businessnews/2011/07/17/Pa-wind-turbines-deadly-to-bats-costly-to-farmers/stories/201107170197.

Thibodeaux, Julie. "Collateral Damage: Bats Getting Caught in Texas Wind Turbines." *GreenSourceDFW*, 31 Oct. 2011, www.greensourcedfw.org/articles/collateral-damage-bats-getting-caught-texas-wind-turbines.

Tracy, Ryan. "Wildlife Slows Wind Power." *The Wall Street Journal,* 10 Dec. 2011, www.wsj.com/articles/SB10001424052970203501304577088593307132850.

RESPOND

1. Select one of the essays from **Chapters 15–19**. Following the guidelines in this chapter, write a paraphrase of the essay that you might use subsequently in an academic argument. Be careful to describe the essay accurately and to note on what pages specific ideas or claims are located. The language of the paraphrase should be entirely your own—though you may include direct quotations of phrases, sentences, or longer passages you would likely use in a paper. Be sure these quotations are introduced and cited in your paraphrase: *Hiltzik leaves no doubt that he rejects Mendelsohn's claim: "This is, of course, exactly wrong" (193).* When you are done, trade your paraphrase with a partner to get feedback on its clarity and accuracy.
2. Summarize three readings or fairly lengthy passages from **Parts 3–5** of this book, following the guidelines in this chapter. Open the item with a correct MLA citation for the piece (see **Chapter 24**). Then provide the summary itself. Follow up with a one- or two-sentence evaluation of the work describing its potential value as a source in an academic argument. In effect, you will be preparing three items that might appear in an annotated bibliography. Here's an example:

   Hiltzik, Michael. "Don't Believe Facebook: The Demise of the Written Word Is Very Far Off." *Everything's an Argument*, by Andrea A. Lunsford and John J. Ruszkiewicz, 8th ed., Bedford, 2019, pp. 193–96. Argues that those who believe that video will soon supplant print as the primary vehicle for news are primarily marketers who underestimate the efficiency and precision of print. The journalistic piece cites studies and provides arguments that suggest print is far from dead.

3. Working with a partner, agree upon an essay that you will both read from **Chapters 15–19**, examining it as a potential source for a research argument. As you read it, choose about a half-dozen words, phrases, or short passages that you would likely quote if you used the essay in a paper and attach a frame or signal phrase to each quotation. Then compare the passages you selected to quote with those your partner culled from the same essay. How do your choices of quoted material create an image or ethos for the original author that differs from the one your partner has created? How do the signal phrases shape a reader's sense of the author's position? Which set of quotations best represents the author's argument? Why?
4. Select one of the essays from **Chapters 15–19** to examine the different ways an author uses source materials to support claims. Begin by highlighting the signal phrases you find attached to borrowed ideas or direct quotations. How well do they introduce or frame this material? Then categorize the various ways the author actually uses particular sources. For example, look for sources that provide context for the topic, review the scholarly literature, define key concepts or terms, explain technical details, furnish evidence, or lay out contrary opinions. When you are done, write a paragraph assessing the author's handling of sources in the piece. Are the borrowed materials integrated well with the author's own thoughts? Do the sources represent an effective synthesis of ideas?

CHAPTER

23

Plagiarism and Academic Integrity

Left to right: Inmagineasia/AGE Fotostock; Jutta Kuss/Getty Images; Dimitri Otis/Getty Images

In many ways, "nothing new under the sun" is more than just a cliché. Most of what you think or write is built on what you've previously read or experienced or learned from others. Luckily, you'll seldom be called on to list every influence on your life. But you do have responsibilities in school and professional situations to acknowledge any intellectual property you've made use of when you create arguments of your own. If you don't, you may be accused of **plagiarism**—claiming as your own the words, research, or creative work of others.

What is intellectual property? It's complicated. But, for academic arguments in Western culture, it is the *expression* of ideas you find in works produced by others that you then use to advance and support your own claims. You have to document not only when you use or reproduce someone's exact words, images, music, or other creations (in whole or in part), but also when you borrow the framework others use to put ideas together in original or creative ways. Needless to say, intellectual property rights have always been contentious, but never more so than today, when digital media make it remarkably easy to duplicate and distribute all sorts of materials. Accustomed to uploading and downloading files, cutting and pasting passages, you may be comfortable working with texts day-to-day in ways that are considered inappropriate, or even dishonest, in school. You may, for example, have patched together sources without putting them in your own words or documenting them fully, practices that will often be seen as plagiarism (see p. 467).

"It's not cheating, it's crowdsourcing."

Mark Anderson/Andertoons.com

So it is essential that you read and understand any policies on academic integrity that your school has set down. In particular, pay attention to how those policies define, prosecute, and punish cheating, plagiarism, and collusion. Some institutions recognize a difference between intentional and unintentional plagiarism, but you don't want the honesty of anything you write to be questioned. You need to learn the rules and understand that the penalties for plagiarism are severe not only for students but for professional writers as well.

But don't panic! Many student writers today are so confused or worried about plagiarism that they shy away from using sources—or end up with a citation for almost every sentence in an essay. There's no reason to go to such extremes. As a conscientious researcher and writer, you simply need to give your best effort in letting readers know what sources you have used. Being careful in such matters will have a big payoff: when you give full credit to your sources, you enhance your ethos in academic arguments—which is why "Academic Integrity" appears in this chapter's title. Audiences will applaud you for saying thanks to those who've helped you. Crediting your sources also proves that you have done your homework: you demonstrate that you understand what others have written about the topic and encourage others to join the intellectual conversation. Finally, citing sources reminds you to think critically about how to use the evidence you've collected. Is it timely and reliable? Have you referenced authorities in a biased or overly selective way? Have you double-checked all quotations and paraphrases? Thinking through such questions helps to guarantee the integrity of your academic work.

Giving Credit

The basic principles for documenting materials are relatively simple. Give credit to all source materials you borrow by following these three steps: (1) placing quotation marks around any words you quote directly, (2) citing your sources according to the documentation style you're using, and (3) identifying all the sources you have cited in a list of references or works cited. Materials to be cited in an academic argument include all of the following:

- direct quotations
- facts that are not widely known
- arguable statements
- judgments, opinions, and claims that have been made by others
- images, statistics, charts, tables, graphs, or other illustrations that appear in any source
- collaboration—that is, the help provided by friends, colleagues, instructors, supervisors, or others

However, three important types of evidence or source material do not need to be acknowledged or documented. They are the following:

1. Common knowledge, which is a specific piece of information most readers in your intended audience will know (that Donald Trump won the 2016 presidential election in the Electoral College, for instance).

2. Facts available from a wide variety of sources (that humans walked on the Moon for the first time on July 20, 1969, for example). If, for instance, you search for a piece of information and find the same information on dozens of different reputable Web sites, you can be pretty sure it is common knowledge.

3. Your own findings from field research (observations, interviews, experiments, or surveys you have conducted), which should be clearly presented as your own.

For the actual forms to use when documenting sources, see **Chapter 24**.

Of course, the devil is in the details. For instance, you may be accused of plagiarism in situations like the following:

- if you don't indicate clearly the source of an idea you obviously didn't come up with on your own
- if you use a paraphrase that's too close to the original wording or sentence structure of your source material (*even* if you cite the source)
- if you leave out the parenthetical in-text reference for a quotation (*even* if you include the quotation marks themselves)

And the accusation can be made even if you didn't intend to plagiarize.

But what about all the sampling and mashups you see all the time in popular culture and social media? And don't some artistic and scholarly works come close to being "mashups"? Yes and no. It's certainly fair to say, for example, that Shakespeare's plays "mash up" a lot of material from *Holinshed's Chronicles*, which he used without acknowledgment. But it's also true that Shakespeare's works are "transformative"—that is, they are made new by Shakespeare's art. Current copyright law protects such works that qualify as transformative and exempts them from copyright violations. But the issues swirling around sampling, mashups, and other creative uses of prior materials (print and online) are far from clear, and far from over. Perhaps Jeff Shaw (in a posting that asks, "Is Mashup Music Protected by Fair Use?") sums up the current situation best:

> Lest we forget, the purpose of copyright law is to help content creators and to enhance creative expression. Fair use is an important step toward those ends, and further legislative work could solidify the step forward that fair use represents.
>
> —Jeff Shaw, "Is Mashup Music Protected by Fair Use?"

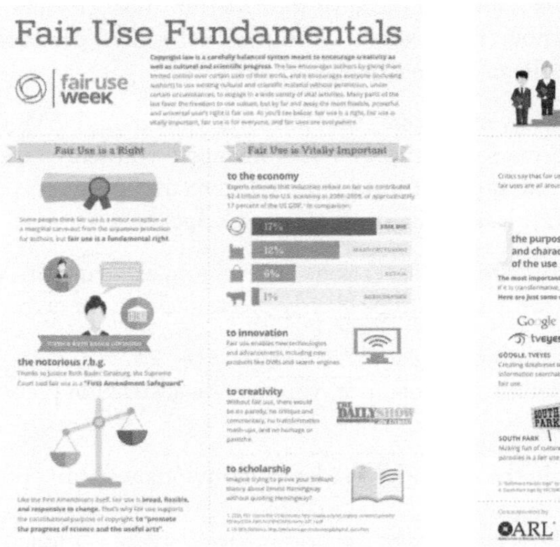

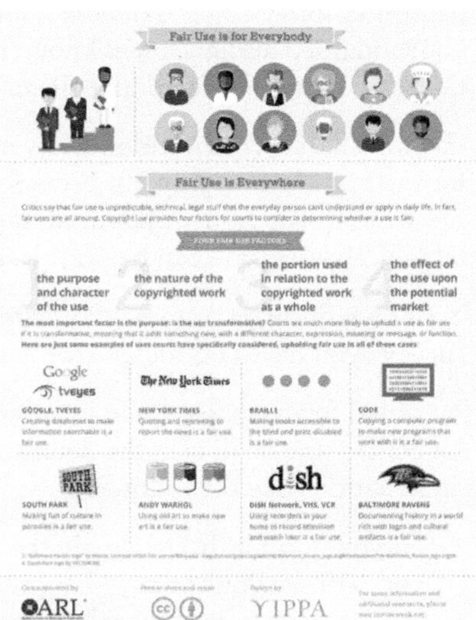

FIGURE 23.1 An infographic from groups supporting "Fair Use Week" defends the importance of the fair use principle.

Getting Permission for and Using Copyrighted Internet Sources

When you gather information from Internet sources and use it in your own work, it's subject to the same rules that govern information gathered from other types of sources.

A growing number of online works, including books, photographs, music, and video, are published under the Creative Commons license, which often eliminates the need to request permission. These works—marked with a Creative Commons license—are made available to the public under this alternative to copyright, which grants permission to reuse or remix work under certain terms if credit is given to the work's creator.

Even if the material does not include a copyright notice or symbol ("© 2019 by Andrea A. Lunsford and John J. Ruszkiewicz," for example), it's likely to be protected by copyright laws, and you may need to request permission to use part or all of it. "Fair use" legal precedents allow writers to quote brief passages from published works without permission from the copyright holder if the use is for educational or personal, noncommercial reasons and if full credit is given to the source. For blog postings or any serious professional uses (especially online), however, you should ask permission of the copyright holder before you include any of his/her ideas, text, or images in your own argument.

If you do need to make a request for permission, here is an example:

From: sanchez.32@stanford.edu
To: litman@mindspring.com
CC: lunsford.2@stanford.edu
Subject: Request for permission

Dear Professor Litman:

I am writing to request permission to quote from your essay "Copyright, Owners' Rights and Users' Privileges on the Internet: Implied Licenses, Caching, Linking, Fair Use, and Sign-on Licenses." I want to quote some of your work as part of an article I am writing for the *Stanford Daily* to explain the complex debates over ownership on the Internet and to argue that students at my school should be participating in these debates. I will give full credit to you and will cite the URL where I first found your work (msen.com/~litman/dayton.htm).

Thank you very much for considering my request.

Raul Sanchez

Acknowledging Your Sources Accurately and Appropriately

While artists, lawyers, and institutions like the film and music industries sort out fair use laws, the bottom line in your academic work is clear: document sources accurately and fully and do not be careless about this very important procedure.

Here, for example, is the first paragraph from a print essay by Russell Platt published in the *Nation*:

> Classical music in America, we are frequently told, is in its death throes: its orchestras bled dry by expensive guest soloists and greedy musicians' unions, its media presence shrinking, its prestige diminished, its educational role ignored, its big record labels dying out or merging into faceless corporate entities. We seem to have too many well-trained musicians in need of work, too many good composers going without commissions, too many concerts to offer an already satiated public.
>
> —Russell Platt, "New World Symphony"

To cite this passage correctly in MLA documentation style, you could quote directly from it, using both quotation marks and some form of note identifying the author or source. Either of the following versions would be acceptable:

> Russell Platt has doubts about claims that classical music is "in its death throes: its orchestras bled dry by expensive guest soloists and greedy musicians unions" ("New World").
>
> But is classical music in the United States really "in its death throes," as some critics of the music scene suggest (Platt)?

You might also paraphrase Platt's paragraph, putting his ideas entirely in your own words but still giving him due credit by ending your remarks with a simple in-text note:

> A familiar story told by critics is that classical music faces a bleak future in the United States, with grasping soloists and unions bankrupting orchestras and classical works vanishing from radio and television, school curricula, and the labels of recording conglomerates. The public may not be willing to support all the talented musicians and composers we have today (Platt).

All of these sentences with citations would be keyed to a works cited entry at the end of the paper that would look like the following in MLA style:

> Platt, Russell. "New World Symphony." *The Nation*, 15 Sept. 2005, www.thenation.com/article/new-world-symphony/.

How might a citation go wrong? As we indicated, omitting either the quotation marks around a borrowed passage or an acknowledgment of the source is grounds for complaint. Neither of the following sentences provides enough information for a correct citation:

> But is classical music in the United States really in its death throes, as some critics of the music scene suggest, with its prestige diminished, its educational role ignored, and its big record labels dying (Platt)?
>
> But is classical music in the United States really in "its death throes," as some critics of the music scene suggest, with "its prestige diminished, its educational role ignored, [and] its big record labels dying"?

Just as faulty is a paraphrase such as the following, which borrows the words or ideas of the source too closely. It represents plagiarism, despite the fact that it identifies the source from which almost all the ideas—and a good many words—are borrowed:

> In "New World Symphony," Russell Platt observes that classical music is thought by many to be in bad shape in America. Its orchestras are being sucked dry by costly guest artists and insatiable unionized musicians, while its place on TV and radio is shrinking. The problem may be that we have too many well-trained musicians who need employment, too many good composers going without jobs, too many concerts for a public that prefers *The Real Housewives of Atlanta.*

Even the fresh idea not taken from Platt at the end of the paragraph doesn't alter the fact that the paraphrase is mostly a mix of Platt's original words, lightly stirred.

Acknowledging Collaboration

Writers generally acknowledge all participants in collaborative projects at the beginning of the presentation, report, or essay. In print texts, the acknowledgment is often placed in a footnote or brief prefatory note.

The eighth edition of the *MLA Handbook* (2016) calls attention to the shifting landscape of collaborative work, noting that

> Today academic work can take many forms other than the research paper. Scholars produce presentations, videos, and interactive Web projects, among other kinds of work...but the aims will remain the same: providing the information that enables a curious reader, viewer, or other user to track down your sources and giving credit to those whose work influenced yours.

RESPOND

1. Define *plagiarism* in your own terms, making your definition as clear and explicit as possible. Then compare your definition with those of two or three other classmates, and write a brief report on the similarities and differences you noted in the definitions. You might research terms such as *plagiarism*, *academic honesty*, and *academic integrity* on the Web. Also be certain to check how your own school defines the words.
2. Spend fifteen or twenty minutes jotting down your ideas about intellectual property and plagiarism. File sharing of music and illegally downloading movies used to be a big deal. Is it simpler/better now just to subscribe to Netflix and Apple Music? Do you agree that forms of intellectual property—like music and films—need to be protected under copyright law? How do you define your own intellectual property, and in what ways and under what conditions are you willing to share it?
3. Come up with your own definition of *academic integrity*, based on what you have observed yourself and other students doing in high school, in college, and, perhaps, on the job. Think about the consequences, for example, of borrowing materials and ideas from each other in a study group or while working on a collaborative project.
4. Not everyone agrees that intellectual material is property that should be protected. The slogan "information wants to be free" has been showing up in popular magazines and on the Internet for a long time, often with a call to readers to take action against protection such as data encryption and further extension of copyright.

   Using a Web search engine, look for pages where the phrase "information wants to be free" or "free information" appears. Find several sites that make arguments in favor of free information, and analyze them in terms of their rhetorical appeals. What claims do the authors make? How do they appeal to their audience? What's the site's ethos, and how is it created? After you've read some arguments in favor of free information, return to this chapter's arguments about intellectual property. Which arguments do you find most persuasive? Why?
5. Although this book is concerned principally with ideas and their written expression, other forms of intellectual property are also legally protected. For example, scientific and technological developments are protectable under patent law, which differs in some significant ways from copyright law (see the "Fair Use Fundamentals" infographic in this chapter on **p. 474**).

   Find the standards for protection under U.S. copyright law and U.S. patent law. You might begin by visiting the U.S. copyright Web site (copyright.gov). Then imagine that you're the president of a small high-tech corporation and are trying to inform your employees of the legal protections available to them and their work. Write a paragraph or two explaining the differences between copyright and patent, and suggest a policy that balances employees' rights to intellectual property with the business's needs to develop new products.

CHAPTER

24

Documenting Sources

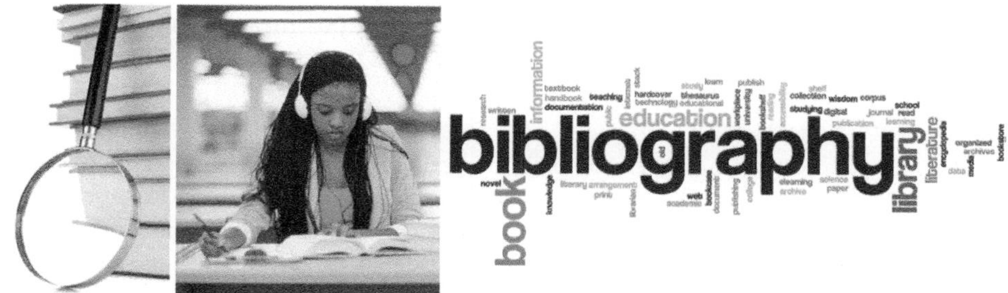

Left to right: Seregam/Shutterstock; Zero Creatives/Image/AGE Fotostock; ibreakstock/Shutterstock

What does documenting sources have to do with argument? First, the sources that a writer chooses become part of any argument, showing that he/she has done some research, knows what others have said about the topic, and understands how to use these items as support for a claim. Similarly, the list of works cited or references makes a statement, saying, "Look at how thoroughly this essay has been researched" or "Note how up-to-date I am!"

Writers working in digital spaces sometimes simply add hotlinks so that their readers can find their sources. If you are writing a multimodal essay that will appear on the Web, such links will be appreciated. But for now, college assignments generally call for full documentation rather than simply a link. You'll find the information you need to create in-text citations and works cited/references lists in this chapter.

Documentation styles vary from discipline to discipline, with one format favored in the social sciences and another in the natural sciences, for example. Your instructor will probably assign a documentation style for you to follow. If not, you can use one of the two covered in this chapter. But note that even the choice of documentation style makes an argument in a subtle way. You'll note in the instructions that follow, for example, that the Modern Language Association (MLA) style requires putting the date of publication of a print source at or near the end of a works cited list entry, whereas the American

Psychological Association (APA) style places that date near the beginning of a references list citation. Such positioning suggests that in MLA style, the author and title are of greater importance than the date for humanities scholars, while APA puts a priority on the date—and timeliness—of sources. Pay attention to such fine points of documentation style, always asking what these choices suggest about the values of scholars and researchers who use a particular system of documentation.

MLA Style

Widely used in the humanities, the latest version of MLA style—described in the *MLA Handbook* (8th edition, 2016)—has been revised significantly "for the digital age." If you have used MLA style in the past, you'll want to check the models here closely and note the differences. Below, we provide guidelines drawn from the *MLA Handbook* for in-text citations, notes, and entries in the list of works cited.

In-Text Citations

MLA style calls for in-text citations in the body of an argument to document sources of quotations, paraphrases, summaries, and so on. For in-text citations, use a signal phrase to introduce the material, often with the author's name (*As Geneva Smitherman explains,* . . .). Keep an in-text citation short, but include enough information for readers to locate the source in the list of works cited. Place the parenthetical citation as near to the relevant material as possible without disrupting the flow of the sentence, as in the following examples.

1. Author Named in a Signal Phrase

Ordinarily, use the author's name in a signal phrase to introduce the material, and cite the page number(s) in parentheses.

> Ravitch chronicles how the focus in education reform has shifted toward privatizing school management rather than toward improving curriculum, teacher training, or funding (36).

2. Author Named in Parentheses

When you don't mention the author in a signal phrase, include the author's last name before the page number(s) in the parentheses. The name and page number are *not* separated by a comma.

> Oil from shale in the western states, if it could be extracted, would be equivalent to six hundred billion barrels, more than all the crude so far produced in the world (McPhee 413).

3. Two Authors

Use both authors' last names.

Gortner and Nicolson maintain that "opinion leaders" influence other people in an organization because they are respected, not because they hold high positions (175).

4. Three or More Authors

When there are three or more authors, brevity (and the MLA) suggests you use the first author's name with *et al.* (in regular type, not italicized).

Similarly, as Goldberger et al. note, their new book builds on their collaborative experiences to inform their description of how women develop cognitively (xii).

5. Organization as Author

Give the full name of a corporate author if it's brief or a shortened form if it's long.

Many global economists assert that the term "developing countries" is no longer a useful designation, as it ignores such countries' rapid economic growth (Gates Foundation 112).

6. Unknown Author

Use the complete title of the work if it's brief or a shortened form if it's long.

"Hype," by one analysis, is "an artificially engendered atmosphere of hysteria" ("Today's Marketplace" 51).

7. Author of Two or More Works

When you use two or more works by the same author, include the title of the work or a shortened version of it in the citation.

Gardner presents readers with their own silliness through his description of a "pointless, ridiculous monster, crouched in the shadows, stinking of dead men, murdered children, and martyred cows" (*Grendel* 2).

8. Authors with the Same Last Name

When you use works by two or more authors with the same last name, include each author's first initial in the in-text citation.

Public health officials agree that the potential environmental risk caused by indoor residual spraying is far lower than the potential risk of death caused by malaria-carrying mosquitoes (S. Dillon 76).

9. Multivolume Work

Note the volume number first and then the page number(s), with a colon and one space between them.

> Aristotle's "On Plants" is now available in a new translation edited by Barnes (2: 1252).

10. Literary Work

Because literary works are often available in many different editions, you need to include enough information for readers to locate the passage in any edition. For a prose work such as a novel or play, first cite the page number from the edition you used, followed by a semicolon; then indicate the part or chapter number (114; ch. 3) or act or scene in a play (42; sc. 2).

> In Ben Jonson's *Volpone*, the miserly title character addresses his treasure as "dear saint" and "the best of things" (1447; act 1).

For a poem, cite the stanza and line numbers. If the poem has only line numbers, use the word *line(s)* in the first reference (lines 33–34) and the number(s) alone in subsequent references.

> On dying, Whitman speculates, "All that goes onward and outward, nothing collapses, / And to die is different from what any one supposed, and luckier" (6.129-30).

For a verse play, omit the page number, and give only the act, scene, and line numbers, separated by periods.

> Before he takes his own life, Othello says he is "one that loved not wisely but too well" (5.2.348).

> As *Macbeth* begins, the witches greet Banquo as "Lesser than Macbeth, and greater" (1.3.65).

11. Works in an Anthology

For an essay, short story, or other short work within an anthology, use the name of the author of the work, not the editor of the anthology; but use the page number(s) from the anthology.

> In the end, if the black artist accepts any duties at all, that duty is to express the beauty of blackness (Hughes 1271).

12. Sacred Text

To cite a sacred text, such as the Qur'an or the Bible, give the title of the edition you used, the book, and the chapter and verse (or their equivalent), separated by a period. In your text, spell out the names of books. In a parenthetical reference, use an abbreviation for books with names of five or more letters (for example, *Gen.* for Genesis).

> He ignored the admonition "Pride goes before destruction, and a haughty spirit before a fall" (*New Oxford Annotated Bible*, Prov. 16.18).

13. Indirect Source

Use the abbreviation *qtd. in* to indicate that what you're quoting or paraphrasing is quoted (as part of a conversation, interview, letter, or excerpt) in the source you're using.

> As Catherine Belsey states, "to speak is to have access to the language which defines, delimits and locates power" (qtd. in Bartels 453).

14. Two or More Sources in the Same Citation

Separate the information for each source with a semicolon.

> Adefunmi was able to patch up the subsequent holes left in worship by substituting various Yoruba, Dahomean, or Fon customs made available to him through research (Brandon 115-17; Hunt 27).

15. Entire Work or One-Page Article

Include the citation in the text without any page numbers or parentheses.

> Kazuo Ishiguro's dystopian novel *Never Let Me Go* explores questions of identity and authenticity.

16. Nonprint or Electronic Source

Give enough information in a signal phrase or parenthetical citation for readers to locate the source in the list of works cited. Usually give the author or title under which you list the source. If the work isn't numbered by page but has numbered sections, parts, or paragraphs, include the name and number(s) of the section(s) you're citing. (For paragraphs, use the abbreviation *par.* or *pars.*; for section, use *sec.*; for part, use *pt.*)

> In his film version of *Hamlet*, Zeffirelli highlights the sexual tension between the prince and his mother.

> Zora Neale Hurston is one of the great anthropologists of the twentieth century, according to Kip Hinton (par. 2).

> Describing children's language acquisition, Pinker explains that "what's innate about language is just a way of paying attention to parental speech" (qtd. in Johnson, sec. 1).

17. Visual Included in the Text

Number all figures (photos, drawings, cartoons, maps, graphs, and charts) and tables separately.

> This trend is illustrated in a chart distributed by the College Board as part of its 2014 analysis of aggregate SAT data (see fig. 1).

Include a caption with enough information about the source to direct readers to the works cited entry. (For an example of an image that a student created, see the sample page from an MLA-style essay on p. 496 in this chapter.)

Explanatory and Bibliographic Notes

We recommend using explanatory notes for information or commentary that doesn't readily fit into your text but is needed for clarification, further explanation, or justification. In addition, bibliographic notes will allow you to cite several sources for one point and to offer thanks to, information about, or evaluation of a source. Use a superscript number in your text at the end of a sentence to refer readers to the notes, which usually appear as endnotes (with the heading *Notes*, not underlined or italicized) on a separate page before the list of works cited. Indent the first line of each note five spaces, and double-space all entries.

Text with Superscript Indicating a Note

> Stewart emphasizes the existence of social contacts in Hawthorne's life so that the audience will accept a different Hawthorne, one more attuned to modern times than the figure in Woodberry.[3]

Note

> [3]Woodberry does, however, show that Hawthorne was often unsociable. He emphasizes the seclusion of Hawthorne's mother, who separated herself from her family after the death of her husband, often even taking meals alone (28). Woodberry seems to imply that Mrs. Hawthorne's isolation rubbed off on her son.

List of Works Cited

A list of works cited is an alphabetical listing of the sources you cite in your essay. The list appears on a separate page at the end of your argument, after any notes, with the heading *Works Cited* centered an inch from the top of the page; don't underline or italicize it or enclose it in quotation marks. Double-space between the heading and the first entry, and double-space the entire list. (If you're asked to list everything you've read as background—not just the sources you cite—call the list *Works Consulted.*) The first line of each entry should align on the left; subsequent lines indent one-half inch or five spaces. See page 497 for a sample works cited page.

Print Books

The basic information for a book includes three elements, each followed by a period:

- the author's name, last name first (for a book with multiple authors, only the first author's name is inverted)
- the title and subtitle, italicized
- the publication information, including the publisher's name (such as Harvard UP) followed by a comma, and the publication date

1. One Author

Larsen, Erik. *Dead Wake: The Last Crossing of the Lusitania*. Crown Publishers, 2015.

2. Two or More Authors

Jacobson, Sid, and Ernie Colón. *The 9/11 Report: A Graphic Adaptation*. Farrar, Straus, and Giroux, 2006.

3. Organization as Author

American Horticultural Society. *The Fully Illustrated Plant-by-Plant Manual of Practical Techniques*. DK, 1999.

4. Unknown Author

National Geographic Atlas of the World. National Geographic, 2004.

5. Two or More Books by the Same Author

List the works alphabetically by title. Use three hyphens for the author's name for the second and subsequent works by that author.

Lorde, Audre. *A Burst of Light*. Firebrand Books, 1988.

---. *Sister Outsider*. Crossings Press, 1984.

6. Editor

Rorty, Amelie Oksenberg, editor. *Essays on Aristotle's Poetics*. Princeton UP, 1992.

7. Author and Editor

Shakespeare, William. *The Tempest*. Edited by Frank Kermode, Routledge, 1994.

8. Selection in an Anthology or Chapter in an Edited Book

List the author(s) of the selection or chapter; its title; the title of the book in which the selection or chapter appears; *edited by* and the name(s) of the editor(s); the publication information; and the inclusive page numbers of the selection or chapter.

Brown, Paul. " 'This thing of darkness I acknowledge mine': *The Tempest* and the Discourse of Colonialism." *Political Shakespeare: Essays in Cultural Materialism*, edited by Jonathan Dollimore and Alan Sinfield, Cornell UP, 1985, pp. 48–71.

9. Two or More Works from the Same Anthology

Include the anthology itself in the list of works cited.

Gates, Henry Louis, Jr., and Nellie McKay, editors. *The Norton Anthology of African American Literature*. Norton, 1997.

Then list each selection separately by its author and title, followed by a cross-reference to the anthology.

Karenga, Maulana. "Black Art: Mute Matter Given Force and Function." Gates and McKay, pp. 1973–77.

Neal, Larry. "The Black Arts Movement." Gates and McKay, pp. 1960–72.

10. Translation

Ferrante, Elena. *The Story of the Lost Child*. Translated by Ann Goldstein, Europa Editions, 2015.

11. Edition Other Than the First

Lunsford, Andrea A., et al. *Everything's an Argument with Readings*. 8th ed., Bedford/St. Martin's, 2019.

12. Graphic Narrative

If the words and images are created by the same person, cite a graphic narrative just as you would a book (see item 1 on p. 485).

Bechdel, Alison. *Are You My Mother?* Houghton Mifflin Harcourt, 2012.

If the work is a collaboration, indicate the author or illustrator who is most important to your research before the title. Then list other contributors in order of their appearance on the title page. Label each person's contribution to the work.

Stavans, Ilan, writer. *Latino USA: A Cartoon History*. Illustrated by Lalo Arcaraz, Basic Books, 2000.

13. One Volume of a Multivolume Work

Byron, Lord George. *Byron's Letters and Journals*. Edited by Leslie A. Marchand, vol. 2, John Murray, 1973. 12 vols.

14. Two or More Volumes of a Multivolume Work

Byron, Lord George. *Byron's Letters and Journals.* Edited by Leslie A. Marchand, John Murray, 1973–82. 12 vols.

15. Preface, Foreword, Introduction, or Afterword

Dunham, Lena. Foreword. *The Liars' Club*, by Mary Karr, Penguin Classics, 2015, pp. xi–xiii.

16. Article in a Reference Work

Robinson, Lisa Clayton. "Harlem Writers Guild." *Africana: The Encyclopedia of the African and African American Experience*, 2nd ed., Oxford UP, 2005.

17. Book That Is Part of a Series

Include the title and number of the series after the publication information.

Moss, Beverly J. *A Community Text Arises.* Hampton, 2003. Language and Social Processes Series 8.

18. Republication

Trilling, Lionel. *The Liberal Imagination.* 1950. Introduction by Louis Menand, New York Review of Books, 2008.

19. Government Document

Canada, Minister of Aboriginal Affairs and Northern Development. *2015–16 Report on Plans and Priorities.* Minister of Public Works and Government Services Canada, 2015.

20. Pamphlet

The Legendary Sleepy Hollow Cemetery. Friends of Sleepy Hollow Cemetery, 2008.

21. Published Proceedings of a Conference

Meisner, Marx S., et al., editors. *Communication for the Commons: Revisiting Participation and Environment.* Proceedings of Twelfth Biennial Conference on Communication and the Environment, 6–11 June 2015, Swedish U of Agricultural Sciences, International Environmental Communication Association, 2015.

22. Title within a Title

Shanahan, Timothy. *Philosophy and* Blade Runner. Palgrave Macmillan, 2014.

Print Periodicals

The basic entry for a periodical includes three elements:

- the author's name, last name first, followed by a period
- the article title, in quotation marks, followed by a period
- the publication information, including the periodical title (italicized), the volume and issue numbers (if any, not italicized), the date of publication, and the page number(s), all followed by commas, with a period at the end of the page numbers

For works with multiple authors, only the first author's name is inverted. Note that the period following the article title goes inside the closing quotation mark.

23. Article in a Print Journal

Give the issue number, if available.

Matchie, Thomas. "Law versus Love in *The Round House.*" *Midwest Quarterly,* vol. 56, no. 4, Summer 2015, pp. 353–64.

Fuqua, Amy. " 'The Furrow of His Brow': Providence and Pragmatism in Toni Morrison's *Paradise.*" *Midwest Quarterly*, vol. 54, no. 1, Autumn 2012, pp. 38–52.

24. Article That Skips Pages

Seabrook, John. "Renaissance Pears." *The New Yorker*, 5 Sept. 2005, pp. 102+.

25. Article in a Print Monthly Magazine

Nijhuis, Michelle. "When Cooking Kills." *National Geographic*, Sept. 2017, pp. 76–81.

26. Article in a Print Weekly Magazine

Grossman, Lev. "A Star Is Born." *Time*, 2 Nov. 2015, pp. 30–39.

27. Article in a Print Newspaper

Bray, Hiawatha. "As Toys Get Smarter, Privacy Issues Emerge." *The Boston Globe,* 10 Dec. 2015, p. C1.

28. Editorial or Letter to the Editor

Posner, Alan. "Colin Powell's Regret." *The New York Times*, 9 Sept. 2005, p. A20.

29. Unsigned Article

"Court Rejects the Sale of Medical Marijuana." *The New York Times*, 26 Feb. 1998, late ed., p. A21.

30. Review

Harris, Brandon. "Black Saints and Sinners." Review of *Five-Carat Soul*, by James McBride. *The New York Review of Books*, 7 Dec. 2017, pp. 50–51.

Digital Sources

Most of the following models are based on the MLA's guidelines for citing electronic sources in the *MLA Handbook* (8th edition, 2016), as well as on up-to-date information available at its Web site (mla.org). The MLA advocates the use of URLs but prefers a Digital Object Indicator (DOI) where available. A DOI is a unique number assigned to a selection, and does not change regardless of where the item is located online. The basic MLA entry for most electronic sources should include the following elements:

- name of the author, editor, or compiler
- title of the work, document, or posting
- publication information (volume, issue, year or date). List page numbers or paragraph numbers only if they are included in the source.
- name of database, italicized
- DOI or URL

31. Document from a Web Site

Begin with the author, if known, followed by the title of the work, title of the Web site, publisher or sponsor (if it is notably different from the title of the Web site), date of publication or last update, and the Digital Object Identifier or URL. If no publication or update date is available, include a date of access at the end.

"Social and Historical Context: Vitality." *Arapesh Grammar and Digital Language Archive Project*, Institute for Advanced Technology in the Humanities, www.arapesh.org/socio_historical_context_vitality.php. Accessed 22 Mar. 2017.

32. Entire Web Site

Include the name of the person or group who created the site, if relevant; the title of the site, italicized; the publisher or sponsor of the site; the date of publication or last update; and the URL.

Barcus, Jane. *What Jane Saw*. Liberals Arts Development Studio/University of Texas at Austin, 2013, whatjanesaw.org.

Halsall, Paul, editor. *Internet Modern History Sourcebook*. Fordham U, 4 Nov. 2011, legacy.fordham.edu/halsall/index.asp.

33. Course, Department, or Personal Web Site

For a course Web site, include the instructor's name; the title of the site, italicized; a description of the site (such as *Course home page*, *Department home page*, or *Home page*—not italicized); the sponsor of the site (academic department and institution); dates of the course or last update to the page; and the URL. Note that the MLA spells *home page* as two separate words. For an academic department, list the name of the department; a description; the academic institution; the date the page was last updated; and the URL.

Film Studies. Department home page. *Wayne State University, College of Liberal Arts and Sciences*, 2016, clas.wayne.edu/FilmStudies/.

Masiello, Regina. 355:101: Expository Writing. *Rutgers School of Arts and Sciences*, 2017, wp.rutgers.edu/courses/55-355101.

34. Online Book

Cite an online book as you would a print book. After the print publication information (if any), give the title of the Web site or database in which the book appears, italicized; and the DOI or URL.

Riis, Jacob A. *How the Other Half Lives: Studies among the Tenements of New York*. Edited by David Phillips, Scribner's, 1890. *The Authentic History Center*, www.authentichistory.com/1898-1913/2-progressivism/2-riis/.

Treat a poem, essay, or other short work within an online book as you would a part of a print book. After the print publication information (if any), give the title of the Web site or database, italicized; and the DOI or URL.

Milton, John. *Paradise Lost: Book I*. *Poetry Foundation*, 2014, www.poetryfoundation.org/poem/174987.

35. Article in a Journal on the Web

For an article in an online journal, cite the same information that you would for a print journal. Then add the DOI or URL.

Wells, Julia. "The 'Terrible Loneliness': Loneliness and Worry in Settler Women's Memoirs from East and South-Central Africa, 1890–1939." *African Studies Quarterly*, vol. 17, no. 2, June 2017, pp. 47–64, africa.ufl.edu/asq/v17/v17i2a3.pdf.

36. Article in a Magazine or Newspaper on the Web

For an article in an online magazine or newspaper, cite the author; the title of the article, in quotation marks; the name of the magazine or newspaper, italicized; the date of publication; and the URL of the page you accessed.

Leonard, Andrew. "The Surveillance State High School." *Salon*, 27 Nov. 2012, www.salon.com/2012/11/27/the_surveillance_state_high_school/.

Crowell, Maddy. "How Computers Are Getting Better at Detecting Liars." *The Christian Science Monitor*, 12 Dec. 2015, www.csmonitor.com/Science/Science-Notebook/2015/1212/How-computers-are-getting-better-at detecting-liars.

37. Entry in a Web Reference Work

Cite the entry as you would an entry from a print reference work (see item 16). Follow with the name of the Web site, the date of publication, and the URL of the site you accessed.

Durante, Amy M. "Finn Mac Cumhail." *Encyclopedia Mythica*, 17 Apr. 2011, www.pantheon.org/articles/f/finn_mac_cumhail.html.

38. Post or Comment on a Web Site

Begin with the author's name; the title of the posting, in quotation marks; the name of the blog, italicized; the sponsor of the blog; the date of the most recent update; and the URL of the page you accessed.

mitchellfreedman. Comment on "*Cloud Atlas's* Theory of Everything," by Emily Eakin. *NYR Daily*, NYREV, 3 Nov. 2012, www.nybooks.com/daily/2012/11/02/ken-wilber-cloud-atlas/.

39. Entry in a Wiki

Since wikis are collectively edited, do not include an author. Treat a wiki as you would a work from a Web site (see item 31). Include the title of the entry; the name of the wiki, italicized; the date of the latest update; and the URL of the page you accessed.

"House Music." *Wikipedia*, 16 Nov. 2017, en.wikipedia.org/wiki/House_music.

40. Post on Social Media

To cite a post on Facebook or another social media site, include the writer's name, a description of the posting, the date of the posting, and the URL of the page you accessed.

Bedford English. "Stacey Cochran Explores Reflective Writing in the Classroom and as a Writer: http://ow.ly/YkjVB." *Facebook*, 15 Feb. 2016, www.facebook.com/BedfordEnglish/posts/10153415001259607.

41. Email or Message on Social Media

Include the writer's name; the subject line, in quotation marks (for email); *Received by* (not italicized or in quotation marks) followed by the recipient's name; and the date of the message. You do not need to include the medium, but may if you are concerned there will be confusion.

Thornbrugh, Caitlin. "Coates Lecture." Received by Rita Anderson, 20 Oct. 2015.

42. Tweet

Include the writer's real name, if known, with the user name (if different) in parentheses. If you don't know the real name, give just the user name. Include the entire tweet, in quotation marks. Include the publisher (Twitter) in italics, follow by the date and time of the message and the URL.

Curiosity Rover. "Can you see me waving? How to spot #Mars in the night sky: https://youtu.be/hv8hVvJlcJQ." *Twitter*, 5 Nov. 2015, 11:00 a.m., twitter.com/marscuriosity/status/672859022911889408.

43. Work from an Online Database or a Subscription Service

For a work from an online database, list the author's name; the title of the work; any print publication information; the name of the database, italicized; and the DOI or URL.

Goldsmith, Oliver. *The Vicar of Wakefield: A Tale*. Philadelphia, 1801. *America's Historical Imprints*, infoweb.newsbank.com.ezproxy.bpl.org/.

Coles, Kimberly Anne. "The Matter of Belief in John Donne's Holy Sonnets." *Renaissance Quarterly*, vol. 68, no. 3, Fall 2015, pp. 899–931. *JSTOR*, doi:10.1086/683855.

44. Computer Software or Video Game

Include the title, italicized; the version number (if given); and publication information. If you are citing material downloaded from a Web site, include the title and version number (if given), but instead of publication information, add the publisher or sponsor of the Web site; the date of publication; and the URL.

Edgeworld. Atom Entertainment, 1 May 2012, www.kabam.com/games/edgeworld.

Words with Friends. Version 5.84, Zynga, 2013.

Other Sources (Including Online Versions)

45. Unpublished Dissertation

Abbas, Megan Brankley. "Knowing Islam: The Entangled History of Western Academia and Modern Islamic Thought." Dissertation, Princeton U, 2015.

46. Published Dissertation

Kidd, Celeste. *Rational Approaches to Learning and Development.* Dissertation, U of Rochester, 2013.

47. Article from a Microform

Sharpe, Lora. "A Quilter's Tribute." *The Boston Globe*, 25 Mar. 1989, p. 13. Microform. *NewsBank*: Social Relations 12, 1989, fiche 6, grids B4–6.

48. Personal, Published, or Broadcast Interview

For a personal interview, list the name of the person interviewed, the label *Personal interview* (not italicized), and the date of the interview.

Cooper, Rebecca. Personal interview. 1 Jan. 2018.

For a published interview, list the name of the person interviewed, the title (if any), along with the label *Interview by* [*interviewer's name*] (not italicized); then add the publication information, including the URL if there is one.

Weddington, Sarah. "Sarah Weddington: Still Arguing for *Roe*." Interview by Michele Kort. *Ms.*, Winter 2013, pp. 32–35.

Jaffrey, Madhur. "Madhur Jaffrey on How Indian Cuisine Won Western Taste Buds." Interview by Shadrach Kabango. *Q*, CBC Radio, 29 Oct. 2015, www.cbc.ca/1.3292918.

For a broadcast interview, list the name of the person interviewed; the title, if any; the label *Interview by* (not italicized); and the name of the interviewer (if relevant). Then list information about the program, the date of the interview, and the URL, if applicable.

Fairey, Shepard. "Spreading the Hope: Street Artist Shepard Fairey." Interview by Terry Gross. *Fresh Air*, National Public Radio, WBUR, Boston, 20 Jan. 2009.

Putin, Vladimir. Interview by Charlie Rose. *Charlie Rose: The Week*, PBS, 19 June 2015.

49. Letter

Treat a published letter like a work in an anthology, but include the date of the letter.

Jacobs, Harriet. "To Amy Post." 4 Apr. 1853. *Incidents in the Life of a Slave Girl,* edited by Jean Fagan Yellin, Harvard UP, 1987, pp. 234–35.

50. Film

For films, ordinarily begin with the title, followed by the director and major performers. If your essay or project focuses on a major person related to the film, such as the director, you can begin with that name or names, followed by the title and performers.

Birdman or (The Unexpected Virtue of Ignorance). Directed by Alejandro González Iñárritu, performances by Michael Keaton, Emma Stone, Zach Galifianakis, Edward Norton, and Naomi Watts, Fox Searchlight, 2014.

Jenkins, Patty, director. *Wonder Woman.* Performances by Gal Gadot, Chris Pine, and Robin Wright, Warner Bros., 2017.

51. Television or Radio Program

"Free Speech on College Campuses." *Washington Journal,* narrated by Peter Slen, C-SPAN, 27 Nov. 2015.

"Take a Giant Step." *Prairie Home Companion,* narrated by Garrison Keillor, American Public Media, 27 Feb. 2016, prairiehome.publicradio.org/listen/full/?name=phc/2016/02/27/phc_20160227_128.

52. Online Video Clip

Cite a short online video as you would a work from a Web site (see item 31).

Nayar, Vineet. "Employees First, Customers Second." *YouTube,* 9 June 2015, www.youtube.com/watch?v=cCdu67s_C5E.

53. Sound Recording

Blige, Mary J. "Don't Mind." *Life II: The Journey Continues (Act 1),* Geffen, 2011.

54. Work of Art or Photograph

List the artist or photographer; the work's title, italicized; and the date of composition. Then cite the name of the museum or other location and the city.

Bradford, Mark. *Let's Walk to the Middle of the Ocean.* 2015, Museum of Modern Art, New York.

Feinstein, Harold. *Hangin' Out, Sharing a Public Bench, NYC.* 1948, Panopticon Gallery, Boston.

To cite a reproduction in a book, add the publication information.

O'Keeffe, Georgia. *Black and Purple Petunias.* 1925, private collection. *Two Lives: A Conversation in Paintings and Photographs*, edited by Alexandra Arrowsmith and Thomas West, HarperCollins, 1992, p. 67.

To cite artwork found online, add the title of the database or Web site, italicized; and the URL of the site you accessed.

Clough, Charles. *January Twenty-First.* 1988–89, Joslyn Art Museum, Omaha, www.joslyn.org/collections-and-exhibitions/permanent-collections/modern-and-contemporary/charles-clough-january-twenty-first/.

55. Lecture or Speech

Smith, Anna Deavere. "On the Road: A Search for American Character." National Endowment for the Humanities, John F. Kennedy Center for the Performing Arts, Washington, 6 Apr. 2015. Address.

56. Performance

The Draft. By Peter Snoad, directed by Diego Arciniegas, Hibernian Hall, Boston, 10 Sept. 2015.

57. Map or Chart

"Map of Sudan." *Global Citizen*, Citizens for Global Solutions, 2011, globalsolutions.org/blog/bashir#.VthzNMfi_FI.

58. Cartoon

Ramirez, Michael P. "Eagle and Loon." Michael P. Ramirez, 31 Aug. 2017, http://www.michaelpramirez.com/loon-and-eagle.html. Cartoon.

59. Advertisement

Louis Vuitton. *Vanity Fair,* Aug. 2017, p. 35. Advertisement.

On p. 496, note the formatting of the first page of a sample essay written in MLA style. On p. 497, you'll find a sample works cited page written for the same student essay.

Sample First Page for an Essay in MLA Style

Lesk 1

Name, instructor, course, date aligned at left

Emily Lesk

Professor Arraéz

Electric Rhetoric

15 November 2014

Title centered

Red, White, and Everywhere

America, I have a confession to make: I don't drink Coke. But don't call me a hypocrite just because I am still the proud owner of a bright red shirt that advertises it. Just call me an American. Even before setting foot in Israel three years ago, I knew exactly where I could find one. The tiny T-shirt shop in the central block of Jerusalem's Ben Yehuda Street did offer other designs, but the one with a bright white "Drink Coca-Cola Classic" written in Hebrew cursive across the chest was what drew in most of the dollar-carrying tourists. While waiting almost twenty minutes for my shirt (depicted in fig. 1), I watched nearly every customer ahead of me ask for "the Coke shirt, *todah rabah* [thank you very much]."

Emily Lesk

Figure number and caption noting the source of the photo

Fig. 1. Hebrew Coca-Cola T-shirt. Personal photograph. Despite my dislike for the beverage, I bought this Coca-Cola T-shirt in Israel.

At the time, I never thought it strange that I wanted one, too. After having absorbed sixteen years of Coca-Cola propaganda through everything from NBC's Saturday morning cartoon lineup to the concession stand at Camden Yards (the Baltimore Orioles' ballpark), I associated the shirt with singing along to the "Just for the Taste of It" jingle and with America's favorite pastime, not with a brown fizzy beverage I refused to consume.

Sample List of Works Cited for an Essay in MLA Style

Lesk 7

Works Cited

Heading centered

Coca-Cola Santa pin. Personal photograph by the author, 9 Nov. 2008.

"The Fabulous Fifties." *Beverage Industry*, vol. 87, no. 6, 1996, p. 16. *General OneFile*, go.galegroup.com/.

"Fifty Years of Coca-Cola Television Advertisements." *American Memory*. Motion Picture, Broadcasting and Recorded Sound Division, Library of Congress, memory.loc.gov/ammem/ccmphtml/colahome.html. Accessed 5 Nov. 2014.

"Haddon Sundblom and Coca-Cola." *The History of Christmas*, 10 Holidays, 2004, www.thehistoryofchristmas.com/sc/coca_cola.htm.

Hebrew Coca-Cola T-shirt. Personal photograph by the author, 8 Nov. 2014.

Ikuta, Yasutoshi, editor. *'50s American Magazine Ads*. Graphic-Sha, 1987.

Pendergrast, Mark. *For God, Country, and Coca-Cola: The Definitive History of the Great American Soft Drink and the Company That Makes It*. 2nd ed., Basic Books, 2000.

Subsequent lines of each entry indented

List is alphabetized by authors' last names (or by title when there is no author)

CHAPTER

25

Composing Arguments Based on Emotion: Pathos

Left to right: Piyaset/Shutterstock; Jan Martin Will/Shutterstock; Blueguy/Shutterstock

Emotional appeals (*appeals to pathos*) are powerful tools for influencing what people think and believe. We all make decisions—even including the most important ones—based on our feelings. That's what many environmental advocates are counting on when they use images like those above to warn of the catastrophic effects of global warming on the earth and its peoples. The first image shows a boy and his boat on what used to be a lake but is now cracked dry earth; the second, a polar bear stranded on a small ice floe as the oceans rise around it; and the third, a graphic design of a melting earth.

Of course, some people don't believe the warnings about climate change, arguing instead that they represent a hoax and that even if the climate is changing, it is not a result of human activities. And, as we would expect, this opposite side of the argument also uses emotionally persuasive images, like the following one from American Patriot, a news commentary YouTube channel.

The arguments packed into these four images all appeal to emotion, and research has shown us that we often make decisions based on just such appeals. So when you hear that formal or academic arguments should rely solely on facts to convince us, remember that facts alone often won't carry the day, even for a worthy cause. The largely successful case made for same-sex marriage provides a notable example of a movement that persuaded people equally by virtue of the reasonableness and the passion of its claims. Like many political and social debates, though, the issue provoked powerful emotions on every side—feelings that sometimes led to extreme words and tactics.

Recent research also shows that images that evoke fear are less effective than those that arouse interest, worry, or hope. When the Yale Center for Climate Change Communication asked both supporters and deniers of climate change what they felt when they thought about this topic, they got the following results:

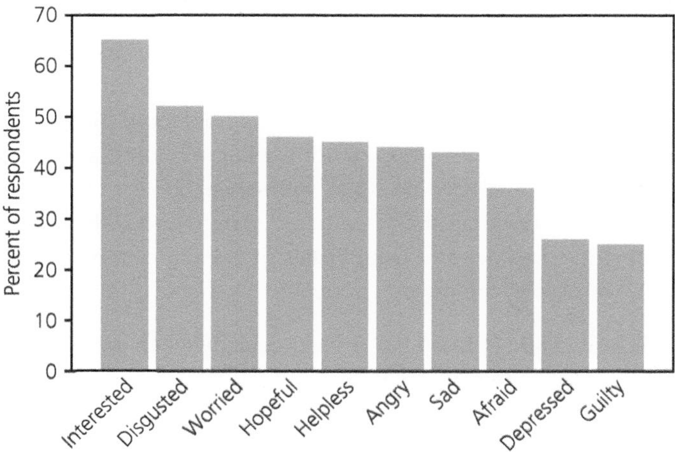

Yale Center for Climate Change Communication

In spite of the findings from such research, we don't have to look hard for arguments that appeal to fear, hatred, envy, and greed, or for campaigns intended to drive wedges between economic or social groups, making them fearful or resentful. For that reason alone, writers should not use emotional appeals rashly or casually. But used carefully and ethically, appeals to emotions—especially ones like worry or hope—can be very helpful in moving an audience to action. (For more about emotional fallacies, see pp. 292–295.

Reading Critically for Pathos

On February 24, 2014, Senator Tom Harkin of Iowa, fresh from two fact-finding trips to Cuba, described his experiences on the Senate floor in a speech praising that island nation's accomplishments in health care and education and urging a normalization of Cuban–American relationships, a recommendation taken up by then-President Obama and Cuban President Raul Castro, who announced on December 17, 2014, that such normalization would begin. Many in the United States applauded this move, but others, including many Cuban Americans in the Miami area, objected strenuously. Florida senator Marco Rubio was one of those speaking most passionately against normalization of relationships. Shortly after Senator Harkin's talk about the "fascinating" socialist experiment ninety miles from the coast of the United States, Rubio delivered a fifteen-minute rejoinder to Harkin without a script or teleprompter. After a sarcastic taunt ("Sounded like he had a wonderful trip visiting what he described as a real paradise"), Rubio quickly turned serious, even angry, as he offered his take on the country Harkin had toured:

> I heard him also talk about these great doctors that they have in Cuba. I have no doubt they're very talented. I've met a bunch of them. You know where I met them? In the United States because they defected. Because in Cuba, doctors would rather drive a taxi cab or work in a hotel than be a doctor. I wonder if they spoke to him about the outbreak of cholera that they've been unable to control, or about the three-tiered system of health care that exists where foreigners and government officials get health care much better than that that's available to the general population.

Language this heated and pointed has risks, especially when a young legislator is taking on a far more experienced colleague. But Rubio, the son of Cuban immigrants, isn't shy about allowing his feelings to show: in the following passage, he uses the kind of emotion-stirring verbal repetition common in oratory to drive home his major concern about Cuba, its influence on other nations:

> Let me tell you what the Cubans are really good at, because they don't know how to run their economy, they don't know how to build, they don't know how to govern a people. What they are really good at is repression. What they are really good at is shutting off information to the Internet and to radio and television and social media. That's what they're really good at. And they're not just good at it domestically, they're good exporters of these things.

When the Obama administration indeed loosened restrictions on travel to Cuba and began establishing diplomatic relations, Rubio stuck to his guns, consistently and emotionally arguing against this move. And while he was a bitter primary campaign rival of Donald Trump, who ridiculed Rubio during the campaign as "little Marco" who was always sweating ("It looked like he had just jumped into a swimming pool with his clothes on"), once Trump was elected president Rubio continued his impassioned campaign to reverse policy on Cuba. So in June 2017, when President Trump announced tightening of restrictions on travel to Cuba and other changes to the Obama policy, Rubio spoke glowingly of the president, saying that "A year and a half ago, an American president landed in Havana and outstretched his hand to a regime. Today, a new president lands in Miami to reach out his hand to the people of Cuba." It's likely that we have not heard the end of this debate, and that we will continue to hear emotion-filled arguments on all sides of this contentious issue.

Lynne Sladky/AP Images

FIGURE 25.1 Senator Rubio with President Trump

RESPOND

Working with a classmate, find a speech or a print editorial that you think uses emotional appeals effectively but sparingly, in an understated way. Make a list of those appeals and briefly explain how each one appeals to an audience. What difference would it have made if the emotional appeals had been presented more forcefully and dramatically? Would doing so have been likely to appeal more strongly to the audience—and why or why not? What is at stake for the writer or speaker in such situations, in terms of credibility and ethos? What are the advantages of evoking emotions in support of your claims or ideas?

Using Emotions to Build Bridges

You may sometimes want to use emotions to connect with readers to assure them that you understand their experiences or "feel their pain," to borrow a sentiment popularized by President Bill Clinton. Such a bridge is especially important when you're writing about matters that readers regard as sensitive. Before they'll trust you, they'll want assurances that you understand the issues in depth. If you strike the right emotional note, you'll establish an important connection. That's what Apple founder Steve Jobs does in a much-admired 2005 commencement address in which he tells the audience that he doesn't have a fancy speech, just three stories from his life:

> My second story is about love and loss. I was lucky. I found what I loved to do early in life. Woz [Steve Wozniak] and I started Apple in my parents' garage when I was twenty. We worked hard and in ten years, Apple had grown from just the two of us in a garage into a $2 billion company with over four thousand employees. We'd just released our finest creation, the Macintosh, a year earlier, and I'd just turned thirty, and then I got fired. How can you get fired from a company you started? Well, as Apple grew, we hired someone who I thought was very talented to run the company with me, and for the first year or so, things went well. But then our visions of the future began to diverge, and eventually we had a falling out. When we did, our board of directors sided with him, and so at thirty, I was out, and very publicly out....
>
> I didn't see it then, but it turned out that getting fired from Apple was the best thing that could have ever happened to me. The heaviness of being successful was replaced by the lightness of being a beginner again, less sure about everything. It freed me to enter one of the most creative periods in my life. During the next five years I started a company named NeXT, another company

> named Pixar and fell in love with an amazing woman who would become my wife. Pixar went on to create the world's first computer-animated feature film, Toy Story, and is now the most successful animation studio in the world.
>
> —Steve Jobs, "You've Got to Find What You Love, Jobs Says"

In no obvious way is Jobs's recollection a formal argument. But it prepares his audience to accept the advice he'll give later in his speech, at least partly because he's speaking from meaningful personal experiences.

A more obvious way to build an emotional tie is simply to help readers identify with your experiences. If, like Georgina Kleege, you were blind and wanted to argue for more sensible attitudes toward blind people, you might ask readers in the first paragraph of your argument to confront their prejudices. Here Kleege, a writer and college instructor who in July 2017 was featured on PBS's "Brief but Spectacular" video series, makes an emotional point by telling a story:

> I tell the class, "I am legally blind." There is a pause, a collective intake of breath. I feel them look away uncertainly and then look back. After all, I just said I couldn't see. Or did I? I had managed to get there on my own—no cane, no dog, none of the usual trappings of blindness. Eyeing me askance now, they might detect that my gaze is not quite focused....They watch me glance down, or towards the door where someone's coming in late. I'm just like anyone else.
>
> —Georgina Kleege, "Call It Blindness"

Given the way she narrates the first day of class, readers are as likely to identify with the students as with Kleege, imagining themselves sitting in a classroom, facing a sightless instructor, confronting their own prejudices about the blind. Kleege wants to put her audience on the edge emotionally.

Let's consider another rhetorical situation: how do you win over an audience when the logical claims that you're making are likely to go against what many in the audience believe? Once again, a slightly risky appeal to emotions on a personal level may work. That's the tack that Michael Pollan takes in bringing readers to consider that "the great moral struggle of our time will be for the rights of animals." In introducing his lengthy exploratory argument, Pollan uses personal experience to appeal to his audience:

> The first time I opened Peter Singer's *Animal Liberation*, I was dining alone at the Palm, trying to enjoy a rib-eye steak cooked medium-rare. If this sounds like a good recipe for cognitive dissonance (if not indigestion), that was sort

of the idea. Preposterous as it might seem to supporters of animal rights, what I was doing was tantamount to reading *Uncle Tom's Cabin* on a plantation in the Deep South in 1852.

—Michael Pollan, "An Animal's Place"

FIGURE 25.2 A visual version of Michael Pollan's rhetorical situation

In creating a vivid image of his first encounter with Singer's book, Pollan's opening builds a bridge between himself as a person trying to enter into the animal rights debate in a fair and open-minded, if still skeptical, way and readers who might be passionate about either side of this argument.

Using Emotions to Sustain an Argument

You can also use emotional appeals to make logical claims stronger or more memorable. In a TV political attack ad, a video clip of a scowling, blustering candidate talking dismissively about an important issue has the potential to damage that candidate considerably. In contrast, a human face smiling or showing honest emotion can sell just about any product—that's why so many political figures now routinely smile at any camera they see. Using emotion is tricky, however, and it can sometimes backfire. Lay on too much feeling—especially sentiments like outrage, pity, or shame, which make people uncomfortable—and you may offend the very audiences you hoped to convince.

Still, strong emotions can add energy to a passage or an entire argument, as they do in Richard Lloyd Parry's *Ghosts of the Tsunami: Death and Life in Japan's Disaster Zone.* In this passage, Parry describes in vivid detail the scene that greeted one mother the day the 2011 earthquake hit:

> On the near side was Hitomi's home village of Magaki and then an expanse of paddies stretching to the Fuji lake; the polished blue and red roofs of other hamlets glittered at the edges of the hills. It was an archetypal view of the Japanese countryside: abundant nature, tamed and cultivated by man. But now she struggled to make sense of what she saw.
>
> Everything up to and in between the hills was water. There was only water: buildings and fields had gone. The water was black in the early light; floating on it were continents and trailing archipelagos of dark scummy rubble, brown in color and composed of tree trunks. Every patch of land that was not elevated had been absorbed by the river, which had been annexed in turn by the sea.
>
> In this new geography, the Fuji lake was no longer a lake....The river was no longer a river....Okawa Elementary School was invisible, hidden from view by the great shoulder of hills from which Hitomi looked down. But the road, the houses, and Magaki, where Hitomi's home and family had been, were washed from the earth.

AP Photo/Wally Santana

FIGURE 25.3 A wrecked car lies submerged in floodwaters after the earthquake and tsunami in Fukushima prefecture, Japan.

As this example suggests, it can be difficult to gauge how much emotion will work in a given argument. Some issues—such as racism, immigration, abortion, and gun control—provoke strong feelings and, as a result, are often argued on emotional terms. But even issues that seem deadly dull—such as reform of federal student loan programs—can be argued passionately when proposed changes in these programs are set in human terms: reduce support for college loans and Kai, Riley, and Jayden end up in dead-end, low-paying jobs; don't reform the program and we're looking at another Wall Street–sized loan bailout and subsequent recession. Both alternatives might scare people into paying enough attention to take political action.

Using Humor

Humor has always played an important role in argument, sometimes as the sugar that makes the medicine go down. You can slip humor into an argument to put readers at ease, thereby making them more open to a proposal you have to offer. It's hard to say *no* when you're laughing. Humor also makes otherwise sober people suspend their judgment and even their prejudices, perhaps because the surprise and naughtiness of wit are combustive: they provoke laughter or smiles, not reflection. Who can resist a no-holds-barred attack on a famous personality, such as this assessment of model/actor Cara Delevingne in the 2017 sci-fi flop *Valerian*:

> As played by model Cara Delevingne with a smirk that just won't quit, Laureline is way ballsier than Valerian, who still looks in need of a mother's love. She can pose and preen like an expert in her space gear—and those eyebrows!—but there's no there there.
>
> —Peter Travers, in *Rolling Stone*

Humor deployed cleverly may be why TV shows like *South Park* and *Modern Family* became popular with mainstream audiences, despite their willingness to explore controversial themes. Similarly, it's possible to make a point through humor that might not work that well in more academic writing. The subject of standardized testing, for instance, has generated much heat and light, as researchers and teachers and policy makers argue endlessly over whether it is helpful—or not. TV talk show host and satirist John Oliver took a crack at the subject in a segment of *Last Week Tonight*, arguing that the testing business in America has gotten way out of hand and that it does not help students but rather funnels money into the coffers of companies such as Pearson, who dominate the testing market.

Frederick M. Brown/Getty Images

After introducing the subject, Oliver goes on one of his signature humorous rampages, skewering the country's obsession with testing:

> Look, standardized tests are the fastest way to terrify any child with five letters outside of just whispering the word "clown."

After showing a video clip of kids rapping about the joys of testing, Oliver continues:

> Standardized tests look like amazing fun. I wish I could take one right now: bring me a pencil please—a number 2 pencil! But it just gets better, because an elementary school in Texas even held a test-themed pep rally featuring a monkey mascot.

Fade to a monkey cavorting around the auditorium stage, swooning over testing fun and yelling "here comes the monkey." Then after a video clip showing teachers describing how many students get physically sick while taking tests ("Something is wrong with our system when we just assume that a certain number of kids will vomit"), Oliver asks,

> Is it any wonder that students are sick of tests?...If standardized tests are bad for teachers and bad for kids, who exactly are they good for? Well, it turns out, they're operated by companies like Pearson, who control forty percent of the testing market.

Pearson, Oliver says, is

> the equivalent of Time Warner Cable: either you never had an interaction with them and don't care, or they ruined your [entire] life.

Viewers may not agree with Oliver's claims about standardized testing, but his use of humor and satire certainly gets him a large viewing audience and keeps them listening to the end.

A writer or speaker can even use humor to deal with sensitive issues. For example, sports commentator Bob Costas, given the honor of eulogizing the great baseball player Mickey Mantle, couldn't ignore problems in Mantle's life. So he argues for Mantle's greatness by admitting the man's weaknesses indirectly through humor:

> It brings to mind a story Mickey liked to tell on himself and maybe some of you have heard it. He pictured himself at the pearly gates, met by St. Peter, who shook his head and said, "Mick, we checked the record. We know some of what went on. Sorry, we can't let you in. But before you go, God wants to know if you'd sign these six dozen baseballs."
>
> —Bob Costas, "Eulogy for Mickey Mantle"

Similarly, politicians may use humor to deal with issues they couldn't acknowledge in any other way. Here, for example, is former president George W. Bush at the 2004 Radio and TV Correspondents' Dinner discussing his much-mocked intellect:

> Those stories about my intellectual capacity do get under my skin. You know, for a while I even thought my staff believed it. There on my schedule first thing every morning it said, "Intelligence briefing."
>
> —George W. Bush

Not all humor is well-intentioned or barb-free. In fact, among the most powerful forms of emotional argument is ridicule—humor aimed at a particular target. Eighteenth-century poet and critic Samuel Johnson was known for his stinging and humorous put-downs, such as this comment to an aspiring writer: "Your manuscript is both good and original, but the part that is good is not original and the part that is original is not good." (Expect your own writing teachers to be kinder.) In our own time, the *Onion* has earned a reputation for its mastery of both ridicule and satire, the art of using over-the-top humor to make a serious point.

But because ridicule is a double-edged sword, it requires a deft hand to wield it. Humor that reflects bad taste discredits a writer completely, as does satire that misses its mark. Unless your target deserves riposte and you can be very funny, it's usually better to steer clear of such humor.

Using Arguments Based on Emotion

You don't want to play puppet master with people's emotions when you write arguments, but it's a good idea to spend some time early in your work thinking about how you want readers to feel as they consider your persuasive claims. For example, would readers of your editorial about campus traffic policies be more inclined to agree with you if you made them envy faculty privileges, or would arousing their sense of fairness work better? What emotional appeals might persuade meat eaters to consider a vegan diet—or vice versa? Would sketches of stage props on a Web site persuade people to buy a season ticket to the theater, or would you spark more interest by featuring pictures of costumed performers?

Consider, too, the effect that a story can have on readers. Writers and journalists routinely use what are called *human-interest stories* to give presence to issues or arguments. You can do the same, using a particular incident to evoke sympathy, understanding, outrage, or amusement. Take care, though, to tell an honest story.

RESPOND

1. To what specific emotions do the following slogans, sales pitches, and maxims appeal?

   "Make America Great Again" (Donald Trump rallying cry)

   "Just do it." (ad for Nike)

   "Think different." (ad for Apple computers)

   "Reach out and touch someone." (ad for AT&T)

   "There are some things money can't buy. For everything else, there's MasterCard." (slogan for MasterCard)

   "Have it your way." (slogan for Burger King)

   "The ultimate driving machine." (slogan for BMW)

   "It's everywhere you want to be." (slogan for Visa)

   "Don't mess with Texas!" (anti-litter campaign slogan)

   "American by Birth. Rebel by Choice." (slogan for Harley-Davidson)

2. Bring a magazine to class, and analyze the emotional appeals in as many full-page ads as you can. Then practice your critical reading skills by classifying those ads by types of emotional appeal, and see whether you can connect the appeals to the subject or target audience of the magazine. Compare your results with those of your classmates, and discuss your findings. For instance, how exactly are the ads in publications such as *Cosmopolitan*, *Wired*, *Sports Illustrated*, *Motor Trend*, and *Smithsonian* adapted to their specific audiences?

3. How do arguments based on emotion work in different media? Are such arguments more or less effective in books, articles, television (both news and entertainment shows), films, brochures, magazines, email, Web sites, the theater, street protests, and so on? You might explore how a single medium handles emotional appeals or compare different media. For example, why do the comments sections of blogs seem to encourage angry outbursts? Are newspapers an emotionally colder source of information than television news programs? If so, why?
4. Spend some time looking for arguments that use ridicule or humor to make their point: check out your favorite Twitter feeds or blogs; watch for bumper stickers, posters, or advertisements; and listen to popular song lyrics. Bring one or two examples to class, and be ready to explain how the humor makes an emotional appeal and whether it's effective.

CHAPTER

26

Composing Arguments Based on Character: Ethos

Whenever you read anything—whether it's a news article, an advertisement, a speech, or a tweet—you no doubt subconsciously analyze the message for a sense of the character and credibility of the sender: *Is this someone I know and trust? Does the Fox News reporter—or the Doctors Without Borders Web site—seem biased, and if so, how? Why should I believe an advertisement for a car? Is this scholar really an authority on the subject?* Our culture teaches us to be skeptical of most messages, especially those that bombard us with slogans, and such reasonable doubt is a crucial skill in reading and evaluating arguments.

For that reason, people and institutions that hope to influence us do everything they can to establish their character and credibility, what ancient rhetors referred to as *ethos.* And sometimes slogans such as "All the News That's Fit to Print," "The Most Trusted Name in News," or "Lean In" can be effective. At the very least, if a phrase is repeated often enough, it begins to sound plausible. Maybe Fox News really IS the most watched and most trusted news source!

But establishing character usually takes more than repetition, as marketers of all kinds know. It arises from credentials actually earned in some way. In the auto industry, for instance, Subaru builds on its customer loyalty by telling buyers that love makes a Subaru, and companies such as Toyota, General Motors, and Nissan are hustling to present themselves as environmentally responsible producers of fuel-efficient, low-emission cars—the Prius, Bolt, and Leaf. BMW, maker of "the ultimate driving machine," points to its fuel-sipping i3 and i8 cars as evidence of its commitment to "sustainable mobility." And Elon Musk (who builds rockets as well as Tesla cars) polishes his good-citizenship bona fides by releasing an affordable mass market electric car and by sharing his electric vehicle patents with other manufacturers. All of these companies realize that their future success is linked to an ability to project a convincing ethos for themselves and their products.

If corporations and institutions can establish an ethos, consider how much character matters when we think about people in the public arena. Perhaps no individual managed a more exceptional assertion of personal ethos than Jorge Mario Bergoglio did after he became Pope Francis on March 13, 2013, following the abdication of Benedict XVI—a man many found scholarly, cold, and out of touch with the modern world. James Carroll, writing for the *New Yorker*, identifies the precise moment when the world realized that it was dealing with a new sort of pope:

> "Who am I to judge?" With those five words, spoken in late July [2013] in reply to a reporter's question about the status of gay priests in the Church, Pope Francis stepped away from the disapproving tone, the explicit moralizing typical of popes and bishops.
>
> —James Carroll, "Who Am I to Judge?"

Carroll goes on to explain that Francis quickly established his ethos with a series of specific actions, decisions, and moments of identification with ordinary people, marking him as someone even nonbelievers might listen to and respect:

> As pope, Francis has simplified the Renaissance regalia of the papacy by abandoning fur-trimmed velvet capes, choosing to live in a two-room apartment instead of the Apostolic Palace, and replacing the papal Mercedes with a Ford Focus. Instead of the traditional red slip-ons, Francis wears ordinary black shoes.... Yet Francis didn't criticize the choices of other prelates. "He makes changes without attacking people," a Jesuit official told me. In his interview with *La Civiltà Cattolica*, Francis said, "My choices, including those related to the day-to-day aspects of life, like the use of a modest car, are related to a spiritual discernment that responds to a need that arises from looking at things, at people, and from reading the signs of the times."

In that last sentence, Francis acknowledges that ethos is gained, in part, through identification with one's audience and era. And this man, movingly photographed embracing the sick and disfigured, also posed for selfies!

Osservatore Romano/ZUMA Press/Vatican City/Holy See/Newscom

You can see, then, why Aristotle treats ethos as a powerful argumentative appeal. Ethos creates quick and sometimes almost irresistible connections between readers and arguments. We observe people, groups, or institutions making and defending claims all the time and inevitably ask ourselves, *Should we pay attention to them? Can we rely on them? Do we dare to trust them?* Consider, though, that the same questions will be asked about you and your work, especially in academic settings.

Thinking Critically about Arguments Based on Character

Put simply, arguments based on character (ethos) depend on *trust*. We tend to accept arguments from those we trust, and we trust them (whether individuals, groups, or institutions) in good part because of their reputations. Three main elements—credibility, authority, and unselfish or clear motives—add up to *ethos.*

To answer serious and important questions, we often turn to professionals (doctors, lawyers, engineers, teachers, pastors) or to experts (those with knowledge and experience) for good advice. Based on their backgrounds, such people come with their ethos already established. Thus, appeals or arguments about character often turn on claims like these:

- A person (or group or institution) is or is not trustworthy or credible on this issue.
- A person (or group or institution) does or does not have the authority to speak to this issue.
- A person (or group or institution) does or does not have unselfish or clear motives for addressing this subject.

Establishing Trustworthiness and Credibility

Trustworthiness and credibility speak to a writer's honesty, respect for an audience and its values, and plain old likability. Sometimes a sense of humor can play an important role in getting an audience to listen to or "like" you. It's no accident that all but the most serious speeches begin with a joke or funny story: the humor puts listeners at ease and helps them identify with the speaker. Writer J. K. Rowling, for example, puts her audience (and herself) at ease early in the commencement address she delivered at Harvard by getting real about such speeches, recalling her own commencement:

> The speaker that day was the distinguished British philosopher Baroness Mary Warnock. Reflecting on her speech has helped me enormously in writing this one, because it turns out that I can't remember a single word she said.
>
> —J. K. Rowling, "The Fringe Benefits of Failure, and the Importance of Imagination"

In just two sentences, Rowling pokes fun at herself and undercuts the expectation that graduation addresses change people's lives. For an audience well disposed toward her already, Rowling has likely lived up to expectations.

But using humor to enhance your credibility may be more common in oratory than in the kind of writing you'll do in school. Fortunately, you have many options, one being simply to make plausible claims and then back them up with evidence. Academic audiences appreciate a reasonable disposition; we will discuss this approach at greater length in the next chapter.

You can also establish trustworthiness by connecting your own beliefs to core principles that are well established and widely respected. This strategy is particularly effective when your position seems to be—at first glance, at least—a threat to traditional values. For example, when former Smith College president Ruth J. Simmons describes her professional self to a commencement audience, she presents her acquired reputation in terms that align perfectly with contemporary values:

> For my part, I was cast as a troublemaker in my early career and accepted the disapproval that accompanies the expression of unpopular views: unpopular views about disparate pay for women and minorities; unpopular views about sexual harassment; unpopular views about exclusionary practices in our universities.
>
> —Ruth J. Simmons

It's fine to be a rebel when you are on the right side of history.

Writers who establish their credibility seem trustworthy. But sometimes, to be credible, you have to admit limitations, too, as *New York Times* columnist Frank Bruni does as he positions himself in relation to issues of oppression and deep-seated bias in an editorial titled "I'm a White Man: Hear Me Out." First acknowledging his racial and socioeconomic privilege as a white man from an upper-class background (private school, backyard swimming pool), Bruni then addresses another, less-privileged facet of his identity:

> But wait. I'm gay....Gay from a different, darker day,...when gay stereotypes went unchallenged, gay jokes drew hearty laughter and exponentially more Americans were closeted than out....Then AIDS spread, and...our rallying cry, "silence = death," defined marginalization as well as any words could.
>
> —Frank Bruni, "I'm a White Man: Hear Me Out"

Making such concessions to readers sends a strong signal that you've looked critically at your own position and can therefore be trusted when you turn to arguing its merits. Speaking to readers directly, using *I* or *you* or *us*, can also help you connect with them, as can using contractions and everyday or colloquial language—both strategies employed by Bruni. In other situations, you may find that a more formal tone gives your claims greater credibility. You'll be making such choices as you search for the ethos that represents you best.

In fact, whenever you write an essay or present an idea, you are sending signals about your credibility, whether you intend to or not. If your ideas are reasonable, your sources are reliable, and your language is appropriate to the project, you suggest to academic readers that you're someone whose ideas *might* deserve attention. Details matter: helpful graphs, tables, charts, or illustrations may carry weight with readers, as will the visual attractiveness of your text, whether in print or digital form. Obviously, correct spelling, grammar, and mechanics are important too. And though you might not worry about it now, at some point you may need letters of recommendation from instructors or supervisors. How will they remember you? Often chiefly from the ethos you have established in your work. Think about that.

Claiming Authority

When you read or listen to an argument, you have every right to ask about the writer's authority: *What does he know about the subject? What experiences does she have that make her especially knowledgeable? Why should I pay attention to this person?* When you offer an argument yourself, you have to anticipate and be prepared to answer questions like these, either directly or indirectly.

How does someone construct an authoritative ethos? In an essay about John McCain's decision to vote against a Senate bill to repeal the Affordable Care Act, AP reporter Laurie Kellman notes some of McCain's experiences that help build his credibility:

> Longtime colleagues...say [McCain] developed his fearlessness as a navy aviator held as a prisoner for more than five years in Vietnam. Resilience, they say, has fueled his long Senate career and helped him overcome two failed presidential campaigns. For some, McCain has become the moral voice of the Republican Party.
>
> —Laurie Kellman, "Cancer Isn't Silencing McCain"

Here Kellman stresses McCain's length of service in the Senate as well as his military service and prisoner of war status, and she refers to him as a "standard bearer" and "moral voice" of the Republican Party. In doing so, she indicates that McCain's ethos is hard won and to be taken seriously.

Justin Sullivan/Getty Images

FIGURE 26.1 Senator John McCain

Of course, writers establish their authority in various ways. Sometimes the assertion of ethos will be bold and personal, as it is when writer and activist Terry Tempest Williams attacks those who poisoned the Utah deserts with nuclear radiation. What gives her the right to speak on this subject? Not scientific expertise, but gut-wrenching personal experience:

> I belong to the Clan of One-Breasted Women. My mother, my grandmothers, and six aunts have all had mastectomies. Seven are dead. The two who survive have just completed rounds of chemotherapy and radiation.
>
> I've had my own problems: two biopsies for breast cancer and a small tumor between my ribs diagnosed as a "borderline malignancy."
>
> —Terry Tempest Williams, "The Clan of One-Breasted Women"

We are willing to listen to Williams because she has lived with the nuclear peril she will deal with in the remainder of her essay.

Other means of claiming authority are less dramatic. By simply attaching titles to their names, writers assert that they hold medical or legal or engineering degrees, or some other important credentials. Or they may mention the number of years they've worked in a given field or the distinguished positions they have held. As a reader, you'll pay more attention to an argument about sustainability offered by a professor of ecology and agriculture at the University of Minnesota than one by your Uncle Sid, who sells tools. But you'll prefer your uncle to the professor when you need advice about a reliable rotary saw.

In our current political climate, the ethos of experts—such as scientists or other academics with deep knowledge about a subject—is being questioned. Matt Grossmann and David A. Hopkins, professors of public policy and political science, identify this trend particularly at the right end of the political spectrum:

> Data from the General Social Survey demonstrate that declining public faith in science is concentrated among conservatives. Compared to Democrats, Republicans are significantly less likely to trust what scientists say, more critical of political bias in academe and less confident in colleges and universities. Negative attitudes toward science and the media also intersect, with one-third of Republicans reporting no trust in journalists to accurately report scientific studies.
>
> —Matt Grossmann and David A. Hopkins, "How Information Became Ideological"

Like the attacks on "fake news," here Grossmann and Hopkins identify an assault on the ethos of scientists and other academic experts.

When readers might be skeptical of both you and your claims, you may have to be even more specific about your credentials. That's exactly the strategy Richard Bernstein uses to establish his right to speak on the subject of "Asian culture." What gives a New York writer named Bernstein the authority to write about Asian peoples? Bernstein tells us in a sparkling example of an argument based on character:

> The Asian culture, as it happens, is something I know a bit about, having spent five years at Harvard striving for a Ph.D. in a joint program called History and East Asian Languages and, after that, living either as a student (for one year) or a journalist (six years) in China and Southeast Asia. At least I know enough to know there is no such thing as the "Asian culture."
>
> —Richard Bernstein, *Dictatorship of Virtue*

When you write for readers who trust you and your work, you may not have to make such an open claim to authority. But making this type of appeal is always an option.

Coming Clean about Motives

When people are trying to convince you of something, it's important (and natural) to ask: *Whose interests are they serving? How will they profit from their proposal?* Such questions go to the heart of ethical arguments.

In a hugely controversial 2014 essay published in the *Princeton Tory*, Tal Fortgang, a first-year student at the Ivy League school, argues that those on campus who used the phrase "Check your privilege" to berate white male students like him for the advantages they enjoy are, in fact, judging him according to gender and race, and not for "all the hard work I have done in my life." To challenge stereotypical assumptions about the "racist patriarchy" that supposedly paved his way to Princeton, Fortgang writes about the experiences of his ancestors, opening the paragraphs with a striking parallel structure:

> Perhaps it's the privilege my grandfather and his brother had to flee their home as teenagers when the Nazis invaded Poland, leaving their mother and five younger siblings behind, running and running....
>
> Or maybe it's the privilege my grandmother had of spending weeks upon weeks on a death march through Polish forests in subzero temperatures, one of just a handful to survive....
>
> Perhaps my privilege is that those two resilient individuals came to America with no money and no English, obtained citizenship, learned the language and met each other....

> Perhaps it was my privilege that my own father worked hard enough in City College to earn a spot at a top graduate school, got a good job, and for 25 years got up well before the crack of dawn, sacrificing precious time he wanted to spend with those he valued most—his wife and kids—to earn that living.
>
> —Tal Fortgang, "Checking My Privilege: Character as the Basis of Privilege"

Fortgang thus attempts to establish his own ethos and win the argument against those who make assumptions about his roots by dramatizing the ethos of his ancestors:

> That's the problem with calling someone out for the "privilege" which you assume has defined their narrative. You don't know what their struggles have been, what they may have gone through to be where they are. Assuming they've benefitted from "power systems" or other conspiratorial imaginary institutions denies them credit for all they've done, things of which you may not even conceive. You don't know whose father died defending your freedom. You don't know whose mother escaped oppression. You don't know who conquered their demons, or may still [be] conquering them now.

As you might imagine, the pushback to "Checking My Privilege" was enormous, some of the hundreds of comments posted to an online version accusing Fortgang himself of assuming the very ethos of victimhood against which he inveighs. Peter Finocchiaro, a reviewer on *Slate*, is especially brutal: "Only a few short months ago he was living at home with his parents. His life experience, one presumes, is fairly limited. So in that sense, he doesn't really know any better. . . . He is an ignorant 19-year-old white guy from Westchester." You can see in this debate how ethos quickly raises issues of knowledge and motives. Fortgang tries to resist the stereotype others would impose on his character, but others regard the very ethos he fashions in his essay as evidence of his naïveté about race, discrimination, and, yes, privilege.

We all, of course, have connections and interests that bind us to other human beings. It makes sense that a young man would explore his social identity, that a woman might be concerned with women's issues, that members of minority groups might define social and cultural conditions on their own terms—or even that investors might look out for their investments. It's simply good strategy, not to mention ethical, to let your audiences know where your loyalties lie when such information does, in fact, shape your work.

Using Ethos in Your Own Writing

- Establish your credibility by listening carefully to and acknowledging your audience's values, showing respect for them, and establishing common ground where (and if) possible. How will you convince your audience you are trustworthy? What will you admit about your own limitations?
- Establish your authority by showing you have done your homework and know your topic well. How will you show that you know your topic well? What appropriate personal experience can you draw on?
- Examine your motives for writing. What, if anything, do you stand to gain from your argument? How can you explain those advantages to your audience?

CULTURAL CONTEXTS FOR ARGUMENT

Ethos

In the United States, students are often asked to establish authority by drawing on personal experiences, by reporting on research they or others have conducted, and by taking a position for which they can offer strong evidence. But this expectation about student authority is by no means universal.

Some cultures regard student writers as novices who can most effectively make arguments by reflecting on what they've learned from their teachers and elders—those who hold the most important knowledge and, hence, authority. When you're arguing a point with people from cultures other than your own, ask questions like:

- Whom are you addressing, and what is your relationship with that person?
- What knowledge are you expected to have? Is it appropriate or expected for you to demonstrate that knowledge—and if so, how?
- What tone is appropriate? And remember: politeness is rarely, if ever, inappropriate.

RESPOND

1. Consider the ethos of these public figures. Then describe one or two products that might benefit from their endorsements as well as several that would not.

    Edward Snowden—whistleblower

    Beyoncé—singer, dancer, actress

    Denzel Washington—actor

    Tom Brady—football player

    Rachel Maddow—TV news commentator

    Ariana Grande—singer

    Seth Meyers—late-night TV host

    Lin-Manuel Miranda—hip hop artist and playwright

    Venus Williams—tennis player

2. Opponents of Richard Nixon, the thirty-seventh president of the United States, once raised doubts about his integrity by asking a single ruinous question: *Would you buy a used car from this man?* Create your own version of the argument of character. Begin by choosing an intriguing or controversial person or group and finding an image online. Then download the image into a word-processing file. Create a caption for the photo that is modeled after the question asked about Nixon: *Would you give this woman your email password? Would you share a campsite with this couple? Would you eat lasagna that this guy fixed?* Finally, write a serious 300-word argument that explores the character flaws or strengths of your subject(s).
3. Practice reading rhetorically and critically by taking a close look at your own Facebook page (or your page on any other social media site). What are some aspects of your character, true or not, that might be conveyed by the photos, videos, and messages you have posted online? Analyze the ethos or character you see projected there, using the advice in this chapter to guide your analysis.

CHAPTER

27

Composing Arguments Based on Facts and Reason: Logos

3
+ 2
12
Schwadron
"IN A POST-FACT WORLD, ANYTHING GOES."

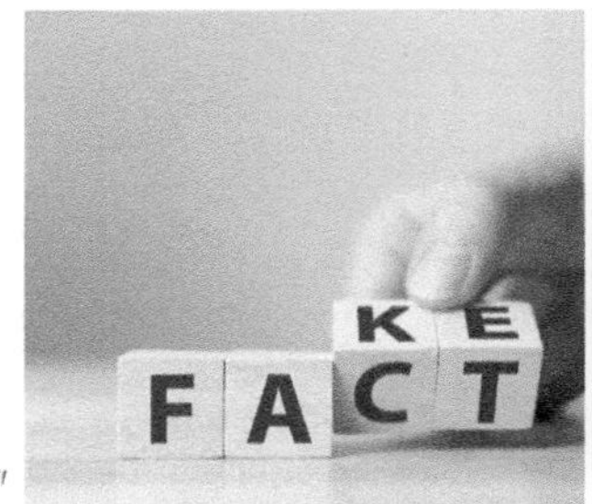

Left to right: Harley Schwadron/CartoonStock.com; Monster Ztudio/Shutterstock; Charles Krupa/AP Images

In 2018, it feels like facts are under siege, as these three images suggest. Cartoonists are having a field day with a "post-fact" world, while serious scientists are hard at work trying to understand "why facts don't change our minds." From Kellyanne Conway's evocation of "alternative facts" to Donald Trump's tendency to label reports that do not support his views as "fake news," we are witnessing a world in which the statement by *Through the Looking-Glass*'s White Queen that "sometimes I've believed as many as six impossible things before breakfast" seems, well, unremarkable. After the 2016 election, for example, President Trump declared that there was "serious voter fraud" in Virginia, in New Hampshire, in California, and elsewhere, although researchers could find no evidence to back up his claim, and fact-checkers across the board found the "fact" to be baseless. In June 2017, three CNN employees resigned after the network retracted a story that claimed Congress was investigating a "Russian investment fund with ties to Trump officials"; the journalists had used only one unreliable source to back up this supposedly factual claim. We could go on and on with such examples from across the political spectrum, and no doubt you could add your own to the list.

In "Why Facts Don't Change Our Minds," Elizabeth Kolbert surveys cognitive science research that's trying to understand why this is so, pointing to a series of experiments at Stanford University that found that "Even after the evidence for their beliefs had been totally refuted, people fail to make appropriate revisions to those beliefs":

> Thousands of subsequent experiments have confirmed (and elaborated on) this finding. As everyone who's followed the research—or even occasionally picked up a copy of *Psychology Today*—knows, any graduate student with a clipboard can demonstrate that reasonable-seeming people are often totally irrational. Rarely has this insight seemed more relevant than it does now.

Scientists working on this issue point to the "confirmation" or "myside" bias, the strong tendency to accept information that supports our beliefs and values and to reject information that opposes them, as well as to our tendency to think we know a whole lot more than we actually do. A study at Yale asked graduate students to rate their knowledge of everyday items, including toilets, and to write up an explanation of how such devices worked. While the graduate students rated their knowledge/understanding as high before they wrote up the explanations, that exercise showed them that they didn't really know how toilets worked, and their self-assessment dropped significantly. The researchers, Steven Sloman and Philip Fernbach, call this effect the "illusion of explanatory depth" and find that it is very widespread. "Where it gets us into trouble," they say, is in "the political domain." As Kolbert writes, "It's one thing for me to flush a toilet without knowing how it operates, and another for me to favor (or oppose) an immigration ban without knowing what I'm talking about." Sloman and Fernbach explain: "As a rule, strong feelings about issues do not emerge from deep understanding.... This is how a community of knowledge can become dangerous."

Such findings are important to all of us, and they suggest several steps all writers, readers, and speakers should take as they deal with arguments based on facts and reason. First, examine your own beliefs in particular facts and pieces of information: do you really know what you're talking about or are you simply echoing what others you know say or think? Second, you need to become a conscientious fact-checker, digging deep to make sure claims are backed by evidence. Doing so is especially important with information you get from social media, where misinformation, disinformation, and even outright lies may be presented as "facts" that you might retweet or post, thus perpetuating false or questionable information.

Finally, don't give up on facts. The researchers discussed above also show that, when given a choice, most people still say they respect and even prefer appeals to claims based on facts, evidence, and reason. Just make sure that the logical appeals you are using are factually correct and ethical as well.

Thinking Critically about Hard Evidence

Aristotle helps us out in classifying arguments by distinguishing two kinds:

Artistic Proofs	Arguments the writer/speaker creates	Constructed arguments	Appeals to reason; common sense
Inartistic Proofs	Arguments the writer/speaker is given	Hard evidence	Facts, statistics, testimonies, witnesses, contracts, documents

We can see these different kinds of logical appeals at work in a passage from a statement made on September 5, 2017, by Attorney General Jeff Sessions:

> Good morning. I am here today to announce that the program known as DACA that was effectuated under the Obama Administration is being rescinded. The DACA program was implemented in 2012 and essentially provided a legal status for recipients for a renewable two-year term, work authorization and other benefits, including participation in the social security program, to 800,000 mostly-adult illegal aliens. This policy was implemented unilaterally to great controversy and legal concern after Congress rejected legislative proposals to extend similar benefits on numerous occasions to this same group of illegal aliens.
>
> In other words, the executive branch, through DACA, deliberately sought to achieve what the legislative branch specifically refused to authorize on multiple occasions. Such an open-ended circumvention of immigration laws was an unconstitutional exercise of authority by the Executive Branch. The effect of this unilateral executive amnesty, among other things, contributed to a surge of unaccompanied minors on the southern border that yielded terrible humanitarian consequences. It also denied jobs to hundreds of thousands of Americans by allowing those same jobs to go to illegal aliens.

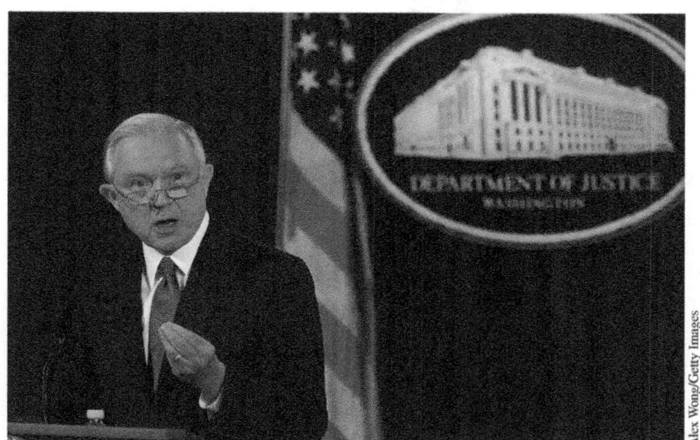

FIGURE 27.1 Jeff Sessions announcing that DACA would be rescinded by the Trump administration

Sessions opens his statement with a simple "good morning" and a direct announcement of his purpose: to rescind the Deferred Action for Childhood Arrivals (DACA) program initiated by the Obama administration in 2012. In the next sentence, he uses "inartistic" evidence of what DACA provided (it was renewable and provided work authorization and other benefits) for "800,000 mostly-adult illegal aliens." Noting that Congress had refused on several occasions to extend benefits to the "same group of illegal aliens," Sessions offers the constructed argument that Obama's "open-ended circumvention of immigration laws was an unconstitutional exercise of authority." Presumably now drawing on hard evidence, Sessions argues that DACA led to "a surge of unaccompanied minors," that it denied jobs to "hundreds of thousands" of Americans, and, by neglecting the "rule of law," it subjected the United States to "the risk of crime, violence, and even terrorism."

Sessions says early on in his statement that DACA was implemented amidst "great controversy," and indeed that fact checks out. Other claims made in the statement, however, were quickly challenged. The nonpartisan FactCheck.org, for example, calls out Sessions's description of DACA recipients as "mostly-adult illegal aliens" (a label he uses several times), citing research by Professor Tom Wong of the University of California, San Diego, whose national survey of 3,063 DACA holders in summer 2017 found that "on average they were six and a half years old when they arrived in the U.S. Most of them—54 percent—were under the age of 7." So while they are adults today, they were *not* adults when they were brought to the United States. Likewise, FactCheck.org points out that Sessions's claim that DACA contributed to a "surge of unaccompanied minors" is, at best, misleading and out of context:

> It is true that there was a surge of unaccompanied children that caught the Obama administration off guard in fiscal 2012. The number of unaccompanied minors crossing the border peaked in fiscal 2014 at 68,541, dropping 42 percent to 39,970 in fiscal 2015 before rising again in fiscal year 2016 to 59,692.
>
> But the children who crossed the border illegally were not eligible for DACA. As we said earlier, the criteria for DACA is continuous residence in the United States since June 15, 2007.

If you were reading or listening to this statement and wanted to do some fact-checking of your own, you might well begin by determining whether DACA really led to the loss of hundreds of thousands of jobs. In today's political climate, in fact, it's important that every one of us read with a critical eye, refusing to accept claims without proof, constructed arguments, or even "hard evidence" that we can't fact-check for ourselves.

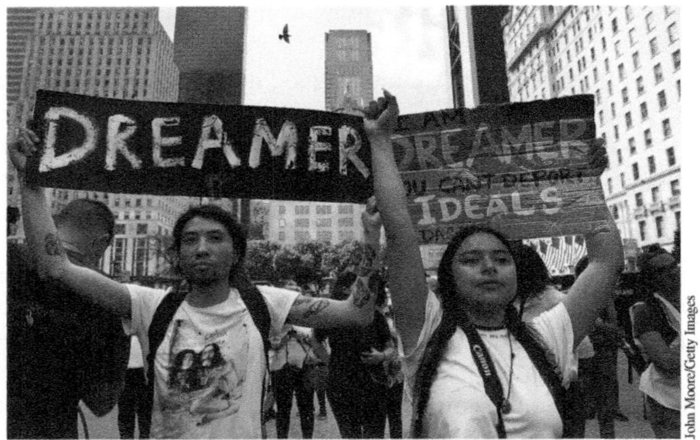

FIGURE 27.2 Two DACA "Dreamers" protesting near Trump Tower in New York the day after Sessions's statement rescinding the program

RESPOND

Discuss whether the following statements are examples of hard evidence or constructed arguments. Not all cases are clear-cut.

1. Drunk drivers are involved in more than 50 percent of traffic deaths.
2. DNA tests of skin found under the victim's fingernails suggest that the defendant was responsible for the assault.
3. A psychologist testified that teenage violence could not be blamed on video games.
4. The crowds at President Trump's inauguration were the largest on record.
5. "The only thing we have to fear is fear itself."
6. Air bags ought to be removed from vehicles because they can kill young children and small-framed adults.

Facts

Gathering factual information and transmitting it faithfully practically define what we mean by professional journalism and scholarship. Carole Cadwalladr, a reviewer for the British newspaper the *Guardian*, praises the research underlying *It's Complicated: The Networked Lives of Teens*. Drawing on almost a decade of research by assistant professor danah boyd of New York University,

> the book is grounded in hard academic research: proper interviews conducted with actual teenagers. What comes across most strongly, more so than the various "myths" and "panics" that the author describes, is just how narrow and circumscribed many of these teenagers' lives have become.

Here the "hard academic research" the reviewer mentions is the ethnographic research that yields an accurate description of these young people's lives.

When your facts are compelling, they might stand on their own in a low-stakes argument, supported by little more than saying where they come from. Consider the power of phrases such as "reported by the *Wall Street Journal*" or "according to FactCheck.org." Such sources gain credibility if they have reported facts accurately and reliably over time. Using such credible sources in an argument can also reflect positively on you.

In scholarly arguments, which have higher expectations for accuracy, what counts is drawing sober conclusions from the evidence turned up through detailed research or empirical studies. The language of such material may seem dryly factual to you, even when the content is inherently interesting. But presenting new knowledge dispassionately is (ideally at least) the whole point of scholarly writing, marking a contrast between it and the kind of intellectual warfare that occurs in many media forums, especially news programs and blogs. Here for example is a portion of a lengthy opening paragraph in the "Discussion and Conclusions" section of a scholarly paper arguing that people who spend a great deal of time on Facebook often frame their lives by what they observe there:

> As expected in the first hypothesis, the results show that the longer people have used Facebook, the stronger was their belief that others were happier than themselves, and the less they agreed that life is fair. Furthermore, as predicted in the second hypothesis, this research found that the more "friends" people included on their Facebook whom they did not know personally, the stronger they believed that others had better lives than themselves. In other words, looking at happy pictures of others on Facebook gives people an impression that others are "always" happy and having good lives, as evident from these pictures of happy moments.
>
> —Hui-Tzu Grace Chou, PhD, and Nicholas Edge, BS,
> "'They Are Happier and Having Better Lives Than I Am':
> The Impact of Using Facebook on Perceptions of Others' Lives"

There are no fireworks in this conclusion, no slanted or hot language, no unfair or selective reporting of data, just a careful attention to the facts and behaviors uncovered by the study. But one can easily imagine these facts being subsequently used to support overdramatized claims about the dangers of social networks. That's often what happens to scholarly studies when they are read and interpreted in the popular media.

Of course, arguing with facts can involve challenging even the most reputable sources if they lead to unfair or selective reporting or if the stories are presented or "framed" unfairly.

In an ideal world, good information—no matter where it comes from—would always drive out bad. But you already know that we don't live in an ideal world, so all too often bad information gets repeated in an echo chamber that amplifies the errors.

Statistics

You've probably heard the old saying "There are three kinds of lies: lies, damned lies, and statistics," and it is certainly possible to lie with numbers, even those that are accurate, because numbers rarely speak for themselves. They need to be interpreted by writers—and writers almost always have agendas that shape the interpretations.

Of course, just because they are often misused doesn't mean that statistics are meaningless, but it does suggest that you need to use them carefully and to remember that your careful reading of numbers is essential. Consider the attention-grabbing map below that went viral in June 2014. Created by Mark Gongloff of the *Huffington Post* in the wake of a school shooting in Oregon, it plotted the location of all seventy-four school shootings that had occurred in the United States since the Sandy Hook tragedy in December 2012, when twenty elementary school children and six adults were gunned down by a rifle-wielding killer. For the graphic, Gongloff drew on a list assembled by the group Everytown for Gun Safety, an organization formed by former New York City mayor and billionaire Michael Bloomberg to counter the influence of the National Rifle Association (NRA). Both the map and Everytown's sobering list of shootings received wide attention in the media, given the startling number of incidents it recorded.

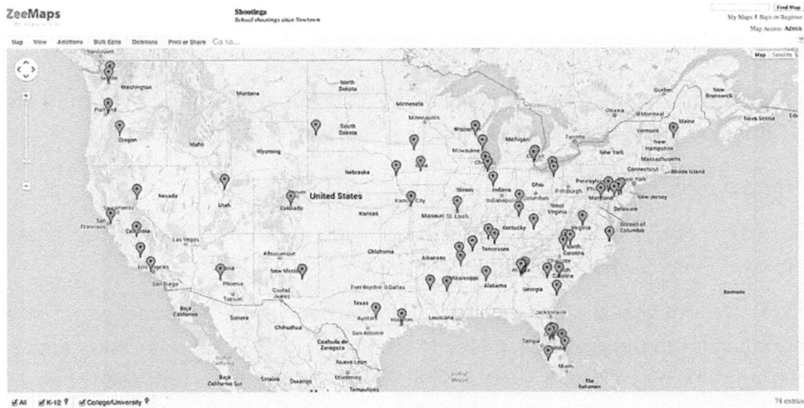

It didn't take long before questions were raised about their accuracy. Were American elementary and secondary school children under such frequent assault as the map based on Everytown's list suggested? Well, yes and no. Guns were going off on and around school campuses, but the firearms weren't always aimed at children. The *Washington Post*, CNN, and other news outlets soon found themselves pulling back on their initial reporting, offering a more nuanced view of the controversial number. To do that, the *Washington Post* began by posing an important question:

> What constitutes a school shooting?
>
> That five-word question has no simple answer, a fact underscored by the backlash to an advocacy group's recent list of school shootings. The list, maintained by Everytown, a group that backs policies to limit gun violence, was updated last week to reflect what it identified as the 74 school shootings since the massacre in Newtown, Conn., a massacre that sparked a national debate over gun control.
>
> Multiple news outlets, including this one, reported on Everytown's data, prompting a backlash over the broad methodology used. As we wrote in our original post, the group considered any instance of a firearm discharging on school property as a shooting—thus casting a broad net that includes homicides, suicides, accidental discharges and, in a handful of cases, shootings that had no relation to the schools themselves and occurred with no students apparently present.
>
> —Niraj Chokshi, "Fight over School Shooting List Underscores Difficulty in Quantifying Gun Violence"

CNN followed the same path, re-evaluating its original reporting in light of criticism from groups not on the same page as Everytown for Gun Safety:

> Without a doubt, that number is startling.
>
> So...CNN took a closer look at the list, delving into the circumstances of each incident Everytown included....
>
> CNN determined that 15 of the incidents Everytown included were situations similar to the violence in Newtown or Oregon—a minor or adult actively shooting inside or near a school. That works out to about one such shooting every five weeks, a startling figure in its own right.
>
> Some of the other incidents on Everytown's list included personal arguments, accidents and alleged gang activities and drug deals.
>
> —Ashley Fantz, Lindsey Knight, and Kevin Wang, "A Closer Look: How Many Newtown-like School Shootings since Sandy Hook?"

Other news organizations came up with their own revised numbers, but clearly the interpretation of a number can be as important as the statistic itself. And what were Mark Gongloff's Twitter reactions to these reassessments? They made an argument as well:

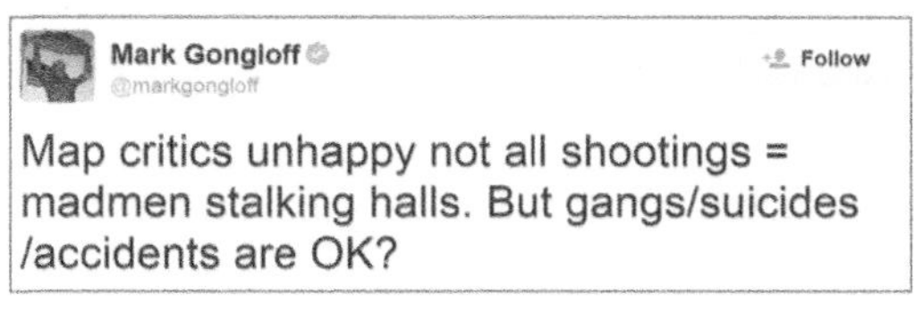
Mark Gongloff @markgongloff Follow

Map critics unhappy not all shootings = madmen stalking halls. But gangs/suicides /accidents are OK?

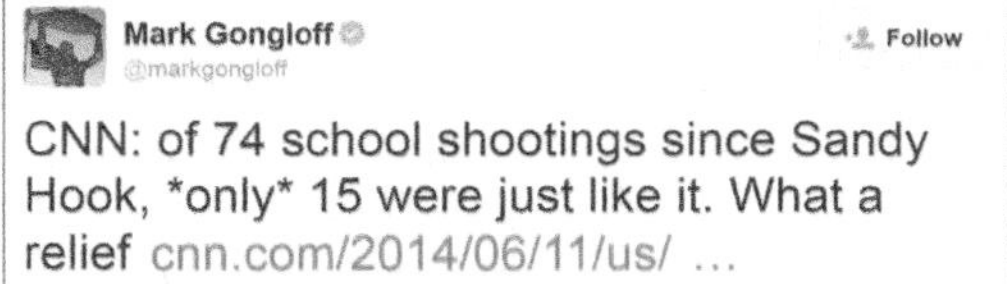
Mark Gongloff @markgongloff Follow

CNN: of 74 school shootings since Sandy Hook, *only* 15 were just like it. What a relief cnn.com/2014/06/11/us/ ...

Arguments over gun violence in schools reached a new peak in 2018 after seventeen students and staff members were killed at Marjory Stoneman Douglas High School in Florida, leading to a nationwide student walkout on March 14 and massive protests at eight hundred sites around the world on March 24 (including over half a million in Washington, D.C., alone), all organized and led by students. Articulate and media savvy, the student leaders knew to rely on "hard evidence" and solid, fact-checked statistics, and they conducted the research necessary to do so. Students across the United States learned a lesson well: when you rely on statistics in your arguments, make sure you understand where they come from, what they mean, and what their limitations might be. Check and double-check them or get help in doing so: you don't want to be accused of using fictitious data based on questionable assumptions.

RESPOND

Statistical evidence becomes useful only when interpreted fairly and reasonably. Go to the *Business Insider* Australia Web site and look for one or more charts of the day (www.businessinsider.com/au/category/chart-of-the-day). Choose one, and use the information in it to support three different claims, at least two of which make very different points. Share your claims with classmates. (The point is not to learn to use data dishonestly but to see firsthand how the same statistics can serve a variety of arguments.)

Surveys and Polls

When they verify the popularity of an idea or a proposal, surveys and polls provide strong persuasive appeals because they come as close to expressing the will of the people as anything short of an election—the most decisive poll of all. However, surveys and polls can do much more than help politicians make decisions. They can be important elements in scientific research, documenting the complexities of human behavior. They can also provide persuasive reasons for action or intervention. When surveys show, for example, that most American sixth-graders can't locate France or Wyoming on a map—not to mention Ukraine or Afghanistan—that's an appeal for better instruction in geography. It always makes sense, however, to question poll numbers, especially when they support our own point of view. Ask who commissioned the poll, who is publishing its outcome, who was surveyed (and in what proportions), and what stakes these parties might have in its outcome.

Are we being too suspicious? Not at all, and especially not today. In fact, this sort of scrutiny is exactly what you might anticipate from your readers whenever you use (or create) surveys to explore an issue. You should be confident that enough subjects have been surveyed to be accurate, that the people chosen for the study were representative of the selected population as a whole, and that they were chosen randomly—not selected because of what they were likely to say. In a splendid article on how women can make research-based choices during pregnancy, economist Emily Oster explores, for example, whether an expectant mother might in fact be able to drink responsibly. She researches not only the results of the data, but also who was surveyed, and how their participation might have influenced the results. One 2001 study of pregnant women's drinking habits and their children's behavior years later cautioned that even a single drink per day while pregnant could cause behavioral issues. However, Oster uncovered a serious flaw in the study, noting that

> 18% of the women who didn't drink at all and 45% of the women who had one drink a day reported using cocaine during pregnancy....[R]eally? Cocaine? Perhaps the problem is that cocaine, not the occasional glass of Chardonnay, makes your child more likely to have behavior problems.
>
> —Emily Oster, "Take Back Your Pregnancy"

Clearly, polls, surveys, and studies need to be examined critically. You can't take even academic research at face value until you have explored its details.

The meaning of polls and surveys is also affected by the way that questions are posed. In the past, research revealed, for example, that polling about same-sex unions got differing responses according to how questions were worded. When people were asked whether gay and lesbian couples should be eligible for the same inheritance and partner health benefits that heterosexual couples receive, a majority of those polled said yes—unless the word *marriage* appeared in the question; then the responses were primarily negative. If anything, the differences here reveal how conflicted people may have been about the issue and how quickly opinions might shift—as they have clearly done. Remember, then, to be very careful in reviewing the wording of survey or poll questions.

Finally, always keep in mind that the date of a poll may strongly affect the results—and their usefulness in an argument. In 2014, for example, a Reuters poll found that 20 percent of California residents said they supported "CalExit," a proposal for California to secede from the United States and become a country in its own right. In 2017, however, the same poll found that figure had jumped from 20 percent to 32 percent. The pollsters note, however, that the "margin of error for the California answers was plus or minus 5 percentage points." On public and political issues, you need to be sure that you are using the most timely information you can get.

RESPOND

Choose an important issue and design a series of questions to evoke a range of responses in a poll. Try to design a question that would make people strongly inclined to agree, another question that would lead them to oppose the same proposition, and a third that tries to be more neutral. Then try out your questions on your classmates and note what you learn about how to improve your questions.

Testimonies and Narratives

Writers often support arguments by presenting human experiences in the form of narrative or testimony—particularly if those experiences are their own. When Republican Senator Orrin Hatch condemned KKK, neo-Nazi, and white nationalist protests in Charlottesville, Virginia, in August 2017, he did so by calling on personal experience:

Senator Hatch Office
@senorrinhatch
Follow
We should call evil by its name. My brother didn't give his life fighting Hitler for Nazi ideas to go unchallenged here at home. -OGH
2:41 PM - 12 Aug 2017

In courts, judges and juries often take into consideration detailed descriptions and narratives of exactly what occurred. In the case of *Doe v. City of Belleville*, the judges of the Seventh Circuit Court of Appeals decided, based on the testimony presented, that a man (known as H.) had been sexually harassed by other men in his workplace. The narrative, in this case, supplies the evidence, noting that one coworker

> constantly referred to H. as "queer" and "fag" and urged H. to "go back to San Francisco with the rest of the queers."...The verbal taunting of H. turned physical one day when [a coworker] trapped [him] against a wall, proceeded to grab H. by the testicles and, having done so, announced to the assemblage of co-workers present, "Well, I guess he's a guy."

Personal perspectives can support a claim convincingly and logically, especially if a writer has earned the trust of readers. In arguing that Tea Party supporters of a government shutdown had no business being offended when some opponents described them as "terrorists," Froma Harrop, one of the writers who used the term, argued logically and from experience why the characterization was appropriate:

> [T]he hurt the tea party writers most complained of was to their feelings. I had engaged in name-calling, they kept saying. One professing to want more civility in our national conversation, as I do, should not be flinging around the *terrorist* word.
>
> May I presume to disagree? Civility is a subjective concept, to be sure, but hurting people's feelings in the course of making solid arguments is fair and square. The decline in the quality of our public discourse results not so much from an excess of spleen, but a deficit of well-constructed arguments. Few things upset partisans more than when the other side makes a case that bats home.
>
> "Most of us know that effectively scoring on a point of argument opens us to the accusation of mean-spiritedness," writes Frank Partsch, who leads the National Conference of Editorial Writers' Civility Project. "It comes with the territory, and a commitment to civility should not suggest that punches will be pulled in order to avoid such accusations."
>
> —Froma Harrop, "Hurt Feelings Can Be a Consequence of Strong Arguments"

This narrative introduction gives a rationale for supporting the claim Harrop is making: we can expect consequences when we argue ineffectively. (For more on establishing credibility with readers, see **Chapter 26**.)

RESPOND

Bring to class a full review of a recent film that you either enjoyed or did not enjoy. Using testimony from that review, write a brief argument to your classmates explaining why they should see that movie (or why they should avoid it), being sure to use evidence from the review fairly and reasonably. Then exchange arguments with a classmate, and decide whether the evidence in your peer's argument helps to change your opinion about the movie. What's convincing about the evidence? If it doesn't convince you, why doesn't it?

Using Reason and Common Sense

If you don't have "hard facts," you can turn to those arguments Aristotle describes as "constructed" from reason and common sense. The formal study of such reasoning is called *logic*, and you probably recognize a famous example of deductive reasoning, called a **syllogism**:

> All human beings are mortal.
>
> Socrates is a human being.
>
> Therefore, Socrates is mortal.

In valid syllogisms, the conclusion follows logically—and technically—from the premises that lead up to it. Many have criticized syllogistic reasoning for being limited, and others have poked fun at it, as in the cartoon below.

Logic: another thing that penguins aren't very good at.

But we routinely see something like syllogistic reasoning operating in public arguments, particularly when writers take the time to explain key principles. Consider the step-by-step reasoning Michael Gerson uses to explain why exactly it was wrong for the Internal Revenue Service in 2010–2011 to target specific political groups, making it more difficult for them to organize politically:

> Why does this matter deserve heightened scrutiny from the rest of us? Because crimes against democracy are particularly insidious. Representative government involves a type of trade. As citizens, we cede power to public officials for important purposes that require centralized power: defending the country, imposing order, collecting taxes to promote the common good. In exchange, we expect public institutions to be evenhanded and disinterested. When the stewards of power—biased judges or corrupt policemen or politically motivated IRS officials—act unfairly, it undermines trust in the whole system.
>
> —Michael Gerson, "An Arrogant and Lawless IRS"

Gerson's criticism of the IRS actions might be mapped out by the following sequence of statements.

> Crimes against democracy undermine trust in the system.
>
> Treating taxpayers differently because of their political beliefs is a crime against democracy.
>
> Therefore, IRS actions that target political groups undermine the American system.

Few writers, of course, think about formal deductive reasoning when they support their claims. Even Aristotle recognized that most people argue perfectly well using informal logic. To do so, they rely mostly on habits of mind and assumptions that they share with their readers or listeners—as Gerson essentially does in his paragraph.

Here, we briefly examine some ways that people use informal logic in their everyday lives. Once again, we begin with Aristotle, who used the term **enthymeme** to describe an ordinary kind of sentence that includes both a claim and a reason but depends on the audience's agreement with an assumption that is left implicit rather than spelled out. Enthymemes can be very persuasive when most people agree with the assumptions they rest on. The following sentences are all enthymemes:

> We'd better cancel the picnic because it's going to rain.
>
> Flat taxes are fair because they treat everyone the same.
>
> I'll buy a PC instead of a Mac because it's cheaper.

Sometimes enthymemes seem so obvious that readers don't realize that they're drawing inferences when they agree with them. Consider the first example:

> We'd better cancel the picnic because it's going to rain.

Let's expand the enthymeme a bit to say more of what the speaker may mean:

> We'd better cancel the picnic this afternoon because the weather bureau is predicting a 70 percent chance of rain for the remainder of the day.

Embedded in this brief argument are all sorts of assumptions and fragments of cultural information that are left implicit but that help to make it persuasive:

> Picnics are ordinarily held outdoors.
>
> When the weather is bad, it's best to cancel picnics.
>
> Rain is bad weather for picnics.
>
> A 70 percent chance of rain means that rain is more likely to occur than not.
>
> When rain is more likely to occur than not, it makes sense to cancel picnics.

For most people, the original statement carries all this information on its own; the enthymeme is a compressed argument, based on what audiences know and will accept.

But sometimes enthymemes aren't self-evident:

> Be wary of environmentalism because it's religion disguised as science.
>
> iPhones are undermining civil society by making us even more focused on ourselves.
>
> It's time to make all public toilets unisex because to do otherwise is discriminatory.

In these cases, you'll have to work much harder to defend both the claim and the implicit assumptions that it's based on by drawing out the inferences that seem self-evident in other enthymemes. And you'll likely also have to supply credible evidence; just calling something a fact doesn't make it one, so a simple declaration of fact won't suffice.

CULTURAL CONTEXTS FOR ARGUMENT

Logos

In the United States, student writers are expected to draw on "hard facts" and evidence as often as possible in supporting their claims: while ethical and emotional appeals are increasingly important and often used in making decisions, logical appeals still tend to hold sway in academic writing. So statistics and facts speak volumes, as does reasoning based on time-honored values such as fairness and equity. In writing to global audiences, you need to remember that not all cultures value the same kinds of appeals. If you want to write to audiences across cultures, you need to know about the norms and values in those cultures. Chinese culture, for example, values authority and often indirect allusion over "facts" alone. Some African cultures value cooperation and community over individualism, and still other cultures value religious texts as providing compelling evidence. So think carefully about what you consider strong evidence, and pay attention to what counts as evidence to others. You can begin by asking yourself questions like:

- What evidence is most valued by your audience: Facts? Concrete examples? Firsthand experience? Religious or philosophical texts? Something else?
- Will analogies count as support? How about precedents?
- Will the testimony of experts count? If so, what kinds of experts are valued most?

Providing Logical Structures for Argument

Some arguments depend on particular logical structures to make their points. In the following pages, we identify a few of these logical structures.

Degree

Arguments based on degree are so common that people barely notice them, nor do they pay much attention to how they work because they seem self-evident. Most audiences will readily accept that *more of a good thing* or *less of a bad thing* is good. In her novel *The Fountainhead*, Ayn Rand asks: "If physical slavery is repulsive, how much more repulsive is the concept of servility of the spirit?" Most readers immediately comprehend the point Rand intends to make about slavery of the spirit because they already know that physical slavery is cruel and would reject any forms of slavery that were even crueler on the principle that *more of a bad thing is bad.* Rand still needs to offer evidence that "servility of the spirit" is, in fact, worse than bodily servitude, but she has begun with a logical structure readers can grasp. Here are other arguments that work similarly:

> If I can get a ten-year warranty on an inexpensive Kia, shouldn't I get the same or better warranty from a more expensive Lexus?

The health benefits from using stem cells in research will surely outweigh the ethical risks.

Better a conventional war now than a nuclear confrontation later.

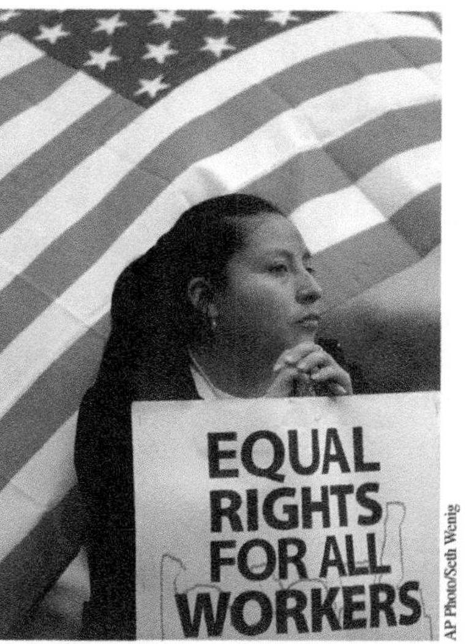

FIGURE 27.3 A demonstrator at an immigrants' rights rally in New York City in 2007. Arguments based on values that are widely shared within a society—such as the idea of equal rights in American culture—have a strong advantage with audiences.

Analogies

Analogies, typically complex or extended comparisons, explain one idea or concept by comparing it to something else.

Here, writer and founder of literacy project 826 Valencia, Dave Eggers, uses an analogy in arguing that we do not value teachers as much as we should:

> When we don't get the results we want in our military endeavors, we don't blame the soldiers. We don't say, "It's these lazy soldiers and their bloated benefits plans! That's why we haven't done better in Afghanistan!" No, if the results aren't there, we blame the planners....No one contemplates blaming the men and women fighting every day in the trenches for little pay and scant recognition. And yet in education we do just that. When we don't like the way our students score on international standardized tests, we blame the teachers.
>
> —Dave Eggers and Nínive Calegari, "The High Cost of Low Teacher Salaries"

Precedent

Arguments from **precedent** and arguments of analogy both involve comparisons. Consider an assertion like this one, which uses a comparison as a precedent:

> If motorists in most other states can pump their own gas safely, surely the state of Oregon can trust its own drivers to be as capable. It's time for Oregon to permit self-service gas stations.

You could tease out several inferences from this claim to explain its reasonableness: people in Oregon are as capable as people in other states; people with equivalent capabilities can do the same thing; pumping gas is not hard; and so forth. But you don't have to because most readers get the argument simply because of the way it is put together. In any case, that argument has begun to have traction: as of January 2018, Oregon began permitting self-service pumps in fifteen rural counties, though doing so called forth virulent pushback on social media. So the debate goes on!

Anadolu Agency/Getty Images

Here is an excerpt from an analytical argument by Kriston Capps that examines attempts by the sculptor of Wall Street's *Charging Bull* to have a new, competing sculpture, *Fearless Girl*, removed on the basis of legal precedents supporting the rights of visual artists. Sculptor Arturo Di Modica's assertion,

> that Visbal's work infringes on his own, is unlikely to hold sway, under recent readings of the Visual Artists Rights Act.... The argument that *Fearless Girl* modifies or destroys *Charging Bull* by blocking its path would represent a leap that courts have been reluctant to take even in clearer cases.
>
> —Kriston Capps, "Why Wall Street's *Charging Bull* Sculptor Has No Real Case against *Fearless Girl*"

You'll encounter additional kinds of logical structures as you create your own arguments. You'll find some of them in **Chapter 13**, "Fallacies of Argument."

CHAPTER

28

Style in Arguments

Left to right: © Photofest, Inc.; © Photofest, Inc.; © Photofest, Inc.; Kevin Mazur/Getty Images

The images above all reflect the notable styles of musicians from different times and musical traditions: Yo-Yo Ma, Count Basie, Kiss, and Beyoncé. One could argue that these performers craft images to define their stage personalities, but how they present themselves also reflects the music they play and the audiences they perform for. Imagine Yo-Yo Ma appearing in Kiss makeup at Carnegie Hall. Weird!

Writers, too, create styles that express their ethos and life experiences. But in persuasive situations, style is also a matter of the specific choices they make—strategically and self-consciously—to influence audiences. And today, style is arguably more important than ever before in getting messages across. In a time when we are overcome with a veritable fire-hose of information 24 hours a day, getting and holding an audience's attention is often difficult. So what can do the job for writers today? STYLE.

It's not surprising, then, that writers take questions of style very seriously, that they adapt their voices to a range of rhetorical situations, from very formal to very casual. At the formal and professional end of the scale, consider the opening paragraph of a dissent by Justice Sonia Sotomayor to a Supreme Court decision affecting affirmative action in Michigan public universities. Writing doesn't get much more consequential than this, and that earnestness is reflected in the justice's sober, authoritative, but utterly clear style:

> We are fortunate to live in a democratic society. But without checks, democratically approved legislation can oppress minority groups. For that reason, our Constitution places limits on what a majority of the people may do. This case implicates one such limit: the guarantee of equal protection of the laws. Although that guarantee is traditionally understood to prohibit intentional discrimination under existing laws, equal protection does not end there. Another fundamental strand of our equal protection jurisprudence focuses on process, securing to all citizens the right to participate meaningfully and equally in self-government. That right is the bedrock of our democracy, for it preserves all other rights.
>
> —Sonia Sotomayor, dissenting opinion, April 22, 2014

Contrast this formal style with the far more casual style in a blog item by *Huffington Post* book editor Claire Fallon, arguing (tongue-in-cheek) that Shakespeare's Romeo is one of those literary figures readers just love to hate. The range of Fallon's vocabulary choices—from "most romantic dude" to "penchant for wallowing"—suggests the (Beyoncé-like?) playfulness of the exercise. Style is obviously a big part of Fallon's game:

> Romeo, Romeo, wherefore art thou such a wishy-washy doofus?...[Romeo] spends his first scene in the play insisting he's heartbroken over a girl he goes on to completely forget about the second he catches a glimpse of Juliet!... Romeo's apparent penchant for wallowing in the romantic misery of unrequited love finds a new target in naive Juliet, who then dies for a guy who probably would have forgotten about her as soon as their honeymoon ended.
>
> —Claire Fallon, "11 Unlikeable Classical Book Characters We Love to Hate"

These examples use different styles but are written in standard English, with a bit of slang mixed into the blog post. In the multilingual, polyglot world we live in today, however, writers are also mixing languages (as Gloria Anzaldúa does when she shifts from English to Spanish to Spanglish in her book *Borderlands: La Frontera*) as well as mixing dialects and languages. This translingual turn recognizes that English itself exists in many forms (Singaporean English, Canadian English, New Zealand English, and so on), that many writers of English speak and write a variety of other languages, and that many if not most writers "code mesh," a term scholar Suresh Canagarajah defines as "a strategy for merging local varieties with standard written Englishes in a move toward more gradually pluralizing academic writing and developing multilingual competence for transnational relationships"

("The Place of World Englishes in Composition," *CCC*, June 2006). Here is an example of code-meshing in an article by Professor Donald McCrary:

> Like my students, I know the value of my native language, black English, and the significance it has played in both my public and private life. However, many would challenge my claim that black English is both a public and private language. For example, in "Aria: A Memoir of a Bilingual Childhood," Richard Rodriguez argues for the separation of home and school languages because he believes the former is private while the latter is public. . . . I, however, view black English as a public language because it is the language with which I learned about the world, including the perils of racism, the importance of education, and the consequences of improper conduct. When Moms told me, "Don't go showin' your ass when I take you in this store," I knew she was telling me to behave respectfully, and I knew what would happen if I didn't. The black English I learned at home is the same black English I used outside the home. It got black people through slavery, and it saved my black behind a thousand times.
>
> Hold up. I know what you gonna say. Talkin' that black English is okay at home and with your friends, but don't be speakin' that foolishness in school or at the j-o-b. And don't be tellin' no students they can speak that mess either. You want people (read: white) to think they ignorant? Right.
>
> Right. I hear you. I hear you. But let's be real. America loves itself some black English. Half the announcers on ESPN speak it, and I'm talking about the white dudes, too. Americans know more black English than they like to admit. Black English is intelligible and intelligent, and just because somebody tells you different, don't necessarily make it so. And that's what I want the academy to understand. My students don't speak no broken English. They speak a legitimate dialect that conveys legitimate meanings.
>
> —Donald McCrary, "Represent, Representin', Representation: The Efficacy of Hybrid Texts in the Writing Classroom"

McCrary, who teaches at Long Island University, "meshes" elements of African American language with "standard" written English to create a style that speaks to both academic and nonacademic audiences. His use of colloquialisms ("I hear you"), features of spoken English ("at the j-o-b"), and what he refers to as "black English" establish a connection between speaker and listener ("But let's be real") as he argues for a more pluralistic and inclusive "translingual approach" to language.

RESPOND

Write a paragraph or two (or three!) about your own use of languages and dialects. In what ways do you ordinarily "mesh" features of different dialects and/or languages? What languages did you grow up speaking and hearing and how do those languages enter into your writing today? How would you describe your own style of writing (and speaking)?

As you might guess from these examples, style always involves making choices about language across a wide range of situations. Style can be public or personal, conventional or creative, and everything in between. When you write, you'll find that you have innumerable tools and options for expressing yourself exactly as you need to. This chapter introduces you to some of them.

Style and Word Choice

Words matter—and those you choose will define the style of your arguments.

In spite of the extensive work on translingualism and code meshing, many academic arguments today still call for a formal or professional style using standard written English. Such language can sound weighty, and it usually is. It often uses technical terms and conventional vocabulary because that's what readers of academic journals or serious magazines and newspapers generally expect. Formal writing also typically avoids contractions, phrases that mimic speech, and sometimes even the pronoun *I*. (For information about the use of pronouns in contemporary writing, see p. 546.) But what may be most remarkable about the style is how little it draws attention to itself—and that's usually deliberate. Here's a paragraph from Annette Vee's *Coding Literacy: How Computer Programming Is Changing Writing*, published by MIT Press in 2017:

> [T]he concept of coding literacy helps to expand access, or to support "transformative access" to programming in the words of rhetorician Adam Banks.[24] For Banks, transformative access allows people "to both change the interfaces of that system and fundamentally change the codes that determine how the system works."[25] Changing the "interface" of programming might entail more widespread education on programming. But changing "how the system works" would move beyond material access to education and into a critical examination of the values and ideologies embedded in that education. Programming

> as defined by computer science or software engineering is bound to echo the values of those contexts. But a concept of coding literacy suggests programming is a literacy practice with many applications beyond a profession defined by a limited set of values. The webmaster, game maker, tinkerer, scientist, and citizen activist can benefit from coding as a means to achieve their goals. As I argue in this book, we must think of programming more broadly—as coding literacy—if the ability to program is to become distributed more broadly. Thinking this way can help change "how the system works."

In this passage, Vee uses conventional standard written English, fairly complex syntax, and abstract terms (transformative access, interfaces, coding literacy) that she expects her readers will make sense of, though she draws the line at employing highly technical terms that only computer scientists would be familiar with. Also note the two footnote markers that identify her sources, also a staple of formal academic discourse. The tone is efficient and cool, the style academic and somewhat distanced.

Colloquial words and phrases, *slang*, and even first- and second-person pronouns (*I*, *me*, *we*, *you*) can create relationships with audiences that feel much more intimate. When you use everyday language in arguments, readers are more likely to identify with you personally and, possibly, with the ideas you represent or advocate. In effect, such vocabulary choices lessen the distance between you and readers.

Admittedly, some colloquial terms simply bewilder readers not tuned in to them. A movie review in *Rolling Stone* or a music review in *Spin* might leave your parents (or some authors) scratching their heads. Writing for the music Web site Pitchfork, Meaghan Garvey has this to say about Spanish R&B singer Bad Gyal's 2018 release:

> On "Blink," slow-winding dancehall rhythms with pulsing bass and staccato hand-claps climax in thumping reggaeton with hypnotic synth washes. Bad Gyal's voice stutters and chops along with the dembow drum loops, her melodies evoking an R-rated lullaby as she sings sweetly about grinding the club ("Me gusta el perreo").
>
> —Meaghan Garvey, "Bad Gyal, 'Blink'"

Huh? we say. But you probably get it.

CULTURAL CONTEXTS FOR ARGUMENT

A Note on Pronoun Preference

Conventions about personal pronouns are in flux right now, and particularly traditional third-person singular pronouns. You may have been asked what pronouns you prefer, since many people identify with neither of the traditional personal pronouns, namely he and she. For this reason, writers and speakers are sensitive to members of their audiences, realizing that some may prefer the use of singular they as in "Jamie called me and I called them back." Others prefer to use an alternate gender-neutral pronoun such as ze or zir. Linguist Peter Smagorinsky notes that it was only several decades ago that women, tired of having to be either Mrs. or Miss, coined the title Ms. It took some time, but eventually caught on:

> It may well be that "ze" and "zir" will replace current pronouns over time. For those who reject "they" as grammatically improper while also recognizing that "he" and "she" are inadequate, it may become a reasonable development.

And of course, still others are just fine with the traditional he or she. The important point for writers and speakers is to be sensitive to these differences and to choose terms appropriately.

You will want to be careful, as Annette Vee is, with the use of *jargon*, the special vocabulary of members of a profession, trade, or field. Although jargon serves as shorthand for experts, it can alienate readers who don't recognize technical words or acronyms.

Another verbal key to an argument's style is its control of **connotation**, the associations that surround many words. Consider the straightforward connotative differences among the following three statements:

> Students from the Labor Action Committee (LAC) carried out a hunger strike to call attention to the below-minimum wages that are being paid to campus temporary workers, saying, "The university must pay a living wage to all its workers."
>
> Left-wing agitators and radicals tried to use self-induced starvation to stampede the university into caving in to their demands.
>
> Champions of human rights put their bodies on the line to protest the university's tightfisted policy of paying temporary workers scandalously low wages.

The style of the first sentence is the most neutral, presenting facts and offering a quotation from one of the students. The second sentence uses loaded terms like *agitators*, *radicals*, and *stampede* to create a negative image of this event, while the final sentence uses other loaded words to create a positive view. As these examples demonstrate, the words you choose can change everything about a sentence.

Watch how Jason Collins, the first openly gay NBA star (see p. 274), uses the connotations of a common sports term to explain why he decided to come out:

> Now I'm a free agent, literally and figuratively. I've reached that enviable state in life in which I can do pretty much what I want. And what I want is to continue to play basketball.…At the same time, I want to be genuine and authentic and truthful.

Collins plays on the professional and figurative meanings of "free agent" to illustrate his desire to be honest about his sexual orientation.

RESPOND

Exercise your critical reading muscles by reviewing the excerpts in this section and choose one or two words or phrases that you think are admirably selected or unusually interesting choices. Then explore the meanings and possibly the connotations of the word or words in a nicely developed paragraph or two.

Sentence Structure and Argument

Writers of effective arguments know that "variety is the spice of life" when it comes to stylish sentences. A strategy as simple as *varying sentence length* can keep readers attentive and interested. For instance, the paragraph from *Coding Literacy* in the preceding section (pp. 544–545) has sentences as short as ten words and as lengthy as twenty-seven. Now the author almost certainly didn't pause as she wrote and think, hmm, I need a little variation here. Instead, as an experienced writer, she simply made sure that her sentences complemented the flow of her ideas and also kept readers engaged.

Sentences, you see, offer you more options and special effects than you can ever exhaust. To pull examples from selections earlier in this chapter, just consider how dramatic, punchy, or even comic short sentences can be:

> Hold up. I know what you gonna say.
>
> —Donald McCrary

Longer sentences can explain ideas, build drama, or sweep readers along:

> I, however, view black English as a public language because it is the language with which I learned about the world, including the perils of racism, the importance of education, and the consequences of improper conduct.
>
> —Donald McCrary

> Bad Gyal's voice stutters and chops along with the dembow drum loops, her melodies evoking an R-rated lullaby as she sings sweetly about grinding the club ("Me gusta el perreo").
>
> —Meaghan Garvey, "Bad Gyal, 'Blink'"

Meanwhile, sentences of medium length handle just about any task assigned without a fuss. They are whatever you need them to be: serviceable, discrete, thoughtful, playful. And they pair up nicely with companions:

> But without checks, democratically approved legislation can oppress minority groups. For that reason, our Constitution places limits on what a majority of the people may do.
>
> —Sonia Sotomayor

Balanced or parallel sentences, in which clauses or phrases are deliberately matched, as highlighted in the following example, draw attention to ideas and relationships:

> Ulysses can be finished. The Internet is never finished.
>
> —Alexis C. Madrigal

And sentences that alternate sentence length can work especially well in much writing. For example, after one or more long sentences, the punch of a short sentence can be dramatic:

> Previously, Ms. Collins was the first woman at *The Times* to hold the post of editorial page editor. The author of six books, she took time off in 2007—between the editorial page editor job and her column—and returned to write about the 2008 presidential election. She's been at it ever since.
>
> —Susan Lehman, *The New York Times*, March 22, 2016

Sentences with complicated structures or interruptions make you pay attention to their motions and, therefore, their ideas:

> As other voting requirements were gradually stripped away—location of birth, property ownership, race, and later sex—literacy and education began to stand in for those qualities in defining what it meant to be an American citizen.
>
> —Annette Vee

Even sentence fragments—which don't meet all the requirements for full sentence status—have their place when used for a specific effect:

> Right. Right. —Donald McCrary

You see, then, that there's *much* more to the rhetoric of sentences than just choosing subjects, verbs, and objects—and far more than we can explain in one section. But you can learn a lot about the power of sentences simply by observing how the writers you admire engineer them—and maybe imitating some of those sentences yourself. You might also make it a habit to read and re-read your own sentences aloud (or in your head) as you compose them to gauge whether words and phrases are meshing with your ideas. And then tinker, tinker, tinker—until the sentences feel and sound right.

RESPOND

Working with a classmate, first find a paragraph you both admire and read it carefully and critically, making sure you understand its structure, syntax, and word choice. Then, individually write paragraphs of your own that imitate the sentences within it—making sure that both these new items are on subjects different from that of the original paragraph. When you are done, compare your paragraphs and pick out a few sentences you think are especially effective.

Punctuation and Argument

In a memorable comment, actor and director Clint Eastwood said, "You can show a lot with a look. . . . It's punctuation." He's certainly right about punctuation's effect, and it is important that as you read and write arguments, you consider punctuation closely.

FIGURE 28.1 "You can show a lot with a look.... It's punctuation."

Eastwood may have been talking about the dramatic effect of end punctuation: the finality of periods; the tentativeness of ellipses (. . .); the query, disbelief, or uncertainty in question marks; or the jolt in the now-appearing-almost-everywhere exclamation point! Yet even exclamations can help create tone if used strategically. In an argument about the treatment of prisoners at Guantánamo, consider how Jane Mayer evokes the sense of desperation in some of the suspected terrorists:

> As we reached the end of the cell-block, hysterical shouts, in broken English, erupted from a caged exercise area nearby. "Come here!" a man screamed. "See here! They are liars!...No sleep!" he yelled. "No food! No medicine! No doctor! Everybody sick here!"
>
> —Jane Mayer, "The Experiment"

Punctuation that works within sentences can also do much to enhance meaning and style. The *semicolon*, for instance, marks a pause that is stronger than a comma but not as strong as a period. Semicolons function like "plus signs"; used correctly, they join items that are alike in structure, conveying a sense of balance, similarity, or even contrast. Do you recall Nathaniel Stein's parody of grading standards at Harvard University (see pp. 273–274)? Watch as he uses a semicolon to enhance the humor in his description of what an A+ paper achieves:

> Nearly every single word in the paper is spelled correctly; those that are not can be reasoned out phonetically within minutes.
>
> —Nathaniel Stein, "Leaked! Harvard's Grading Rubric"

In many situations, however, semicolons, with their emphasis on symmetry and balance, can feel stodgy, formal, and maybe even old-fashioned, and lots of writers avoid them, perhaps because they are very difficult to get right. Check a writing handbook before you get too friendly with semicolons.

Much easier to manage are colons, which function like pointers within sentences: they say *pay attention to this*. Philip Womack's London *Telegraph* review of *Harry Potter and the Deathly Hallows, Part 2* demonstrates how a colon enables a writer to introduce a lengthy illustration clearly and elegantly:

> The first scene of David Yates's film picks up where his previous installment left off: with a shot of the dark lord Voldemort's noseless face in triumph as he steals the most powerful magic wand in the world from the tomb of Harry's protector, Professor Dumbledore.
>
> —Philip Womack

And Paul Krugman of the *New York Times* shows how to use a colon to catch a reader's attention:

> Recently two research teams, working independently and using different methods, reached an alarming conclusion: The West Antarctic ice sheet is doomed.
>
> —Paul Krugman, "Point of No Return"

Colons can serve as lead-ins for complete sentences, complex phrases, or even single words. As such, they are versatile and potentially dramatic pieces of punctuation.

Like colons, dashes help readers focus on important, sometimes additional details. But they have even greater flexibility since they can be used singly or in pairs. Alone, dashes function much like colons to add information. Here's the *Washington Post*'s Eugene Robinson commenting pessimistically on a political situation in Iraq, using a single dash to extend his thoughts:

> The aim of U.S. policy at this point should be minimizing the calamity, not chasing rainbows of a unified, democratic, pluralistic Iraq—which, sadly, is something the power brokers in Iraq do not want.
>
> —Eugene Robinson, "The 'Ungrateful Volcano' of Iraq"

And here are paired dashes used to insert such information in the opening of the Philip Womack review of *Deathly Hallows 2* cited earlier:

> *Harry Potter and the Deathly Hallows, Part 2*—the eighth and final film in the blockbusting series—begins with our teenage heroes fighting for their lives, and for their entire world.

As these examples illustrate, punctuation often enhances the rhythm of an argument. Take a look at how Maya Angelou uses a dash along with another punctuation mark—ellipsis points—to create a pause or hesitation, in this case one that builds anticipation:

> Then the voice, husky and familiar, came to wash over us—"The winnah, and still heavyweight champeen of the world...Joe Louis."
>
> —Maya Angelou, "Champion of the World"

It's probably worth mentioning that today we are seeing an upsurge in the use of ellipses on social media—a virtual onslaught of these little dots. Of course, in the very informal style of many texts and tweets, writers may be likely to omit end punctuation entirely. The use of ellipsis dots can signal a trailing off of a thought, leave open the possibility of further communication, or mimic conversational-style pauses. But they can also be a sign of laziness, as Matthew J. X. Malady points out in "Why Everyone and Your Mother Started Using Ellipses...Everywhere":

> Ellipses, then,...can help carefully structure a bit of written communication so that it mimics some of the more subtle, meaningful elements of face-to-face conversation. But when we want to be lazy, they also allow us to avoid thinking too much while crafting a message.

RESPOND

First, read several movie reviews carefully and critically. Then try writing a brief movie review for your campus newspaper, experimenting with punctuation as one way to create an effective style. See if using a series of questions might have a strong effect, whether exclamation points would add or detract from the message you want to send, and so on. When you've finished the review, compare it to one written by a classmate, and look for similarities and differences in your choices of punctuation.

Special Effects: Figurative Language

You don't have to look hard to find examples of figurative language adding style to arguments. When a writing teacher suggests you take a weed whacker to your prose, she's using a figure of speech (in this case, a *metaphor*) to suggest you cut the wordiness. To indicate how little he trusts the testimony of John Koskinen, head of the Internal Revenue Service, political pundit Michael Gerson takes the metaphor of a "witch hunt" and flips it on the bureaucrat, relying on readers to recognize an *allusion* to Shakespeare's *Macbeth*:

> Democrats were left to complain about a Republican "witch hunt"—while Koskinen set up a caldron, added some eye of newt and toe of frog and hailed the Thane of Cawdor.
>
> —Michael Gerson, "An Arrogant and Lawless IRS"

Chronicle/Alamy Stock Photo

FIGURE 28.2 The three witches from *Macbeth*, at their cauldron

Figurative language like this—indispensable to our ability to communicate effectively—dramatizes ideas, either by clarifying or enhancing the thoughts themselves or by framing them in language that makes them stand out. As a result, figurative language makes arguments attractive, memorable, and powerful. An apt simile, a timely rhetorical question, or a wicked understatement might do a better job bringing an argument home than whole paragraphs of evidence. Figurative language is not the icing on the cake: it's the cake itself!

Figures of speech are usually classified into two main types: **tropes**, which involve a change in the ordinary meaning of a word or phrase; and **schemes**, which involve a special arrangement of words. Here is a brief alphabetical listing—with examples—of some of the most familiar kinds.

Tropes

To create tropes, you often have to think of one idea or claim in relationship to others. Some of the most powerful—one might even say *inevitable*—tropes involve making purposeful comparisons between ideas: analogies, metaphors, and similes. Other tropes such as irony, signifying, and understatement are tools for expressing attitudes toward ideas: you might use them to shape the way you want your audience to think about a claim that you or someone else has made.

Allusion

An **allusion** is a connection that illuminates one situation by comparing it to another similar but usually more famous one, often with historical or literary connections. Allusions work with events, people, or concepts—expanding and enlarging them so readers better appreciate their significance. For example, a person who makes a career-ending blunder might be said to have met her *Waterloo*, the famous battle that terminated Napoleon's ambitions. Similarly, every impropriety in Washington brings up mentions of *Watergate*, the only scandal to lead to a presidential resignation; any daring venture becomes a *moon shot*, paralleling the ambitious program that led to a lunar landing in 1969. Using allusions can be tricky: they work only if readers get the connection. But when they do, they can pack a wallop. When on page 553 Michael Gerson mentions "eye of newt" and "toe of frog" in the same breath as IRS chief John Koskinen, he knows what fans of *Macbeth* are thinking. But other readers might be left clueless.

Analogy

Analogies compare two things, often point by point, either to show similarity or to suggest that if two concepts, phenomena, events, or even people are alike in one way, they are probably alike in other ways as well. Often extended in length, analogies can clarify or emphasize points of comparison, thereby supporting particular claims.

Here's the first paragraph of an essay in which a writer who is also a runner thinks deeply about the analogies between the two tough activities:

> When people ask me what running and writing have in common, I tend to look at the ground and say it might have something to do with discipline: You do both of those things when you don't feel like it, and make them part of your regular routine. You know some days will be harder than others, and on some

you won't hit your mark and will want to quit. But you don't. You force yourself into a practice; the practice becomes habit and then simply part of your identity. A surprising amount of success, as Woody Allen once said, comes from just showing up.

—Rachel Toor, "What Writing and Running Have in Common"

FIGURE 28.3 This cartoon creates an analogy in the way it depicts the relationship between North Korea and the United States.

To be effective, an analogy has to make a good point and hold up to scrutiny. If it doesn't, it can be criticized as a faulty analogy, a fallacy of argument (see p. 303).

Antonomasia

Antonomasia is an intriguing trope that simply involves substituting a descriptive phrase for a proper name. It is probably most familiar to you from sports or entertainment figures: "His Airness" still means Michael Jordan; Aretha Franklin remains "The Queen of Soul"; Cleveland Cavaliers star LeBron James is "the King"; and Superman, of course, is "The Man of Steel." In politics, antonomasia is sometimes used neutrally (Ronald Reagan as "The Gipper"), sometimes as a back-handed compliment (Margaret Thatcher as "The Iron Lady"), and occasionally as a crude and racist put-down (Elizabeth Warren as "Pocahontas"). As you well know if you have one, nicknames can pack potent arguments into just one phrase.

Hyperbole

Hyperbole is the use of overstatement for special effect, a kind of fireworks in prose. The tabloid gossip magazines that scream at you in the checkout line survive by hyperbole. Everyone has seen these overstated arguments and perhaps marveled at the way they sell.

Hyperbole can, however, serve both writers and audiences when very strong opinions need to be registered. One senses exasperation in this excerpt from a list of the worst movies of 2017, which ranks *Pirates of the Caribbean: Dead Men Tell No Tales* as one of the most boring and worst films of that year:

> The (sigh) fifth movie in Disney's deathless series finds Johnny Depp and co. dead in the water. Remember when we loved the star's loose-and-boozy portrayal of Capt. Jack Sparrow, so fresh and charismatic 14 years ago? He was a joy. Now, you just want to smack the tri-cornered hat off his head and see him stranded on a godforsaken rock somewhere near the Marianas Trench.
>
> —John Serba, mlive.com

Irony

Irony is a complex trope in which words convey meanings that are in tension with or even opposite to their literal meanings. Readers who catch the irony realize that a writer is asking them (or someone else) to think about all the potential connotations in their language. One of the most famous uses of satiric irony in literature occurs in Shakespeare's *Julius Caesar* when Antony punctuates his condemnation of Caesar's assassins with the repeated word *honourable*. He begins by admitting, "So are they all, honourable men" but ends railing against "the honourable men / Whose daggers have stabb'd Caesar." Within just a few lines, Antony's funeral speech has altered the meaning of the term.

In popular culture, irony often takes a humorous bent in publications such as the *Onion* and the appropriately named *Ironic Times*. Yet even serious critics of society and politics use satiric devices to undercut celebrities and politicians, particularly when such public figures ignore the irony in their own positions.

louiselinton
UNITED STATES OF AMERICA
10 likes
louiselinton Great #daytrip to #Kentucky! #nicest #people #beautiful #countryside #rolandmouret pants #tomford sunnies, #hermesscarf #valentinorockstudheels #valentino #usa

> Louise Linton, the Scottish actress, made news on Monday when she posted a photo to her Instagram account showing her and her husband [Secretary of the Treasury Steven Mnuchin] deplaning on an official trip to Kentucky. In her white wide-legged trousers and slim blouse, handbag held as though being presented in the crook of her arm, she looked every bit the jet-setting style-grammer. As any aspiring social media celebrity would, she took the opportunity to let her followers know not only what she thought of the bluegrass state, but also who she was wearing.
>
> —Tony Bravo, "Louise Linton's Fashion Instagram Post Reveals Her Entitlement"

The ironically negative responses to Linton came instantly: "Glad we could pay for your little getaway," Instagram user @jennimiller29 replied to Linton, ending with the hashtag "#deplorable." "Please don't tag your Hermes scarf," @emily.e.dickey responded, calling the hashtagging "Distasteful."

Metaphor

A bedrock of our language, **metaphor** creates or implies a comparison between two things, illuminating something unfamiliar by correlating it to something we usually know much better. For example, to explain the complicated structure of DNA, scientists Watson and Crick famously used items people would likely recognize: a helix (spiral) and a zipper. Metaphors can clarify and enliven arguments. In the following passage, novelist and poet Benjamin Sáenz uses several metaphors (highlighted) to describe his relationship to the southern border of the United States:

> It seems obvious to me now that I remained always a son of the border, a boy never quite comfortable in an American skin, and certainly not comfortable in a Mexican one. My entire life, I have lived in a liminal space, and that space has both defined and confined me. That liminal space wrote and invented me. It has been my prison, and it has also been my only piece of sky.
>
> —Benjamin Sáenz, "Notes from Another Country"

In an example from Andrew Sullivan's blog, he quotes an 1896 issue of *Munsey's Magazine* that uses a metaphor to explain what, at that time, the bicycle meant to women and to clarify the new freedom it gave women who weren't accustomed to being able to ride around on their own:

> To men, the bicycle in the beginning was merely a new toy, another machine added to the long list of devices they knew in their work and play. To women, it was a steed upon which they rode into a new world.

And here is Kurt Andersen in the *Atlantic* writing about what he calls America's "lurch toward fantasy":

> For all the fun, and all the many salutary effects of the 1960s—the main decade of my childhood—I saw that those years had also been the big-bang moment for truthiness. And if the '60s amounted to a national nervous breakdown, we are probably mistaken to consider ourselves over it.

Metonymy

Metonymy is a rhetorical trope in which a writer uses a particular object to stand for a general concept. You'll recognize the move immediately in the expression "The *pen* is mightier than the *sword*"—which obviously is not about Bics and sabers. Metonyms are vivid and concrete ways of compacting big concepts into expressive packages for argument: the term *Wall Street* can embody the nation's whole complicated banking and investment system, while all the offices and officials of the U.S. military become the *Pentagon*. You can quickly think of dozens of expressions that represent larger, more complex concepts: *Nashville, Hollywood, Big Pharma, the Press, the Oval Office*, even perhaps *the electorate*.

FIGURE 28.4 It's not just a street; it's a metonym!

Oxymoron

Oxymoron is a rhetorical trope that states a paradox or contradiction. John Milton created a classic example when he described Hell as a place of "darkness visible." We may be less poetic today, but we nevertheless appreciate the creativity (or arrogance) in expressions such as *light beer, sports utility vehicle, expressway gridlock*, or *negative economic growth*. You might not have much cause to use this figure in your writing, but you'll get credit for noting and commenting on oxymoronic ideas or behaviors.

Rhetorical Question

Rhetorical questions, which we use frequently, are questions posed by a speaker or writer that don't really require answers. Instead, an answer is implied or unimportant. When you say "Who cares?" or "What difference does it make?" you're using such questions.

Rhetorical questions show up in arguments for many reasons, most often perhaps to direct readers' attention to the issues a writer intends to explore. For example, Erin Biba asks a provocative, open-ended rhetorical question in her analysis of Facebook "friending":

> So if we're spending most of our time online talking to people we don't even know, how deep can the conversation ever get?
>
> —Erin Biba, "Friendship Has Its Limits"

Signifying

Signifying, in which a speaker or writer cleverly and often humorously needles another person, is a distinctive trope found extensively in African American English. In the following passage, two African American men (Grave Digger and Coffin Ed) signify on their white supervisor (Anderson), who has ordered them to discover the originators of a riot:

> "I take it you've discovered who started the riot," Anderson said.
>
> "We knew who he was all along," Grave Digger said.
>
> "It's just nothing we can do to him," Coffin Ed echoed.
>
> "Why not, for God's sake?"
>
> "He's dead," Coffin Ed said.
>
> "Who?"
>
> "Lincoln," Grave Digger said.
>
> "He hadn't ought to have freed us if he didn't want to make provisions to feed us," Coffin Ed said. "Anyone could have told him that."
>
> —Chester Himes, *Hot Day, Hot Night*

Coffin Ed and Grave Digger demonstrate the major characteristics of effective signifying—indirection, ironic humor, fluid rhythm, and a surprising twist at the end. Rather than insulting Anderson directly by pointing out that he's asked a dumb question, they criticize the question indirectly by ultimately blaming a white man for the riot (and not just any white man, but one they're supposed to revere). This twist leaves the supervisor speechless, teaching him something and giving Grave Digger and Coffin Ed the last word—and last laugh.

Take a look at the example of signifying from a *Boondocks* cartoon (see facing page). Note how Huey seems to be sympathizing with Jazmine and then, in two surprising twists, reveals that he has been needling her all along.

FIGURE 28.5 In these *Boondocks* strips, Huey signifies on Jazmine, using indirection, ironic humor, and two surprising twists.

Simile

A **simile** uses *like* or *as* to compare two things. Here's a simile from an essay about visiting Montana in the August 2017 *Hemispheres Magazine*:

> By now we've driven the cows to an open pasture. The wranglers teach me how to cut a cow from the herd, as real cowboys do. I find it's a lot like parallel parking, except the curb keeps moving to join the other curbs, and my car has lost respect for me.
>
> —Jacob Baynham, "Three Perfect Days: Montana"

And here is a series of similes, from an excerpt of a *Wired* magazine review of a new magazine for women:

> Women's magazines occupy a special niche in the cluttered infoscape of modern media. Ask any *Vogue* junkie: no girl-themed Web site or CNN segment on women's health can replace the guilty pleasure of slipping a glossy fashion rag into your shopping cart. Smooth as a pint of chocolate Häagen-Dazs, feckless as a thousand-dollar slip dress, women's magazines wrap culture, trends, health, and trash in a single, decadent package. But like the diet dessert recipes they print, these slick publications can leave a bad taste in your mouth.
>
> —Tiffany Lee Brown, "En Vogue"

Here, three similes—*smooth as a pint of chocolate Häagen-Dazs* and *feckless as a thousand-dollar slip dress* in the third sentence, and *like the diet dessert recipes* in the fourth—add to the image of women's magazines as a mishmash of "trash" and "trends."

Understatement

Understatement uses a quiet message to make its point. In her memoir, Rosa Parks—the civil rights activist who made history in 1955 by refusing to give up her bus seat to a white passenger—uses understatement so often that it becomes a hallmark of her style. She refers to her lifelong efforts to advance civil rights as just a small way of "carrying on."

Understatement can be particularly effective in arguments that might seem to call for its opposite. Outraged that New York's Metropolitan Opera has decided to stage *The Death of Klinghoffer*, a work depicting the murder by terrorists of a wheelchair-bound Jewish passenger on a cruise ship in 1985, writer Eve Epstein in particular points to an aria in which a terrorist named Rambo blames all the world's problems on Jews, and then, following an evocative dash, she makes a quiet observation:

> Rambo's aria echoes the views of *Der Stürmer*, Julius Streicher's Nazi newspaper, without a hint of irony or condemnation. The leitmotif of the morally and physically crippled Jew who should be disposed of has been heard before—and it did not end well.
>
> —Eve Epstein, "The Met's Staging of *Klinghoffer* Should Be Scrapped"

"It did not end well" alludes, of course, to the Holocaust.

RESPOND

Use online sources (such as American Rhetoric's Top 100 Speeches at **americanrhetoric.com/top100speechesall.html**) to find the text of an essay or a speech by someone who uses figures of speech liberally. Pick a paragraph that is rich in figures and read it carefully and critically. Then rewrite it, eliminating every bit of figurative language. Then read the original and your revised version aloud to your class. Can you imagine a rhetorical situation in which your pared-down version would be more appropriate?

Schemes

Schemes are rhetorical figures that manipulate the actual word order of phrases, sentences, or paragraphs to achieve specific effects, adding stylistic power or "zing" to arguments. The variety of such devices is beyond the scope of this work. Following are schemes that you're likely to see most often, again in alphabetical order.

Anaphora

Anaphora, or effective repetition, can act like a drumbeat in an argument, bringing the point home. Sometimes an anaphora can be quite obvious, especially when the repeated expressions occur at the beginning of a series of sentences or clauses. Here is President Lyndon Johnson urging Congress in 1965 to pass voting rights legislation:

> There is no constitutional issue here. The command of the Constitution is plain.
>
> There is no moral issue. It is wrong—deadly wrong—to deny any of your fellow Americans the right to vote in this country.
>
> There is no issue of States rights or national rights. There is only the struggle for human rights.
>
> I have not the slightest doubt what will be your answer.

Repetitions can occur within sentences or paragraphs as well. Here, in an argument about the future of Chicago, Lerone Bennett Jr. uses repetition to link Chicago to innovation and creativity:

> [Chicago]'s the place where organized Black history was born, where gospel music was born, where jazz and the blues were reborn, where the Beatles and the Rolling Stones went up to the mountaintop to get the new musical commandments from Chuck Berry and the rock'n'roll apostles.
>
> —Lerone Bennett Jr. "Blacks in Chicago"

Antithesis

Antithesis is the use of parallel words or sentence structures to highlight contrasts or opposition:

> Marriage has many pains, but celibacy has no pleasures.
>
> —Samuel Johnson

> Those who kill people are called murderers; those who kill animals, sportsmen.

Inverted Word Order

Inverted word order is a comparatively rare scheme in which the parts of a sentence or clause are not in the usual subject-verb-object order. It can help make arguments particularly memorable:

> Into this grey lake plopped the thought, I know this man, don't I?
>
> —Doris Lessing

> Hard to see, the dark side is.
>
> —Yoda

Parallelism

Parallelism involves the use of grammatically similar phrases or clauses for special effect. Among the most common of rhetorical effects, parallelism can be used to underscore the relationships between ideas in phrases, clauses, complete sentences, or even paragraphs. You probably recognize the famous parallel clauses that open Charles Dickens's *A Tale of Two Cities*:

> It was the best of times,
>
> it was the worst of times...

The author's paralleled clauses and sentences go on and on through more than a half-dozen pairings, their rhythm unforgettable. Or consider how this unattributed line from the 2008 presidential campaign season resonates because of its elaborate and sequential parallel structure:

> Rosa sat so that Martin could walk. Martin walked so that Obama could run. Obama ran so that our children could fly.

RESPOND

Identify the figurative language used in the following slogans. Note that some slogans may use more than one device.

"A day without orange juice is like a day without sunshine." (Florida Orange Juice)

"Taste the Feeling" (Coca-Cola)

"Be all that you can be." (U.S. Army)

"Breakfast of champions." (Wheaties)

"America runs on Dunkin'." (Dunkin' Donuts)

"Like a rock." (Chevrolet trucks)

CULTURAL CONTEXTS FOR ARGUMENT

Levels of Formality and Other Issues of Style

At least one important style question needs to be asked when arguing across cultures: what level of formality is most appropriate? In the United States, a fairly informal style is often acceptable and even appreciated. Many cultures, however, tend to value formality. If in doubt, err on the side of formality:

- Take care to use proper titles as appropriate (*Ms.*, *Mr.*, *Dr.*, etc.).
- Don't use first names unless you've been invited to do so.
- Steer clear of slang and jargon. When you're communicating with members of other cultures, slang may not be understood, or it may be seen as disrespectful.
- Avoid potentially puzzling pop cultural allusions, such as sports analogies or musical references, if your audience might not understand them.

When arguing across cultures or languages, another stylistic issue might be clarity. When communicating with people whose native languages are different from your own, analogies and similes almost always aid in understanding. Likening something unknown to something familiar can help make your argument forceful—and understandable.

CHAPTER

29

Visual Rhetoric

Left to right: Junior Gonzalez/Getty Images; H. Armstrong Roberts/ClassicStock/Getty Images; Grzegorz Knec/Alamy Stock Photo

During the summer of 2017, protesters and counterprotesters and counter-counterprotesters gathered across the United States in attempts to "unite the right," to "say no to white supremacy," to "make fascists afraid again," to rally for "blood and soil," to claim that "you will not replace us." Often the protesters carried symbols or flags, including the three depicted above: the Confederate flag, the American flag, and the flag of Nazi Germany (others carried a wide range of flags or banners, from Black Lives Matter and the Anti-Defamation League's "No Place for Hate" to the National Socialist Movement flag, the Southern Nationalist Flag, and the Identity Evropa flag, all three associated with white nationalism).

These banners and flags are powerful examples of visual rhetoric and the arguments such images can make. Even so small a sampling of visual rhetoric underscores what you doubtless already know: images grab and hold our attention, stir our emotions, tease our imaginations, provoke intense responses, and make arguments. In short, they have clout.

RESPOND

Choose a flag or banner that speaks strongly to you and then study it carefully and critically. What arguments—implicit and explicit—does the banner or flag make? What are its appeals and who does it seem to address? How do you respond to the image or symbol, and why? Are your responses based primarily on emotion, on logic and reason, on ethical considerations? Then write a paragraph in which you analyze your connection to this imagery.

The Power of Visual Arguments

Even in everyday situations, images—from T-shirts to billboards to animated films and computer screens—influence us. Media analyst Kevin Kelly ponders the role screens and their images now play in our lives:

> Everywhere we look, we see screens. The other day I watched clips from a movie as I pumped gas into my car. The other night I saw a movie on the backseat of a plane. We will watch anywhere. Screens playing video pop up in the most unexpected places—like ATM machines and supermarket checkout lines and tiny phones; some movie fans watch entire films in between calls. These ever-present screens have created an audience for very short moving pictures, as brief as three minutes, while cheap digital creation tools have empowered a new generation of filmmakers, who are rapidly filling up those screens. We are headed toward screen ubiquity.
>
> —Kevin Kelly, "Becoming Screen Literate"

Of course, visual arguments weren't invented by YouTube, and their power isn't novel either. The pharaohs of Egypt lined the banks of the Nile River with statues of themselves to assert their authority, and there is no shortage of monumental effigies in Washington, D.C., today.

© Mel Longhurst/Photoshot

FIGURE 29.1 Not only the high and mighty: sculpture of a Great Depression–era breadline at the Franklin Delano Roosevelt Memorial in Washington, D.C.

Still, the ease with which all of us make and share images *is* unprecedented: people are uploading three billion shots a *day* to Snapchat. And most of us have easily adjusted to instantaneous multichannel, multimedia connectivity. We expect it to be seamless too. The prophet of this era was Marshall McLuhan, who nearly fifty years ago proclaimed that "the medium is the massage," with the play on *message* and *massage* intentional. As McLuhan says, "We shape our tools and afterwards our tools shape us. All media works us over completely."

McLuhan was certainly prescient, as legendary filmmaker Werner Herzog makes clear in his 2016 documentary, *Lo and Behold: Reveries of the Connected World*. Herzog conducted interviews with a range of people— from computer scientists at UCLA and Carnegie Mellon to Silicon Valley denizens like Elon Musk and Sebastian Thrun to ordinary citizens caught up in use, abuse, and overuse— associated with the Internet. Herzog's instantly recognizable voice-over narrates the film's ten sections: as a reviewer for the *New Yorker* puts it, "It should be impossible to sound simultaneously droning and clipped, but somehow Herzog manages it, and it's delicious to watch the expressions on the faces of neuroscientists as he inquires, 'Could it be that the Internet starts to dream of itself?'"

The poster on the facing page aims to capture the complexity of "the connected world" as well as to suggest that we may well have lost our minds in the enormously complex, hugely wired world that now seems to "work us over" perhaps more than even McLuhan imagined. Take a close look at the poster and do some critical thinking about it and its effects. Note the four stars at the top under the heading, the figure dominating the poster (which appears to be a male wearing a suit and tie), the use of color to highlight the scramble in our Internet-filled heads, the change in font in the title, and the bottom caption "The human side of the digital revolution." How do image and text work together to create an argument and how would you express that argument? Certainly the poster intends to entice viewers to take in Herzog's film, but what other arguments can you detect there? Look back to **Chapter 12** for more information on analyzing texts and images.

FIGURE 29.2 "Herzog weaves a fantastical tale. For those looking for a ride through our modern technological world, or indeed a preview of what is to come, this is it."

RESPOND

Find an advertisement, poster, or flyer—either print or digital—that uses both verbal and visual elements. Analyze its argument first by pointing out the claims the ad makes (or implies) and then by identifying the ways it supports them verbally and/or visually. (If it helps, go over the questions about multimodal texts offered in **Chapter 12** on **pp. 288–290**.) Then switch ads with a classmate and discuss his/her analysis. Compare your responses to the two ads. If they're different—and they probably will be—how might you account for the differences?

Using Visuals in Your Own Arguments

Given the power of images, it's only natural that you would use them in your own composing. In fact, many college instructors now expect projects for their courses to be posted to the Web, where digital photos, videos, and design elements are native. Other instructors invite or even require students to do multimedia reports or to use videos, photo collages, cartoons, or other media to make arguments. Using visual media in your academic writing can have all the reach and versatility of more conventional verbal appeals to pathos, ethos, and logos. Often even more.

Using Images and Visual Design to Create Pathos

Many advertisements, YouTube videos, political posters, rallies, marches, and even church services use visual images to trigger emotions. You can't flip through a magazine, watch a video, or browse the Web without being cajoled or seduced by figures or design elements of all kinds—most of them fashioned in some way to attract your eye and attention.

Technology has also made it incredibly easy for you to create on-the-spot photographs and videos that you can use for making arguments of your own. With a GoPro camera strapped to your head, you could document transportation problems in and around campus and then present your visual evidence in a paper or an oral report. You don't have to be a professional these days to produce poignant, stirring, or even satirical visual texts.

Yet just because images are powerful doesn't mean they always work. When you compose visually, you have to be certain to generate impressions that support your arguments, not weigh against them.

Shape Visuals to Convey Appropriate Feelings

To appeal visually to your readers' emotions, think first of the goal of your writing: you want every image or use of multimedia to advance that purpose. Consider, for a moment, the iconic *Apollo 8* "earthrise" photograph of our planet hanging above the horizon of the moon. You could adapt this image to introduce an appeal for additional investment in the space program. Or it might become part of an argument about the need to preserve frail natural environments, or a stirring appeal against nationalism: *From space, we are one world.* Any of these claims might be supported successfully without the image, but the photograph—like most visuals—will probably touch members of your audience more strongly than words alone could.

NASA

FIGURE 29.3 Still striking almost fifty years later, this 1968 *Apollo 8* photograph of the earth shining over the moon can support many kinds of arguments.

Consider Emotional Responses to Color

As the "earthrise" photo demonstrates, color can have great power too: the beautiful blue earth floating in deep black space carries a message of its own. Indeed, our response to color is part of our biological and cultural makeup. So it makes sense to consider what shades are especially effective with the kinds of arguments you're making, whether they occur in images themselves or in elements such as headings, fonts, backgrounds, screens, banners, and so on. And remember that a black-and-white image can also be a memorable design choice.

Here's an image of the box cover for one of the iconic Zelda games for Nintendo. Note its simplicity and the use of vivid color: red dominates, signaling strength and adventure; the gold background and the gold-emblazoned shield and sword suggest fantasy. This particular game (*A Link to the Past*) was released in the United States in 1992.

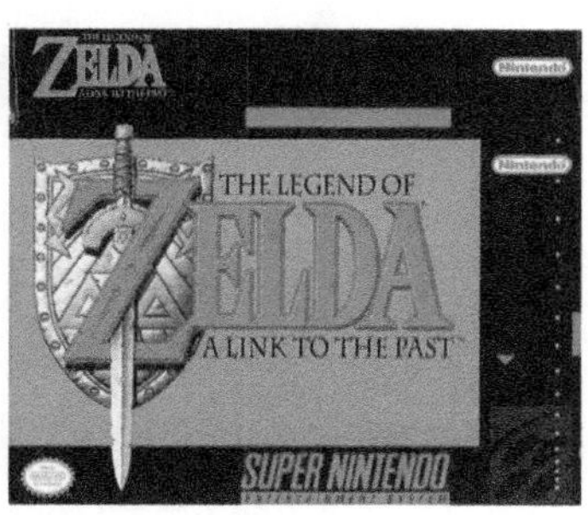

Compare the 1992 box cover art with the most recent Zelda game, *Breath of the Wild* (2017). Here the cooler green and blue colors speak of the natural world and the adventures Link will encounter there.

When you think about using images like these in your writing, do some critical analysis of the image before you definitely decide on it. How does the image, and its use of color, help to support the argument you are making? Is it a good fit?

If you are creating images of your own, let your selection of colors be guided by your own good taste, by designs you admire, or by the advice of friends or helpful professionals. Some design and presentation software will even help you choose colors by offering dependable "default" shades or an array of pre-existing designs and compatible colors (for example, of presentation slides). To be emotionally effective, the colors you choose for a design should follow certain commonsense principles. If you're using background colors on a political poster, Web site, or slide, the contrast between words and background should be vivid enough to make reading easy. For example, white letters on a yellow background are not usually legible. Similarly, bright background colors should be avoided for long documents because reading is easiest with dark letters against a light or white background. Avoid complex patterns; even though they might look interesting and be easy to create, they often interfere with other more important elements of a presentation.

When you use visuals—either ones you've created or those you have taken from other sources—in your college projects, test them on prospective readers. That's what professionals do because they appreciate how delicate the choices of visual and multimedia texts can be. These responses will help you analyze your own arguments and improve your success with them.

© Eve Arnold/Magnum Photos

FIGURE 29.4 Eve Arnold took this powerful black-and-white photograph in 1958 at a party in Virginia for students being introduced to mixed-race schools. How might a full-color image have changed the impact of the scene?

Using Images to Establish Ethos

If you are on Instagram, Twitter, LinkedIn, or other social networking sites, you no doubt chose photographs for those sites with an eye to creating a sense of who you are, what you value, and how you wish to be perceived. You fashioned a self-image. So it shouldn't come as a surprise that you can boost your credibility as a writer by using visual design strategically: we know one person whose Facebook presentation of images and media so impressed a prospective employer that she got a job on the spot. So whether you are using photographs, videos, or other media on your personal pages or in your college work, it pays to attend to how they construct your ethos.

Understand How Images Enhance Credibility and Authority

You might have noticed that just about every company, organization, institution, government agency, or club now sports a logo or an emblem. Whether it's the Red Cross, the Canadian Olympic Committee, or perhaps the school you attend, such groups use carefully crafted images to signal their authority and trustworthiness. An emblem or a logo can also carry a wealth of cultural and historical implications. That's why university Web sites typically include the seal of the institution somewhere on the homepage (and always on its letterhead) or why the president of the United States travels with a presidential seal to hang on the speaker's podium.

What do the following posters, which circulated during the 2016 presidential election, suggest about each candidate's ethos? Based on these images, how would you describe each candidate as a politician?

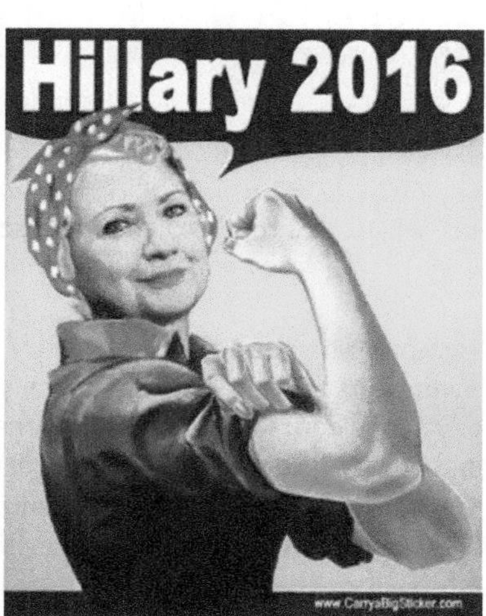

FIGURE 29.5 Posters from the 2016 election

Though you probably don't have a personal logo or trademark, your personal ethos functions the same way when you make an argument. You can establish it by offering visual evidence of your knowledge or competence. In an essay on safety issues in competitive biking, you might include a photo of yourself in a key race, embed a video showing how often serious accidents occur, or include an audio file of an interview with an injured biker. The photo proves that you have personal experience with biking, while the video and audio files show that you have done research and know your subject well, thus helping to affirm your credibility.

Predictably, your choice of *medium* also says something important about you. Making an appeal on a Web site sends signals about your technical skills, contemporary orientation, and personality. So if you direct people to a Facebook or Flickr page, be sure that any materials there present you favorably. Be just as careful in a classroom that any handouts or slides you use for an oral report demonstrate your competence. And remember that you don't always have to be high-tech to be effective: when reporting on a children's story that you're writing, the most sensible medium of presentation might be cardboard and paper made into an oversized book and illustrated by hand.

FIGURE 29.6 Take a look at these three government logos, each of which intends to convey credibility, authority, and maybe more. Do they accomplish their goals? Why or why not?

You demonstrate your ethos simply by showing an awareness of the basic design conventions for any kind of writing you're doing. It's no accident that lab reports for science courses are sober and unembellished. Visually, they reinforce the professional ethos of scientific work. The same is true of a college research paper. So whether you're composing an essay, a résumé, a film, an animated comic, or a Web site, look for successful models and follow their design cues.

Consider How Details of Design Reflect Your Ethos

As we have just suggested, almost every design element you use in a paper or project sends signals about character and ethos. You might resent the tediousness of placing page numbers in the appropriate corner, aligning long quotations just so, and putting footnotes in the right place, but these details prove that you are paying attention. Gestures as simple as writing on official stationery (if, for example, you are representing a club or campus organization) or dressing up for an oral presentation matter too: suddenly you seem more mature and competent.

Even the type fonts that you select for a document can mark you as warm and inviting or as efficient and contemporary. The warm and inviting fonts often belong to a family called *serif*. The serifs are those little flourishes at the ends of the strokes that make the fonts seem handcrafted and artful:

warm and inviting (Bookman Old Style)

warm and inviting (Times New Roman)

warm and inviting (Georgia)

Cleaner, modern fonts go without those little flourishes and are called *sans serif*. These fonts are cooler, simpler, and, some argue, more readable on a computer screen (depending on screen resolution):

efficient and contemporary (Helvetica)

efficient and contemporary (Verdana)

efficient and contemporary (Comic Sans MS)

Other typographic elements send messages as well. The size of type can make a difference. If your text or headings are in boldface and too large, you'll seem to be shouting:

LOSE WEIGHT! PAY NOTHING!*

Tiny type, on the other hand, might make you seem evasive:

*Excludes the costs of enrollment and required meal purchases. Minimum contract: 12 months.

Finally, don't ignore the signals you send through your choice of *illustrations* and *photographs* themselves. Images communicate your preferences, sensitivities, and inclusiveness—sometimes inadvertently. Conference planners, for example, are careful to create brochures that represent all participants, and they make sure that the brochure photos don't show only women, only men, or only members of one racial or ethnic group.

FIGURE 29.7 In March 2017, journalist Tim Murphy asked, "Who's missing from this photo of politicians deciding the future of women's health?" Notice anyone other than white men here?

RESPOND

Choose a project or an essay you have written recently and read it critically for how well *visually* it establishes your credibility and how well it is designed. Ask a classmate or friend to look at it and describe the ethos you convey through the item. Then go back to the drawing board with a memo to yourself about how you might use images or media to improve it.

Using Visual Images to Support Logos

To celebrate the Fourth of July in 2017, ancestry.com, the online company that helps people identify their ancestors through DNA, aired a commercial called "Declaration Descendants." A still from one of the frames appears below.

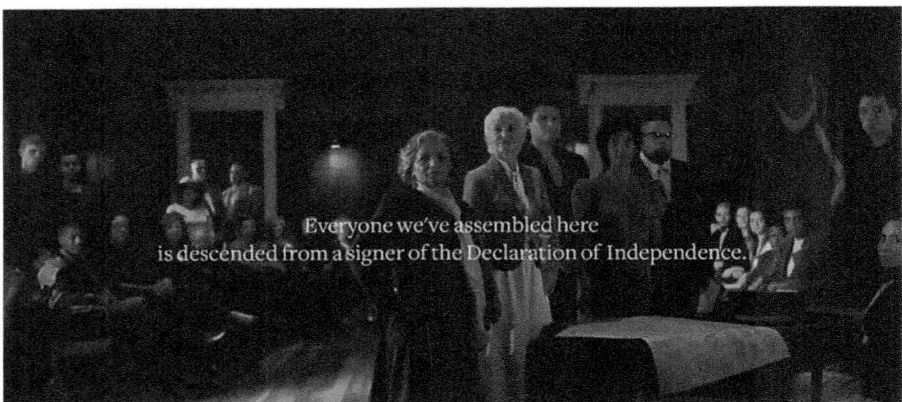

In the commercial, people from a wide range of ethnicities recite parts of the American Declaration of Independence. At the conclusion, viewers learn that each of those readers is a descendent of someone who signed the Declaration. As the CEO of ancestry.com Vineet Mehra said about the advertisement, "We're all much more similar than you think. And we're using facts and data to prove it. This is not fluffy marketing. These are facts." Thus an online ancestry service uses images, facts, and data to support its major claim.

As this example shows, we get information from visual images of all kinds, including commercials we see on television and online every day. Today, much information comes to us in graphic presentations that use images along with words. Such images work well to gather information efficiently and persuasively. In fact, readers now expect evidence to be presented graphically, and we are learning to read such graphic representations more and more critically.

Organize Information Visually

Graphic presentation calls for design that enables readers and viewers to look at an item and understand what it does. A brilliant, much-copied example of such an intuitive design is a seat adjuster invented many years ago by Mercedes-Benz (see below). It's shaped like a tiny seat. Push any element of the control, and the real seat moves in that direction—back and forth, up and down. No instructions are necessary.

© Ron Kimball/KimballStock

FIGURE 29.8 Mercedes-Benz's seat adjuster

Good visual design can work the same way in an argument by conveying evidence, data, and other information without elaborate instructions. Titles, headings, subheadings, enlarged quotations, running heads, and boxes are some common visual signals:

- Use headings to guide your readers through your print or electronic document. For long and complex pieces, use subheadings as well, and make sure they are parallel.
- Use type font, size, and color to show related information among headings.
- Arrange headings or text on a page to enforce relationships among comparable items, ideas, or bits of evidence.
- Use a list or a box to set off material for emphasis or to show that it differs from the rest of the presentation. You can also use shading, color, and typography for emphasis.
- Place your images and illustrations strategically. What you position front and center will appear more important than items in less conspicuous places. Images of comparable size will be treated as equally important.

Remember, too, that design principles evolve and change from medium to medium. A printed text or presentation slide, for example, ordinarily works best when its elements are easy to read, simply organized, and surrounded by restful white space. But some electronic texts thrive on visual clutter, packing a grab bag of data into a limited space (see the "Infographic of Infographics" on the following page). Look closely, though, and you'll probably find the logic in these designs.

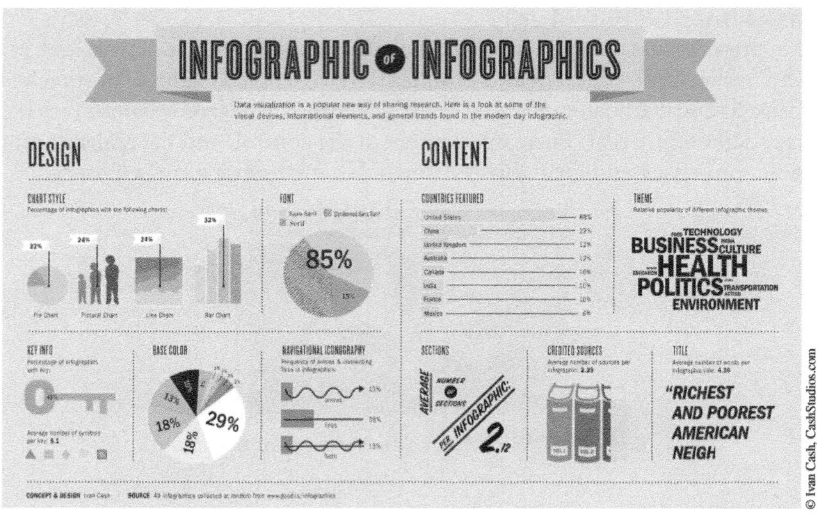

FIGURE 29.9 An infographic

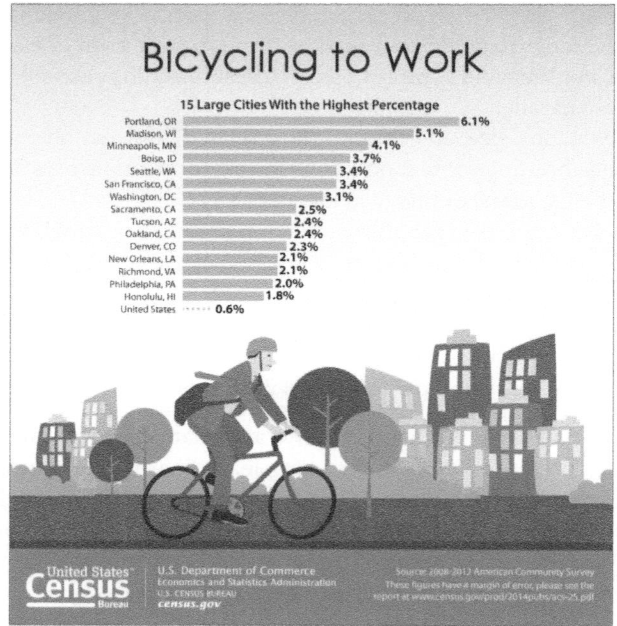

FIGURE 29.10 A bar graph

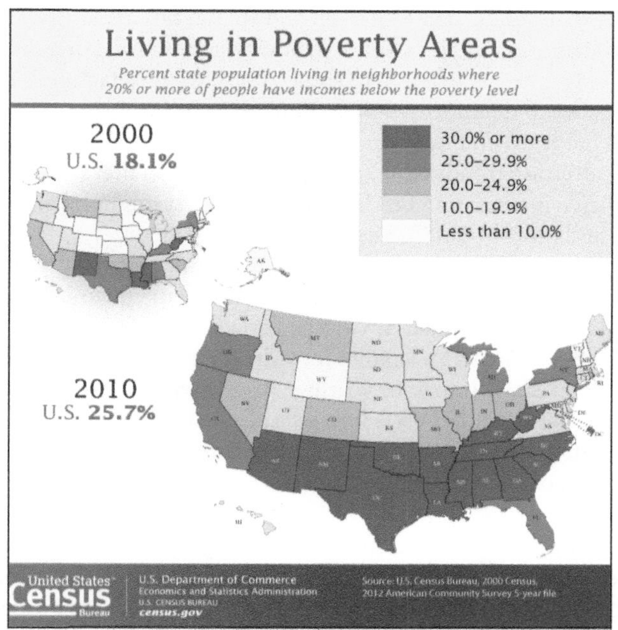

FIGURE 29.11 A map

Use Visuals to Convey Data Efficiently

Words are capable of great precision and subtlety, but some information is conveyed far more effectively by charts, graphs, drawings, maps, or photos—as several items in Chapter 27 illustrate. When making an argument, especially to a large group, consider what information might be more persuasive and memorable in nonverbal form.

A *pie chart* is an effective way of comparing parts to the whole. You might use a pie chart to illustrate the ethnic composition of your school, the percentage of taxes paid by people at different income levels, or the consumption of energy by different nations. Pie charts depict such information memorably.

A *graph* is an efficient device for comparing items over time or according to other variables. You could use a graph to trace the rise and fall of test scores over several decades, to show college enrollment by sex, race, and Hispanic origin, or to track bicycle usage in the United States, as in the bar graph on p. 578.

Diagrams or *drawings* are useful for attracting attention to details. Use drawings to illustrate complex physical processes or designs of all sorts. After the 2001 attack on the World Trade Center, for example, engineers prepared drawings and diagrams to help citizens understand precisely what led to the total collapse of the buildings.

You can use *maps* to illustrate location and spatial relationships—something as simple as the distribution of office space in your student union or as complex as poverty in the United States, as in the map shown on p. 579. In fact, scholars in many fields now use geographic information system (GIS) technology to merge maps with databases in all fields to offer new kinds of arguments about everything from traffic patterns and health care trends to character movements in literary works. Plotting data this way yields information far different from what might be offered in words alone. You can find more about GIS applications online.

Timelines allow you to represent the passage of time graphically, and online tools like Sutori or Our Story or Office Timeline can help you create them for insertion into your documents. Similarly, Web pages can make for valuable illustrations. Programs like ShrinkTheWeb's Snapito let you create snapshots of Web sites that can then be inserted easily into your writing. And when you want to combine a variety of graphs, charts, and other texts into a single visual argument, you might create an *infographic* using free software such as Canva Infographic Maker, Google Charts, Easel.ly, Venngage, or Pictochart.

Follow Professional Guidelines for Presenting Visuals

Charts, graphs, tables, illustrations, timelines, snapshots of Web sites, and video clips play such an important role in many fields that professional groups have come up with guidelines for labeling and formatting these items. You need to become familiar with those conventions as you advance in a field. A guide such as the *Publication Manual of the American Psychological Association*, Sixth Edition, or the *MLA Handbook*, Eighth Edition, describes these rules in detail.

Remember to Check for Copyrighted Material

You also must be careful to respect copyright rules when using visual items that were created by someone else. If you do introduce any borrowed items into academic work, be careful to document them fully. It's relatively easy these days to download visual texts of all kinds from the Web. Some of these items—such as clip art or government documents—may be in the *public domain*, meaning that you're free to use them without requesting permission or paying a royalty. But other visual texts may require permission, especially if you intend to publish your work or use the item commercially. Remember: anything you place on a Web site is considered "published." (See Chapter 23 for more on intellectual property and fair use.)

part 6

Public Speaking: Getting Started

CHAPTER

30

Becoming a Public Speaker

The ability to speak confidently and convincingly in front of others is a crucial skill for anyone who wants to take an active role in life. This pocket guide offers the tools you need to create and deliver effective speeches, from presentations to fellow students to speeches delivered in virtually any setting—including those presented online. Here you will find the basic components of any good speech and acquire the skills to deliver presentations in a variety of specialized contexts—from the college classroom to the civic, business, and professional arenas. You'll also find proven techniques to build your confidence by overcoming the anxiety associated with public speaking.

Gain a Vital Life Skill

Public speaking provides a sense of empowerment and satisfaction rarely found elsewhere. More than ever, it has become both a vital life skill and a potent weapon in career development. Business magnate Warren Buffett passionately extols the role that public speaking has played in his success:

> Be sure to do it, whether you like it or not...do it until you get comfortable with it....Public speaking is an asset that will last you 50 or 60 years, and it's a necessary skill; and if you don't like doing it, that will also last you 50 or 60 years....Once you tackle the fear and master the skill, you can run the world. You can walk into rooms, command people, and get them to listen to you and your great ideas.[1]

Advance Your Professional Goals

Skill in public speaking will give you an unmistakable edge professionally. Employers of new college graduates consistently reveal that ability in oral and written communication is among the most important skills they look for in new hires—more so even than leadership, quantitative, technical, or interpersonal skills. Survey after survey confirms the value of skill in oral communication, making the public speaking course potentially the most valuable one you can take during your undergraduate career.

SKILLS EMPLOYERS RATE AS MOST IMPORTANT

1. Ability to work in a team
2. Problem-solving skills
3. Communication skills (written)
4. Strong work ethic
5. **Communication skills (verbal)**
6. Leadership
7. Initiative
8. Analytical/quantitative skills
9. Flexibility/adaptability
10. Detail-oriented
11. Interpersonal skills (relates well to others)
12. Technical skills

Source: National Association of Colleges and Employers, *Job Outlook 2017*, **www.naceweb.org/about-us/press/2017/employers-seek-teamwork-problem-solving-skills-on-resumes/**

Enhance Your Career as a Student

Preparing speeches calls upon numerous skills that you will need in other college courses. As in the speech class, many courses also require that you research and write about topics, analyze audiences, outline and organize ideas, and support claims. These and other skill sets covered in this guide, including working with presentation media and controlling voice and body during delivery, are valuable in any course that includes an oral-presentation component, from English composition to engineering.

Find New Opportunities for Civic Engagement

Public speaking also offers you ways to enter the public conversation about social concerns and become a more engaged citizen. Public speaking gives you a voice that can be heard and can be counted.

Climate change, immigration reform, gun violence—such large civic issues require our considered judgment and action. Yet today too many of us leave it up to politicians, journalists, and other "experts" to make decisions about critical issues such as these. Voter turnout in the United States is much lower than in most established democracies, with only about 50 percent of young persons ages 18–29 voting in the 2016 presidential election.[2] This same age group barely shows up at the polls at all for congressional, state, and local elections. When we as citizens speak up in sufficient numbers, democracy functions better and change that truly reflects the will of the people occurs. For example, the students who survived the 2018 school shooting in Parkland, Florida, have emerged as powerful voices in favor of gun control. Speaking passionately at rallies and in public forums, the Parkland students have made a real impact on civic discourse: they helped pressure state lawmakers into passing new restrictions on gun purchases.

As you study public speaking, you will have the opportunity to research topics that are meaningful to you, consider alternate viewpoints, and choose a course of action.[3] You will learn to distinguish between argument that advances constructive goals and uncivil speech that serves merely to inflame and demean others. You will learn, in short, the "rules of engagement" for effective public discourse.[4] As you do, you will gain confidence in your ability to join your voice with others in pursuit of issues you care about.

The Classical Roots of Public Speaking

Originally, the practice of giving speeches was known as **rhetoric** or **oratory**. Rhetoric flourished in the Greek city-state of Athens in the fifth century B.C.E. and referred to making effective speeches, particularly those of a persuasive nature.

Athens was the site of the world's first direct democracy, and public speaking was the vehicle that allowed it to succeed. Meeting in a public square called the **agora**, Athenians routinely spoke with great skill on the issues of public policy; and their belief that citizenship demands active participation in public affairs endures in modern democracies to this day.

Greek, and later Roman, teachers divided the process of preparing a speech into five parts—*invention*, *arrangement*, *style*, *memory*, and *delivery*—called the **canons of rhetoric**. These parts correspond to the order in which these teachers believed a speech should be put together.

- *Invention* refers to discovering the types of evidence and arguments you will use to make your case.
- *Arrangement* is organizing the evidence and arguments in ways best suited to the topic and audience (see **Chapter 40**).
- *Style* is the way the speaker uses language to express the speech ideas (see **Chapter 43**).
- *Memory* is the practice of the speech until it can be delivered artfully (see **Chapter 44**).
- *Delivery* is the vocal and nonverbal behavior you use when speaking (see **Chapters 45 and 46**).

Although founding scholars such as the great Greek rhetorician Aristotle (384–322 B.C.E.) and the Roman statesman and orator Cicero (106–43 B.C.E.) surely did not anticipate the ever-present PowerPoint or Prezi slideshow that accompanies contemporary speeches, the speechmaking structure they bequeathed to us as the canons of rhetoric remains remarkably intact. Often identified by terms other than the original, these canons nonetheless continue to be taught in current books on public speaking, including this pocket guide.

QUICK TIP

Voice Your Ideas in a Public Forum

The Greeks called it the *agora*; the Romans, the *forum*. Today, the term **public forum** denotes a variety of venues for the discussion of issues of public interest, including traditional physical spaces such as town halls as well as virtual forums streamed to listeners online. Participation in any of these forums offers an excellent opportunity to pose questions and deliver brief comments, thereby providing you with exposure to an audience and building confidence. To find a forum in your area, check with your school or local town government, or online at the National Issues Forums Institute (**www.nifi.org**).

Learning to Speak in Public

None of us is born knowing how to deliver a successful speech. Rather, public speaking is an acquired skill that improves with practice. It is also a skill that shares many features with other familiar activities, such as conversing and writing, and it can be much less daunting when you realize that you can draw on expertise you already have.

Draw on Conversational Skills

In several respects, planning and delivering a speech resembles engaging in a particularly important conversation. When speaking with a friend, you automatically check to make certain you are understood and adjust your meaning accordingly. You also discuss issues that are appropriate to the circumstances. When a stranger is involved, however, you try to get to know his or her interests and attitudes before revealing any strong opinions. These instinctive adjustments to *audience*, *topic*, and *occasion* represent critical steps in creating a speech. Although public speaking requires more planning, both the conversationalist and the public speaker try to uncover the audience's interests and needs before speaking.

Draw on Skills in Composition

Preparing a speech also has much in common with writing. Both depend on having a focused sense of who the audience is.[5] Both speaking and writing often require that you research a topic, offer credible evidence, employ effective transitions, and devise persuasive appeals. The principles of organizing a speech parallel those of organizing an essay, including offering a compelling introduction, a clear thesis statement, supporting ideas, and a thoughtful conclusion.

Develop an Effective Oral Style

Although public speaking has much in common with everyday conversation and with writing, a speech is a unique form of communication characterized by an oral style of language. Language as used in a speech is simpler, more rhythmic, more repetitious, and more interactive than either conversation or writing.[6] Effective speakers use familiar words, easy-to-follow sentences, and frequent repetition to emphasize ideas and help listeners follow along.

Language in a speech also is often more interactive and inclusive of the audience than written language. Audience members want to know what the speaker thinks and feels and that he or she recognizes them and relates the message to them. Speakers accomplish this by making specific references to themselves and to the audience. Yet in contrast to conversation, in order to develop an effective oral style you must practice the words you will say and the way you will say them.

Effective public speakers, engaging conversationalists, and compelling writers share an important quality: They keep their focus on offering something of value to their audience.

Demonstrate Respect for Difference

Every audience member wants to feel that the speaker has his or her particular needs and interests at heart, and to feel recognized and included in the message. To create this sense of inclusion, a public speaker must be able to address diverse audiences with sensitivity, demonstrating respect for differences in culture and identity. Striving for inclusion and adopting an audience-centered perspective will bring you closer to the goal of every public speaker—establishing a genuine connection with the audience.

Public Speaking as a Form of Communication

Public speaking is one of four categories of human communication: dyadic, small group, mass, and public speaking.

- **Dyadic communication** happens between two people, as in a conversation.
- **Small group communication** involves a small number of people who can see and speak directly with one another.
- **Mass communication** occurs between a speaker and a large audience of unknown people who usually are not present with the speaker, or who are part of such an immense crowd that there can be little or no interaction between speaker and listener.
- In **public speaking**, a speaker delivers a message with a specific purpose to an audience of people who are present during the delivery of the speech. Public speaking always includes a speaker who has a reason for speaking, an audience that gives the speaker its attention, and a message that is meant to accomplish a specific purpose. Public speakers address audiences largely without interruption and take responsibility for the words and ideas being expressed.

Public Speaking as an Interactive Communication Process

In any communication event, several elements are present. These include the source, the receiver, the message, the channel, and shared meaning (see Figure 30.1).

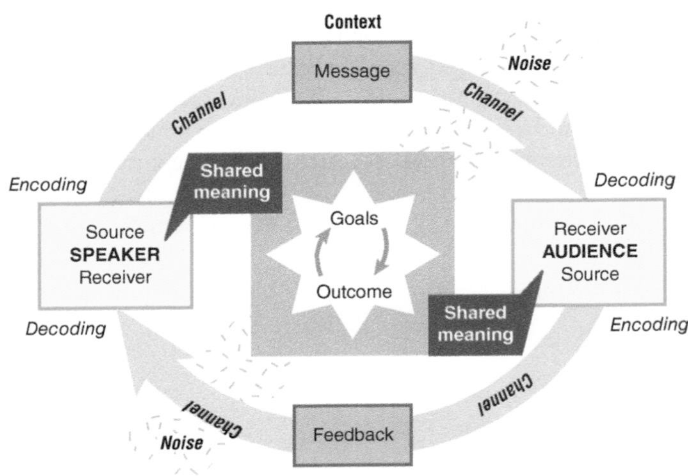

FIGURE 30.1 The Communication Process

The **source**, or sender, creates a message. Creating, organizing, and producing the message is called **encoding**—the process of converting thoughts into words. The recipient of the source's message is the **receiver**, or audience; interpreting the message is called **decoding**. Audience members decode the meaning of the message selectively, based on their own experiences and attitudes.

Feedback, the audience's response to a message, can be conveyed both verbally and nonverbally. The **message** is the content of the communication process: thoughts and ideas put into meaningful expressions, expressed verbally and nonverbally.

The medium through which the speaker sends a message is the **channel**. If a speaker delivers a message in front of a live audience, the channel is the air through which sound waves travel. Among other channels are phones, televisions, and the internet. **Noise** is any interference with the message. Noise can disrupt the communication process through physical sounds such as cell phones ringing and people talking or texting, through psychological distractions such as heated emotions, or through environmental interference such as a too-cold room or the presence of unexpected people.

Shared meaning is the mutual understanding of a message between speaker and audience. The lowest level of shared meaning exists when the speaker has merely caught the audience's attention. As the message develops, a higher degree of shared meaning is possible. Thus listener and speaker together truly make a speech a speech—they "co-create" its meaning.

Two other factors are critical to consider when preparing and delivering a speech—context and goals. *Context* includes anything that influences the speaker, the audience, or the occasion—and thus, ultimately, the speech. In classroom speeches, the context would include (among other things) the physical setting, the order and timing of speeches, and the cultural orientations of audience members. Part of the context of any speech is the situation that created the need for the speech in the first place. All speeches are delivered in response to a specific **rhetorical situation**, or a circumstance calling for a public response.[7] Is the speech in response to a recent event affecting the audience? Bearing the rhetorical situation in mind ensures that you maintain an **audience-centered perspective**—that is, that you keep the needs, values, attitudes, and wants of your listeners firmly in focus.

A final prerequisite for any effective speech is a clearly defined **specific speech purpose** or goal—what you want the audience to learn or do as a result of the speech. Establishing a specific speech purpose early on will help you proceed through speech preparation and delivery with a clear focus in mind (see pp. 634–635).

CHAPTER

31

From A to Z: Overview of a Speech

Public speaking is an applied art, and every speaking opportunity, including that provided by the classroom, offers you valuable hands-on experience. To help you get started quickly, this chapter previews the steps involved in putting together any speech or presentation. Subsequent chapters expand on these steps. **Figure 31.1** illustrates the process of preparing for a speech.

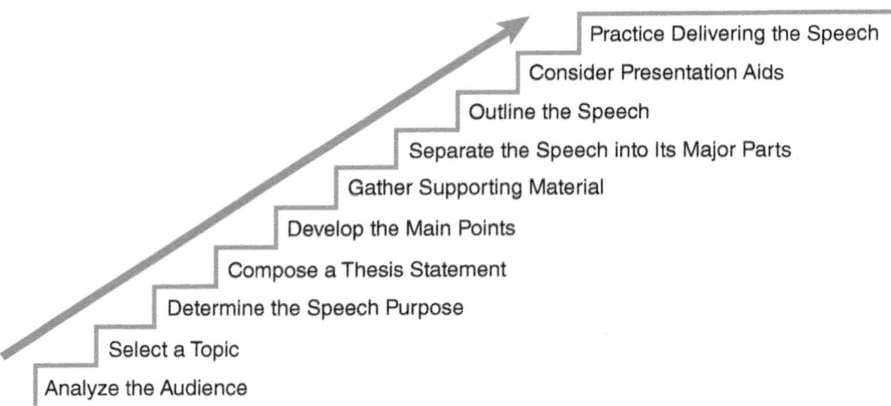

FIGURE 31.1 Steps in the Speechmaking Process

Analyze the Audience

The first step in preparing any speech is to consider the audience—how their interests, needs, and opinions will influence their responses toward a given topic, speaker, and occasion. *Audience analysis* is a process of learning about audience members' attributes and motivations using tools such as interviews and questionnaires (see **Chapter 35**). For a brief first speech, however, especially one delivered in the classroom, start with your own powers of observation. Consider some simple demographic characteristics: ratio of males to females, age ranges, and apparent cultural and socioeconomic backgrounds. Take these characteristics into account as you select a topic and draft the speech, focusing on ways you can relate it meaningfully to this particular audience.

Select a Topic

Unless the topic is assigned, the next step is to decide what you want to speak about. First, consider the speech occasion and reason for speaking. What topics will be suitable to your audience's needs and wants in these circumstances? Using these parameters, let your interests and expertise guide you in selecting something to speak about (see **Chapter 36** on selecting a topic and purpose).

Determine the Speech Purpose

A speech without a purpose is like a car without fuel—it won't get you anywhere. Actually, a speech requires that you fix *two* purposes in your mind. First, for any given topic, you should direct your speech toward one of three general speech purposes—to *inform*, to *persuade*, or to *mark a special occasion*. Thus you need to decide whether your goal is simply to give your audience information about the topic, to persuade them to accept one position to the exclusion of other positions, or to help them memorialize an occasion such as a wedding, a funeral, or an awards event.

You should also mentally formulate a specific speech purpose—a statement of what you want the audience to learn, agree with, or perhaps act upon as a result of your speech. For example, if your general purpose is to inform, your specific purpose might be "to inform my audience about how self-driving cars will impact insurance policies." If your general purpose is to persuade, the specific purpose might be "to persuade my audience that they should support tighter regulations on insuring self-driving vehicles."

Compose a Thesis Statement

Next, compose a thesis statement that clearly expresses the central idea of your speech. While the specific purpose focuses your attention on the outcome you want to achieve with the speech, the thesis statement concisely identifies, in a single sentence, what the speech is about:

General Purpose:	To inform
Specific Purpose:	To inform my audience about three critical steps we can take to combat identity theft
Thesis Statement:	The best ways to combat identity theft are to review your monthly financial statements, periodically check your credit report, and secure your personal information in both digital and print form.

From this point forward in the development of your speech, refer to the thesis statement often to make sure that you are on track to illustrate or prove it.

QUICK TIP

Speak with Purpose

To ensure that the audience learns or does what you want them to as a result of your speech, keep your thesis and speech goals in sight. Write your thesis statement and general and specific speech purposes on a sticky note and place it on the edge of your computer screen. It will be an important guide in developing your speech.

Develop the Main Points

Organize your speech around two or three main points. These are the primary pieces of knowledge (in an informative speech) or the key claims (in a persuasive speech). If you create a clear thesis for your speech, the main points will be easily identifiable.

Thesis:	The best ways to combat identity theft are to review your monthly financial statements, periodically check your credit report, and secure your personal information in both digital and print form.
	I. Review your monthly bank statements, credit card bills, and similar financial records to be aware of all transactions.
	II. Check your consumer credit report at least twice a year.
	III. Keep your personal identifying digital and print information highly secure.

Gather Supporting Materials

Use supporting material to illustrate or prove your main points. Supporting material potentially includes the entire world of information available to you—from personal experiences to every conceivable kind of credible source. Plan to research your topic to provide evidence for your assertions and lend credibility to your message.

Arrange the Speech into Its Major Parts

Every speech will have an introduction, a body, and a conclusion. Develop each part separately, then bring them together using transition statements (see **Chapter 39**). The **introduction** serves to draw the audience's interest to the topic, speaker, and thesis. The speech **body** contains the speech's main points and subpoints. The **conclusion** restates the speech thesis and reiterates how the main points confirm it (see **Chapter 42** on the introduction and conclusion).

DEVELOPING SPEECH PARTS

Introduction

- Pique the audience's interest with a quotation, short story, example, or other means of gaining their attention described in **Chapter 42**.
- Introduce yourself and your topic.
- Preview the thesis and main points.

(Use a transition statement to signal the start of the speech body.)

Body

- Develop the main points and illustrate each one with relevant supporting material.
- Organize your ideas and evidence in a structure that suits the topic, audience, and occasion.

(Use transitions to move between main points and to the conclusion.)

Conclusion

- Review the thesis and reiterate how the main points confirm it.
- Leave the audience with something to think about.

Outline the Speech

An outline is a plan for arranging the elements of your speech in support of your thesis. Outlines are based on the principle of coordination and subordination—the logical placement of ideas relative to their importance to one another. Coordinate points are of equal importance and are indicated by their parallel alignment. Subordinate points are given less weight than the points they support and are placed to the right of them. (For a full discussion of outlining, see **Chapter 41**.)

Coordinate Points	I. Main Point 1
	II. Main Point 2
	    A. Subpoint 1
	    B. Subpoint 2

Subordinate Points	I. Main Point 1
	    A. First level of subordination
	        1. Second level of subordination
	        2. Second level of subordination
	            a. Third level of subordination
	            b. Third level of subordination

As your speeches become more detailed, you will need to select an appropriate **organizational pattern** (see **Chapter 40**). You will also need to familiarize yourself with developing both working and speaking outlines (see **Chapter 41**). To allow for the full development of your ideas, a working outline generally contains points stated in close-to-complete sentences. A speaking outline is far briefer and uses either short phrases or key words.

Consider Presentation Aids

As you prepare your speech, consider whether using visual, audio, or a combination of different presentation aids will help the audience understand points. (See **Chapters 47–49**.)

Practice Delivering the Speech

Preparation and practice are necessary for the success of even your first speech in class. You will want to feel and appear natural to your listeners, an effect best achieved by rehearsing both the verbal and nonverbal **delivery** of your speech (see **Chapters 45 and 46**). So practice your speech at least six times. For a four- to six-minute speech, that's only about one-half hour of actual practice time.

QUICK TIP

Be Aware of Your Nonverbal Delivery

Audiences are highly attuned to a speaker's facial expressions, gestures, and general body movement. As you rehearse, practice smiling and otherwise animating your face in ways that feel natural to you. Audiences want to feel that you care about what you are saying, so avoid a deadpan, or blank, expression. Make eye contact with your practice audience. Doing so will make audience members feel that you recognize and respect them. Practice gestures that feel natural to you, steering clear of exaggerated movements.

CHAPTER

32

Managing Speech Anxiety

Contrary to what most of us think, feeling nervous about giving a speech is not only normal but desirable. Channeled properly, nervousness (or more specifically, the adrenaline that accompanies it) can actually boost performance. The key is knowing how to make this state work *for* rather than *against* us. This chapter introduces specific anxiety-reducing techniques that speakers use to minimize their tension and maximize their speaking experience.

> I focus on the information rather than being graded. I also practice my speech a ton to really make sure I do not speak too quickly. I time myself so that I can develop an average time. This makes me more confident [in dealing] with time requirements. And, because I know that I am well prepared, I really try to just relax.
>
> —Kristen Obracay, student

Identify What Makes You Anxious

Anxiety is a state of uneasiness brought on by uncertainty and fear about the outcome of an event. Lacking positive public-speaking experience, feeling different from members of the audience, or feeling uneasy about being the center of attention—each of these factors can lead to the onset of **public-speaking anxiety** (PSA), a situation-specific social anxiety that arises from anticipating giving an oral presentation.[1] Fortunately, we can learn techniques to tame this anxiety in each of these situations and make it work for us. An important first step is to identify what makes us anxious.

Lack of Positive Experience

If you are new to public speaking or have had unpleasant experiences, anxiety about what to expect is only natural. Without positive experiences to draw on, it's hard to put this anxiety into perspective. It's a bit of a vicious circle. Some people react by deciding to avoid speeches altogether, yet gaining more experience is key to overcoming speech anxiety.

Feeling Different

The prospect of being in front of an audience makes many of us extra-sensitive to our perceived personal shortcomings, such as a less-than-perfect haircut or an accent. We may believe that no one could be interested in anything we have to say.

As inexperienced speakers, we become anxious because we assume that being different somehow means being inferior. Actually, each of us is different from everyone else. However, nearly everyone experiences nervousness about giving a speech.

> I control my anxiety by mentally viewing myself as being 100 percent equal to my classmates.
>
> —Lee Morris, student

Being the Center of Attention

Certain audience behaviors—such as chatting with a neighbor or checking text messages—can cause us as speakers to think we've lost the audience's attention by doing something wrong; we wonder about our mistakes and whether others noticed these supposed flaws. Left unchecked, this kind of thinking can distract us from the speech itself, with all our attention now focused on "me." Our self-consciousness makes us feel even more conspicuous and sensitive to even the smallest faults, which increases our anxiety! Actually, an audience rarely notices anything about us that we don't want to reveal.

> It's always scary to speak in front of others, but you just have to remember that everyone is human....Nobody wants you to fail; they're not waiting on you to mess up.
>
> —Mary Parrish, student

Pinpoint the Onset of Anxiety

Different people become anxious at different times during the speechmaking process.[2] Depending on when anxiety strikes, the consequences can include everything from procrastination to poor speech performance. But by pinpointing the onset of speech anxiety, you can manage it promptly with specific anxiety-reducing techniques.

Pre-Preparation Anxiety

Some people feel anxious the minute they know they will be giving a speech. **Pre-preparation anxiety** can be a problem when we delay planning for the speech, or when it so preoccupies us that we miss vital information needed to fulfill the speech assignment. If this form of anxiety affects you, start very early using the stress-reducing techniques described later in this chapter.

Preparation Anxiety

For a few people, anxiety arises only when they actually begin to prepare for the speech. These individuals might feel overwhelmed by the time and planning required or hit a roadblock that puts them behind schedule. Preparation pressures produce a cycle of stress, procrastination, and outright avoidance, all of which contribute to **preparation anxiety**. If you find yourself feeling anxious during this stage, immerse yourself in the speech's preparation but calm your nerves by taking short, relaxing breaks to regain your confidence and focus.

Pre-Performance Anxiety

Some people experience anxiety as they rehearse their speech. This is when the reality of the situation sets in: They worry that the audience will be watching and listening only to them, feel that their ideas aren't expressed ideally, or sense that time is short. If this **pre-performance anxiety** is strong enough, some may even decide to stop rehearsing. If you experience heightened anxiety at this point, practice **positive self-talk**, turning negative thoughts to positive ones (see "Modify Thought and Attitudes" on pp. 599–600).

> I experience anxiety before, during, and after the speech. My "before speech" anxiety begins the night before my speech, but then I begin to look over my notecards, and I start to realize that I am ready for this speech. I practice one more time and I tell myself I am going to be fine.
>
> —Paige Mease, student

Performance Anxiety

For most people, anxiety is highest just as a speech begins.[3] **Performance anxiety** usually is most pronounced during the introduction of the speech when we are most aware of the audience's attention. Audiences we perceive as negative usually cause us to feel more anxious than those we sense are positive or neutral.[4] But experienced speakers agree that by controlling their nervousness during the introduction, the rest of the speech goes quite smoothly.

Regardless of when anxiety about a speech strikes, the important thing to remember is that you can manage the anxiety and not let it manage you—by harming your motivation or by causing you to avoid investing the time and energy required to deliver a successful speech.

Use Proven Strategies to Build Your Confidence

A number of proven strategies exist to help you rein in your fears about public speaking, from positive self-talk and visualization to various relaxation techniques. The first step in taming speech anxiety is to have a thorough plan for each presentation.

Prepare and Practice

If you know your material and have adequately rehearsed your delivery, you're far more likely to feel confident. Once you have prepared the speech, be sure to rehearse it several times.

> Knowing your material is crucial! The worst anxiety comes when you feel unprepared. You just can't help but be nervous, at least a little. If you are confident about what you're speaking, the anxiety fades and you'll feel more comfortable.
>
> —Shea Michelle Allen, student

Modify Thoughts and Attitudes

Negative thoughts about speechmaking increase speech anxiety, but positive thoughts reduce it.[5] A positive attitude actually results in lowered heart rate and reduced anxiety during the delivery of the speech.[6] As you prepare for and deliver your speech, envision it as a valuable, worthwhile, and challenging activity. Use these steps to challenge negative beliefs and encourage positive self-talk:

1. Identify your negative self-talk.
2. Examine the beliefs underlying the negative thoughts.

3. Replace negative self-talk and beliefs with positive statements and mental images.
4. Continue practicing these steps until you feel confident about your speech.

QUICK TIP

Envision Your Speech as a Conversation

Rather than thinking of your speech as a formal performance where you will be judged and critiqued, try thinking of it as a kind of ordinary conversation. In this way, you will feel less threatened and more relaxed about the process. Here's what Virgin airlines founder and entrepreneur Richard Branson recommends:

> Close your mind to the fact that you're on a stage with hundreds of people watching you and instead imagine yourself in a situation where you'd be comfortable speaking to a group...in your dining room at home, telling a story to friends over dinner....This trick has certainly removed some of the anxiety for me.[7]
>
> —Richard Branson, entrepreneur

Visualize Success

Visualization—the practice of summoning feelings and actions consistent with successful performance—is a highly effective method of reducing speech anxiety.[8]

Like positive self-talk, visualization is a form of **cognitive restructuring**—training your mind to think in a more positive way about something that makes you anxious. It requires you to close your eyes and visualize a series of positive feelings and actions that will occur on the day of your speech.

> Close your eyes and allow your body to get comfortable in the chair in which you are sitting. Take a deep, comfortable breath and hold it...now slowly release it through your nose. Now take another deep breath and make certain that you are breathing from the diaphragm...hold it...now slowly release it and note how you feel while doing this. Now one more deep breath...hold it...and release it slowly...and begin your normal breathing pattern.
>
> Now begin to visualize the beginning of a day in which you are going to give an informative speech. See yourself getting up in the morning, full of energy, full of confidence, looking forward to the day's challenges. As you dress, think about how the clothes you choose make you look and feel good about yourself. As you are drive, ride, or walk to the speech setting, note how clear and confident you feel. You feel thoroughly prepared for the topic you will be presenting today.

Now you see yourself standing or sitting in the room where you will present your speech, talking very comfortably and confidently with others in the room. The people to whom you will be presenting your speech appear to be quite friendly and are very cordial in their greetings and conversations prior to the presentation. You feel absolutely sure of your material and of your ability to present the information in a forceful, convincing, positive manner.

Now you see yourself approaching the area from which you will present. You are feeling very good about this presentation and see yourself move eagerly forward. All of your audiovisual materials are well organized, well planned, and clearly aid your presentation.[9]

Activate the Relaxation Response

Before, during, and sometimes after a speech you may experience rapid heart rate and breathing, dry mouth, faintness, freezing-up, or other uncomfortable sensations. These physiological reactions result from the **"fight-or-flight" response**—the body's automatic response to threatening or fear-inducing events. Research shows that you can counteract these sensations by activating a *relaxation response*[10] using techniques such as meditation and controlled breathing.

Briefly Meditate

You can calm yourself considerably before a presentation with this brief meditation exercise:

1. Sit comfortably in a quiet space.
2. Relax your muscles, moving from neck to shoulders to arms to back to legs.
3. Choose a word, phrase, or prayer (e.g., "*Namaste,*" "*Om,*" "Hail Mary, full of grace"). Breathe slowly and say it until you become calm (about ten to twenty minutes).

QUICK TIP

Stretch Away Stress

You can significantly lessen pre-speech jitters by stretching. A half-hour to one-hour session of whole-body stretches and simple yoga poses, combined with deep breathing, will help discharge nervous energy and sharpen mental focus.

Use Stress-Control Breathing

When you feel stressed, the center of your breathing tends to move from the abdomen to the upper chest, leaving you with a reduced supply of air. The chest and shoulders rise, and you feel out of breath. *Stress-control breathing* gives you more movement in the stomach than in the chest.[11] Try it in two stages.

Stage One

Inhale air and let your abdomen go out. Exhale air and let your abdomen go in. Do this for a while until you get into the rhythm of it.

Stage Two

As you inhale, use a soothing word such as *calm* or *relax*, or use a personal mantra like this: "Inhale *calm*, abdomen out, exhale *calm*, abdomen in." Go slowly, taking about three to five seconds with each inhalation and exhalation.

Begin stress-control breathing *several days* before a speech. Then, once the occasion arrives, perform it while awaiting your turn at the podium and just before you start your speech.

> I have two ways to cope with my nervousness before I'm about to speak. I take a couple of deep breaths from my stomach; I breathe in through my nose and out through my mouth. This allows more oxygen to the brain so you can think clearly. I also calm myself down by saying, "Everything will be okay, and the world is not going to crumble before me if I mess up."
>
> —Jenna Sanford, student

Use Movement to Minimize Anxiety

During delivery, you can use controlled movements with your hands and body to release nervousness (see **Chapter 46**):

- Practice natural gestures, such as holding up your index finger when stating your first main point. Think about what you want to say as you do this, instead of thinking about how you look or feel.
- Move as you speak. You don't have to stand perfectly still behind the podium when you deliver a speech. Walk around as you make some of your points. Movement relieves tension and helps hold the audience's attention.

QUICK TIP

Enjoy the Occasion

Most people ultimately find that giving speeches can indeed be fun. It's satisfying and empowering to influence people, and a good speech is a sure way to do this. Think of giving a speech in this way, and chances are you will find much pleasure in it.

Learn from Feedback

Speech evaluations help to identify ways to improve what you do. You can learn a lot through self-evaluation, but self-perceptions can be distorted,[12] so objective evaluations by others often are more helpful. Ultimately, all speakers rely on audience feedback to evaluate the effectiveness of their speeches.

CHECKLIST

Steps in Gaining Confidence

- ☐ Prepare and practice, early and often.
- ☐ Modify thoughts and attitudes—practice positive self-talk.
- ☐ Practice visualization.
- ☐ Use stress-control breathing, meditation, and other relaxation techniques.
- ☐ Incorporate natural, controlled movements.
- ☐ Learn from the experience of public speaking and enjoy it.

CHAPTER

33

Ethical Public Speaking

When we have an audience's attention, we are in the unusual position of being able to influence or persuade listeners and, at times, to move them to act—for better or worse. With this power to affect the minds and hearts of others comes *responsibility*—"a moral obligation to behave correctly towards or in respect of a person or thing."[1] Taking responsibility for your words lies at the heart of being an ethical speaker.

Ethics is the study of moral conduct. Applied to public speaking, **communication ethics** addresses our responsibilities when seeking influence over other people and for which there are positive and negative, or "right" and "wrong," choices of action.[2] For example, should you show a gory photograph without warning to convince audience members to support animal rights? Should you bother to check the credibility of a suspect source before offering it to the audience? Is it ethical to present only one side of an argument?

Demonstrate Competence and Character

Ethics is derived from the Greek word **ethos**, meaning "character." As Aristotle first noted, the foremost duty speakers have toward their audience is to demonstrate *positive ethos*, or good character. Speakers in ancient Greece were regarded positively when they displayed the "virtues" of *competence*, *good moral character*, and *goodwill*. Today, surprisingly little has changed. Modern research on source credibility (a contemporary term for ethos) reveals that people place their greatest trust in speakers who

- Have a solid grasp of the subject (Aristotle's *competence*).
- Are honest and straightforward (*good moral character*).
- Are genuinely respectful of and interested in the welfare of their listeners[3] (*goodwill*).

Respect Your Listeners' Values

Our sense of ethics, of right and wrong actions, is reflected in our **values**—our most enduring judgments or standards of what's good and bad in life and of what's important to us. Values shape how we see the world and form the basis on which we judge the actions of others.[4]

Because values are so central to who we are, consideration of the audience's values is an important aspect of preparing an ethical speech. No member of an audience wants his or her values attacked, treated without respect, or even merely unacknowledged. Yet conflicting values lie at the heart of many controversies that today's public speakers might address, making it difficult to speak about certain topics without challenging cherished beliefs. The United States is a country of immigrants, for example, but a sizable minority (34 percent) of the population views newcomers as a threat to American customs and values. Attitudes vary considerably by age—68 percent of young adults ages 18–29 believe immigrants strengthen the country—and by education, race, religion, and other variables.[5] As you plan speeches on controversial topics, anticipate that audience members will hold a range of values that will differ not only from your own, but from each other's. Audience analysis is key to discovering and planning for these differences (see **Chapter 35**).

Contribute to Positive Public Discourse

An important measure of ethical speaking is whether it contributes something positive to **public discourse**—speech involving issues of importance to the larger community, such as race relations or immigration reform.

Perhaps the most important contribution you can make to public debates of this nature is the advancement of constructive goals. An ethical speech appeals to the greater good rather than to narrow self-interest. It steers clear of **invective**, or verbal attacks, designed to discredit and belittle those with whom you disagree. Ethical speakers avoid arguments that target a person instead of the issue at hand (*ad hominem* attack) or that are built upon other fallacies of reasoning.

Use Your Rights of Free Speech Responsibly

The United States vigorously protects **free speech**—defined as the right to be free from unreasonable constraints on expression[6]—thereby assuring protection both to speakers who treat the truth with respect and to those whose words are inflammatory and offensive. But while offensive speech is often legally protected under the **First Amendment**, racist, sexist, or ageist slurs, gay-bashing, and other forms of negative or hate speech clearly are unethical. **Hate speech** is any offensive communication—verbal or nonverbal—directed against people's race, ethnicity, national origin, gender, religion, sexual orientation, disability, and the like.

Be aware that even under the First Amendment, certain types of speech are not only unethical but actually illegal:

- Speech that incites people to imminent violence, or so-called **"fighting words."**
- Speech that expresses blackmail, perjury, child pornography, or obscenity.[7]
- Speech that can be proved to be defamatory or potentially harmful to an individual's reputation at work or in the community, called **slander.**

If you are talking about public figures or matters of public concern, you will not be legally liable for defamation unless it can be shown that you spoke with a **reckless disregard for the truth**—that is, if you knew that what you were saying was false but said it anyway. If your comments refer to private persons, it will be easier for them to assert a claim against you. You will have the burden of proving that what you said was true.

QUICK TIP

Beware the Heckler's Veto

Drowning out a speaker's message with which you disagree—called a **heckler's veto**—demonstrates disrespect both to the speaker and to fellow listeners. It robs audience members of the ability to make up their own minds about an issue and silences the free expression of ideas. Tolerance for opposing viewpoints is a necessary ingredient of an ethical—and democratic—society. How is your school community doing on this score?

Observe Ethical Ground Rules

Ethical speech rests on a foundation of dignity and integrity. **Dignity** refers to bearing and conduct that is respectful to self and others. **Integrity** signals the speaker's incorruptibility—that he or she will avoid compromising the truth for the sake of personal expediency.[8] Speaking ethically also requires that we adhere to certain moral ground rules, or "pillars of character," including being *trustworthy, respectful, responsible, fair,* and *civic-minded.*[9]

Be Trustworthy

Trustworthiness is a combination of honesty and dependability. Speakers demonstrate their trustworthiness by supporting their points truthfully and by not presenting misleading or false information.

Demonstrate Respect

Speakers demonstrate **respect** by treating audience members with civility and courtesy.[10] Respectful speakers address listeners as unique human beings and avoid **ethnocentrism** and **stereotyping** (see Chapter 43). They refrain from any form of personal attack, and focus on issues rather than on personalities.

Make Responsible Speech Choices

Responsibility means being accountable for what you say. Ask yourself: Will learning about my topic in some way benefit my listeners? Do I use sound evidence and reasoning? Do I make emotional appeals because they are appropriate, rather than to shore up otherwise weak arguments?

Demonstrate Fairness

Fairness refers to making a genuine effort to see all sides of an issue and acknowledging the information listeners need in order to make informed decisions.[11] Bear in mind that most subjects are complicated and multifaceted; rarely is there only one right or wrong way to view a topic.

Be Civic-Minded

Being **civic-minded** means caring about your community, as expressed in your speeches and your deeds. At the broadest level, being civic-minded is essential to the democratic process because democracy depends on our participation.

Avoid Plagiarism

Crediting sources is a crucial aspect of any speech. **Plagiarism**—the use of other people's ideas or words without acknowledging the source—is unethical. You are obviously plagiarizing when you simply "cut and paste" material from sources into your speech and represent it as your own. But it is also plagiarism to copy material into your speech draft from a source (such as a magazine article or website) and then change and rearrange words and sentence structure here and there to make it appear as if it were your own.

Orally Acknowledge Your Sources

The rule for avoiding plagiarism as a public speaker is straightforward: *Any source that requires credit in written form should be acknowledged in oral form.* These sources include direct quotations, as well as paraphrased and summarized information—any facts and statistics, ideas, opinions, or theories gathered and reported by others (see Chapter 38). More than any other single action, acknowledging sources lets listeners know you are trustworthy and will represent both fact and opinion fairly and responsibly.

Citing Quotations, Paraphrases, and Summaries

When citing other people's ideas, you can present them in one of three ways:

- **Direct quotations** are verbatim—or word for word—presentations of statements made by someone else. Direct quotes should always be acknowledged in a speech.
- A **paraphrase** is a restatement of someone else's ideas, opinions, or theories in the speaker's own words. Because paraphrases alter the *form* but not the *substance* of another person's ideas, you must acknowledge the original source.
- A **summary** is a brief overview of someone else's ideas, opinions, or theories. While a paraphrase contains approximately the same number of words as the original source material stated in the speaker's own words, a summary condenses the same material, distilling only its essence.

Note how a speaker could paraphrase and summarize, *with credit*, the following excerpt from an article published in the *New Yorker* titled "Strange Fruit: The Rise and Fall of Açai," by John Colapinto.

Original Version:	Açai was virtually unknown outside Brazil until 10 years ago, when Ryan and Jeremy Black, two brothers from Southern California, and their friend Edmund Nichols began exporting it to the United States. Since then, the fruit has followed a cycle of popularity befitting a teenage pop singer: a Miley Cyrus–like trajectory from obscurity to hype, critical backlash, and eventual ubiquity. Embraced as a "superfruit"—a potent combination of cholesterol-reducing fats and anti-aging antioxidants—açai became one of the fastest-growing foods in history. . . ."

Compare the original version of the excerpt to how it could be properly quoted, paraphrased, or summarized in a speech. Oral citation language is bolded for easy identification.

Direct Quotation:	**As John Colapinto states in an article titled "Strange Fruit: The Rise and Fall of Açai," published in the May 30, 2011, issue of the *New Yorker*,** "The fruit has followed a cycle of popularity befitting a teenage pop singer: a Miley Cyrus–like trajectory from obscurity to hype, critical backlash, and eventual ubiquity."
Oral Paraphrase:	**In an article titled "Strange Fruit: The Rise and Fall of Açai," published in the May 30, 2011, issue of the *New Yorker*, John Colapinto explains that** until two brothers from Southern California named Ryan and Jeremy Black, along with their friend Edmund Nichols, began exporting açai to the United States ten years ago, it was unknown here. Now, says Colapinto, açai is seen as a "superfruit" that can help with everything from lowering cholesterol to fighting aging through its antioxidant properties.
Oral Summary:	**In an article titled "Strange Fruit: The Rise and Fall of Açai," published in the May 30, 2011, issue of the *New Yorker*, John Colapinto says that** açai, a fruit grown in Brazil that was unknown in this country until ten years ago, is now marketed as a "superfruit" that has powerful health benefits.

For detailed directions on crediting sources in your speech, see **Chapter 38**, "Citing Sources in Your Speech."

Fair Use, Copyright, and Ethical Speaking

Copyright is a legal protection afforded the creators of original literary and artistic works.[12] When including copyrighted materials in your speeches—such as reproductions of graphs or photographs, a video or sound clip—you must determine when and if you need permission to use such works.

When a work is copyrighted, you may not reproduce, distribute, or display it without the permission of the copyright holder. For any work created from 1978 to the present, a copyright is good during the author's lifetime plus fifty years. After that, unless extended, the work falls into the **public domain**, which means anyone may reproduce it. Not subject to copyright are federal (but *not* state or local) government publications, common knowledge, and select other categories.

An exception to the prohibitions of copyright is the doctrine of fair use, which permits the limited use of copyrighted works without permission for the purposes of scholarship, criticism, comment, news reporting, teaching, or research.[13] This means that when preparing speeches for the classroom, you have much more latitude to use other people's creative work without seeking permission, but *with* credit in all cases, including display of the copyright symbol (©) on any copyrighted handouts or presentation aids you include in your speech. (For more information, see www.copyright.gov.)

Creative Commons is an organization that allows creators of works to decide how they want other people to use their copyrighted works. It offers creators six types of licenses, three of which are perhaps most relevant to students in the classroom: *attribution* (lets you use the work if you give credit the way the author requests); *noncommercial* (lets you use the work for *noncommercial purposes* only); and *no derivative works* (lets you use only verbatim—exact—versions of the work).

The rules of fair use apply equally to works licensed under Creative Commons and the laws of copyright. Student speakers may search the Creative Commons website for suitable materials for their speech at creativecommons.org.

CHECKLIST

Correctly Quote, Paraphrase, and Summarize Information

- ☐ If *directly* quoting a source, repeat the source word for word and acknowledge whose words you are using.
- ☐ If *paraphrasing* someone else's ideas, restate the ideas in your own words and acknowledge the source.
- ☐ If *summarizing* someone else's ideas, briefly describe their essence and acknowledge the source.

CHAPTER

34

Listeners and Speakers

Imagine giving a speech that no one heard. Merely considering such a circumstance points to the central role of the listener in a speech. In fact, all successful communication is two-way, including that of public speaking.

Connecting with a speaker takes effort and commitment. We can bring our full attention and critical faculties to bear on the speech event, tune out, or automatically reject the message. For the speaker, connecting with audience members also entails work, requiring that we learn about, or listen to, their concerns—by analyzing the audience before delivering the speech (see **Chapter 35**) and by being responsive to listeners during it. Thus it is listener and speaker together who truly make a speech possible.

Recognize the Centrality of Listening

More than any other single communication act, we listen—to *gain understanding*, to *evaluate and act on information*, and to *provide support*.[1] Many of us assume that these and other listening acts come naturally, but listening is an intentional act. While **hearing** is the physiological, largely involuntary process of perceiving sound, **listening** is the conscious act of receiving, constructing meaning from, and responding to spoken and nonverbal messages.[2] Listening involves consciously *selecting* what you will listen to, *giving it your attention*, *processing* and *understanding* it, *remembering* the information, and *responding* to it—either verbally, nonverbally, or through both channels.[3]

Chapter 34, "Listeners and Speakers," from *A Pocket Guide to Public Speaking*, Sixth Edition, by Dan O'Hair, Hannah Rubenstein, and Rob Stewart, pp. 28–33 (Chapter 5).

QUICK TIP

Succeed by Listening

College students in the United States spend more time listening (about 24 percent) than they do on any other communication activity, such as speaking (20 percent), using the internet (13 percent), writing (9 percent), or reading (8 percent).[4] Listening is also the number one activity employees do during the work day.[5] Managers overwhelmingly associate listening skills with competence, efficiency, and leadership potential, and they promote employees who display those skills and hire new entrants who possess them.[6] In both college and work arenas, skill in listening leads to success.

Recognize That We Listen Selectively

In any given situation, no two audience members will process the information in exactly the same way. The reason lies in **selective perception**—people pay attention selectively to certain messages while ignoring others.[7] Two major factors influence what we listen to and what we ignore:

1. We pay attention to what we hold to be important.
2. We pay attention to information that touches our beliefs and expectations and we ignore, downplay, or even belittle messages that contradict them.

To a certain extent, selective perception is simple human nature, but both as listener and speaker, there are steps you can take to counter it.

- As a *listener*, evaluate the speaker's message without prejudgment and avoid screening out parts of the message that don't immediately align with your views.
- As a *speaker*, give the audience good reasons to care about your message. Demonstrate the topic's relevance to them, and anticipate and address audience attitudes and beliefs.

Anticipate Obstacles to Listening

Selective perception is hardly our only obstacle to listening. Numerous distractions keep us from listening in a way that is focused and purposeful. In any listening situation, including that of listening to speeches, try to identify and overcome common obstacles, whether stemming from the environment or our own behavior.

Minimize External and Internal Distractions

A **listening distraction** is anything that competes for the attention we are trying to give to something else. *External distractions* can originate outside of us, in the environment, while *internal distractions* arise from our own thoughts and feelings.

External listening distractions, such as the din of jackhammers or competing conversations, can significantly interfere with our ability to listen, so try to anticipate and plan for them. If you struggle to see or hear over noise or at a distance, arrive early and sit in the front. To reduce internal listening distractions, avoid daydreaming, be well rested, monitor yourself for lapses in attention, and consciously focus on listening.

CHECKLIST

Dealing with Distractions While Delivering a Speech

- ☐ *Problem:* Passing distractions (chatting, entry of latecomers)
  Solution: Pause until distraction recedes
- ☐ *Problem:* Ongoing noise (construction)
  Solution: Raise speaking volume
- ☐ *Problem:* Sudden distraction (collapsing chair, falling object)
  Solution: Minimize response and proceed
- ☐ *Problem:* Audience interruption (raised hand, prolonged comment)
  Solution: Acknowledge audience reaction and either follow up or defer response to conclusion of speech

Refrain from Multitasking

You cannot actively listen well while multitasking. Activities such as checking a cell phone or calendar, finishing an assignment, or responding to a text divert our attention from the message and reduce our ability to interpret it accurately.

Guard against Scriptwriting and Defensive Listening

When we, as listeners, engage in *scriptwriting*, we focus on what we, rather than the speaker, will say next.[8] Similarly, people who engage in **defensive listening** decide either that they won't like what the speaker is going to say or that they know better. Remind yourself that effective listening precedes effective rebuttal. Try waiting for the speaker to finish before devising your own arguments.

Beware of Laziness and Overconfidence

Laziness and overconfidence can manifest themselves in several ways: We may expect too little from speakers, ignore important information, or display an arrogant attitude. Later, we discover we missed important information.

Work to Overcome Cultural Barriers

Differences in dialects or accents, nonverbal cues, word choices, and even physical appearance can serve as barriers to listening, but they need not if you keep your focus on the message rather than the messenger. Refrain from judging a speaker on the basis of his or her accent, appearance, or demeanor; focus instead on what is actually being said. Whenever possible, reveal your needs to him or her by asking questions.

QUICK TIP

Listening Styles and Cultural Differences

Research suggests a link between our listening styles and a culture's predominant communication style.[9] A study of young adults in the United States, Germany, and Israel found distinct listening style preferences that mirrored key value preferences, or preferred states of being, of each culture. Germans tended toward action-oriented listening, Israelis displayed a content-oriented style, and Americans exhibited both people- and time-oriented styles. While preliminary in nature and not valid as a means of stereotyping a given culture's group behavior, these findings confirm the cultural component of all forms of communication, including listening. They also point to the need to focus on intercultural understanding as you learn about your audience.

Practice Active Listening

Active listening—listening that is focused and purposeful—is a skill you can cultivate. Setting listening goals, listening for main ideas, watching for nonverbal cues (see **Chapter 46**), and using critical thinking strategies will help you become a more adept listener.

Set Listening Goals

Determine ahead of time what you need and expect from the listening situation.

1. **Identify your listening needs:** "I must know my classmate's central idea, purpose in speaking, main points, and organizational pattern in order to complete a required written evaluation."

2. **Identify why listening will help you:** "I will get a better grade on the evaluation if I am able to identify and evaluate the major components of Sara's speech."
3. **Make an action statement (goal):** "I will minimize distractions, practice the active listening steps during the speech, take notes, and ask questions about anything I do not understand."
4. **Assess goal achievement:** "I did identify the components of the speech I decided to focus upon and wrote about them in class."

Listen for Main Ideas

To ensure that you retain the speaker's key points, try these strategies:

- Listen for introductions, transitions, and conclusions to alert you to the main points. Most speakers preview their main points in the introduction. Transitions often alert you to an upcoming point. Conclusions often recap main points.
- Take notes on the speaker's main points. Several different methods of note taking—bullet, column, and outline—can be helpful.

QUICK TIP

Listen Responsibly

As listeners, we are ethically bound to refrain from disruptive and intimidating tactics—such as heckling, name-calling, interrupting out of turn, and other breaches of civility—as a means of silencing those with whom we disagree. The ability to dissent is a hallmark of a free society, but to preserve that freedom, we must refrain from using disruptive and intimidating tactics in place of civil dialogue.

Strive for the Open and Respectful Exchange of Ideas

In contrast to *monologue*, in which we try merely to impose what we think on another person or group of people, **dialogic communication** is the open sharing of ideas in an atmosphere of respect.[10] True dialogue encourages both listener and speaker to reach conclusions together. For listeners, this means maintaining an open mind and listening with empathy.[11] For the speaker, this means approaching a speech not as an argument that must be "won," but as an opportunity to achieve understanding with audience members.

Evaluate Evidence and Reasoning

Purposeful, focused listening and **critical thinking**—the ability to evaluate claims on the basis of well-supported reasons—go hand in hand. As you listen to speeches, use your critical faculties to do the following:

- *Evaluate the speaker's evidence.* Is it accurate? Are the sources credible and can they be located?
- *Analyze the speaker's assumptions and biases.* What lies behind the assertions? Does the evidence support them?
- *Assess the speaker's reasoning.* Does it betray faulty logic? Does it rely on fallacies in reasoning?
- *Consider multiple perspectives.* Is there another way to view the argument? How do other viewpoints compare with the speaker's?
- *Summarize and assess the relevant facts and evidence.* If the speaker asks for action (as in some persuasive speeches), decide how you will act on the basis of the evidence rather than acting just to "go along" with what other people do.

Offer Constructive and Compassionate Feedback

Follow these guidelines when evaluating the speeches of others:

- *Be honest and fair in your evaluation of the speech.* Assess the speech as a whole and remain open to ideas and beliefs that differ from your own.
- *Adjust to the speaker's style.* Each of us has a unique communication style, a way of presenting ourselves through a mix of verbal and nonverbal signals. Don't judge the content of a speaker's message by his or her style.
- *Be compassionate in your criticism.* Always start by saying something positive, and focus on the speech, not the speaker.
- *Be selective in your criticism.* Make specific rather than global statements. Rather than statements such as, "I just couldn't get into your topic," give the speaker something he or she can learn from: "I wanted more on why the housing market is falling...."

part 7

Public Speaking: Development

CHAPTER

35

Analyzing the Audience

Advertisers are shrewd analysts of people's needs and wants, extensively researching our buying habits and lifestyle choices to identify what motivates us. To engage your listeners and sustain their involvement in your message, you too must investigate your audience. **Audience analysis** is the process of gathering and analyzing information about audience members' attributes and motivations with the explicit aim of preparing your speech in ways that will be meaningful to them. This is the single most important aspect of preparing for any speech.

Taking the measure of the audience is critical because audience members, and people in general, tend to evaluate information in terms of their own—rather than the speaker's— point of view, at least until they are convinced to take a second look.[1] You may want listeners to share your enthusiasm about an issue, but unless you know something about their perspectives on the topic, you won't be able to appeal to them effectively. Thus, assuming an **audience-centered perspective** throughout the speech preparation process—from selection and treatment of the speech topic to making decisions about how you will organize, word, and deliver it—will help you prepare a presentation that your audience will want to hear.

Adapt to Audience Psychology: Who Are Your Listeners?

To analyze an audience, speakers investigate both psychological and demographic factors. **Psychographics** focuses on the audience's attitudes, beliefs, and values—their *feelings and opinions,* including those related to the topic, speaker, and occasion. (See p. 622 for *demographics*—the statistical characteristics of an audience, such as age, ethnic or cultural background, and socioeconomic status.)

Attitudes, beliefs, and values, while intertwined, reflect distinct mental states that reveal a great deal about us. **Attitudes** are our general evaluations of people, ideas, objects, or events.[2] To evaluate something is to judge it as relatively good or bad, desirable or undesirable. People generally act in accordance with their attitudes (although the degree to which they do so depends on many factors).[3]

Attitudes are based on **beliefs**—the ways in which people perceive reality.[4] Beliefs are our feelings about what is true or real. The less faith listeners have that something exists—a UFO, for instance—the less open they are to hearing about it.

Both attitudes and beliefs are shaped by *values*—our most enduring judgments about what's good in life, as shaped by our culture and our unique experiences within it. We feel our values strongly and strive to realize them.

As a rule, audience members are more interested in and pay greater attention to topics toward which they have positive attitudes and that are in keeping with their values and beliefs. The less we know about something, the more indifferent we tend to be. It is easier (though not simple) to spark interest in an indifferent audience than it is to turn negative attitudes around.

"If the Value Fits, Use It"

Evoking some combination of the audience's values, attitudes, and beliefs in the speeches you deliver will make them more personally relevant and motivating. Many advocacy groups recognize the power of appealing to their constituents' values. For example, the Biodiversity Project, an organization that helps environmental groups raise public awareness, counsels speakers to appeal directly to the three foremost values their audience members hold about the environment (discovered in nationally representative surveys commissioned by the Project), offering the following as an example:

> You care about your family's health (value #1 as identified in survey) and you feel a responsibility to protect your loved ones' quality of life (value #2). The local wetland provides a sanctuary to many plants and animals. It helps clean our air and water and provides a space of beauty and serenity (value #3). All of this is about to be destroyed by irresponsible development.[5]

Gauge Listeners' Feelings toward the Topic

Consideration of the audience's attitudes (and beliefs and values) about a topic is key to offering a speech that will resonate with them. Is your topic one with which the audience is familiar, or is it new to them? Do listeners hold positive, negative, or neutral attitudes toward the topic? Once you have this information (using tools such as interviews and surveys; see p. 627), adjust the speech accordingly (see also the checklist on p. 622 for additional strategies for appealing to different audiences).

If the topic is *new* to listeners,

- Start by showing why the topic is relevant to them.
- Relate the topic to familiar issues and ideas about which they already hold positive attitudes.

If listeners know *relatively little* about the topic,

- Stick to the basics and include background information.
- Steer clear of jargon, and define unclear terms.
- Repeat important points, summarizing information often.

If listeners are *negatively disposed* toward the topic,

- Focus on establishing rapport and credibility.
- Don't directly challenge listeners' attitudes; instead begin with areas of agreement.
- Discover why they have a negative bias in order to tactfully introduce the other side of the argument.
- Offer solid evidence from sources they are likely to accept.
- Give good reasons for developing a positive attitude toward the topic.[6]

If listeners hold *positive attitudes* toward the topic,

- Stimulate the audience to feel even more strongly by emphasizing the side of the argument with which they already agree.
- Tell stories with vivid language that reinforce listeners' attitudes.[7]

If listeners are a *captive audience* (see p. 622),

- Motivate listeners to pay attention by stressing what is most relevant to them.
- Pay close attention to the length of your speech.

Gauge Listeners' Feelings toward You as the Speaker

How audience members feel about you will also have significant bearing on their responsiveness to the message. A speaker who is well liked can gain an initial hearing even when listeners are unsure what to expect from the message itself.

To create positive audience attitudes toward you, first display the characteristics of speaker credibility (*ethos*) described in **Chapter 33**. Listeners have a natural desire to identify with the speaker and to feel that he or she shares their perceptions,[8] so establish a feeling of commonality, or **identification**, with them. Use eye contact and body movements to include the audience in your message. Share a personal story, emphasize a shared role, and otherwise stress mutual bonds. Word your speech with inclusive language such as the personal pronouns *we*, *you*, *I*, and *me* (see p. 700).

CHECKLIST

Appeal to Audience Attitudes, Beliefs, and Values

Have you...

- ☐ Investigated audience members' attitudes, beliefs, and values toward your topic?
- ☐ Assessed the audience's level of knowledge about the topic?
- ☐ Considered strategies to address positive, negative, and neutral responses to your speech topic?
- ☐ Considered appealing directly to audience members' attitudes and values in your speech?

Gauge Listeners' Feelings toward the Occasion

Depending on the circumstances calling for the speech (the rhetorical situation), people will bring different sets of expectations and emotions to it. Members of a **captive audience**, who are required to hear the speaker, may be less positively disposed to the occasion than those of a **voluntary audience** who attend of their own free will. Whether planning a wedding toast or a business presentation, failure to anticipate and adjust for the audience's expectations risks alienating them.

QUICK TIP

Rise to the Top of the Applicant Pool with Audience Analysis

Audience analysis is a potent tool when preparing for job interviews. Discover how many people will meet with you, their roles in the organization, and their areas of expertise. Research the company's background and its culture. Visit the company's website, investigate employees' LinkedIn profiles, and research news articles on the company. During the interview, use inclusive language to put the focus on the company: "*Your* product saw tremendous growth this year...." Earn the interviewers' respect by gathering key details and anticipating what they will want and need to know from you.

Adapt Your Message to Audience Demographics

Demographics are the statistical characteristics of a given population. At least eight characteristics are typically considered when analyzing speech audiences: *age*, *ethnic and cultural background*, *socioeconomic status* (including *income*, *occupation*, and *education*), *religious and political affiliations*, *gender and sexual orientation*, and *group affiliations*. Any number of other traits—for example, disability or place of residence—may be important to investigate as well. Knowing where audience members fall in relation to audience demographics will help you identify your **target audience**—those individuals within the broader audience whom you are most likely to influence in the direction you seek. You may not be able to please everyone, but you should be able to establish a connection with your target audience.

Age

Each age group has its own concerns, psychological drives, and motivations. Thus being aware of the **generational identity** of your audience—such as Generation Z (those born since 2000) or Generation Y (also called Millennials, those born between 1980 and 1999)—allows you to develop points that are relevant to the experiences and interests of the widest possible cross section of your listeners. The table below lists some of the prominent characteristics of today's generations.

Generational Identity and Today's Generations

GENERATION	CHARACTERISTICS
Traditional 1925–1945	Respect for authority and duty, disciplined, strong sense of right and wrong
Baby Boomer 1946–1964	Idealistic, devoted to career, self-actualizing, values health and wellness
Generation X 1965–1979	Seeks work-life balance, entrepreneurial, technically savvy, flexible, questions authority figures, skeptical
Generation Y/ Millennials 1980–1999	Technically savvy, optimistic, self-confident, appreciative of diversity, entrepreneurial
Generation Z 2000–	Comfortable with the highest level of technical connectivity, naturally inclined to collaborate online, boundless faith in power of technology to make things possible[9]

Ethnic and Cultural Background

An understanding of and sensitivity to the ethnic and cultural composition of your listeners are key factors in delivering a successful (and ethical) speech. Some audience members may have a great deal in common with you. Others may be fluent in a language other than yours and must struggle to understand you. Some members of the audience may belong to a distinct **co-culture**, or social community whose perspectives and style of communicating differ significantly from yours. All will want to feel recognized by the speaker. (See pp. 626–627 for guidelines on adapting to diverse audiences.)

Socioeconomic Status

Socioeconomic status (SES) includes income, occupation, and education. Knowing roughly where an audience falls in terms of these key variables can be critical in effectively targeting your message.

Income

Income determines people's experiences on many levels, from how they are housed, clothed, and fed, to what they can afford. Beyond this, income has a ripple effect, influencing many other aspects of life. Given how pervasively income affects people's life experiences, insight into this aspect of an audience's makeup can be quite important.

Occupation

In many speech situations, the *occupation* of audience members can be an important demographic characteristic to know. Occupational interests often are tied to other areas of social concern, such as politics, the economy, education, and social reform. Personal attitudes, beliefs, and goals are also closely tied to occupational standing.

Education

Level of *education* strongly influences people's perspectives and range of abilities. Higher levels of education have been linked to greater flexibility of opinions and often lead to increased lifetime earnings, better health outcomes, and greater civic engagement;[10] such factors may be important to consider when preparing a speech. Depending upon audience members' level of education, your speech may treat topics at a higher or lower level of sophistication, with fewer or more clarifying examples.

QUICK TIP

Addressing On-the-Job Audiences

On the job, presentations ranging from business reports to scientific talks are typically delivered to fellow workers, colleagues, managers, clients, or others. Audiences include the *expert or insider audience, colleagues within the field*, the *lay audience*, and the *mixed audience*.

Religion

Beliefs, practices, and sometimes social and political views vary among religious traditions, making *religion* another key demographic variable. At least a dozen major religious traditions coexist in the United States.[11] Not all members of the same religious tradition will agree on all religiously based issues. Catholics disagree on birth control and divorce, Jews disagree on whether to recognize same-sex unions, and so forth. Awareness of an audience's general religious orientation can be critical when your speech touches on controversial topics with religious implications, such as capital punishment, same-sex marriage, and teaching about the origins of humankind.

Political Affiliation

As with religion, beware of making unwarranted assumptions about the sensitive issue of an audience's political values and beliefs. Some people avoid anything that smacks of politics while others enjoy a lively debate. Conservative individuals hold certain views that liberals dispute, and the chasm between far right and far left is great indeed. If your topic involves politics, you'll need to obtain background information on the audience's views.

Gender and Sexual Orientation

Distinct from the fixed physical characteristics of biological sex, **gender** is our social and psychological sense of ourselves as males or females.[12] Making assumptions about the preferences, abilities, and behaviors of your audience members based on their presumed gender or sexual orientation (e.g., their romantic preferences) can seriously undermine their receptivity to your message. To ensure that you treat issues of gender and sexual orientation evenly, use language sensitive to them (e.g., "spouse or partner") and avoid gender stereotypes and sexist language (see p. 704).

Group Affiliations

The various groups to which audience members belong—whether social, civic, work-related, or religiously or politically affiliated—reflect their interests and values and so provide insight into what they care about. Investigating the audience members' group affiliations will help you craft a message that will appeal to them.

QUICK TIP

Be Sensitive to Disability When Analyzing an Audience

More than 19 percent of the population have some sort of physical, mental, or employment disability; more than half of these have a severe disability.[13] About 9 percent of undergraduates (not including veterans) are counted as disabled.[14] Disabilities range from sight and hearing impairments to constraints on physical mobility and employment. Keep *persons with disabilities (PWD)* in mind when you speak, and use language and examples that afford them respect and dignity.

Adapt to Diverse Audiences

In the United States, one-third of the population, or 116 million people, belong to a racial or an ethnic minority group,[15] and about 43 million people, or over 13 percent, are foreign born.[16] Nationwide, 21 percent of the population speaks a language other than English in the home; about two-thirds of these speak Spanish.[17] These figures suggest that audience members will hold different cultural perspectives and employ different styles of communicating that may or may not mesh with your own.

How might you prepare to speak in front of an ethnically and culturally diverse audience, including that of your classroom? In any speaking situation, your foremost concern should be to treat your listeners with dignity and to act with integrity (see **Chapter 34**). As described below, since values are central to who we are, identifying your listeners' values with respect to your topic can help you to avoid ethnocentrism (see **p. 607**) and deliver your message in a culturally sensitive manner.

Adapt to Cross-Cultural Values

People in every culture possess **cultural values** related to their personal relationships, religion, occupation, and so forth, and these values can significantly influence how audience members respond to a speaker's message. For example, while dominant cultural values in U.S. society include *achievement and success, equal opportunity, material comfort*, and *democracy*,[18] in Mexico, *famillismo (family loyalty), respecto* (respect), and *fatalismo* (fatalism) are strongly held cultural values. Surveys of several Asian societies identify *a spirit of harmony, humility toward superiors, awe of nature*, and *desire for prosperity* as important values.[19] Becoming familiar with differences, as well as points of similarity, in cultural values can help you frame messages effectively and with sensitivity.

Individual audience analysis is always the first step when seeking to learn about an audience. But public speakers will also benefit by sensitizing themselves to broader national differences in cultural values, especially when time and opportunity constraints make it difficult to gather detailed information on an audience. Cultural researcher Geert Hofstede's wide-ranging research reveals six major "value dimensions," or "broad preferences for one state of affairs over another," as being significant across all cultures, but in widely varying degrees. To find out how eighty-six countries rank in terms of these values and to compare your home culture with another culture, see www.hofstede-insights.com/product/compare-countries/.

Several other global surveys can also be extremely useful for learning about cultural values, including the *Pew Global Attitudes Project* (www.pewglobal.org), *Gallup World Poll* (worldview.gallup.com), and the World Values Survey (www.worldvaluessurvey.org).

Focus on Universal Values

As much as possible, try to determine the attitudes, beliefs, and values of audience members. At the same time, you can focus on certain values that, if not universally shared, are probably universally aspired to in the human heart. These include love, truthfulness, fairness, freedom, unity, tolerance, responsibility, and respect for life.[20]

CHECKLIST

Reviewing Your Speech in the Light of Audience Demographics

- ☐ Does your speech acknowledge potential differences in values and beliefs and address them sensitively?
- ☐ Have you reviewed your topic in light of the age range and generational identity of your listeners? Do you use examples they will recognize and find relevant?
- ☐ Have you tried to create a sense of identification between yourself and audience members?
- ☐ Are your explanations and examples at a level appropriate to the audience's sophistication and education?
- ☐ Do you make any unwarranted assumptions about the audience's political or religious values and beliefs?
- ☐ Does your topic carry religious or political overtones that are likely to stir your listeners' emotions in a negative way?

Tools for Learning About Your Audience

You can discover information about your audience through personal interviews, surveys, and published sources. Often, it takes just a few questions to get some idea of audience members' opinions and demographic characteristics.

Conduct Interviews

Interviews, even brief ones, can reveal a lot about the audience's interests and needs. You can conduct interviews one-on-one or in a group, in person or by telephone or online. Consider interviewing a sampling of the audience, or even just one knowledgeable representative of the group that you will address. As with questionnaires (see "Survey the Audience," which follows), interviews usually consist of a mix of open- and closed-ended questions.

Survey the Audience

Surveys can be as informal as a poll of several audience members or as formal as the pre-speech distribution of a written survey, or **questionnaire**—a series of fixed-alternative, scale, or open-ended questions. **Fixed-alternative questions** contain a limited choice of answers, such as "Yes," "No," or "For *x* years":

> "Do you smoke cigarettes?"
>
> Yes ______ No ______ I quit, but I smoked for ______ years.

Scale questions—also called *attitude scales*—measure the respondents' level of agreement or disagreement with specific positions or indicate how important listeners judge something to be:

> "Flag burning should be outlawed."
>
> Strongly Agree____ Agree____ Disagree____
> Strongly Disagree____ Undecided____
>
> "How important is religion in your life?"
>
> Very Important____ Important____ Moderately Important____
> Of Minor Importance____ Unimportant____

Open-ended questions (also called *unstructured questions*) begin with a *how, what, when, where,* or *why,* and they are particularly useful for probing beliefs and opinions. This style of question allows respondents to elaborate as much as they wish:

> "How do you feel about using the results of DNA testing to prove innocence or guilt in criminal proceedings?"

Often, it takes just a few fixed-alternative and scale questions to draw a fairly clear picture of audience members' backgrounds and attitudes and where they fall in demographic categories. You may wish to use web-based survey software, such as SurveyMonkey or QuestionPro, to generate surveys electronically using premade templates and distribute them online.

Consult Published Sources

Organizations of all kinds publish information describing their missions, operations, and achievements. Sources include websites and related online articles, brochures, newspaper and magazine articles, and annual reports.

Although published opinion polls won't specifically reflect your particular listeners' responses, they too can provide valuable insight into how a representative state, national, or international sample feels about the issue in question. Consider consulting these and other polling organizations:

- National Opinion Research Center (NORC): www.norc.uchicago.edu
- Roper Center for Public Opinion Research: ropercenter.cornell.edu
- Gallup: www.gallup.com
- Pew Research Center U.S. Politics and Policy: www.people-press.org

Analyze the Speech Setting and Context

As important as analyzing the audience is assessing (and then preparing for) the setting in which you will give your speech—size of audience; location; time; length of speech; and rhetorical situation (the particular circumstances or reasons why you are delivering the speech about this topic at this time), as seen in the following checklist.

CHECKLIST

Analyzing the Speech Situation

- ☐ Where will the speech take place?
- ☐ How long am I expected to speak?
- ☐ What special events or circumstances of concern to my audience should I acknowledge?
- ☐ How many people will attend?
- ☐ Will I need a microphone?
- ☐ How will any projecting equipment I plan to use in my speech, such as an LCD projector, function in the space?
- ☐ Where will I stand or sit in relation to the audience?
- ☐ Will I be able to interact with listeners?

CHAPTER

36

Selecting a Topic and Purpose

Perhaps no folk saying was ever truer for the public speaker than this one: "You've got to know where you are going in order to get there." That is, unless you can clearly identify *what* you want to say and *why* you want to say it—your topic and purpose—you won't be able to get *there*—giving a speech that works. **Figure 36.1** demonstrates the steps involved in selecting a topic and purpose and forming a thesis for your speech; this chapter explains these steps. Once they are completed, you will be ready to flesh out the speech with the supporting material described in **Chapter 37**.

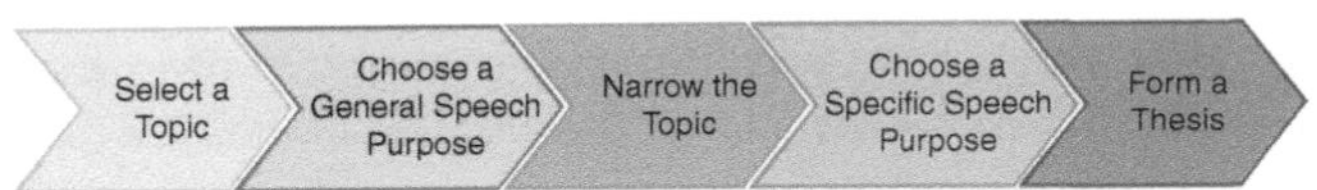

FIGURE 36.1 Selecting a Topic and Purpose

Explore Topics for Your Speech

A good topic must stir the audience's curiosity as well as your own. You must feel excited enough about it to devote the necessary time to research and organization, so allow yourself the space to discover topics to which you are genuinely drawn. Focus on topics about which you can speak competently and bring fresh information to your listeners. At the same time, consider each potential topic's appeal to the audience (based on audience analysis, including psychological and demographic information; see **Chapter 35**).

Identify Personal Interests

Personal interests run the gamut from favorite activities and hobbies to deeply held goals and values. You can translate personal experiences into powerful topics, especially if sharing them in some way benefits the audience. "What it's like" stories, for example, yield captivating topics: What is it like to be part of a medical mission team working

Chapter 36, "Selecting a Topic and Purpose," from *A Pocket Guide to Public Speaking*, Sixth Edition, by Dan O'Hair, Hannah Rubenstein, and Rob Stewart, pp. 47–55 (Chapter 7).

in Uganda? What have you learned as a longtime practitioner of spinning, biking, hiking, or yoga? How have managed your health complications to live a full life?

Consider Current Events and Controversial Issues

Think about events and issues that most affect you and your audience, and see if you can make a difference. Black Lives Matter, opioid addiction, Confederate memorials, Cuba-U.S. relations, minimum wage laws, the DACA program—the list of pressing and controversial topics is long. Which ones matter to you and your audience?

Survey Grassroots Issues: Engage the Community

Audience members, including college students, respond enthusiastically to local issues that may affect them directly. Review your community's news, including your school's paper and press releases, and read news blogs for the local headlines. What social, environmental, health, political, or other issues are affecting your community?

Steer Clear of Overused and Trivial Topics

To avoid boring your classmates and instructor, stay away from tired issues, such as drunk driving and the health risks of cigarettes, as well as trite topics such as "how to change a tire." Instead, seek out subject matter that yields new information or different perspectives. For ideas, consult your favorite print or online publications. One way to find fresh topics is to check websites that provide information on search trends, hot topics, and ideas that are trending now, such as Google Trends (www.google.com/trends), Zeitgeist Minds (www.zeitgeistminds.com), Twitter Trends (www.twitter.com), and Facebook Trending (www.facebook.com).

Try Brainstorming to Generate Ideas

Brainstorming is a method of spontaneously generating ideas through word association, topic (mind) mapping, or internet browsing. Brainstorming works! It is a structured and effective way to identify topic ideas in a relatively brief period of time.

To brainstorm by **word association**, write down *one* topic that might interest you and your listeners. Then jot down the first thing that comes to mind related to it. Repeat the process until you have fifteen to twenty items. Narrow the list to two or three, and then select a final topic:

energy → solar energy → solar panels → Elon Musk's SolarCity company

Topic (mind) mapping is a brainstorming technique in which you lay out words in diagram form to show categorical relationships among them. Put a potential topic in the middle of a piece of paper. As related ideas come to you, write them down, as shown in **Figure 36.2**.

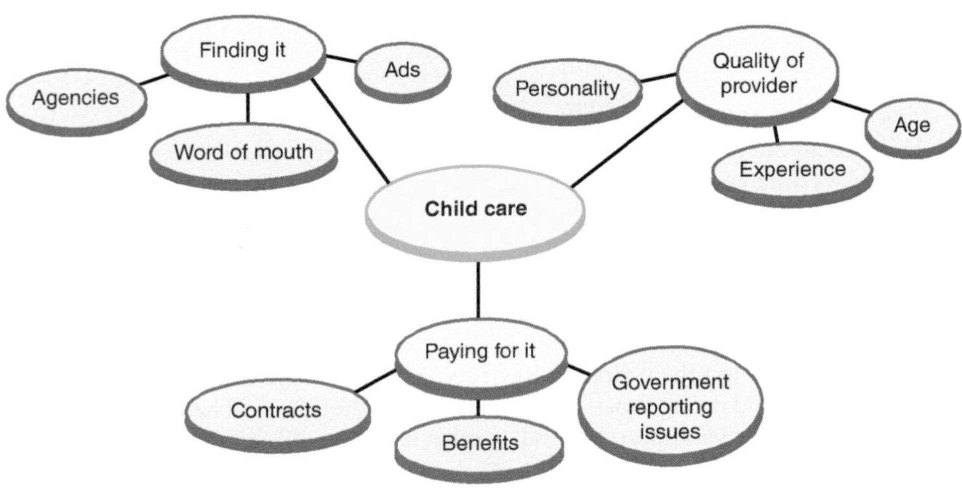

FIGURE 36.2 A Topic Map

Use Internet Tools

Yet other online means for finding (and narrowing) a topic are the databases available on a library's home page. Consult *general databases* such as Academic OneFile (for browsing and starting the search process) and *subject-specific databases* such as Ethnic NewsWatch (for in-depth research on a topic). Popular internet search engines such as Google also offer a wealth of resources to discover and narrow topics. Each search engine offers options for specialized searches within books, news, blogs, images, and other sources. You can narrow topics by limiting searches to within a range of dates (e.g., 1900–1950), to a geographic region (e.g., Europe), or to a particular language.

QUICK TIP

Jump-Start Your Search Using Trusted Websites

Sites on your library's home page, such as *Opposing Viewpoints in Context* and *Issues and Controversies Online*, can help you select and narrow topics on vital issues. In addition, for trustworthy background information on pressing social, political, environmental, and regional issues, librarians often refer students to two related online publications—CQ *Researcher* (published weekly) and *CQ Global Researcher* (published monthly). Each topic entry includes an overview of the current situation, pro/con statements from opposing positions, and bibliographies of key sources. Ask your librarian about related resources.

Identify the General Purpose of Your Speech

Once you have an idea for a topic, you'll need to refine and adapt it to your general speech purpose. The **general speech purpose** for any speech answers the question, "What is my objective in speaking on this topic to this audience on this occasion?" Public speakers typically accomplish one of three general purposes: to inform, to persuade, or to mark a special occasion.

- Do you aim primarily to educate or inform listeners about your topic? The general purpose of an **informative speech** is *to increase the audience's awareness and understanding of a topic by defining, describing, explaining, or demonstrating your knowledge of the subject.*
- Is your goal to influence listeners to accept your position on a topic and perhaps to take action (e.g., "only eat sustainably farmed beef")? The general purpose of the persuasive speech is *to effect some degree of change in the audience's attitudes, beliefs, or even specific behaviors.*
- Are you there to mark a special occasion, such as an awards ceremony, funeral, or wedding? The special occasion speech serves the general purpose of *entertaining, celebrating, commemorating, inspiring, or setting a social agenda*, and includes speeches of introduction, acceptance, and presentation; roasts and toasts; eulogies; and after-dinner speeches, among others.

Note that there is always some overlap in these three types of speeches. An informative speech will have aspects of persuasion in it, and a persuasive speech will also inform. A special occasion speech will include informational and persuasive aspects. Nevertheless, identifying the *primary* function as one of these three purposes will help you narrow your topic and meet your speech goals.

QUICK TIP

To Identify the General Speech Purpose, Consider the Occasion

The speech occasion itself often suggests an appropriate general speech purpose. A town activist, invited to address a civic group about installing solar panels in town buildings, may choose a *persuasive purpose* to encourage the group to get behind the effort. If invited to describe the initiative to the town finance committee, the activist may choose an *informative purpose*, in which the goal is to help the committee understand project costs. If asked to speak at an event celebrating the project's completion, the speaker will choose a *special occasion purpose*. Addressing the same topic, the speaker selects a different general speech purpose to suit each audience and occasion.

Refine the Topic and Purpose

Once you have an idea for a topic and have established a general speech purpose, the next step is to narrow the topic, using your time constraints, audience, occasion, and other relevant factors as guideposts.

Narrow Your Topic

Just as brainstorming and internet tools can be used to discover a topic, they can be instrumental in narrowing one. Using *topic mapping*, you can brainstorm by category (e.g., subtopic). Say your general topic is internships. Some related categories are paid internships, unpaid internships, and cooperative (co-op) education. Ask yourself, "What questions do I have about the topic? Am I more interested in cooperative education or one of the two types of internships? What aspect of internships is my audience most likely to want to hear about?" You can also use trend searching (see p. 631) to narrow your topic.

CHECKLIST

Narrowing Your Topic

- ☐ What is my audience most likely to know about the subject?
- ☐ What do my listeners most likely want to learn?
- ☐ What aspects of the topic are most relevant to the occasion?
- ☐ Can I develop the topic using just two or three main points?
- ☐ How much can I competently research and report on in the time I am given to speak?

Form a Specific Speech Purpose

Once you've narrowed the topic, you need to refine your speech goal beyond the general speech purpose. You know you want to give an informative speech, a persuasive speech, or a special occasion speech, but now you should be able to identify more specifically what you want the speech to accomplish. The **specific speech purpose** describes in action form what you want to achieve with the speech. It does this by spelling out, in a single sentence, what you want the audience to learn, agree with, or perhaps act upon as a result of your speech.

Formulating the specific speech purpose is straightforward. Ask yourself, "What is it about my topic that I want the audience to learn, do, reconsider, or agree with?" Be specific about your aim, and then state it in action form, as in the following, written for a persuasive speech:

Topic (before narrowing):	Binge Drinking
Narrowed Topic:	Describe the nature and prevalence of binge drinking on U.S. campuses and offer solutions to avoid it
General Speech Purpose:	To persuade
Specific Speech Purpose:	To persuade my audience that binge drinking is harmful and convince listeners to consume alcohol safely or not at all

Although the specific purpose statement need not be articulated in the actual speech, it is important to formulate it for yourself in order to keep in mind exactly what you are working to accomplish. Remember the old saying: You've got to know where you are going in order to get there.

Compose a Thesis Statement

While the specific purpose focuses your attention on the outcome you want to achieve with the speech, the **thesis statement** (also called *central idea*) concisely identifies what the speech is *about*. It states the theme of the speech in a single declarative statement, succinctly expressing what the speech will attempt to demonstrate or prove. The main points, the supporting material, and the conclusion all serve to flesh out the thesis. By clearly stating your speech thesis (what it's about), you set in your mind exactly what outcome you want to accomplish (the specific purpose).

The difference between the thesis and specific purpose can be clearly seen in the following examples.

Example 1

Speech Topic:	Blogs
General Speech Purpose:	To inform
Specific Speech Purpose:	To inform my audience of three benefits of keeping a blog
Thesis Statement:	Maintaining a blog provides the opportunity to practice writing, a means of networking with others who share similar interests, and the chance to develop basic website management skills.

Example 2

Speech Topic:	Service learning courses
General Speech Purpose:	To persuade
Specific Speech Purpose:	To persuade my audience that service learning courses are beneficial for gaining employment after schooling.
Thesis Statement:	Taking service learning courses is a good way to build your résumé and increase your chances of gaining employment after graduation.

In an informative speech, the thesis conveys the scope of the topic, the steps associated with the topic, or the underlying elements of it. It describes what the audience will learn.

In a persuasive speech, the thesis represents what you are going to prove in the address. Notice, too, that in both examples, after you read the thesis you find yourself asking "Why?" or thinking "Prove it!" This will be accomplished by the evidence you give in the speech points (see **Chapter 39**).

CHECKLIST

Identifying the Speech Topic, Purpose, and Thesis

- ☐ Is the topic appropriate to the occasion?
- ☐ Will the topic appeal to the audience's interests and needs?
- ☐ Will I be able to offer a fresh perspective on the topic?
- ☐ Have I identified the general speech purpose—to inform, persuade, or mark a special occasion?
- ☐ Have I identified what I want the audience to gain from the speech—the specific speech purpose?
- ☐ Have I narrowed my topic in line with how much I can competently research and then report on in the time I am given to speak?
- ☐ Does my thesis statement sum up in a single sentence what my speech is about?
- ☐ Does my thesis statement make the claim I intend to make about my topic?

FROM SOURCE TO SPEECH

Narrowing Your Topic to Fit Your Audience

How do you narrow a topic to fit the audience and the speech occasion? Consider the following case study.

A Case Study

Jenny is a member of the campus animal rights club and a student in a public speaking class. She is giving two persuasive speeches this semester: one to her public speaking class and one to the student council, as a representative of her club. For both presentations, Jenny plans to speak on the broad topic of animal rights. But she must narrow this topic considerably to fit each audience and speech occasion.

First, Jenny draws a topic map to generate ideas.

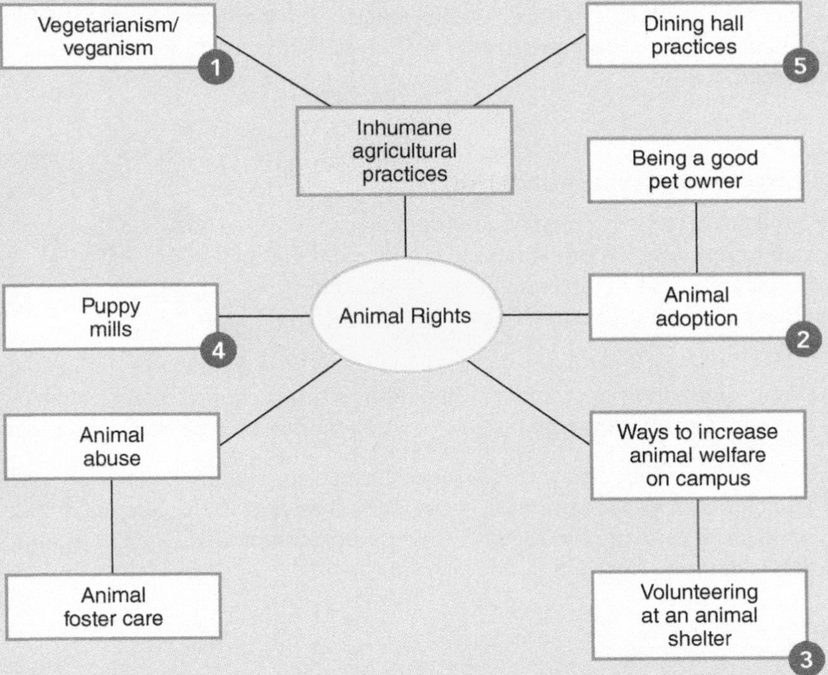

For each presentation, Jenny narrows her topic after considering her audience and the speech occasion.

Public Speaking Class (25–30 people):

- Mixed ages, races, and ethnicities, and an even mix of males and females
- Busy with classes, jobs, sports, and clubs
- Half live in campus housing, where pets are not allowed

Anderson Ross/Getty Images

1. Jenny eliminates vegetarianism because she will be unlikely to change listeners' minds in a six-minute speech.
2. She eliminates animal adoption because it may not be feasible for many students.
3. Volunteering at an animal shelter is an option for all animal lovers, even those who are not allowed to have pets on campus. Jenny argues that students should donate an hour a week to a nearby shelter, so that busy students can still participate.

Student Council (8–10 people):

- Mixed demographic characteristics
- Similar interests: government, maintaining a rich campus life, an investment in ethics and the honor code, and an interest in keeping student affairs within budget

Manfred Rutz/Getty Images

4. Jenny eliminates puppy mills—though the student council may agree that the mills are harmful, they are not in a position to directly address the problem.
5. Jenny zeroes in on dining hall practices, which are directly tied to campus life. Her club's proposed resolution to use free-range eggs in the campus dining hall benefits all students and requires the support of the council—an ideal topic for this audience.

CHAPTER

37

Developing Supporting Material

Good speeches contain relevant, motivating, and audience-centered **supporting material** in the form of examples, stories, testimony, facts, and statistics. (In a persuasive speech, these same supporting materials are referred to as evidence.) Supporting material, such as you might discover in a magazine or journal article, engages the audience in your topic, illustrates and elaborates upon your ideas, and provides evidence for your arguments.

Offer Examples

Examples are indispensable tools speakers use to clarify their ideas. An **example** is a typical instance of something. Without examples to illustrate the points a speaker wants to convey, listeners would get lost in a sea of abstract statements. Examples can be *brief* or *extended* and may be either *factual* or *hypothetical*.

Brief examples offer a single illustration of a point. In a speech about restrictions on freedom of expression in China, author Ian McEwan uses the following brief factual example.

> In China, state monitoring of free expression is on an industrial scale. To censor daily the internet alone, the Chinese government employs as many as fifty thousand bureaucrats—a level of thought repression unprecedented in human history.[1]

Sometimes it takes more than a brief example to effectively illustrate a point. **Extended examples** offer extended illustrations of the idea, item, or event being described, thereby allowing the speaker to create a more detailed picture for the audience.

Chapter 37, "Developing Supporting Material," from *A Pocket Guide to Public Speaking*, Sixth Edition, by Dan O'Hair, Hannah Rubenstein, and Rob Stewart, pp. 56–61 (Chapter 8). Copyright © 2019 by Bedford/ St. Martin.

Here, TED speaker Jonathan Drori uses an extended example to illustrate how pollen (the fertilizing element of plants) can link criminals to their crimes:

> [Pollen forensics] is being used now to track where counterfeit drugs have been made, where banknotes have come from.... And murder suspects have been tracked using their clothing....Some of the people were brought to trial [in Bosnia] because of the evidence of pollen, which showed that bodies had been buried, exhumed, and then reburied somewhere else.[2]

In some speeches, you may need to make a point about something that could happen in the future if certain events were to occur. Since it hasn't happened yet, you'll need a **hypothetical example** of what you believe the outcome might be. Republican Representative Vernon Ehlers of Michigan offered the following hypothetical example at a congressional hearing on human cloning:

> What if in the cloning process you produce someone with two heads and three arms? Are you simply going to euthanize and dispose of that person? The answer is no. We're talking about human life.[3]

Share Stories

One of the most powerful means of conveying a message and connecting with an audience is through a **story**—the telling of a chain of events. Stories (also called **narratives**) help us make sense of our experiences;[4] they tell tales, both real and imaginary, about practically anything under the sun. Stories can be relatively short and simple descriptions of incidents worked into the speech or they can form most of the presentation (see narrative pattern of organization, p. 664). A successful story will strike a chord with and create an emotional connection between speaker and audience members.

All stories possess the essential storytelling elements of *character* (or "protagonist"), *challenge* or *conflict*, and *resolution*, or means of dealing with the challenge. Using these elements, many stories, and especially those that describe overcoming obstacles, work well when they follow a three-part trajectory. First, introduce the protagonist (perhaps yourself) in his or her story setting, or context. Next, recount the challenge or conflict the character faces. A compelling description of the challenge or conflict is crucial in storytelling since everyone can relate to struggle and even failure and how to overcome it. Finally, reveal how the challenge was either dealt with or overcome.

In a speech on helping more young Americans earn college degrees, Melinda French Gates used this format in the following very brief story to illustrate that although some students encounter many barriers to completing degrees, they persevere.

> Last year, we met a young man named Cornell at Central Piedmont Community College in Charlotte, North Carolina. We asked him to describe his typical day. He clocks into work at 11 P.M. When he gets off at 7 the next morning, he sleeps for an hour. In his car. Then he goes to class until 2 o'clock. "After that," Cornell said, "I just crash."[5]

QUICK TIP

Share Stories That Make an Impact

When you include a compelling story in a speech, you will reach the deeper parts of audience members' brains—the hippocampus and amygdala—where emotion and memory work together. Audience members will be more likely to pay attention, remember, and even act on information conveyed in this way.[8]

In just six sentences, Gates includes the elements of character (the student Cornell), challenge (taking classes while working difficult hours), and resolution (getting enough sleep to continue).

Many speakers liberally sprinkle their speeches with **anecdotes**—brief stories of interesting and often humorous incidents based on real life, with a recognizable *moral*—the lesson the speaker wishes to convey. With its offering of wisdom gained through life experiences, the moral is the most important part of an anecdote.[6] For example, in a speech to students at Maharishi University, comedian Jim Carrey talked about how his father's fear of being impractical led him to become an accountant instead of the comedian he wanted to be. This spurred Carrey to take another path:

> So many of us choose our path out of fear disguised as practicality.... I learned many great lessons from my father, not the least of which was that you can fail at what you don't want, so you might as well take a chance on doing what you love.[7]

Draw on Testimony

Another potentially powerful source of support for your speech is **testimony**—firsthand findings, eyewitness accounts, and people's opinions. **Expert testimony** includes information from trained professionals in the field. **Lay testimony** is testimony supplied by nonexperts (such as eyewitnesses).

Credibility plays a key role in the effectiveness of testimony, so establish the qualifications of the person whose testimony you use, and inform listeners when and where the testimony was offered (see p. 650 for an example).

QUICK TIP

Use a Variety of Supporting Materials

Listeners respond most favorably to a variety of supporting materials derived from multiple sources to illustrate each main point.[9] Alternating among different types of supporting material—moving from a story to a statistic, for example—will make the presentation more interesting and credible while simultaneously appealing to your audience members' different learning styles.

Provide Facts and Statistics

Most people require some type of evidence before they will accept someone else's claims or position.[10] In Western societies, people especially tend to trust evidence that is based on facts and statistics. **Facts** represent documented occurrences, including actual events, dates, times, people, and places. Listeners are not likely to accept your statements as factual unless you back them up with credible sources.

Statistics are quantified evidence that summarizes, compares, and predicts things. Statistics can clarify complex information and help make abstract concepts concrete for listeners. Audience members will appreciate some statistics in support of your assertions, but they don't want an endless parade of them.

Use Statistics Accurately

Statistics add precision to speech claims—*if* you know what the numbers actually mean and use terms that describe them accurately. Following are some basic statistical terms commonly used in speeches that include statistics.

Use Frequencies to Indicate Counts

A *frequency* is simply a count of the number of times something occurs:

On the midterm exam there were 8 A's, 15 B's, 7 C's, 2 D's, and 1 F.

Frequencies can indicate size, describe trends, or help listeners understand comparisons between two or more categories:

- Inside the cabin, the Airbus A380 has room for 525 passengers.[11] *(shows size)*
- Deaths due to opioid overdoses rose from 52,404 in 2015 to roughly 64,000 in 2016.[12] *(describes a trend)*
- In July 2016, the population of the state of Colorado was 49.7 percent female and 50.3 percent male.[13] *(compares two categories)*

Use Percentages to Express Proportion

As informative as counts can be, the similarity or difference in magnitude between things may be more meaningfully indicated as a *percentage*—the quantified portion of a whole. Informing an audience that deaths due to opioid overdoses rose in the United States between 2015 and 2016 by nearly 19 percent more quickly shows them the magnitude of the problem than does offering a count.[14] Percentages also help audience members easily grasp comparisons between things, such as the unemployment rate in several states:

> In August 2017, Alaska had the highest rate of unemployment, at 7.2 percent. At 2.3 percent, North Dakota had the lowest rate.[15]

Audience members cannot take the time to pause and reflect on the figures as they would with written text, so consider how you can help listeners interpret the numbers, as in this example:

> As you can see, Alaska's unemployment rate is more than three times greater than that of North Dakota.

Use Types of Averages Accurately

An *average* describes information according to its typical characteristics. Usually we think of the average as the sum of the scores divided by the number of scores. This is the *mean,* the computed average. But there are two other kinds of averages—the *median* and the *mode.*

Consider a teacher whose nine students scored 5, 19, 22, 23, 24, 26, 28, 28, and 30, with 30 points being the highest possible grade. The following illustrates how she would calculate the three types of averages:

- The *mean* score is 22.8, the *arithmetic average,* the sum of the scores divided by 9.
- The *median* score is 24, *the center-most score in a distribution* or the point above and below which 50 percent of the nine scores fall.
- The *mode* score is 28, the *most frequently occurring score* in the distribution.

As a matter of accuracy, in your speeches you should distinguish among these three kinds of averages. Always try to find out whether "average" refers to the mean, median, or mode.

Use Statistics Selectively—and Memorably

Rather than overwhelm the audience with numbers, put a few figures in context to make your message more compelling. For example, instead of only mentioning the actual number of persons using Instagram worldwide (over seven hundred million active monthly users and counting), use a simple ratio to drive home the company's growing reach: "Today, at least 70 percent of businesses in the U.S. use Instagram, nearly double that of one year ago."[16]

Present Statistics Ethically

Offering listeners inaccurate statistics is unethical. Following are steps you can take to reduce the likelihood of using false or misleading statistics:

- *Use only reliable statistics.* Include statistics from the most authoritative source you can locate, and evaluate the methods used to generate the data.
- *Present statistics in context.* Inform listeners of when the data were collected and by whom, the method used to collect the data, and the scope of the research:

    > These figures represent data collected by the U.S. Department of Education during 2018 from questionnaires distributed to all public and private schools in the United States with students in at least one of grades 9–12 in the fifty states and the District of Columbia.

- *Avoid cherry-picking.* Politicians are often accused of **cherry-picking**—selecting only those statistics that buttress their own arguments while ignoring competing data.[17] Avoid misrepresenting the truth by offering only one-sided data.
- *Avoid confusing statistics with "absolute truth."* Even the most recent data available will change the next time data are collected. Nor are statistics necessarily any more accurate than the human who collected them. Offer data as they appropriately represent your point, but refrain from declaring that these data are definitive.

CHAPTER

38

Citing Sources in Your Speech

Alerting the audience to the sources you use and offering ones that they will find authoritative is a critical aspect of delivering a presentation. When you credit speech sources, you:

- Increase the odds that audience members will believe in your message.
- Demonstrate the quality and range of your research to listeners.
- Demonstrate that reliable sources support your position.
- Avoid plagiarism and gain credibility as an ethical speaker who acknowledges the work of others.
- Enhance your own authority by demonstrating how your own ideas fit into the larger intellectual conversation about the topic.
- Enable listeners to locate your sources and pursue their own research on the topic.

Ethically you are bound to attribute any information drawn from other people's ideas, opinions, and theories—as well as any facts and statistics gathered by others—to their original sources. That is, you are bound to be honest. You need not credit sources for ideas that are **common knowledge**—information that is likely to be known by many people and described in multiple places (though such information must *truly* be widely disseminated; see the "Quick Tip" on the following page).

Chapter 38, "Citing Sources in Your Speech," from *A Pocket Guide to Public Speaking*, Sixth Edition, by Dan O'Hair, Hannah Rubenstein, and Rob Stewart, pp. 71–76 (Chapter 10). Copyright © 2019 by Bedford/St. Martin.

QUICK TIP

Common Knowledge and Uncommon Facts

One exception to needing to give credit for material in a speech (or a written work) is the use of **common knowledge**. For example, it is common knowledge that Thomas Jefferson was the third president of the United States. It is not common knowledge that he had a personal library of 6,487 books, which he donated to the Library of Congress after it was attacked and burned down by British troops in 1814. This fact does require acknowledgment of a source—in this case, an article entitled "10 Things You Didn't Know about Thomas Jefferson," published (without a byline) on June 30, 2011, in the *Washington Post*.

Alert Listeners to Key Source Information

An **oral citation** credits the source of speech material that is derived from other people's ideas. For each source, plan on briefly alerting the audience to the following:

1. The *author* or *origin of the source* ("documentary filmmaker Ken Burns..." or "On the *National Science Foundation* website...")
2. The *type of source* (journal article, book, personal interview, website, blog, online video, etc.)
3. The *title* or a *description of the source* ("In the book *Endangered Minds*..."; or "*In an article on sharks*...")
4. The *date of the source* ("The article, published in the *October 10th, 2018*, issue..." or "According to a report on choosing a college major, posted online *September 28, 2018*, on the *Chronicle of Higher Education* website...")

Of course, spoken citations need not include complete references (exact titles, full names of all authors, volume and page numbers); doing so will interrupt the flow of your presentation and distract listeners' attention. However, do keep a list of complete references for a bibliography to appear at the end of your speech.

Establish the Source's Trustworthiness

Focus on presenting your sources in a way that will encourage audience members to process and believe in the source material. Too often, inexperienced speakers credit their sources in bare-bones fashion, offering a rote recitation of citation elements. For example, a student might cite a source's name, but leave out key details about the source's background that could convince the audience to trust the source.

Discerning listeners will only accept the information you offer if they believe that the sources for it are reliable and accurate, or *credible*. **Source credibility** refers to our level of trust in a source's credentials and track record for providing accurate information. If you support a scientific claim by crediting it to an unknown student's personal blog, for example, listeners won't find it nearly as reliable as if you credited it to a scientist affiliated with a reputable institution.

Be aware that while a source that is credible is usually accurate, this is not always so.[1] Sometimes we have information that contradicts what we are told by a credible source. For instance, a soldier might read an article in the *Washington Post* about a conflict in which he or she participated. The soldier knows the story contains inaccuracies because the soldier was there. In general, however, the soldier finds the *Washington Post* a credible source. Therefore, *since even the most credible source can sometimes be wrong, it is always better to offer a variety of sources, rather than a single source, to support a major point.* This is especially the case when your claims are controversial.

QUICK TIP

Consider Audience Perception of Sources

Not every trustworthy source is necessarily appropriate for every audience. For example, a politically conservative audience may reject information from a liberal publication. Readers of the *Nation*, for example, tend to be liberal, while those who read the *National Review* tend to be more conservative. Thus, audience analysis should factor in your choice of sources. In addition to checking that your sources are reliable, consider whether they will be seen as credible by your particular audience.[2]

Qualify the Source

A simple and straightforward way to demonstrate a source's trustworthiness is to include a brief description of the source's qualifications to address the topic (a **source qualifier**), along with your oral citation—for example, "researcher at Duke Cancer Institute," "columnist for the *Economist*". This will allow the audience to put the source in perspective. To see how you can orally cite sources in ways that listeners will accept and believe, see "Types of Sources and Sample Oral Citations" (p. 648).

Avoid a Mechanical Delivery

Acknowledging sources need not interrupt the flow of your speech. On the contrary, audience members will welcome information that adds backing to your assertions. The key is to avoid a formulaic, or mechanical, delivery. Audience members expect a natural style of delivery of your speech, and this includes delivery of speech sources.

Vary the Wording

Avoid a rote delivery of sources by varying your wording. If you introduce one source with the phrase "According to...," switch to another construction ("As reported by...") for the next one. Alternating introductory phrases provides necessary variety.

Vary the Order

Vary the order in which you introduce a citation. Occasionally discuss the findings first, before citing the source. For example, you might state that "Caffeine can cause actual intoxication" and provide evidence to back up this claim before revealing your source—"A chief source for this argument is a report in the July 5, 2018, issue of the *New England Journal of Medicine*...."

Types of Sources and Sample Oral Citations

Following are common types of sources cited in a speech, the specific citation elements to mention, and examples of how you might refer to these elements in a presentation. Each example includes a boldfaced source qualifier describing the source's qualifications to address the topic—for instance, "director of undergraduate studies for four years" or "research scientist at Smith-Kline." Qualifying a source can make the difference between winning or losing acceptance for your arguments.

Book

If a book has *two* or *fewer* authors, state first and last names, title, and date of publication. If *three* or *more authors*, state first and last name of first author and "co-authors."

> *Example:* In his book *Thinking, Fast and Slow*, published in *2011*, **psychologist and Nobel Prize winner** Daniel Kahneman claims that...
>
> *Example:* In *The Civic Potential of Video Games*, published in 2009, Joseph Kahne, **noted professor of education and director of the Civic Education Research Group at Mills College**, and his two co-authors, **both educators,** wrote that...

Reference Work

For a reference work (e.g., encyclopedia, almanac, directory), note title, date of publication, and author or sponsoring organization.

> *Example:* According to *Literary Market Place 2018*, **the foremost guide to the U.S. book publishing industry**, Karen Hallard and her co-editors report that...

Article in a Journal, Newspaper, or Magazine

When citing from an article either online or in print, use the same guidelines as you do for a book.

> *Example:* In an article titled "The False Promise of DNA Testing," published in the June 2016 edition of *Atlantic Monthly* magazine, **journalist and *New York Times* contributing writer** Matthew Shaer argues that forensic testing is becoming ever less reliable.

Website

Name the website, section of website cited (if applicable), and last update.

> *Example:* On its website, last updated November 8, 2017, the Society of Interventional Radiology, **a national organization of physicians and scientists**, explains that radio waves are harmless to healthy cells....

If website content is undated or not regularly updated, review the site for credibility before use. (If you are citing an online article, use the guidelines under "Article in a Journal, Newspaper, or Magazine" above.)

Blog

Name the blogger, affiliated website (if applicable), and date of posting.

> *Example:* In an April 26, 2017, posting on *Talking Points Memo*, **a news blog that specializes in original reporting on government and politics**, editor Josh Marshall notes that...

Television or Radio Program

Name the program, segment, reporter, and date aired.

> *Example:* Judy Woodruff, **PBS NewsHour anchor**, described in a segment on sexual harassment aired on November 14, 2017...

Online Video

Name the online video source, program, segment, and date aired (if applicable).

> *Example:* In a session on mindfulness delivered at the University of Miami on October 9, 2015, and broadcast on YouTube, Jon Kabat-Zinn, **scientist, renowned author, and founding director of the Stress Reduction Clinic**...

QUICK TIP

Credit Sources in Presentation Aids

Just as you acknowledge the ideas of others in the verbal portion of your speech, be sure to credit such material used in any accompanying presentation aids. When reproducing copyrighted material, such as a table or photograph, label it with a copyright symbol (©) and the source information. Even if it is not copyrighted, supporting material listed on a visual aid may require citation. You may cite this material orally, print the citation unobtrusively on the aid, or both.

Testimony (Lay or Expert)

Name the person, date, and context in which information was offered.

> *Example:* On June 7, 2016, in congressional testimony before the U.S. Senate Foreign Relations Committee, Victoria Nuland, **Assistant Secretary of State for European and Eurasian Affairs**, revealed that Russian violations of borders...

Interview and Other Personal Communication

Name the person and date of the interview or personal communication.

> *Example:* In an interview I conducted last week, Tim Zeutenhorst, **chairman of the Orange City Area Health System Board, at Orange City Hospital in Iowa,** said...

> *Example:* In a June 23, 2018, email/Twitter post/letter/memorandum from Ron Jones, **a researcher at the Cleveland Clinic**...

CHECKLIST

Offering Key Source Information

- ☐ Have I identified the author or origin of the source?
- ☐ Have I indicated the type of source?
- ☐ Have I offered the title or description of the source?
- ☐ Have I noted the date of the source?
- ☐ Have I qualified the source to establish its reliability and credibility?

part 8

Public Speaking: Organization

CHAPTER

39

Organizing the Body of the Speech

A speech structure is simple, composed of just three basic parts: an introduction, a body, and a conclusion. The **introduction** establishes the purpose of the speech and shows its relevance to the audience. The **body** of the speech presents main points that are intended to fulfill the speech purpose. The **conclusion** brings closure to the speech by restating the purpose, summarizing main points, and reiterating the thesis and its relevance to the audience. In essence, the introduction of a speech tells listeners where they are going, the body takes them there, and the conclusion lets them know the journey has ended.

Chapter 42 describes how to create effective introductions and conclusions. Here we focus on the elements of the speech body—*main points, supporting points,* and *transitions*—and how to arrange them in an outline. In an **outline,** you separate main and supporting points—the major speech claims and the evidence to support them—into larger and smaller divisions and subdivisions. (See also **Chapter 41** on Preparing Outlines for the Speech.)

Use Main Points to Make Your Major Claims

Main points express the key ideas of the speech. Their function is to represent each of the major ideas or claims being made in support of the speech thesis. To create main points, identify the most important ideas of the speech, as reflected in your thesis. What ideas can you demonstrate with supporting material? Each of these ideas or claims should be expressed as a main point.

Restrict the Number of Main Points

Research indicates that audiences can comfortably take in only between two and seven main points.[1] For most speeches, and especially those delivered in the classroom, between two and five main points should be sufficient. As a rule, the fewer main points in a speech, the greater the odds that you will maintain your listeners' attention. If you have too many main points, further narrow your topic (see Chapter 36) or check the points for proper subordination (see p. 656).

QUICK TIP

Save the Best for Last—or First

Listeners have the best recall of speech points made at the beginning of a speech (the "primacy effect") and at the end of a speech (the "recency effect") than of those made in between (unless the ideas made in between are much more striking than the others).[2] If it is especially important that listeners remember certain ideas, introduce those ideas near the beginning of the speech and reiterate them at the conclusion.

Restrict Each Main Point to a Single Idea

A main point should not introduce more than one idea. If it does, split it into two (or more) main points:

Incorrect:	I. We have more free speech on earth than at any previous time in recorded history, but free speech is under serious threat from extremes on all sides, even though freedom of speech sustains all the other freedoms we enjoy.
Correct:	I. We have more free speech than at any previous time in recorded history. II. Free speech is under serious threat from extremes on all sides. III. Freedom of speech sustains all the other freedoms we enjoy.[3]

Main points should be mutually exclusive of one another. If they are not, consider whether a main point more properly serves as a subpoint.

Express each main point as a *declarative sentence*—one that asserts or claims something. In addition, state your main points (and supporting points; see p. 655) in *parallel form*—that is, in similar grammatical form and style (see p. 657). Phrasing points in parallel form helps listeners understand and retain the points (by providing consistency) and lends power and elegance to your words.

Incorrect:	I. After college, female students who were athletes are more likely to be employed full time than female students who did not engage in athletics. II. They are also more likely to thrive physically. III. Social well-being is another aspect in which female student athletes score better.
Correct:	I. After college, female student athletes are more likely to be employed full time. II. Post graduation, female student athletes are also more likely to thrive in their physical well-being. III. After they graduate, female student athletes are more likely to thrive in their social well-being.

Use the Purpose and Thesis Statements as Guides

Main points should flow directly from your specific purpose and thesis statements (see pp. 630–633), as in the following example:

Specific Purpose: What you want the audience to learn or do as a result of your speech	"I want my audience to understand the reasons why meditation is helpful for mental and physical health."
Thesis: The central idea of the speech	"Meditation is an effective means of reducing stress and improving overall mental and physical health."
Main Points:	I. Meditation helps you gain inner peace. II. Meditation helps you increase self-awareness. III. Regular meditation can improve heart health.

Use Supporting Points to Substantiate Your Claims

Supporting points organize the evidence you have gathered to explain (in an informative speech) or justify (in a persuasive speech) the main points. It is here that you substantiate or prove the main points with examples, narratives, testimony, facts, and statistics discovered in your research (see Chapter 37).

In an outline, supporting points appear in a subordinate position to main points. This is indicated by **indentation**. Just as with main points, order supporting points according to their importance or relevance to the main point.

The most common format for outlining points is the **roman numeral outline**. Main points are enumerated with uppercase roman numerals (I, II, III...), supporting points are enumerated with capital letters (A, B, C...), sub-supporting points are enumerated with Arabic numerals (1, 2, 3...), and sub-subsupporting points are enumerated with lowercase letters (a, b, c...), as seen in the following:

- I. Main point
    - A. Supporting point
        - 1. Subsupporting point
            - a. Sub-subsupporting point
            - b. Sub-subsupporting point
        - 2. Subsupporting point
            - a. Sub-subsupporting point
            - b. Sub-subsupporting point
    - B. Supporting point
- II. Main point

Pay Close Attention to Coordination and Subordination

Outlines reflect the principles of **coordination and subordination**—the logical placement of ideas relative to their importance to one another. Ideas that are *coordinate* are given equal weight; **coordinate points** are indicated by their parallel alignment. An idea that is *subordinate* to another is given relatively less weight; **subordinate points** are indicated by their indentation below the more important points.

Principles of Coordination and Subordination

- Assign equal weight to ideas that are coordinate.
- Assign relatively less weight to ideas that are subordinate.
- Indicate coordinate points by their parallel alignment.
- Indicate subordinate points by their indentation below the more important points.
- Every point must be supported by at least two points or none at all (consider how to address one "dangling" point by including it in the point above it).

Strive for a Unified, Coherent, and Balanced Organization

A well-organized speech is characterized by unity, coherence, and balance. Try to adhere to these principles as you arrange your speech points.

A speech exhibits *unity* when it contains only those points implied by the specific purpose and thesis statements. The thesis is supported by main points, main points are strengthened by supporting points, and supporting points consist of carefully chosen evidence and examples.

A speech exhibits *coherence* when it is organized clearly and logically, with speech points aligned in order of importance (see "Principles of Coordination and Subordination," p. 656). Main points should support the thesis statement, and supporting points should enlarge upon the main points. Transitions serve as mental bridges that help establish coherence.

The principle of *balance* suggests that appropriate emphasis or weight be given to each part of the speech relative to the other parts and to the thesis. Inexperienced speakers may devote overly lengthy coverage to one point and insufficient attention to the others, or may provide scanty evidence in the body of the speech after presenting an impressive introduction. The body of a speech should always be the longest part, and the introduction and conclusion should be of roughly the same length. Stating the main points in parallel form is one aspect of balance. Assigning each main point at least two supporting points is another. If you have only one subpoint, consider how you might incorporate it into the superior point. Think of a main point as a tabletop and supporting points as table legs; without at least two legs, the table cannot stand.

CHECKLIST

Reviewing Main and Supporting Points

- ☐ Do the main points flow directly from the speech goal and thesis?
- ☐ Do the main points express the key points of the speech?
- ☐ Is each main point truly a main point or a subpoint of another main point?
- ☐ Is each main point substantiated by at least two supporting points—or none?
- ☐ Do you spend roughly the same amount of time on each main point?
- ☐ Are the supporting points truly subordinate to the main points?
- ☐ Does each main point and supporting point focus on a single idea?
- ☐ Are the main and supporting points stated in parallel form?

Use Transitions to Give Direction to the Speech

Transitions are words, phrases, or sentences that tie the speech ideas together and enable the listener to follow the speaker as he or she moves from one point to the next. Transitions (also called *connectives*) are a truly critical component of speeches because listeners cannot go back and re-read what they might have missed. Focus on creating transitions to shift listeners from one point to the next. Transitions can take the form of full sentences, phrases, or single words.

Use Transitions between Speech Points

Use transitions to move between speech points—from one main point to the next, and from one subpoint to another.

When moving from one main point to another, full-sentence transitions are especially effective. For example, to move from main point I in a speech about sales contests (*"Top management should sponsor sales contests to halt the decline in sales"*) to main point II (*"Sales contests will lead to better sales presentations"*), the speaker might use the following transition:

> Next, let's look at exactly what sales contests can do for us.

Transitions between supporting points can be handled using single words, phrases, or full sentences as in the following:

> Next, ...
>
> First, ... (second, third, and so forth)
>
> Similarly, ...
>
> We now turn...
>
> If you think that's shocking, consider this...

FROM POINT TO POINT

Using Transitions to Guide Your Listeners

Transitions direct your listeners from one point to another in your speech, leading them forward along a logical path while reinforcing key ideas along the way. Plan on using transitions to move between:

- The introduction and the body of the speech
- The main points
- The subpoints, whenever appropriate
- The body of the speech and the conclusion

Introduction

I. Today I'll explore the steps you can take to help achieve carbon neutrality on your campus...

(**Transition:** *So how do you go carbon-neutral?)*

Body

I. Get informed—examine the steps that other campuses have already taken toward carbon neutrality

(**Transition:** *Looking at what other campuses have done is only part of carbon neutrality, however. Perhaps most important,...)*

II. Recognize that change starts here, on campus, with you....

While transitions help guide your listeners from point to point, they can also do a lot more, including:

- Introduce main points
- Illustrate cause and effect
- Signal explanations and examples
- Emphasize, repeat, compare, or contrast ideas
- Summarize and preview information
- Suggest conclusions from evidence

Following is an excerpt from a working outline on a speech about achieving carbon neutrality on campus. Note how the student edits himself to ensure that he (1) uses transitions to help listeners follow along and retain his speech points and (2) uses transitions strategically to achieve his goal of persuading the audience.

(**Transition:** *Why is it important for college campuses to become carbon-neutral?)*

I. College campuses generate the carbon equivalent of many large towns...

(**Transition:** *As a result...)*

A. Colleges have a moral responsibility to their students and their surrounding communities to reduce carbon emissions...

B. Administrators face decisions about mounting energy costs...

(**Transition:** *Following are some ideas to create a carbon-neutral campus. First . . .)*

I. Launch a campus-wide campaign to encourage students to reduce their energy use

(**Transition:** *For example...)*

A. Provide energy-efficient lightbulbs to students

B. Encourage students to use bikes and public transit as much as possible, instead of personal cars

C. Emphasize the importance of shutting off lights and electronic devices when leaving a room...

(**Transition:** *Pushing students to take action is a critical part of achieving carbon neutrality. But another key aspect is action by school administrators, who have the power to implement wide-ranging sustainable energy policies...)*

II. Lobby administrators to investigate biomass facilities and offshore wind and solar energy sources...

A. Ensure that new campus buildings meet renewable energy standards...

B. Take necessary steps to retrofit older campus buildings...

C. Explore alternative heating...

(**Transition:** *So far, we've talked about practical actions we can take to move toward carbon neutrality on campus, but what about beyond the campus?)*

III. Get involved at the town government level

A. Town-gown communities...

B. Speak up and voice your concerns...

(**Transition:** *As you can see, we have work to do...*

Conclusion

I. If we want our children and our children's children to see a healthy earth, we must take action now...

Use Internal Previews and Summaries as Transitions

Previews briefly introduce audience members to the ideas that the speaker will address. In a speech introduction, the **preview statement** briefly mentions the main points and thesis of the speech (see p. 592). Within the body itself, speakers use an **internal preview** to draw the audience in with a glimpse of what they will discuss next. An **internal summary** draws together ideas to reinforce them before proceeding to another speech point. Often, a speaker will transition from one major idea or main point to the next using an internal summary and internal preview together.

> We've seen that mountain bikes differ from road bikes in the design of the tires, the seat, the gears, the suspension systems, and the handlebars. (*internal summary*) Now let's take a look at the different types of mountain bikes themselves. As you will see, mountain bikes vary according to the type of riding they're designed to handle—downhill, trails, and cross-country. Let's begin with cross-country. (*internal preview*)

See Chapter 41 for guidance on including transitions in the outline of your speech.

CHECKLIST

Use Transitional Words and Phrases

- ☐ **To show comparisons:** *similarly; in the same way; likewise; just as*
- ☐ **To contrast ideas:** *on the other hand; and yet; at the same time; in spite of; however; in contrast*
- ☐ **To illustrate cause and effect:** *as a result; hence; because; thus; consequently*
- ☐ **To illustrate sequence of time or events:** *first, second, third…; following this; later; earlier; at present; in the past*
- ☐ **To indicate explanation:** *for example; to illustrate; in other words; to simplify; to clarify*
- ☐ **To indicate additional examples:** *not only; in addition to; let's look at*
- ☐ **To emphasize significance:** *most important; above all; remember; keep in mind*
- ☐ **To summarize:** *in conclusion; in summary; finally; let me conclude by saying*

CHAPTER

40

Selecting an Organizational Pattern

Of all of the aspects of speechmaking, the idea of organizational arrangements may seem the most confusing. But selecting and organizing speech points into a pattern is easier and more natural than it might seem. An organizational pattern helps you link points together to maximum effect for your topic and purpose and lets the audience follow your ideas as you wish. Studies confirm that the way you organize your ideas affects your audience's understanding of them, so you'll want to make use of a pattern.[1] A good time to select one is after you've researched the speech and prepared main points.

Speeches make use of at least a dozen different organizational arrangements of main and supporting points. Here we look at six commonly used patterns, five of which are used for all forms of speeches: chronological, spatial, causal (cause-effect), topical, and narrative, and one, the problem-solution pattern, which is typically used for persuasive speeches.

Arranging Speech Points Chronologically

Some topics lend themselves well to the arrangement of main points according to their occurrence in time relative to one another. The **chronological pattern of arrangement** (also called the *temporal pattern*) follows the natural sequential order of the main points. Topics that describe a series of events in time (such as events leading to development of a vaccine) or develop in line with a set pattern of actions or tasks (such as steps in installing solar panels) call out for this pattern. A speech describing the development of the World

Wide Web, for example, immediately calls for a time-ordered sequence of main points:

Thesis Statement:	The internet evolved from a small network designed for military and academic scientists into a vast array of networks used by billions of people around the globe.
Main Points:	I. The internet was first conceived in 1962 as the ARPANET to promote the sharing of research among scientists in the United States. II. In the 1980s, a team created TCP/IP, a language that could link networks, and the internet as we know it was born. III. At the end of the Cold War, the ARPANET was decommissioned, and the World Wide Web constituted the bulk of internet traffic.

ONE TOPIC (PATTERNS OF IMMIGRATION) ORGANIZED SIX WAYS

Chronological Pattern

Thesis Statement: "Immigration to the U.S. has ebbed and flowed, from the first large wave in 1820 to the most recent wave beginning in 1965."

Sample Main Points:

I. First large wave occurred between 1790 and 1820: English, Scottish, Irish, Germans, and Spanish.
II. Second wave, largely German, British, and Irish, arrived between 1820 and 1860.
III. Asian immigrants arrived in Western states between 1880 and 1914 in the third wave.
IV. Fourth wave, 1965-present: Asians, Mexicans, South and Central Americans, and Europeans.

Spatial Pattern

Thesis Statement: "Border Patrol sectors—from westernmost San Diego to easternmost Brownsville—have highest apprehension rates for undocumented migrants."[2]

Sample Main Points:

I. For many years, highest migrant apprehension rates occurred, from west to east, for San Diego, Tucson, and El Paso sectors, but these sectors have seen steep declines in recent years.
II. Along the middle of the border, two Texas sectors—Del Rio and Laredo—have shown modest increases in migrant apprehensions since 2010.
III. Recently, the Rio Grande Valley Sector, at east end of Texas border, has seen increased apprehensions, leading all sectors.

Causal Pattern
Thesis Statement: "U.S. children whose parents are unauthorized immigrants (*cause*) are exposed to risks, including lower preschool enrollment, poverty, and reduced socioeconomic progress." (*effects*) **Sample Main Points:** I. Children ages 3–4 with unauthorized immigrant parents are less likely to attend preschool.[3] II. Three-quarters of children with unauthorized parents have incomes under 185 percent of the poverty line.[4] III. Children with unauthorized parents are more likely to stay in poverty.[5]
Problem-Solution Pattern
Thesis Statement: "Persons who overstay their visas account for about 40 percent of undocumented immigrants in the U.S.[6] (*problem*) To address the issue, we need a biometric (fingerprint) exit system that will identify visa overstayers." (*solution*) **Sample Main Points:** I. Up to five million persons who entered the United States legally remain here with expired visas.[7] II. The Department of Homeland Security takes fingerprints and photos of entering visitors with visas but has no similar system to track their exits. III. DHS plans to launch a biometric exit system at high-volume airports in 2018.[8]
Topical Pattern
Thesis Statement: "Debates about immigration often focus on immigrants' role in the labor force, admissions policies, and enforcement policies." **Sample Main Points:** I. Immigrants accounted for nearly 17 percent of the civilian labor force in 2014.[9] II. Immigration admissions policies are based on reuniting families, admitting skilled workers, and protecting refugees.[10] III. The Criminal Alien Program (CAP) is the primary immigration enforcement channel.[11]
Narrative Pattern
Thesis Statement: "I came to the U.S. illegally as the child of undocumented immigrants. I am about to graduate high school and want to go to college, but because I am undocumented I cannot apply for aid." **Sample Main Points:** I. I was brought to the United States at age 3 by undocumented parents. II. I attended U.S. schools through high school. III. I remain undocumented and cannot apply for college aid.

Arranging Speech Points Using a Spatial Pattern

When describing the physical arrangement of a place, a scene, or an object, logic suggests that the main points can be arranged in order of their physical proximity or direction relative to one another. This calls for a **spatial pattern of arrangement**. For example, you can select a spatial arrangement when your speech provides the audience with a "tour" of a particular place:

Thesis Statement:	El Morro National Monument in New Mexico is captivating for its variety of natural and historical landmarks.
Main Points:	I. Visitors first encounter an abundant variety of plant life native to the high-country desert. II. Soon visitors come upon an age-old watering hole that has receded beneath the 200-foot cliffs. III. Beyond are the famous cliff carvings made by hundreds of travelers over several centuries of exploration in the Southwest.

In a speech describing a geothermal heating and cooling company's market growth across regions of the country, a speaker might use the spatial arrangement as follows:

Thesis Statement:	Sales of geothermal systems have grown in every region of the country.
Main Points:	I. Sales are strongest in the Eastern Zone. II. Sales are growing at a rate of 10 percent quarterly in the Central Zone. III. Sales are up slightly in the Mountain Zone.

Arranging Speech Points Using a Causal (Cause-Effect) Pattern

Some speech topics represent cause-effect relationships. Examples include (1) events leading to higher interest rates, (2) reasons students drop out of college, and (3) causes of a disease. The main points in a **causal (cause-effect) pattern** of arrangement usually take the following form:

I. Cause

II. Effect

Sometimes a topic can be discussed in terms of multiple causes for a single effect, or a single cause for multiple effects:

MULTIPLE CAUSES FOR A SINGLE EFFECT	SINGLE CAUSE FOR MULTIPLE EFFECTS
(Reasons Students Drop Out of College)	(Reasons Students Drop Out of College)
I. Cause 1 (lack of funds) II. Cause 2 (unsatisfactory social life) III. Cause 3 (unsatisfactory academic performance) IV. Effect (drop out of college)	I. Cause (lack of funds) II. Effect 1 (lowered earnings over lifetime) III. Effect 2 (decreased job satisfaction over lifetime) IV. Effect 3 (increased stress level)

Some topics are best understood by presenting listeners with the effect(s) before the cause(s). In a speech on health care costs, a student speaker arranges his main points as follows:

Thesis Statement:	In response to rising health care costs, large employers are shifting part of the expense to workers.
Main Points:	I. (*effect*) Workers are now seeing higher co-pays and deductibles. II. (*effect*) Raising the amount employees must contribute has restricted employer costs to just 5 percent this year. III. (*cause*) The Affordable Care Act mandates that large employers offer more of their workers health care plans. IV. (*cause*) Rising health care costs have led to more expensive plans at all levels of coverage.

QUICK TIP

Blend Organizational Patterns

The pattern of organization for your subpoints can differ from the pattern you select for your main points. Do keep your main points in one pattern—this will be the predominant pattern for the speech—but feel free to use other patterns for subpoints when it makes sense to do so. For instance, for a speech about the history of tattooing in the United States, you may choose a chronological pattern to organize the main points but use a cause-effect arrangement for some of your subpoints regarding why tattooing is so popular today.

Arranging Speech Points Using a Problem-Solution Pattern

The **problem-solution pattern** organizes main points to demonstrate the nature and significance of a problem followed by a proposed solution. Most often used in persuasive speeches, the problem-solution pattern can be arranged as simply as two main points:

I. Problem (define what it is)

II. Solution (offer a way to overcome the problem)

But many problem-solution speeches require more than two points to adequately explain the problem and to substantiate the recommended solution:

I. The nature of the problem (identify its causes, incidence, etc.)

II. Effects of the problem (explain why it's a problem, for whom, etc.)

III. Unsatisfactory solutions (discuss those that have not worked)

IV. Proposed solution (explain why it's expected to work)

Following is a partial outline of a persuasive speech about cyberbullying arranged in a problem-solution format.

Thesis Statement:	To combat cyberbullying, we need to educate the public about it, report it when it happens, and punish the offenders.
Main Point:	I. Nature of cyberbullying A. Types of activities involved 1. Name-calling, insults 2. Circulation of embarrassing pictures 3. Sharing of private information 4. Threats B. Incidence of bullying C. Profile of offenders
Main Point:	II. Effects of cyberbullying on victims A. Acting out in school B. Feeling unsafe in school C. Skipping school D. Experiencing depression
Main Point:	III. Unsuccessful attempts at solving cyberbullying A. Let offenders and victims work it out on their own B. Ignore problem, assuming it will go away
Main Point:	IV. Ways to solve cyberbullying A. Educate in schools B. Report incidents to authorities C. Suspend or expel offenders

Arranging Speech Points Topically

When each of the main points is a subtopic or category of the speech topic, try the **topical pattern** of arrangement (also called **categorical pattern**). Consider an informative speech about choosing Chicago as a place to establish a career. You plan to emphasize three reasons for choosing Chicago: the strong economic climate of the city, its cultural variety, and its accessible public transportation. Since these three points are of relatively equal importance, they can be arranged in any order without affecting one another or the speech purpose negatively. For example:

Thesis Statement:	Chicago is an excellent place to establish a career.
Main Points:	I. Accessible transportation II. Cultural variety III. Multiple industries

This is not to say that when using a topical arrangement, you should arrange the main points without careful consideration. Any number of considerations can factor into your ordering of points, not least of which should be the audience's most immediate needs and interests. Perhaps you have determined that listeners' main concern is the city's attractions for young professionals, followed by an interest in its cultural variety and accessible transportation.

QUICK TIP

Find Freedom with the Topical Pattern

Topical arrangements give you the greatest freedom to structure main points according to the way you wish to present your topic. You can approach a topic by dividing it into two or more categories, for example. You can lead with your strongest evidence or leave your most compelling points until you near the conclusion. If your topic does not call out for one of the other patterns described in this chapter, be sure to experiment with the topical pattern.

Arranging Speech Points Using a Narrative Pattern

Storytelling is often a natural and effective way to get your message across. In the **narrative pattern**, the speech consists of a story or series of short stories, replete with characters, conflict or complications, and resolution (see p. 664).

In practice, a speech built largely upon a story (or series of stories) is likely to incorporate elements of other designs. You might organize the main points of the story in an effect-cause design, in which you first reveal the outcome of what happened (such as a man-made disaster) and then describe the events that led up to the accident (the causes).

Whatever the structure, simply telling a story is no guarantee of giving a good speech. Any speech should include an introduction with a preview and clear thesis, well-organized main points, effective transitions, and a conclusion.

CHECKLIST

Determining an Organizational Pattern

Does your speech...

- ☐ Describe a series of developments in time or a set of actions that occur sequentially? Use the *chronological pattern*.
- ☐ Describe or explain the physical arrangement of a place, a scene, or an object? Use the *spatial pattern*.
- ☐ Explain or demonstrate a topic in terms of its underlying causes or effects? Use the *causal pattern*.
- ☐ Demonstrate the nature and significance of a problem and justify a proposed solution? Use the *problem-solution pattern*.
- ☐ Stress natural divisions or categories of a topic, in which points can be moved to emphasize audience needs and interests? Use a *topical pattern*.
- ☐ Convey ideas through a story, using character, conflict, and resolution? Use a *narrative pattern*, perhaps in combination with another pattern.

CHAPTER

41

Preparing Outlines for the Speech

Outlines are enormously helpful in putting together and delivering a successful speech, providing a framework for your speech materials and a blueprint for your presentation. Plotting points into hierarchical fashion based on their relative importance to one another and using indentation to visually represent this hierarchy will allow you to examine the underlying logic and relationship of ideas to one another.

Speakers can choose among several different types of outline formats. (For a review of the principles and of the mechanics of outlining, see Chapter 39.)

Plan on Creating Two Outlines

As you develop a speech, plan on creating two outlines: a working outline and a speaking, or delivery, outline. Use the **working outline** (also called a *preparation outline*) to organize and firm up main points and, with the research you've gathered, develop supporting points to substantiate them. Completed, the working outline should contain your entire speech, organized and supported to your satisfaction.

Use a **speaking outline** to practice and actually present the speech. Speaking outlines contain the working outline in condensed form and are much briefer. Figure 41.1 provides an overview of the steps involved in outlining a speech.

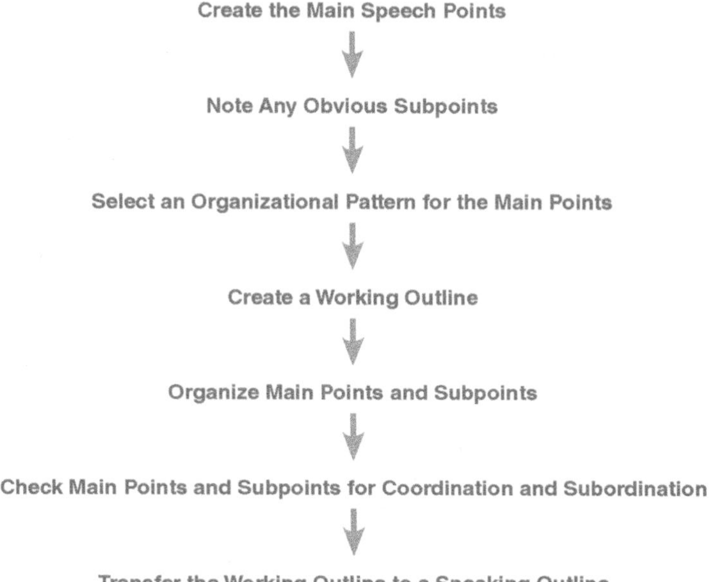
Create the Main Speech Points
Note Any Obvious Subpoints
Select an Organizational Pattern for the Main Points
Create a Working Outline
Organize Main Points and Subpoints
Check Main Points and Subpoints for Coordination and Subordination
Transfer the Working Outline to a Speaking Outline

FIGURE 41.1 Steps in Organizing and Outlining the Speech

Use Sentences, Phrases, or Key Words

Speeches can be outlined in sentences, phrases, or key words. (Working outlines typically contain partial or full sentences, reflecting much of the text of the speech; speaking outlines use key words or short phrases.)

In the **sentence outline format**, each main and supporting point is stated in sentence form as a declarative statement (e.g., one that states a fact or an argument) in much the same way you will express the idea during delivery. Following is an excerpt in sentence format from a speech by Mark B. McClellan on keeping prescription drugs safe:[1]

I. The prescription drug supply is under attack from a variety of increasingly sophisticated threats.
   A. Technologies for counterfeiting—ranging from pill molding to dyes—have improved across the board.
   B. Inadequately regulated internet sites have become major portals for unsafe and illegal drugs.

A **phrase outline** uses partial construction of the sentence form of each point. McClellan's sentence outline would appear as follows in phrase outline form:

I. Drug supply under attack
   A. Counterfeiting technologies more sophisticated
   B. Unregulated internet sites

The **key-word outline** uses the smallest possible units of understanding to outline the main and supporting points. Key-word outlines encourage you to become familiar enough with your speech points that a glance at a few words is enough to remind you of exactly what to say.

I. Threats
   A. Counterfeiting
   B. Internet

Use a Key-Word Outline for Optimal Eye Contact

The type of outline you select will affect how you deliver a speech. The less you rely on reading any outline, the more eye contact you can have with audience members—an essential aspect of a successful speech. For this reason, experts recommend using key-word or phrase outlines over sentence outlines, with key-word outline often being the preferred format. Key-word outlines permit not only the greatest degree of eye contact but also greater freedom of movement and better control of your thoughts and actions than either sentence or phrase outlines. With adequate practice, the key words will jog your memory so that the delivery of your ideas becomes more natural.

Create a Working Outline First

Begin with a working outline before transferring your ideas to a speaking outline containing key words or shortened phrases. Edit and rearrange items in the working outline as necessary as you work through the mass of information you've collected.

Prepare the body of the speech *before* the introduction, keeping the introduction (and the conclusion) *separate from* the main points (see sample outlines in this chapter). Since introductions serve to preview main points, you will first need to finalize the main points in the body. Introductions must also gain the audience's attention, introduce the topic and thesis, and establish the speaker's credibility (see **Chapter 42**). To ensure that you address these elements, use such labels as *Attention Getter, Topic and Thesis, Credibility Statement*, and *Preview Statement* (see the Sample Working Outline that follows).

Sample Working Outline

The following working outline is from a speech delivered by public speaking student Zachary Dominque. It includes all elements of the speech, including transitions and reminders to show presentation aids (SHOW SLIDE) in red. (In practice, working outlines may or may not include delivery cues; speaking outlines do include them. See p. 670). Next to each mention of a source requiring credit is a note in parentheses (e.g., "For bibliography: ABC of Mountain Biking"). This allows you to maintain a bibliography. The speech is organized topically, according to natural subdivisions of a topic (see p. 668).

The History and Sport of Mountain Biking

ZACHARY DOMINQUE

St. Edwards University

Topic:	Mountain Biking
General Speech Purpose:	To inform my listeners about the sport of mountain biking
Specific Purpose:	To help my audience gain an overview of and appreciation for mountain biking
Thesis Statement:	Mountain biking is a relatively new, exciting, and diverse sport.

Introduction

(Attention getter)

I. Imagine that you're on a bike, plunging down a steep, rock-strewn mountain, yet fully in control.

II. Adrenaline courses through your body as you hurtle through the air, touch down on glistening pebbled streams and tangled grasses, and rocket upward again.

III. You should be scared, but you're not; in fact, you're having the time of your life.

IV. Like we say, Nirvana.

V. How many of you like to bike—ride to campus, bike for fitness, or cycle just for fun?

VI. You might own a bike with a lightweight frame and thin wheels, and use it to log some serious mileage—or possibly a comfort bike, with a nice soft seat and solid tires.

(Credibility statement:)

VII. Good morning, folks. My name is Zachary Dominque, and I'm a mountain biker.

VIII. I've been racing since I was eight years old and won state champion three years ago, so this topic is close to my heart.

(Preview)

IX. Today, I'm going to take you on a tour of the exciting sport of mountain biking: I'll be your engine—your driver—in mountain bike-speak.

X. Our ride begins with a brief overview of mountain biking; then we'll do a hopturn—a turn in reverse—to learn about the sport's colorful history.

XI. Pedalling ahead in this beautiful autumn air, we'll chat about the various differences in design and function between mountain bikes and road bikes.

XII. We'll conclude our tour at a local bike shop, where you can compare downhill, trail, and cross-country mountain bikes.

XIII. These are the three main types of mountain bikes, designed for the three major types of mountain biking.

XIV. I hope by then that you'll catch a little bit of mountain biking fever and see why I find it such an exciting, intense, and physically challenging sport.

(TRANSITION) Mountain biking is a sport that can be extreme, recreational, or somewhere in between. But no matter what kind of rider you are, it's always a great way to get out in the natural world and get the adrenaline going. To start, let me briefly define mountain biking.

Body

I. The website ABC of Mountain Biking offers a good basic definition: "Mountain biking is a form of cycling on off-road or unpaved surfaces such as mountain trails and dirt roads; the biker uses a bicycle with a sturdy frame and fat tires." (**For bibliography:** ABC of Mountain Biking)

  A. The idea behind mountain biking is to go where other bikes won't take you.

    1. Mountain bikers ride on backcountry roads and on single-track trails winding through fields or forests.

    2. They climb up steep, rock-strewn hills and race down over them.

    3. The focus is on self-reliance, because these bikers often venture miles from help.

  B. According to the National Bicycle Dealers Association website, in 2012 mountain bikes accounted for 25 percent of all bikes sold in the United States.

    1. If you factor in sales of the comfort bike, which is actually a mountain bike modified for purely recreational riders, sales jump to nearly 38 percent of all bikes sold. (**For bibliography:** National Bicycle Dealers Assn)

    2. Some 50 million Americans love riding their mountain bikes, according to data collected by the New England Mountain Bike Association. (**For bibliography:** New England Mountain Bike Assn)

(TRANSITION) So you see that mountain biking is popular with a lot of people. But the sport itself is fairly new.

II. The history of mountain biking is less than 50 years old, and its founders are still around.

  A. The man in this picture is Gary Fisher, one of the founders of mountain biking. **(SHOW GF SLIDE 1)**

  B. According to *The Original Mountain Bike Book*, written in 1998 by pioneering mountain bikers Rob van der Plas and Charles Kelly, they, along with Fisher, Joe Breeze, and other members of the founding posse from the Marin County, California, area, were instrumental in founding the modern sport of mountain biking in the early 1970s. (**For bibliography:** *Original MB Book*)

C. Mountain bikes—called MTBs or ATBs (for all-terrain bikes)—didn't exist then as we now know them, so as you can see in this picture of Gary Fisher, he's riding a modified one-speed Schwinn cruiser. **(SHOW SCHWINN SLIDE 2)**

   1. Cruisers, or "ballooners," aren't made to go off road at all.
   2. Nothing equips them to navigate trails, and their brakes aren't remotely equipped to handle stops on steep descents.
   3. But this is the type of bike Fisher and others started out with.

D. By the mid-1970s, growing numbers of bikers in California got into using modified cruisers to race downhill on rocky trails.

   1. They'd meet at the bottom of Mount Tamalpais, in Corte Madera, California. **(SHOW MT TAM SLIDE 3)**
   2. They'd walk their bikes a mile or two up its steep slopes, and hurl on down.

E. As even more people got involved, Charles Kelly and others organized the famed Repack Downhill Race on Mt. Tam.

   1. Held from 1976 to 1979, the Repack race became a magnet for enthusiasts and put the sport on the map, according to *The Original Mountain Bike Book*.

(TRANSITION) The reason why the race was called "Repack" is a story in itself.

   2. The trail in the Repack race plummeted 1,300 feet in less than 2 miles.

      a. Such a steep drop meant constant braking, which in turn required riders to replace, or "repack," their bikes' grease after nearly each run, according to the Marin Museum of Biking website. (**For bibliography:** Marin Museum)

      b. As Breeze recounts in his own words: "The bikes' antiquated hub coaster brake would get so hot that the grease would vaporize, and after a run or two, the hub had to be repacked with new grease." **(SHOW BIKE SLIDE 4)**

(TRANSITION) As you might imagine, these early enthusiasts eventually tired of the routine.

F. The bikers had tinkered with their bikes from the start, adding gearing, drum brakes, and suspension systems.

G. In 1979, Joe Breeze designed a new frame—called the "Breezer"—which became the first actual mountain bike.

H. By 1982, as van der Plas and Kelly write in *The Original Mountain Bike Book*, standardized production of mountain bikes finally took off.

(TRANSITION) Now that you've learned a bit of the history of mountain biking, let's look at what today's mountain bike can do. To make things clearer, I'll compare them to road bikes. Road bikes are the class of bikes that cyclists who compete in the Tour de France use.

III. Mountain bikes and road bikes are built for different purposes. **(SHOW MB & RB SLIDE 5)**

A. Mountain bikes are built to tackle rough ground, while road bikes are designed to ride fast on paved, smooth surfaces.

1. To accomplish their task, mountain bikes feature wide tires with tough tread.

2. In contrast, road bike tires are ultrathin and their frames extremely lightweight.

a. If you take a road bike off-road, chances are you'll destroy it.

b. Without the knobby tread and thickness found on mountain bike tires, road bike tires can't grip onto the rocks and other obstacles that cover off-road courses.

B. The handlebars on the bikes also differ, as you can see here.

1. Mountain bikes feature flat handlebars; these keep us in an upright stance, so that we don't flip over when we hit something.

2. The drop handlebars on road bikes require the cyclist to lean far forward; this position suits road cycling, which prizes speed.

C. The gears and suspension systems also differentiate mountain bikes from road bikes.

1. Mountain bikes use lower gears than road bikes and are more widely spaced, giving them more control to ride difficult terrain.

2. As for suspension, road bikes generally don't have any kind of suspension system that can absorb power.

 a. That is, they don't have shock absorbers because they're not supposed to hit anything.

 b. Imagine riding over rocks and roots without shocks; it wouldn't be pretty.

3. Many mountain bikes have at least a great front shock absorbing suspension system.

 a. Some have rear-suspension systems.

 b. Some bikes have dual systems.

(TRANSITION) I hope by now you have a sense of the mountain bike design. But there are finer distinctions to draw.

IV. There are actually three different types of mountain bikes, designed to accommodate the three major kinds of mountain biking—downhill, trails, and cross-country.

(TRANSITION) Let's start with downhill. **(SHOW DH SLIDE 6)**

A. Downhill bikes have the fewest gears of the three types of mountain bikes and weigh the most.

1. That's because downhill biking is a daredevil sport—these bikers are crazy!

2. They slide down hills at insane speeds, and they go off jumps.

B. As described on the website Trails.com, downhill racers catch a shuttle going up the mountain, then speed downhill while chewing up obstacles. (**For Bibliography:** Trails.com)

C. Think of downhill racing as skiing with a bike.

(TRANSITION) Now let's swing by trail biking. **(SHOW TB SLIDE 7)**

D. Trail bikes look quite different than either downhill or cross-country bikes.

   1. They have very small wheels, measuring either 20, 24, or 26 inches, and smaller frames.
   2. These differences in design help trail bikers do what they do best: jump over obstacles—cars, rocks, and large logs.

E. The trail biker's goal is to not put a foot down on the ground.

F. Trail bike racing is one of the few types of biking that's done by time, not all at a mass start.

(TRANSITION) The third major type of mountain biking, cross-country, or XC cycling, is my sport. **(SHOW XC SLIDE 8)**

G. Cross-country biking is also the most common type of mountain biking—and the one sponsored by the Olympics.

   1. That's right. According to Olympic.org, in 1996, mountain biking became an Olympic sport. (**For Bibliography:** Olympic.org)
   2. This was just two decades after its inception.

H. With cross-country, you get the best of all worlds, at least in my humble opinion.

   1. The courses are creative, incorporating hills and valleys and rough to not-so-rough terrain.
   2. If done competitively, cross-country biking is like competing in a marathon.
   3. Done recreationally, it offers you the chance to see the great outdoors while getting, or staying, in great shape.

I. Cross-country bikes come in two forms.

   1. XC bikes are very lightweight, with either full or partial suspension.
   2. The Trails/Marathon XC hybrid bikes are a bit heavier, with full suspension; XC bikes are designed for seriously long rides.

(TRANSITION) Well, it has been quite a tour, folks. (***Signals close of speech***)

Conclusion

I. Our course began with an overview of mountain biking and a hopturn into a brief history of the sport.

II. We also learned about the differences between mountain bikes and road bikes, and the three major categories of mountain bikes. (***Summarizes main points***)

III. To me, mountain biking, and especially cross-country, is the perfect sport—fulfilling physical, spiritual, and social needs.

IV. It's a great sport to take up recreationally. (***Leaves audience with something to think about***)

V. And if you decide to mountain bike competitively, just remember: Ride fast, drive hard, and leave your blood on every trail. (***Memorable close***)

Works Cited

International Olympic Committee. 2015. "Cycling, Mountain Biking." March 2015. www.stillmed.olympic.org/AssetsDocs/OSC%20Section/pdf/QR_sports_summer/Sports_Olympiques_VTT_eng.pdf.

Marin Museum of Biking. n.d. "History of Mountain Biking." Accessed October 11, 2017. www.mmbhof.org/mtn-bike-hall-of-fame/history.

National Bicycle Dealers Association. 2015. "Industry Overview, 2015." Accessed November 28, 2017. www.nbda.com/articles/industry-overview-2012-pg34.htm.

New England Mountain Bike Association. 2013. "CT NEMBA's Trail School." April 7, 2013. www.nemba.org/news/ct-nembas-trail-school.

Trails.com. n.d. "Mountain Bikes and Biking." Accessed October 11, 2017. www.trails.com/mountain-bikes-and-biking.html.

Van der Plas, Rob, and Charles Kelly. 1998. *The Original Mountain Bike Book.* Minneapolis: Motorbooks.

Prepare a Speaking Outline for Delivery

Using the same numbering system as the working outline, condense long phrases or sentences into key words or short phrases, including just enough words to jog your memory. Include any **delivery cues** that will be part of the speech (see below). Place the speaking outline on large (at least 4 × 6-inch) notecards, 8.5 × 11-inch sheets of paper, or in a speaker's notes software program or app. Print large enough, or use large enough fonts, so that you can see the words at a glance. (For accuracy's sake, even in phrase or key-word outlines, direct quotations may be written out verbatim, as seen in this outline.)

DELIVERY CUE	EXAMPLE
Transitions	(TRANSITION)
Timing	(PAUSE) (SLOW DOWN)
Speaking Rate/ Volume	(SLOWLY) (LOUDER)
Presentation Aids	(SHOW MODEL)(SLIDE 3)
Source	(ATLANTA CONSTITUTION, August 2, 2018)
Statistic	(2018, boys to girls = 94,232; U.S. Health & Human Services)
Quotation	Eubie Blake, 100: "If I'd known I was gonna live this long, I'd have taken better care of myself."

Sample Speaking Outline

The History and Sport of Mountain Biking

ZACHARY DOMINQUE

St. Edwards University

Introduction

I. Imagine on bike, plunging rock-strewn, yet control.

II. Adrenaline, hurtle, touch downstream, rocket.

III. Scared, but not—time of life.

IV. Nirvana.

V. How many bike, fitness, fun?

VI. Might own lightweight, thin wheels, serious mileage—or comfort, soft seat, solid tires.

VII. Morning, Zachary, MTBer.

VIII. Eight; champion, heart.

IX. Today, tour, exciting sport of…engine, driver, MTB-speak.

X. Ride begins brief overview; do hopturn—colorful history.

XI. Pedaling ahead autumn, chat differences between mountain, road.

XII. Conclude shop, compare MTBs.

XIII. Three types bikes, designed for three…

XIV. Hope catch fever, exciting, intense, and physically.

(TRANSITION) MTB sport extreme…in-between. But no matter, always great way natural world, adrenaline. Start, define.

Body

I. *ABC/MB def*: "MTB is a form of cycling on off-road or unpaved surfaces such as mountain trails and dirt roads; the biker uses a bicycle with a sturdy frame and fat tires."

   A. The idea—go where others.

      1. MTBs ride backcountry, single-track winding fields, forests.
      2. Climb steep, rock-strewn, race down.
      3. Self-reliance, miles from help.

   B. National Bicycle Dealers Assoc., 2013 MTBs 25 percent sold.

      1. Factor comfort, actually MTB modified recreational, sales 38 percent.
      2. 50 million love riding, data gathered NE MTB Assn.

(TRANSITION) So MTB popular people. But fairly new.

II. History MTB less 50, founders.

   A. Gary Fisher, founders MTB. **(SHOW GF SLIDE 1)**

   B. *Original Mountain Bike Book*, written 1998 by van der Plas, Kelly; they, along with Fisher, Breeze, other members posse Marin, instrumental founding modern sport early 1970s.

   C. MTBs or ATBs (terrain)—didn't exist, so picture Fisher, modified Schwinn cruiser. **(SHOW SCHWINN SLIDE 2)**

      1. Cruisers, "ballooners," off-road.
      2. Nothing equips navigate, brakes equipped stops descents.
      3. But bike Fisher, others started.

   D. Mid-1970s, growing numbers using modified race downhill.

      1. Meet bottom Tamalpais, CA. **(SHOW MT TAM SLIDE 3)**
      2. Walk bikes mile up steep, hurl.

   E. Even involved, Kelly, others organized Repack.

      1. 1976–1979, magnet enthusiasts, on map, *Original MTB*.

(TRANSITION) Reason called "Repack" story itself.

2. Trail plummeted 1,300 feet 2 miles, Breeze article MTB Fame website.
    a. Such drop constant braking, required riders replace, "repack," grease each run.
    b. Breeze recounts: "The bikes' antiquated hub coaster brake would get so hot that the grease would vaporize, and after a run or two, the hub had to be repacked with new grease." **(SHOW BIKE SLIDE 4)**

(TRANSITION) Might imagine, early enthusiasts tired.

F. Bikers tinkered, gearing, drum, suspension.

G. 1979, Breeze new frame—"Breezer"—first actual MTB.

H. 1982, as van der Plas, Kelly write in *Original MTB,* standardized took off.

(TRANSITION) Now learned history, let's look today's can do. Clearer, compare road. Class cyclists Tour de France use.

III. MTB, road built different purposes. **(SHOW MB & RB SLIDE 5)**

A. MTB tackle rough, road designed fast, paved, smooth.
  1. Accomplish task, wide tire, tough tread.
  2. In contrast, road ultrathin, frames lightweight.
    a. Take off-road, destroy.
    b. Without knobby tread, thickness MTB tires, road can't grip rocks, obstacles.

B. Handlebars differ.
  1. MTB flat; upright stance, don't flip.
  2. Drop handlebars require forward; suits road cycling, prizes speed.

C. Gears, suspension also differ.
  1. MTB lower gears, widely spaced—more control difficult terrain.

2. As for suspension, road don't, absorb power.
    a. That is, don't have shock, not supposed to.
    b. Imagine without shocks; wouldn't be pretty.
3. Many MTBs at least a great front.
    a. Some rear.
    b. Some dual.

(TRANSITION) Hope sense MTB design, but finer distinction...

IV. Actually three types MTB, accommodate three kinds.

(TRANSITION) Let's start with downhill. **(SHOW DH SLIDE 6)**

A. Downhill fewest gears, weigh most.
    1. Because downhill daredevil—crazy!
    2. Slide insane, off jumps.
B. Trails.com, downhill racers catch shuttle going up, speed downhill chewing up.
C. Think racing skiing bike.

(TRANSITION) Now let's swing by trail biking. **(SHOW TB SLIDE 7)**

D. Trail bikes look different than either.
    1. Small wheels, 20, 24, or 26, smaller frames.
    2. Differences design help trail do best—jump obstacles—cars, rocks, large logs.
E. Trail goal not foot on ground.
F. Trail racing few types done by time, not mass.

(TRANSITION) Third major type MTB, cross-country, or XC. **(SHOW XC SLIDE 8)**

G. Cross-country most common—Olympics.
    1. That's right. In 1996...
    2. Just two decades inception.

H. With XC, best all worlds, humble.

   1. Courses creative, incorporating hills, valleys, rough, not-so.
   2. Competitively, XC like marathon.
   3. Recreationally, chance see outdoors, shape.

I. XC two forms.

   1. Lightweight, full or partial.
   2. Trails/Marathon XC hybrids heavier, full suspension; designed seriously long.

(TRANSITION) Quite tour.

Conclusion

I. Course began overview, hopturn history sport.

II. Also learned differences: mountain, road, three major categories of MTB, three types MTB accommodate fans.

III. To me, MTB, especially XC, perfect—fulfilling physical, spiritual, social needs.

IV. Great take up recreationally.

V. Decide bike competitively, remember: ride fast, drive hard, leave blood.

CHECKLIST

Steps in Creating a Speaking Outline

- ☐ Create the outline on sheets of paper, large notecards, or software app.
- ☐ Write large and legibly using at least a 14-point font or easy-to-read ink and large letters.
- ☐ For each main and subpoint, choose a key word or phrase that will jog your memory accurately.
- ☐ Include delivery cues.
- ☐ Write out full quotations or other critical information.
- ☐ Using the speaking outline, practice the speech at least five times, or as needed.

part 9

Public Speaking: Starting, Finishing, and Styling

CHAPTER

42

Developing the Introduction and Conclusion

A compelling introduction and conclusion, although not a substitute for a well-developed speech body, are nevertheless essential to the success of any speech. A good opening previews what's to come in a way that engages listeners in the topic and speaker. An effective conclusion ensures that the audience remembers key points and reacts in a way that the speaker intends.

Preparing the Introduction

The choices you make about the introduction can affect the outcome of the entire speech. In the first several minutes (one speaker pegs it at twenty seconds),[1] audience members will decide whether they are interested in the topic of your speech and whether they will believe what you say. A speech introduction serves to:

- Arouse the audience's attention and willingness to listen.
- Introduce the topic, purpose, and main points.
- Establish your credibility to speak on the topic.
- Motivate the audience to accept your speech goals.

CHECKLIST

Guidelines for Preparing the Introduction

- ☐ Prepare the introduction after you've completed the speech body so you will know exactly what you need to preview.
- ☐ Keep the introduction brief—as a rule, no more than 10–15 percent of the entire speech.
- ☐ Practice delivering your introduction until you feel confident you've got it right.

Gain Audience Attention

An introduction must first of all win the audience's attention. They must believe the speech will interest them and offer them something of benefit. Techniques for doing this include sharing a compelling quotation or story, establishing common ground, providing unusual information, posing a question, and using humor.

Use a Quotation

In a recent commencement address, Twitter executive Wayne Chang advised graduates: "Make your own rules, hack the system, and change the world."[2] Quotations such as this, which touch upon a theme of the speech, will likely arouse interest. Quotations can be drawn from literature, poetry, and film, or directly from people you know.

Tell a Story

Noted speechwriter William Safire once remarked that stories are "surefire attention getters."[3] Stories, or *narratives*, personalize issues by encouraging audience identification and involvement. Speeches that begin with brief stories of meaningful and entertaining incidents can boost speaker credibility and promote greater understanding and retention of the speaker's message[4] (**see also p. 640**). You can relate an entire story (if brief) in the introduction or, alternatively, offer part of a longer one, indicating you will return to it further on in the speech.

> **QUICK TIP**
>
> **Show Them the Transformation**
>
> Stories often feature transformation—how people overcome obstacles or otherwise experience change.[5] One powerful means of gaining audience involvement is to tell a story in which others were changed by adopting beliefs and behaviors similar to those you are proposing in your speech. If you can think of a story that does this, your message is likely to be doubly persuasive.

Establish Common Ground

Audiences are won over when speakers express interest in them and show that they share in the audience's concerns and goals. Refer to the occasion that has brought you together, and use your knowledge of the audience to touch briefly on areas of shared experience. This creates goodwill and a feeling of common ground (or *identification;* see also **Chapter 35**).

Offer Unusual Information

"Nearly one in 100 people are now displaced from their homes."[6] Surprising audience members with startling facts and statistics is one of the surest ways to get their attention. Offering statistics, for example, is a powerful means of illustrating consequences and relationships that can quickly bring points into focus, as in this opener by Chef James Oliver: "Sadly, in the next eighteen minutes when I do our chat, four Americans that are alive will be dead from the food they eat."[7]

Pose Questions

"How long do you think our water supply will last?" Posing questions such as this can be an effective way to draw the audience's attention to what you are about to say. Questions can be real or rhetorical. **Rhetorical questions** do not invite actual responses. Instead, they make the audience think.

Use Humor—Perhaps

Handled well, humor can build rapport and set a positive tone for the speech. But humor can also easily backfire. Simply telling a series of unrelated jokes without making a relevant point will detract from your purpose, and few things turn an audience off more quickly than tasteless humor. Strictly avoid humor or sarcasm that belittles others—whether on the basis of race, sex, ability, or otherwise. A good rule of thumb is that speech humor should always match the rhetorical situation.

Preview the Topic, Purpose, and Main Points

Once you've gained the audience's attention, use the introduction to provide a **preview**, or brief overview, of the speech *topic*, *purpose*, and *main points*. First, declare what your speech is about (topic) and what you hope to accomplish (purpose).

Topic and purpose are clearly revealed in this introduction by Marvin Runyon, former postmaster general of the United States:

> This afternoon, I want to examine the truth of that statement—"Nothing moves people like the mail, and no one moves the mail like the U.S. Postal Service." I want to look at where we are today as a communications industry, and where we intend to be in the days and years ahead.[8]

Once you've revealed the topic and purpose, briefly preview the main points of the speech. This helps audience members mentally organize the speech as they follow along. Simply tell the audience what the main points will be and in what order you will address them. Save your in-depth discussion of each one for the body of your speech.

Robert L. Darbelnet, former CEO of the American Automobile Association, effectively introduces his topic, purpose, and main points with this preview:

> My remarks today are intended to give you a sense of AAA's ongoing efforts to improve America's roads. Our hope is that you will join your voices to ours as we call on the federal government to do three things:
>
> Number one: Perhaps the most important, provide adequate funding for highway maintenance and improvements.
>
> Number two: Play a strong, responsible, yet flexible role in transportation programs.
>
> And number three: Invest in highway safety.
>
> Let's see what our strengths are, what the issues are, and what we can do about them.[9]

Establish Credibility as a Speaker

During the introduction, audience members make a decision about whether they are interested not just in your topic but also in you. They want to feel that they can trust what you have to say—that they can believe in your *ethos*, or good character. To build credibility, offer a simple statement of your qualifications for speaking on the topic. Briefly emphasize some experience, knowledge, or perspective you have that is different from or more extensive than that of your audience: "I've felt passionate about preserving open space ever since I started volunteering with the Land Trust four summers ago."

Motivate the Audience to Accept Your Goals

A final, and critical, function of the introduction is to motivate the audience to care about your topic and make it relevant to them. You may choose to convey what the audience stands to gain by the information you will share or convince audience members that your speech purpose is consistent with their motives and values. A student speech about the value of interview training shows how this can be accomplished:

> Why do you need interview training? It boils down to competition. As in sports, when you're not training, someone else is out there training to beat you. All things being equal, the person who has the best interviewing skills has got the edge.

CHECKLIST

How Effective Is Your Introduction?

Does your introduction...

- ☐ Capture the audience's attention?
- ☐ Stimulate their interest in what's to come?
- ☐ Establish a positive bond with listeners?
- ☐ Alert listeners to the speech topic, purpose, and main points?
- ☐ Establish your credibility?
- ☐ Motivate listeners to accept your speech goals?

Preparing the Conclusion

Just as a well-crafted introduction gets your speech effectively out of the starting gate, a well-constructed conclusion lets you drive home your purpose and leave the audience inspired to think about and even to act upon your ideas. The conclusion serves to:

- Signal the end of the speech and provide closure.
- Summarize the key points.
- Reiterate the thesis or central idea of the speech.
- Challenge the audience to remember and possibly act upon your ideas.
- End the speech memorably.

Signal the End of the Speech and Provide Closure

People who listen to speeches are taking a journey of sorts, and they want and need the speaker to acknowledge the journey's end. They look for logical and emotional closure.

One signal that a speech is about to end is a transitional word or phrase: *finally, looking back, in conclusion, let me close by saying* (see **Chapter 39**). You can also signal closure by adjusting your manner of delivery; for example, you can vary your tone, pitch, rhythm, and rate of speech to indicate that the speech is winding down (see **Chapters 45 and 46**).

CHECKLIST

Guidelines for Preparing the Conclusion

- ☐ As with the introduction, prepare the conclusion after you've completed the speech body.
- ☐ Do not leave the conclusion to chance. Include it with your speaking outline.
- ☐ Keep the conclusion brief—as a rule, no more than 10–15 percent, or about one-sixth, of the overall speech. Conclude soon after you say you are about to end.
- ☐ Carefully consider your use of language. More than in other parts of the speech, the conclusion can contain words that inspire and motivate (see **Chapter 43** on use of language).
- ☐ Practice delivering your conclusion until you feel confident you've got it right.
- ☐ Once you've signaled the end of your speech, conclude in short order (though not abruptly).

Summarize the Key Points

One bit of age-old advice for giving a speech is "Tell them what you are going to tell them (in the introduction), tell them (in the body), and tell them what you told them (in the conclusion)." The idea is that emphasizing the main points three times will help the audience remember them. A restatement of points in the conclusion brings the speech full circle and gives the audience a sense of completion. Consider how executive Holger Kluge, in a speech titled "Reflections on Diversity," summarizes his main points:

> I have covered a lot of ground here today. But as I draw to a close, I'd like to stress three things.
>
> First, diversity is more than equity....
>
> Second, weaving diversity into the very fabric of your organization takes time....
>
> Third, diversity will deliver bottom line results to your businesses and those results will be substantial....[10]

Reiterate the Topic and Speech Purpose

The conclusion should reiterate the topic and speech purpose—to imprint it on the audience's memory. In the conclusion to a speech about the U.S. immigration debate, civil defense lawyer Elpidio Villarreal reminds his listeners of his central idea:

> Two paths are open to us. One path would keep us true to our fundamental values as a nation and a people. The other would lead us down a dark trail; one marked by 700-mile-long fences, emergency detention centers and vigilante border patrols. Because I really am an American, heart and soul, and because that means never being without hope, I still believe we will ultimately choose the right path. We have to.[11]

Challenge the Audience to Respond

A strong conclusion challenges audience members to put to use what the speaker has shared with them. In an *informative speech*, the speaker challenges audience members to use what they've learned in a way that benefits them. In a *persuasive speech*, the challenge usually comes in the form of a call to action. Here the speaker challenges listeners to act in response to the speech, see the problem in a new way, or change both their actions and their beliefs about the problem.

Emma Watson, United Nations Women Goodwill Ambassador, makes a strong call to action at the conclusion of her speech at a special event for the HeForShe campaign.

> We are struggling for a uniting word, but the good news is we have a uniting movement. It is called HeForShe. I am inviting you to step forward, to be seen to speak up, to be the "he" for "she." And to ask yourself if not me, who? If not now, when?[12]

QUICK TIP

Bring Your Speech Full Circle

Picking up on a story or an idea you mentioned in the introduction can be a memorable way to conclude a speech and bring the entire presentation full circle. You can provide the resolution of the story or reiterate the link between the moral (lesson) of the story and the speech theme.

Make the Conclusion Memorable

A speech that makes a lasting impression is one that listeners are most likely to remember and act on. To accomplish this, make use of the same devices for capturing attention described for use in introductions—quotations, stories, startling statements, questions, references to the audience and the occasion, and humor.

CHECKLIST

How Effective Is Your Conclusion?

Does your conclusion...

- ☐ Alert the audience, with a transition, that the speech is ending?
- ☐ Actually come to an end soon after you say you will finish?
- ☐ Last no more than about one-sixth of the time spent on the body of the speech?
- ☐ Remind listeners of the speech topic, purpose, and main points?
- ☐ Include a challenge or call to action to motivate the audience to respond to your ideas or appeals?
- ☐ Provide a sense of closure and make a lasting impression?

CHAPTER 43

Using Language

Words are the public speaker's tools of the trade, and the ones you choose to style your speech will play a crucial role in creating a dynamic connection with your audience. The right words and **rhetorical devices** (techniques of language) will help your listeners understand, believe in, and retain your message.

Use an Oral Style

Speeches require an **oral style**—the use of language that is simpler, more repetitious, more rhythmic, and more interactive than written language.[1] As Jayne Benjulian, former chief speechwriter at Apple, has noted, "Every speech has language meant to be spoken. They are monologues. . . .Speeches are an oral medium."[2] Speeches therefore must be prepared for the ear—to be *heard* rather than read. This is particularly important because unlike readers, listeners have only one chance to get the message.

Strive for Simplicity

To ensure understanding, express yourself simply, without pretentious language or unnecessary **jargon** (the specialized, "insider" language of a given profession). Speak in commonly understood terms and choose the simpler of two synonyms: *guess* rather than *extrapolate*; *use* rather than *utilize*. Use fewer rather than more words, and shorter sentences rather than longer ones. As speechwriter Peggy Noonan notes in her book *Simply Speaking*:

> Good hard simple words with good hard clear meanings are good things to use when you speak. They are like pickets in a fence, slim and unimpressive on their own but sturdy and effective when strung together.[3]

Former First Lady Michelle Obama, in a speech at the Democratic Convention, used the simplest, jargon-free language to describe her party's response to its opponents: "When they go low, we go high."[4] Each word contains just one syllable, yet the audience roared with understanding and approval.

Make Frequent Use of Repetition

Repetition is key to oral style, serving to compensate for natural lapses in listening and to reinforce information. Even very brief speeches repeat key words and phrases. Repetition adds emphasis to important ideas, helps listeners follow your logic, and infuses language with rhythm and drama.

QUICK TIP

Experiment with Phrases and Sentence Fragments

In line with an oral style, experiment with using phrases and sentence fragments in place of full sentences. This speaker, a physician, demonstrates how short phrases can add punch to a speech: "I'm just a simple bone-and-joint guy. I can set your broken bones. Take away your bunions. Even give you a new hip. But I don't mess around with the stuff between the ears.…That's another specialty."[5]

Use Personal Pronouns

Audience members want to know what the speaker thinks and feels, and to be assured that he or she recognizes them and relates them to the message. The direct form of address, using the personal pronouns such as *we*, *us*, *I*, and *you*, helps to create this feeling of recognition and inclusion. Note how Sheryl Sandberg, Chief Operating Officer of Facebook, uses personal pronouns to begin a speech on why there are too few women leaders (italics added):

> So for any of *us* in this room today, let's start out by admitting *we're* lucky. *We* don't live in the world *our* mothers lived in, *our* grandmothers lived in, where career choices for women were so limited.…But all that aside, *we* still have a problem.…Women are not making it to the top of any profession anywhere in the world.[6]

Choose Concrete Language and Vivid Imagery

Concrete words and vivid imagery engage audience members' senses, making a speech come alive for listeners. **Concrete language** is specific, tangible, and definite. Concrete nouns such as *iceberg*, *stone*, *lawn*, and *butter* describe things we can physically sense (see, hear, taste, smell, and touch). In contrast, **abstract language** is general or nonspecific, leaving meaning open to interpretation. Abstract nouns, such as *peace*, *freedom*, and *love*, are purely conceptual; they have no physical reference. Politicians use abstract language to appeal to mass audiences, or to be noncommittal: "We strive for peace." In most speaking situations, however, listeners will appreciate concrete nouns and verbs.

Note how concrete nouns and adjectives that modify them add precision and color:

Abstract:	The old road needed repair.
Concrete:	The rutted road was pitted with muddy craters.

Offer Vivid Imagery

Imagery is concrete language that brings into play the senses of smell, taste, sight, hearing, and touch to paint mental pictures. Vivid imagery is more easily recalled than colorless language,[7] and speeches containing ample imagery also elicit more positive responses than those that do not.[8]

Adding imagery into your speech need not be difficult if you focus on using strong, active verbs and colorful adjectives. Rather than *walk*, you can say *saunter*; in place of *look*, use *gaze*. Replace passive forms of the verb "to be" (e.g., *is*, *are*, *was*, *were*, *will be*...) with more active verb forms. Rather than "the houses were empty," use "the houses *stood* empty." You can use descriptive adjectives to modify nouns (as in "*dilapidated* house") and use adverbs to modify verbs. President Franklin D. Roosevelt famously did this when he characterized the nation's struggles during World War II as "this dark hour,"[9] conveying with one simple adjective the gravity of the times.

CHOOSE STRONG VERBS	
Mundane Verb	**Colorful Alternative**
look	*behold, gaze, glimpse, peek, stare*
walk	*stride, amble, stroll, skulk*
throw	*hurl, fling, pitch*
sit	*sink, plop, settle*
eat	*devour, inhale, gorge*

Use Figures of Speech

Figures of speech make striking comparisons that help listeners visualize, identify with, and understand the speaker's ideas. Such figures as similes, metaphors, and analogies are key to making a speech both memorable and persuasive.

A **simile** explicitly compares one thing to another, using *like* or *as*: "He works *like a dog*," and "rusted-out factories scattered *like tombstones across the landscape*."[10]

A **metaphor** also compares two things, but does so by describing one thing as actually *being* the other: "Time is a thief" and "Drain the swamp" (with government bureaucracy being the swamp).

An **analogy** is simply an extended metaphor or simile that compares an unfamiliar concept or process to a more familiar one. For example, African American minister Phil Wilson used metaphoric language when he preached about the dangers of AIDS:

> Our house is on fire! The fire truck arrives, but we won't come out, because we're afraid the folks from next door will see that we're in that burning house. AIDS is a fire raging in our community and it's out of control![11]

Avoid Clichés, Mixed Metaphors, and Faulty Analogies

Used properly, similes and metaphors express ideas compactly and cleverly. However, avoid those that are predictable and stale, known as **clichés**, such as "sold like hotcakes" (a clichéd simile) and "pearly white teeth" (a clichéd metaphor). Beware, too, of using **mixed metaphors**, or combining two or more unrelated (and incompatible) images: For example, "Burning the midnight oil at both ends" incorrectly joins the metaphor "burning the midnight oil" and "burning the candle at both ends."

Analogies, too, can mislead audience members if used carelessly. A **faulty analogy** is an inaccurate or misleading comparison suggesting that because two things are similar in some ways, they are necessarily similar in others.

Choose Words That Build Credibility

Audiences expect speakers to be competent and credible. To project these qualities, use language that is appropriate, accurate, assertive, and unbiased.

Use Words Appropriately

The language you use in a speech should be appropriate to the audience, the occasion, and the subject matter. Formal occasions call for more formal language, but no matter what the occasion, listeners will expect you to avoid obvious grammatical errors and substandard usage (as well as any form of suggestive language, bathroom humor, and obscene references). Done carefully, it may be appropriate to mix regionalisms or **vernacular language** (language specific to particular regions of a country) or even slang into your speech. Even alternating between two languages, called *code-switching*, may be appropriate. The key is to ensure that your meaning is clear and your use is suitable for your audience. Consider the following excerpt:

> On the gulf where I was raised, *el valle del Rio Grande* in South Texas—that triangular piece of land wedged between the river *y el golfo* which serves as the Texas–U.S./Mexican border—is a Mexican *pueblito* called Hargill.[12]

Use Words Accurately

Audiences lose confidence in speakers who misuse words. Check that your words mean what you intend, and beware especially of **malapropisms**—the inadvertent, incorrect uses of a word or phrase in place of one that sounds like it[13] ("It's a strange receptacle" for "It's a strange spectacle").

Use the Active Voice

Voice is the feature of verbs that indicates the subject's relationship to the action. Speaking in the active rather than passive voice will make your statements—and the audience's perception of you as the speaker—clear and assertive instead of indirect and weak. A verb is in the *active voice* when the subject performs the action, and in the *passive voice* when the subject is acted upon or is the receiver of the action:

Passive:	A test was announced by Ms. Carlos for Tuesday. A president is elected every four years.
Active:	Ms. Carlos announced a test for Tuesday. The voters elect a president every four years.

Use Inclusive, Unbiased Language

Focus on using language that reflects respect for audience members' cultural beliefs, norms, and traditions. Review and eliminate any language that reflects unfounded assumptions, negative descriptions, or stereotypes of a given group's age, class, gender identity, sexual orientation, ability, and ethnic, racial, or religious characteristics. Consider whether certain seemingly well-known names and terms may be foreign to some listeners, and include brief explanations for them. Sayings specific to a certain region or group of people—termed **colloquial expressions** or *idioms*—such as "back the wrong horse" and "ballpark figure" can add color and richness to a speech, but only if listeners understand them.

Word your speech with gender-neutral language: Avoid the third-person generic masculine pronouns (*his, he*) in favor of inclusive pronouns such as *his or her, he or she, they, their, we, our, you, your*, or other gender-neutral terms that your audience will understand.

QUICK TIP

Denotative versus Connotative Meaning

When drafting your speech, choose words that are both denotatively and connotatively appropriate to the audience. The **denotative meaning** of a word is its literal, or dictionary, definition. The **connotative meaning** of a word is the special (often emotional) association that different people bring to bear on it. For example, you may agree that you are *angry* but not *irate*, and *thrifty* but not *cheap*. Consider how the connotative meanings of your word choices might affect the audience's response to your message, including those of non-native speakers of English.

Choose Words That Create a Lasting Impression

Oral speech that is artfully arranged and infused with rhythm draws listeners in and leaves a lasting impression on audience members. It is surprisingly easy to achieve this effect with rhetorical devices such as repetition, alliteration, and parallelism.

Use Repetition to Create Rhythm

Repeating key words, phrases, or even sentences at various intervals throughout a speech creates a distinctive rhythm and thereby implants important ideas in listeners' minds. Repetition works particularly well when delivered with the appropriate voice inflections and pauses.

In a form of repetition called **anaphora**, the speaker repeats a word or phrase at the beginning of successive phrases, clauses, or sentences. In his speech delivered in 1963 in Washington, DC, Dr. Martin Luther King Jr. repeated the phrase "I have a dream" eleven times in eight successive sentences, each with an upward inflection followed by a pause. Speakers have made use of anaphora since earliest times. For example, Jesus preached (italics added):

> *Blessed are* the poor in spirit...
>
> *Blessed are* the meek...
>
> *Blessed are* the peacemakers...[14]

Repetition can focus attention on the theme of the speech. Speakers may do this by using both anaphora and *epiphora* in the same speech. In **epiphora** (also called *epistrophe*), the repetition of a word or phrase appears at the end of successive statements. In a speech to his New Hampshire supporters, former President Barack Obama used both anaphora and epiphora to establish a theme of empowerment (italics added):

> *It was* a creed written into the founding documents that declared the destiny of a nation: *Yes, we can.*
>
> *It was* whispered by slaves and abolitionists as they blazed a trail toward freedom through the darkest of nights: *Yes, we can.*
>
> *It was* sung by immigrants as they struck out from distant shores and pioneers who pushed westward against an unforgiving wilderness: *Yes, we can.*[15]

Use Alliteration for a Poetic Quality

Alliteration is the repetition of the same sounds, usually initial consonants, in two or more neighboring words or syllables. Alliteration lends speeches a poetic, musical rhythm. A classic example is Jesse Jackson's "Down with dope, up with hope." More recently, President Donald J. Trump threatened to respond to North Korean aggression with "fire and fury."

Experiment with Parallelism

Parallelism is the arrangement of words, phrases, or sentences in a similar form. Parallel structure helps emphasize important ideas, and can be as simple as orally numbering points ("first, second, and third"). Like repetition, parallelism also creates a sense of steady or building rhythm. Speakers often make use of three parallel elements, called a *triad*, as in Abraham Lincoln's famous "...of the people, by the people, and for the people...."

Parallelism in speeches often makes use of **antithesis**—setting off two ideas in balanced (parallel) opposition to each other to create a powerful effect:

> One small step for a man, one giant leap for mankind.
>
> —*Neil Armstrong on the moon, 1969*

> For many are called, but few are chosen.
>
> —*Matthew 22:14*

CHECKLIST

Using Effective Oral Style

- ☐ Use familiar words and easy-to-follow sentences.
- ☐ Root out biased language.
- ☐ Avoid unnecessary jargon.
- ☐ Use fewer rather than more words to express your thoughts.
- ☐ Clarify meaning and make memorable comparisons with ***similes***, ***metaphors***, and ***analogies***.
- ☐ Use the active voice.
- ☐ Repeat key words, phrases, or sentences at the beginning of successive sentences (***anaphora***) and at their close (***epiphora***).
- ☐ Experiment with ***alliteration***—words that repeat the same sounds, usually initial consonants, in two or more neighboring words or syllables.
- ☐ Experiment with ***parallelism***—arranging words, phrases, or sentences in similar form.

part 10

Public Speaking: Delivery

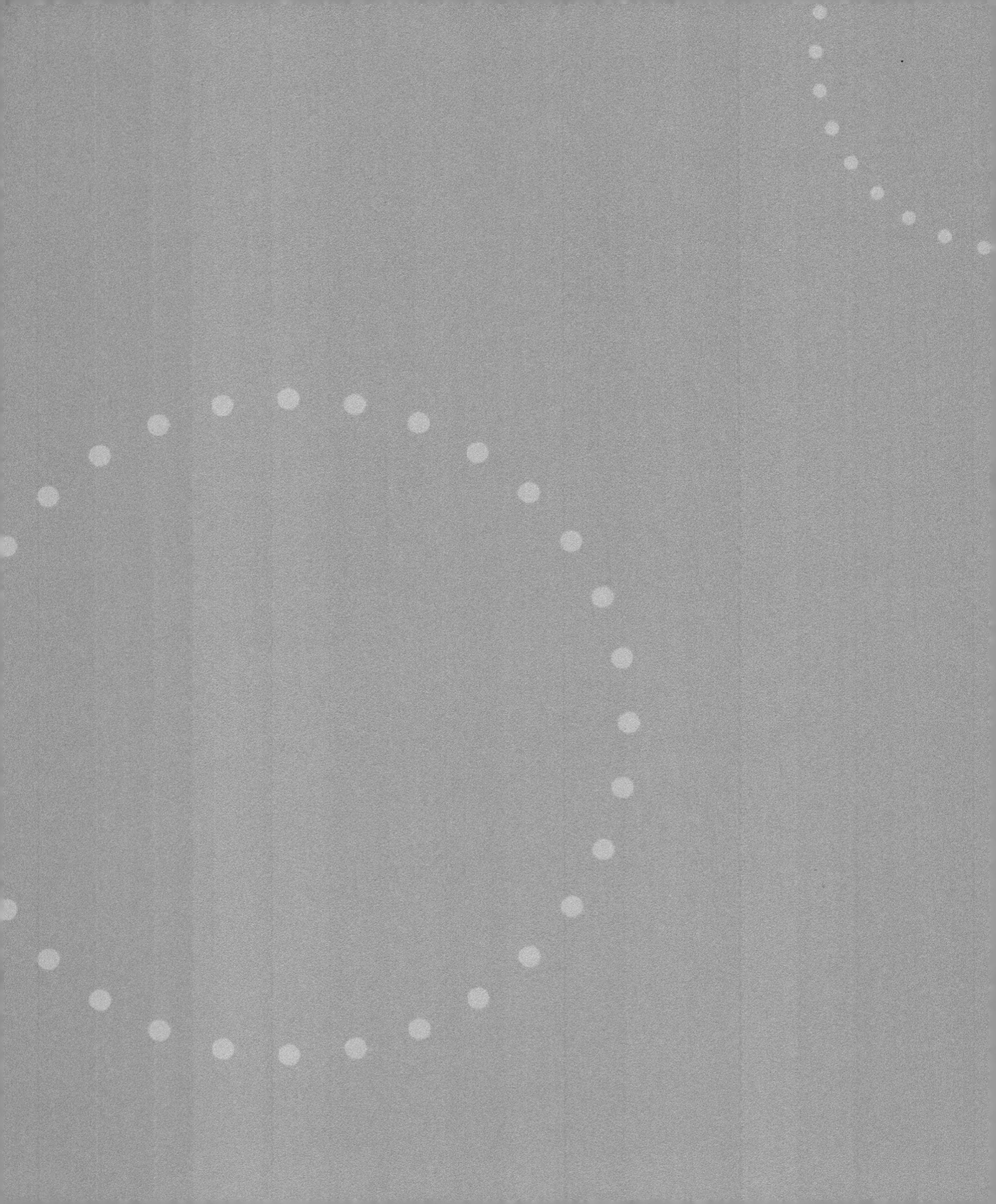

CHAPTER

44

Methods of Delivery

For most of us, anticipating the actual delivery of a speech feels unnerving. In fact, effective delivery rests on the same natural foundation as everyday conversation, except, obviously, that it is more rehearsed and purposeful. By focusing on four key qualities of effective delivery, you can reduce your fears and make your presentations more authentic.

Keys to Effective Delivery

Effective delivery is the controlled use of voice and body to express the qualities of naturalness, enthusiasm, confidence, and directness.[1] Audiences respond most favorably to speakers who project these characteristics during delivery. As you practice delivering your speech, focus on these key qualities:

- *Strive for naturalness.* Rather than behaving theatrically, act naturally. Think of your speech as a particularly important conversation.
- *Show enthusiasm.* Inspire your listeners by showing enthusiasm for your topic and for the occasion. An enthusiastic delivery helps you feel good about your speech, and it focuses your audience's attention on the message.
- *Project a sense of confidence.* Focus on the ideas you want to convey rather than on yourself. Inspire the audience's confidence in you by appearing confident to them.
- *Be direct.* Engage directly with audience members. Demonstrate your interest and concern for listeners by establishing eye contact, using a friendly tone of voice, and animating your facial expressions, especially positive ones such as smiling and nodding whenever appropriate. (See **Chapters 45 and 46** on techniques for using voice and body in a speech.)

Select a Method of Delivery

For virtually any type of speech or presentation, you can choose from four basic methods of delivery: speaking from manuscript, speaking from memory, speaking impromptu, and speaking extemporaneously.

Speaking from Manuscript

When **speaking from manuscript**, you read a speech *verbatim*—that is, from prepared written text that contains the entire speech, word for word. As a rule, speaking from manuscript restricts eye contact and body movement, and may also limit expressiveness in vocal variety and quality. Watching a speaker read a speech can be monotonous and boring for the audience.

If you must read from prepared text—for example, when you need to convey a precise message, when you will be quoted and must avoid misinterpretation, or when addressing an emergency and conveying exact descriptions and direction—do what you can to deliver the speech naturally:

- Vary the rhythm of your words (see Chapter 45).
- Become familiar enough with the speech so that you can establish some eye contact.
- Use a large font and double- or triple-space the manuscript so that you can read without straining.
- Consider using some compelling presentation aids (see Chapter 48).

Speaking from Memory

The formal name for **speaking from memory** is *oratory*. In oratorical style, you put the entire speech, word for word, into writing and then commit it to memory. Memorization is not a natural way to present a message. True eye contact with the audience is unlikely, and the potential for disaster exists because there is always the possibility of forgetting. Some kinds of brief speeches, however, such as toasts and introductions, can be well served by memorization. Sometimes it's helpful to memorize a part of the speech, especially when you use direct quotations as a form of support. If you do use memorization, practice that portion of your speech so completely that you can convey enthusiasm and directness.

Speaking Impromptu

Speaking impromptu is a type of delivery that is unpracticed, spontaneous, or improvised, and involves speaking on relatively short notice with little time to prepare. Many occasions require that you make remarks on the spur of the moment. An instructor may ask you to summarize key points from an assignment, for example, or a boss may invite you to take the place of an absent co-worker who was scheduled to speak on a new project.

Try to anticipate situations that may require you to speak impromptu, and prepare some remarks beforehand. Otherwise, maximize the time you do have to prepare on the spot:

- *Think first about your listeners.* Consider their interests and needs, and try to shape your remarks accordingly. For example, who are the people present, and what are their views on the topic?
- *Listen to what others around you are saying.* Take notes in a key-word or phrase format (see p. 681) and arrange them into main points from which you can speak.
- *Acknowledge the previous speaker.* If your speech follows someone else's, acknowledge that person's statements. Then make your points.
- *Stay on the topic.* Don't wander off track.
- *Use transitions.* Use signal words such as *first, second,* and *third* to organize points and help listeners follow them.

As much as possible, try to organize your points into a discernible pattern. If addressing a problem, for example, such as a project failure or glitch, consider the *problem-solution pattern*—state problem(s), then offer solution(s); or the *cause-effect pattern* of organizational arrangement—state cause(s) first, then address effect(s); see Chapter 40 for various ways of using these patterns. If called upon to defend one proposal as superior to another, consider using the *comparative advantage pattern* to illustrate various advantages of your favored proposal over the other options.

Speaking Extemporaneously

When **speaking extemporaneously**, you prepare and practice in advance, giving full attention to all facets of the speech—content, arrangement, and delivery alike. However, instead of memorizing or writing the speech word for word, you speak from an outline of key words and phrases that isolates the main ideas that you want to communicate (see Chapter 41).

Because extemporaneous delivery is most conducive to achieving a natural, conversational quality, most speakers prefer it among the four types of delivery. Knowing your ideas well enough to present them without memorization or manuscript gives you greater flexibility in adapting to the specific speaking situation. You can modify wording, rearrange your points, change examples, or omit information in keeping with the audience and the setting. You can have more eye contact, more direct body orientation, greater freedom of movement, and generally better control of your thoughts and actions than any of the other delivery methods allow.

Speaking extemporaneously does present a possible drawback. Occasionally, even a glance at your speaking notes may fail to jog your memory on a point you wanted to cover, and you find yourself searching for what to say next. The remedy for this potential pitfall is frequent practice—rehearsing the speech about six times—using a key word or phrase outline (see p. 681).

CHOOSING A METHOD OF DELIVERY	
When...	**Method of Delivery**
You want to avoid being misquoted or misconstrued, or you need to communicate exact descriptions and directions...	Consider *speaking from manuscript* (read the part of your speech requiring precise wording from fully prepared text).
You must deliver a short special occasion speech, such as a toast or an introduction, or you plan on using direct quotations...	Consider *speaking from memory* (memorize part or all of your speech).
You are called upon to speak without prior planning or preparation...	By definition, you will be *speaking impromptu*—(organizing your thoughts with little or no lead time). Follow the guidelines on **p. 710**.
You have time to prepare and practice developing a speech or presentation that achieves a natural conversational style...	Consider *speaking extemporaneously* (develop your speech in working outline and then practice and deliver it with a phrase or key-word speaking outline).

CHECKLIST

Tips for Successful Delivery

- ☐ Strive for naturalness.
- ☐ Show enthusiasm.
- ☐ Project a sense of confidence and composure.
- ☐ Engage your audience by being direct.
- ☐ If you must read from a prepared text, do so naturally.
- ☐ In general, don't try to memorize entire speeches.
- ☐ When speaking impromptu, maximize any preparation time.

CHAPTER 45

Your Voice in Delivery

Used properly in the delivery of a speech, your voice is a powerful instrument of expression that conveys who you are and delivers your message with confidence. As you practice, you can learn to control each of the elements of vocal delivery: volume, pitch, speaking rate, pauses, vocal variety, and pronunciation and articulation.

Adjust Your Speaking Volume

Volume, the relative loudness of a speaker's voice while delivering a speech, is usually the most obvious vocal element we notice about a speaker, and with good reason. We need to hear the speaker at a comfortable level. The proper volume for delivering a speech is somewhat louder than that of normal conversation. Just how much louder depends on three factors: (1) the size of the room and of the audience, (2) whether or not you use a microphone, and (3) the level of background noise. Speaking at the appropriate volume is critical to how credible your listeners will perceive you to be, so check that audience members can hear you. Be alert to signals that your volume is slipping or is too loud and make the necessary adjustments.

Vary Your Intonation

Pitch is the range of sounds from high to low (or vice versa). Anatomy determines a person's natural pitch—a bigger or smaller voice box produces a lower- or higher-pitched voice. But within these natural constraints, you can and should control pitch through **intonation**—the rising and falling of sound across phrases and sentences. Intonation is important in speechmaking because it powerfully affects the meaning associated with spoken words. For example, say "Stop." Now, say "Stop!" Varying intonation conveys two very distinct meanings.

As you speak, intonation conveys your mood, level of enthusiasm, and commitment to the audience and occasion. Without intonation, speaking becomes monotonous—a death knell to any speech.

To avoid a monotone voice, practice and listen to your speeches with a recording device, such as a smart phone or computer. You will readily identify instances that require better intonation.

QUICK TIP

Breathe from Your Diaphragm

To project your voice so that it is loud enough to be heard by everyone in the audience, breathe deeply from your diaphragm rather than more shallowly from your vocal cords. The reason? The strength of your voice depends on the amount of air the diaphragm—a large, dome-shaped muscle encasing the inner rib cage—pushes from the lungs to the vocal cords. With full but relaxed breaths, the depth of your voice will improve and help your voice sound more confident.

Adjust Your Speaking Rate

Speaking rate is the pace at which you convey speech. The normal rate of speech in face-to-face conversation for native English-speaking adults is roughly between 120–130 and 160–170 words per minute, but there is no standard or ideal rate. If the overall rate is too slow, the audience will get fidgety, bored, and even sleepy. If too fast, listeners will appear irritated and confused, because they can't catch what you're saying. The audience may see you as unsure about your control of the speech.[1] If you tend to speak either too quickly or too slowly, choose 160 words from your speech and time yourself for one minute as you speak them aloud. If you fall very short of finishing, increase your pace. If you finish well before the minute is up, slow down. Practice until you achieve a comfortable speaking rate.

QUICK TIP

Use a Natural Conversational Pace

Experts recommend using your natural conversational pace when delivering a speech, but varying the pace and vocal emphasis at different points.[2] Focus on slowing your pace during serious points and picking it up during lighter ones. Think about "punching" key phrases with emphatic intonation. Experiment with and practice these variations in pacing and vocal emphasis until they feel natural.

Use Strategic Pauses

Many novice speakers are uncomfortable with pauses. Like intonation, however, pauses can be important strategic elements of a speech. **Pauses** enhance meaning by providing a type of punctuation, emphasizing a point, drawing attention to a thought, or just allowing listeners a moment to contemplate what is being said.

As you practice delivering your speech, focus on avoiding unnecessary and undesirable **vocal fillers** such as *uh, hmm, you know, I mean,* and *it's like*. These so-called disfluencies will make you appear unprepared and cause audience members to be distracted from the message. Rather than vocal fillers, use silent pauses for strategic effect.

Strive for Vocal Variety

Rather than operating separately, all the vocal elements described so far—volume, pitch, speaking rate, and pauses—work together to create **vocal variety**. Indeed, the real key to effective vocal delivery is to vary all these elements with a tone of enthusiasm. For example, as the great civil rights leader Martin Luther King Jr. spoke the now famous words "I have a dream," his pauses were immediately preceded by a combination of reduced speech rate and increased volume and pitch. Vocal variety comes quite naturally when you are excited about what you are saying to an audience, when you feel it is important and want to share it with them.

CHECKLIST

Practice Check for Vocal Effectiveness

- ☐ As you practice, is your vocal delivery effective?
- ☐ Is your voice too loud? Too soft?
- ☐ Do you avoid speaking in a monotone? Do you vary the stress or emphasis you place on words to clearly express your meaning?
- ☐ Is your rate of speech comfortable for listeners?
- ☐ Do you avoid unnecessary vocal fillers, such as *uh, hmm, you know, I mean,* and *it's like*?
- ☐ Do you use silent pauses for strategic effect?
- ☐ Does your voice reflect a variety of emotional expressions? Do you convey enthusiasm?

Carefully Pronounce and Articulate Words

Few things distract an audience more than improper pronunciation or unclear articulation of words. **Pronunciation** is the correct formation of word sounds—examples of mispronunciation include, *aks* for *asked* (askt), and *jen-yu-wine* for *genuine* (jen yu in). **Articulation** is the clarity or forcefulness with which the sounds are made, regardless of whether they are pronounced correctly. Incorrect pronunciation and poor articulation are largely a matter of habit.

A common pattern of poor articulation is **mumbling**—slurring words together at a low level of volume and pitch so that they are barely audible. Sometimes the problem is **lazy speech**. Common examples are saying *fer* instead of *for* and *wanna* instead of *want to.*

Like any habit, poor articulation can be overcome by unlearning the problem behavior:

- If you mumble, practice speaking more loudly and with emphatic pronunciation.
- If you tend toward lazy speech, put more effort into your articulation.
- Consciously try to say each word clearly and correctly.
- Practice clear and precise enunciation of proper word sounds. Say *articulation* several times until it rolls off your tongue naturally.
- Do the same for these words: *want to, going to, Atlanta, chocolate, sophomore, California.*

Use Dialect (Language Variation) with Care

Every culture has subcultural variations on the preferred pronunciation and articulation of its languages, called **dialects**. In the United States, there is so-called Standard English, Black English, regional varieties of Spanglish (a mix of Spanish and English, such as Tex-Mex), and other regional variations in the South, New England, and along the Canadian border. Although dialects are neither superior nor inferior to standard language patterns, the audience must be able to understand and relate to the speaker's language. As you practice your delivery, ensure that your pronunciation and word usage can be understood by all audience members, or take the time to share with them any special meanings you may wish to convey.

CHECKLIST

Tips on Using a Microphone

- ☐ Learn how to use and perform a sound check with the microphone well before delivering your speech.
- ☐ When you first speak into the microphone, ask listeners if they can hear you clearly.
- ☐ Speak directly into the microphone; with many mics, if you turn your head or body, you won't be heard.
- ☐ When wearing a hands-free ***lavaliere microphone*** (also called a ***lapel microphone*** or ***personal microphone***) clipped to clothing, speak as if you were addressing a small group. The amplifier will do the rest.
- ☐ When using a ***handheld*** or ***fixed microphone***, beware of ***popping***, a sound that occurs when you use sharp consonants, such as *p*, *t*, and *d*, and the air hits the mike. To prevent popping, move the microphone slightly below your mouth and several inches away.

CHAPTER

46

Your Body in Delivery

As we listen to a speaker, we simultaneously use our eyes and ears to evaluate messages sent by his or her **nonverbal communication**—body movements, physical appearance, and qualities of voice. As we listen to a speaker's words, we respond at the same time to his or her visual and vocal cues. Thus it is vital to plan not only the words you will say but also the physical manner in which you will deliver them.

Pay Attention to Body Language

Research confirms the importance of **body language**—facial expressions, eye behavior, gestures, and general body movements during the delivery of a speech. For example, audiences are more readily persuaded by speakers who emphasize eye contact, nod at listeners, and stand with an open body position than by those who minimize these nonverbal cues.[1]

Animate Your Facial Expressions

From our facial expressions, audiences can gauge whether we are excited about, disenchanted by, or indifferent to our speech—and the audience to whom we are presenting it.

Few behaviors are more effective for building rapport with an audience than *smiling*.[2] A smile is a sign of mutual welcome at the start of a speech, of mutual comfort and interest during the speech, and of mutual goodwill at the close of a speech. In addition, smiling when you feel nervous or otherwise uncomfortable can help you relax and gain heightened composure. Of course, facial expressions need to correspond to the tenor of the speech. Doing what is natural and normal for the occasion should be the rule.

CHECKLIST

Tips for Using Effective Facial Expressions

- ☐ Use animated expressions that feel natural and express your meaning.
- ☐ Never use expressions that are out of character for you or inappropriate to the speech occasion.
- ☐ In practice sessions, loosen your facial features with exercises such as widening your eyes and moving your mouth.
- ☐ Establish rapport with the audience by smiling naturally when appropriate.

Maintain Eye Contact

If smiling is an effective way to build rapport, maintaining eye contact is mandatory in establishing a positive relationship with your listeners. Having eye contact with the audience is one of the most, if not *the* most, important physical actions in public speaking, at least in Western cultures. Eye contact does the following:

- Maintains the quality of directness in speech delivery.
- Lets people know they are recognized.
- Indicates acknowledgment and respect.
- Signals to audience members that you see them as unique human beings.

While it may be impossible to look at every listener, you can make the audience feel recognized by using a technique called **scanning**—moving your gaze from one listener to another and from one section to another, pausing to gaze at one person long enough to complete one thought. Be certain to give each section of the room equal attention. Some experienced speakers recommend that your eyes should focus on the back row, giving the audience the impression you are taking them all in.

Use Gestures That Feel Natural

Words alone seldom suffice to convey what we want to express. Physical gestures fill in the gaps, as in illustrating the size or shape of an object (e.g., by showing the size of it by extending two hands, palms facing each other), or expressing the depth of an emotion (e.g., by pounding a fist on a podium). Gestures should arise from genuine emotions and should conform to your personality.[3]

CHECKLIST

Using Gestures Effectively

- ☐ Use natural, spontaneous gestures.
- ☐ Avoid exaggerated gestures, but use gestures that are broad enough to be seen by each audience member.
- ☐ Eliminate distracting gestures, such as fidgeting with pens, jingling coins in pockets, drumming your fingers on a podium or table, or brushing back hair from your eyes.
- ☐ Analyze your gestures for effectiveness in practice sessions.
- ☐ Practice movements that feel natural to you.

Create a Feeling of Immediacy

In most Western cultures, listeners learn more from and respond most positively to speakers who create a perception of physical and psychological closeness, called **nonverbal immediacy**, between themselves and audience members.[4] The following behaviors encourage immediacy:

- Make frequent eye contact.
- Animate your facial expressions.
- Smile when appropriate.
- Use natural body movements.
- Use vocal variety.
- Maintain upright but not stiff posture.
- Use natural hand and arm gestures.

QUICK TIP

Use Movement to Connect

Audience members soon tire of listening to a **talking head** who remains steadily positioned in one place behind a microphone or a podium, so even in formal situations, use natural body movements. Use your physical position vis-à-vis audience members to adjust your relationship with them, establishing a level of familiarity and closeness that is appropriate to the rhetorical situation. Movement toward listeners stimulates a sense of informality and closeness; remaining behind the podium fosters a more formal relationship of speaker to audience.

Maintain Good Posture

A speaker's posture sends a definite message to the audience. Listeners perceive speakers who slouch as being sloppy, unfocused, or even weak. Strive to stand erect, but not ramrod straight. The goal should be to appear authoritative but not rigid.

Practice the Delivery

Practice is essential to effective delivery. The more you practice, the greater your comfort level will be when you actually deliver the speech. More than anything, it is uncertainty that breeds anxiety. By practicing your speech using a fully developed speaking outline (see **Chapter 41**), you will know what to expect when you actually stand in front of an audience.

Focus on the Message

The primary purpose of any speech is to get a message across, not to display extraordinary delivery skills. Keep this goal foremost in your mind. Psychologically, too, focusing on your message is likely to make your delivery more natural and confident.

Plan Ahead and Practice Often

If possible, begin practicing your speech at least several days before you are scheduled to deliver it.

- Practice with your speaking notes, revising those parts of the speech that aren't satisfactory, and altering the notes as you go.
- Record the speech (see the Quick Tip below).
- Time each part of your speech—introduction, body, and conclusion (see **Chapter 42** for guidelines).
- Include any presentation aids you plan to use.
- Practice the speech about five times in its final form.
- Try to simulate the actual speech setting, paying particular attention to seating arrangement and projecting your voice to fill the space.
- Practice in front of at least one volunteer, and seek constructive criticism.
- Schedule your practice sessions early in the process so that you have time to prepare.
- Dress appropriately for the rhetorical situation.

QUICK TIP

Record Two Practice Sessions

Videorecording two practice sessions can provide valuable feedback. As you watch your initial recording, make notes of the things you'd like to change. Before rerecording, practice several more times until you are comfortable with the changes you've incorporated. No one is ever entirely thrilled with his or her image on video, so try to avoid unnecessary self-criticism. Videorecord your speech a second time, paying close attention to the areas of speech delivery that you want to improve.

FROM WEAK TO CONFIDENT DELIVERY

Enhancing Your Delivery with Body Language

Positive and natural nonverbal behaviors—including frequent eye contact, animated facial expressions (including smiling), natural hand and arm gestures, relaxed but erect posture, and vocal variety that avoids a monotone—encourage audience members' trust and willingness to seriously consider your message.

In her first speech (left), student speaker Teresa stood behind a podium. The audience couldn't see her gestures, and her delivery was stiff and uninspired. After practicing the speech about six times (right), Teresa improved her delivery by assuming a more confident posture, using open hand and arm gestures, and moving from the podium.

The first time she delivered her speech (left), student speaker Charlotte read continuously from notecards and failed to make eye contact and engage nonverbally with the audience. After practice (right), Charlotte effectively connects with her audience with eye contact, a smile, and a gesture toward her presentation aid. She keeps her hands and arms around the middle of her body, above the waistline, which helps speakers project a sense of confidence and authority.

part 11

Public Speaking: Presentation Aids

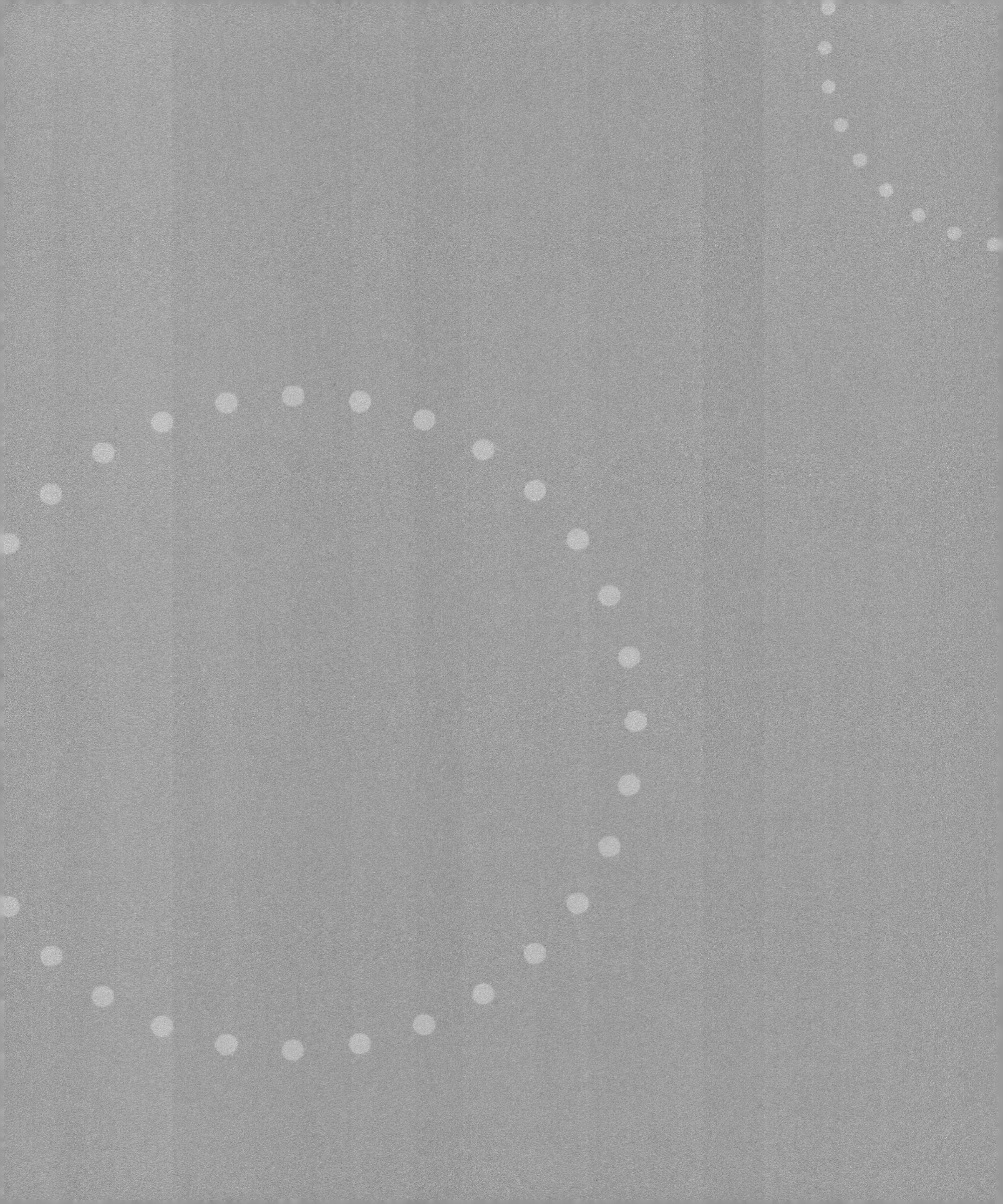

CHAPTER

47

Speaking with Presentation Aids

Used judiciously, presentation aids can help listeners to understand and retain information that is otherwise difficult or timeconsuming to convey in words. Indeed, research confirms that most people process information best when it is presented both with words and graphics—a principle dubbed the **multimedia effect**.[1] However, no matter how powerful a photograph, chart, or other aid may be, if it is unrelated to a speech point, is poorly designed, or simply duplicates what the speaker says, the audience will become distracted and actually retain *less* information than without it.[2]

Select an Appropriate Aid

A **presentation aid** can be an object, model, picture, graph, chart, table, audio, video, or multimedia. Choose the aid, or combination of aids, that will help your audience grasp information most effectively.

Props and Models

A **prop** can be any object, inanimate or even live, that helps demonstrate the speaker's points. A **model** is a three-dimensional, scale-size representation of an object. Presentations in engineering, architecture, and many other disciplines often make use these aids. When using a prop or model:

- In most cases, keep the prop or model hidden until you are ready to use it.
- Make sure it is big enough for everyone to see (and read, if applicable).
- Practice your speech using the prop or model.

Pictures

Pictures (two-dimensional representations) include photographs, line drawings, diagrams, maps, and posters. A *diagram* or *schematic drawing* explains how something works or is constructed or operated. *Maps* help listeners visualize geographic areas and understand relationships among them; they also illustrate the proportion of one thing to something else in different areas. Pictures, including photographs, can strengthen many types of presentations, including those using persuasive appeals, but avoid using shocking images that will upset viewers.

Graphs, Charts, and Tables

A **graph** represents relationships among two or more things. A *line graph* uses points connected by lines to demonstrate how something changes or fluctuates in value. A *bar and column graph* uses bars of varying lengths to compare quantities or magnitudes. *Pie graphs* depict the division of a whole into slices. Each slice constitutes a percentage of the whole.

Pictograms use picture symbols (icons) to illustrate relationships and trends; for example, a generic-looking human figure repeated in a row can demonstrate increasing enrollment in college over time.

CHECKLIST

Create Effective Line, Bar, and Pie Graphs

- ☐ Label the axes of line graphs, bar graphs, and pictograms.
- ☐ Start the numerical axis of the line or bar graph at zero.
- ☐ Compare only like variables.
- ☐ Assign a clear title to the graph.
- ☐ Clearly label all relevant points of information in the graph.
- ☐ When creating multidimensional bar graphs, do not compare more than three kinds of information.
- ☐ In pie graphs, restrict the number of pie slices to a maximum of seven.
- ☐ Identify and accurately represent the values or percentages of each pie slice.
- ☐ In pictograms, clearly indicate what each icon symbolizes.
- ☐ Make all pictograms the same size.

A **chart** visually organizes complex information into compact form. A **flowchart** diagrams the progression of a process or relationship, helping viewers visualize a sequence or directional flow. A **table** (tabular chart) systematically groups data in column form, allowing viewers to examine and make comparisons about information quickly.

Audio, Video, and Multimedia

Audio and video clips—including short recordings of sound, music, or speech; video clips; and multimedia, which combines audio, video, stills, animation, and text into a single production—can powerfully engage audience members and and help them understand and relate to your message.[3] (See Chapter 49 for guidelines on embedding audio and video into a slide deck.)

When incorporating audio and video into your presentation:

- Cue the audio or video clip to the appropriate segment before the presentation.
- Keep clips short—total 30–60 seconds per clip.
- As with any type of presentation aid, use clips to support one or more key points, but don't rely on them to replace your role as speaker.
- Embed video clips directly into your slides.
- Alert audience members beforehand to what will be played, and discuss its relevance to speech points when it concludes.
- Use the audio or video clip in a manner consistent with copyright.

QUICK TIP

Reasons to Use Video as an Aid

Video adds more drama, engages more senses, and communicates more information in less time than other media—*if* it is relevant to the speech. When deciding to include video as a presentation aid, consider whether it will serve one or more of these functions:

- Encourage audience identification with the topic
- Elicit a desired emotional response
- Make an idea tangible (by, for example, demonstrating it)
- Provide testimony that adds credibility to your claims

Options for Showing Presentation Aids

Today, nearly all presenters generate tables, charts, and other aids using presentation software programs such as Microsoft PowerPoint and Apple Keynote (and their online counterparts such as Prezi). They then project slides using LCD panels and projectors or a DLP (digital light processing) device. On the more traditional side, display options include flip charts, chalkboards and whiteboards, and handouts.

Flip Charts

A **flip chart** is simply a large pad of paper on which you can write or draw. This aid is often prepared in advance; then, as you progress through the speech, you flip through the pad to the next exhibit. You can also write and draw on the pad as you speak. Sometimes a simple drawing or word written for emphasis can be as or more powerful than a highly polished slide.

Chalkboards and Whiteboards

On the lowest-tech end of the spectrum lies the writing board on which you can write with chalk (on a chalkboard) or with nonpermanent markers (on a whiteboard). Reserve the writing board for impromptu explanations, such as presenting simple processes that are done in steps, or for engaging the audience in short brainstorming sessions. If you have the time to prepare a speech properly, however, don't rely on a writing board. They force the speaker to turn his or her back to the audience, make listeners wait while you write, and require legible handwriting that will be clear to all viewers.

QUICK TIP

Hold the Handouts

A **handout** conveys information that either is impractical to give to the audience in another manner or is intended to be kept by audience members after the presentation. To avoid distracting listeners, unless you specifically want them to read the information as you speak, wait until you are finished before you distribute the handout. If you do want the audience to view a handout during the speech, pass it out only when you are ready to talk about it.

CHECKLIST

Incorporating Presentation Aids into Your Speech

- ☐ Practice with the aids and the equipment used to display them until you are confident that you can handle them without causing undue distractions.
- ☐ Talk to your audience rather than to the screen or object—avoid turning your back to the audience.
- ☐ Maintain eye contact with the audience.
- ☐ Place the aid to one side rather than behind you, so that the entire audience can see it.
- ☐ Display the aid only when you are ready to discuss it.
- ☐ If you use a pointer, once you've indicated your point, put it down.
- ☐ In case problems arise, be prepared to give your presentation without the aids.

CHAPTER

48

Designing Presentation Aids

The quality of a speaker's presentation aids is a critical factor in the audience's perception of his or her credibility, or *ethos*. Well-designed aids signal that the speaker is prepared and professional; poorly designed aids create a negative impression that is difficult to overcome.

As you prepare aids (such as slides made with Microsoft PowerPoint or similar programs), focus on keeping elements easy to view and designed in a consistent manner. Audience members can follow only one piece of information at a time, and visuals that are crowded or difficult to decipher will divert attention from your message.[1]

Keep the Design Simple

Audience members should be able to process the message in your slides quickly—master presenter Nancy Duarte suggests in three seconds—so that they can return their attention to the speaker.[2] Thus it is important to restrict text to a minimum and present only one major idea per slide:

- *Follow the six-by-six rule.* Use no more than six words in a line and six lines on one slide. This will keep the audience's attention on you (see the table on p. 731).
- *Word text in active verb form.* Use the active voice and parallel grammatical structure, for example "Gather Necessary Documents; Apply Early" (see Chapter 43 on language).
- *Avoid clutter.* Allow plenty of white space, or "visual breathing room" for viewers.[3]
- *Create concise titles.* Use titles that summarize content and reinforce your message.

CLUTTERED AID	EASY-TO-READ AID
Buying a Used Car	**Buying a Used Car**
1. Prepare in advance—know the market value of several cars you are interested in before going to shop.	1. Know the car's market value.
2. Do not get into a hurry about buying the first car you see—be patient, there will be others.	2. Don't hurry to buy.
3. It is recommended that you shop around for credit before buying the car.	3. Shop for credit before buying.
4. Inspect the car carefully, looking for funny sounds, stains, worn equipment, dents, etc.	4. Inspect the car carefully.
5. Ask for proof about the history of the car, including previous owners.	5. Get proof of the car's history.

QUICK TIP

Beware of "Chartjunk"

Certain kinds of information—especially statistical data and sequences of action—are best understood when visually presented. However, avoid what design expert Edward Tufte coined as *"chartjunk"*[4]—slides jammed with too many graphs, charts, and meaningless design elements that obscure rather than illuminate information. Use fewer rather than more slides and only those design elements that truly enhance meaning.

Use Design Elements Consistently

Apply the same design decisions you make for one presentation aid to all of the aids you display; this will ensure that viewers aren't distracted by a jumble of unrelated visual elements. Carry your choice of design elements—color, fonts, upper- and lowercase letters, styling (boldface, underlining, italics), general page layout, and repeating elements such as titles and logos—through each aid.

Select Appropriate Typeface Styles and Fonts

A *typeface* is a specific style of lettering, such as Arial or Times New Roman. Typefaces come in a variety of *fonts*, or sets of sizes (called the *point size*), and upper and lower cases. Designers divide the thousands of available typefaces into two major categories: serif and sans serif. *Serif typefaces* include small flourishes, or strokes, at the tops and bottoms of each letter. *Sans serif typefaces* are more blocklike and linear; they are designed without these tiny strokes.

Consider these design guidelines when selecting type:

- Check the lettering for legibility, taking into consideration the audience's distance from the visual. On slides, experiment with 36-point type for major headings, 24-point type for subheadings, and *at least* 18-point type for text.
- Lettering should stand apart from the background. Use either dark text on light background or light text on dark background.
- Use a common typeface that is simple and easy to read and is not distracting.
- Use standard upper- and lowercase type rather than all capitals.
- Use no more than two different typefaces in a single aid.
- Use **boldface**, underlining, or *italics* sparingly.

QUICK TIP

Using Serif and Sans Serif Type

For reading a block of text, serif typefaces are easier on the eye. Small amounts of text, however, such as headings, are best viewed in sans serif type. Thus, consider a sans serif typeface for the heading and a serif typeface for the body of the text. If you include only a few lines of text, use sans serif type throughout.

Use Color Carefully

Skillful use of color can draw attention to key points, influence the mood of a presentation, and make things easier to see. Conversely, poor color combinations will set the wrong mood, render an image unattractive, or make it unreadable. Note the effect of these color combinations:

EFFECTS OF COLOR COMBINATIONS

Color	Effect in Combination
Yellow	Warm on white, harsh on black, fiery on red, soothing on light blue
Blue	Warm on white, hard to see on black
Red	Bright on white, warm or difficult to see on black

Color affects both the legibility of text and the mood conveyed. Following are some tips for using color effectively in your presentation aids:

- Keep the *background color* constant across all slides or other aids.
- Use *bold, bright colors* to emphasize important points.
- For typeface and graphics, use colors that contrast rather than clash with or blend into the background color; check for visibility when projecting. Audiences will remember information just as easily if white text appears on dark background or dark text on light background, so long as the design is appealing.[5]
- Limit colors to no more than three, with maximum of four in complex and detailed aids.

Consider Subjective Interpretations of Color

Colors can evoke distinct associations for people, so take care not to summon an unintended meaning or mood. For example, control engineers see red and think danger, while a financial manager will think unprofitability.

Consider, too, that the meanings associated with certain colors may differ across cultures. Western societies don black for funerals, while the Chinese use white. If you are presenting in a cross-cultural context, check the meanings of colors for the relevant nationalities.

CHECKLIST

Apply the Principles of Simplicity and Continuity

- ☐ Concentrate on presenting one major idea per visual aid.
- ☐ Apply design decisions consistently to each aid.
- ☐ Use type that is large enough for audience members to read comfortably.
- ☐ Use color judiciously to highlight key ideas and enhance readability.
- ☐ Check that colors contrast rather than clash.

CHAPTER

49

Using Presentation Software

Public speakers can use a variety of powerful software tools to create and display high-quality visual aids. These programs include the familiar Microsoft PowerPoint and its Apple counterpart, Keynote, and online programs such as Prezi.

Give a Speech, Not a Slide Show

Frequently we hear someone say, "I'm giving a PowerPoint (or a Prezi or Keynote) presentation today," instead of "I'm giving a speech." Some speakers hide behind presentation media, focusing attention on their aids rather than on the audience. They might mistakenly believe that the display itself is the presentation, or that it will somehow save an otherwise poorly planned speech. It can be easy to become so involved in generating fancy aids that you forget your primary mission: to communicate through the spoken word and your physical presence. Speaker and message must take center stage.

Develop a Plan

Often the best place to begin planning your slides is your speaking outline (see p. 682). Think through which points might be better explained with some kind of visual: Decide what the content of your slides should be, how many slides you'll need, and how to arrange them. Review and edit slides as necessary using *Slide Sorter* view (in PowerPoint), *Light table* or *Outline* view (in Keynote), or *path tool* (in Prezi).

Avoid Technical Glitches

Technical errors are always a hazard with presentation software and any hardware required to run it. Common risks include a projector malfunctioning, a presentation file being incompatible with an operating system, an internet connection failing, or a computer drive freezing. Follow these steps to avoid such problems.

1. Save all presentation files to a reliable source—flash drive, CD, DVD, website, or email—that you can access on the presentation computer.
2. Save all presentation files (images, sound, videos) into the same folder in the source location.
3. Familiarize yourself with the presentation computer before you give the speech to facilitate smooth operation during the presentation.
4. Check that the operating system of the presentation computer (e.g., Windows 10, Mac OS High Sierra) is compatible with the the aids.
5. Confirm that the version of the software used to create the aids corresponds to the software on the presentation computer; this will prevent distortions in your graphics, sound, and video.
6. Prepare both a digital backup and a set of printed handouts of the aids.

Find Media for Presentations

You can import photos, illustrations, clip art, video, or sound directly into your aids by downloading your own files or those from the internet. For downloadable digital images, try the following websites:

- Google images (images.google.com)
- Getty Images (www.gettyimages.com)
- Flickr Creative Commons (www.flickr.com/creativecommons): access to photographs shared by amateur and hobbyist photographers
- American Memory (memory.loc.gov/ammem/index.html): free access to still and moving images depicting the history of the American experience

The following sites offer downloadable music files and audio clips:

- SoundCloud (www.soundcloud.com)
- Jamendo (www.jamendo.com)
- MP3.com (www.mp3.com)
- SoundClick (www.soundclick.com)
- Audio Archive (www.archive.org/details/audio)
- The Daily.WAV (www.dailywav.com)

The following sites contain useful video clips:

- YouTube (www.youtube.com)
- CNN Video (www.cnn.com/video) and ABC News Video (abcnews.go.com/video): especially useful for speech topics on current events or timely social issues
- New York Times (www.nytimes.com/video)
- Google Videos (video.google.com)

Avoid Copyright Infringement

Abide by copyright restrictions when using visual and audio materials from the internet or other sources. Some material is available under fair-use provisions (see p. 609). Even if fair use applies, cite the source of the material in your presentation. Consult your school's information technology (IT) office for statements of policy pertaining to copyrighted and fair-use materials, especially from undocumented sources such as peer-to-peer (P2P) sharing.

- Cite the source of all copyrighted material in your presentation. For example, include a bibliographic footnote on the slide containing the material.
- Be wary of sites purporting to offer "royalty free" media objects; there might actually be other costs associated with the materials.
- When time, resources, and ability allow, create and use your own pictures, video, or audio for your presentation slides.

CHECKLIST

Tips for Successfully Using Presentation Software in Your Speech

- ☐ Don't let the technology get in the way of relating to your audience.
- ☐ Talk to your audience rather than to the screen.
- ☐ Maintain eye contact as much as possible.
- ☐ Have a backup plan in case of technical errors.
- ☐ If you use a pointer (laser or otherwise), turn it off and put it down as soon as you have made your point.
- ☐ Incorporate the aids into your practice sessions until you are confident that they strengthen, rather than detract from, your core message.

FROM SLIDE SHOW TO PRESENTATION

Getting Ready to Deliver a PowerPoint, Keynote, or Prezi Presentation

To avoid technical glitches, practice delivering your speech with your presentation software and ensure compatibility with the venue's equipment.

Check the Venue

Before your speech, take stock of the equipment and room layout. See the annotated photo for tips on achieving a smooth delivery with digital aids.

1. **Power sources.** Ensure that cords can reach the presentation equipment, and consider taping them to the floor to keep them out of the way.

2. **Computer needs and compatibility.** Check that you can display all aids, from the slide show to audio and video clips, on the presentation computer. If possible, practice at least once on this computer.

(top) Purestock/Getty Images; (bottom left) Jeff Presnail/Getty Images/Getty Images; (bottom center) cinoby/Getty Images; (bottom right) Caspar Benson/Getty Images

3. **Internet access.** Have wireless log-in information available and/or a cable that reaches the internet jack.

4. **Backup plan.** Create a contingency plan in case of computer failure; for example, print overhead transparencies from slide show, prepare to put information on a whiteboard, or create handouts.

5. **Audio.** Determine how you will broadcast any audio aids, and check speaker volume before the speech.

Position Yourself Carefully

Choose a place to stand that gives the audience clear sightlines to you and your slide show. Stand so that you can face forward even when changing slides or gesturing toward your aids. This helps you connect with your audience and project your voice clearly, and it prevents you from reading off your slides.

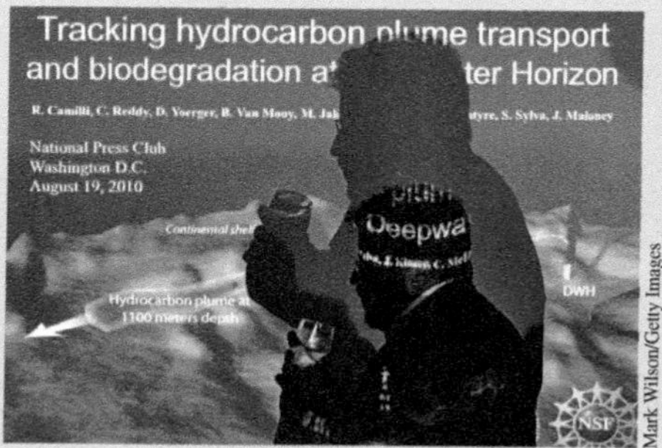

Mark Wilson/Getty Images

Needs improvement: This speaker's sideways stance discourages eye contact and indicates that he may be reading off his slides.

Macmillan Learning

Good placement: This speaker can access the computer or gesture toward the slides without blocking the audience's sightlines.

Notes

A Pocket Guide to Public Speaking, Sixth Edition

Chapter 30

1. "Why Warren Buffett's Most Valuable Skill Wasn't from a Diploma," Fox on Stocks, December 19, 2012, www.foxonstocks.com/why-warrenbuffetts-most-valuable0skill-wasn't-from-a-diploma/.
2. "Youth Voting," Center for Information and Research on Civic Learning and Engagement (CIRCLE), accessed November 8, 2017, civicyouth.org/quick-facts/youth-voting.
3. For a discussion of Daniel Yankelovich's three-step process by which public judgments occur, see Yankelovich, *Coming to Public Judgment: Making Democracy Work in a Complex World* (Syracuse, NY: Syracuse University Press, 1991).
4. For a discussion of conversation stoppers and rules of engagement, see W. Barnett Pearce, "Toward a National Conversation about Public Issues," in *The Changing Conversation in America: Lectures from the Smithsonian,* eds. William F. Eadie and Paul E. Nelson (Thousand Oaks, CA: Sage, 2002), 16.
5. Robert Perrin, "The Speaking-Writing Connection: Enhancing the Symbiotic Relationship," *Contemporary Education* 65 (1994): 62–64.
6. Kristine Bruss, "Writing for the Ear: Strengthening Oral Style in Manuscript Speeches," Communication *Teacher* 26, no. 2 (April 2012): 76–81.
7. Lloyd F. Bitzer, "The Rhetorical Situation," *Philosophy and Rhetoric* (Winter 1968): 1–14.

Chapter 32

1. Michael J. Beatty, "Situational and Predispositional Correlates of Public Speaking Anxiety," *Communication Education* 37 (1988): 28–39; Ralph Behnke and Chris R. Sawyer, "Milestones of Anticipatory Public Speaking Anxiety," *Communication Education* 48 (1999): 165–72; Graham D. Bodie, "A Racing Heart, Rattling Knees, and Ruminative Thoughts: Defining, Explaining, and Treating Public Speaking Anxiety," *Communication Education* 59 (2010): 70–105.
2. Behnke and Sawyer, "Milestones of Anticipatory Public Speaking Anxiety."
3. Behnke and Sawyer, "Milestones of Anticipatory Public Speaking Anxiety."
4. David-Paul Pertaub, Mel Slater, and Chris Barker, "An Experiment on Public Speaking Anxiety in Response to Three Different Types of Virtual Audience," *Presence: Teleoperators and Virtual Environments* 11 (2002): 670–78.
5. Joe Ayres, "Coping with Speech Anxiety: The Power of Positive Thinking," *Communication Education* 37 (1988): 289–96; Joe Ayres, "An Examination of the Impact of Anticipated Communication and Communication Apprehension on Negative Thinking, Task-Relevant Thinking, and Recall," *Communication Research Reports* 9 (1992): 3–11.

6. Pamela J. Feldman, Sheldon Cohen, Natalie Hamrick, and Stephen J. Lepore, "Psychological Stress, Appraisal, Emotion, and Cardiovascular Response in a Public Speaking Task," *Psychology and Health* 19 (2004): 353–68; Senqi Hu and Juong-Min Romans-Kroll, "Effects of Positive Attitude toward Giving a Speech on Cardiovascular and Subjective Fear Responses during Speech on Anxious Subjects," *Perceptual and Motor Skills* 81 (1995): 609–10.
7. Richard Branson, "Richard Branson on How to Calm Public Speaking Jitters," *Fortune*, January 12, 2015, fortune.com/2015/01/12/richard-branson-on-how-to-calm-public-speaking-jitters/.
8. Joe Ayres and Tim Hopf, "Visualization: Is It More Than Extra Attention?" *Communication Education* 38 (1989): 1–5; Joe Ayers and Tim Hopf, *Coping with Speech Anxiety* (Norwood, NJ: Ablex, 1993); Joe Ayres, Chia-Fang "Sandy" Hsu, and Tim Hopf, "Does Exposure to Visualization Alter Speech Preparation Processes?" *Communication Research Reports* 17 (2000): 366–74.
9. Ayres and Hopf, "Visualization," 2–3.
10. Herbert Benson and Miriam Z. Klipper, *The Relaxation Response* (New York: HarperCollins, 2000).
11. Laurie Schloff and Marcia Yudkin, *Smart Speaking* (New York: Plume, 1991), 91–92.
12. Lars-Gunnar Lundh, Britta Berg, Helena Johansson, Linda Kjellén Nilsson, Jenny Sandberg, and Anna Segerstedt, "Social Anxiety Is Associated with a Negatively Distorted Perception of One's Own Voice," *Cognitive Behavior Therapy* 31 (2002): 25–30.

Chapter 33

1. *Oxford English Dictionary,* s. v. "responsibility," accessed September 26, 2017, www.oed.com/view/Entry/163862?redirectedFrom=responsibility.
2. Richard L. Johannesen, Kathleen S. Valde, and Karen E. Whedbee, *Ethics in Human Communication*, 6th ed. (Long Grove, IL: Waveland Press, 2007).
3. Edward P. J. Corbett, *Classical Rhetoric for the Modern Student* (New York: Oxford University Press, 1990).
4. Shalom H. Schwartz, "An Overview of the Schwartz Theory of Basic Values," *Online Readings in Psychology and Culture* 2, no. 1 (2012), dx.doi.org/10.9707/2307-0919.1116.
5. Betsy Cooper et al., "How Americans View Immigrants and What They Want from Immigration Reform: Findings from the 2015 American Values Atlas," *Public Religion Research Institute,* March 29, 2016, www.prri.org/research/poll-immigration-reform-views-on-immigrants/.
6. Douglas M. Fraleigh and Joseph S. Tuman, *Freedom of Speech in the Marketplace of Ideas* (New York: Bedford/St. Martin's, 1997).
7. Newseum Institute, "First Amendment FAQ," www.newseuminstitute.org/first-amendment-center/first-amendment-faq/#speech.
8. William B. Gudykunst et al., *Building Bridges: Interpersonal Skills for a Changing World* (Boston: Houghton Mifflin, 1995), 92.
9. Michael Josephson, *Making Ethical Decisions: The Six Pillars of Character* (Josephson Institute of Ethics, 2002).
10. Josephson, *Making Ethical Decisions.*
11. Josephson, *Making Ethical Decisions.*
12. U.S. Copyright Office, accessed September 26, 2017, www.copyright.gov.

13. U.S. Copyright Office, "Fair Use," accessed September 26, 2017, www.copyright.gov/fair-use/more-info.html.

Chapter 34

1. Andrew D. Wolvin and Carolyn G. Coakley, "A Listening Taxonomy," in *Perspectives on Listening*, eds. Andrew D. Wolvin and Carolyn G. Coakley (Norwood, NJ: Ablex, 1993), 15–22.
2. "An ILA Definition of Listening," *Listening Post* 53, no. 1 (1995): 4–5.
3. Ethel Glenn, "A Content Analysis of Fifty Definitions of Listening," *Journal of the International Listening Association* 3 (1989): 21–31.
4. Laura A. Janusik and Andrew D. Wolvin, "24 Hours in a Day: Listening Update to the Time Studies," *International Journal of Listening* 23 (2009): 104–20; see also Richard Emanuel et al., "How College Students Spend Their Time Communicating," *International Journal of Listening* 22 (2008): 13–28.
5. Janusik and Wolvin, "24 Hours in a Day."
6. Avraham N. Kluger and Keren Zaidel, "Are Listeners Perceived as Leaders?" *International Journal of Listening* 27, no. 2 (2013): 73–84; S. A. Welch and William T. Mickelson, "A Listening Competence Comparison of Working Professionals," *International Journal of Listening* 27, no. 2 (2013): 85–99.
7. Albert H. Hastorf and Hadley Cantril, "They Saw a Game: A Case Study," *Journal of Abnormal and Social Psychology* 49, no. 1 (1954): 129–34; Gordon W. Allport and Lee J. Postman, "The Basic Psychology of Rumor," *Transactions of the New York Academy of Sciences* 8 (1945): 61–81.
8. Thomas E. Anastasi Jr., *Listen! Techniques for Improving Communication Skills* (Boston: CBI Publishing, 1982).
9. Christian Kiewitz et al., "Cultural Differences in Listening Style Preferences: A Comparison of Young Adults in Germany, Israel, and the United States," *International Journal of Public Opinion Research* 9, no. 3 (1997): 233–47, search.proquest.com/docview/60068159?accountid=10965; M. Imhof and L. A. Janusik, "Development and Validation of the Imhof Janusik Listening Concepts Inventory to Measure Listening Conceptualization Differences between Cultures," *Journal of Intercultural Communication Research* 35, no. 2 (2006): 79–98.
10. Ronald D. Gordon, "Communication, Dialogue, and Transformation," *Human Communication* 9, no. 1 (2006): 17–30.
11. James Floyd, "Provocation: Dialogic Listening as Reachable Goal," *International Journal of Listening* 24 (2010): 170–73.

Chapter 35

1. Pablo Briñol and Richard E. Petty, "The History of Attitudes and Persuasion Research," *Handbook of the History of Social Psychology*, eds. Arie Kruglanski and Wolfgang Stroebe (New York: Psychology Press, 2011).
2. Richard E. Petty and John T. Cacioppo, *Attitudes and Persuasion: Classic and Contemporary Approaches* (Dubuque, IA: Wm. C. Brown, 1981); M. Fishbein and I. Ajzen, *Belief, Attitude, Intention, and Behavior: An Introduction to Theory and Research* (Reading, MA: Addison-Wesley, 1975); I. Ajzen and M. Fishbein, "The Influence of Attitudes on Behavior," *The Handbook of Attitudes*, eds. Dolores Albarracín, Blair T. Johnson, and Mark P. Zanna (Mahwah, NJ: Erlbaum, 2005), 173–221.

3. Richard E. Petty, S. Christian Wheeler, and Zakary L. Tormala, "Persuasion and Attitude Change," *Handbook of Psychology, Personality, and Social Psychology,* Vol. 5, eds. Theodore Millon, Melvin Lerner, and Irving B. Weiner (New York: John Wiley & Sons, 2003).
4. *The Stanford Encyclopedia of Philosophy,* s.v. "Belief," Winter 2011 edition, plato.stanford.edu/archives/win2011/entries/belief/.
5. N. Belden, J. Russonello, and V. Breglio, "Human Values and Nature's Future: Americans' Attitudes on Biological Diversity," 1995, public opinion survey analysis conducted for the Communications Consortium Media Center.
6. Herbert Simon, *Persuasion in Society,* 2nd ed. (New York: Routledge, 2011).
7. Simon, *Persuasion in Society.*
8. Kenneth Burke, *A Rhetoric of Motives* (Berkeley, CA: University of California Press, 1969).
9. See, for example, "Millennials, Gen X and Baby Boomers: Who's Working at Your Company and What Do They Think about Ethics?" Ethics Resource Center, 2009 National Business Ethics Survey Supplemental Research Brief, http://observgo.uquebec.ca/observgo/fichiers/53123_DAEPI%202.pdf; Dennis McCafferty, "Workforce Preview: What to Expect from Gen Z," *Baseline Magazine,* April 4, 2013, www.baselinemag.com/it-management/slideshows/workforce-preview-what-to-expect-from-gen-z; "Generations: Demographic Trends in Population and Workforce," Catalyst, May 1, 2012, www.catalyst.org/knowledge/generations-demographic-trends-population-and-workforce.
10. Jere R. Behrman and Nevzer Stacey, eds., *The Social Benefits of Education* (Ann Arbor, MI: University of Michigan Press, 2000).
11. "America's Changing Religious Landscape," Pew Research Center, May 12, 2015, www.pewforum.org/2015/05/12/americas-changing-religious-landscape/.
12. Daniel Canary and Kathryn Dindia, eds., *Sex Differences and Similarities in Communication,* 2nd ed. (Mahwah, NJ: Erlbaum, 2006).
13. U.S. Census Bureau Newsroom, June 2, 2016, accessed September 6, 2016, www.census.gov/newsroom/facts-for-features/2016/cb16-ff12.html.
14. U.S. Department of Education, National Center for Education Statistics, April 2016, "Digest of Education Statistics, 2014," nces.ed.gov/pubs2016/2016006.pdf.
15. U.S. Census Bureau, June 2, 2016, accessed January 25, 2018, www.census.gov/quickfacts/fact/table/US/PST045217.
16. "Facts on U.S. Immigrants, 2015," Pew Research Center, May 3, 2017, www.pewhispanic.org/2017/05/03/facts-on-u-s-immigrants/.
17. Steven A. Camarota and Karen Zeigler, "Nearly 65 Million U.S. Residents Spoke a Foreign Language at Home in 2015," Center for Immigration Studies, October 18, 2016, https://cis.org/Report/Nearly-65-Million-US-Residents-Spoke-Foreign-Language-Home-2015.
18. Edward D. Steele and W. Charles Redding, "The American Value System: Premises for Persuasion," *Western Speech* 26 (1962): 83–91; Robin M. Williams Jr., *American Society: A Sociological Interpretation,* 3rd ed. (New York: Alfred A. Knopf, 1970).

19. World Values Survey Wave 2 1990-1994 OFFICIAL AGGREGATE v.20140429. World Values Survey Association (www.worldvaluessurvey.org). Aggregate File Producer: Asep/JDS, Madrid SPAIN.
20. Rushworth M. Kidder, *Shared Values for a Troubled World: Conversations with Men and Women of Conscience* (San Francisco: Jossey-Bass Publishers, 1994).

Chapter 37

1. Ian McEwan, "Freedom of Expression Sustains All Other Freedoms We Enjoy," *Vital Speeches of the Day,* Vol. XXXI, No. 8, August 2015, pp. 245–47.
2. Jonathan Drori, "Every Pollen Grain Has a Story," TED Talks, February 2010, www.ted.com/talks/jonathan_drori_every_pollen_grain_has_a_story.html.
3. Quoted in Katharine Q. Seelye, "Congressman Offers Bill to Ban Cloning of Humans," *New York Times,* March 6, 1997, sec. A.
4. Mark Turner, *The Literary Mind* (New York: Oxford University Press, 1996).
5. Melinda French Gates, "Raising the Bar on College Completion," Keynote Address, American Association of Community Colleges, April 20, 2010, www.gatesfoundation.org/media-center/speeches/2010/04/raising-the-bar-on-college-completion.
6. Steven D. Cohen, "The Art of Public Narrative: Teaching Students How to Construct Memorable Anecdotes," *Communication Teacher* 25, no. 4, (2011): 197–204, doi: 10.1080/17404622.2011.601726.
7. Jim Carrey, Commencement Address, Maharishi University of Management, May 24, 2014, www.mum.edu/whats-happening/graduation-2014/full-jim-carrey-address-video-and-transcript/.
8. Nick Morgan, "Why You Must Tell Stories, Not Dump Information, in Your Presentations," *Forbes,* May 9, 2013, www.forbes.com/sites/nickmorgan/2013/05/09/why-you-must-tell-stories-not-dump-information-in-your-presentations/#426926dd78bb; Kurt Braddock and James Price Dillard, "Meta-analytic Evidence for the Persuasive Effect of Narratives on Beliefs, Attitudes, Intentions, and Behaviors," *Communication Monographs,* 2016, doi:10.1080/03637.
9. Yaacov Schul and Ruth Mayo, "Two Sources Are Better Than One: The Effects of Ignoring One Message on Using a Different Message from the Same Source," *Journal of Experimental Social Psychology* 35 (1999): 327–45; Mike Allen et al., "Testing the Persuasiveness of Evidence: Combining Narrative and Statistical Forms," *Communication Research Reports* 17 (2000): 331–36, cited in Rodney A. Reynolds and J. Lynn Reynolds, "Evidence," in *The Persuasion Handbook: Developments in Theory and Practice,* eds. James Price Dillard and Michael Pfau (Thousand Oaks, CA: Sage, 2002), 427–44, doi: 10.4135/9781412976046.n22.
10. Reynolds and Reynolds, "Evidence."
11. "Airbus delivers 110th A380," Airbus, March 14, 2013, http://www.airbus.com/newsroom/press-releases/en/2013/03/airbus-delivers-100th-a380.html.
12. Josh Katz, "Drug Deaths in America Are Rising Faster Than Ever," *New York Times,* June 5, 2017, www.nytimes.com/interactive/2017/06/05/upshot/opioid-epidemic-drug-overdose-deaths-are-rising-faster-than-ever.html.
13. "State and County QuickFacts," U.S. Census Bureau, accessed October 3, 2017, https://www.census.gov/quickfacts/fact/table/CO/PST045217# viewtop.

14. Katz, "Drug Deaths in America Are Rising Faster Than Ever."
15. Bureau of Labor Statistics, "State Employment and Unemployment Summary," Sept. 15, 2017, www.bls.gov/news.release/laus.nr0.htm.
16. Maddy Osman, "18 Instagram Stats Every Marketer Should Know for 2017," Sprout Social, August 2, 2017, sproutsocial.com/insights/instagram-stats/.
17. Roger Pielke Jr., "The Cherry Pick," *Ogmius: Newsletter for the Center for Science and Technology Research* 8 (2004), sciencepolicy.colorado.edu/ogmius/archives/issue_8/intro.html.

Chapter 38

1. Ralph Underwager and Hollida Wakefield, "The Taint Hearing," paper presented at the 13th Annual Symposium in Forensic Psychology, Vancouver, BC, April 17, 1997, www.ipt-forensics.com/journal/volume10/j10_7.htm#en0.
2. Institute for Writing and Rhetoric, "Sources and Citation at Dartmouth College," produced by the Committee on Sources, May 2008, writing-speech.dartmouth.edu/learning/materials/sources-and-citations-dartmouth#3A.

Chapter 39

1. Gordon H. Bower, "Organizational Factors in Memory," *Cognitive Psychology* 1 (1970): 18–46.
2. Ian McEwan, "Freedom of Expression Sustains All the Other Freedoms We Enjoy," *Vital Speeches of the Day*, Vol. LXXXI, No. 8, August 2015.
3. Hermann Ebbinghaus, *On Memory: A Contribution to Experimental Psychology* (New York: Teachers College, 1813); Murray Glanzer and Anita R. Cunitz, "Two Storage Mechanisms in Free Recall," *Journal of Verbal Learning and Verbal Behavior* 5 (1966): 351–60.

Chapter 40

1. Raymond G. Smith, "Effects of Speech Organization upon Attitudes of College Students," *Speech Monographs* 18 (1951): 547–49; Ernest Thompson, "An Experimental Investigation of the Relative Effectiveness of Organizational Structure in Oral Communication," *Southern Speech Journal* 26 (1960): 59–69.
2. Melissa Del Bosque, "Beyond the Border: Into the Wilderness," *The Guardian*, August 6, 2014, www.theguardian.com/world/ng-interactive/2014/aug/06/-sp-texas-border-deadliest-state-undocumented-migrants.
3. Randy Capps, Michael Fix, and Jie Zong, "A Profile of U.S. Children with Unauthorized Immigrant Parents," Migration Policy Institute Fact Sheet, January, 2016, www.migrationpolicy.org/research/profile-us-children-unauthorized-immigrant-parents.
4. Capps, Fix, and Zong, "A Profile of U.S. Children with Unauthorized Immigrant Parents."
5. Capps, Fix, and Zong, "A Profile of U.S. Children with Unauthorized Immigrant Parents."
6. Brian Eakin, "Homeland Security Grilled on Visa Overstays," Courthouse News Service, June 14, 2016, www.courthousenews.com/2016/06/14/homeland-security-grilled-on-visa-overstays.htm.

7. Eakin, "Homeland Security Grilled on Visa Overstays."
8. Joe Davidson, "Visa Overstays a Security Risk When 99% of Foreigners Leave U.S. on Time?" *Washington Post,* June 15, 2016, www.washingtonpost.com/news/powerpost/wp/2016/06/15/visa-overstays-a-security-risk-when-99-of-foreigners-leave-u-s-on-time/.
9. Jie Zong and Jeanne Batalova, "Frequently Requested Statistics on Immigrants and Immigration in the United States," Migration Policy Institute, March 8, 2017, www.migrationpolicy.org/article/frequently-requested-statistics-immigrants-and-immigration-united-states.
10. "How the United States Immigration System Works: A Fact Sheet," American Immigration Council, August 12, 2016, www.immigrationpolicy.org/just-facts/how-united-states-immigration-system-works-fact-sheet.
11. Guillermo Cantor, Mark Noferi, and Daniel E. Martinez, "Enforcement Overdrive: A Comprehensive Assessment of ICE's Criminal Alien Program," American Immigration Council, November 1, 2015, www.immigrationpolicy.org/special-reports/enforcement-overdrive-comprehensive-assessment-criminal-alien-program.
12. "Life on the Internet Timeline," Public Broadcasting System, accessed April 3, 2000, www.pbs.org/internet/timeline/index.html.

Chapter 41

1. Mark B. McClellan, fifth annual David A. Winston lecture, National Press Club, Washington, DC, October 20, 2003, www.fda.gov/newsevents/speeches/speecharchives/ucm053609.htm.

Chapter 42

1. Jeremey Donovan, *How to Deliver a TED Talk* (CreateSpace Independent Publishing Platform, 2012).
2. Laurie Loisel, "Twitter Exec tells UMASS Amherst Grads to 'Hack the System,'" *Boston Globe,* May 6, 2016, www.bostonglobe.com/metro/2016/05/06/twitter-exec-tells-umass-amherst-grads-hack-system/uAYypkmN3v1QlHMSsaIyaJ/story.html.
3. William Safire, *Lend Me Your Ears: Great Speeches in History* (New York: Norton, 1992), 676.
4. Bas Andeweg and Jap de Jong, "May I Have Your Attention? Exordial Techniques in Informative Oral Presentations," *Technical Communication Quarterly* 7, no. 3 (Summer 1998): 271–84.
5. Nancy Duarte, *Harvard Business Review Guide to Persuasive Presentations* (Boston: Harvard Business Review Press, 2012).
6. Phillip Connor and Jens Manuel Krogstad, "Key Facts About the World's Refugees," Pew Research Center FactTank, October 5, 2016, www.pewresearch.org/fact-tank/2016/10/05/key-facts-about-the-worlds-refugees/.
7. Jamie Oliver, "Teach Every Child about Food," filmed February 2010, TED video, www.ted.com/talks/jamie_oliver.
8. Marvin Runyon, "No One Moves the Mail Like the U.S. Postal Service," *Vital Speeches of the Day* 61, no. 2 (1994): 52–55.

9. Robert L. Darbelnet, "U.S. Roads and Bridges: Highway Funding at a Crossroads," *Vital Speeches of the Day* 63, no. 12 (1997): 379.
10. Holger Kluge, "Reflections on Diversity," *Vital Speeches of the Day* 63, no. 6 (1997): 171–72.
11. Elpidio Villarreal, "Choosing the Right Path," *Vital Speeches of the Day* 72, no. 26 (2007): 784–86.
12. Emma Watson, "Gender Equality Is Your Issue Too," UN Women, September 20, 2014, www.unwomen.org/en/news/stories/2014/9/emma-watson-gender-equality-is-your-issue-too.

Chapter 43

1. Kristine Bruss, "Writing for the Ear: Strengthening Oral Style in Manuscript Speeches," *Communication Teacher* 26, no.2 (April 2012): 76–81.
2. Bourree Lam, "What It Was Like to Write Speeches for Apple Executives," *The Atlantic,* June 10, 2016, www.theatlantic.com/business/archive/2016/06/speechwriter-poet/486329/.
3. Peggy Noonan, *Simply Speaking: How to Communicate Your Ideas with Style, Substance, and Clarity* (New York: Regan Books, 1998), 51.
4. Michelle Obama, "Remarks by the First Lady at the Democratic National Convention," delivered at the Wells Fargo Center, Philadelphia, PA. The White House Briefing Room, July 25, 2016.
5. Dan Hooley, "The Lessons of the Ring," *Vital Speeches of the Day* 70, no. 20 (2004): 660–63.
6. Sheryl Sandberg, "Why We Have Too Few Women Leaders," TED Talks, December 2010, www.ted.com/talks/sheryl_sandberg_why_we_have_too_few_women_leaders.html.
7. Susan T. Fiske and Shelley E. Taylor, "Vivid Information Is More Easily Recalled Than Dull or Pallid Stimuli," *Social Cognition,* 2nd ed. (New York: McGraw Hill), quoted in Jennifer Jerit and Jason Barabas, "Bankrupt Rhetoric: How Misleading Information Affects Knowledge about Social Security," *Public Opinion Quarterly* 70, no. 3 (2006): 278–304.
8. Loren J. Naidoo and Robert G. Lord, "Speech Imagery and Perceptions of Charisma: The Mediating Role of Positive Affect," *Leadership Quarterly* 19, no. 3 (2008): 283–96.
9. Franklin D. Roosevelt, address delivered on July 4, 1942, Fourth of July Celebrations Database, gurukul.american.edu/heintze/Roosevelt.htm.
10. Donald J. Trump, Inaugural Address, January 20, 2017, www.whitehouse.gov/inaugural-address.
11. L. Clemetson and J. Gordon-Thomas, "Our House Is on Fire," *Newsweek,* June 11, 2001, 50.
12. Gloria Anzaldúa, "Entering into the Serpent," in *The St. Martin's Handbook,* eds. Andrea Lunsford and Robert Connors, 3rd ed. (New York: St. Martin's Press, 1995), 25.
13. P. H. Matthews, *The Concise Oxford Dictionary of Linguistics* (New York: Oxford University Press, 1997).
14. Cited in William Safire, *Lend Me Your Ears: Great Speeches in History* (New York: Norton, 1992), 22.
15. "Barack Obama's New Hampshire Primary Speech," *New York Times,* January 8, 2008, www.nytimes.com/2008/01/08/us/politics/08text-obama.html?r=0.

Chapter 44

1. James A. Winans, *Public Speaking* (New York: Century, 1925). Professor Winans was among the first Americans to contribute significantly to the study of rhetoric. His explanation of delivery is considered by many to be the best coverage of the topic in the English language. His perspective infuses this chapter.

Chapter 45

1. Kyle James Tusing and James Price Dillard, "The Sounds of Dominance: Vocal Precursors of Perceived Dominance during Interpersonal Influence," *Human Communication Research* 26 (2000): 148–71.
2. Carmine Gallo, *Talk Like TED* (New York: St Martin's Press, 2014), 97.

Chapter 46

1. C. F. Bond and the Global Deception Research Team, "A World of Lies," *Journal of Cross-Cultural Psychology* 37 (2006): 60–74; Timothy R. Levine, Kelli Jean K. Asada, and Hee Sun Park, "The Lying Chicken and the Gaze Avoidant Egg: Eye Contact, Deception, and Causal Order," *Southern Communication Journal* 71 (2006): 401–11.
2. Eva Krumburger, "Effects of Dynamic Attributes of Smiles in Human and Synthetic Faces: A Simulated Job Interview Setting," *Journal of Nonverbal Behavior* 33 (2009): 1–15.
3. Alissa Melinger and Willem M. Levelt, "Gesture and the Communicative Intention of the Speaker," *Gesture* 4 (2004): 119–41.
4. Virginia P. Richmond, James C. McCroskly, and Aaron D. Johnson, "Development of the Nonverbal Immediacy Scale (NIS): Measures of Self- and Other-Perceived Nonverbal Immediacy," *Communication Quarterly* 51, no. 4 (2003): 504–17.

Chapter 47

1. Richard E. Mayer, *The Multimedia Principle* (New York: Cambridge University Press, 2001).
2. See discussion of the redundancy effect in Richard E. Mayer, ed., *The Cambridge Handbook of Multimedia Learning* (New York: Cambridge University Press, 2005).
3. Gary Jones, "Message First: Using Films to Power the Point," *Business Communication Quarterly* 67, no. 1 (2004): 88–91.

Chapter 48

1. Nancy Duarte, "Avoiding the Road to PowerPoint Hell," *Wall Street Journal,* January 22, 2011, https://www.wsj.com/articles/SB10001424052748703954004576090053995594270.
2. Nancy Duarte, *slide:ology: The Art and Science of Creating Great Presentations* (Sebastopol, CA: O'Reilly Media, 2008), 140.
3. Duarte, "Avoiding the Road to PowerPoint Hell."
4. Edward Tufte, *The Visual Display of Quantitative Information* (Cheshire, CT: Graphics Press, 2001); Edward Tufte, "PowerPoint Is Evil," *Wired* 11 (2003), www.wired.com/wired/archive/11.09/ppt2_pr.html.
5. Ronald Larson, "Slide Composition for Electronic Presentations," *Journal of Educational Computing Research,* 31, no. 1 (2004): 61–76.

Works Cited

Habits of the Creative Mind

"About the Project." *7 Billion Others*. The GoodPlanet Foundation, n.d. Web. 27 Dec. 2013.

Abumrad, Jad, and Robert Krulwich. "An Equation for Good." *Radiolab*. WNYC. 15 Dec. 2010. Podcast. 21 Dec. 2013.

Alexander, Michelle. *The New Jim Crow: Mass Incarceration in the Age of Color Blindness*. New York: New Press, 2010. Print.

The Aristocrats. Dir. Paul Provenza. Think Film Company, 2005. Film.

Armstrong, Elizabeth M., and Ernest L. Abel. "Fetal Alcohol Syndrome: The Origins of a Moral Panic." *Alcohol and Alcoholism* 35.3 (May 2000): 276–82. Web. 29 Dec. 2013.

Arthus-Bertrand, Yann. *6 Billion Others: Portraits of Humanity from Around the World*. New York: Abrams, 2009. Print.

---. *Earth from Above*. 3rd ed. New York: Abrams, 2005. Print.

Bain, Ken. *What the Best College Students Do*. Cambridge, MA: Harvard UP, 2012. Print.

---. *What the Best College Teachers Do*. Cambridge, MA: Harvard UP, 2004. Print.

Bechdel, Alison. "Comics Reporter Interview #1—Alison Bechdel." Interview by Tom Spurgeon. Comicsreporter.com. *The Comics Reporter*, 18 Dec. 2012. Web. 8 Nov. 2014.

---. *Fun Home: A Family Tragicomic*. New York: Mariner, 2006. Print.

---. MacArthur Fellow Biography. MacArthur Foundation. Web. 8 Nov 2014.

---. quoted in Dwight Garner. "The Days of Their Lives: Lesbians Star in Funny Pages." Books of the Times. *New York Times*, 2 Dec. 2008. Web. 8 Nov. 2014.

Berger, John. "Why Look at Animals?" *About Looking*. New York: Random, 2011. Print.

Berthoff, Ann E. *Forming/Thinking/Writing: The Composing Imagination*. Montclair, NJ: Boynton/Cook, 1982. Print.

Blake, William. "Auguries of Innocence." *The Poetry Foundation*. Web. 16 Jan. 2014.

Bulwer-Lytton, Edward. *Paul Clifford. Gutenberg.org*. Project Gutenberg, 6 Nov. 2012. Web. 16 Jan. 2014.

---. *Richelieu, or, The Conspiracy: A Play in Five Acts. Openlibrary.org*. Web. 16 Jan. 2014.

The Bulwer-Lytton Fiction Contest. English Dept. San Jose State U, n.d. Web. 16 Jan. 2014.

Burke, Kenneth. *The Philosophy of Literary Form*. U of California. Berkeley: UP of California, 1941. Print.

Cain, Susan. *Quiet: The Power of Introverts in a World that Can't Stop Talking*. New York: Crown, 2012. Print.

Capote, Truman. *In Cold Blood*. New York: Random, 1965. Print.

---. "The Story Behind a Nonfiction Novel." Interview by George Plimpton. *New York Times,* 16 Jan. 1966. Web. 21 Dec. 2013.

Carroll, Lewis. *Alice's Adventures in Wonderland. Gutenberg.org*. Project Gutenberg, 8 Mar. 1994. Web. 18 Dec. 2013.

CK, Louis. "About Tig Notaro." *Louis CK*, 5 Oct. 2012. Web. 24 Jan. 2014.

Coates, Ta-Nehisi. "Considering the President's Comments on Racial Profiling." *Theatlantic.com.* Atlantic Monthly Group, 19 July 2013. Web. 27 Dec. 2013.

---. "Fear of a Black President." *Theatlantic.com*. Atlantic Monthly Group, 22 Aug. 2012. Web. 27 Dec. 2013.

Colette. quoted in Emily Temple. "'My Pencils Outlast their Erasers': Great Writers on the Art of Revision." *Theatlantic.com*. Atlantic Monthly Group, 14 Jan. 2013. Web. 27 Dec. 2013.

Crutchfield, Susan. "Play[ing] her Part Correctly: Helen Keller as Vaudevillian Freak." *Disability Studies Quarterly* 25.3 (2005): n.pag. Web. 17 Jan. 2013.

Csikszentmihalyi, Mihaly. *Creativity: Flow and the Psychology of Discovery and Invention*. New York: Harper, 1996. Print.

Delbanco, Andrew. *College: What it Was, Is, and Should Be*. Princeton, NJ: Princeton UP, 2012. Print.

"Diane Arbus." *Wikipedia*. Wikimedia Foundation, 8 Dec. 2013. Web. 16 Jan. 2014.

Dissanayake, Ellen. "The Arts After Darwin: Does Art Have an Origin and Adaptive Function?" *Ellendissanayake.com*. U of Washington P, n.d. Web. 16 Jan. 2014.

Dreisinger, Baz. "Marching On: James McBride's *'Good Lord Bird.'*" *NYTimes.com*. New York Times, 15 Aug. 2013. Web. 4 Jan. 2014.

Duncker, Karl. "On Problem Solving." *Psychological Monographs* 58:5 (1945) Whole no. 270. Web. 3 June 2015.

Edwards, Betty. *Drawing on the Right Side of the Brain: A Course in Enhancing Creativity and Artistic Confidence*. New York: Tarcher, 1979. Print.

Ericsson, K. Anders, Ralf Th. Krampe, and Clemens Tesch-Römer. "The Role of Deliberate Practice in the Acquisition of Expert Performance." *Psychological Review* 100.3 (1993): 363–406. Web. 3 June 2015.

Fitzgerald, F. Scott. "Appendix A: Fitzgerald's Correspondence about The Great Gatsby (1922–25)." *The Great Gatsby*. Ed. Michael Nowlin. Peterborough, ON, Canada: Broadview, 2007. 185–87. Print.

Framework for Success in Postsecondary Writing. *Wpacouncil.org*. Council of Writing Program Administrators, n.d. Web. 27 Jan. 2014.

Freeza, Bill. "Is Drug War Driven Mass Incarceration the New Jim Crow?" *Forbes.com*. Forbes Media, 28 Feb. 2012. Web. 2 Jan. 2014.

Frost, Robert. "The Road Not Taken." The Poetry Foundation. Web. 4 June 2015.

Gaiman, Neil. "Advice to Authors." *Neilgaiman.com*. Harper Collins, n.d. Web. 6 Nov. 2014.

Galileo. *The Dialogue Concerning the Two Chief World Systems*. Trans. Stillmann Drake. New York: Modern Library, 2001. Print.

Gazzaniga, Michael S. "The Split Brain in Man." *Scientific American* 217.2 (1967): 24–29. Web. 3 June 2015.

"Genesis." *The English Standard Version Bible*. *ESVBible.org*. Crossway, 2015. Web. 16 Jan. 2014.

Gibson, William. *The Miracle Worker*. Playhouse 90, 1957. Teleplay.

---. *The Miracle Worker*. Dir. Arthur Penn. Playfilm Productions, 1962. Film.

---. *The Miracle Worker*. Samuel French, 1961. Play.

---. *Monday After the Miracle*. New York: Dramatists Play Service, 1983. Play.

Gladwell, Malcolm. *Outliers: The Story of Success*. New York: Little, 2008. Print.

---. *What the Dog Saw: And Other Adventures*. New York: Little, 2009. Print.

Gladwell, Malcolm, and Robert Krulwich. "Secrets of Success." *Radiolab*. WNYC. 26 July 2010. Podcast. 21 Dec. 2013.

Gonzales, Laurence. *Deep Survival: Who Lives, Who Dies, and Why*. New York: Norton, 2004. Print.

Gutkind, Lee. "Home." Lee Gutkind. Web. 5 Nov. 2014.

Hochschild, Adam. "'Why's This So Good?' No. 61: John McPhee and the Archdruid." *Nieman Storyboard*. Nieman Foundation for Journalism at Harvard, 2 Oct. 2012. Web. 4 Jan. 2014.

Hohn, Donovan. *Moby-Duck: The True Story of 28,800 Bath Toys Lost at Sea and the Beachcombers, Oceanographers, Environmentalists, and Fools, Including the Author, Who Went in Search of Them*. New York: Viking, 2011. Print.

Johnson, Harriet McBryde. "Unspeakable Conversations." *NYTimes.com*. New York Times Magazine, 16 Feb. 2003. Web. 4 Jan. 2014.

Keller, Helen. *The Story of My Life*. *Gutenberg.org*. Project Gutenberg, 4 Feb. 2013. Web. 17 Jan. 2014.

---. *Teacher: Anne Sullivan Macy*. Garden City, New York: Doubleday, 1955. Print.

---. "Vaudeville Speech." quoted in Dorothy Hermann, *Helen Keller: A Life*. Chicago: U of Chicago P, 1998. Print.

---. *The World I Live In*. *Gutenberg.org*. Project Gutenberg, 1 Jan. 2009. Web. 17 Jan. 2014.

Kolbert, Elizabeth. *Field Notes from a Catastrophe: Man, Nature, and Climate Change*. New York: Bloomsbury, 2006. Print.

Lamotte, Anne. *Bird by Bird: Some Instructions on Writing and Life*. New York: Anchor, 1995. Print.

Lee, Colonel Robert E. "Colonel Robert E. Lee's Report Concerning the Attack at Harper's Ferry." 1859. *Famous Trials: The Trial of John Brown*. U of Missouri Coll. of Law, n.d. Web. 7 Jan. 2014.

Lepore, Jill. "Battleground America: One Nation, Under the Gun." *Newyorker.com*. New Yorker, 23 Apr. 2012. Web. 21 Jan. 2014.

---. *Book of Ages: The Life and Opinions of Jane Franklin*. New York: Knopf, 2013. Print.

---. Interview by Sasha Weiss and Judith Thurman. "Out Loud: Jane Franklin's Untold American Story." *Newyorker.com*. New Yorker, 30 June 2013. Podcast. 5 June 2015.

---. "Poor Jane's Almanac." *NYTimes.com*. New York Times, 23 Apr. 2011. Web. 23 Dec. 2013.

---. "The Prodigal Daughter: Writing, History, Mourning." *New Yorker,* 8 July 2013: 34–40. Print.

Lethem, Jonathan. "The Ecstasy of Influence: A Plagiarism." *Harpers.org*. Harper's Magazine, Feb. 2007. Web. 21 Jan. 2014.

Lightman, Alan. "The Accidental Universe." *Harpers.org*. Harper's Magazine, Dec. 2011. Web. 31 Dec. 2013.

Lincoln, Abraham. "Gettysburg Address." *Gutenberg.org*. Project Gutenberg, Web. 24 Jan. 2014.

The Matrix. Dir. Andy Wachowski and Lana Wachowski. Warner Bros., 1999. Film.

McBride, James. *The Good Lord Bird*. New York: Riverhead, 2013. Print.

---. Quoted in Julie Bosman. "Traveling with John Brown Along the Road to Literary Celebrity." *NYTimes.com*. New York Times, 24 Nov. 2013. Web. 7 Jan. 2014.

McPhee, John. "John McPhee, The Art of Nonfiction No. 3." Interview by Peter Hessler. *Paris Review* 192 (Spring 2010). Web. 1 Jan. 2014.

---. "Structure." *Newyorker.com*. New Yorker, 14 Jan. 2013. Web. 4 Jan. 2014.

Morrison, Toni. Interview by Elissa Schappell. "Toni Morrison, The Art of Fiction No. 134." *Theparisreview.org*. Paris Review 128 (Fall 1993). Web. 26 Dec. 2013.

Notaro, Tig. *LIVE*. Secretlycanadian.com. 3 Aug. 2012. MP3 file.

Obama, Barack. "Remarks by the President on the Nomination of Dr. Kim Jim for World Bank President." *Whitehouse.gov*. 23 Mar. 2012. Web. 27 Dec. 2013.

---. "Remarks by the President on Trayvon Martin." *Whitehouse.gov*. 19 July 2013. Web. 27 Dec. 2013.

Osifchin, Chris. "Abu Ghraib Ruminations." Message to Richard E. Miller. 29 Jan. 2014. E-mail.

Pink, Daniel. "The Puzzle of Motivation." TED. July 2009. Web. 11 Nov. 2014.

---. *A Whole New Mind: Why Right-Brainers Will Rule the Future*. New York: Riverhead, 2005. Print.

Plato. "The Apology." *Plato: Complete Works*. Eds. John M. Cooper and D. S. Hutchinson. Indianapolis: Hackett, 1997. 17–36. Print.

---. *The Republic*. Trans. G.M.E. Grube. 2nd ed. Indianapolis: Hackett, 1992. Print.

Pollan, Michael. "An Animal's Place." *NYTimes.com.* New York Times, 10 Nov. 2002. Web. 31 Dec. 2013.

---. *The Botany of Desire: A Plant's Eye View of the World.* New York: Random, 2001. Print.

Rose, Erik. Student Writing. n.d. TS. Rutgers UP. Contacted 12 Jan. 2014.

Sacks, Oliver. "The Mind's Eye." *Newyorker.com.* New Yorker, 28 July 2003. Web. 18 Jan. 2014.

Sagan, Carl. *Cosmos.* New York: Ballantine, 2013. Print.

Said, Edward. *Orientalism.* 2nd ed. New York: Vintage, 1994. Print.

Saint Anselm. *Basic Writings: Proslogium, Mologium, Gaunilo's In Behalf of the Fool, Cur Deus Homo.* Trans. S. N. Deane. 2nd ed. Peru, IL: Open Court, 1998. Print.

Schlosser, Eric. "Eric Schlosser." Interview by Robert Boynton. *The New New Journalism.* New York: Random, 2005. Print.

Shakespeare, William. *Romeo and Juliet. Gutenberg.org.* Project Gutenberg, 25 May 2012. Web. 24 Jan. 2014.

Simon, David. "HBO's 'Treme' Creator David Simon Explains It All for You." *Nola.com.* Times-Picayune, 11 Apr. 2010. Web. 15 Nov. 2014.

Singer, Peter. *Animal Liberation: A New Ethic for Our Treatment of Animals.* New York: Random, 1975. Print.

Skloot, Rebecca. "How Rebecca Skloot Built *The Immortal Life of Henrietta Lacks.*" Interview by David Dobbs. *Theopennotebook.com.* The Open Notebook, 22 Nov. 2011. Web. 4 Jan. 2014.

---. *The Immortal Life of Henrietta Lacks.* New York: Crown, 2010. Print.

---. "What's the Most Important Lesson You Learned from a Teacher?" *Rebeccaskloot.com.* Rebecca Skloot, 8 May 2012. Web. 29 Dec. 2013.

Smith, Zadie. "Fail Better." *Theguardian.com.* Guardian, 13 Jan. 2007. Web. 20 Dec. 2013.

---. *NW.* London: Penguin, 2012. Print.

Sontag, Susan. "America Seen through Photographs, Darkly." *On Photography.* New York: Farrar, 1977. 27–50. Print.

---. "Looking at War." *New Yorker,* Dec. 2002: 82–98. Print.

---. "Regarding the Torture of Others." *NYTimes.com.* New York Times Magazine, 23 May 2004. Web. 20 Dec. 2013.

Sotomayor, Sonia. *My Beloved World.* New York: Knopf, 2013. Print.

Spiotta, Dana. *Stone Arabia.* New York: Scribner, 2012. Print.

Stern, Daniel. "Life Becomes a Dream." Rev. of *The Benefactor* by Susan Sontag. *NYTimes.com.* New York Times, 8 Sept. 1963. Web. 3 June 2015.

Stiver, Annie. "The Time is Ripe." Apr. 2012. TS. Rutgers UP. Contacted 29 Jan. 2014.

Talbot, Margaret. "Stealing Life." *Newyorker.com.* New Yorker, 22 Oct. 2007. Web.

Tharp, Twyla. *The Creative Habit: Learn It and Use It for Life.* New York: Simon, 2003. Print.

Thoreau, Henry David. "Walden." *Walden, and On the Duty of Civil Disobedience.* Project Gutenberg. Jan. 1995. Web. 26 Dec. 2013.

Toy Story. Dir. John Lasseter. Pixar Animation Studios, 1995. Film.

Trainer, Laureen. "The Missing Photographs: An Examination of Diane Arbus's Images of Transvestites and Homosexuals from 1957 to 1965." *Americansuburbx.com.* American Suburb X, 2 Oct. 2009. Web. 16 Jan. 2014.

Tremmel, Michelle. "What to Make of the Five-Paragraph Theme: History of the Genre and Implications." *TETYC* Sept. 2011. 29–41. Print.

Waking Life. Dir. Richard Linklater. Fox Searchlight, 2001. Film.

Walk, Kerry. "Teaching with Writing." Princeton Writing Program. Princeton U, n.d. Web. 27 Dec. 2013.

Wallace, David Foster. *This is Water: Some Thoughts, Delivered on a Significant Occasion, About Living a Compassionate Life.* Transcription of 2005 Kenyon Commencement Address—May 21, 2005. Purdue U, n.d. Web. 23 Dec. 2013.

Walzer, Michael. "Political Action: The Problem of Dirty Hands." *Philosophy and Public Affairs* 2.2 (1973): 160–80. Print.

Webster, Daniel W., and Jon S. Vernick. "Introduction." *Reducing Gun Violence in America: Informing Policy with Evidence and Analysis.* Eds. Daniel W. Webster and Jon S. Vernick. Baltimore, MD: Johns Hopkins UP, 2013. Print.

Woolf, Virginia. Letter to Vita Sackville-West. 26 Feb. 1939. MS. *Woolf in the World: A Pen and Press of Her Own.* Mortimer Rare Book Room. Smith College. Web. 31 Dec. 2013.

---. *A Room of One's Own. Gutenberg.org.* Project Gutenberg Australia. Web. 11 Nov. 2014.

---. "Street Haunting: A London Adventure." *Virginia Woolf: Selected Essays.* Oxford: Oxford UP, 2008. 177–87. Print.

---. *Three Guineas.* 1938. Blackwell Publishing. Web. 20 Dec. 2013.

"WPA Outcomes Statement for First-Year Composition." *Wpacouncil.org.* Council of Writing Program Administrators, n.d. Web. 27 Jan. 2014.

Zakaria, Fareed. "The Case for Gun Control: Why Limiting Access to Guns is Intelligent and American." *Time.com.* Time, 20 Aug. 2012. Web. 27 Jan. 2014.

---. "A Statement from Fareed." Fareed Zakaria GPS. *Globalpublicsquare.blogs.cnn.com.* CNN, 10 Aug. 2012. Web. 3 June 2015.

Acknowledgments

Habits of the Creative Mind

Edward W. Said. Excerpt from *Orientalism*. Copyright © 1978 by Edward W. Said. Used by permission of Pantheon Books, an imprint of the Knopf Doubleday Publishing Group, a division of Penguin Random House LLC. All rights reserved.

Michael Walzer. "Political Action: The Problem of Dirty Hands." Philosophy and Public Affairs 2.2 (1973): 160–180. Republished with permission of Blackwell Publishing, Inc.; permission conveyed through Copyright Clearance Center, Inc.

Daniel W. Webster & Jon S. Vernick, eds. Foreword by Michael R. Bloomberg. *Reducing Gun Violence in America: Informing Policy with Evidence and Analysis*. pp. xxv–xxvi. © 2013 The Johns Hopkins University Press. Reprinted with permission of Johns Hopkins University Press.

FieldWorking: Reading and Writing Research, Fourth Edition

Beth Campbell. "Reading an Artifact." Reprinted by permission.

Julie Cheville. "From Ethos to Ethics." Reprinted by permission.

Jennifer S. Cook. "Writing a Verbal Portrait." Reprinted by permission of Moira Collins.

Nancy Hauserman. "Taking Care." Reprinted by permission.

David Isay, ed. Excerpt from *Listening Is an Act of Love: A Celebration of American Life from the StoryCorps Project*, edited by David Isay. Copyright © 2007 by Sound Portraits Productions, Inc. Used by permission of Penguin Press, an imprint of Penguin Publishing Group, a division of Penguin Random House LLC. All rights reserved.

Gloria Naylor. Excerpt from *Mama Day*. Copyright © 1988 by Gloria Naylor. Reprinted by permission of Houghton Mifflin Harcourt Publishing Company. All rights reserved.

Donna Niday. "One Family Story: The Core and Its Variants." Reprinted by permission.

Kathleen Ryan. "FieldWorking Book Clubs." Reprinted by permission.

Oliver Sacks. Excerpt from *An Anthropologist on Mars: Seven Paradoxical Tales*. Copyright © 1995 by Oliver Sacks. Used by permission of Alfred A. Knopf, an imprint of the Knopf Doubleday Publishing Group, a division of Penguin Random House LLC. All rights reserved.

Alice Walker. "Everyday Use." *In Love & Trouble: Stories Of Black Women*. Copyright © 1973 by Alice Walker. Reprinted by permission of Houghton Mifflin Harcourt Publishing Company. All rights reserved.

Everything's an Argument, Eighth Edition

Kate Beispel. "The Snacktivities and Musings of a Millennial Foodie." Reprinted by permission.

James Carroll. "Who Am I to Judge?" *New Yorker*, December 23–30, 2013. Copyright © 2013. Reprinted by permission of the author.

Tal Fortgang. "Checking My Privilege: Character as the Basis of Privilege." *Princeton Tory*, April 2, 2014. Copyright © 2014. Reprinted by permission.

Cameron Hauer. "Appeal, Audience, and Narrative in Kristof's Wilderness." Reprinted by permission.

Michael Hiltzik. "Don't Believe Facebook: The Demise of the Written Word Is Very Far Off." *Los Angeles Times*, June 17, 2016. Copyright © 2016 Los Angeles Times. Reprinted by permission.

Rob Jenkins. "Defining the Relationship." *Chronicle of Higher Education*, August 9, 2016. Used with the permission of the *Chronicle of Higher Education*. Copyright © 2016. All rights reserved.

Jenny Kim. "The Toxicity in Learning." Reprinted by permission.

Nicholas Kristof. "Fleeing to the Mountains." *New York Times*, August 13, 2017. Copyright © 2017 The New York Times. All rights reserved. Used by permission and protected by the Copyright Laws of the United States. The printing, copying, redistribution, or retransmission of this Content without express written permission is prohibited.

Barry LePatner. Excerpt from *Too Big to Fall: America's Failing Infrastructure and the Way Forward* by Barry B. LePatner (Foster Publishing, 2010). Copyright © 2010. Reprinted by permission.

Sidra Montgomery. "The Emotion Work of 'Thank You for Your Service.'" Reprinted by permission.

Kathryn Schulz. "Dead Certainty: How 'Making a Murderer' Goes Wrong." *New Yorker*, January 25, 2016. Copyright © 2016. Reprinted by permission.

Ruth J. Simmons. Smith College commencement speech. May 18, 2014. Reprinted by permission.

Lenore Skenazy. "My Free-Range Parenting Manifesto." *Politico*, July 22, 2015. Copyright © 2015 Politico: Politics, Political News. Reproduced with permission of Capitol News Company LLC in the format Republish in a book via Copyright Clearance Center.

Becca Stanek. "I took vitamins every day for a decade. Then I found out they're useless." *The Week*, March 28, 2017. Copyright © 2017. Reprinted by permission.

Jean M. Twenge. "Have Smartphones Destroyed a Generation?" *The Atlantic*, August 5, 2017. © 2017 The Atlantic Media Co., as first published in the *Atlantic Magazine*. All rights reserved. Distributed by Tribune Content Agency, LLC.

Diane Weathers. "Speaking Our Truth" (excerpt). *Essence* 33.6 (October 2002), p. 24. Reprinted by permission.

Caleb Wong. "Addiction to Social Media: How to Overcome It." Reprinted by permission.

A Pocket Guide to Public Speaking, Sixth Edition

Joe Ayres & Theodore S. Hopf. "Visualization: Is it more than extra-attention?" *Communication Education*. Copyright © National Communication Association, reprinted by permission of Taylor & Francis Ltd., http://www.tandfonline.com on behalf of National Communication Association.

Index

A

I

J

K

L

M